P9-AQK-407

D-DAY

UNDER FIRE 1 STORMING FORTRESS EUROPE

OSPREY
PUBLISHING

OSPREY PUBLISHING
Bloomsbury Publishing Plc
PO Box 883, Oxford, OX1 9PL, UK
1385 Broadway, 5th Floor, New York, NY 10018, USA
E-mail: info@ospreypublishing.com
www.ospreypublishing.com

OSPREY is a trademark of Osprey Publishing Ltd

First published in Great Britain in 2020

© Osprey Publishing, 2020

All rights reserved. No part of this publication may be
reproduced or transmitted in any form or by any means,
electronic or mechanical, including photocopying, recording,
or any information storage or retrieval system, without prior
permission in writing from the publishers.

A catalogue record for this book is available from
the British Library.

ISBN: PB 9781472838780
eBook 9781472838803
ePDF 9781472838810
XML 9781472838827

20 21 22 23 24   10 9 8 7 6 5 4 3 2 1

Originated by PDQ Digital Media Solutions, Bungay, UK
Printed and bound in India by Replika Press Private Ltd.

MIX
Paper from
responsible sources
FSC® C016779
www.fsc.org

Osprey Publishing supports the Woodland Trust, the UK's leading
woodland conservation charity.

To find out more about our authors and books visit
www.ospreypublishing.com. Here you will find extracts,
author interviews, details of forthcoming events and the
option to sign up for our newsletter

CREDITS

WRITERS:
Jack Chambers
Erik Hendrix

ARTISTS:
Esteve Polls
IHQ Studios
George Papadakis
Kostas Tsiakos
Jason Baroody

COVER DESIGN:
Stewart Larking

FINISHES:
Anwar Hanano
Victor Castro
Michael David Nelson
Team Comfort and Adam
Malena Salinas
Dylan Klingler
Alyssa Aman
Krystal Hertlein
Drew Norman
Alex Sophabmisay
Kelsey Neveu
Sarah Drews
Sarah Puett
Alysia Schmidt
Hanna Al-Shaer

COLOURISTS:
German Torres
IHQ Studios
Malena Salinas

LETTER:
Amanda Hendrix

EDITORS:
Erik Hendrix
Laura Callaghan
Amanda Hendrix

HISTORICAL CONSULTANT:
Gordon L. Rottman

PORTMANTEAUX PUBLISHING:
Adam Fortier
Erik Hendrix

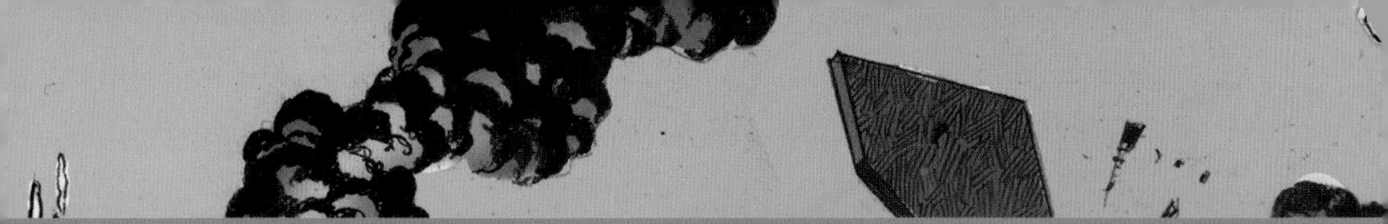

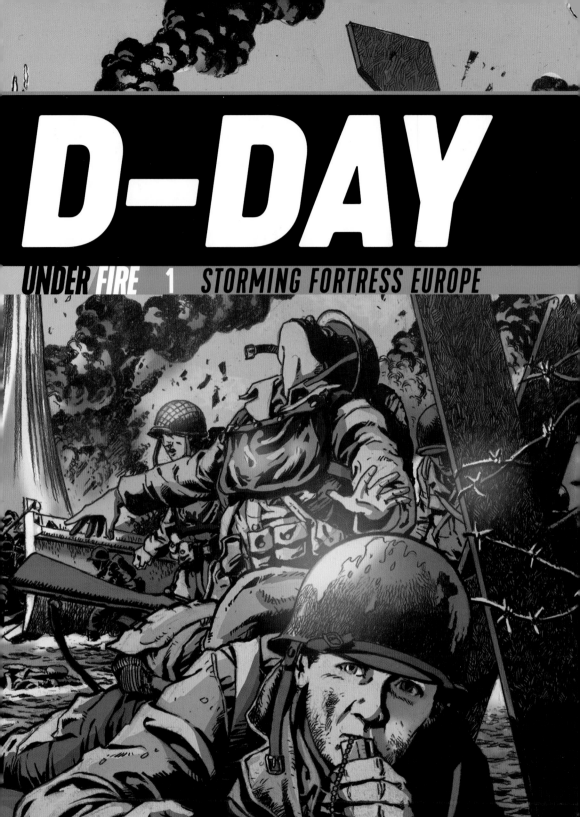

D-DAY

UNDER FIRE 1 STORMING FORTRESS EUROPE

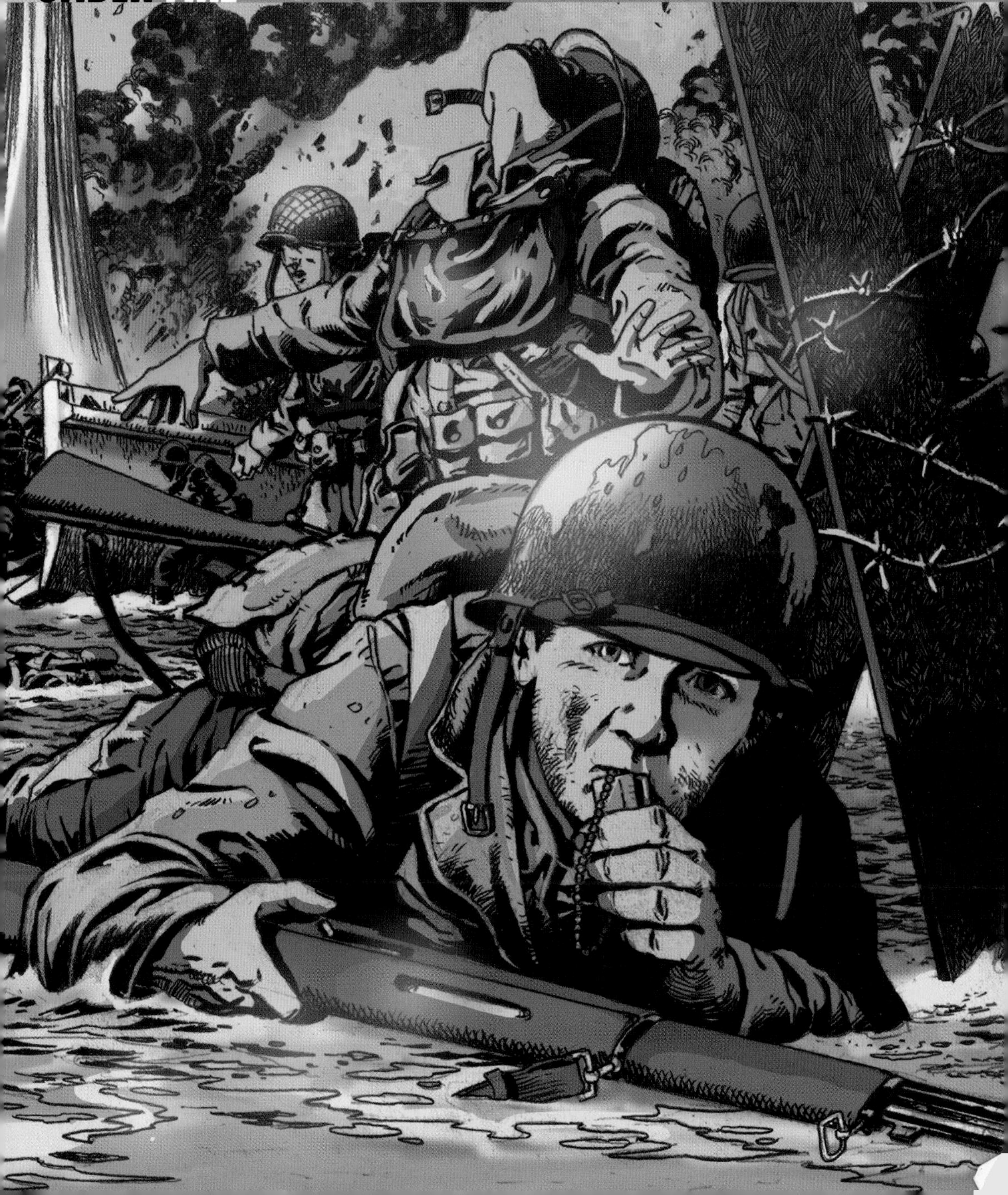

UNDER *FIRE*

INTRODUCTION TO D-DAY

STORMING FORTRESS EUROPE

It is spring 1944, and the war against Hitler's Germany has dragged on into its fifth year. France has suffered under German occupation since 1940, and since the evacuation of the British Expeditionary Force from Dunkirk in June 1940, no serious effort has been made to return Allied troops to the continent. A disastrous commando raid on Dieppe in 1942 taught the Allies a costly lesson: a frontal attack against a defended port would result in catastrophic losses.

Germany is under pressure from the Soviet Union in the east, which is beginning to press the attack after blunting Hitler's offensive at Kursk in 1943 and inflicting a major defeat at Stalingrad. The western Allies have been urged by Stalin to open a 'second front' that would force Germany to divert troops and equipment from the east, but Britain and the US were not ready for the invasion of the Continent originally planned for 1943. Until now, British Prime Minister Winston Churchill and US President Franklin D. Roosevelt have pressed the fight in other theatres around the world, while training soldiers and increasing production of the equipment and landing craft needed to prepare for a decisive invasion.

Now the Allies are committed, and a vast international task force under General Dwight D. Eisenhower has been assembled in the south of England, ready to embark for the

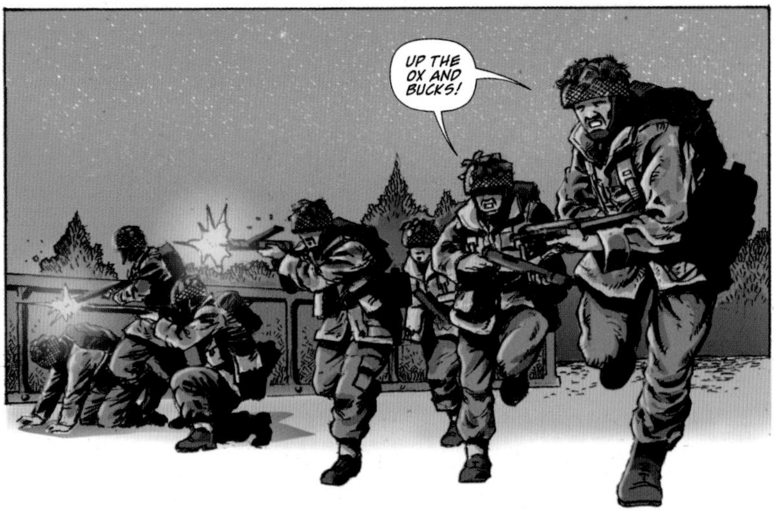
UP THE OX AND BUCKS!

beaches of Normandy, the chosen landing area. Relatively less well defended, these beaches are nonetheless part of Field Marshal Erwin Rommel's 'Atlantic Wall': fortified with strongpoints, mines and obstacles and defended by batteries inland. A huge intelligence operation, codenamed Fortitude, has also been under way to convince the German command that the blow will come elsewhere on the French coast: the Pas-de-Calais. This operation will prove incredibly successful, throwing the German military leadership into confusion and helping bring about catastrophic delays in the response.

On the night of 5/6 June, 1944, taking advantage of an unexpected break in bad weather, the vast force of over 5,000 ships, battleships, destroyers, minesweepers and landing craft stealthily approaches the coast of France down five channels swept clear of mines, heading for beaches codenamed Utah, Omaha, Gold, Juno and Sword. Ahead of them have gone British and American airborne assault troops, tasked with securing key bridges and roads behind the landing area to protect the invasion from the inevitable armoured counterattack. This is the Allies' one chance: if it succeeds, it will turn the tide of the war and

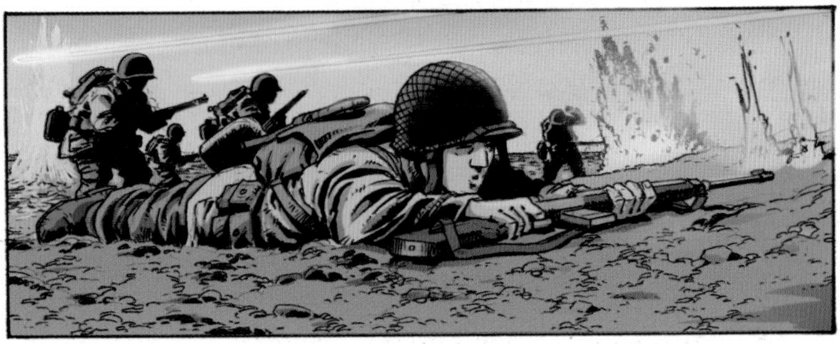

ensure Hitler's eventual defeat; if it fails, Germany will gain another year to strengthen the defences of Fortress Europe, develop the secret weapons to which Hitler attaches such importance, and turn against the advancing armies of the Soviet Union on the Eastern Front. History has nothing to offer more dramatic.

A NOTE FROM THE EDITOR

To convey the story of so complex an operation on such a vast scale is an ambitious undertaking, and to do so, we have focused on the stories of just a handful individuals and units from among the many thousands who played their part in the invasion and in the German response.

The story ranges from the airborne assaults against the town of Sainte-Mère-Église, the gun battery at Merville and the vital bridges at Bénouville and Ranville, to the German defence on the ground, the horrifically costly beach landings themselves, the US Rangers' assault on the sheer cliffs of Pointe du Hoc, the race by the 1st Special Service Brigade to relieve the exhausted paratroopers at the bridges, the chaotic response of the German command structure, the part played by French civilians and the fate of the long-awaited armoured counterattack by the 21st Panzer Division.

Although the dialogue is of course fictionalised, with the exception of the French commando, Léon Faivre, all those people named in the caption boxes are real historical figures, and their actions are reconstructed as closely as we could – with a little leeway for narrative and artistic licence.

00:00 -
MIDNIGHT

FRANCE, 6TH JUNE 1944

UTAH BEACH

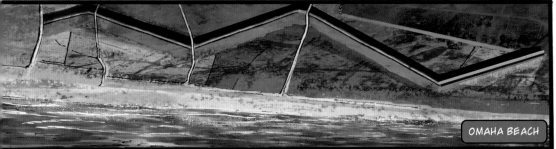

OMAHA BEACH

GOLD BEACH

JUNO BEACH

SWORD BEACH

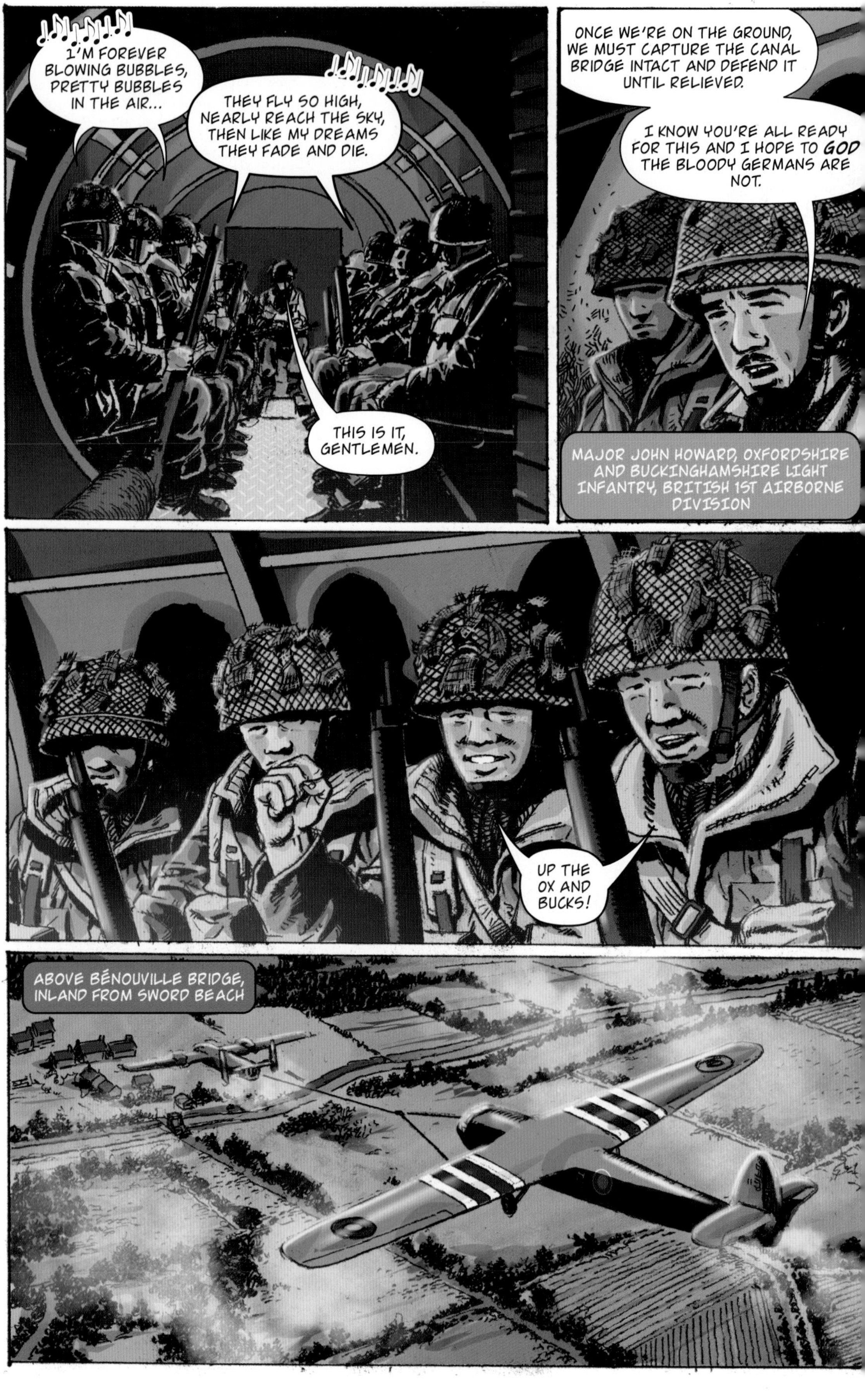
I'M FOREVER BLOWING BUBBLES, PRETTY BUBBLES IN THE AIR...
THEY FLY SO HIGH, NEARLY REACH THE SKY, THEN LIKE MY DREAMS THEY FADE AND DIE.
THIS IS IT, GENTLEMEN.
ONCE WE'RE ON THE GROUND, WE MUST CAPTURE THE CANAL BRIDGE INTACT AND DEFEND IT UNTIL RELIEVED.
I KNOW YOU'RE ALL READY FOR THIS AND I HOPE TO **GOD** THE BLOODY GERMANS ARE NOT.
MAJOR JOHN HOWARD, OXFORDSHIRE AND BUCKINGHAMSHIRE LIGHT INFANTRY, BRITISH 1ST AIRBORNE DIVISION
UP THE OX AND BUCKS!
ABOVE BÉNOUVILLE BRIDGE, INLAND FROM SWORD BEACH

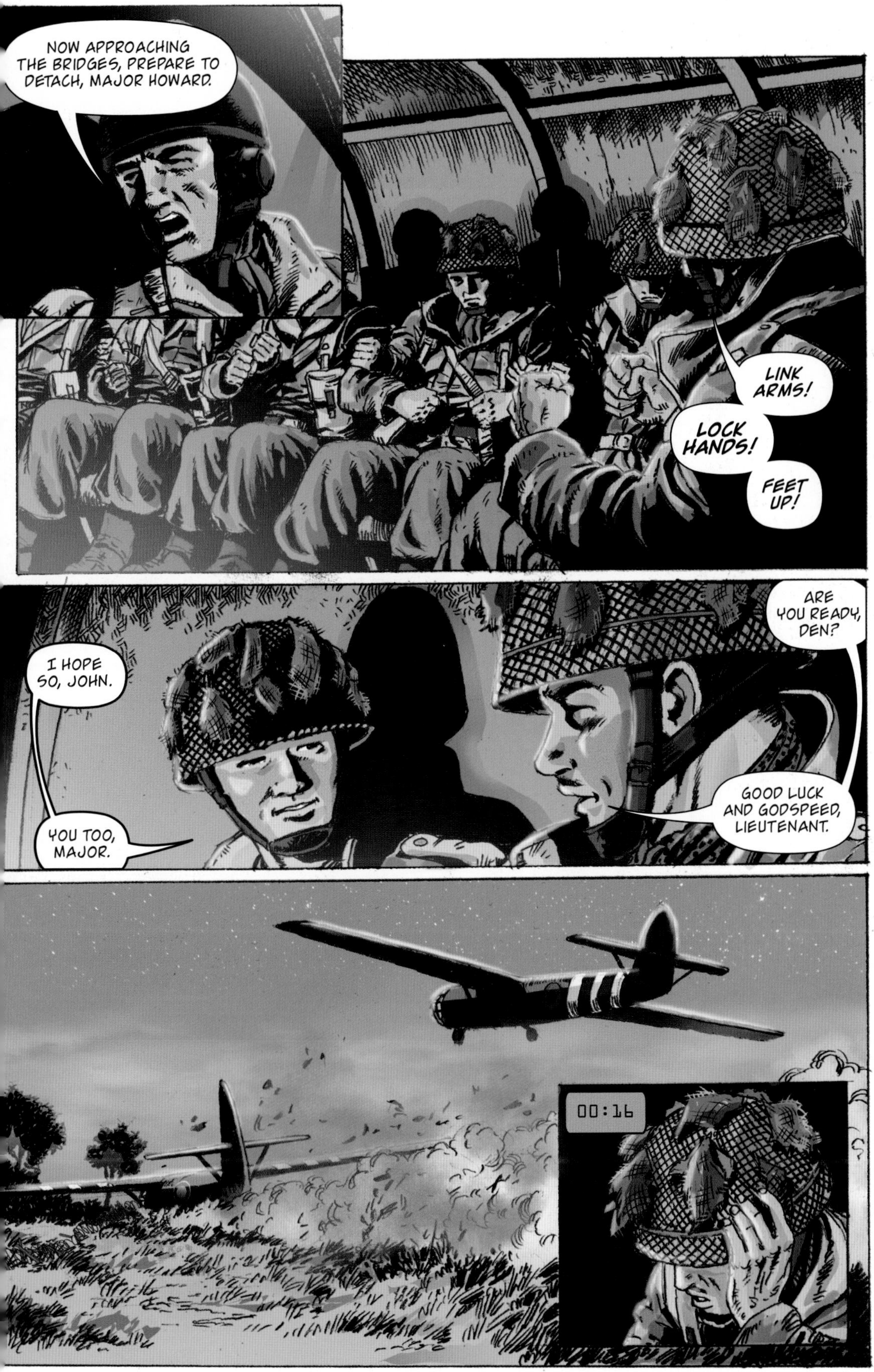
NOW APPROACHING THE BRIDGES, PREPARE TO DETACH, MAJOR HOWARD.
LINK ARMS!
LOCK HANDS!
FEET UP!
ARE YOU READY, DEN?
I HOPE SO, JOHN.
GOOD LUCK AND GODSPEED, LIEUTENANT.
YOU TOO, MAJOR.
00:16

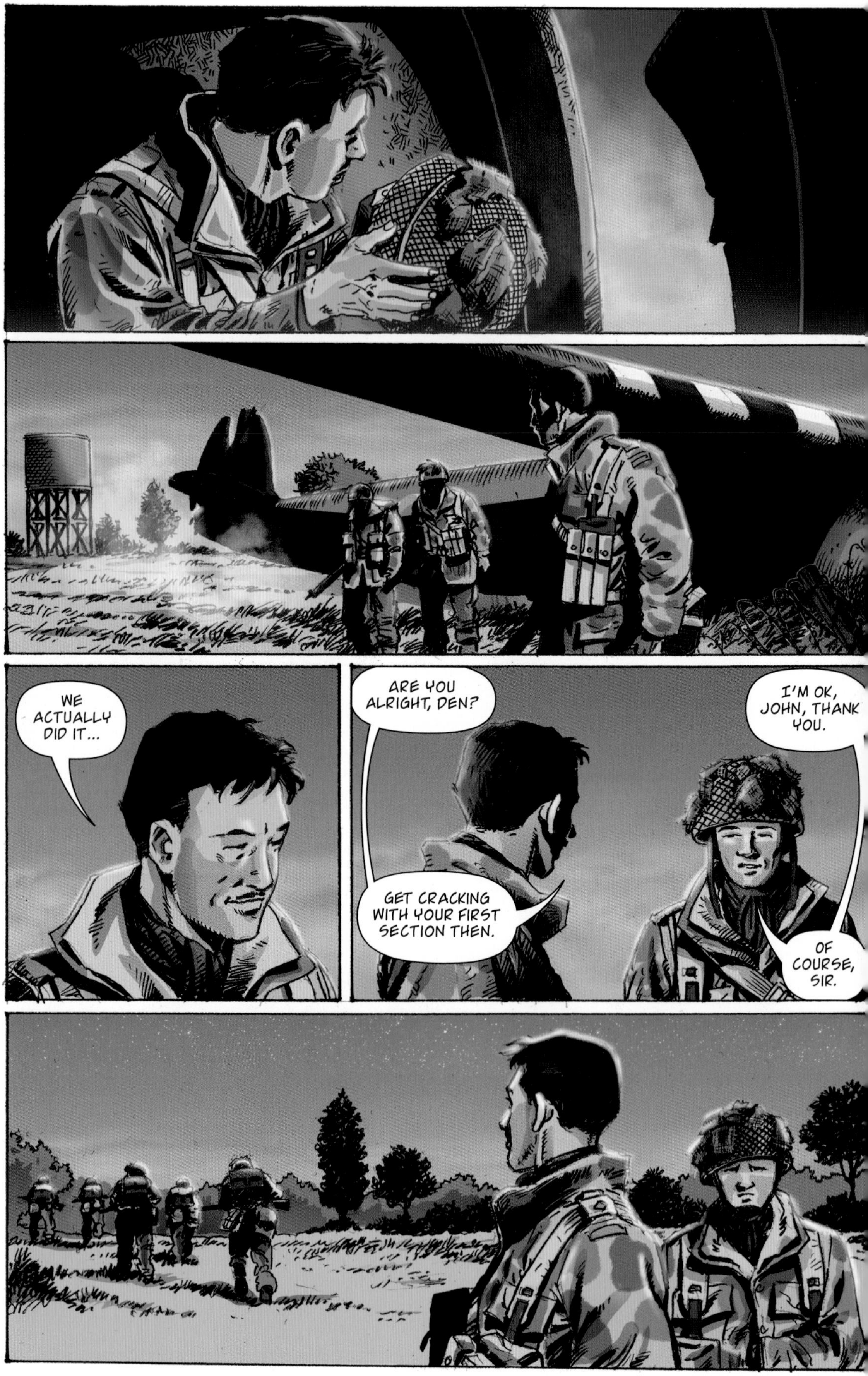
WE ACTUALLY DID IT...
ARE YOU ALRIGHT, DEN?
I'M OK, JOHN, THANK YOU.
GET CRACKING WITH YOUR FIRST SECTION THEN.
OF COURSE, SIR.

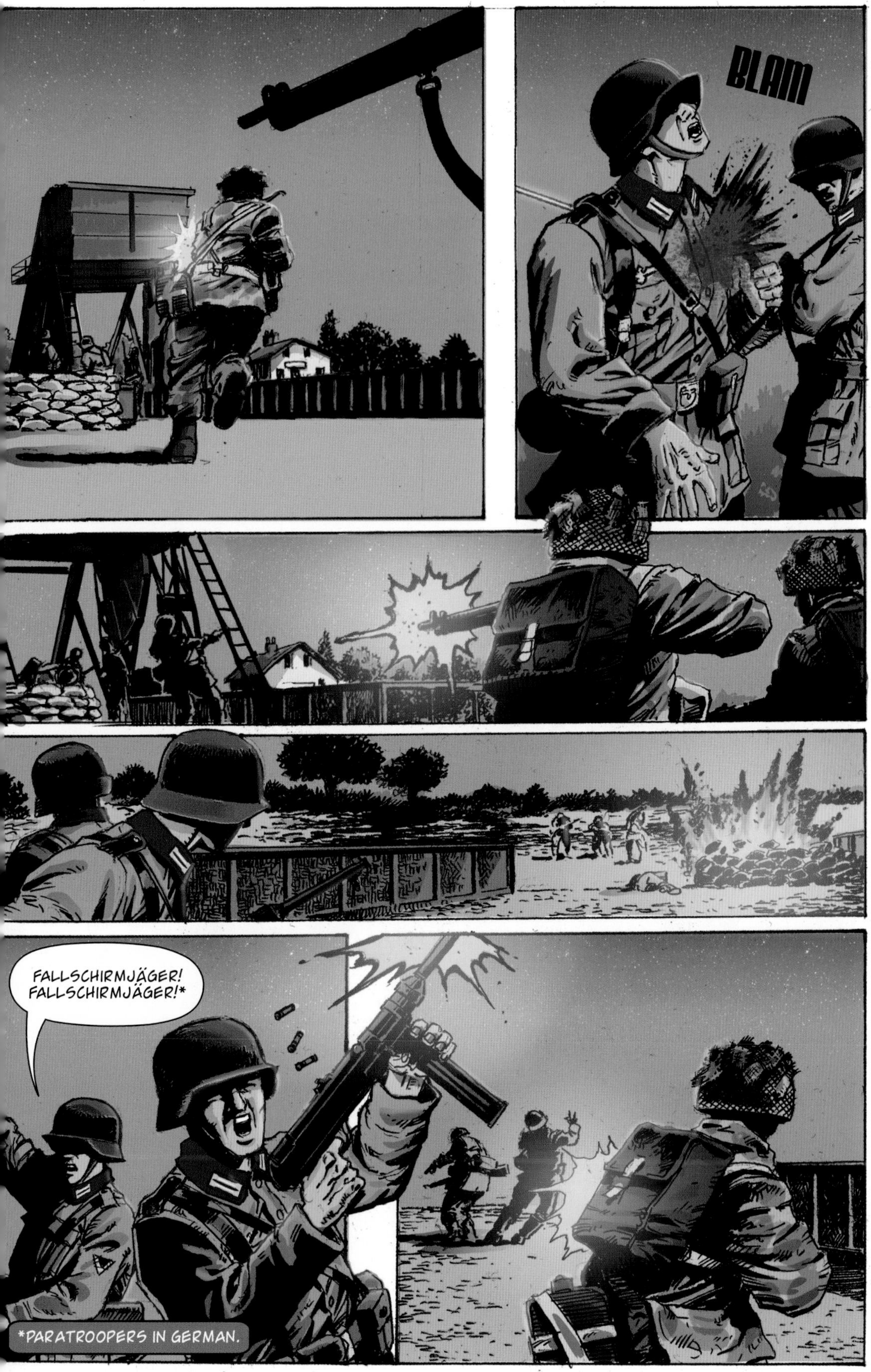
BLAM
FALLSCHIRMJÄGER! FALLSCHIRMJÄGER!*
*PARATROOPERS IN GERMAN.

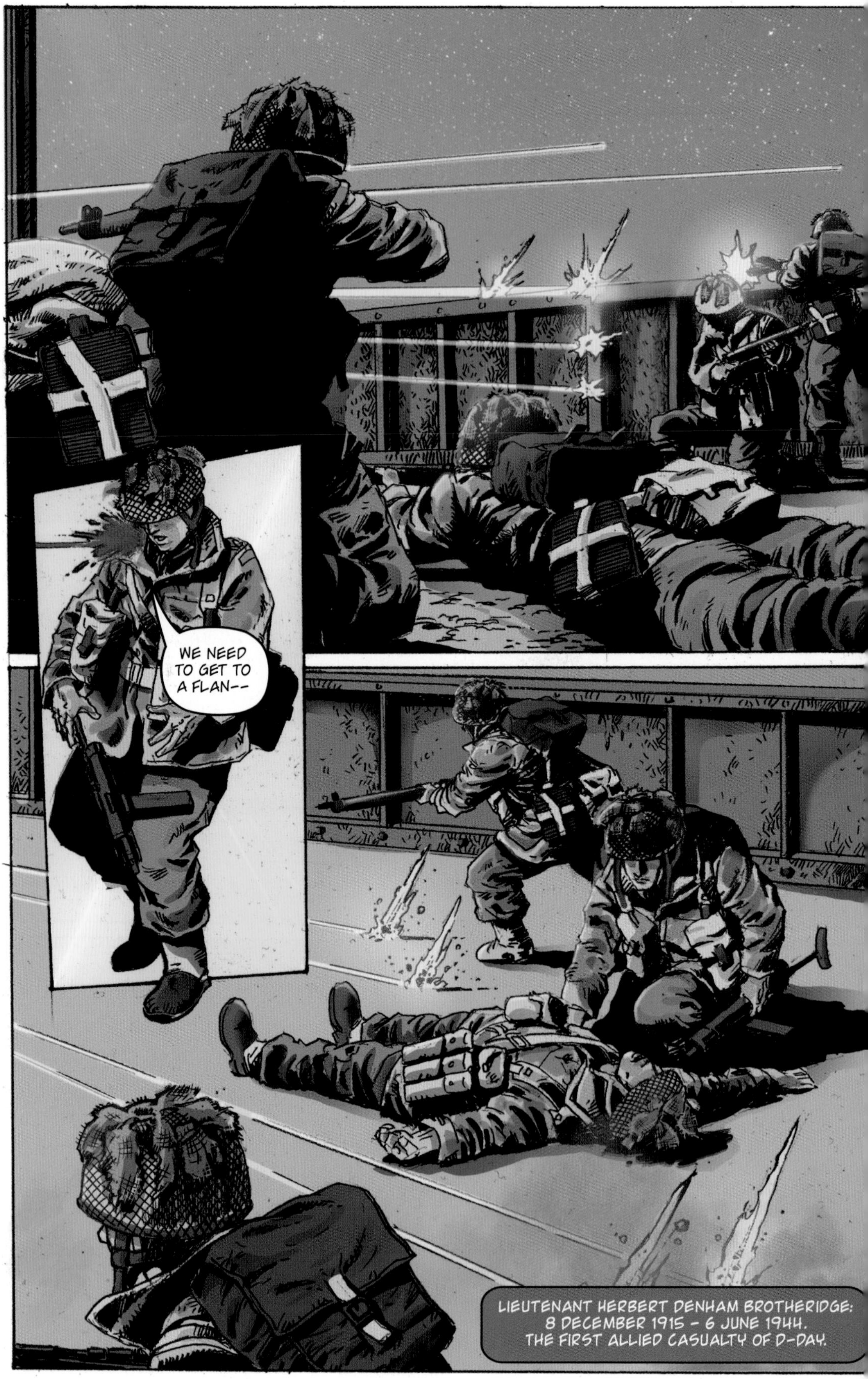
WE NEED TO GET TO A FLAN--
LIEUTENANT HERBERT DENHAM BROTHERIDGE: 8 DECEMBER 1915 – 6 JUNE 1944. THE FIRST ALLIED CASUALTY OF D-DAY.

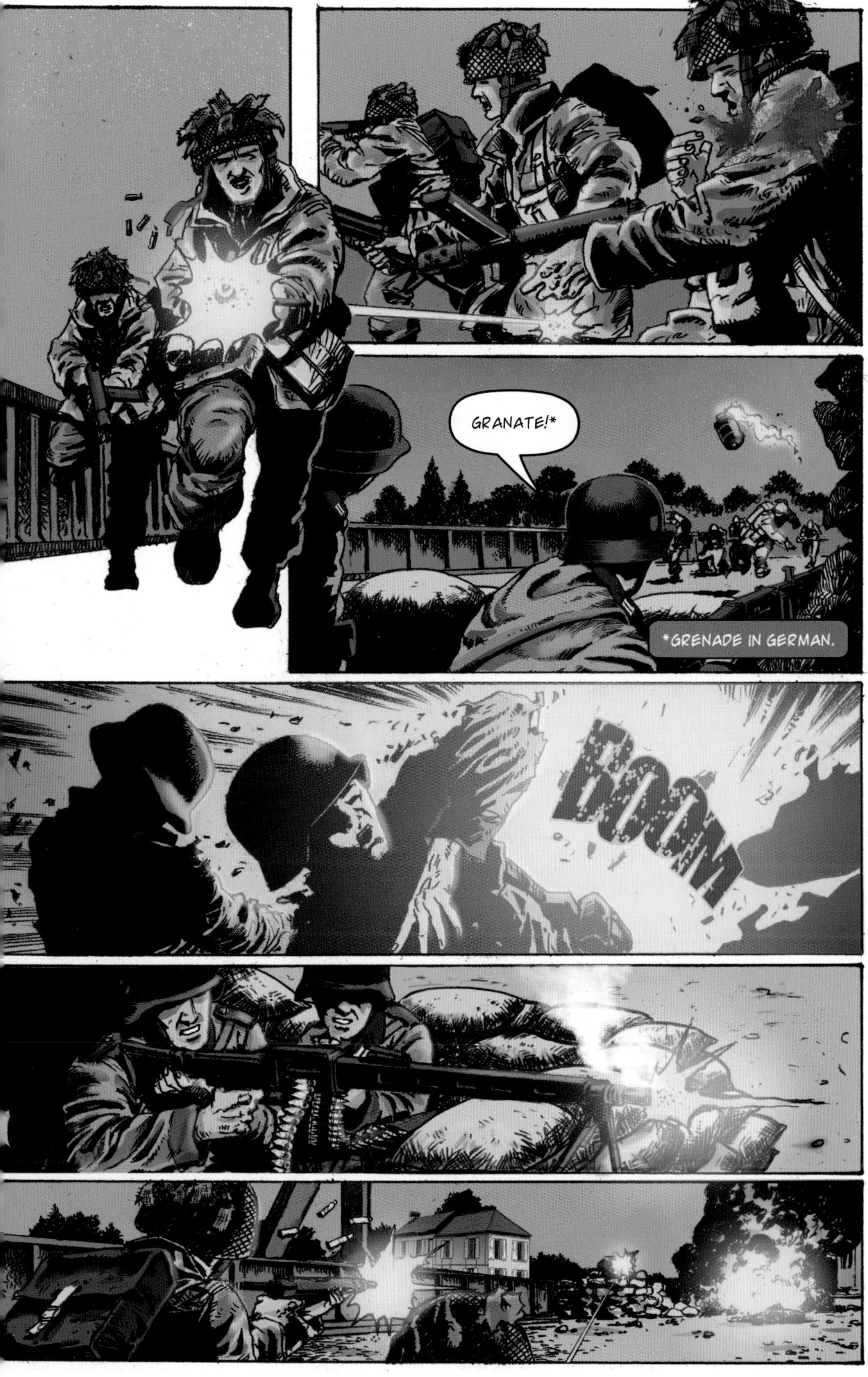
GRANATE!*
*GRENADE IN GERMAN.
BOOM

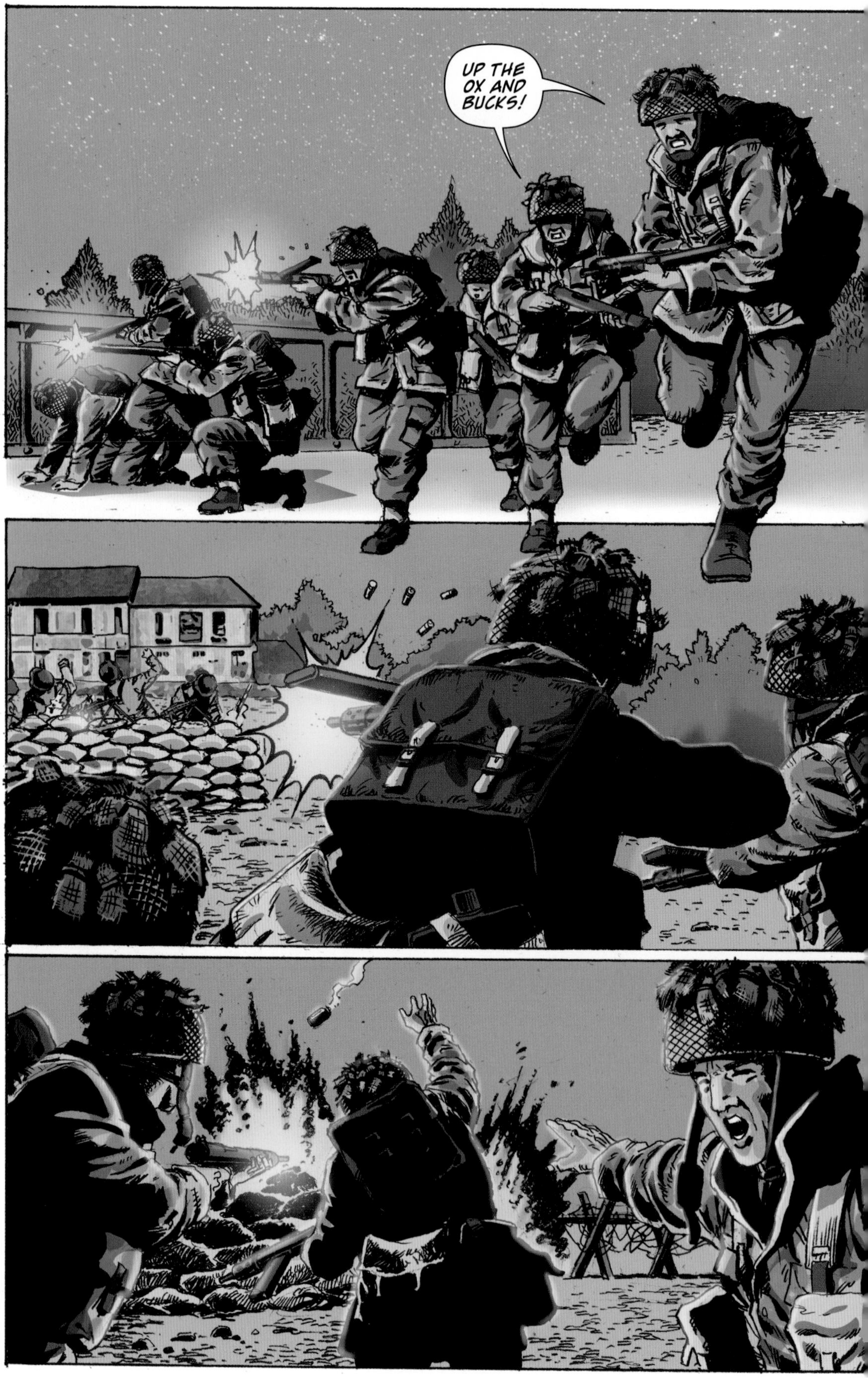
UP THE OX AND BUCKS!

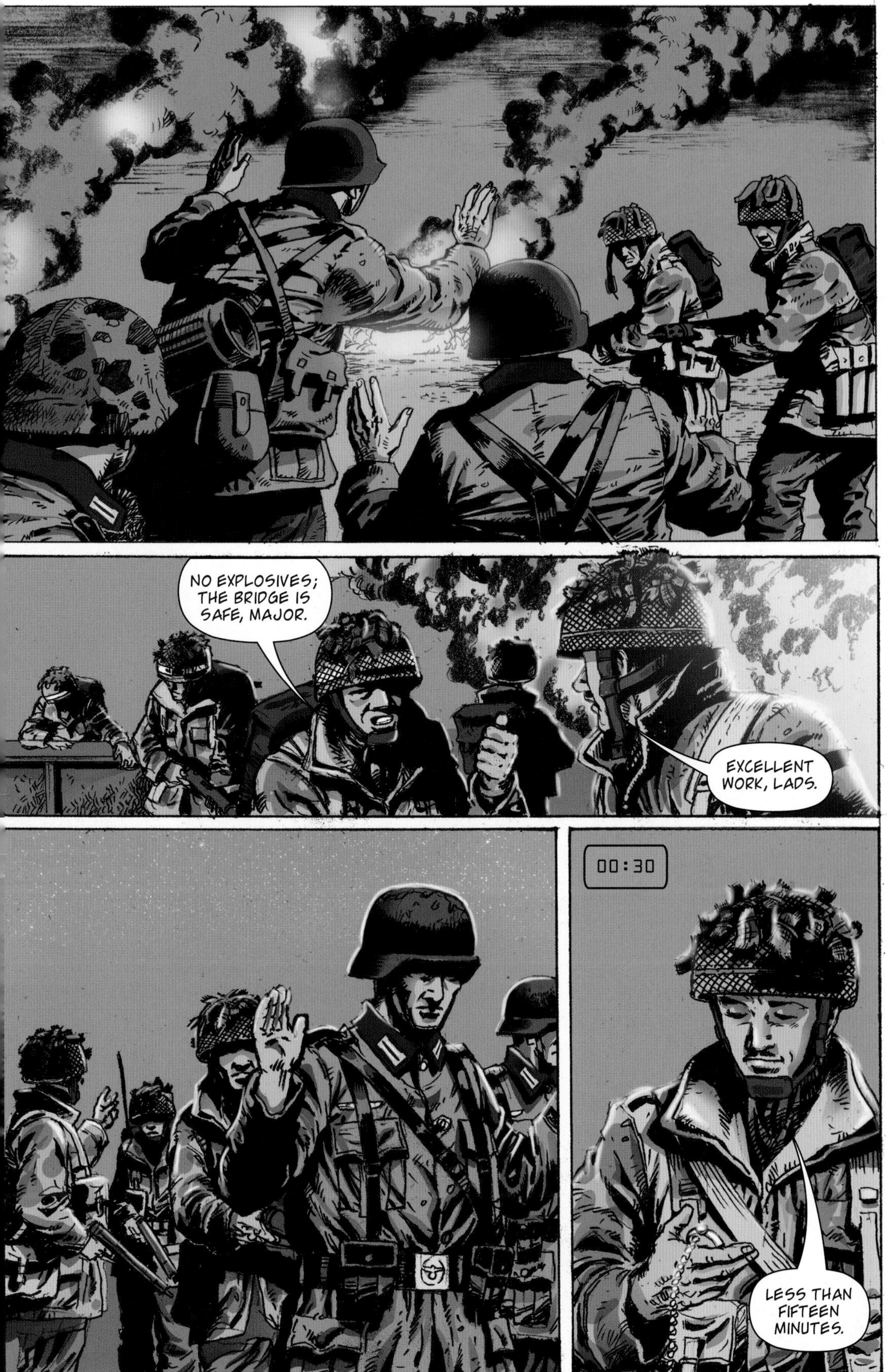
NO EXPLOSIVES; THE BRIDGE IS SAFE, MAJOR.
EXCELLENT WORK, LADS.
00:30
LESS THAN FIFTEEN MINUTES.

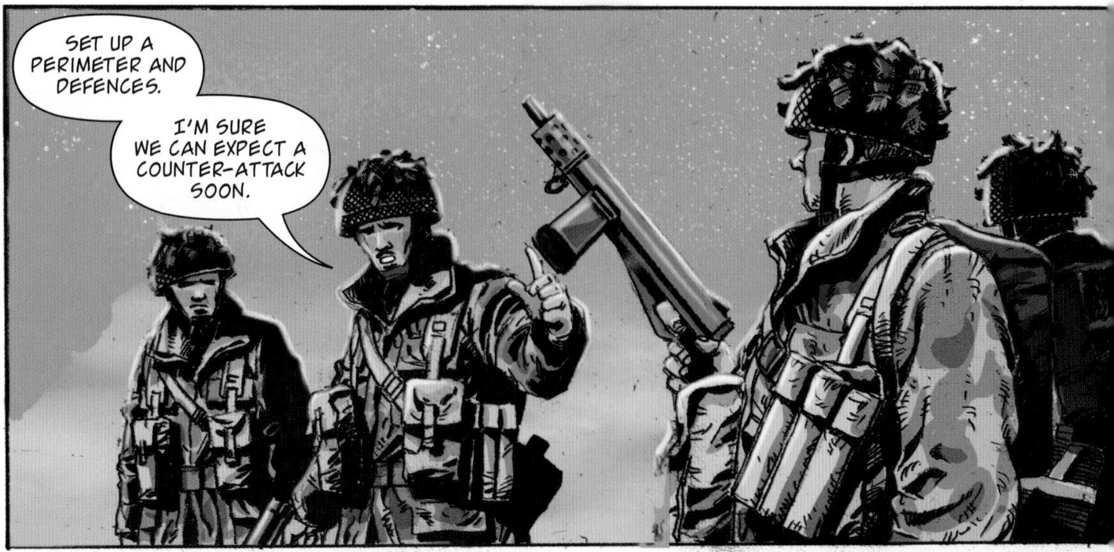
SET UP A PERIMETER AND DEFENCES.
I'M SURE WE CAN EXPECT A COUNTER-ATTACK SOON.

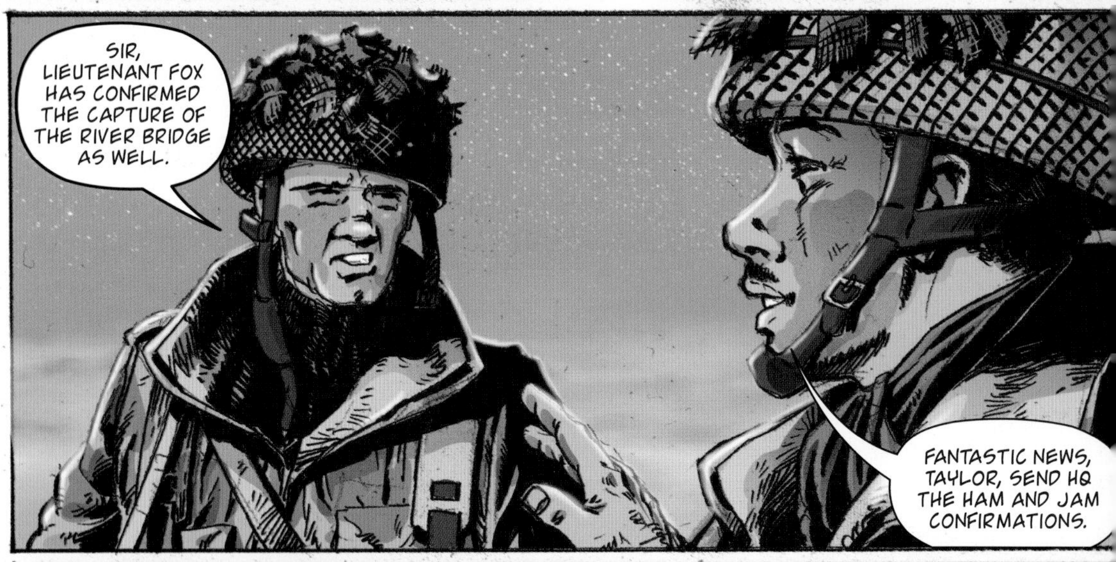
SIR, LIEUTENANT FOX HAS CONFIRMED THE CAPTURE OF THE RIVER BRIDGE AS WELL.
FANTASTIC NEWS, TAYLOR, SEND HQ THE HAM AND JAM CONFIRMATIONS.

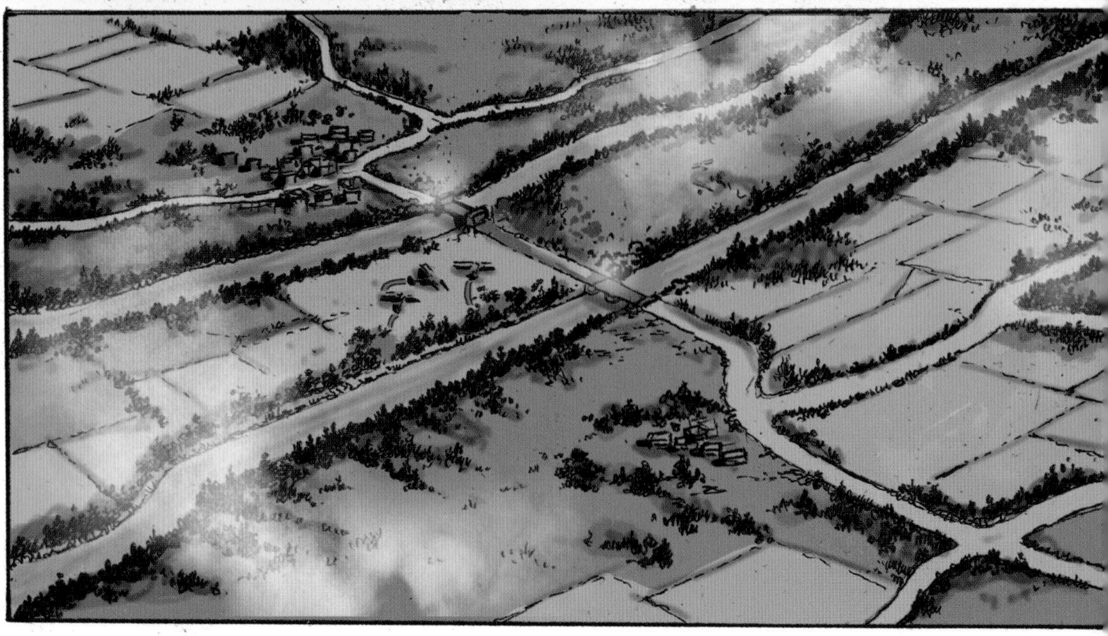

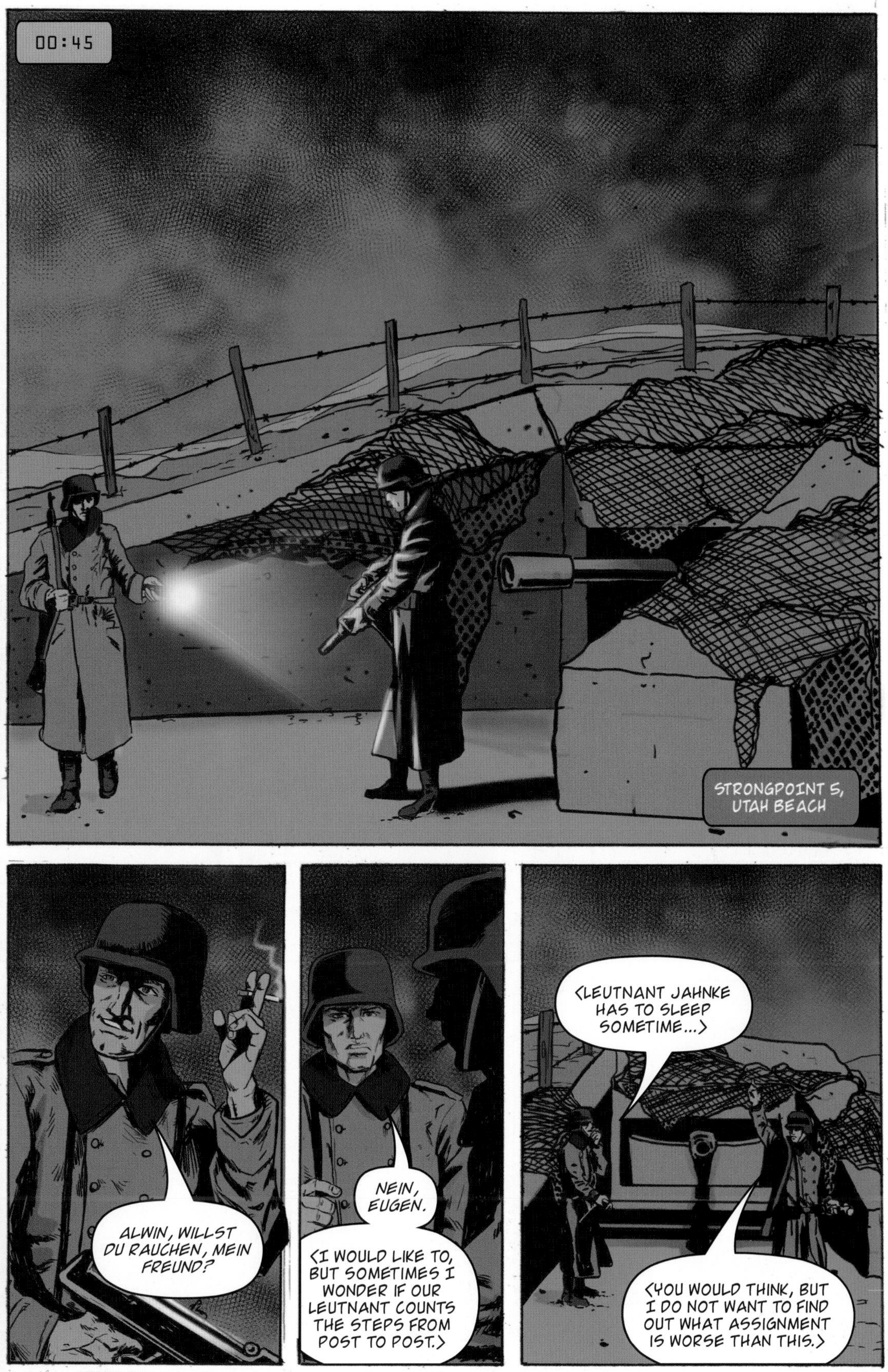

00:45
STRONGPOINT 5, UTAH BEACH
ALWIN, WILLST DU RAUCHEN, MEIN FREUND?
NEIN, EUGEN.
<I WOULD LIKE TO, BUT SOMETIMES I WONDER IF OUR LEUTNANT COUNTS THE STEPS FROM POST TO POST.>
<LEUTNANT JAHNKE HAS TO SLEEP SOMETIME...>
<YOU WOULD THINK, BUT I DO NOT WANT TO FIND OUT WHAT ASSIGNMENT IS WORSE THAN THIS.>

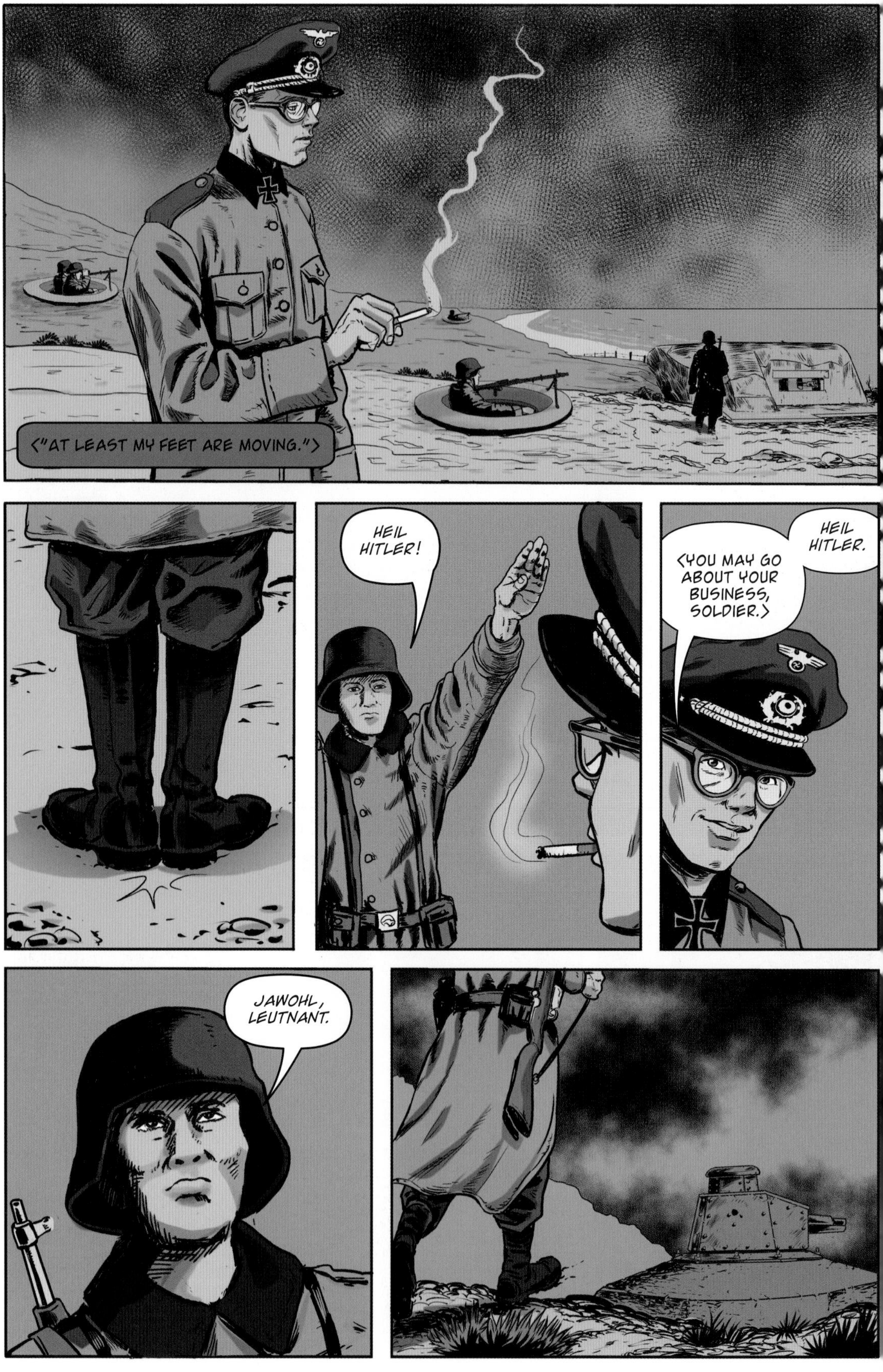

<"AT LEAST MY FEET ARE MOVING.">
HEIL HITLER!
HEIL HITLER.
<YOU MAY GO ABOUT YOUR BUSINESS, SOLDIER.>
JAWOHL, LEUTNANT.

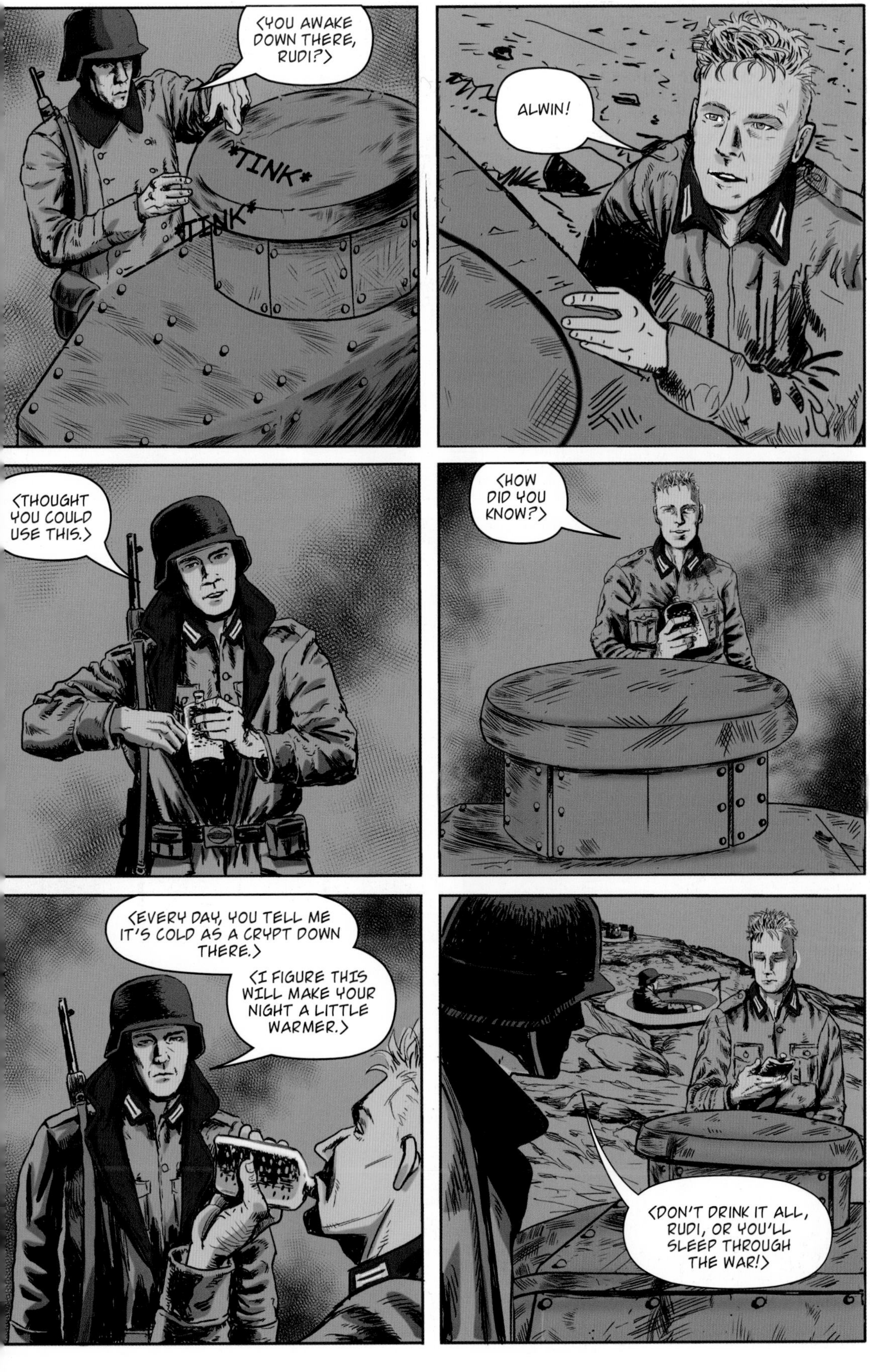
<YOU AWAKE DOWN THERE, RUDI?>
TINK
TINK
ALWIN!
<THOUGHT YOU COULD USE THIS.>
<HOW DID YOU KNOW?>
<EVERY DAY, YOU TELL ME IT'S COLD AS A CRYPT DOWN THERE.>
<I FIGURE THIS WILL MAKE YOUR NIGHT A LITTLE WARMER.>
<DON'T DRINK IT ALL, RUDI, OR YOU'LL SLEEP THROUGH THE WAR!>

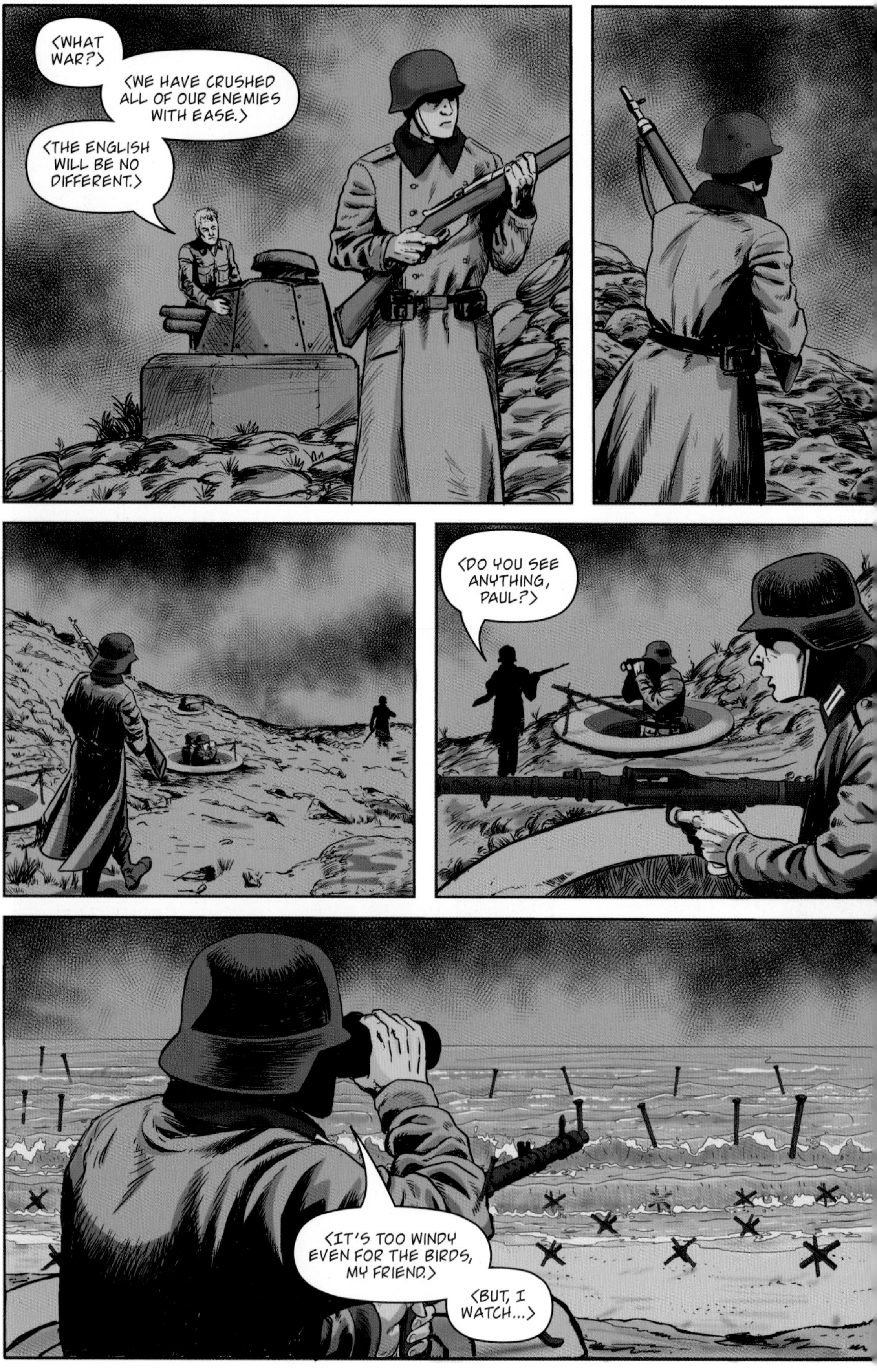

<WHAT WAR?>
<WE HAVE CRUSHED ALL OF OUR ENEMIES WITH EASE.>
<THE ENGLISH WILL BE NO DIFFERENT.>
<DO YOU SEE ANYTHING, PAUL?>
<IT'S TOO WINDY EVEN FOR THE BIRDS, MY FRIEND.>
<BUT, I WATCH...>

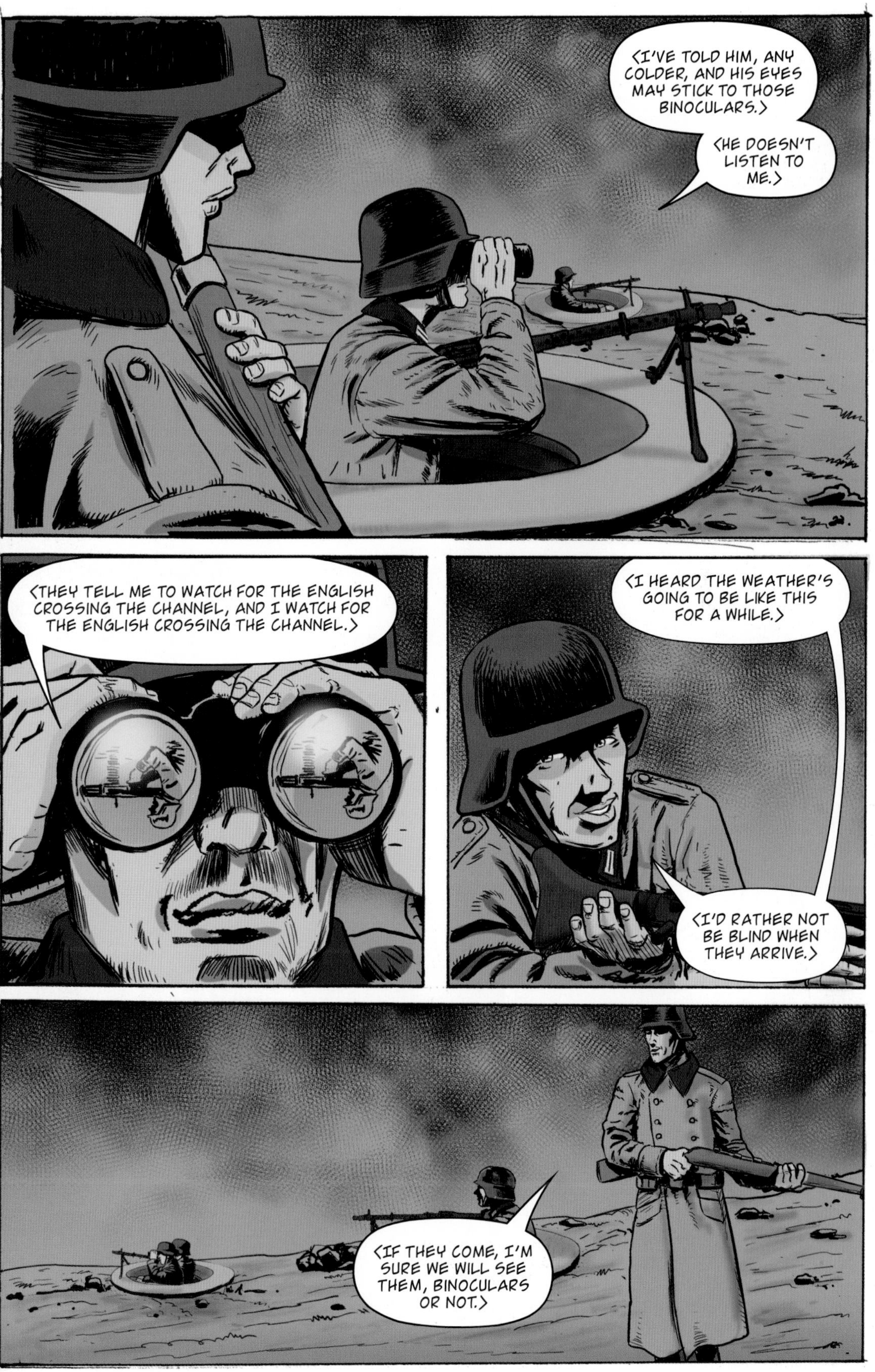

<I'VE TOLD HIM, ANY COLDER, AND HIS EYES MAY STICK TO THOSE BINOCULARS.>
<HE DOESN'T LISTEN TO ME.>
<THEY TELL ME TO WATCH FOR THE ENGLISH CROSSING THE CHANNEL, AND I WATCH FOR THE ENGLISH CROSSING THE CHANNEL.>
<I HEARD THE WEATHER'S GOING TO BE LIKE THIS FOR A WHILE.>
<I'D RATHER NOT BE BLIND WHEN THEY ARRIVE.>
<IF THEY COME, I'M SURE WE WILL SEE THEM, BINOCULARS OR NOT.>

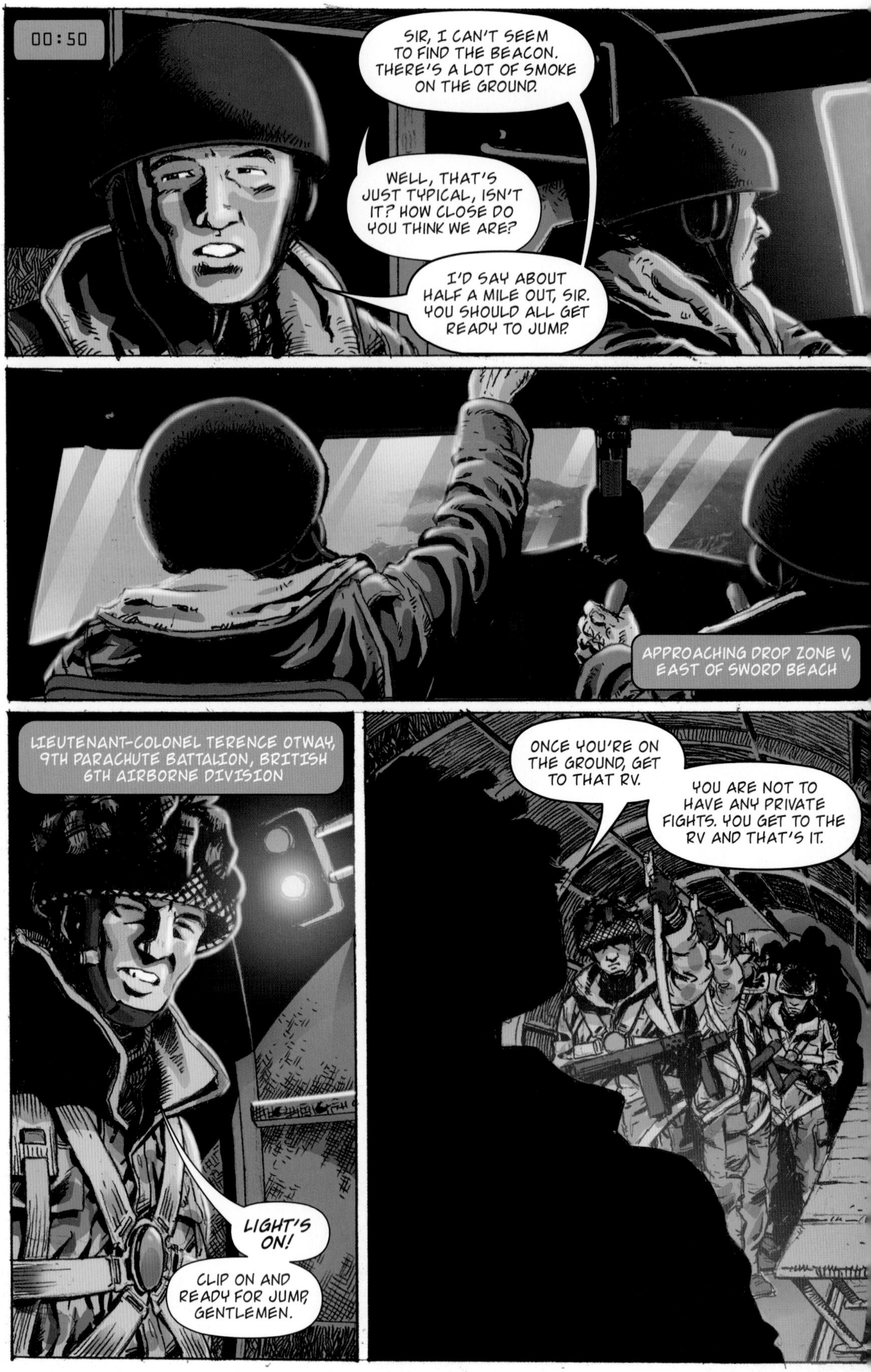
00:50
SIR, I CAN'T SEEM TO FIND THE BEACON. THERE'S A LOT OF SMOKE ON THE GROUND.
WELL, THAT'S JUST TYPICAL, ISN'T IT? HOW CLOSE DO YOU THINK WE ARE?
I'D SAY ABOUT HALF A MILE OUT, SIR. YOU SHOULD ALL GET READY TO JUMP.
APPROACHING DROP ZONE V, EAST OF SWORD BEACH
LIEUTENANT-COLONEL TERENCE OTWAY, 9TH PARACHUTE BATTALION, BRITISH 6TH AIRBORNE DIVISION
LIGHT'S ON!
CLIP ON AND READY FOR JUMP, GENTLEMEN.
ONCE YOU'RE ON THE GROUND, GET TO THAT RV.
YOU ARE NOT TO HAVE ANY PRIVATE FIGHTS. YOU GET TO THE RV AND THAT'S IT.

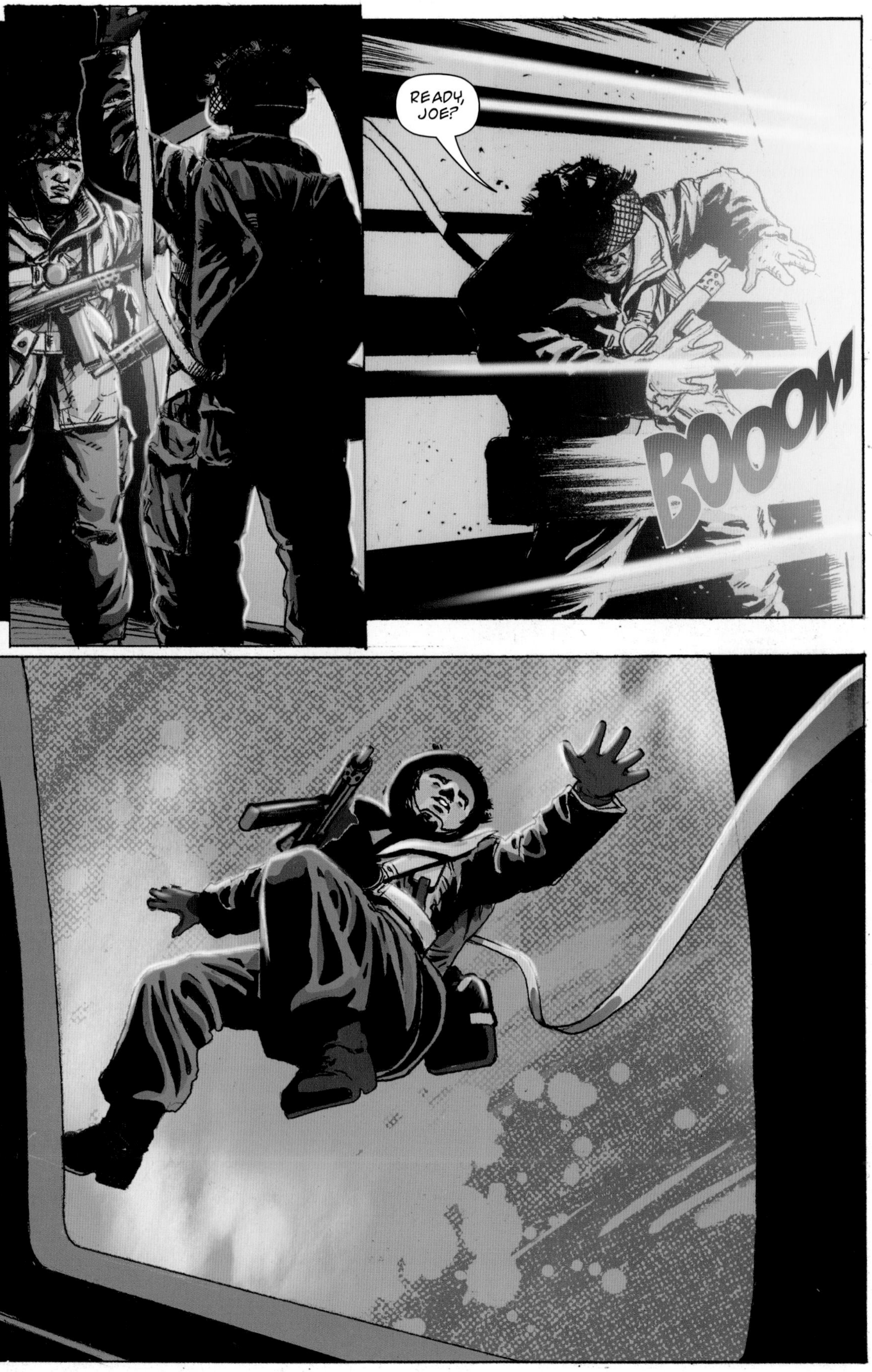
READY, JOE?
BOOOM

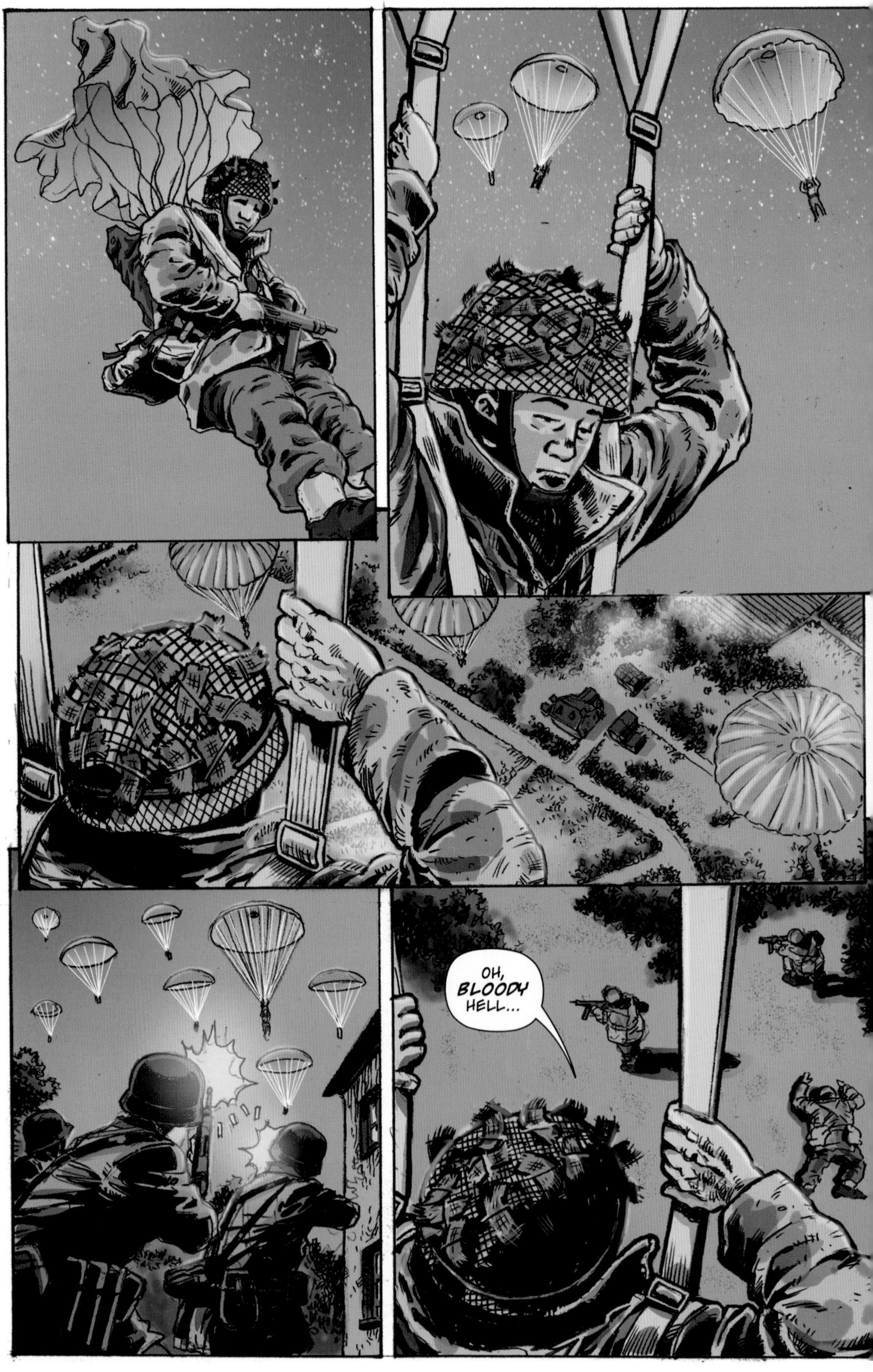
OH, BLOODY HELL...

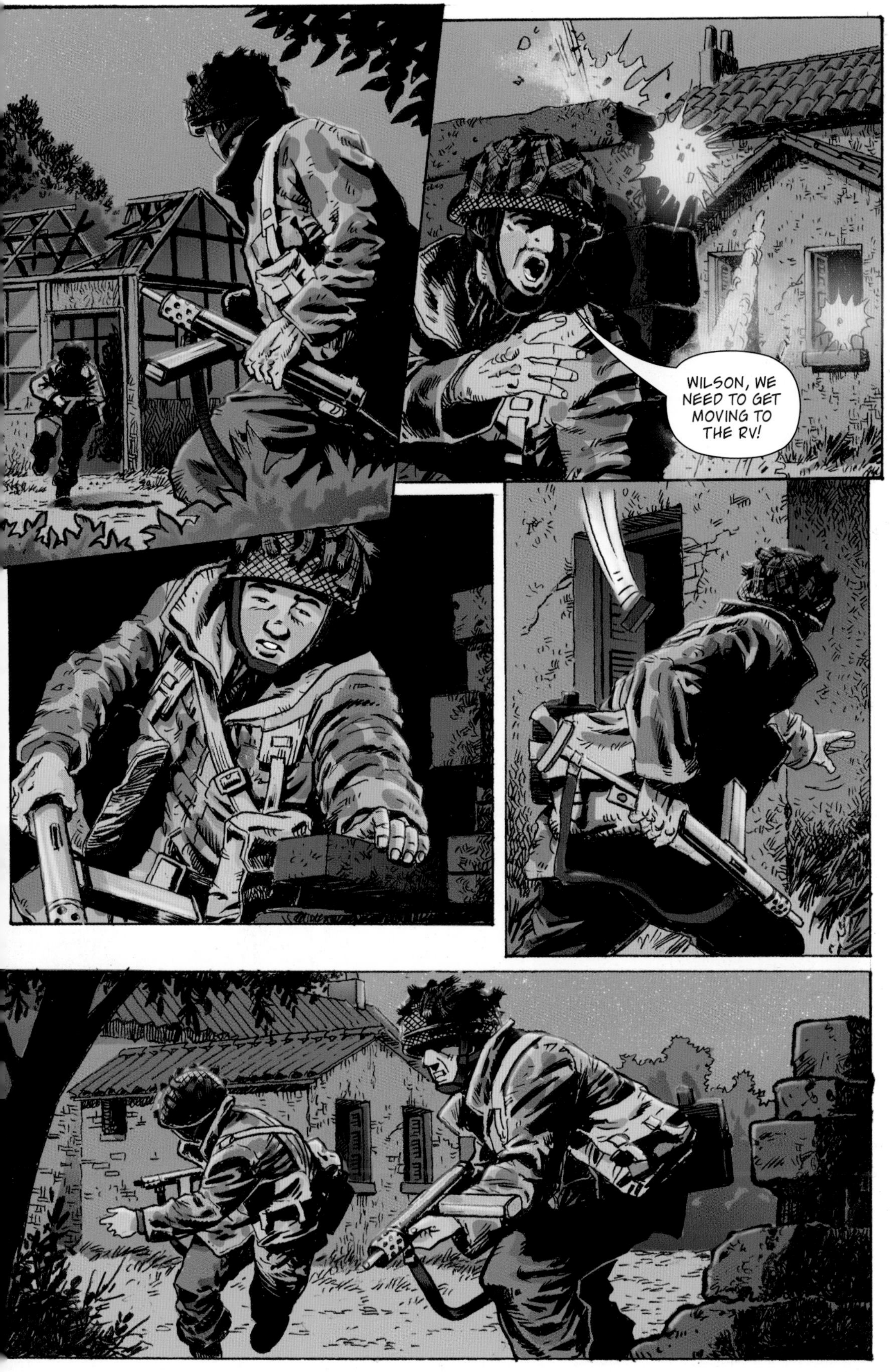
WILSON, WE NEED TO GET MOVING TO THE RV!

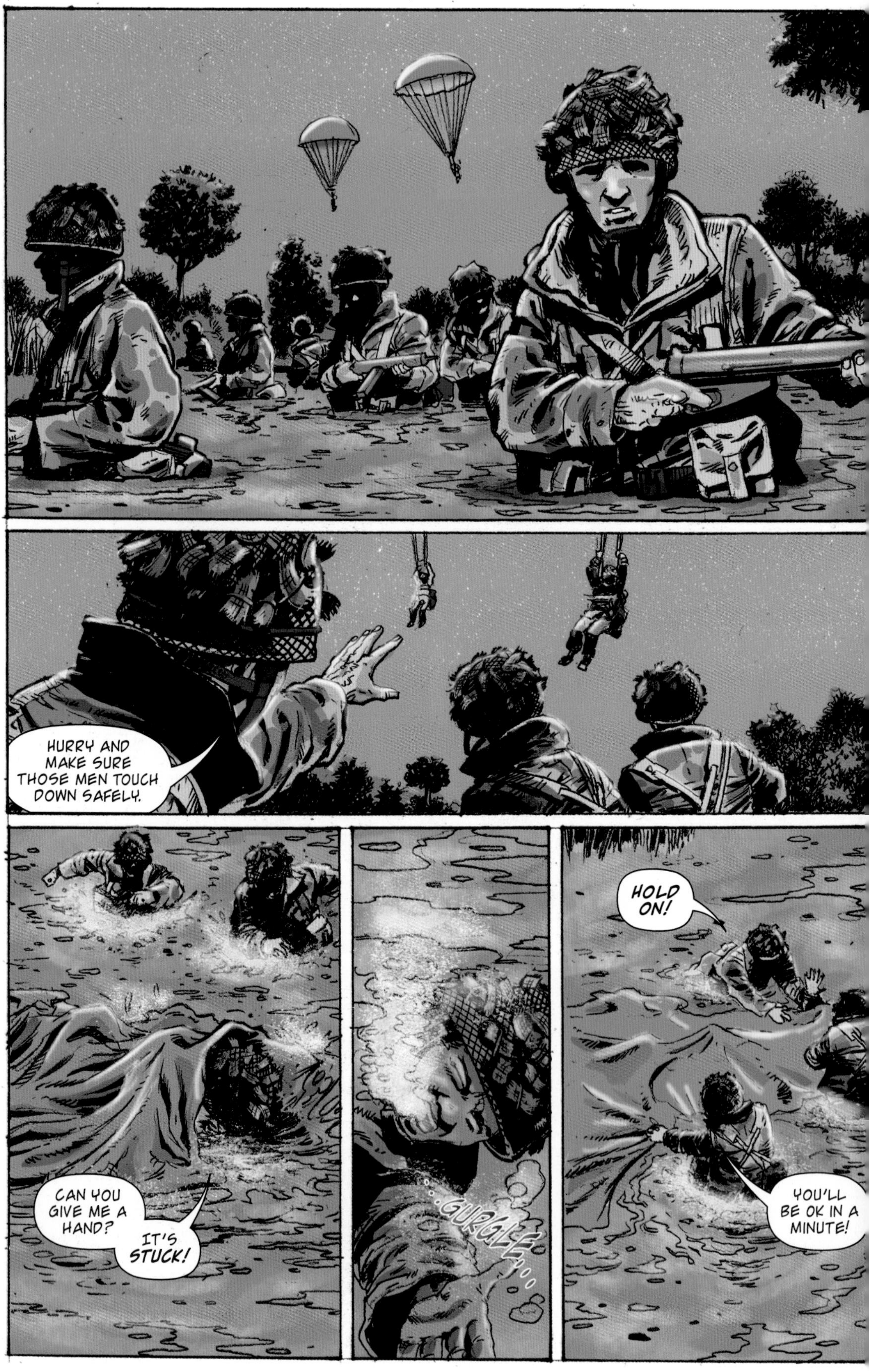
HURRY AND MAKE SURE THOSE MEN TOUCH DOWN SAFELY.
CAN YOU GIVE ME A HAND?
IT'S STUCK!
GURGLE
HOLD ON!
YOU'LL BE OK IN A MINUTE!

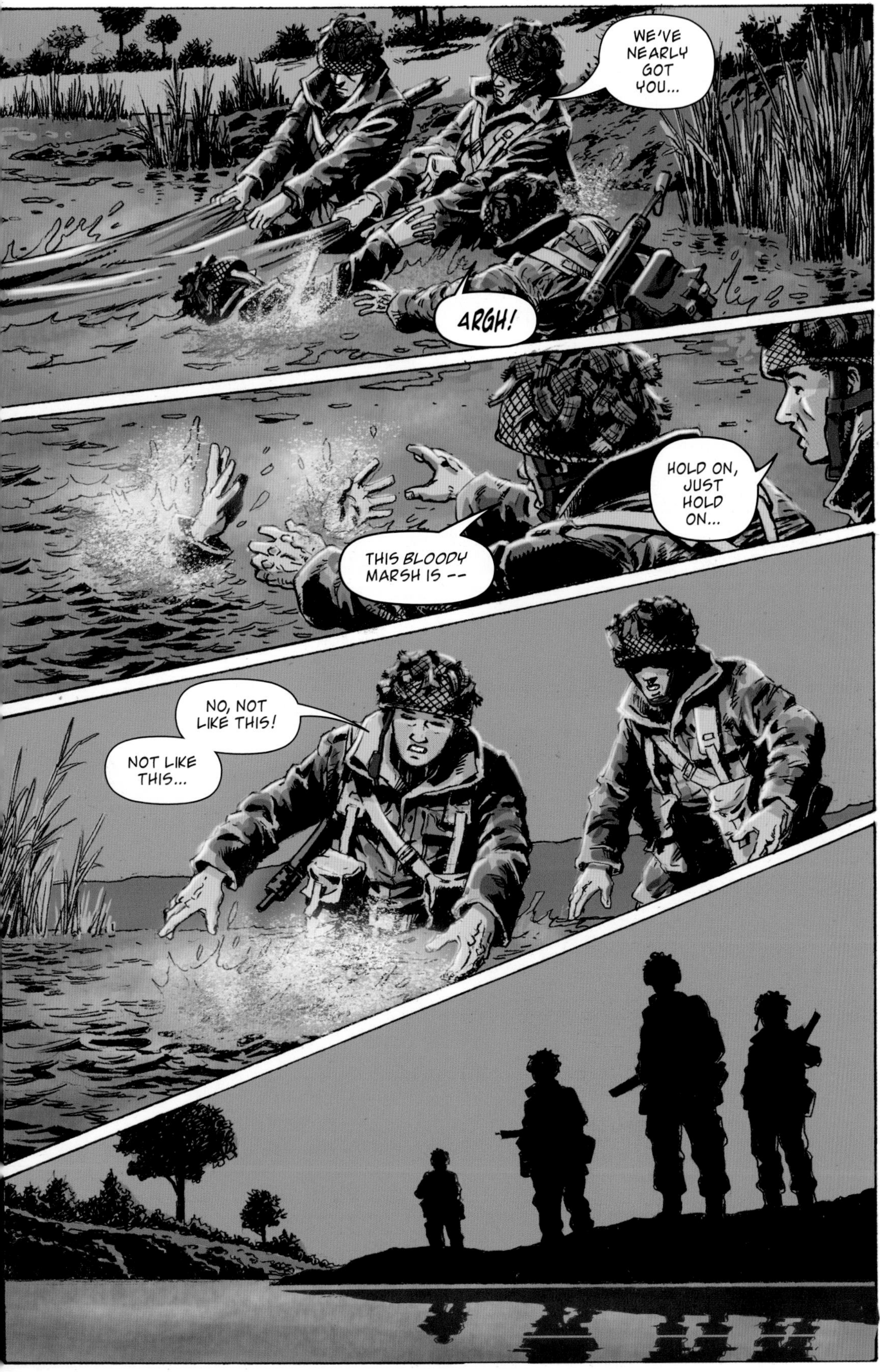
WE'VE NEARLY GOT YOU...
ARGH!
HOLD ON, JUST HOLD ON...
THIS BLOODY MARSH IS --
NO, NOT LIKE THIS!
NOT LIKE THIS...

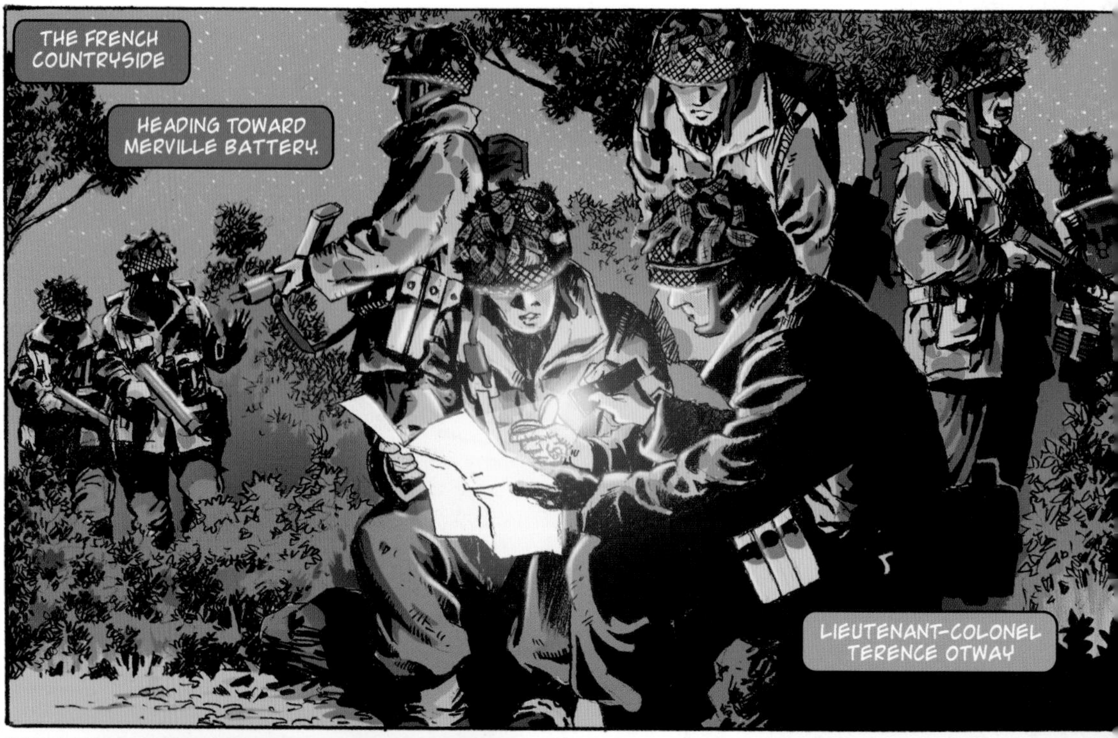
THE FRENCH COUNTRYSIDE
HEADING TOWARD MERVILLE BATTERY.
LIEUTENANT-COLONEL TERENCE OTWAY

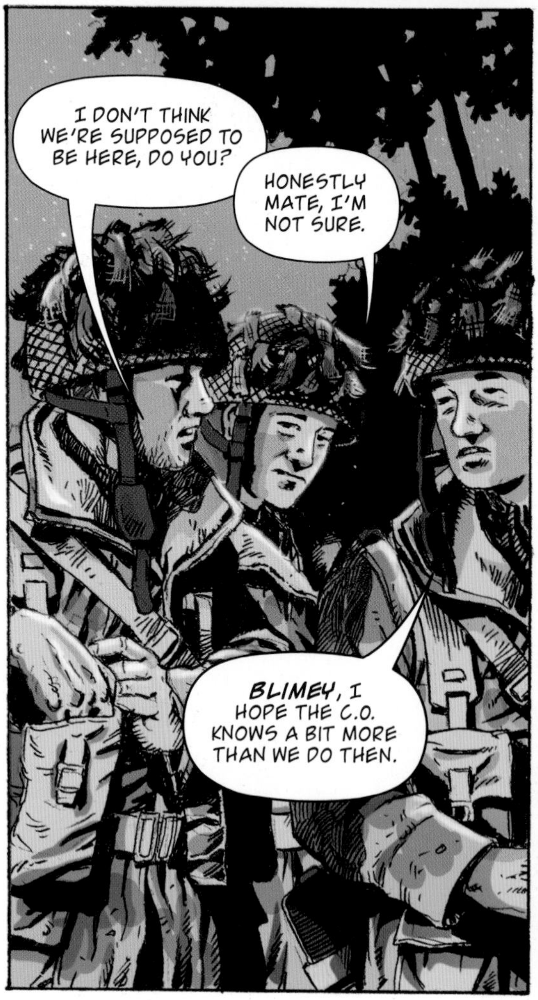
I DON'T THINK WE'RE SUPPOSED TO BE HERE, DO YOU?
HONESTLY MATE, I'M NOT SURE.
BLIMEY, I HOPE THE C.O. KNOWS A BIT MORE THAN WE DO THEN.

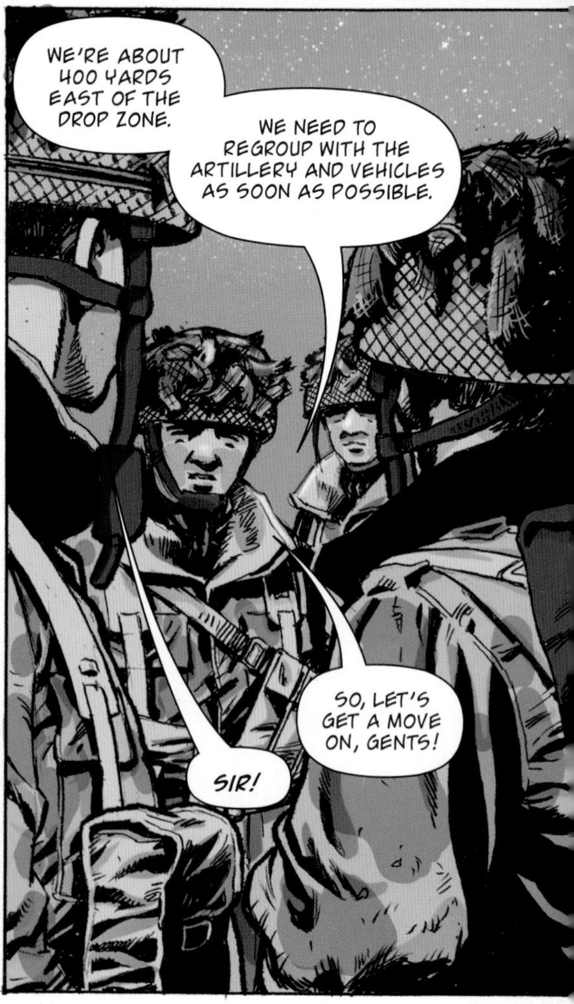
WE'RE ABOUT 400 YARDS EAST OF THE DROP ZONE.
WE NEED TO REGROUP WITH THE ARTILLERY AND VEHICLES AS SOON AS POSSIBLE.
SO, LET'S GET A MOVE ON, GENTS!
SIR!

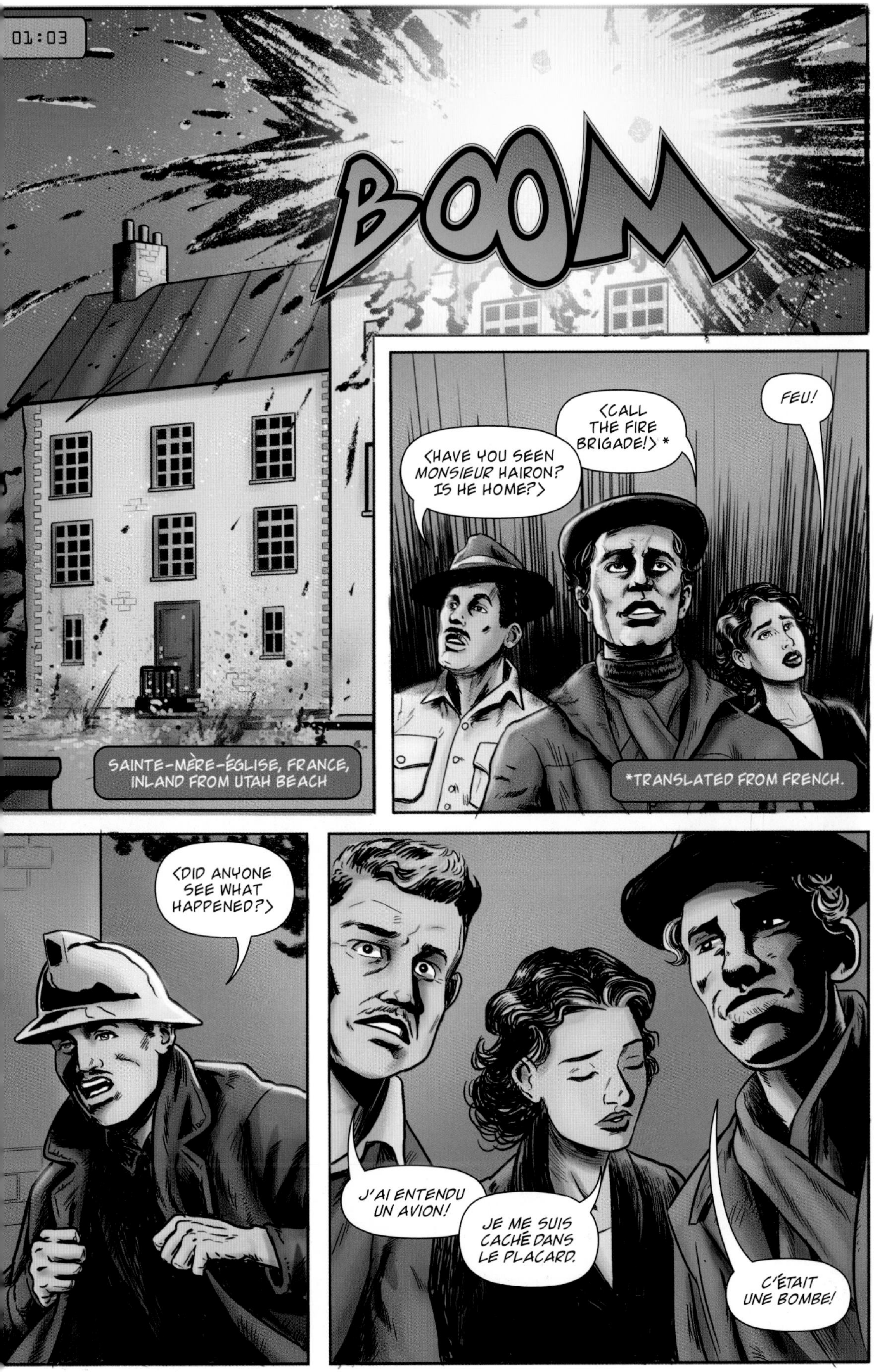
01:03
BOOM
SAINTE-MÈRE-ÉGLISE, FRANCE, INLAND FROM UTAH BEACH
<HAVE YOU SEEN MONSIEUR HAIRON? IS HE HOME?>
<CALL THE FIRE BRIGADE!> *
FEU!
*TRANSLATED FROM FRENCH.
<DID ANYONE SEE WHAT HAPPENED?>
J'AI ENTENDU UN AVION!
JE ME SUIS CACHÉ DANS LE PLACARD.
C'ÉTAIT UNE BOMBE!

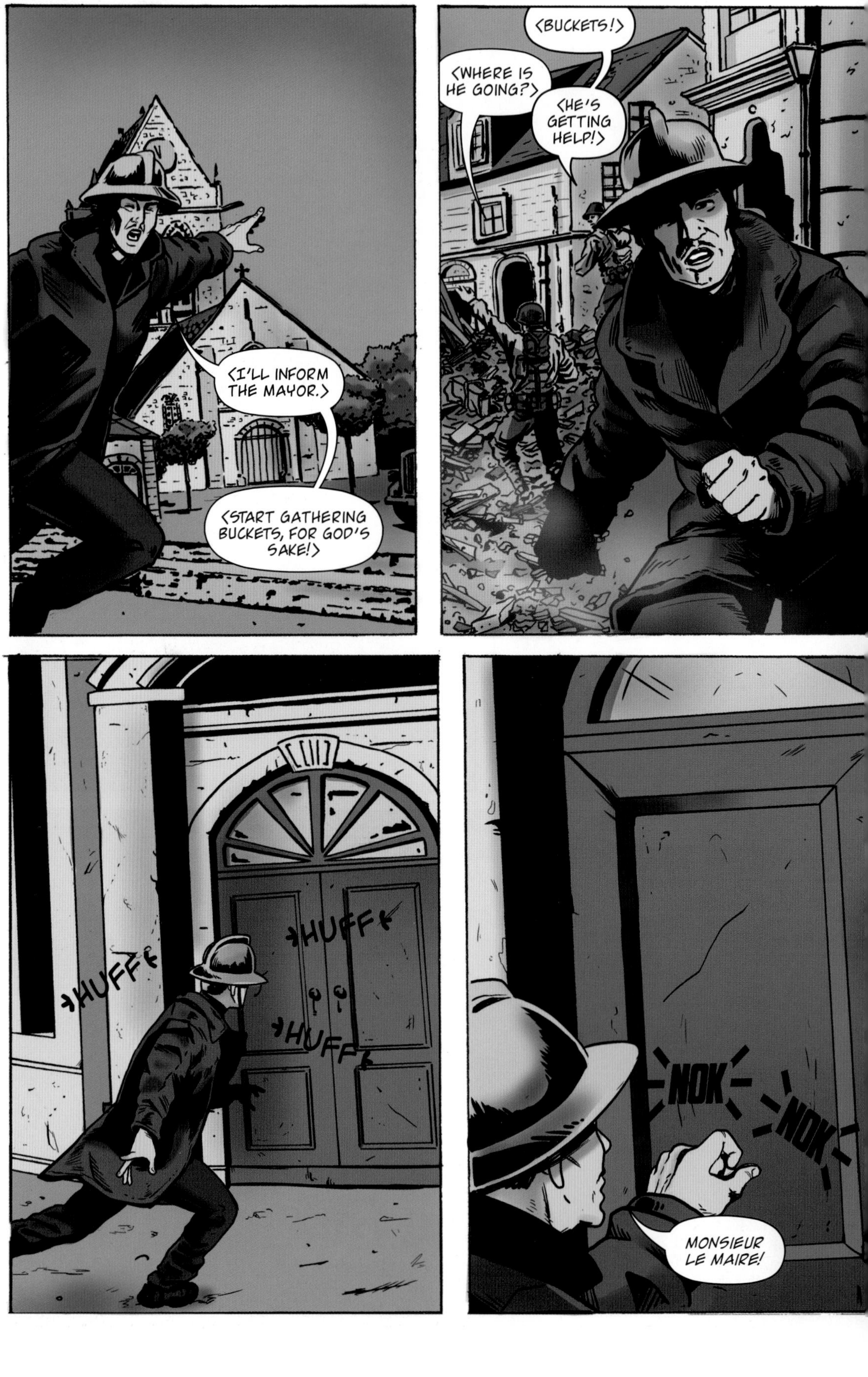

<I'LL INFORM THE MAYOR.>
<START GATHERING BUCKETS, FOR GOD'S SAKE!>
<WHERE IS HE GOING?>
<BUCKETS!>
<HE'S GETTING HELP!>
HUFF
HUFF
HUFF
NOK
NOK
MONSIEUR LE MAIRE!

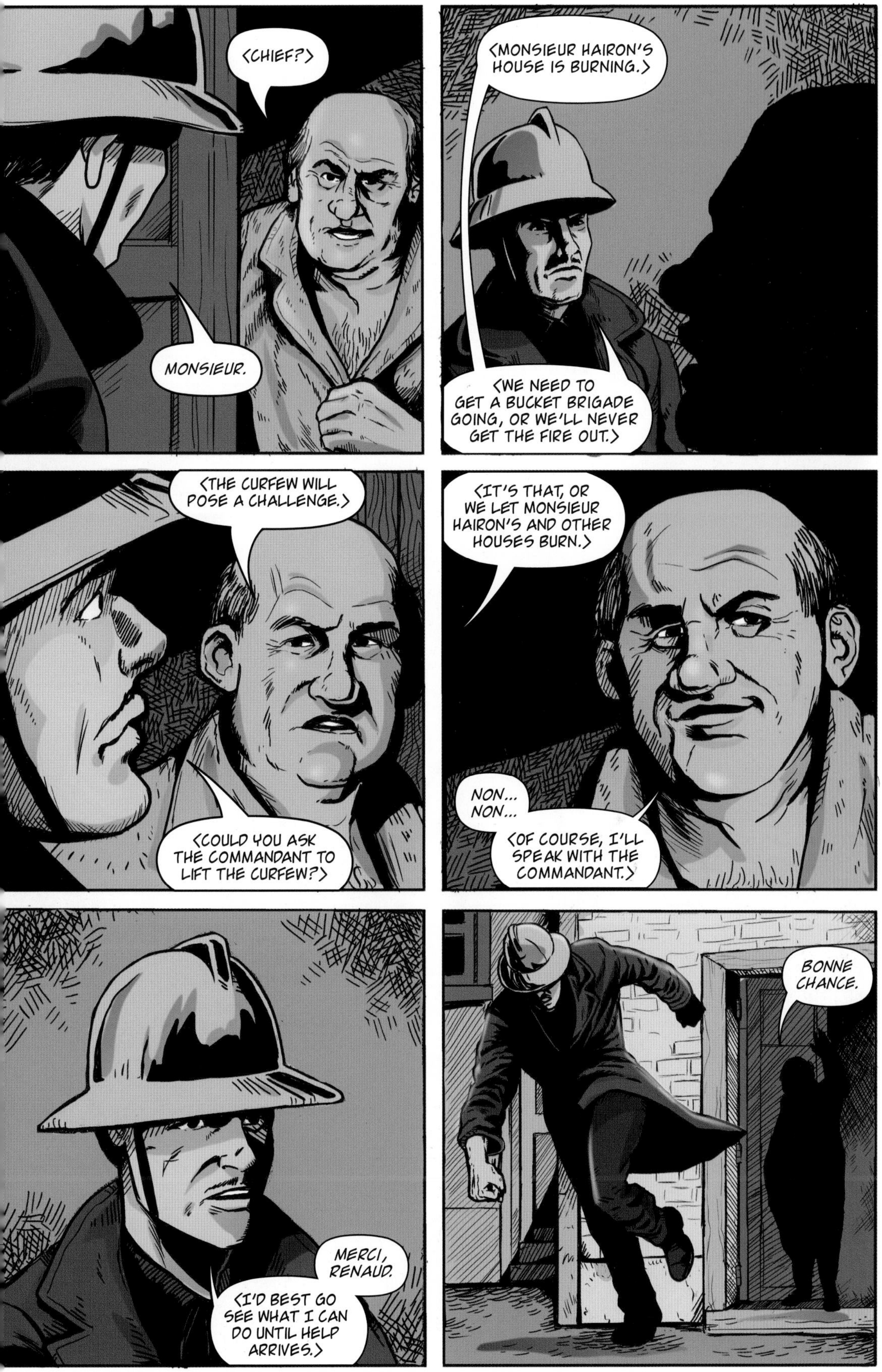
<CHIEF?>
MONSIEUR.
<MONSIEUR HAIRON'S HOUSE IS BURNING.>
<WE NEED TO GET A BUCKET BRIGADE GOING, OR WE'LL NEVER GET THE FIRE OUT.>
<THE CURFEW WILL POSE A CHALLENGE.>
<COULD YOU ASK THE COMMANDANT TO LIFT THE CURFEW?>
<IT'S THAT, OR WE LET MONSIEUR HAIRON'S AND OTHER HOUSES BURN.>
NON... NON...
<OF COURSE, I'LL SPEAK WITH THE COMMANDANT.>
MERCI, RENAUD.
<I'D BEST GO SEE WHAT I CAN DO UNTIL HELP ARRIVES.>
BONNE CHANCE.

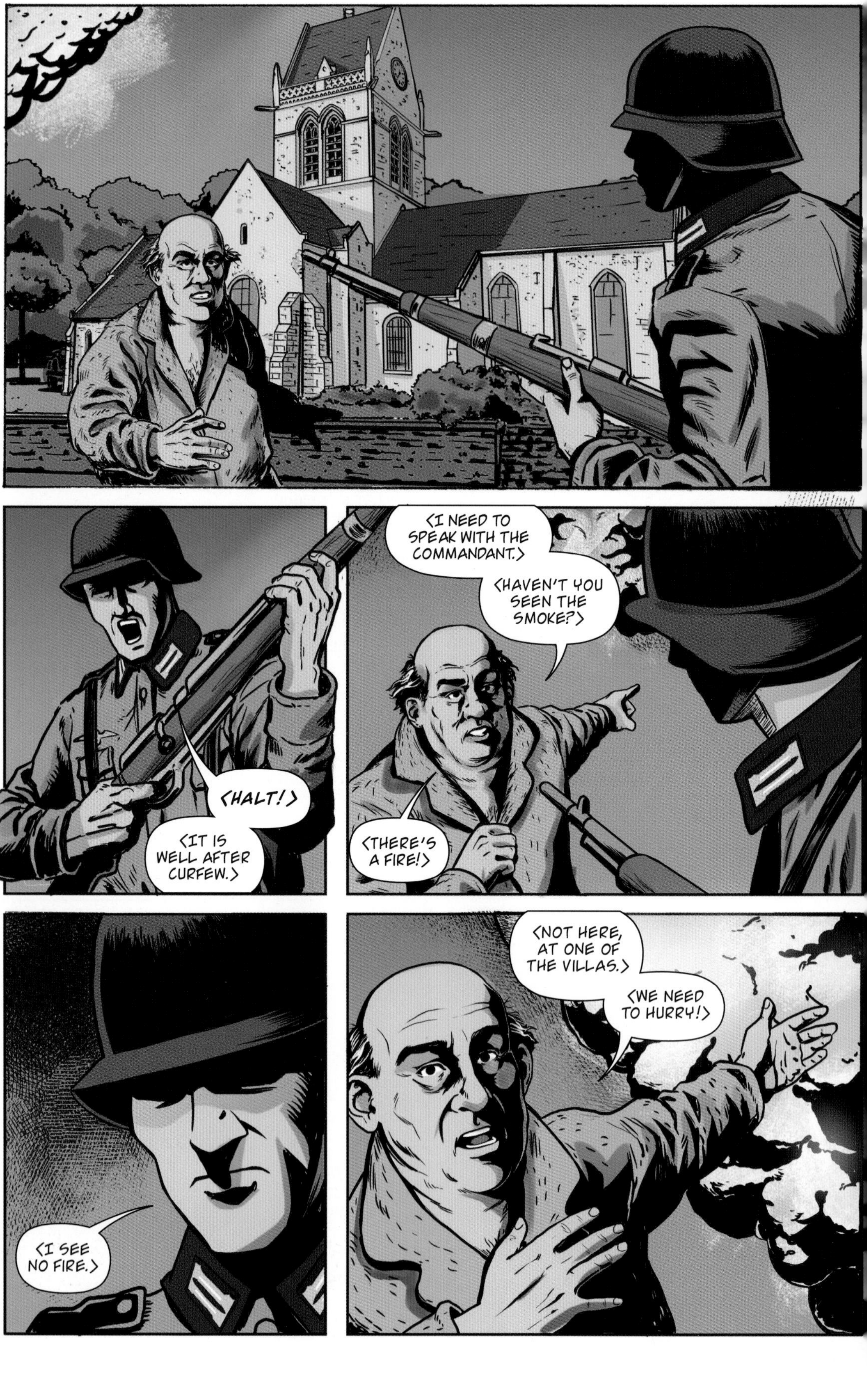
<HALT!>
<IT IS WELL AFTER CURFEW.>
<I NEED TO SPEAK WITH THE COMMANDANT.>
<HAVEN'T YOU SEEN THE SMOKE?>
<THERE'S A FIRE!>
<I SEE NO FIRE.>
<NOT HERE, AT ONE OF THE VILLAS.>
<WE NEED TO HURRY!>

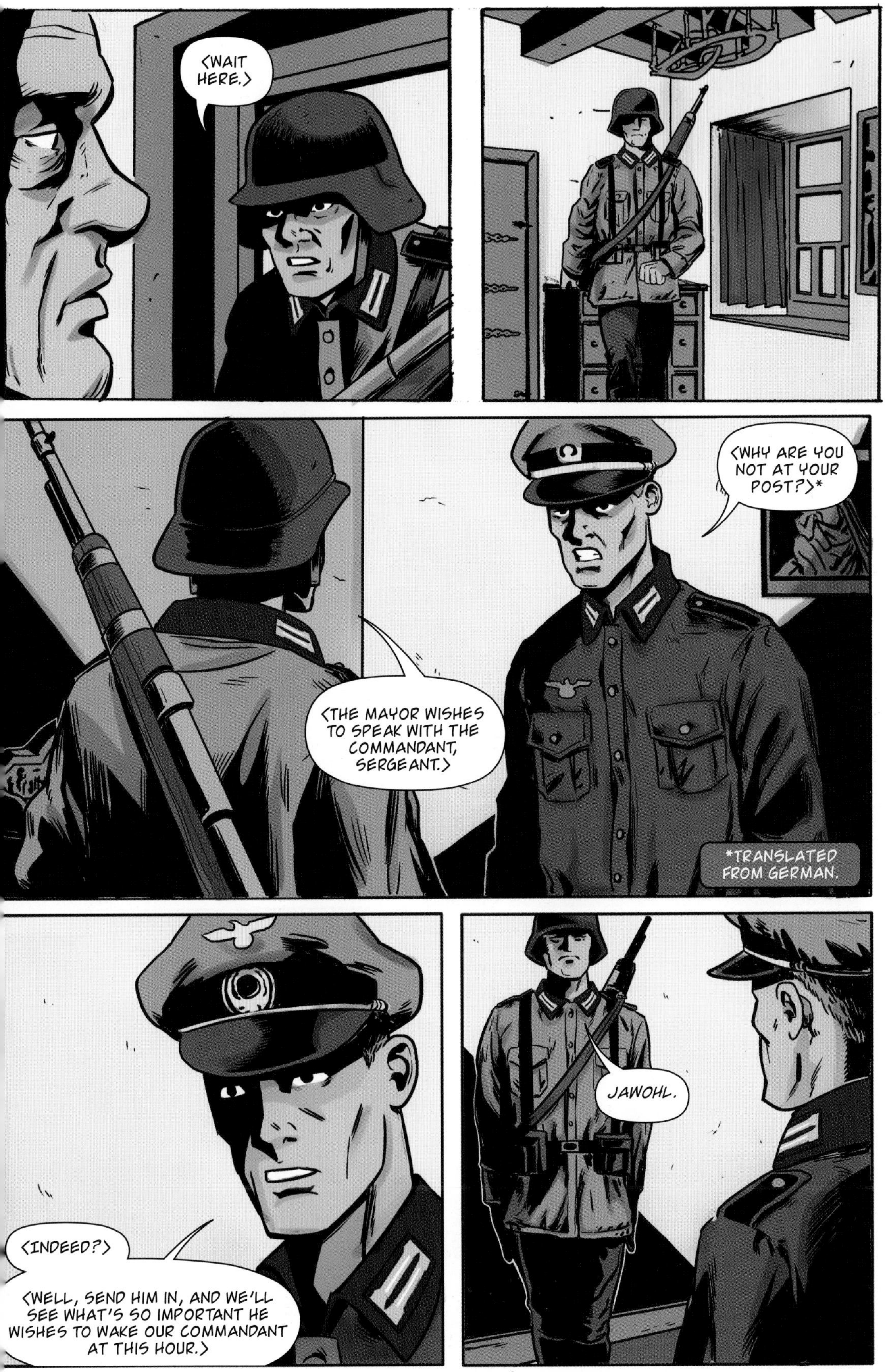
<WAIT HERE.>
<WHY ARE YOU NOT AT YOUR POST?>*
<THE MAYOR WISHES TO SPEAK WITH THE COMMANDANT, SERGEANT.>
*TRANSLATED FROM GERMAN.
<INDEED?>
<WELL, SEND HIM IN, AND WE'LL SEE WHAT'S SO IMPORTANT HE WISHES TO WAKE OUR COMMANDANT AT THIS HOUR.>
JAWOHL.

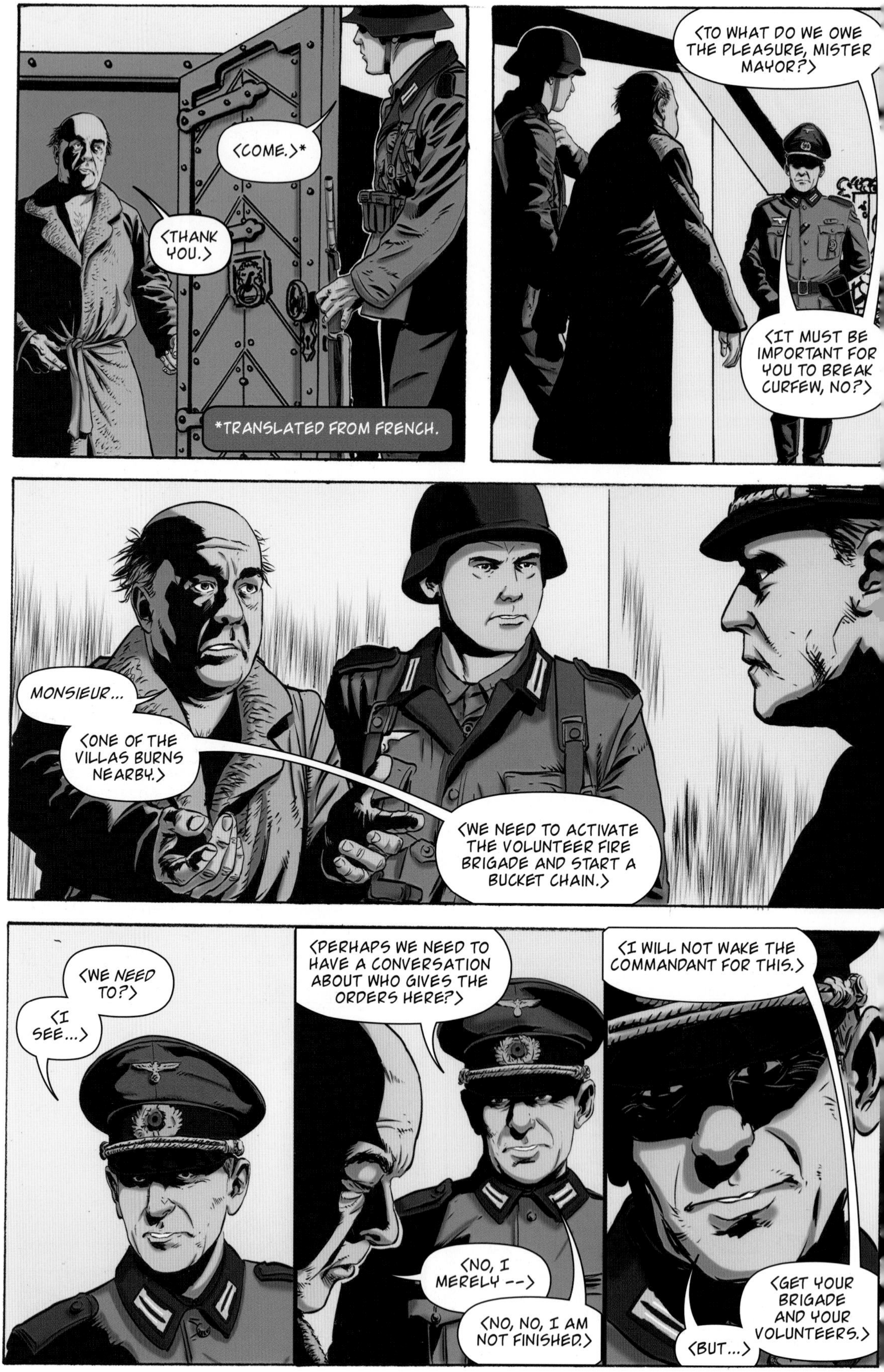

<COME.>*
<THANK YOU.>
*TRANSLATED FROM FRENCH.
<TO WHAT DO WE OWE THE PLEASURE, MISTER MAYOR?>
<IT MUST BE IMPORTANT FOR YOU TO BREAK CURFEW, NO?>
MONSIEUR...
<ONE OF THE VILLAS BURNS NEARBY.>
<WE NEED TO ACTIVATE THE VOLUNTEER FIRE BRIGADE AND START A BUCKET CHAIN.>
<WE NEED TO?>
<I SEE...>
<PERHAPS WE NEED TO HAVE A CONVERSATION ABOUT WHO GIVES THE ORDERS HERE?>
<NO, I MERELY -->
<NO, NO, I AM NOT FINISHED.>
<I WILL NOT WAKE THE COMMANDANT FOR THIS.>
<BUT...>
<GET YOUR BRIGADE AND YOUR VOLUNTEERS.>

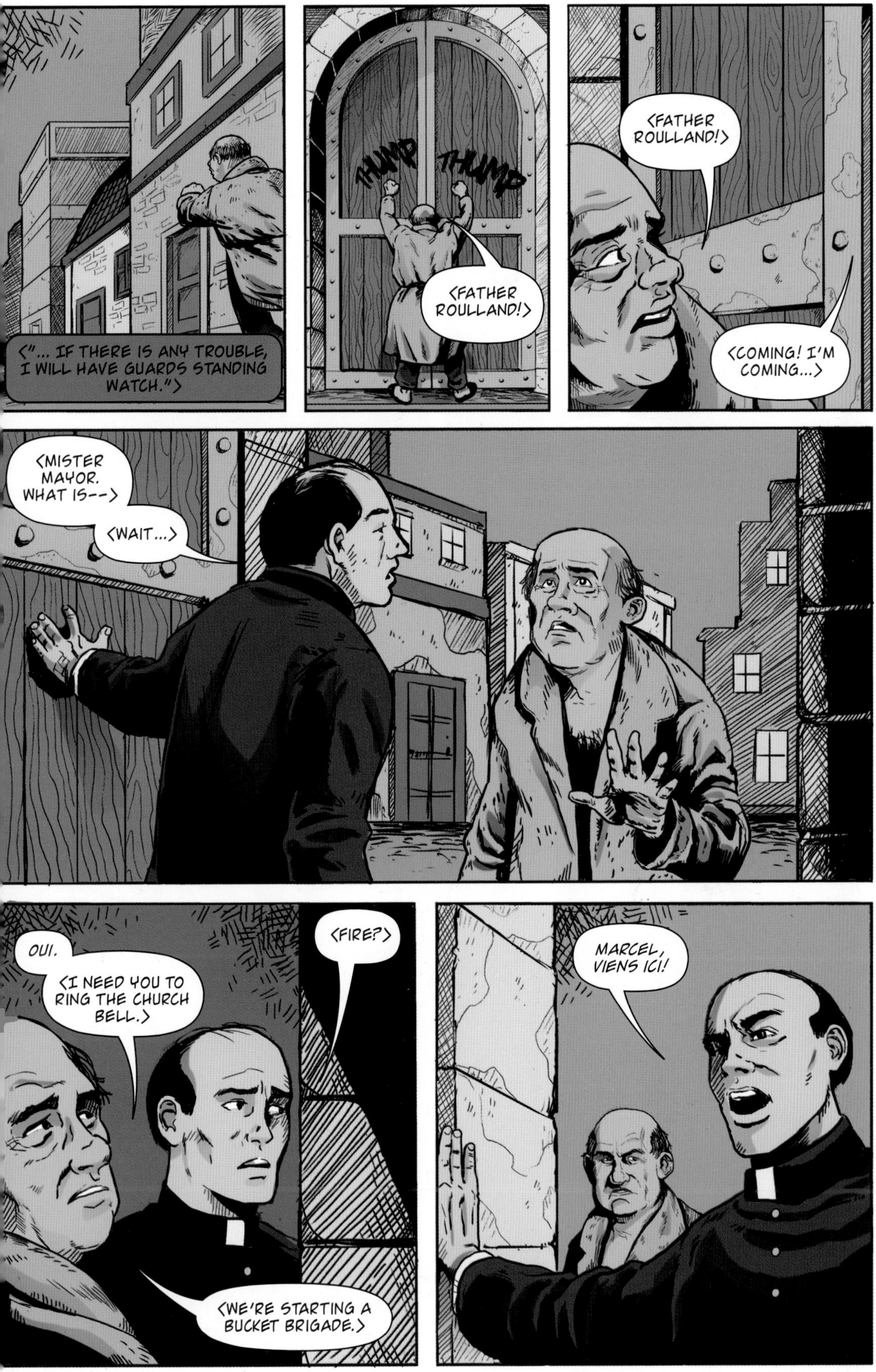
<"... IF THERE IS ANY TROUBLE, I WILL HAVE GUARDS STANDING WATCH.">
THUMP THUMP
<FATHER ROULLAND!>
<FATHER ROULLAND!>
<COMING! I'M COMING...>
<MISTER MAYOR. WHAT IS-->
<WAIT...>
OUI.
<I NEED YOU TO RING THE CHURCH BELL.>
<FIRE?>
<WE'RE STARTING A BUCKET BRIGADE.>
MARCEL, VIENS ICI!

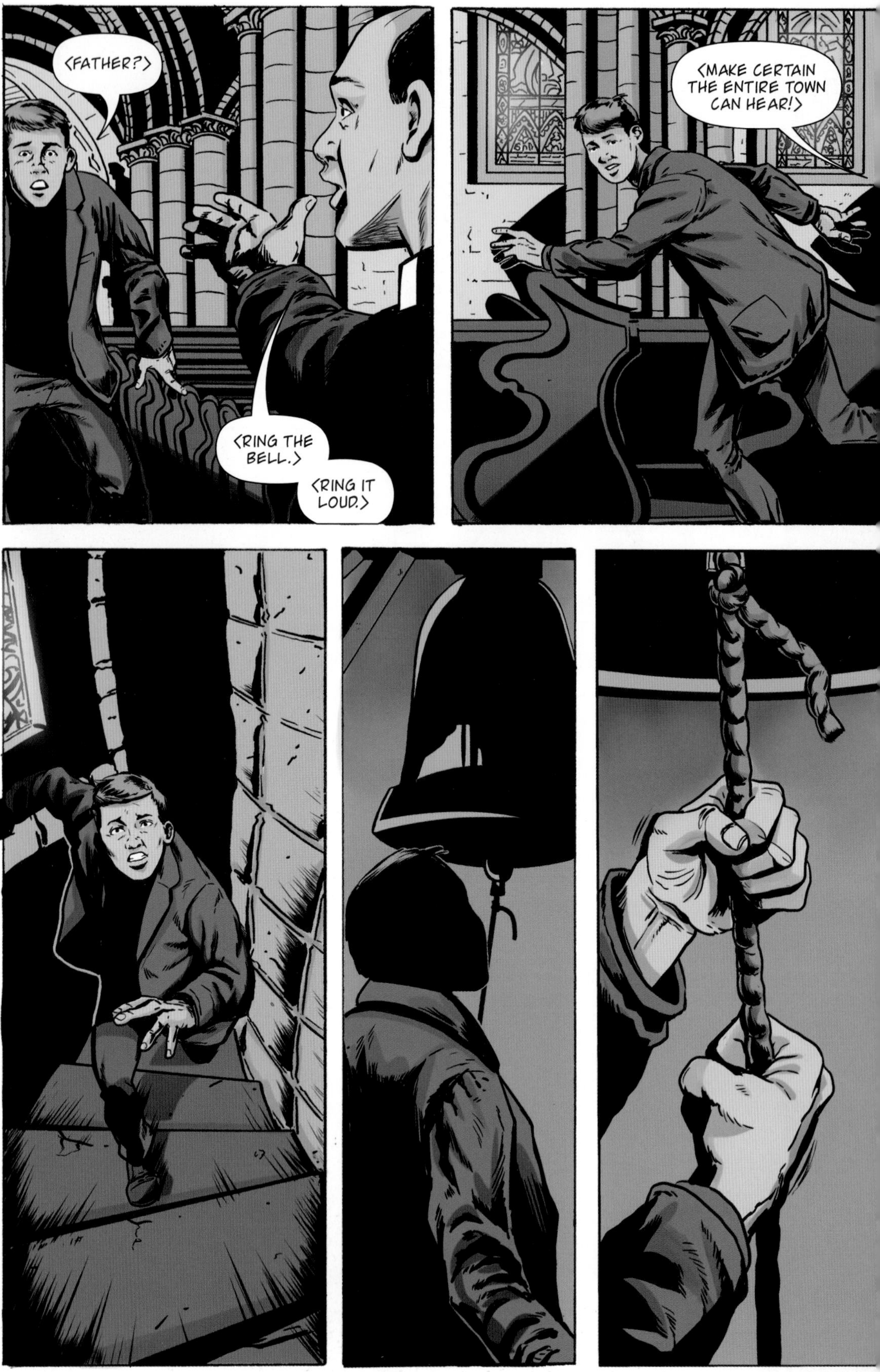
<FATHER?>
<RING THE BELL.>
<RING IT LOUD.>
<MAKE CERTAIN THE ENTIRE TOWN CAN HEAR!>

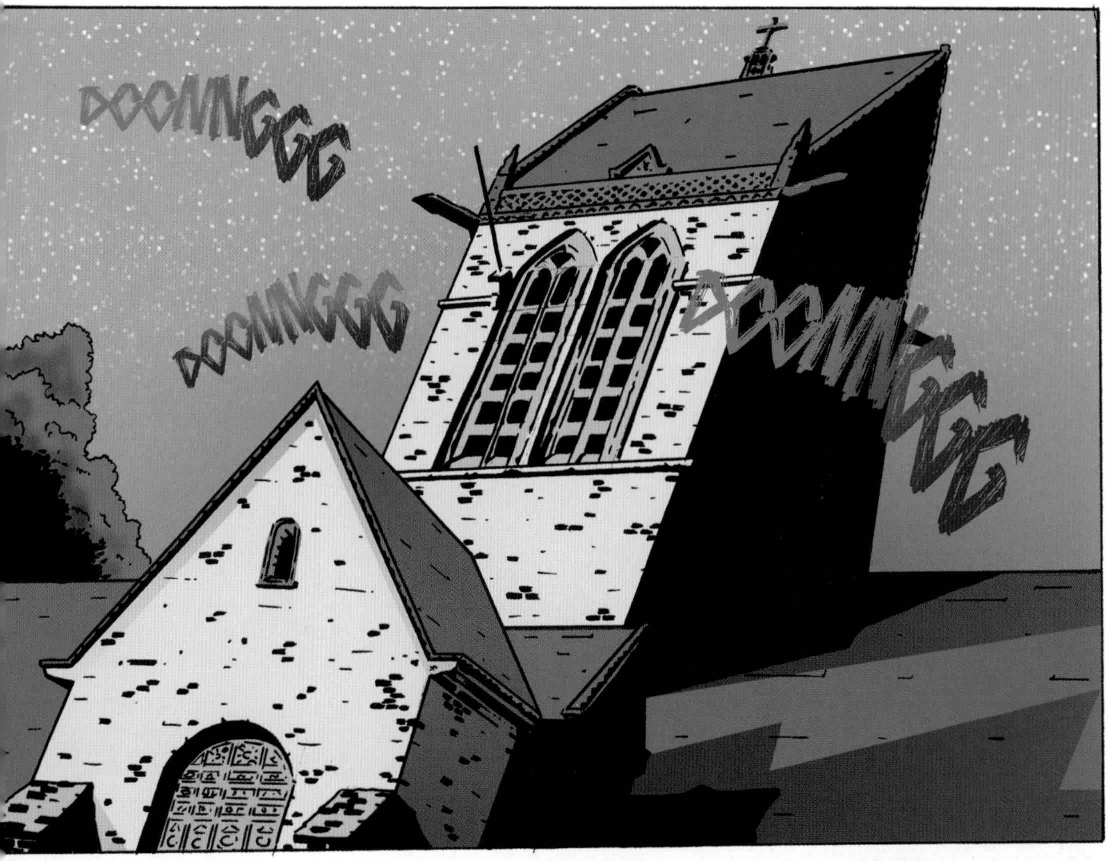
DOONNGGG
DOONNGGG
DOONNGGG

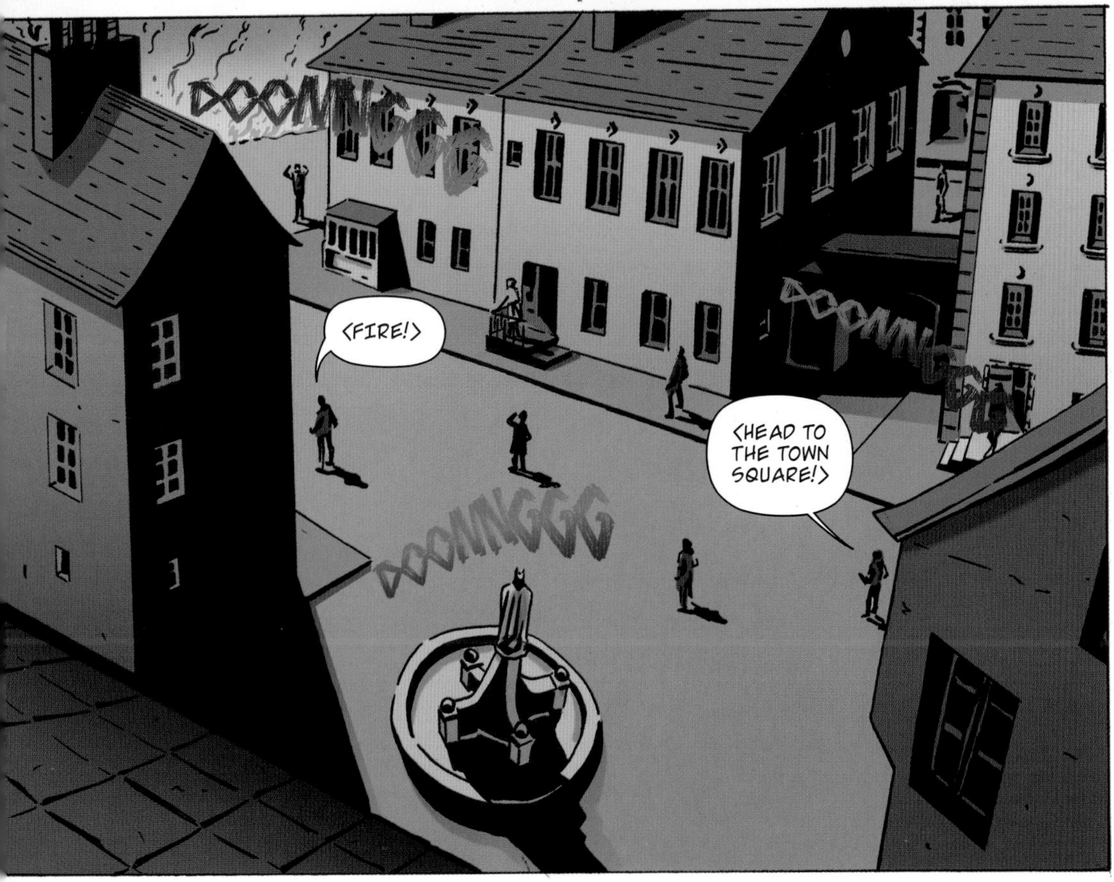
DOONNGGG
DOONNGGG
<FIRE!>
<HEAD TO THE TOWN SQUARE!>
DOONNGGG

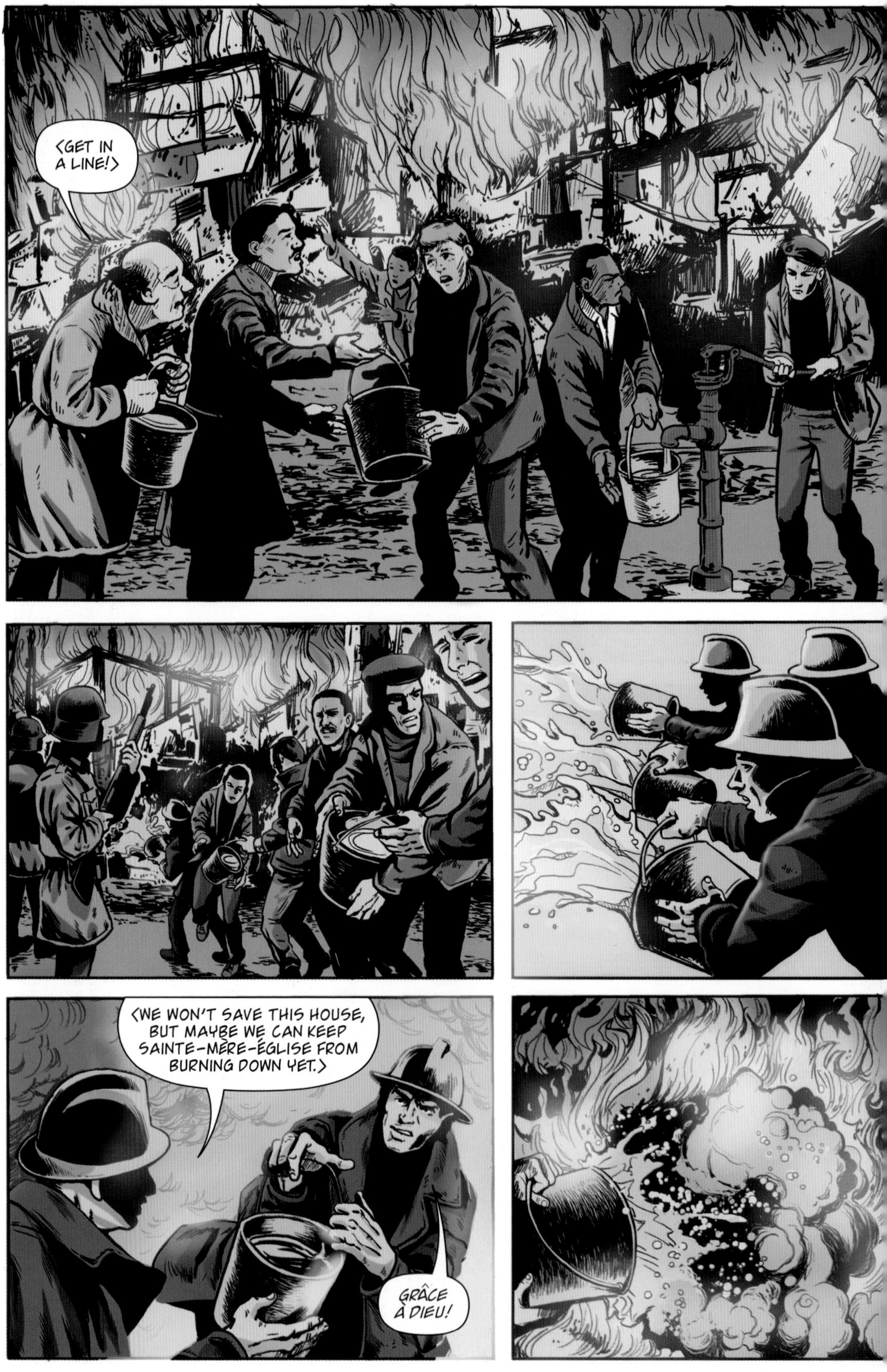
<GET IN A LINE!>
<WE WON'T SAVE THIS HOUSE, BUT MAYBE WE CAN KEEP SAINTE-MÈRE-ÉGLISE FROM BURNING DOWN YET.>
GRÂCE À DIEU!

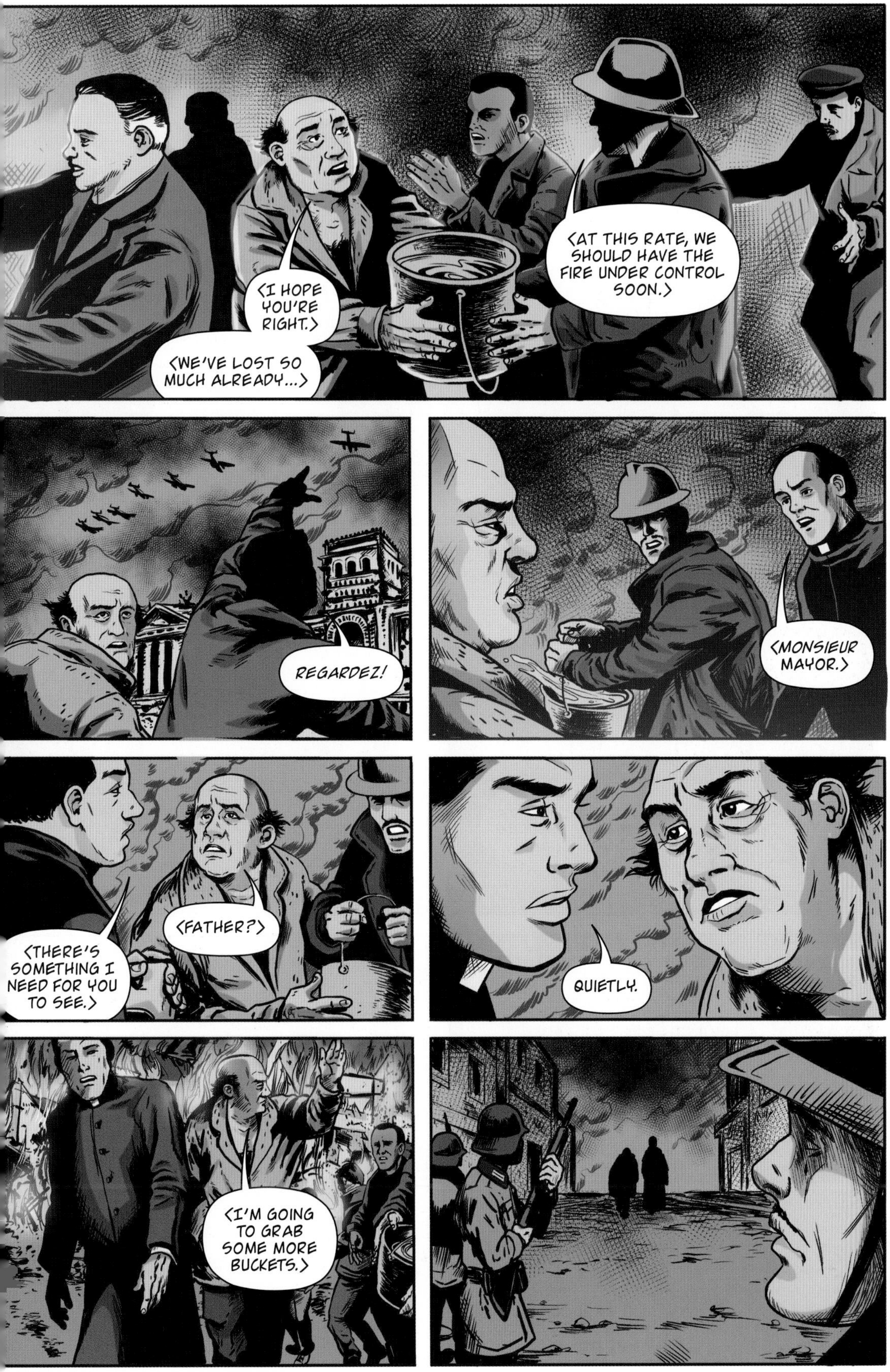

<I HOPE YOU'RE RIGHT.>
<WE'VE LOST SO MUCH ALREADY...>
<AT THIS RATE, WE SHOULD HAVE THE FIRE UNDER CONTROL SOON.>
REGARDEZ!
<MONSIEUR MAYOR.>
<FATHER?>
<THERE'S SOMETHING I NEED FOR YOU TO SEE.>
QUIETLY.
<I'M GOING TO GRAB SOME MORE BUCKETS.>

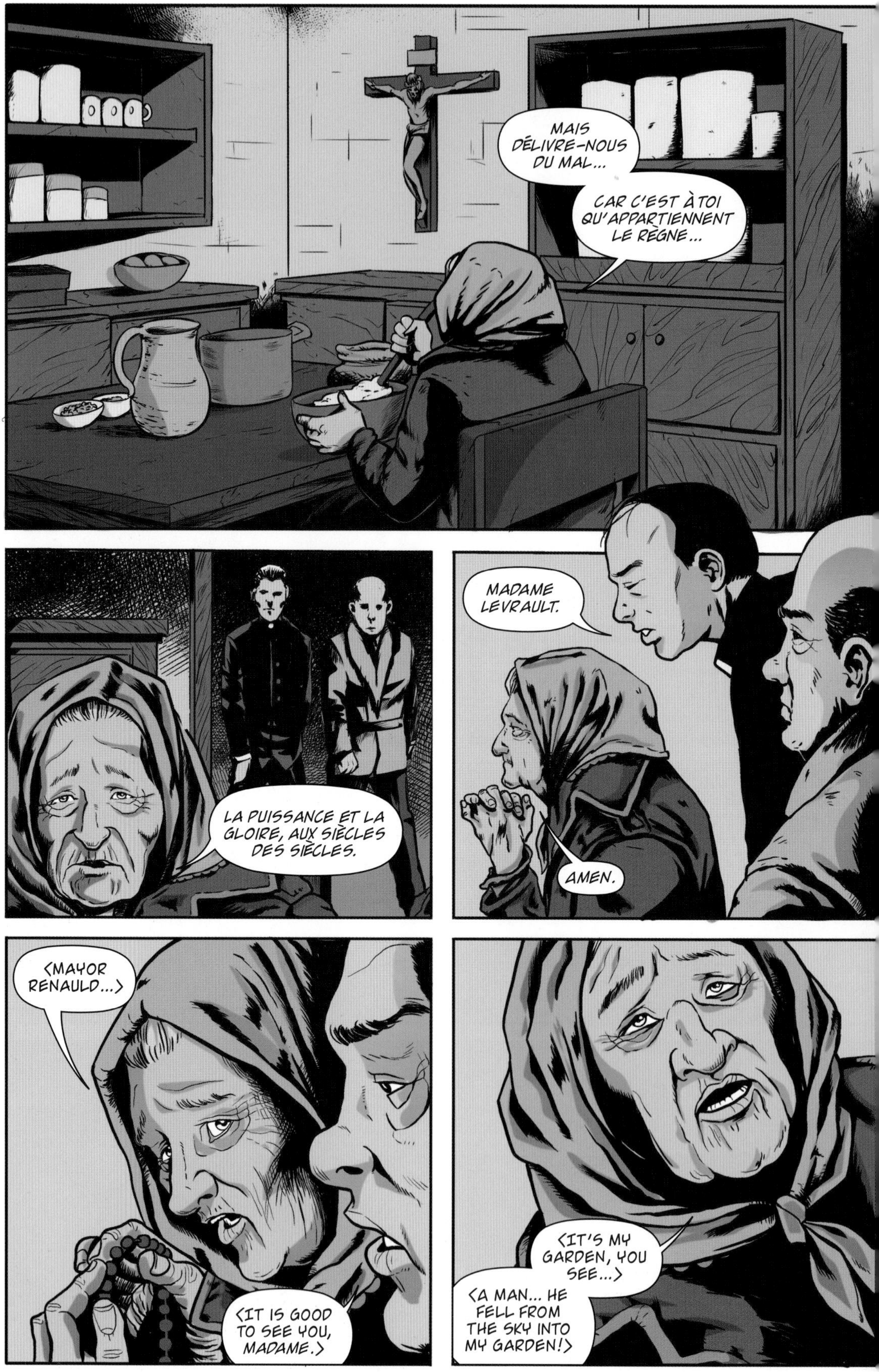
MAIS DÉLIVRE-NOUS DU MAL...
CAR C'EST À TOI QU'APPARTIENNENT LE RÈGNE...
LA PUISSANCE ET LA GLOIRE, AUX SIÈCLES DES SIÈCLES.
MADAME LEVRAULT.
AMEN.
<MAYOR RENAULD...>
<IT IS GOOD TO SEE YOU, MADAME.>
<IT'S MY GARDEN, YOU SEE...>
<A MAN... HE FELL FROM THE SKY INTO MY GARDEN!>

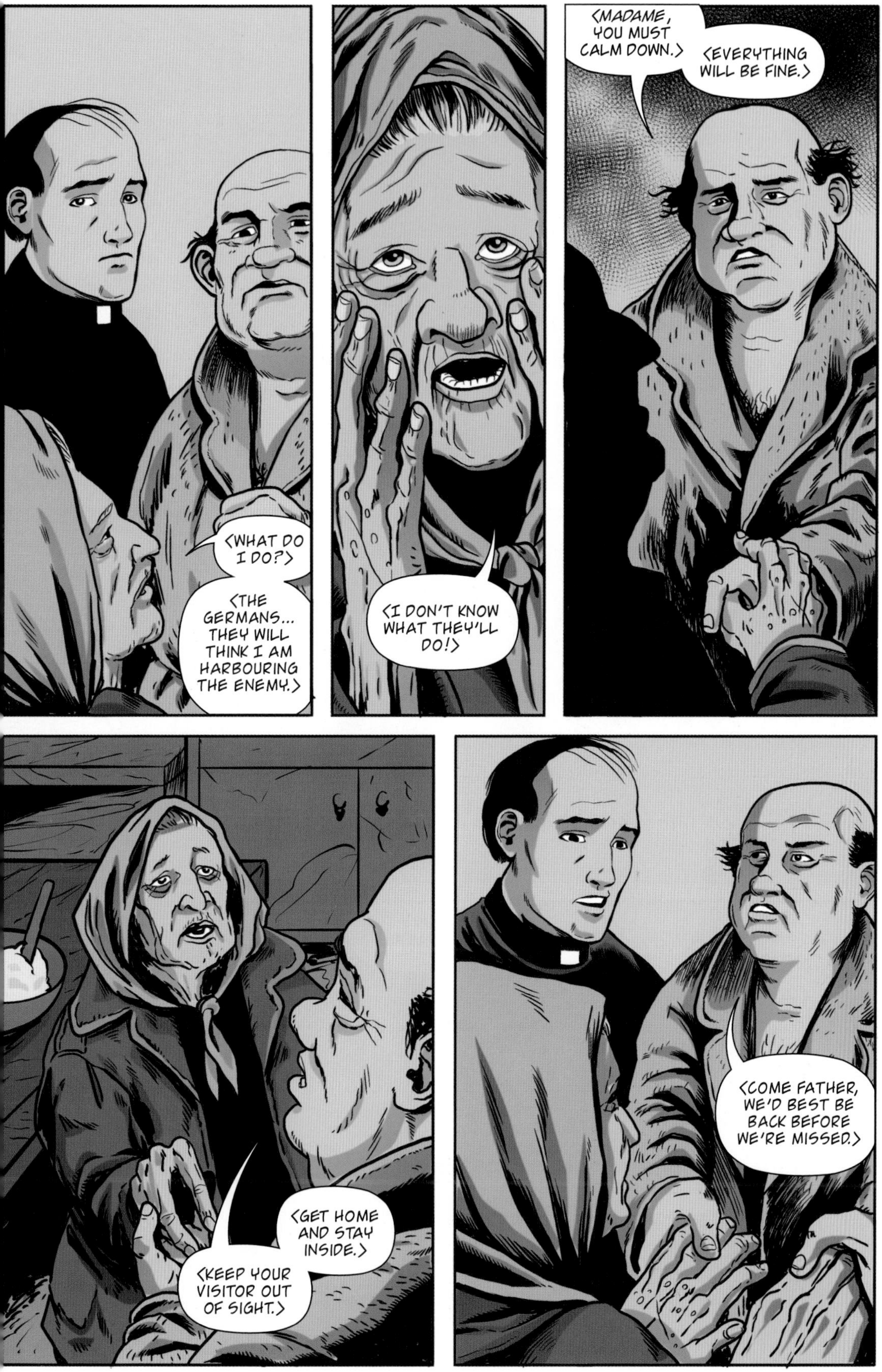
<WHAT DO I DO?>
<THE GERMANS... THEY WILL THINK I AM HARBOURING THE ENEMY.>
<I DON'T KNOW WHAT THEY'LL DO!>
<MADAME, YOU MUST CALM DOWN.>
<EVERYTHING WILL BE FINE.>
<GET HOME AND STAY INSIDE.>
<KEEP YOUR VISITOR OUT OF SIGHT.>
<COME FATHER, WE'D BEST BE BACK BEFORE WE'RE MISSED.>

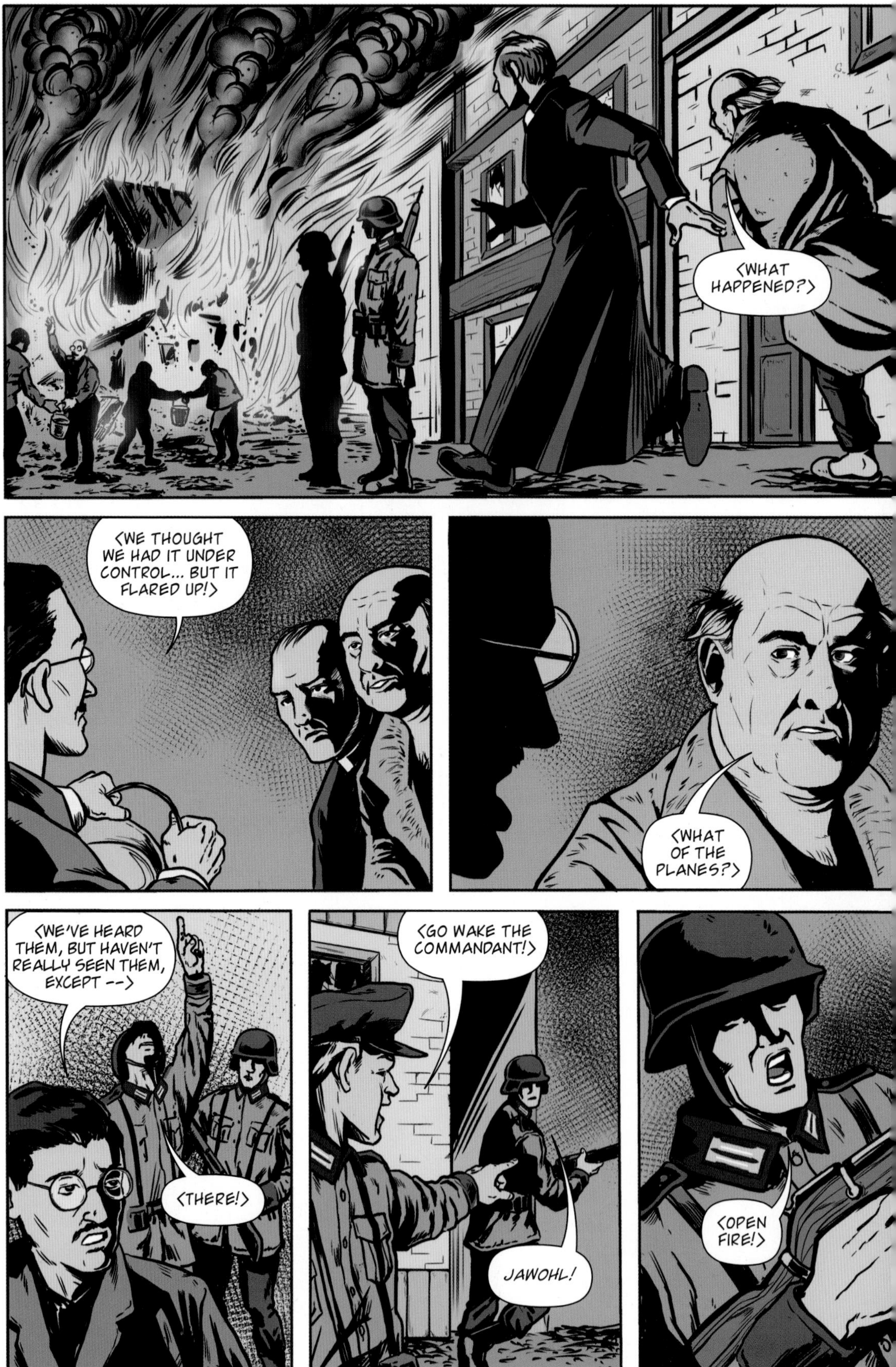
<WHAT HAPPENED?>
<WE THOUGHT WE HAD IT UNDER CONTROL... BUT IT FLARED UP!>
<WHAT OF THE PLANES?>
<WE'VE HEARD THEM, BUT HAVEN'T REALLY SEEN THEM, EXCEPT -->
<THERE!>
<GO WAKE THE COMMANDANT!>
JAWOHL!
<OPEN FIRE!>

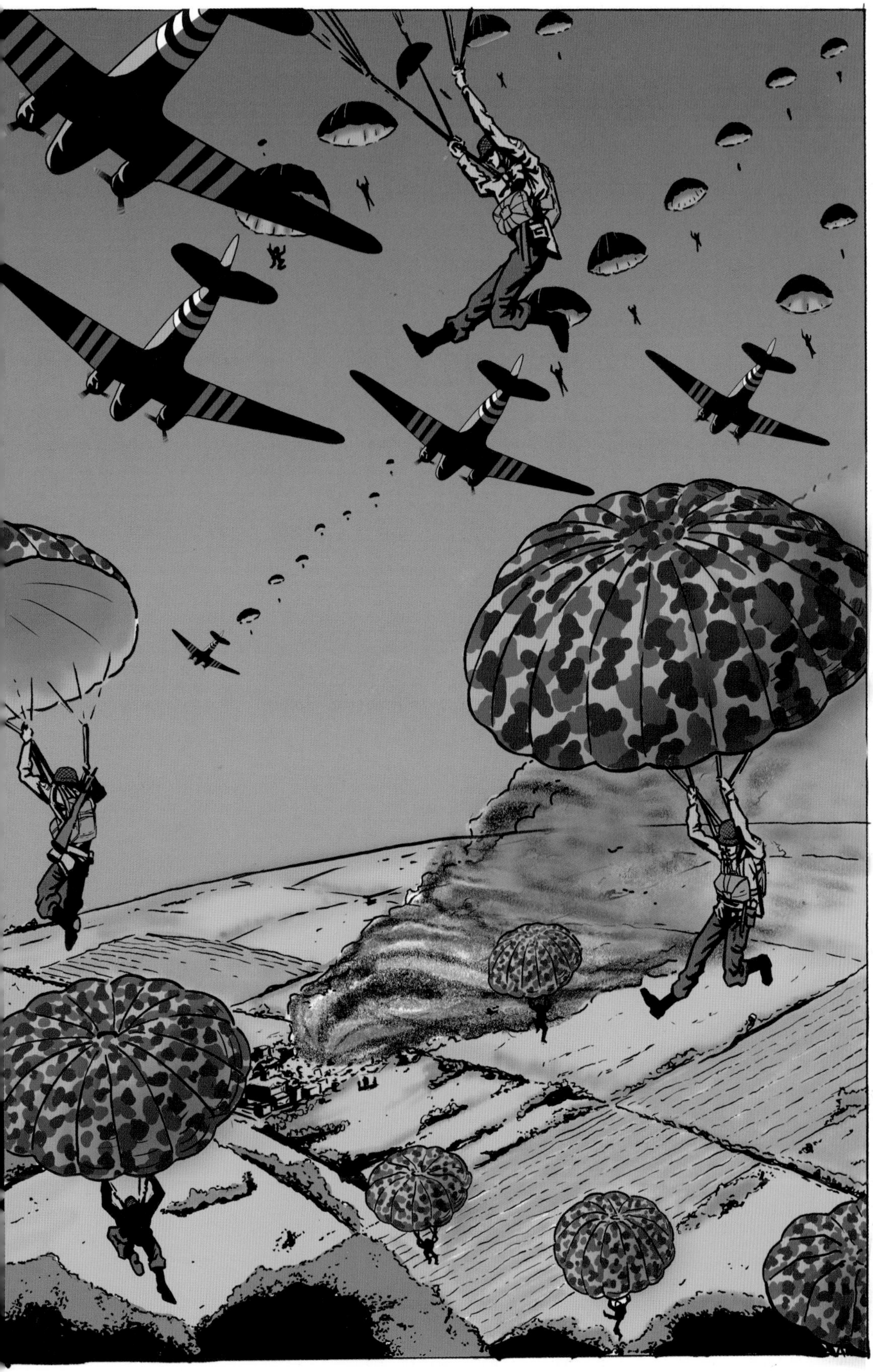

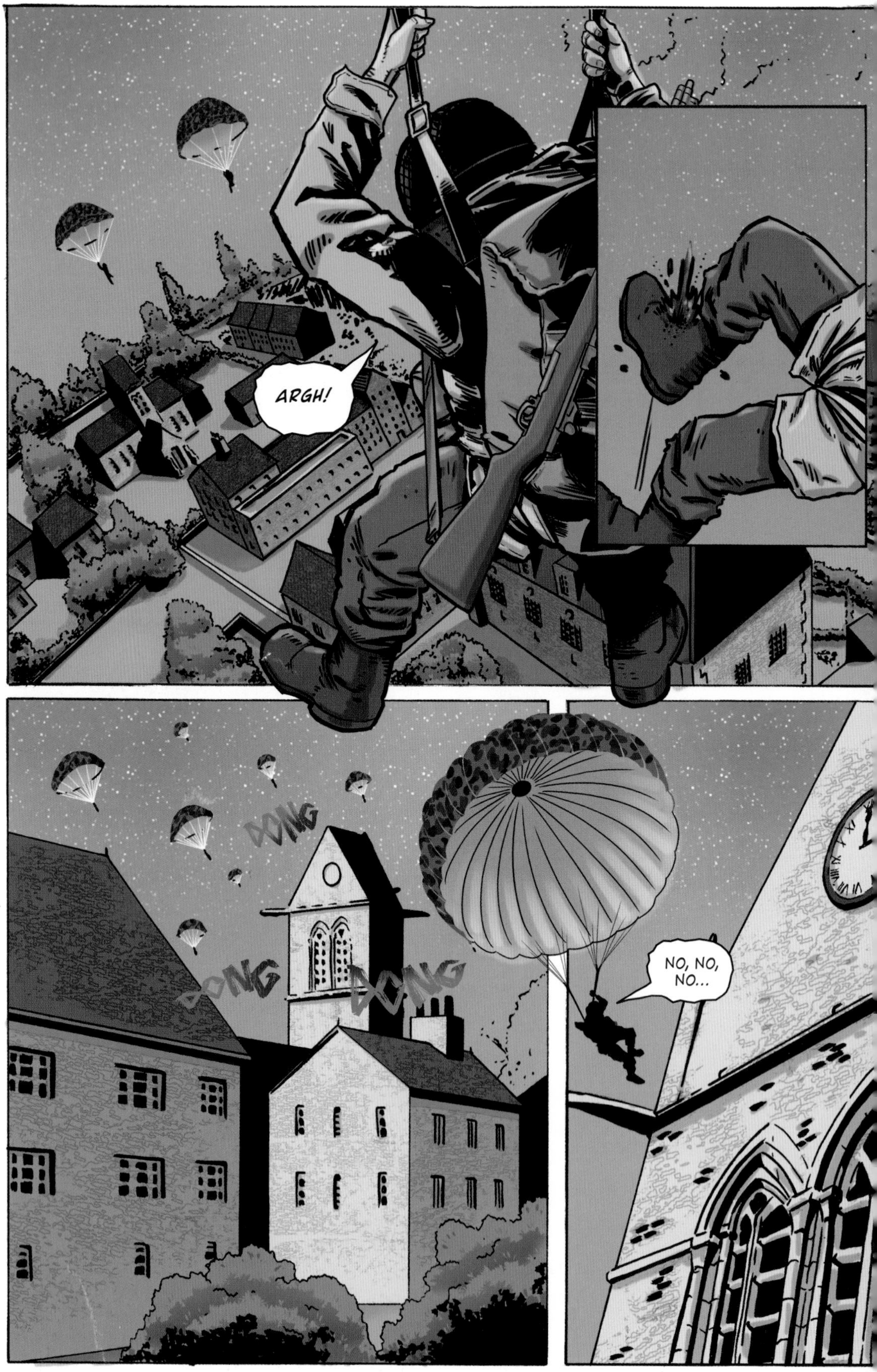
ARGH!
DONG
DONG
DONG
NO, NO, NO...

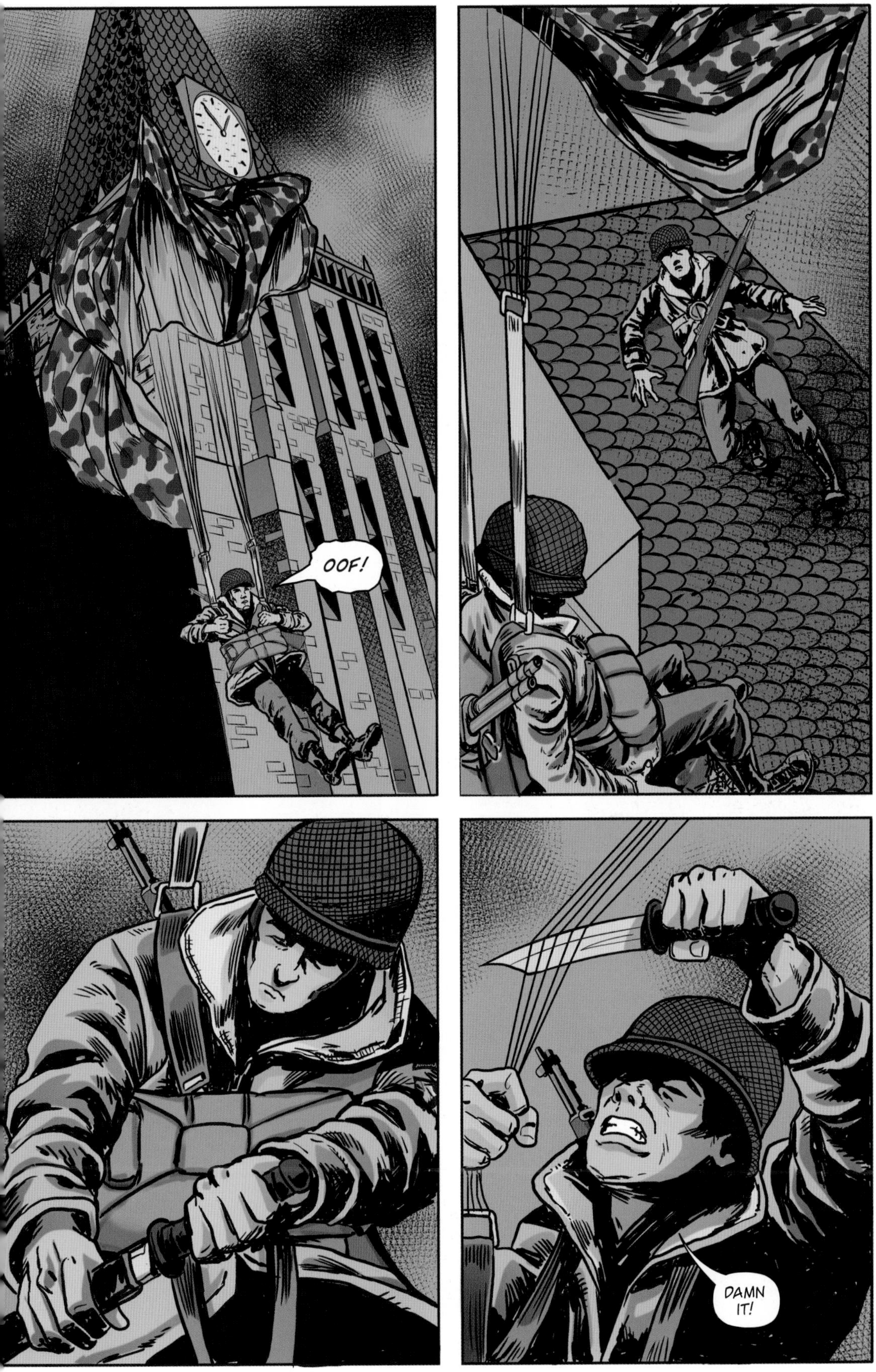
OOF!
DAMN IT!

NO...

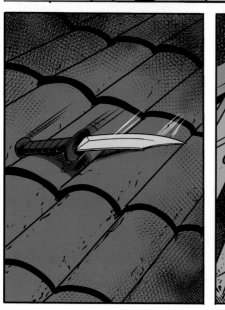

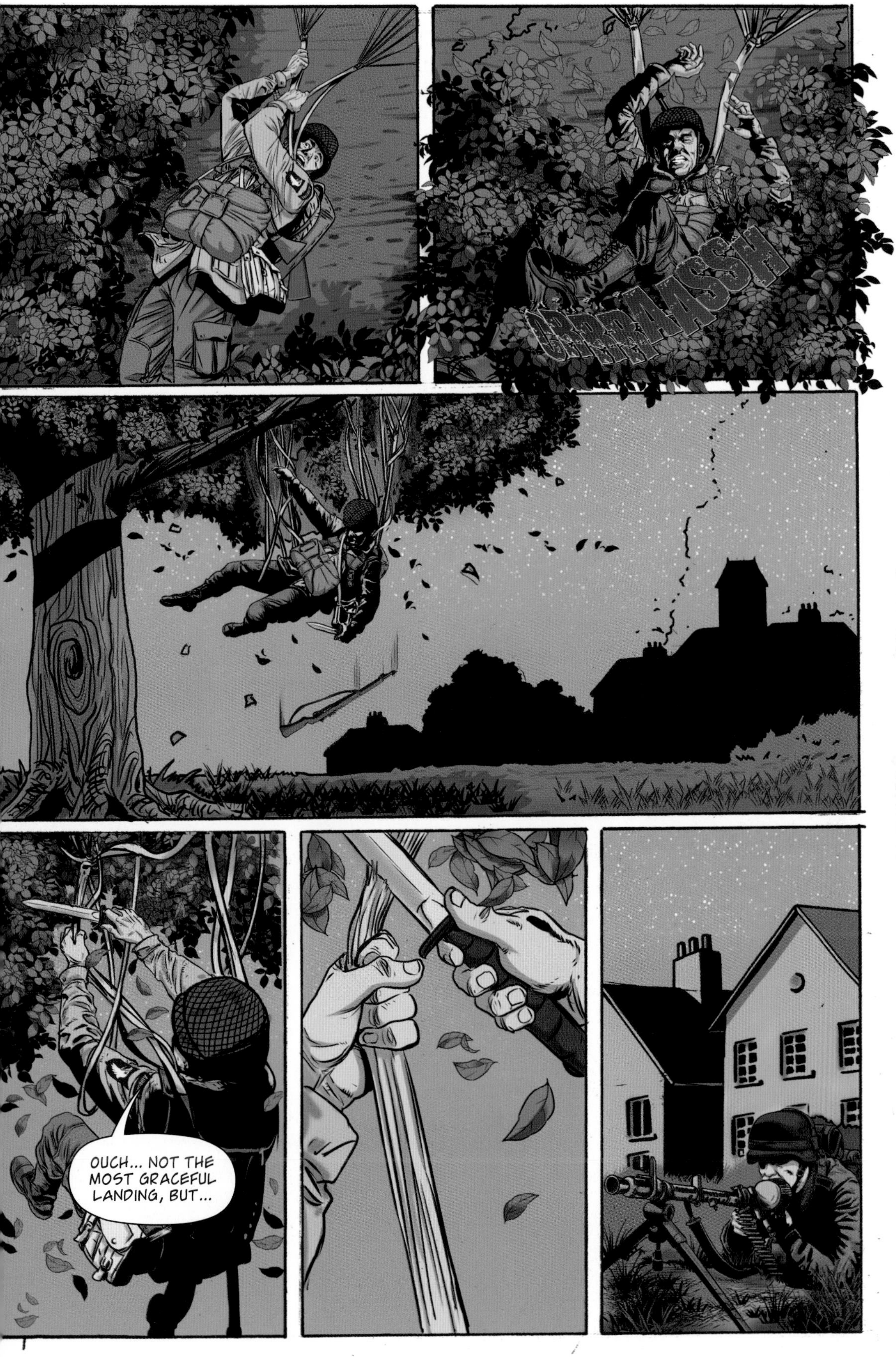
CRRRAASSH
OUCH... NOT THE MOST GRACEFUL LANDING, BUT...

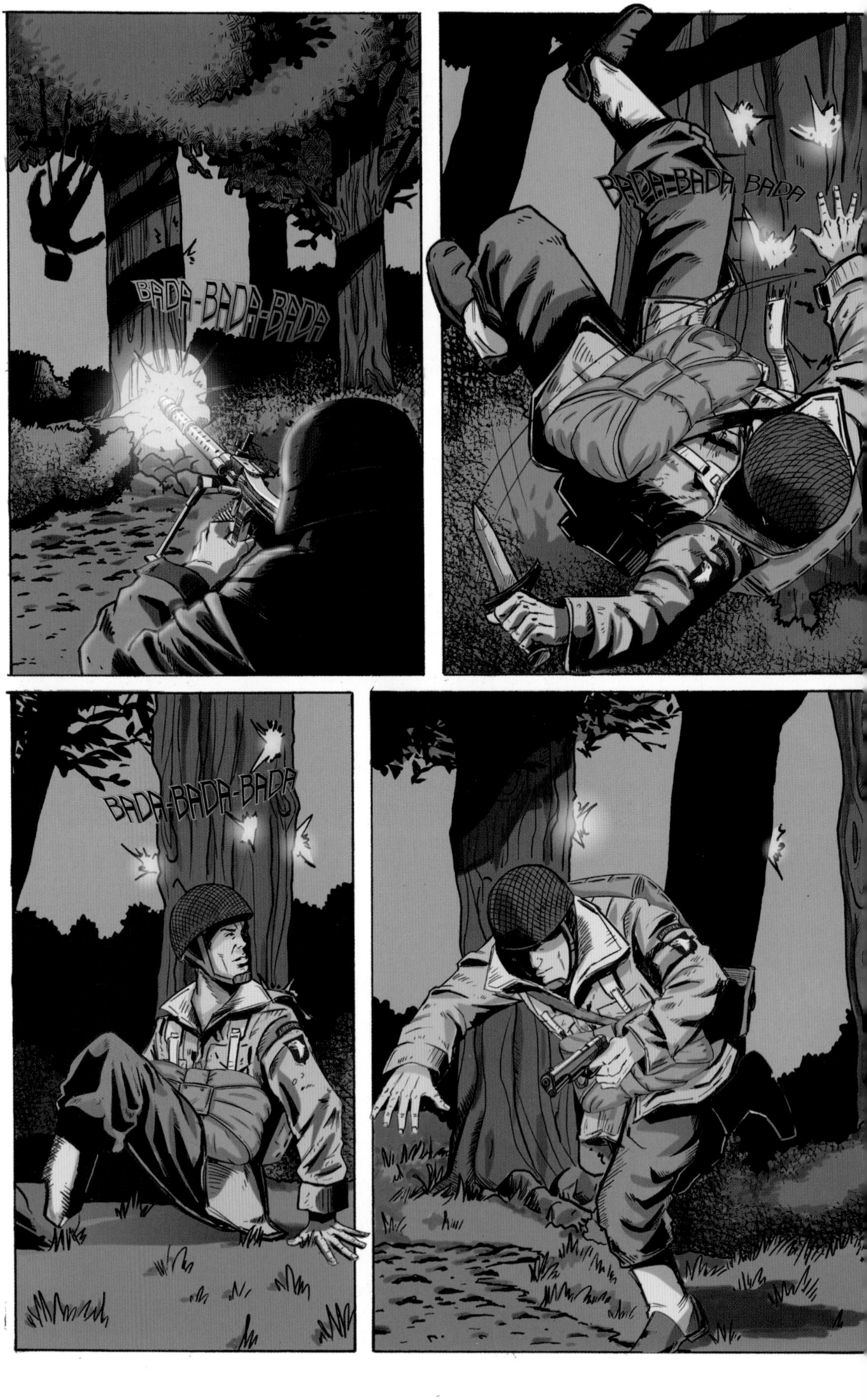
BADA-BADA-BADA
BADA-BADA BADA
BADA-BADA-BADA

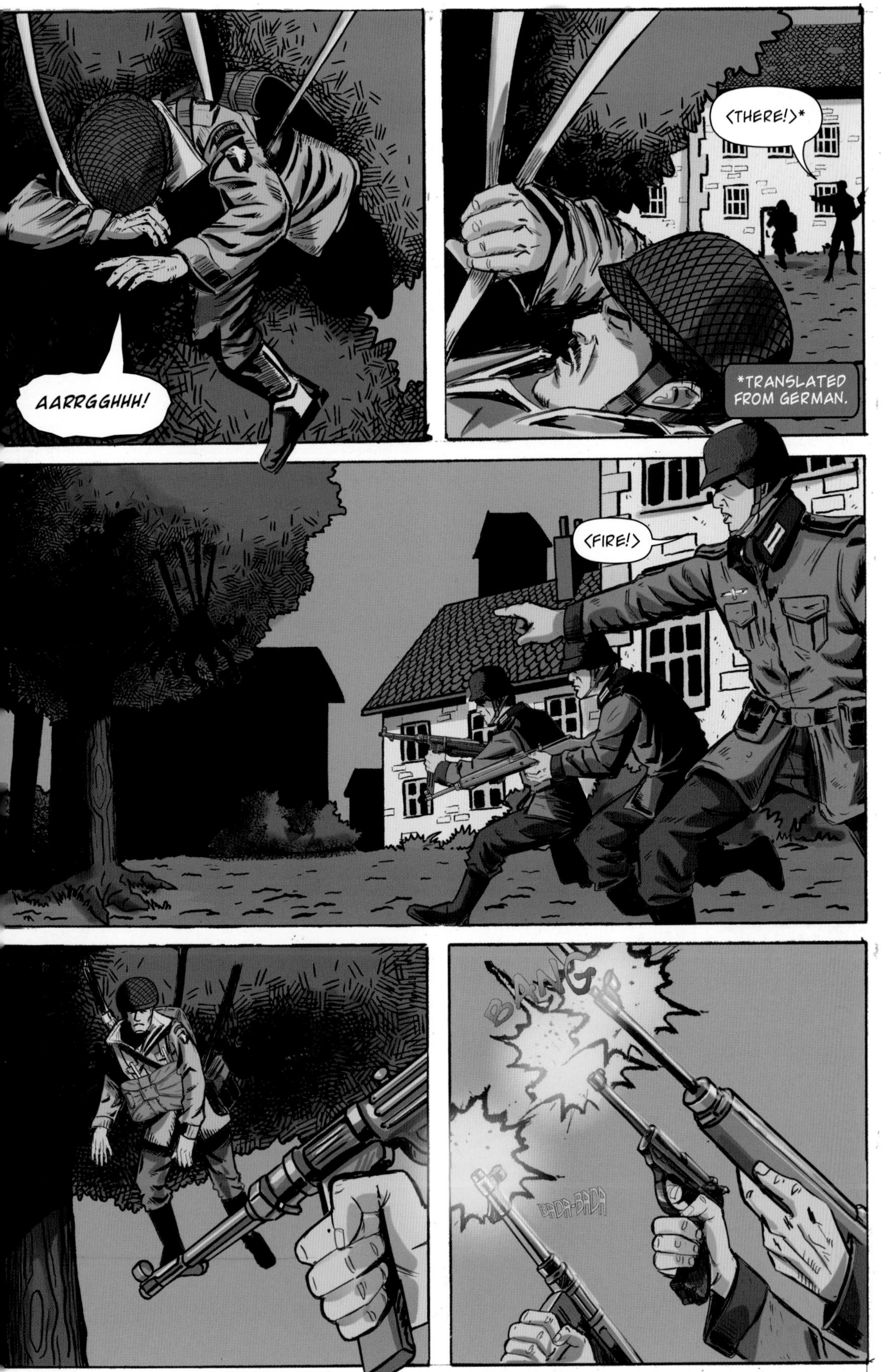
AARRGGHHH!
<THERE!>*
*TRANSLATED FROM GERMAN.
<FIRE!>
BANG
BADA-BADA

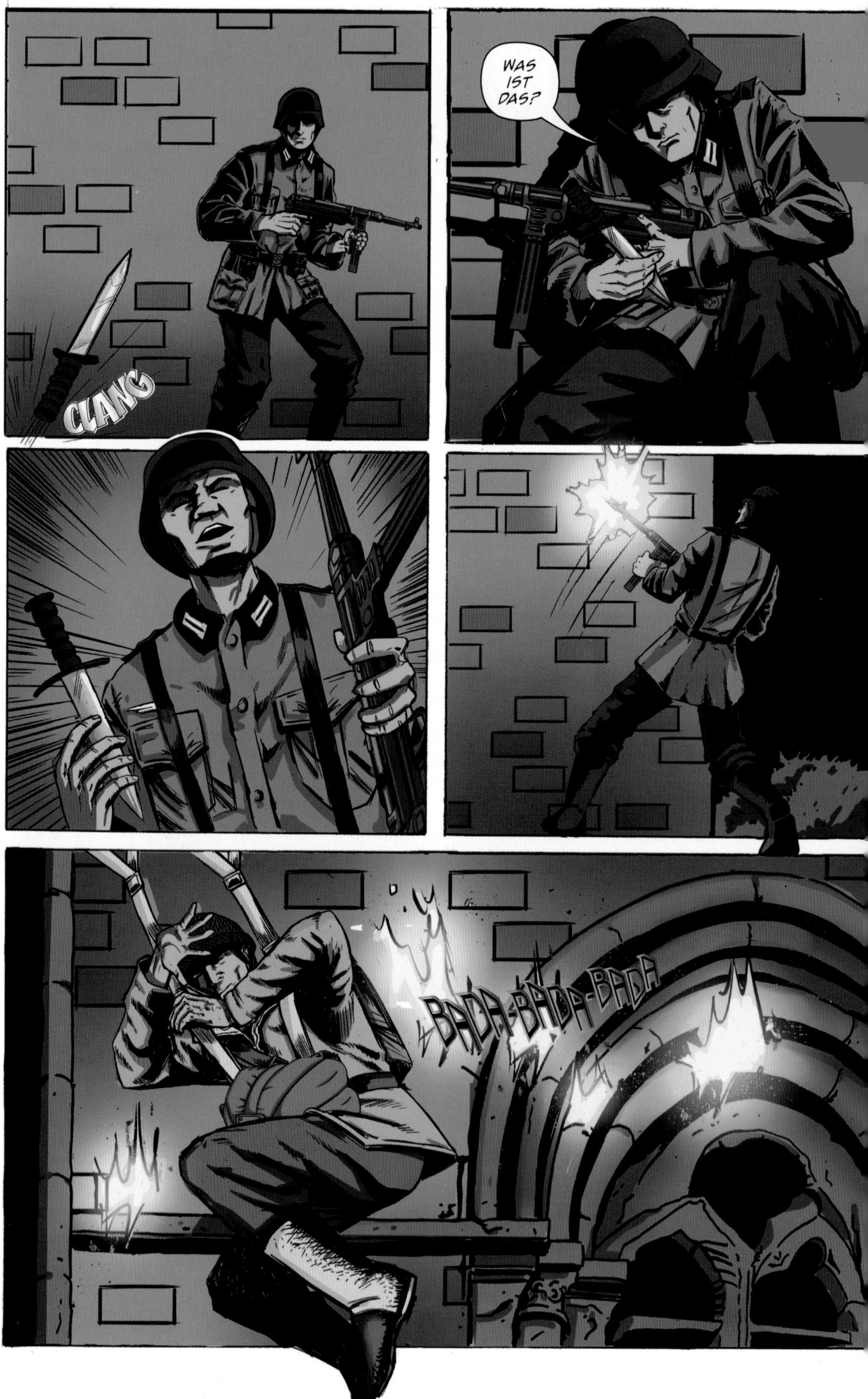
CLANG
WAS IST DAS?
BADA-BADA-BADA

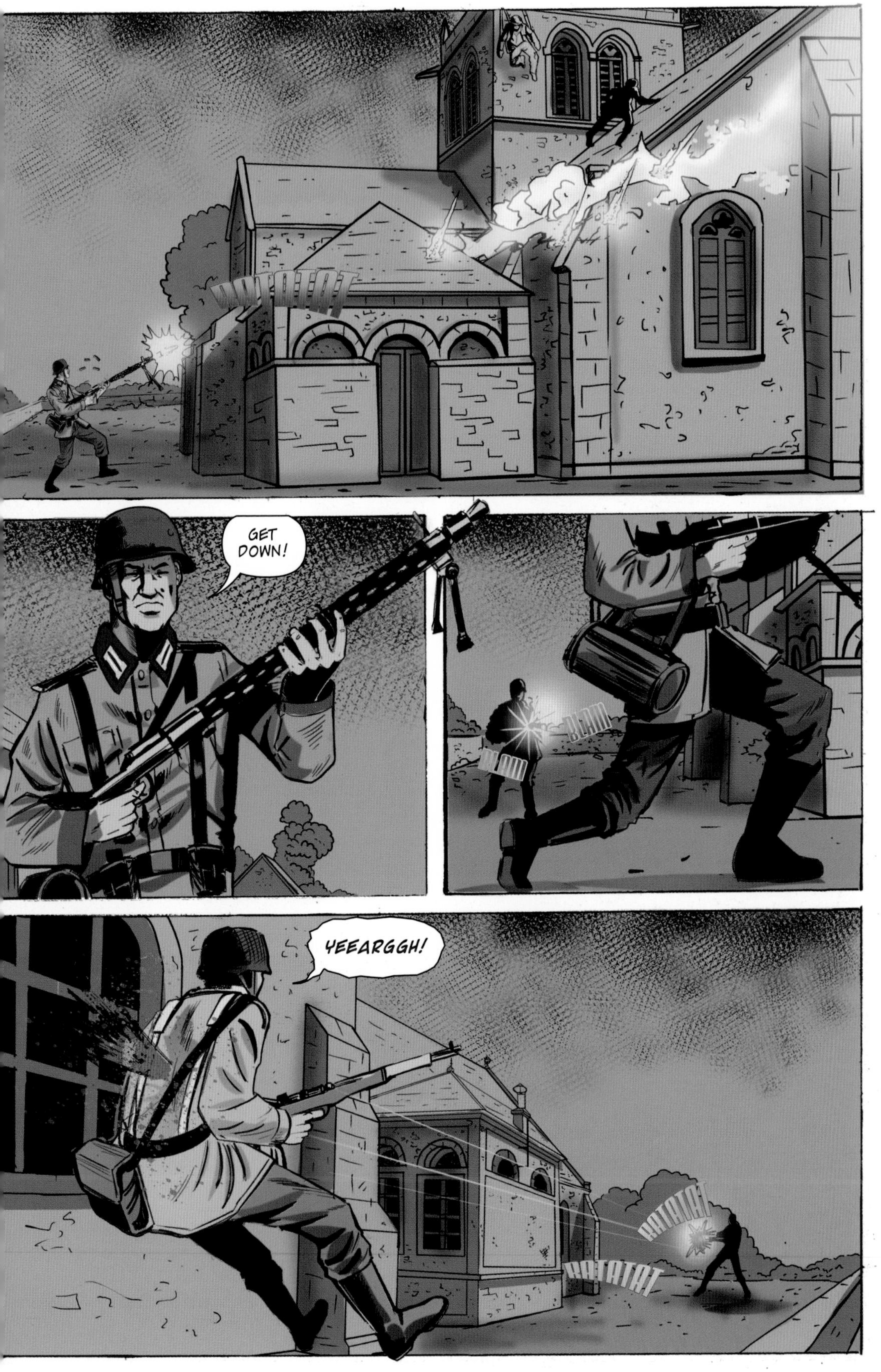
GET DOWN!
BLAM
BLAM
YEEARGGH!
RATATAT
RATATAT

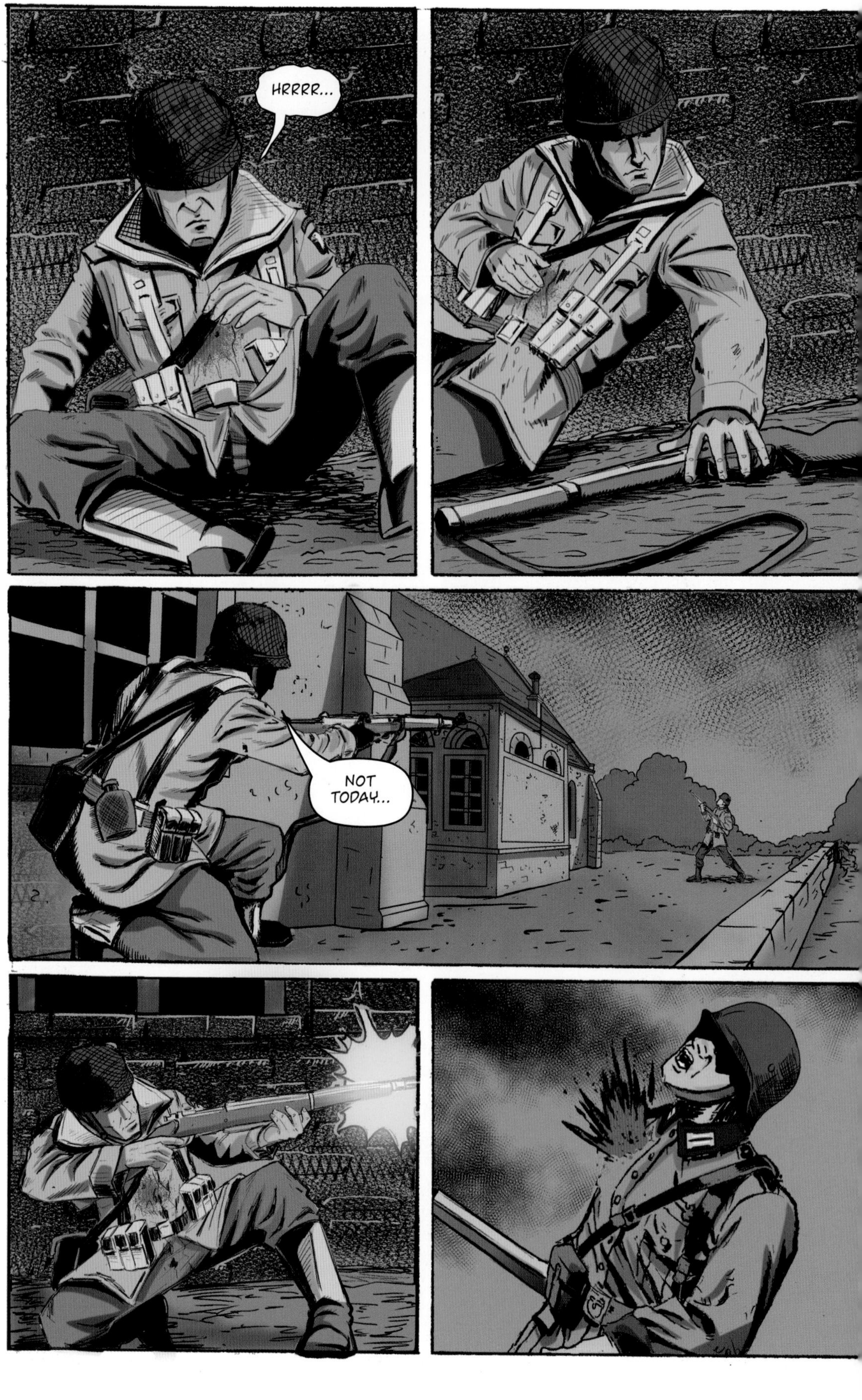
HRRRR...
NOT TODAY...

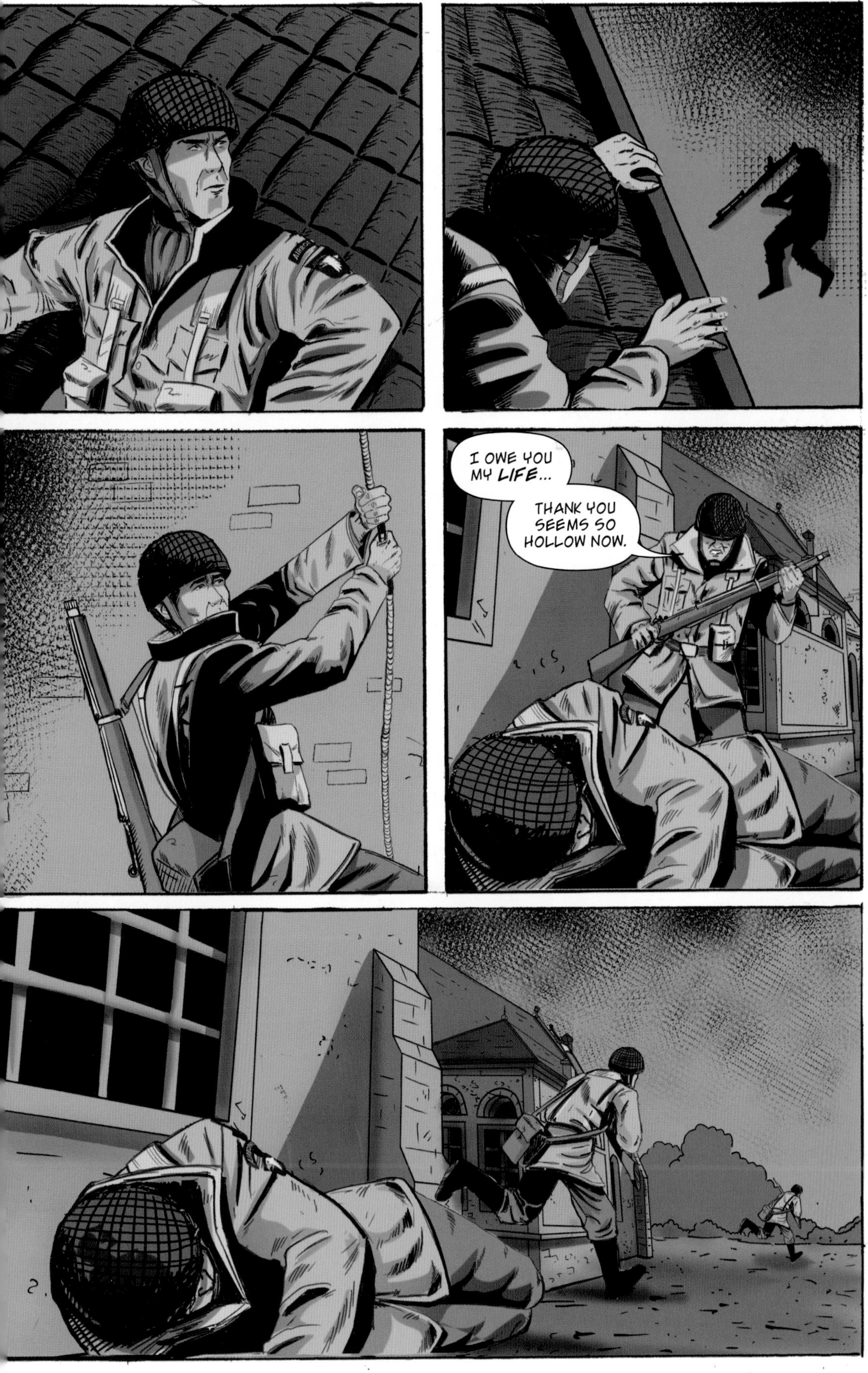

I OWE YOU MY *LIFE*...
THANK YOU SEEMS SO HOLLOW NOW.

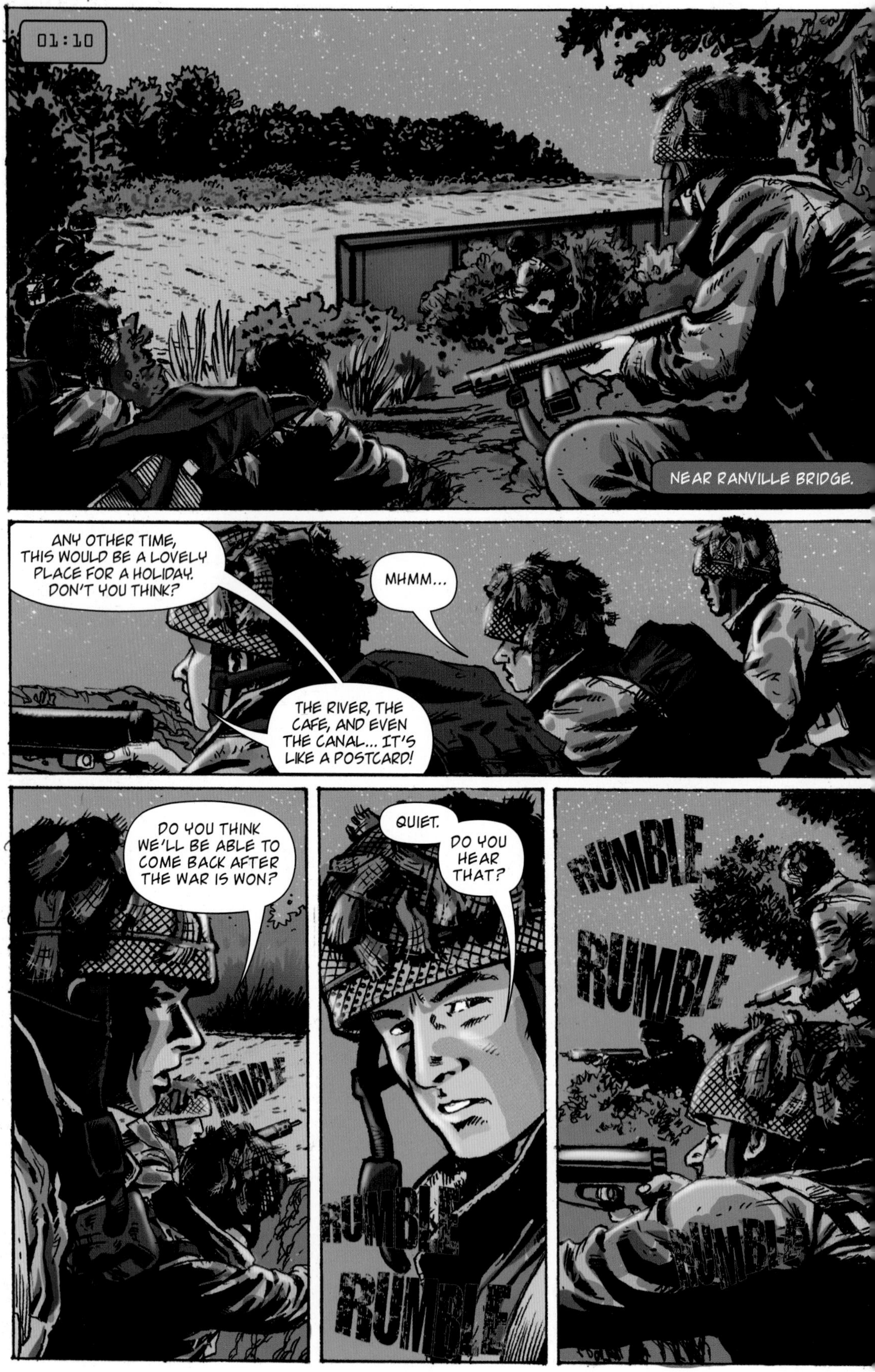

01:10
NEAR RANVILLE BRIDGE.
ANY OTHER TIME, THIS WOULD BE A LOVELY PLACE FOR A HOLIDAY. DON'T YOU THINK?
MHMM...
THE RIVER, THE CAFE, AND EVEN THE CANAL... IT'S LIKE A POSTCARD!
DO YOU THINK WE'LL BE ABLE TO COME BACK AFTER THE WAR IS WON?
RUMBLE
QUIET.
DO YOU HEAR THAT?
RUMBLE
RUMBLE
RUMBLE
RUMBLE
RUMBLE

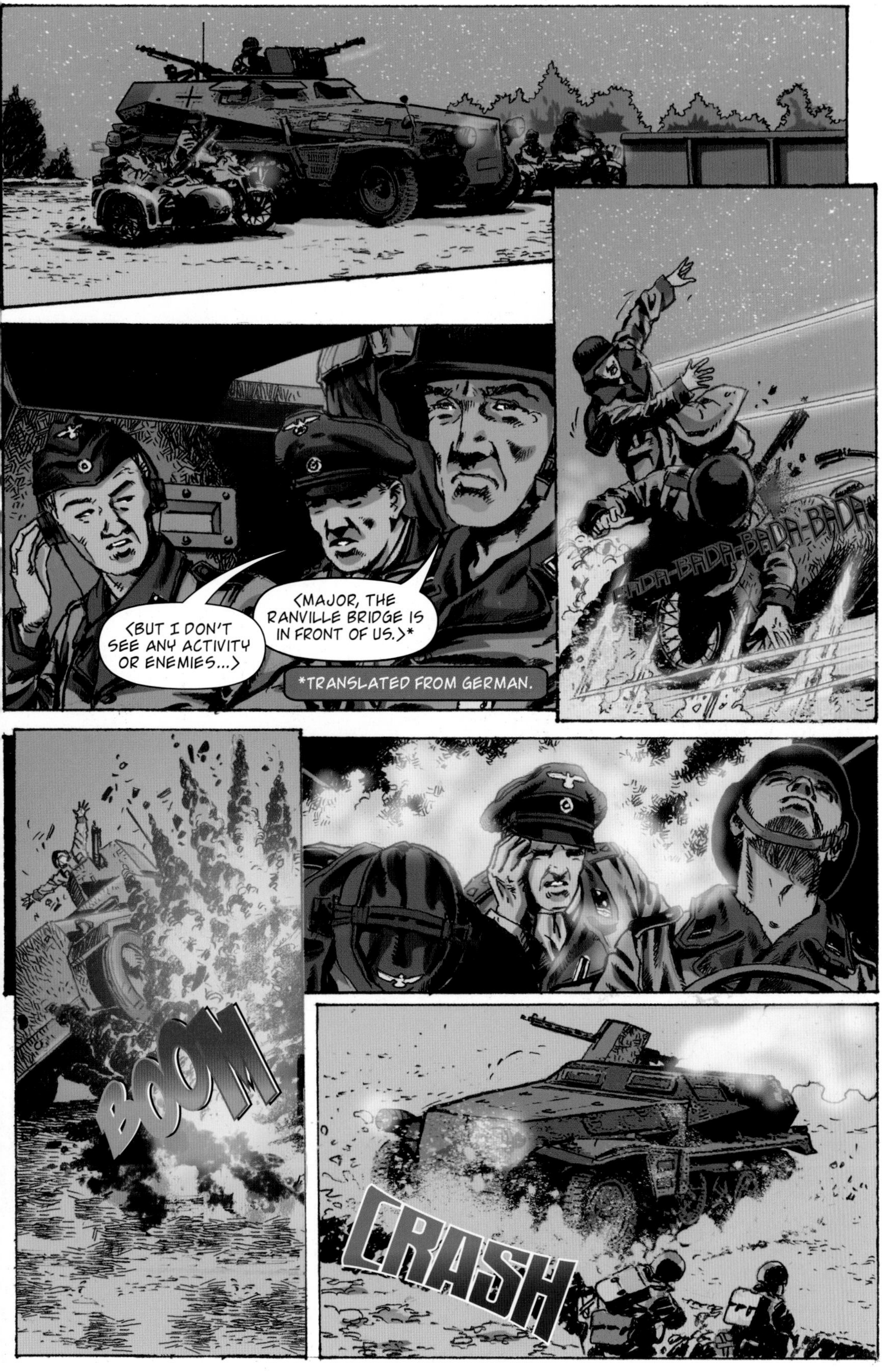

<MAJOR, THE RANVILLE BRIDGE IS IN FRONT OF US.>*
<BUT I DON'T SEE ANY ACTIVITY OR ENEMIES...>
*TRANSLATED FROM GERMAN.
BADA-BADA-BADA-BADA
BOOM
CRASH

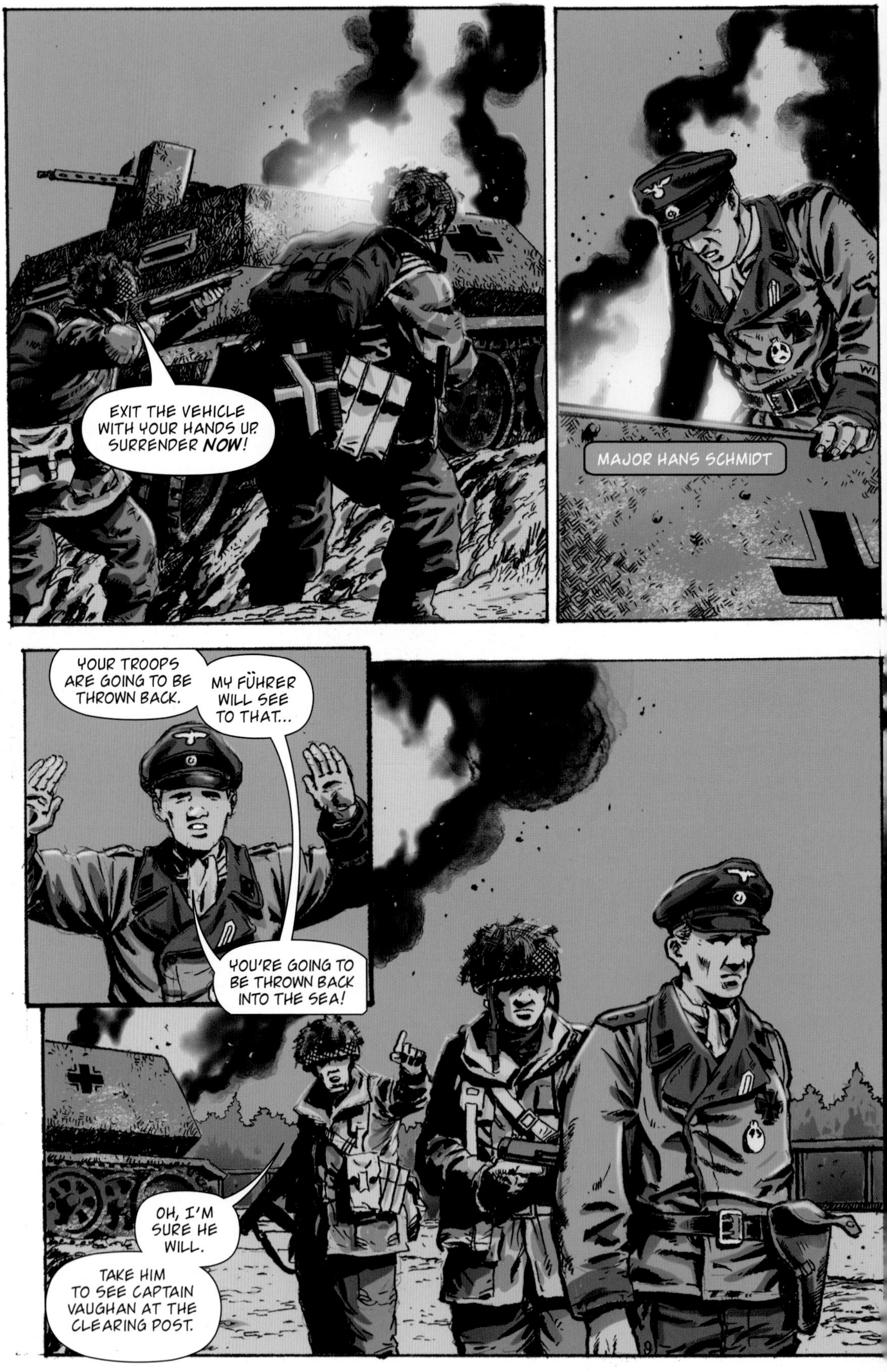
EXIT THE VEHICLE WITH YOUR HANDS UP. SURRENDER NOW!
MAJOR HANS SCHMIDT
YOUR TROOPS ARE GOING TO BE THROWN BACK.
MY FÜHRER WILL SEE TO THAT...
YOU'RE GOING TO BE THROWN BACK INTO THE SEA!
OH, I'M SURE HE WILL.
TAKE HIM TO SEE CAPTAIN VAUGHAN AT THE CLEARING POST.

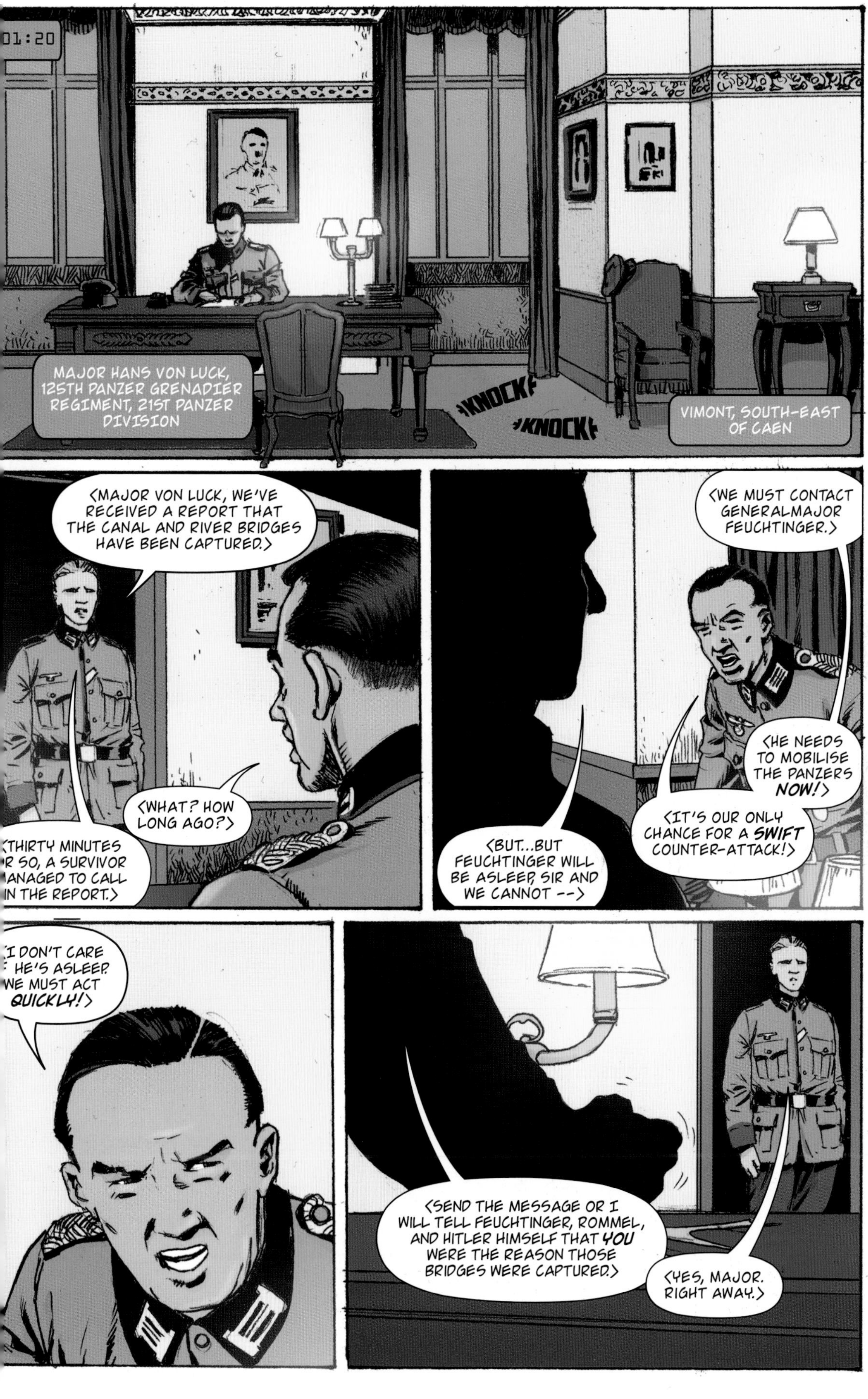
01:20
MAJOR HANS VON LUCK, 125TH PANZER GRENADIER REGIMENT, 21ST PANZER DIVISION
KNOCK
KNOCK
VIMONT, SOUTH-EAST OF CAEN
<MAJOR VON LUCK, WE'VE RECEIVED A REPORT THAT THE CANAL AND RIVER BRIDGES HAVE BEEN CAPTURED.>
<WHAT? HOW LONG AGO?>
<THIRTY MINUTES R SO, A SURVIVOR ANAGED TO CALL IN THE REPORT.>
<WE MUST CONTACT GENERALMAJOR FEUCHTINGER.>
<HE NEEDS TO MOBILISE THE PANZERS NOW!>
<BUT...BUT FEUCHTINGER WILL BE ASLEEP, SIR AND WE CANNOT -->
<IT'S OUR ONLY CHANCE FOR A SWIFT COUNTER-ATTACK!>
<I DON'T CARE HE'S ASLEEP. WE MUST ACT QUICKLY!>
<SEND THE MESSAGE OR I WILL TELL FEUCHTINGER, ROMMEL, AND HITLER HIMSELF THAT YOU WERE THE REASON THOSE BRIDGES WERE CAPTURED.>
<YES, MAJOR. RIGHT AWAY.>

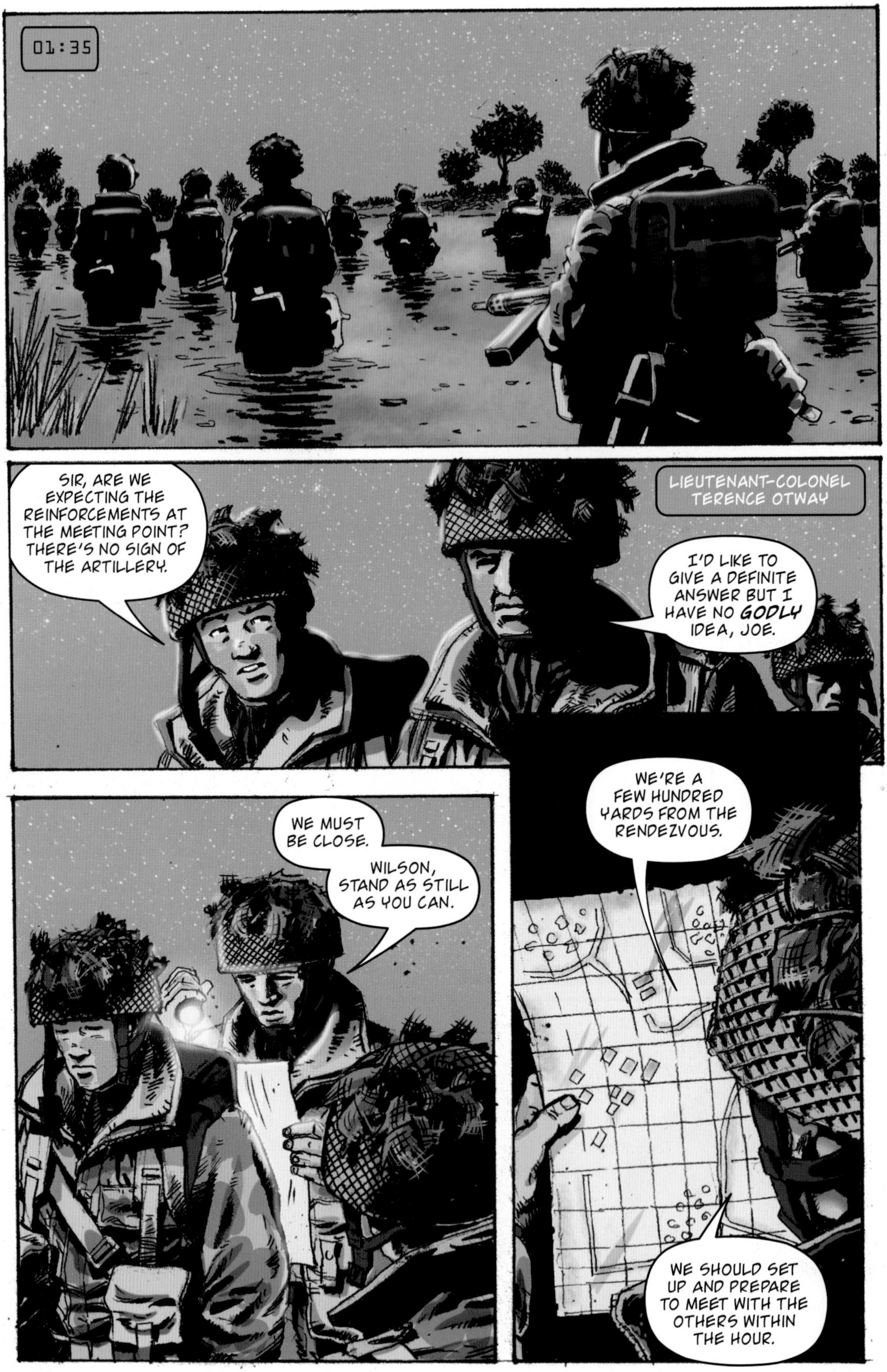
01:35
SIR, ARE WE EXPECTING THE REINFORCEMENTS AT THE MEETING POINT? THERE'S NO SIGN OF THE ARTILLERY.
LIEUTENANT-COLONEL TERENCE OTWAY
I'D LIKE TO GIVE A DEFINITE ANSWER BUT I HAVE NO GODLY IDEA, JOE.
WE MUST BE CLOSE.
WILSON, STAND AS STILL AS YOU CAN.
WE'RE A FEW HUNDRED YARDS FROM THE RENDEZVOUS.
WE SHOULD SET UP AND PREPARE TO MEET WITH THE OTHERS WITHIN THE HOUR.

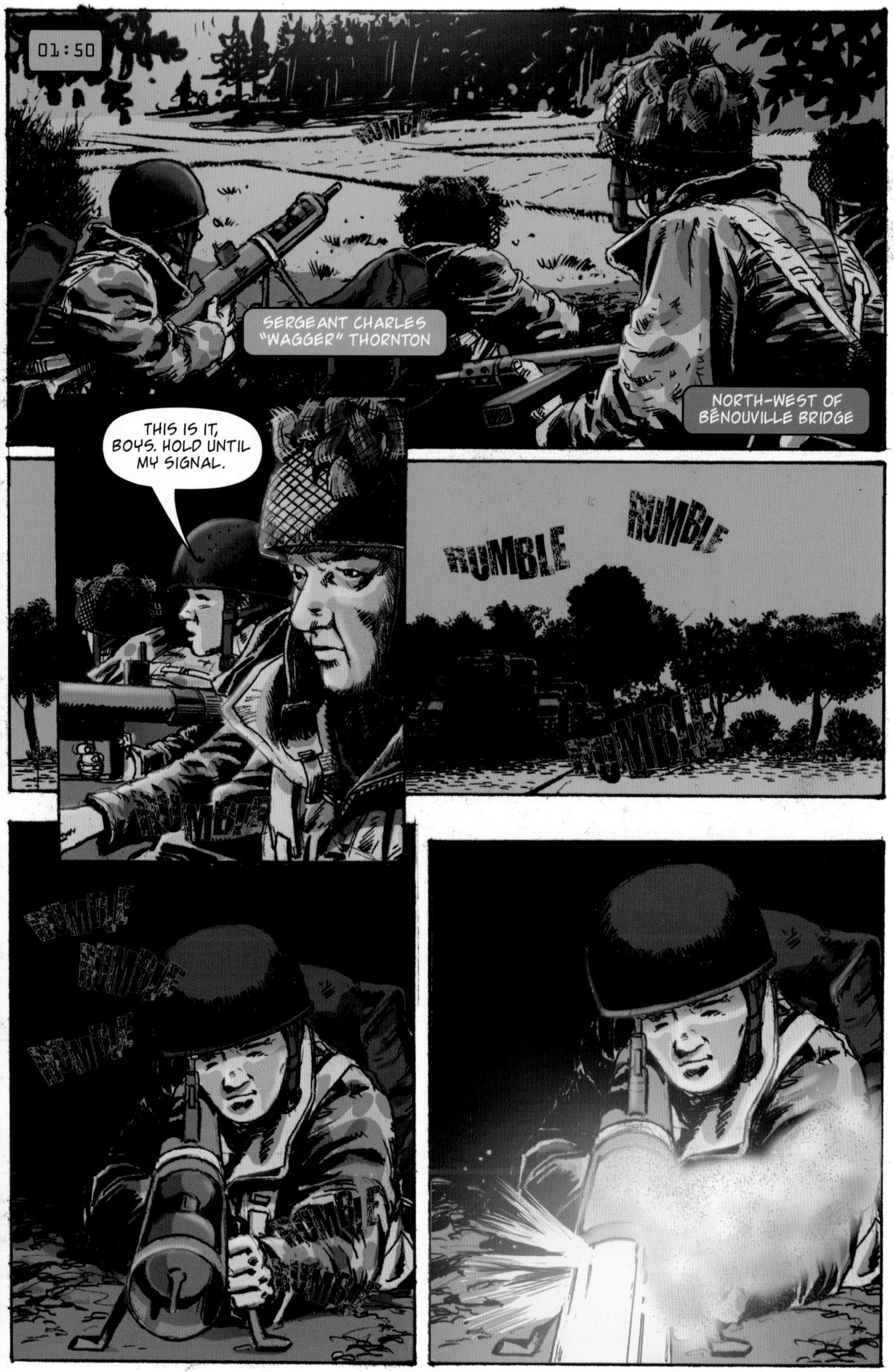
01:50
RUMBLE
SERGEANT CHARLES "WAGGER" THORNTON
NORTH-WEST OF BÉNOUVILLE BRIDGE
THIS IS IT, BOYS. HOLD UNTIL MY SIGNAL.
RUMBLE
RUMBLE
RUMBLE
RUMBLE
RUMBLE
RUMBLE
RUMBLE
RUMBLE
RUMBLE

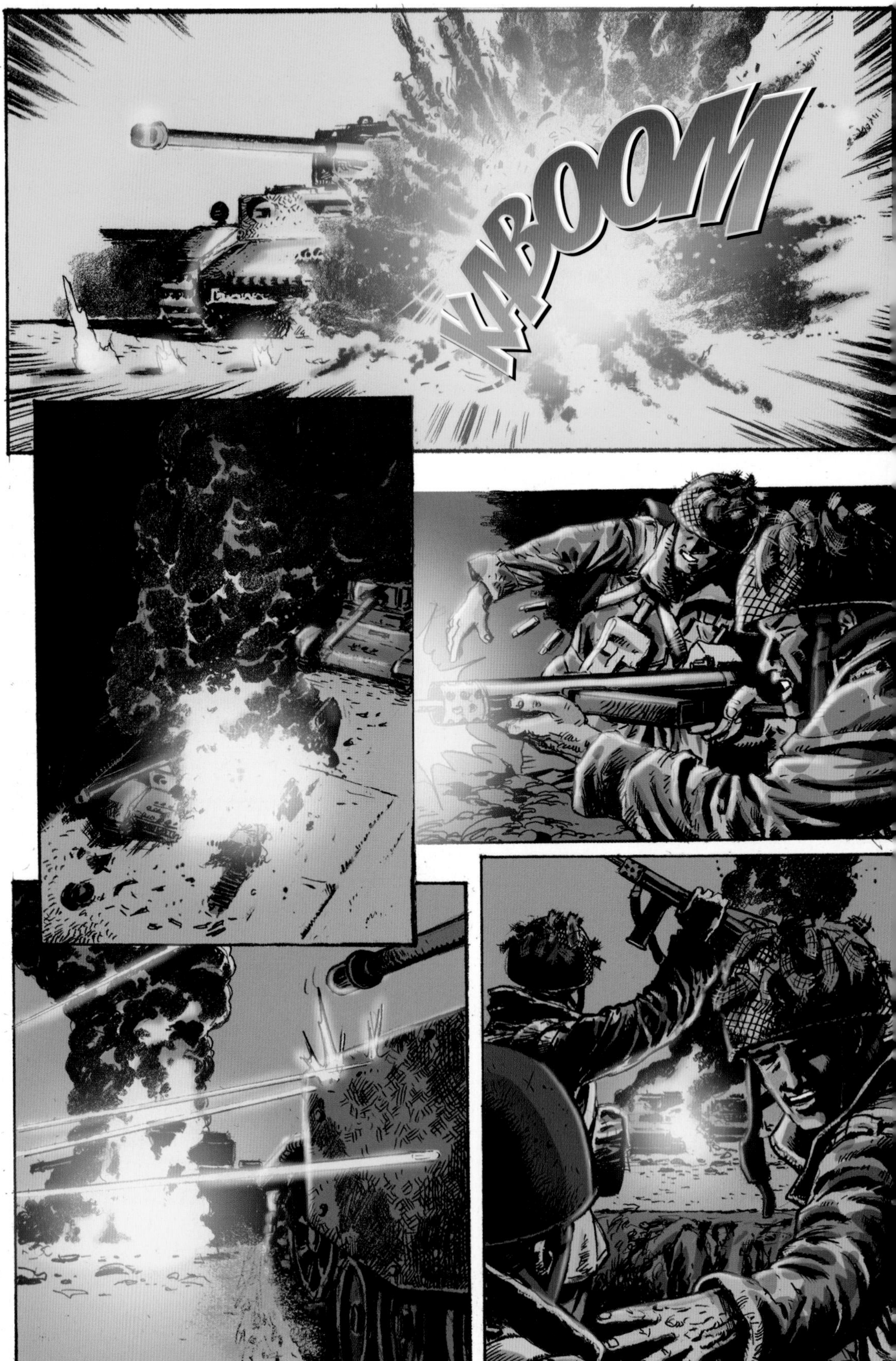
KABOOM

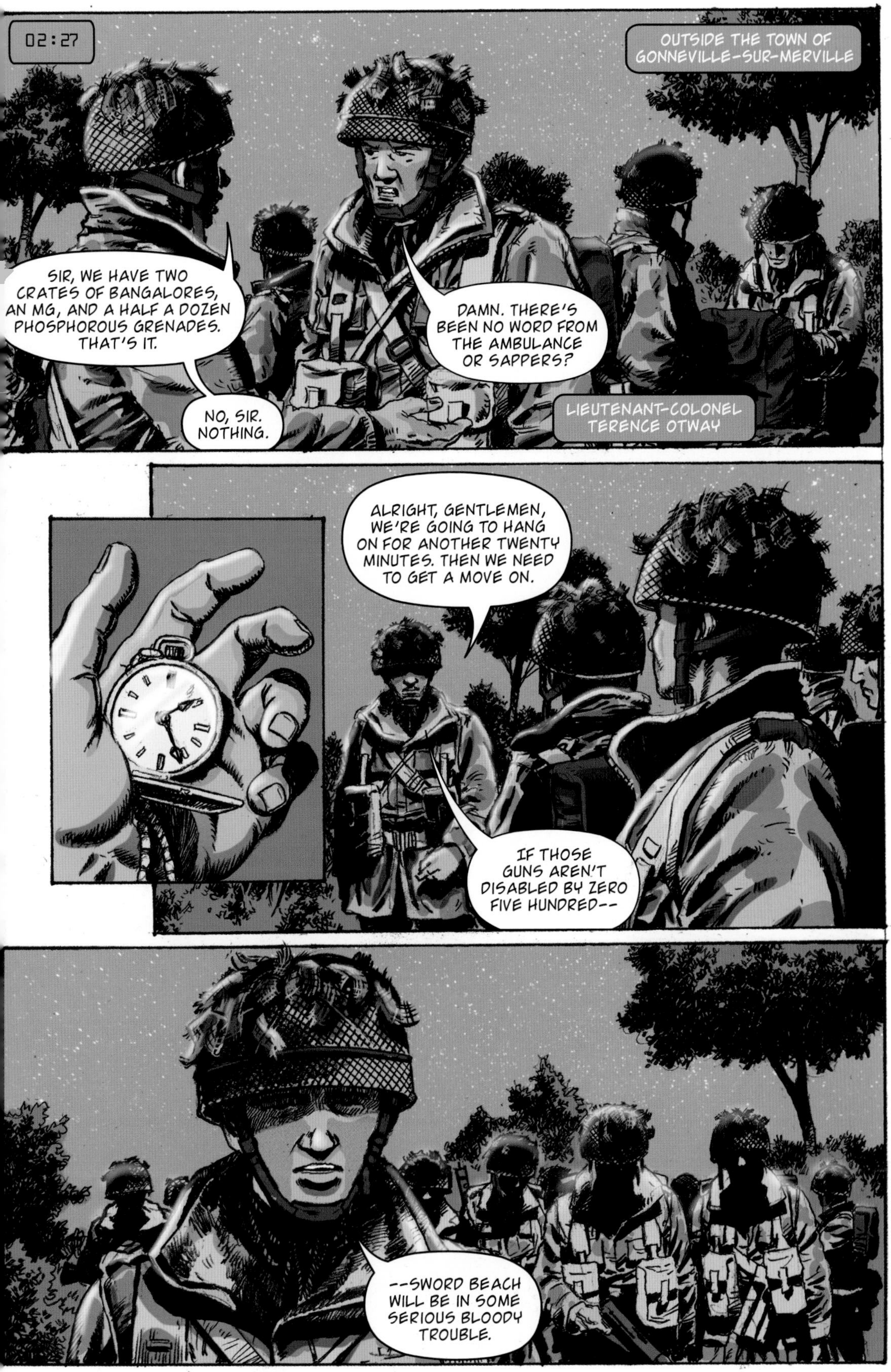
02:27
OUTSIDE THE TOWN OF GONNEVILLE-SUR-MERVILLE
SIR, WE HAVE TWO CRATES OF BANGALORES, AN MG, AND A HALF A DOZEN PHOSPHOROUS GRENADES. THAT'S IT.
DAMN. THERE'S BEEN NO WORD FROM THE AMBULANCE OR SAPPERS?
NO, SIR. NOTHING.
LIEUTENANT-COLONEL TERENCE OTWAY
ALRIGHT, GENTLEMEN, WE'RE GOING TO HANG ON FOR ANOTHER TWENTY MINUTES. THEN WE NEED TO GET A MOVE ON.
IF THOSE GUNS AREN'T DISABLED BY ZERO FIVE HUNDRED--
--SWORD BEACH WILL BE IN SOME SERIOUS BLOODY TROUBLE.

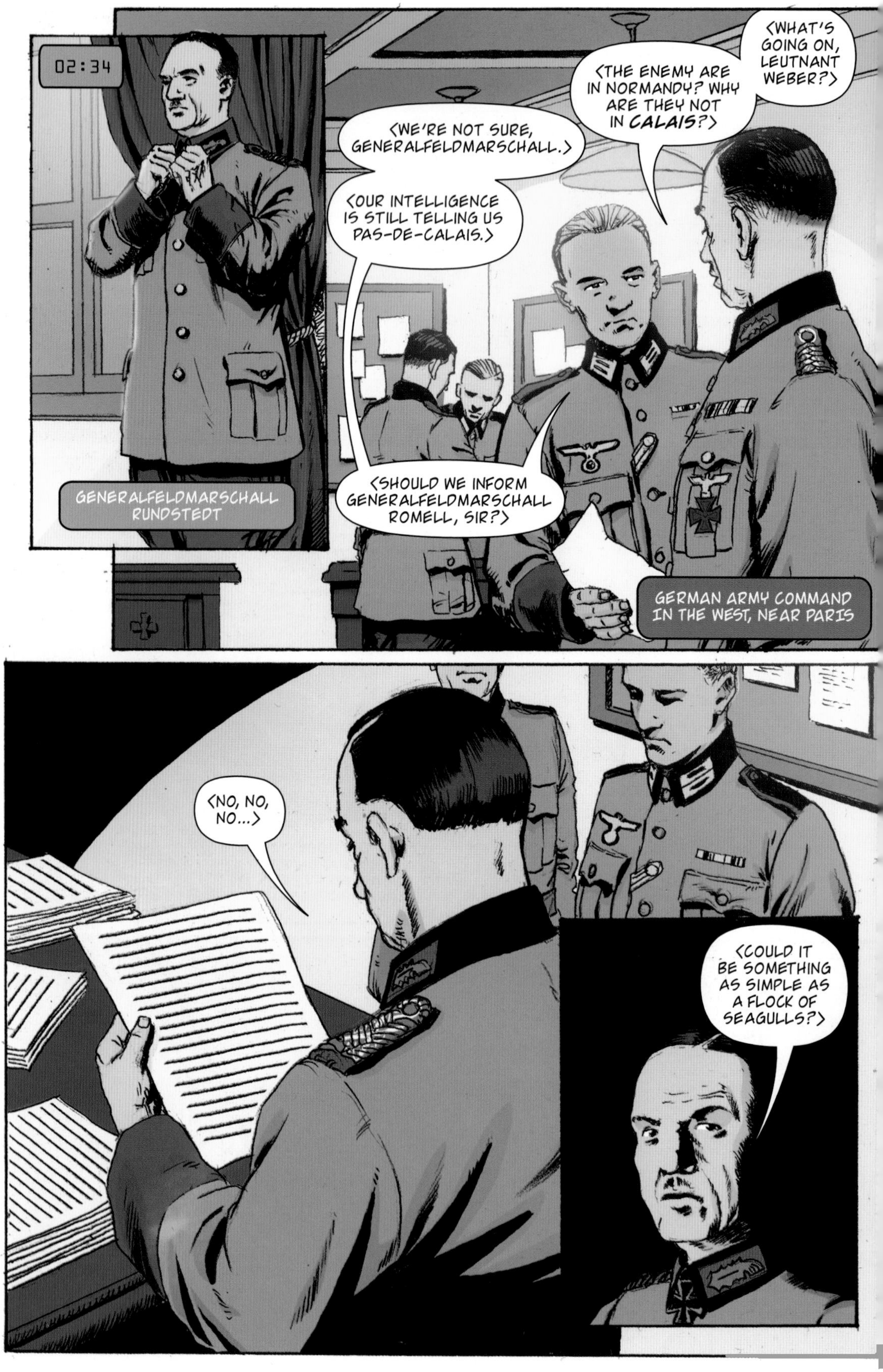

02:34
GENERALFELDMARSCHALL RUNDSTEDT
<WHAT'S GOING ON, LEUTNANT WEBER?>
<THE ENEMY ARE IN NORMANDY? WHY ARE THEY NOT IN CALAIS?>
<WE'RE NOT SURE, GENERALFELDMARSCHALL.>
<OUR INTELLIGENCE IS STILL TELLING US PAS-DE-CALAIS.>
<SHOULD WE INFORM GENERALFELDMARSCHALL ROMELL, SIR?>
GERMAN ARMY COMMAND IN THE WEST, NEAR PARIS
<NO, NO, NO...>
<COULD IT BE SOMETHING AS SIMPLE AS A FLOCK OF SEAGULLS?>

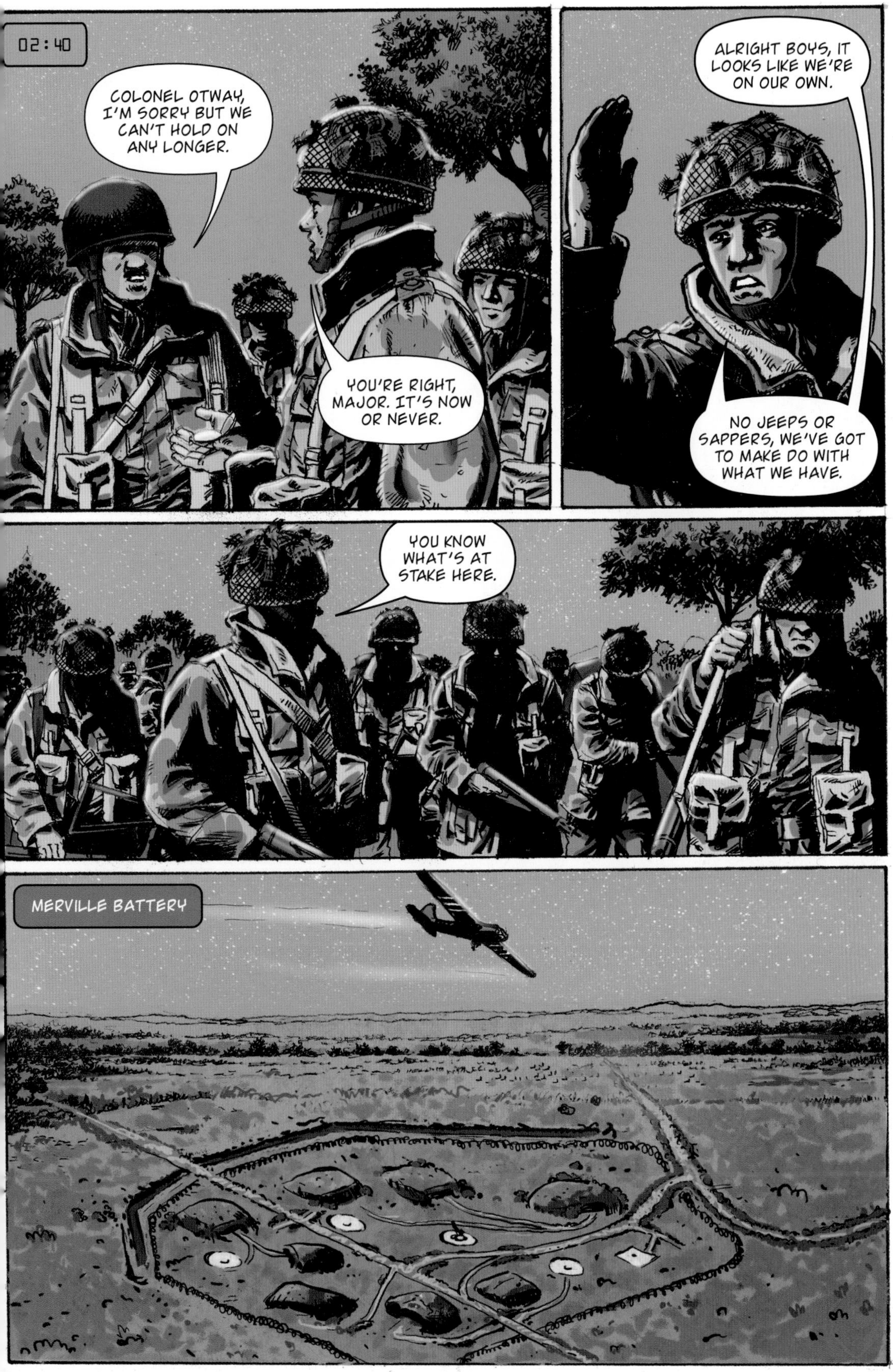
02:40
COLONEL OTWAY, I'M SORRY BUT WE CAN'T HOLD ON ANY LONGER.
YOU'RE RIGHT, MAJOR. IT'S NOW OR NEVER.
ALRIGHT BOYS, IT LOOKS LIKE WE'RE ON OUR OWN.
NO JEEPS OR SAPPERS, WE'VE GOT TO MAKE DO WITH WHAT WE HAVE.
YOU KNOW WHAT'S AT STAKE HERE.
MERVILLE BATTERY

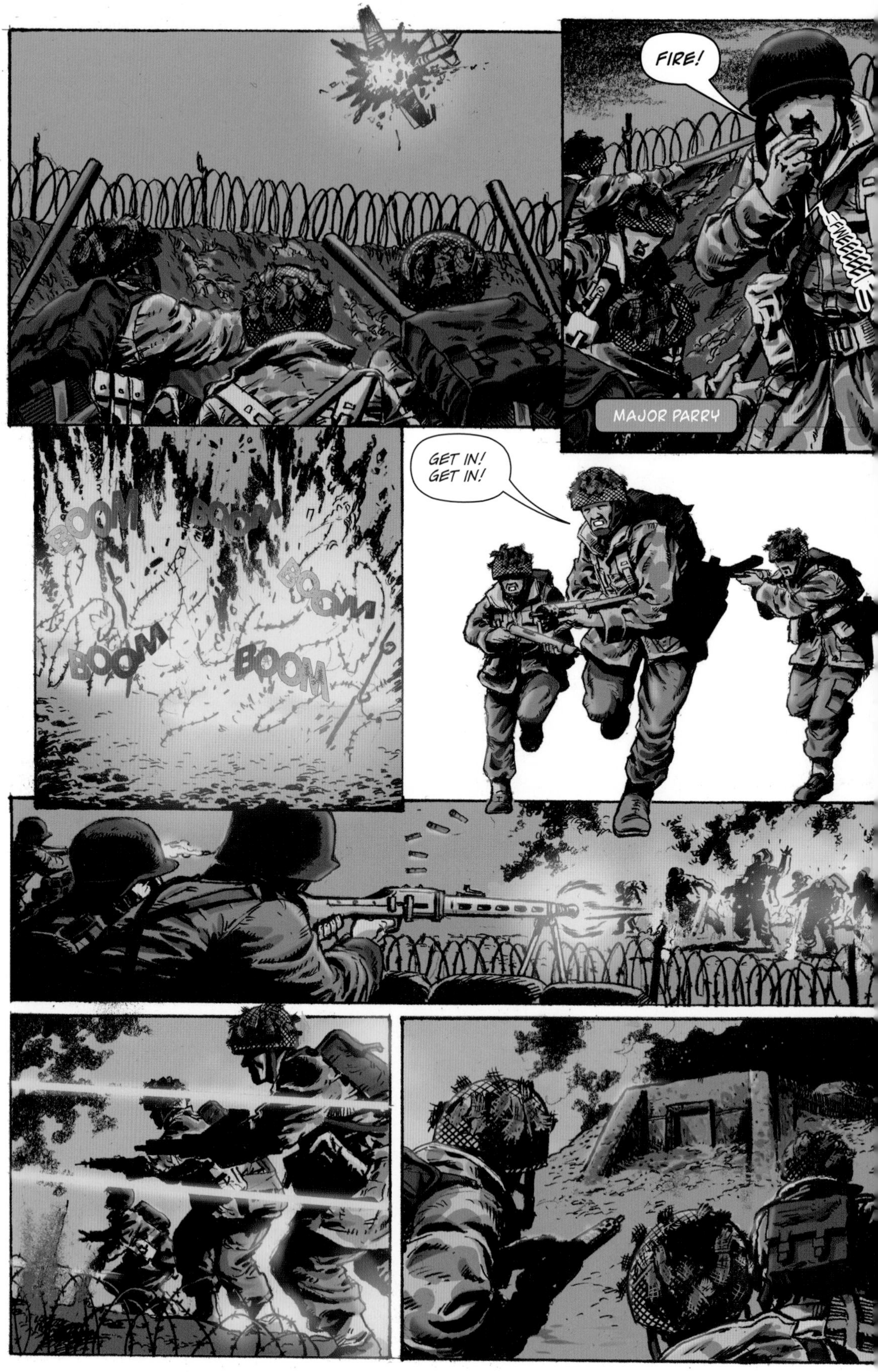
FIRE!
FWEEEEE!
MAJOR PARRY
BOOM BOOM BOOM BOOM BOOM
GET IN! GET IN!

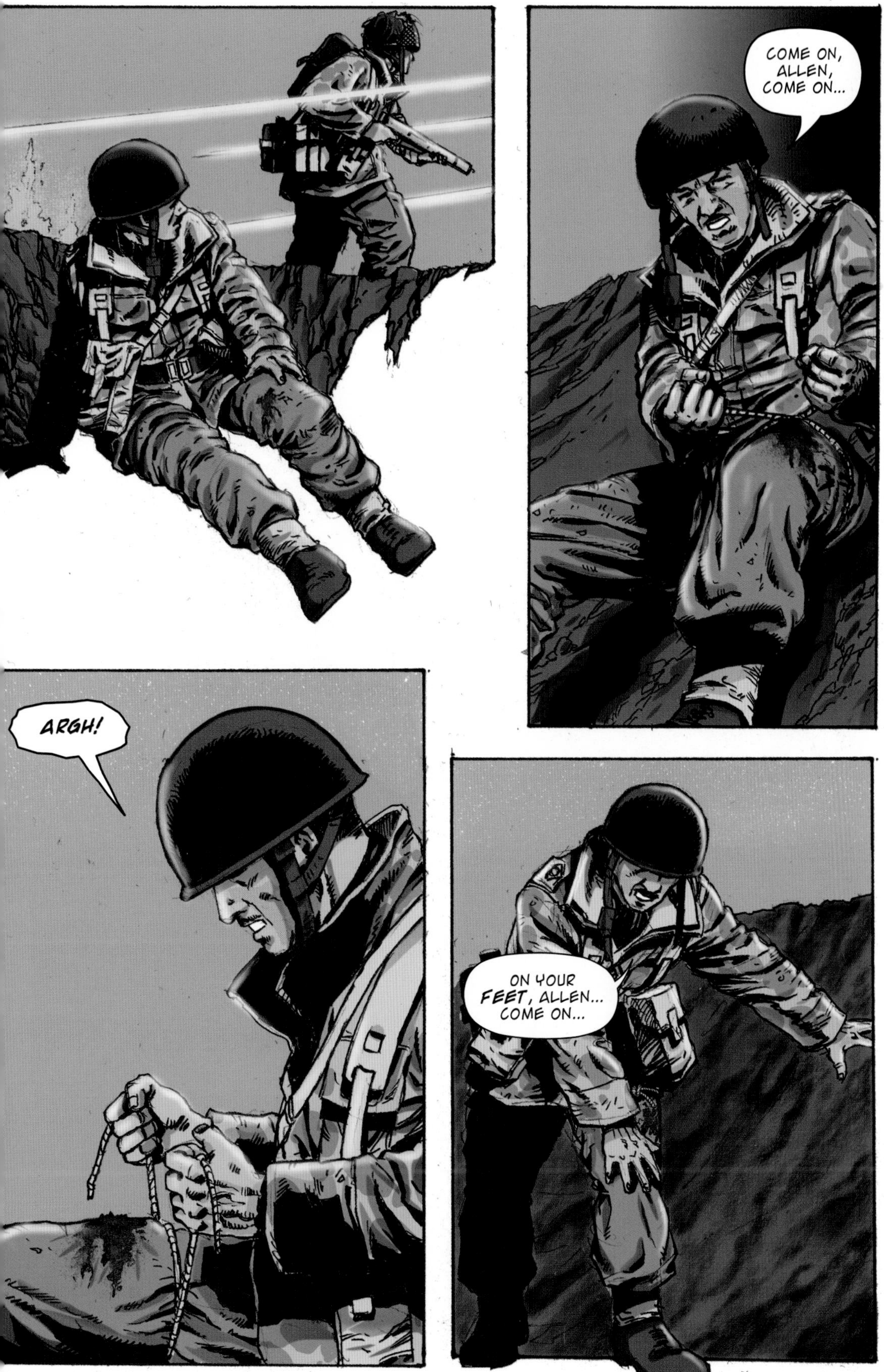
COME ON, ALLEN, COME ON...
ARGH!
ON YOUR FEET, ALLEN... COME ON...

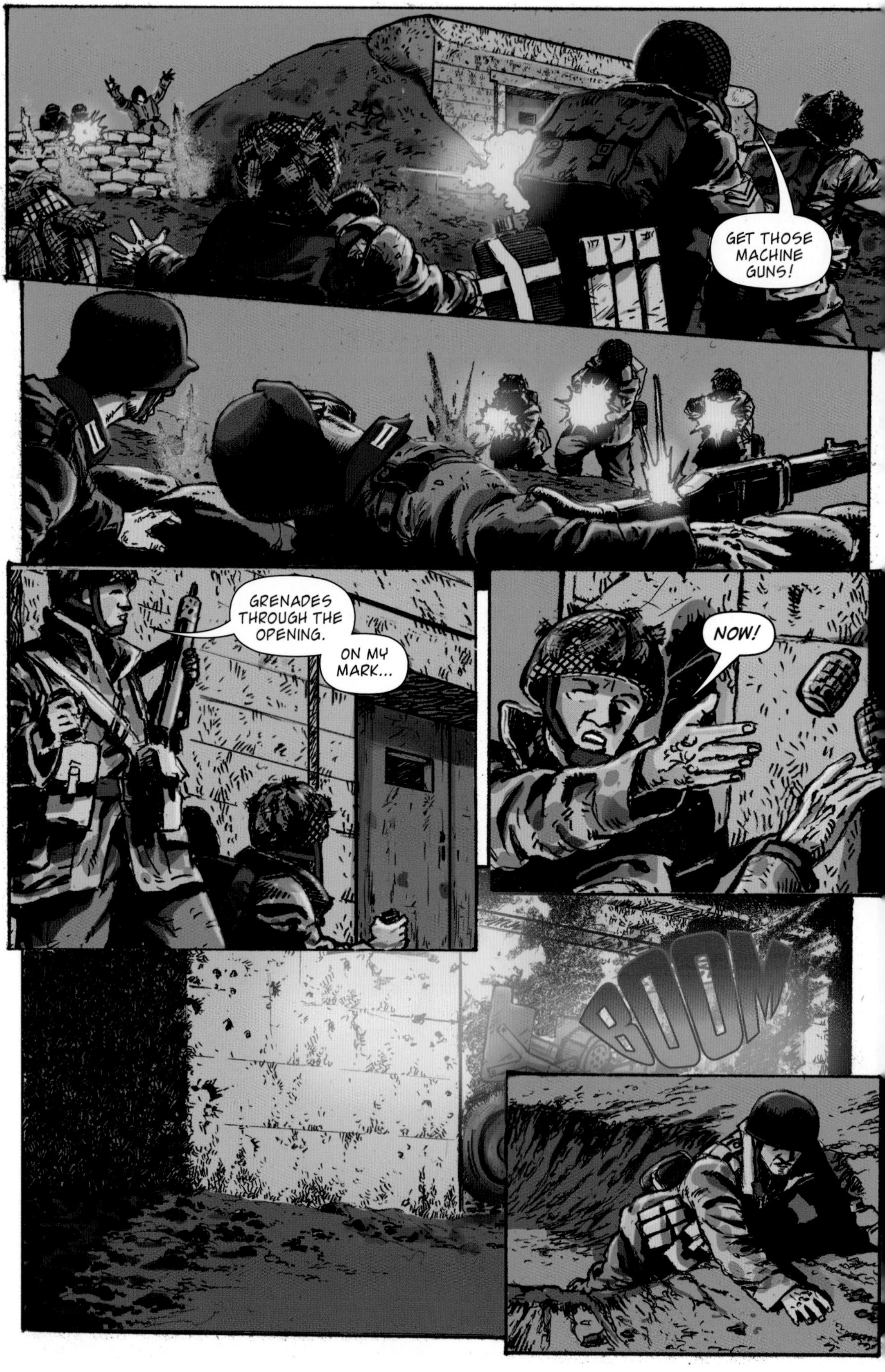
GET THOSE MACHINE GUNS!
GRENADES THROUGH THE OPENING.
ON MY MARK...
NOW!
BOOM

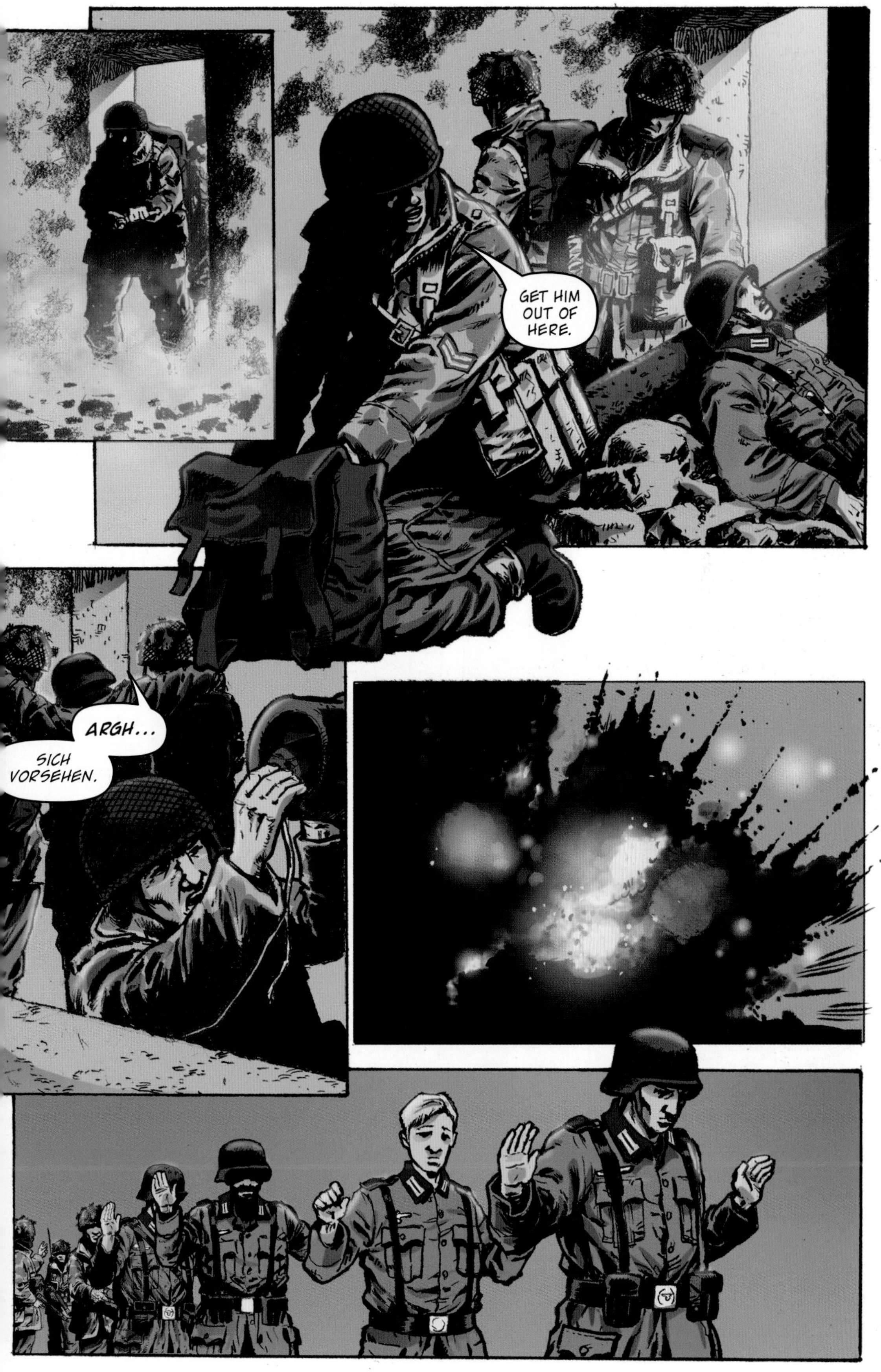
GET HIM OUT OF HERE.
ARGH...
SICH VORSEHEN.

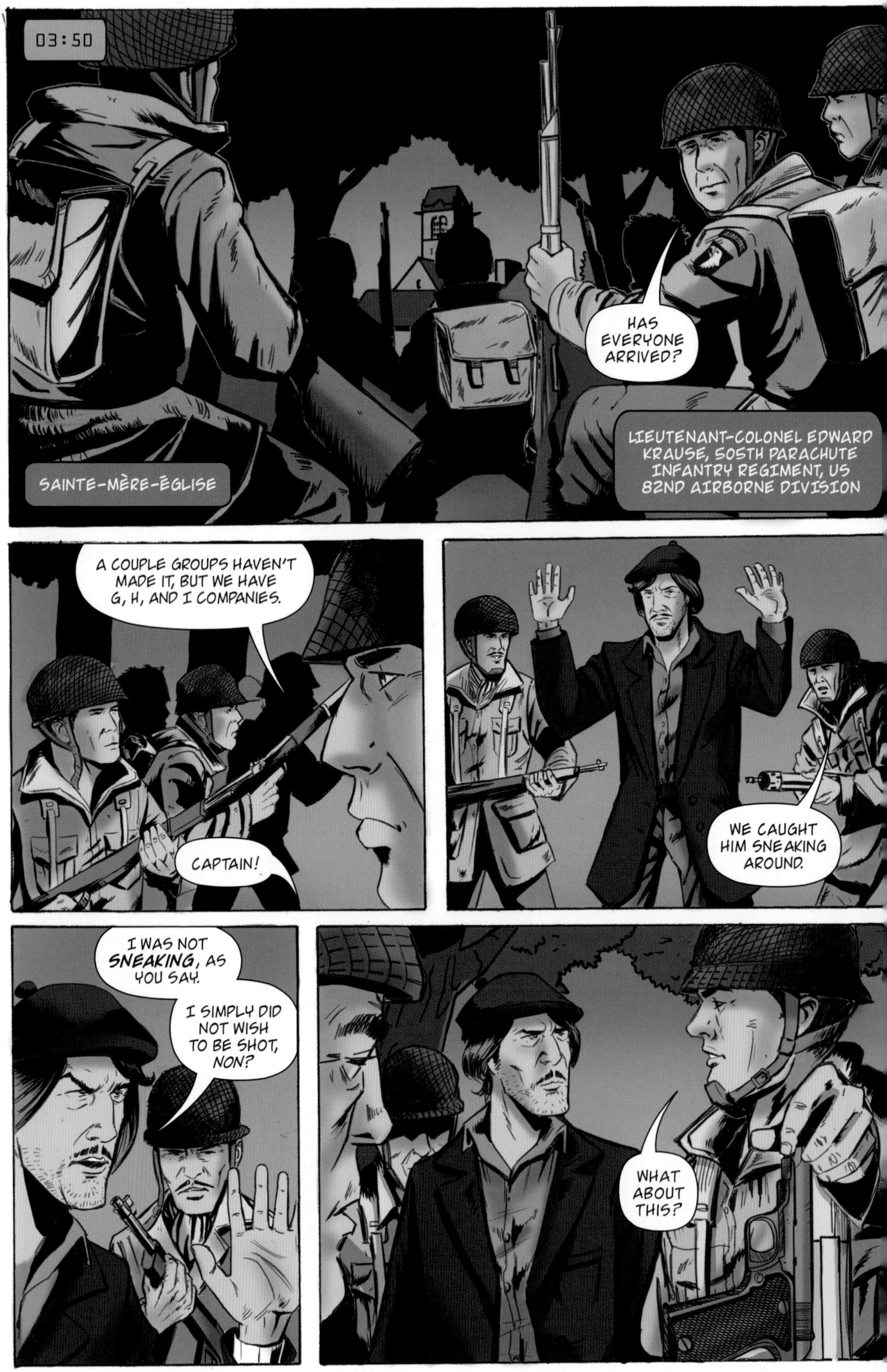
03:50
SAINTE-MÈRE-ÉGLISE
HAS EVERYONE ARRIVED?
LIEUTENANT-COLONEL EDWARD KRAUSE, 505TH PARACHUTE INFANTRY REGIMENT, US 82ND AIRBORNE DIVISION
A COUPLE GROUPS HAVEN'T MADE IT, BUT WE HAVE G, H, AND I COMPANIES.
CAPTAIN!
WE CAUGHT HIM SNEAKING AROUND.
I WAS NOT **SNEAKING**, AS YOU SAY.
I SIMPLY DID NOT WISH TO BE SHOT, *NON?*
WHAT ABOUT THIS?

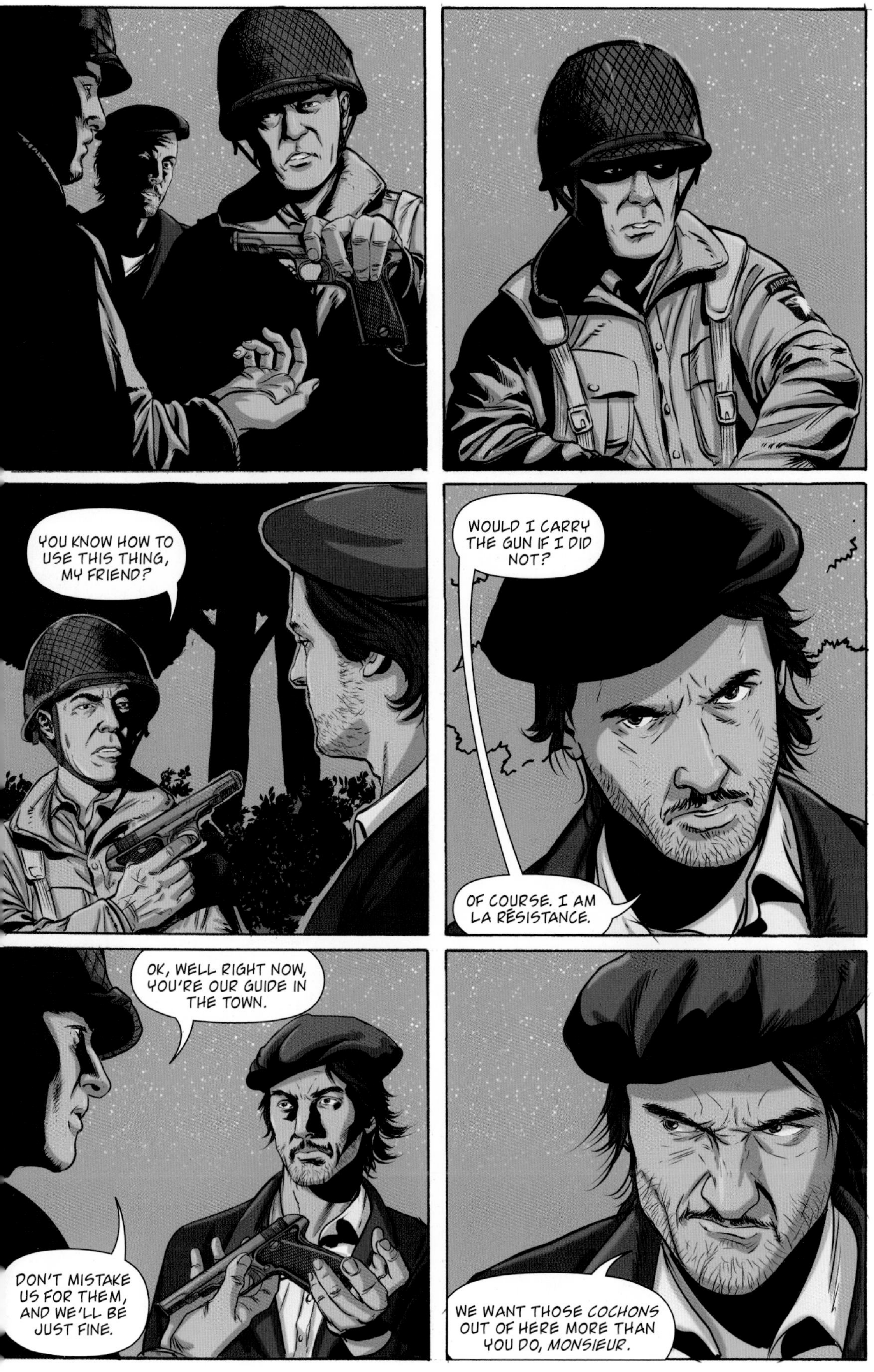
YOU KNOW HOW TO USE THIS THING, MY FRIEND?
WOULD I CARRY THE GUN IF I DID NOT?
OF COURSE. I AM LA RÉSISTANCE.
OK, WELL RIGHT NOW, YOU'RE OUR GUIDE IN THE TOWN.
DON'T MISTAKE US FOR THEM, AND WE'LL BE JUST FINE.
WE WANT THOSE COCHONS OUT OF HERE MORE THAN YOU DO, MONSIEUR.

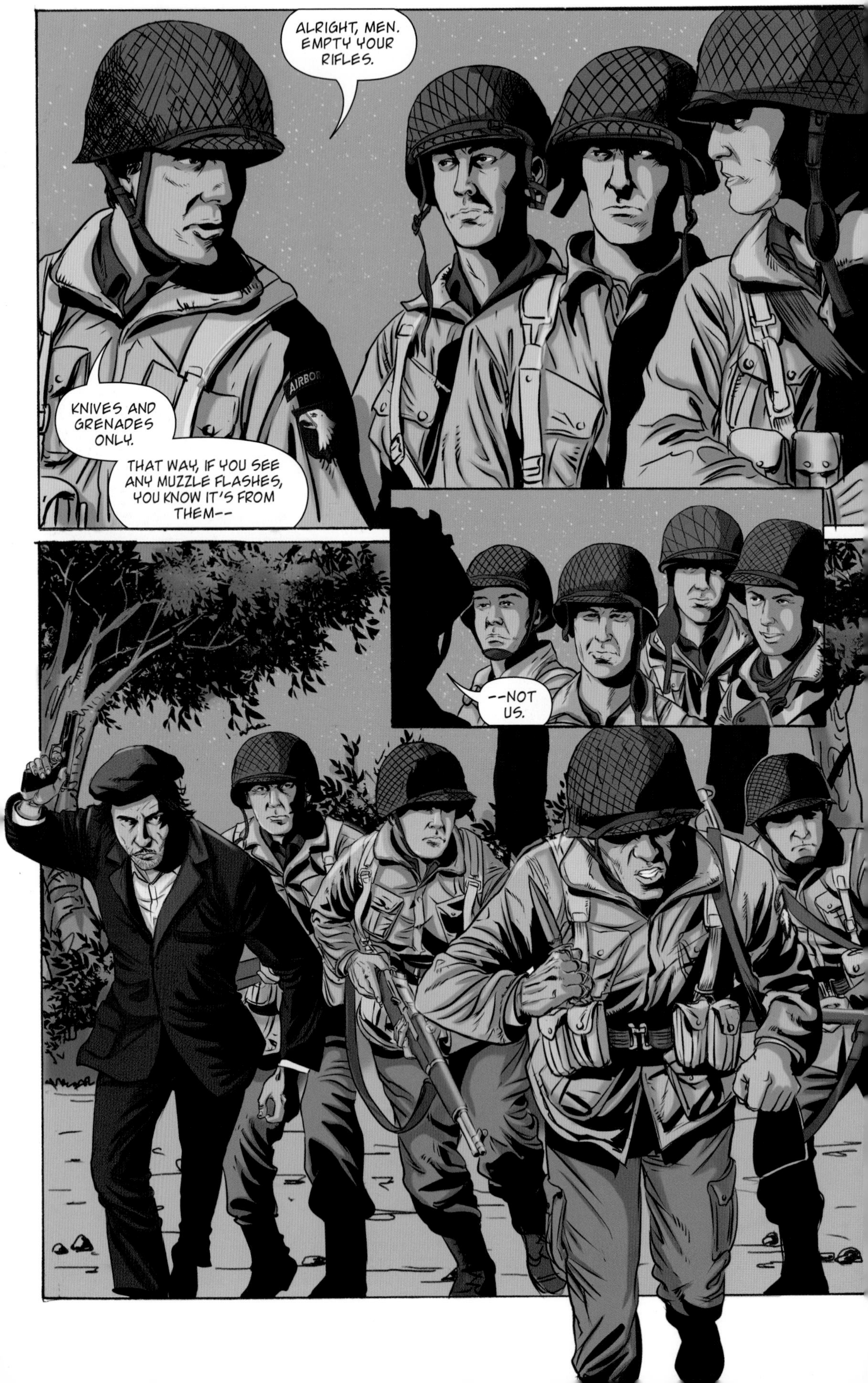
ALRIGHT, MEN. EMPTY YOUR RIFLES.
KNIVES AND GRENADES ONLY.
THAT WAY, IF YOU SEE ANY MUZZLE FLASHES, YOU KNOW IT'S FROM THEM--
--NOT US.
AIRBOR

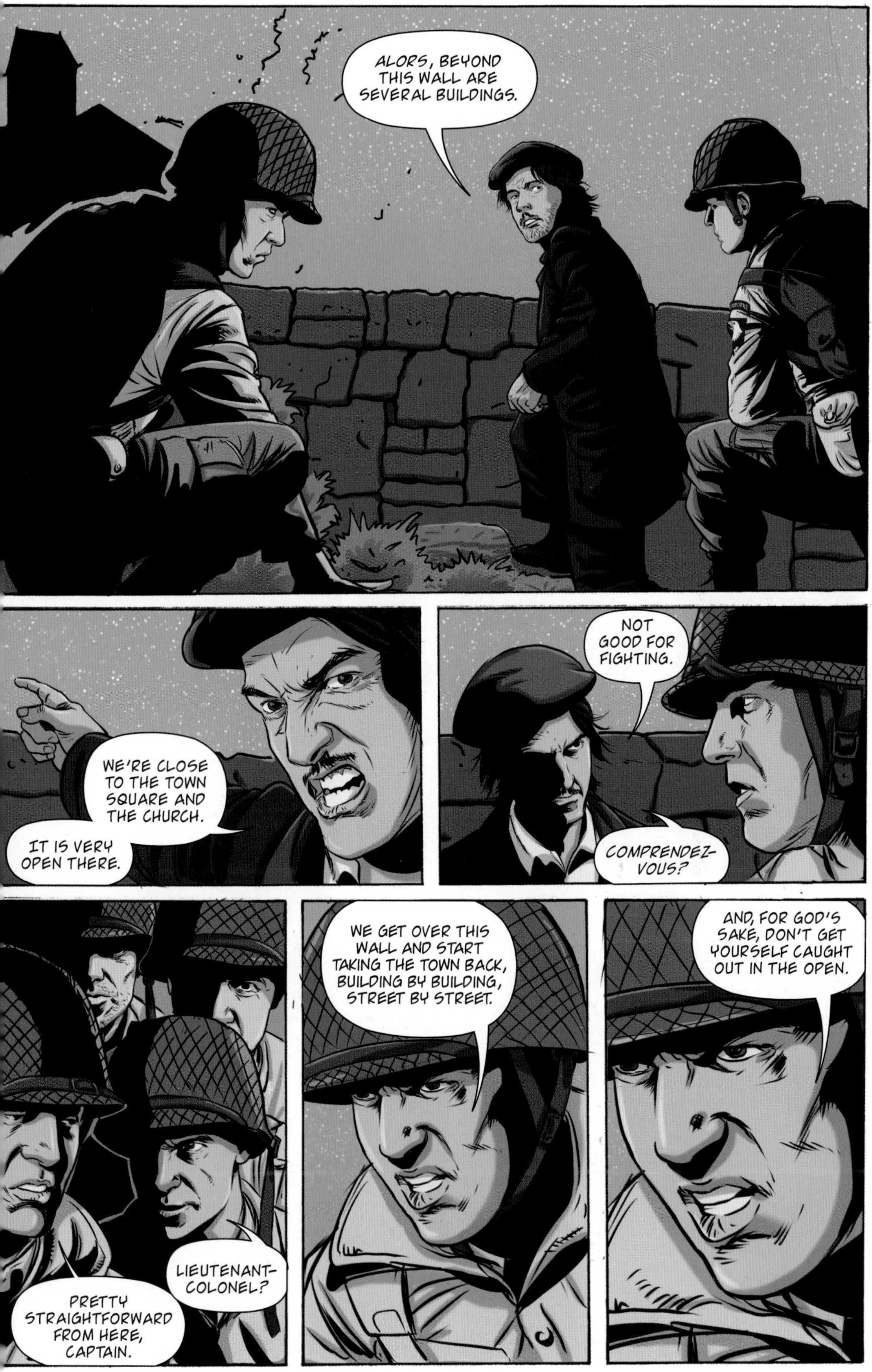
ALORS, BEYOND THIS WALL ARE SEVERAL BUILDINGS.
WE'RE CLOSE TO THE TOWN SQUARE AND THE CHURCH.
IT IS VERY OPEN THERE.
NOT GOOD FOR FIGHTING.
COMPRENDEZ-VOUS?
PRETTY STRAIGHTFORWARD FROM HERE, CAPTAIN.
LIEUTENANT-COLONEL?
WE GET OVER THIS WALL AND START TAKING THE TOWN BACK, BUILDING BY BUILDING, STREET BY STREET.
AND, FOR GOD'S SAKE, DON'T GET YOURSELF CAUGHT OUT IN THE OPEN.

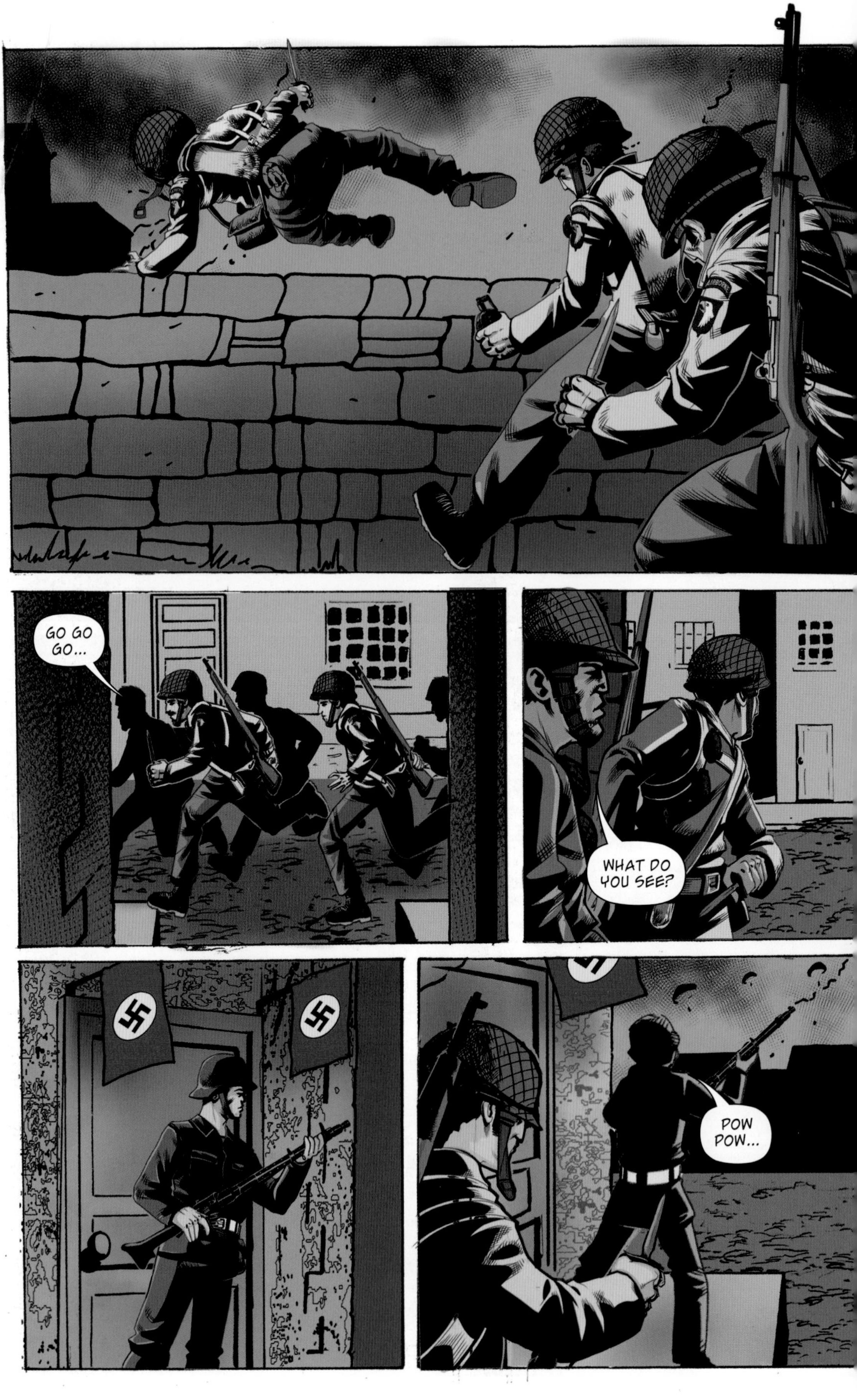
GO GO GO...
WHAT DO YOU SEE?
POW POW...

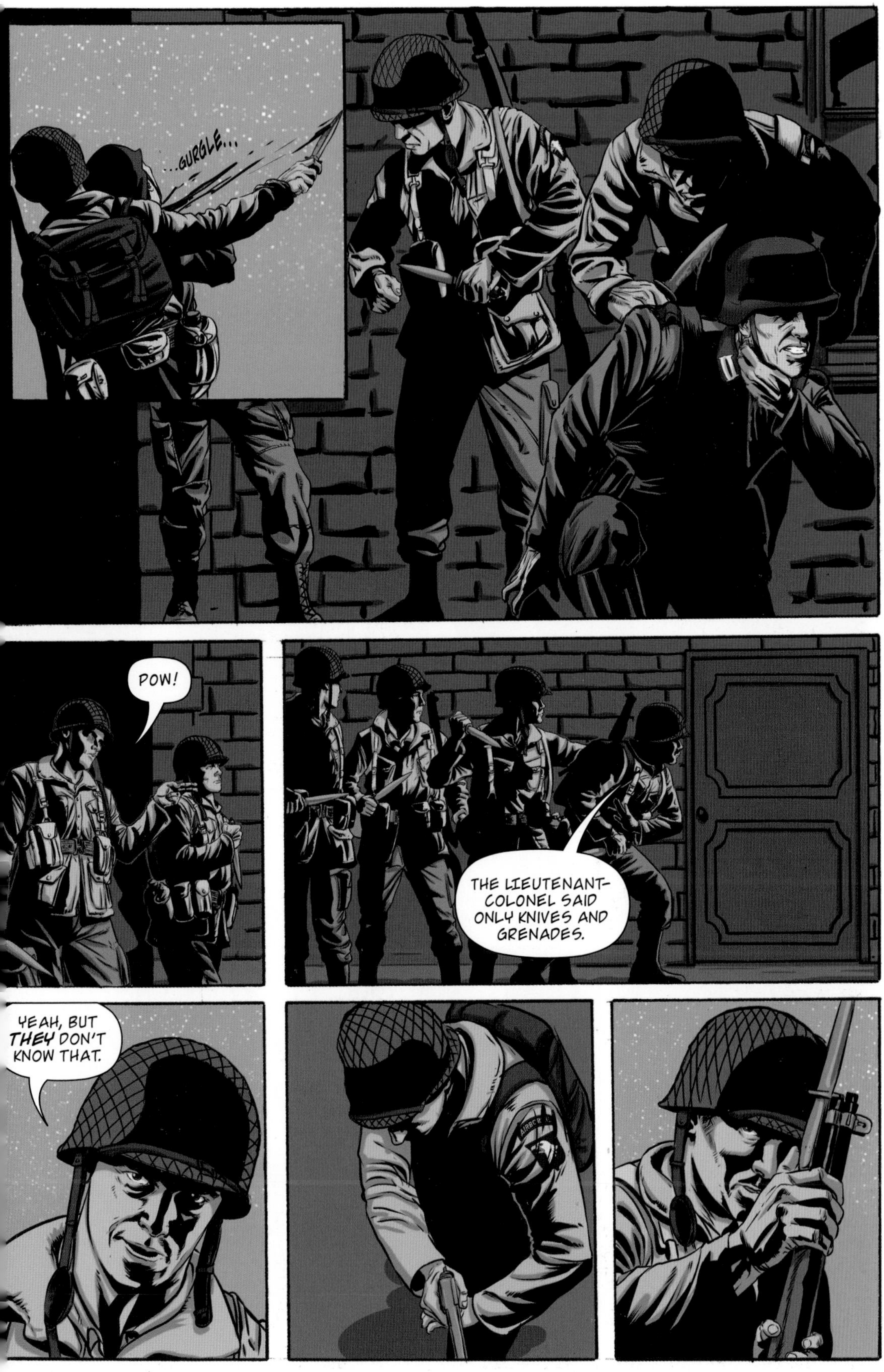
...GURGLE...
POW!
THE LIEUTENANT-COLONEL SAID ONLY KNIVES AND GRENADES.
YEAH, BUT THEY DON'T KNOW THAT.

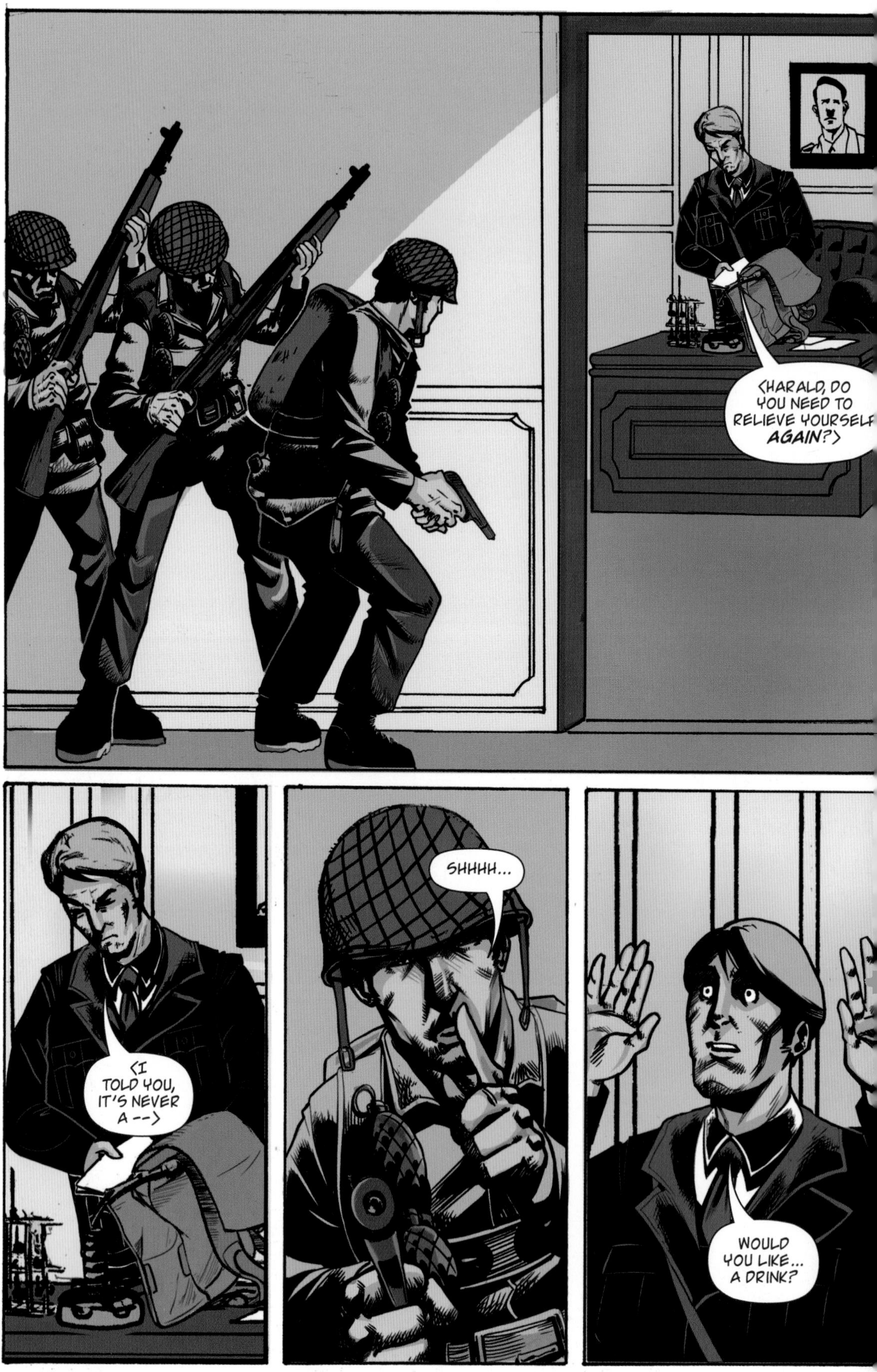
<HARALD, DO YOU NEED TO RELIEVE YOURSELF AGAIN?>
<I TOLD YOU, IT'S NEVER A -->
SHHHH...
WOULD YOU LIKE... A DRINK?

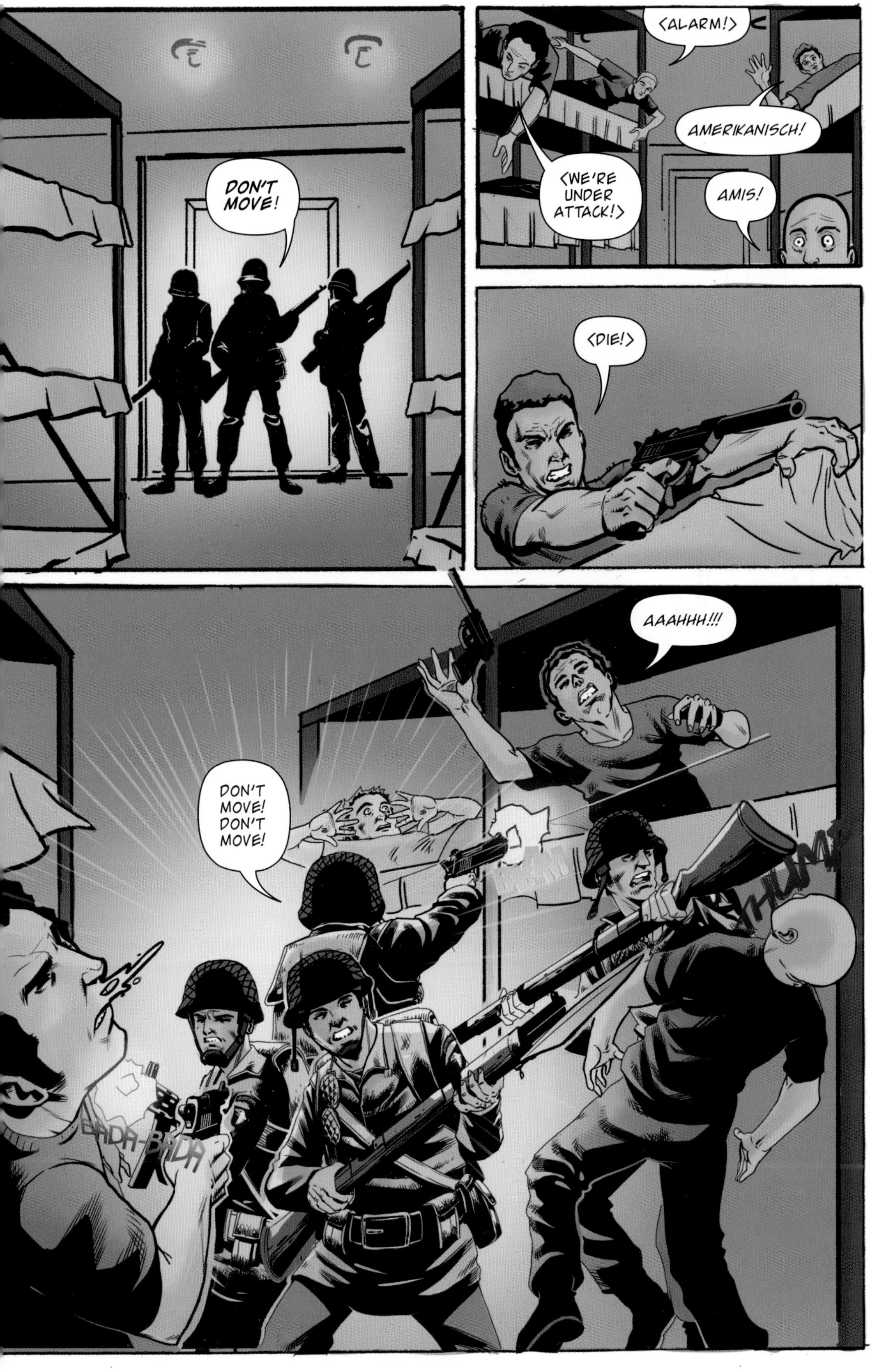

DON'T MOVE!
<ALARM!>
<WE'RE UNDER ATTACK!>
AMERIKANISCH!
AMIS!
<DIE!>
AAAHHH!!!
DON'T MOVE! DON'T MOVE!
BADA-BADA

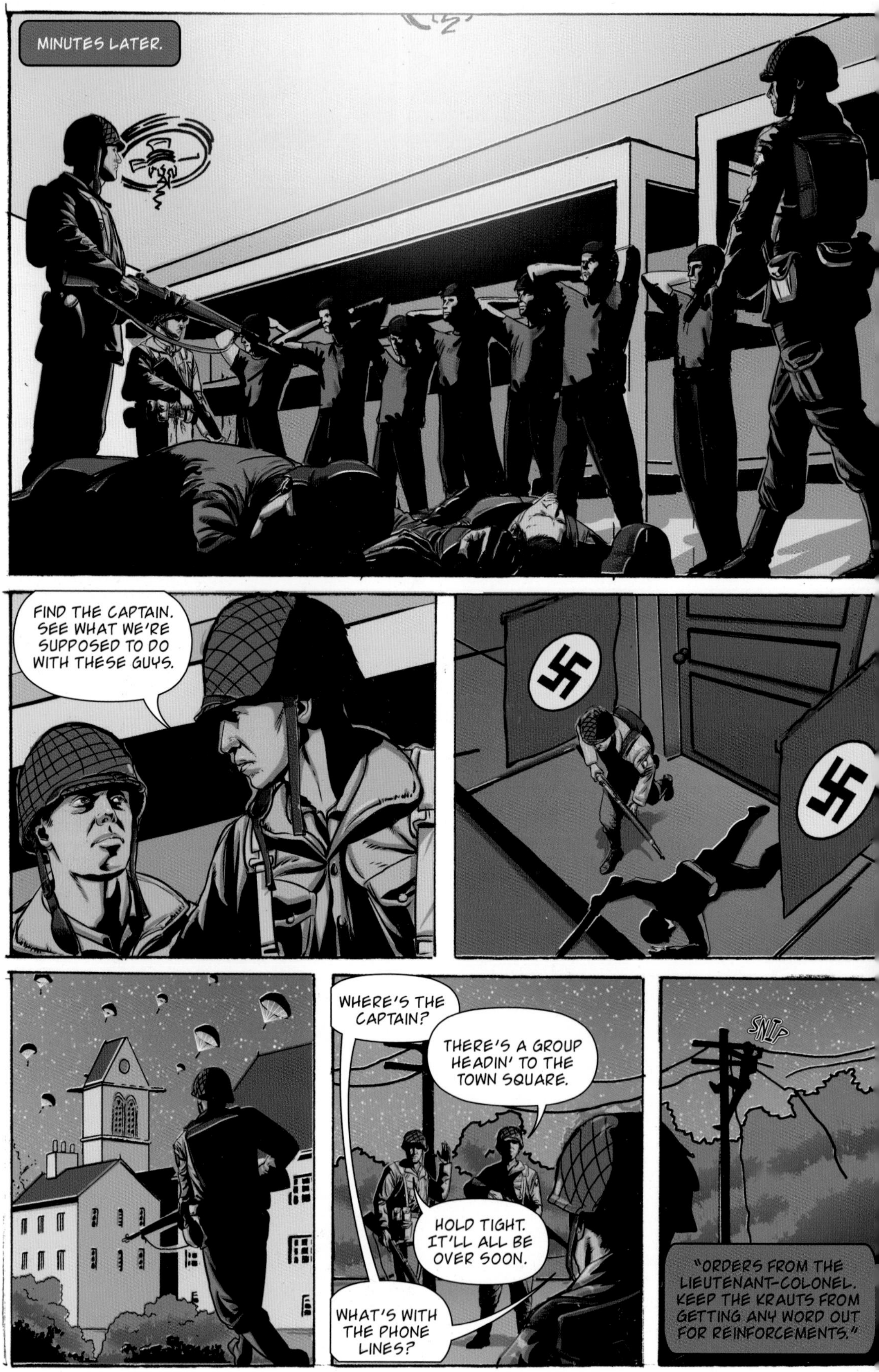
MINUTES LATER.
FIND THE CAPTAIN. SEE WHAT WE'RE SUPPOSED TO DO WITH THESE GUYS.
WHERE'S THE CAPTAIN?
THERE'S A GROUP HEADIN' TO THE TOWN SQUARE.
HOLD TIGHT. IT'LL ALL BE OVER SOON.
WHAT'S WITH THE PHONE LINES?
SNIP
"ORDERS FROM THE LIEUTENANT-COLONEL. KEEP THE KRAUTS FROM GETTING ANY WORD OUT FOR REINFORCEMENTS."

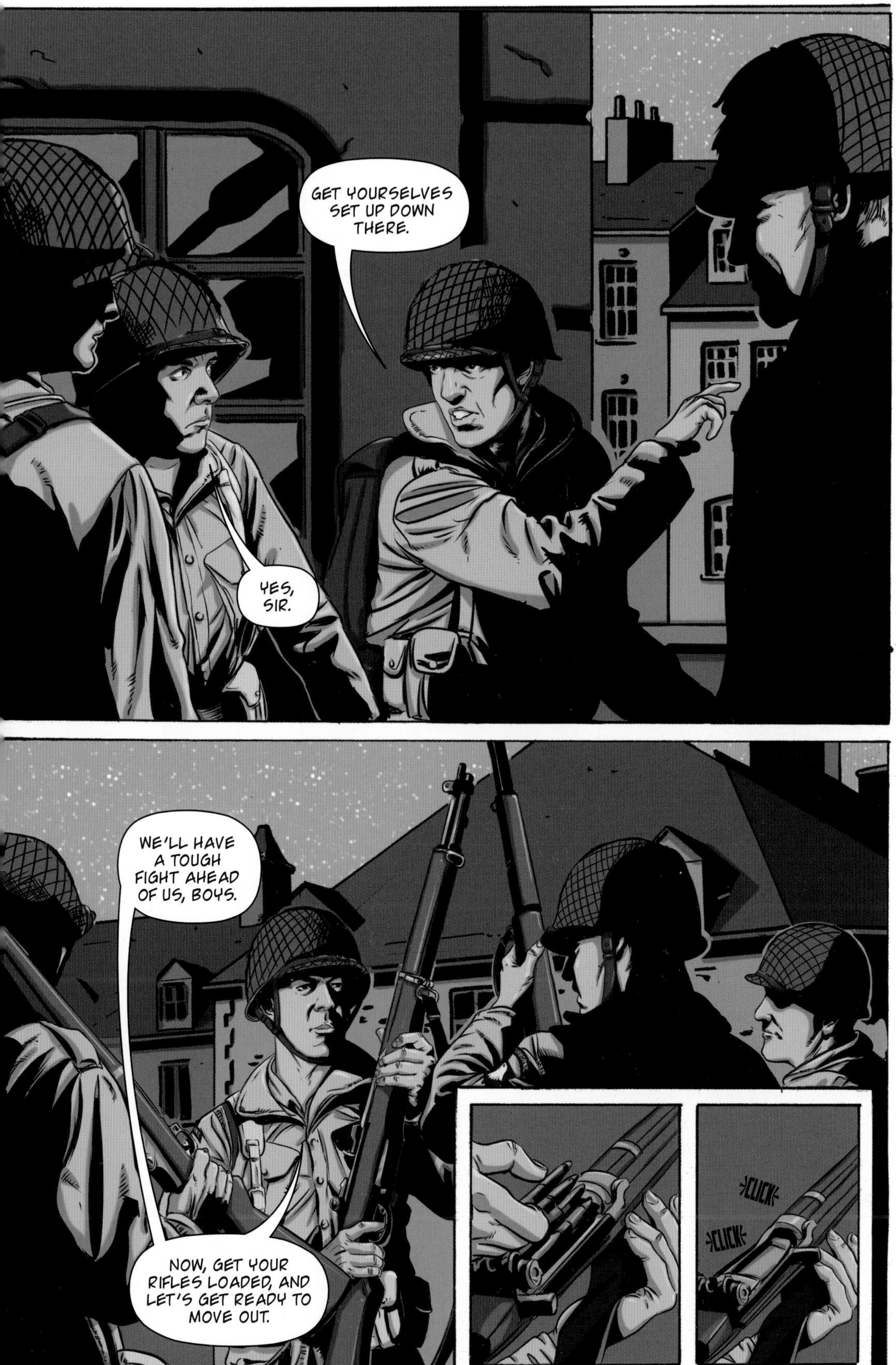
GET YOURSELVES SET UP DOWN THERE.
YES, SIR.
WE'LL HAVE A TOUGH FIGHT AHEAD OF US, BOYS.
NOW, GET YOUR RIFLES LOADED, AND LET'S GET READY TO MOVE OUT.
CLICK
CLICK

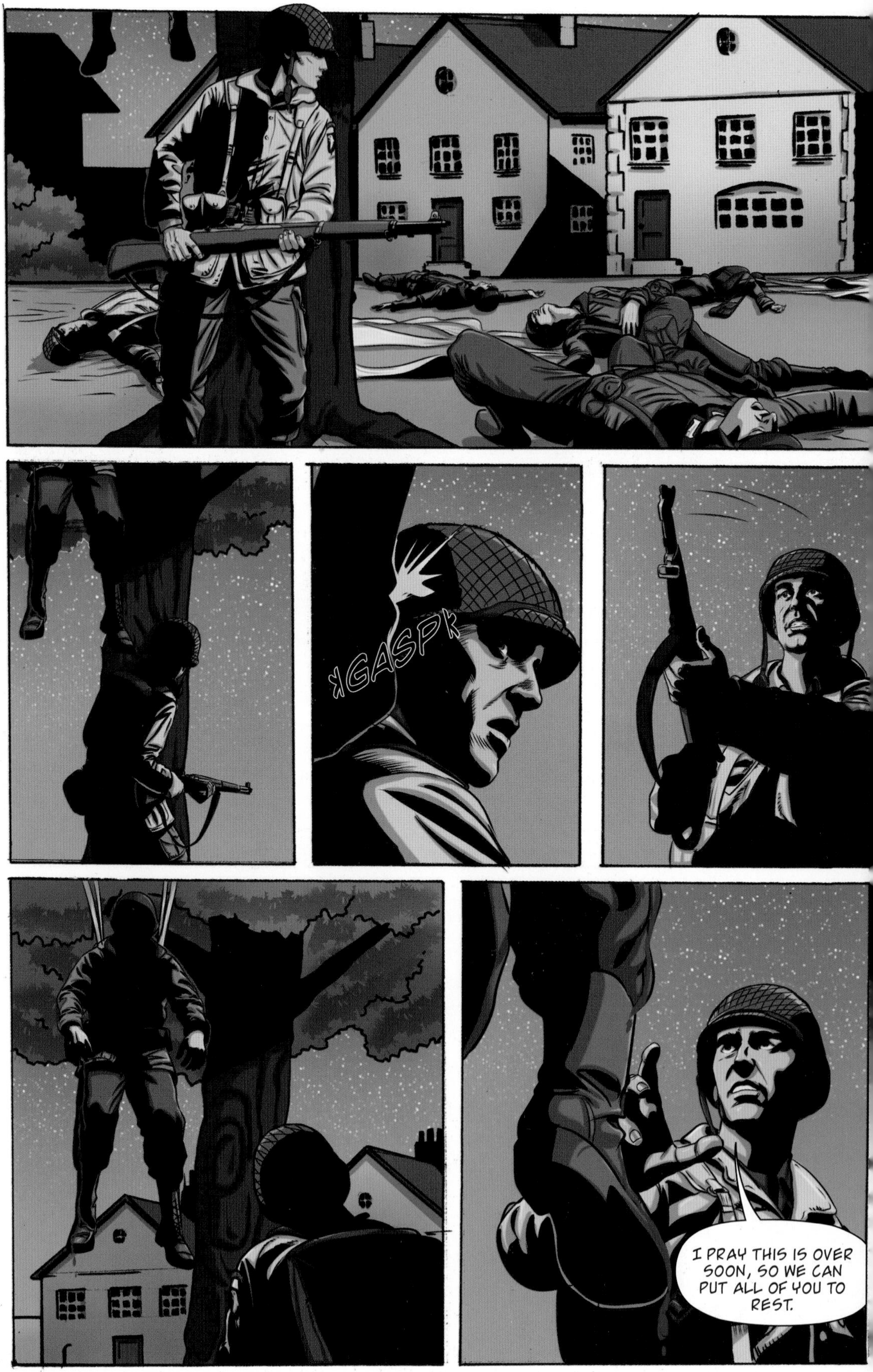
KGASPK
I PRAY THIS IS OVER SOON, SO WE CAN PUT ALL OF YOU TO REST.

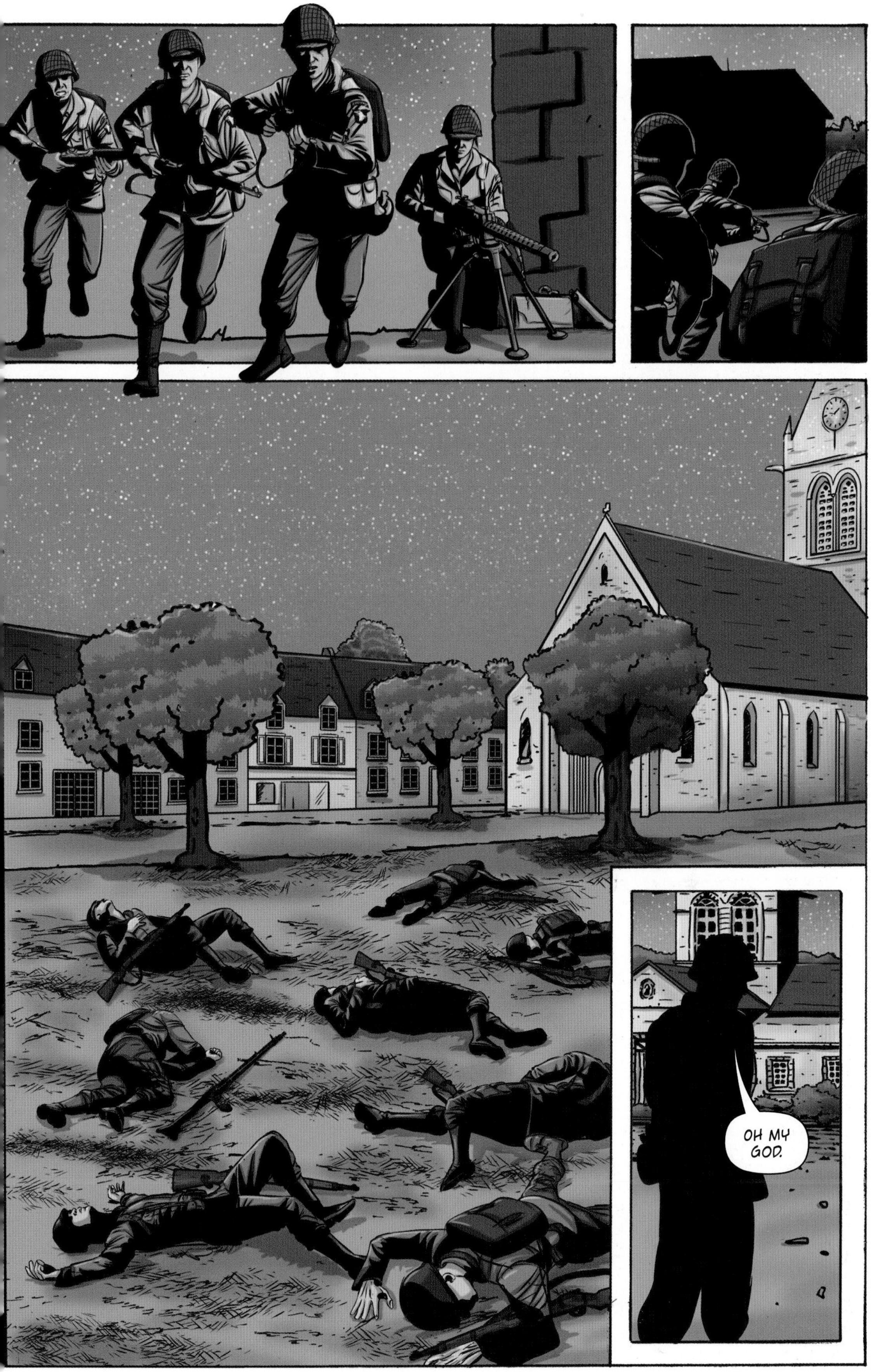
OH MY GOD.

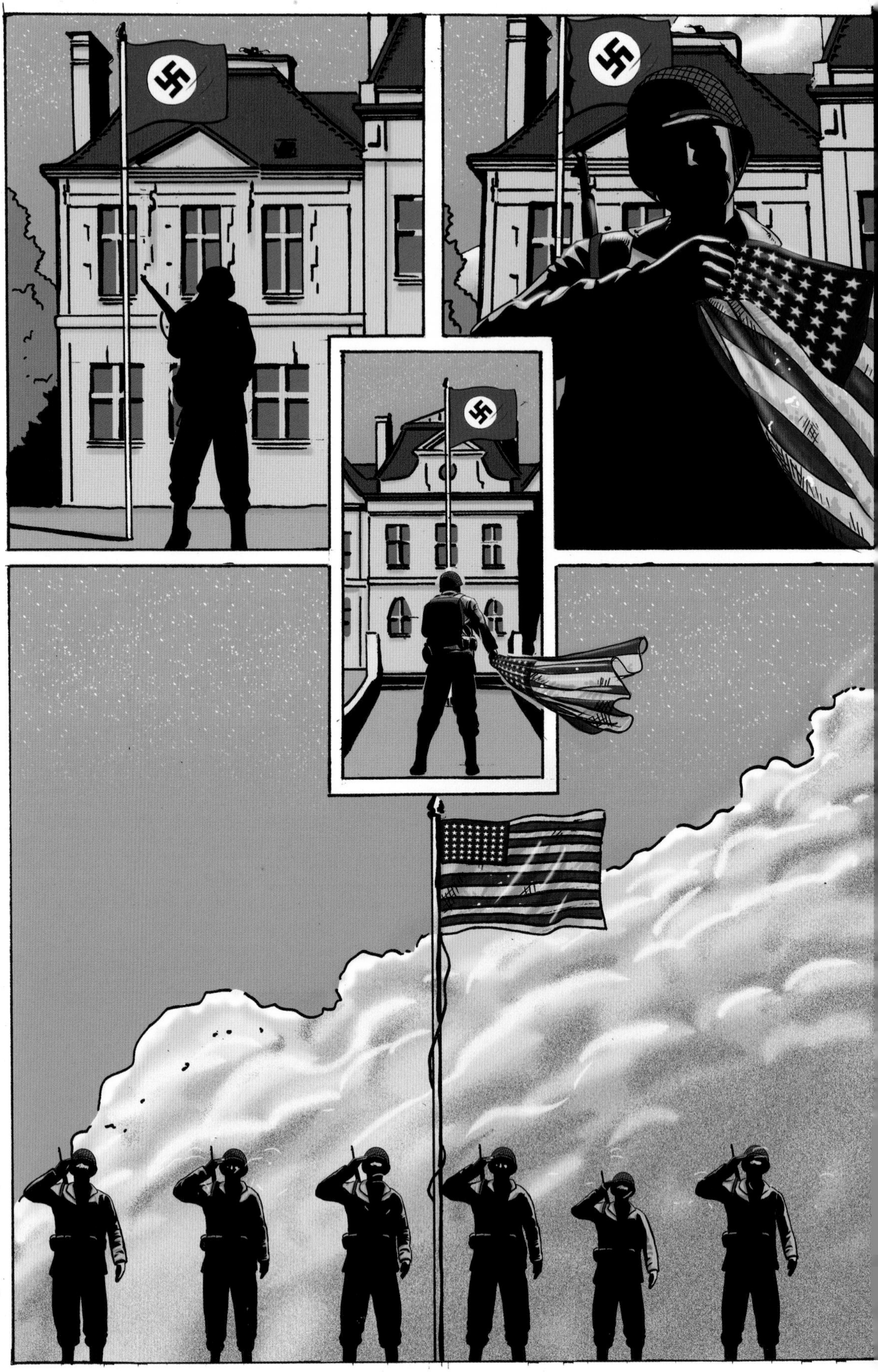

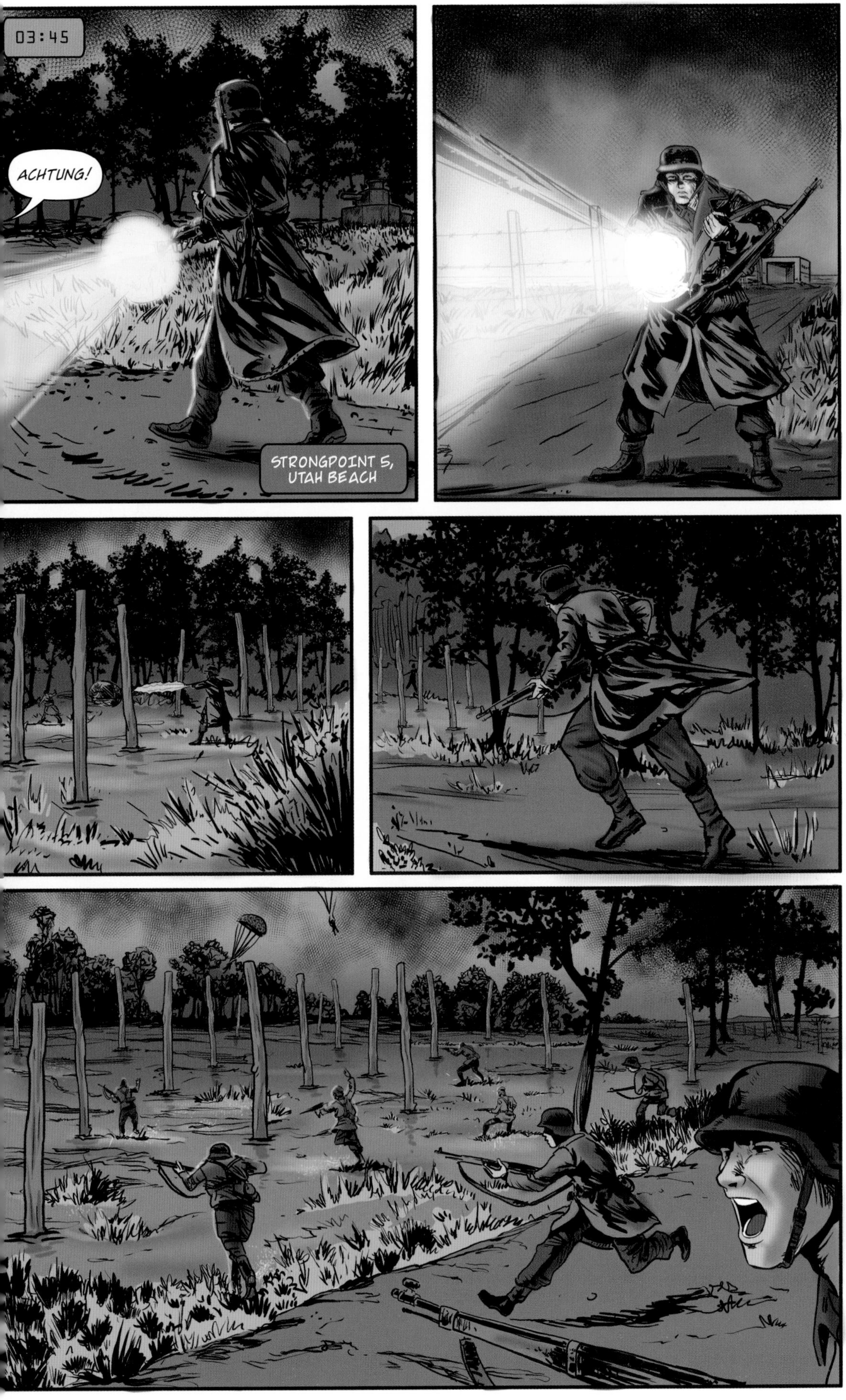
03:45
ACHTUNG!
STRONGPOINT 5, UTAH BEACH

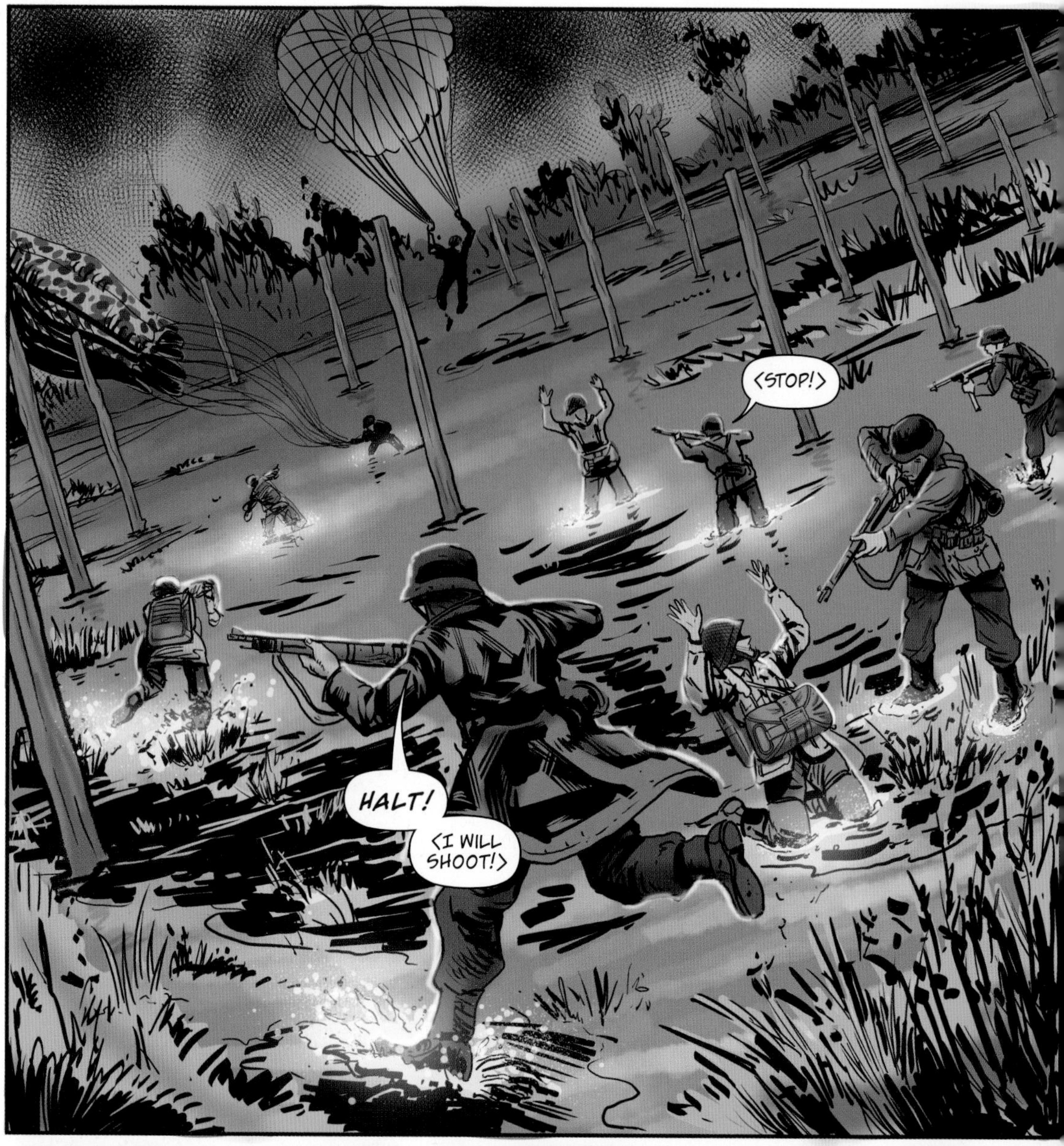

<STOP!>
HALT!
<I WILL SHOOT!>

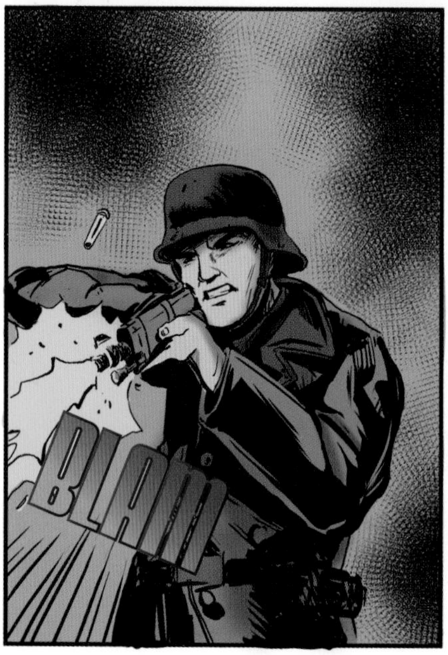

BLAM

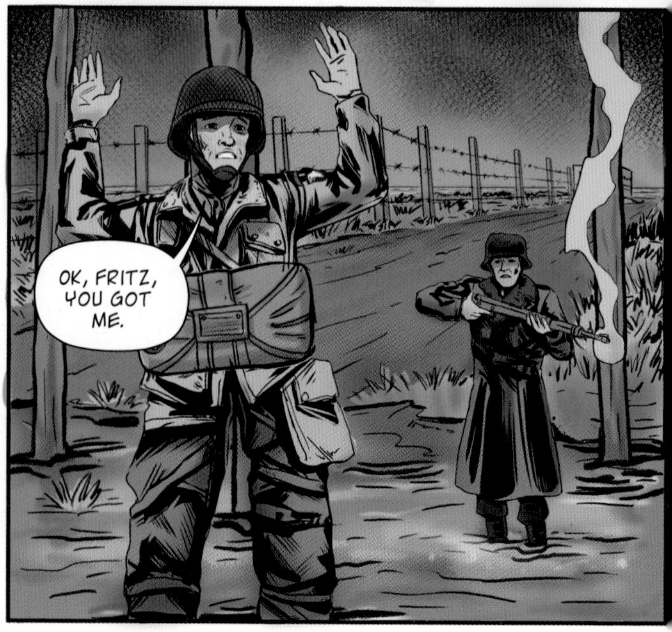

OK, FRITZ, YOU GOT ME.

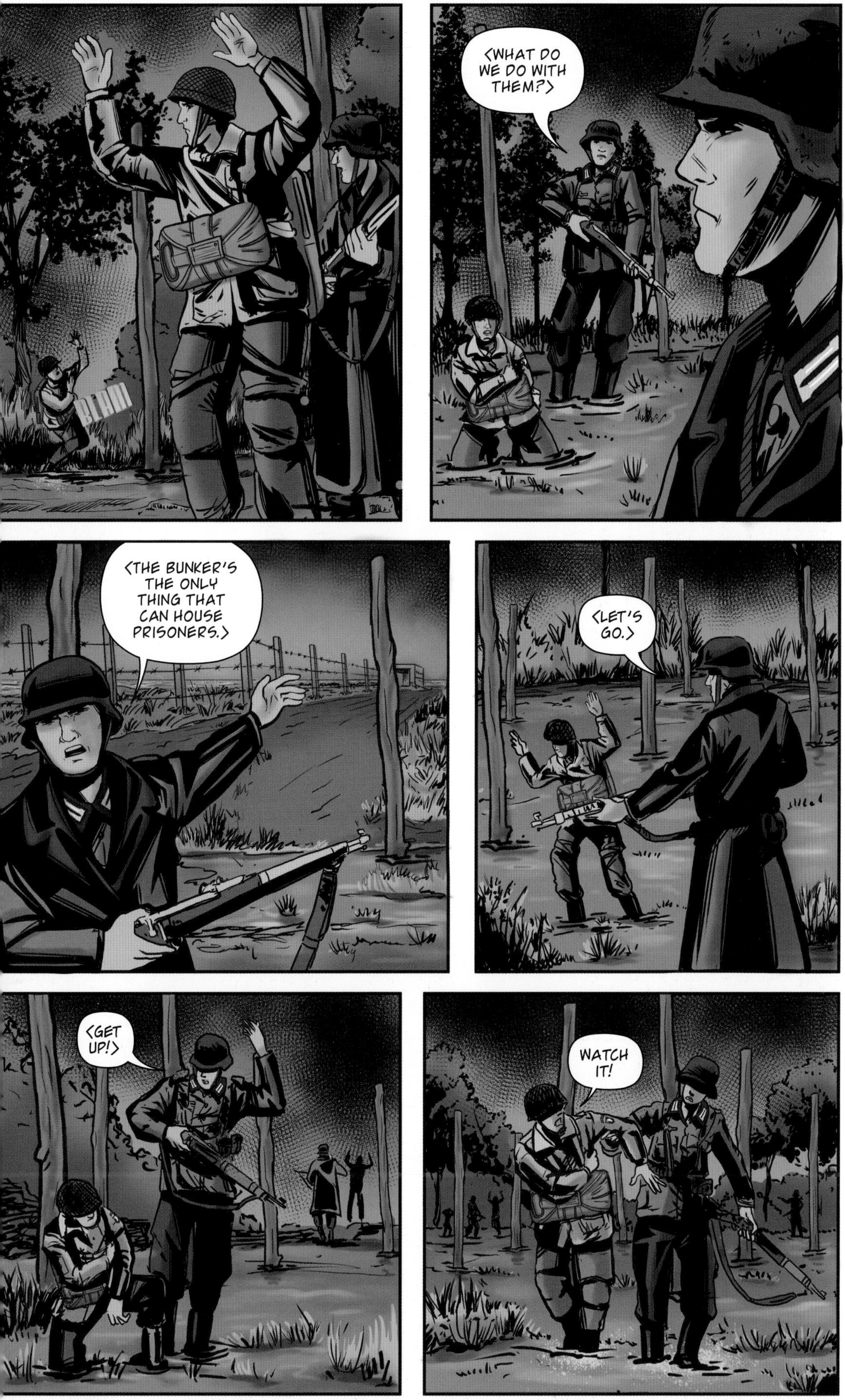
BLAM
<WHAT DO WE DO WITH THEM?>
<THE BUNKER'S THE ONLY THING THAT CAN HOUSE PRISONERS.>
<LET'S GO.>
<GET UP!>
WATCH IT!

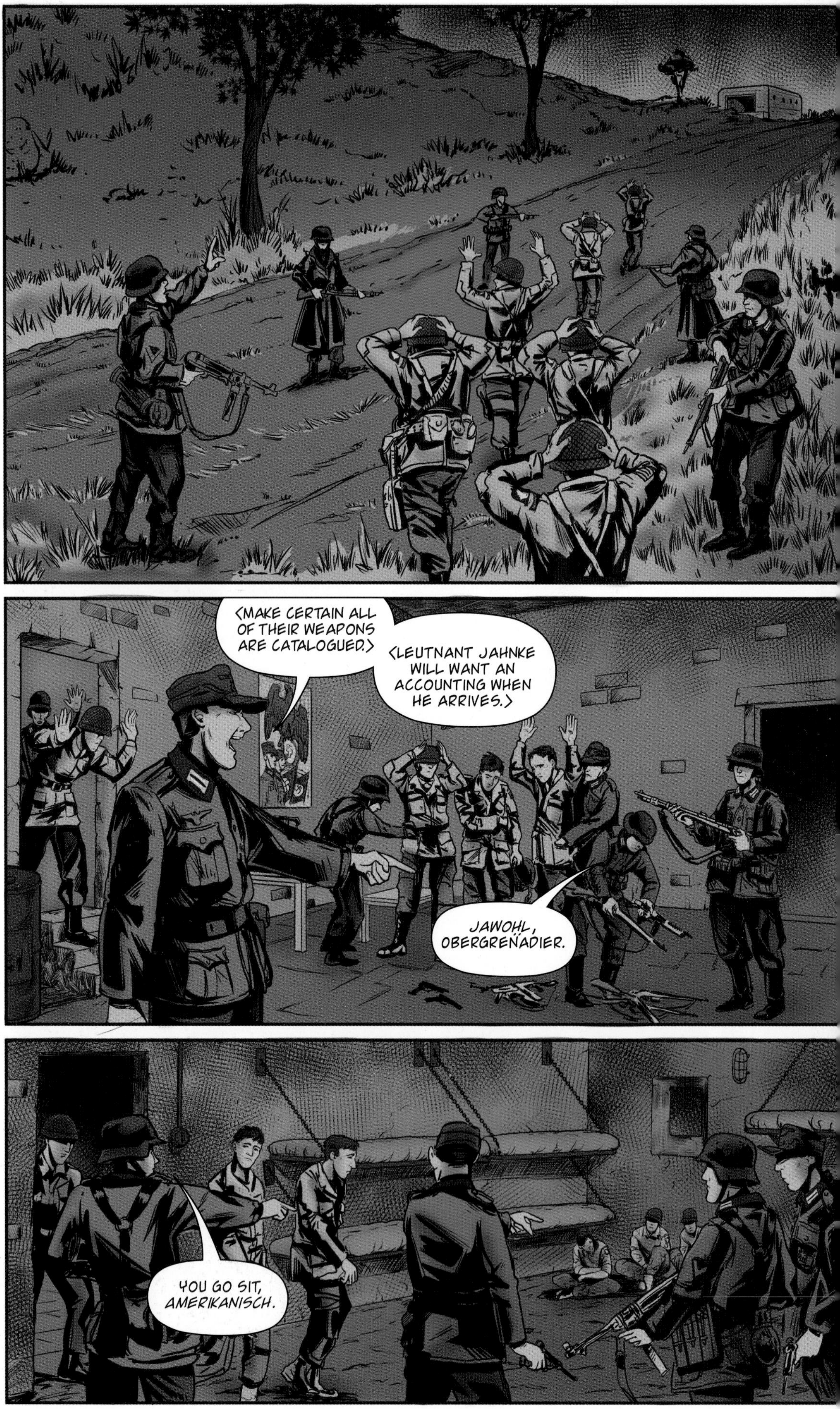

<MAKE CERTAIN ALL OF THEIR WEAPONS ARE CATALOGUED.>
<LEUTNANT JAHNKE WILL WANT AN ACCOUNTING WHEN HE ARRIVES.>
JAWOHL, OBERGRENADIER.
YOU GO SIT, AMERIKANISCH.

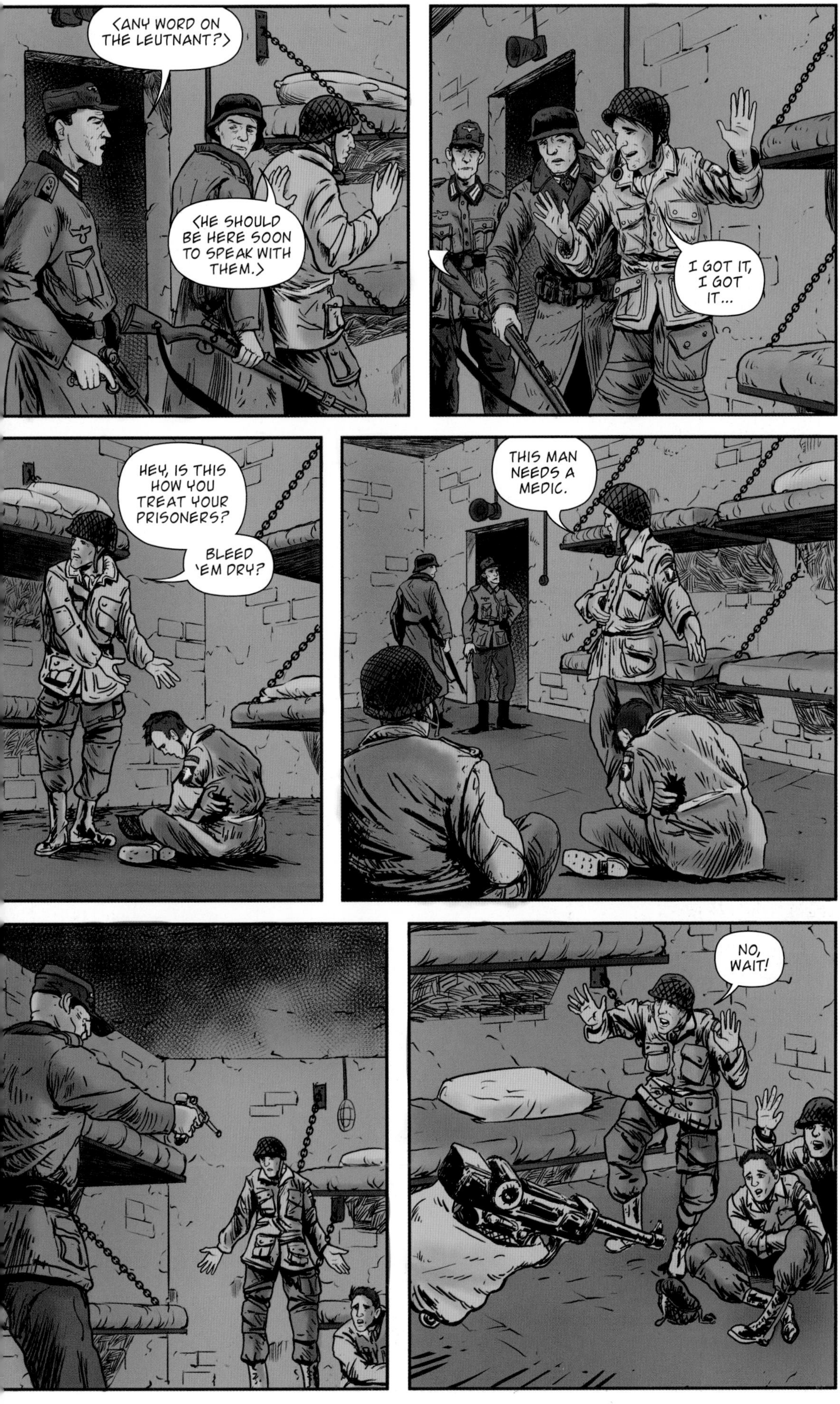
<ANY WORD ON THE LEUTNANT?>
<HE SHOULD BE HERE SOON TO SPEAK WITH THEM.>
I GOT IT, I GOT IT...
HEY, IS THIS HOW YOU TREAT YOUR PRISONERS?
BLEED 'EM DRY?
THIS MAN NEEDS A MEDIC.
NO, WAIT!

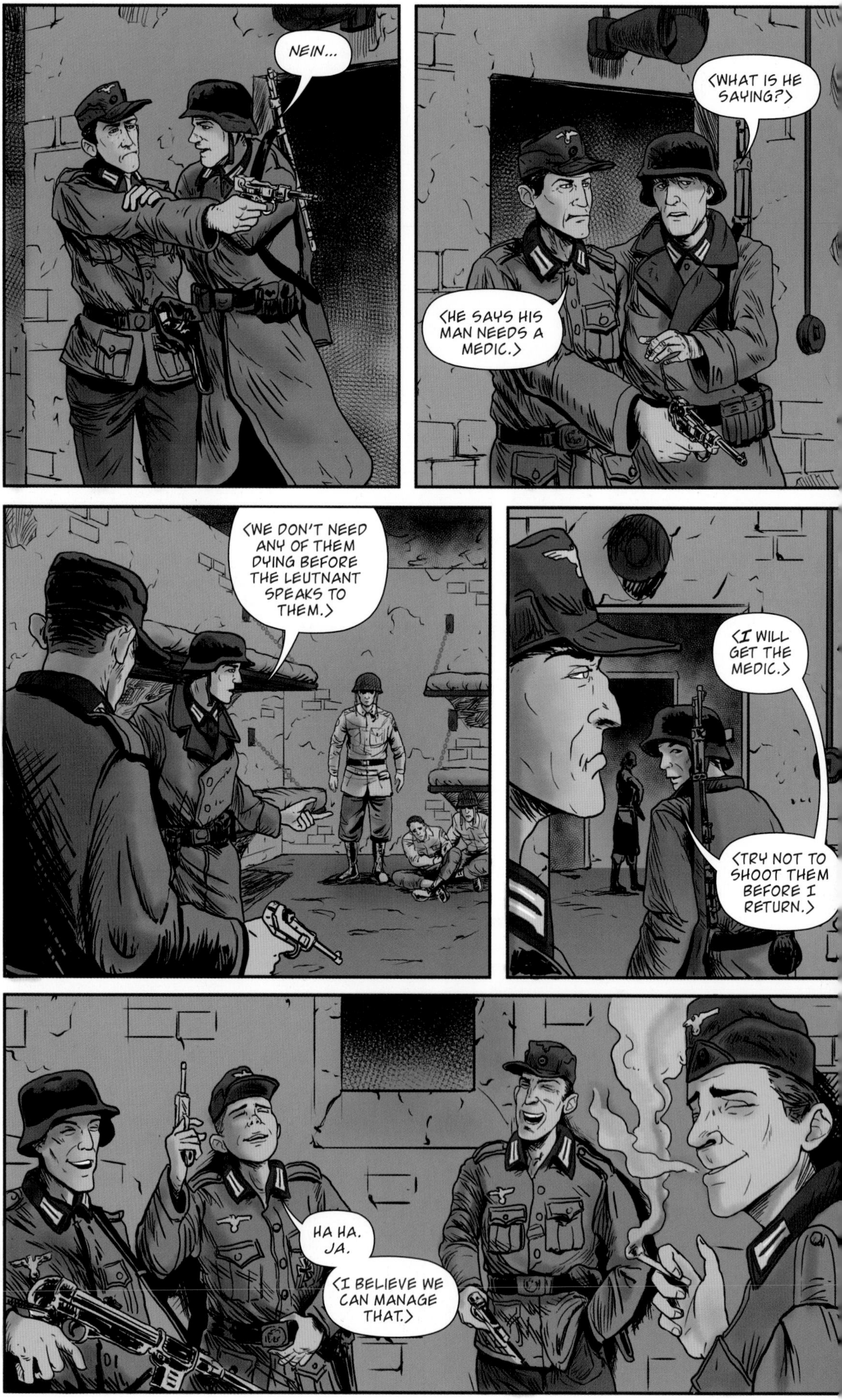
NEIN...
<WHAT IS HE SAYING?>
<HE SAYS HIS MAN NEEDS A MEDIC.>
<WE DON'T NEED ANY OF THEM DYING BEFORE THE LEUTNANT SPEAKS TO THEM.>
<I WILL GET THE MEDIC.>
<TRY NOT TO SHOOT THEM BEFORE I RETURN.>
HA HA. JA.
<I BELIEVE WE CAN MANAGE THAT.>

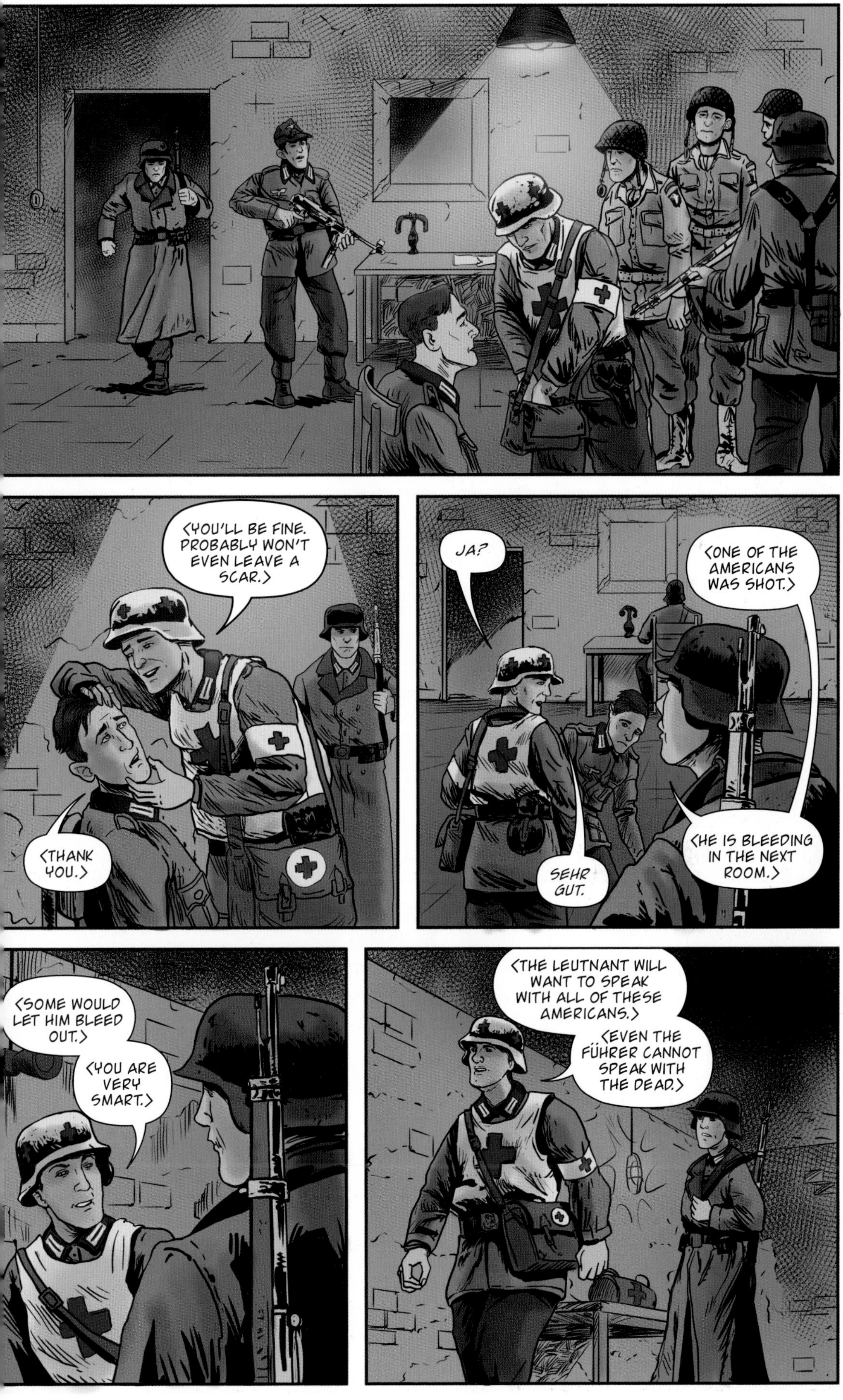
<YOU'LL BE FINE. PROBABLY WON'T EVEN LEAVE A SCAR.>
<THANK YOU.>
JA?
<ONE OF THE AMERICANS WAS SHOT.>
<HE IS BLEEDING IN THE NEXT ROOM.>
SEHR GUT.
<SOME WOULD LET HIM BLEED OUT.>
<YOU ARE VERY SMART.>
<THE LEUTNANT WILL WANT TO SPEAK WITH ALL OF THESE AMERICANS.>
<EVEN THE FÜHRER CANNOT SPEAK WITH THE DEAD.>

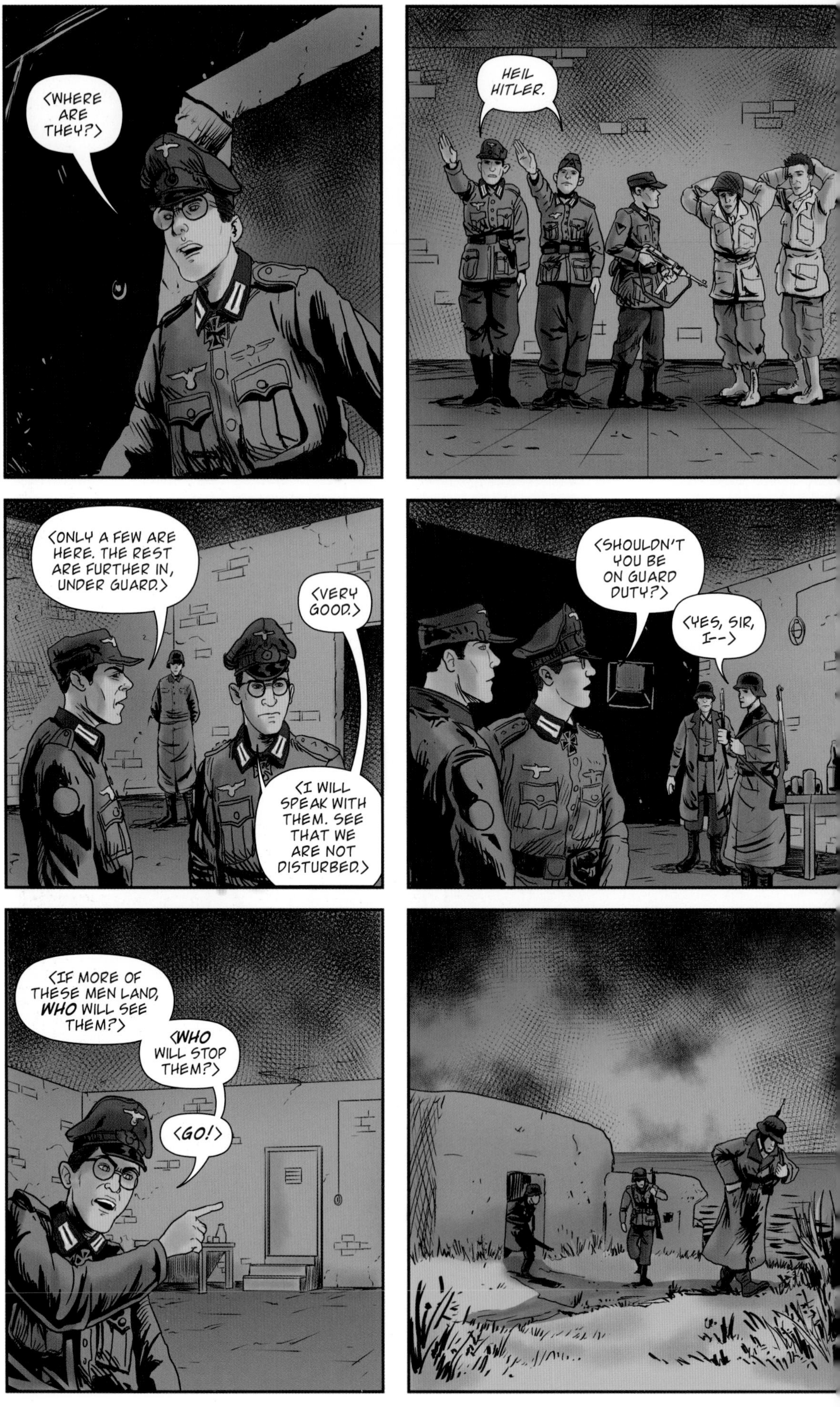
<WHERE ARE THEY?>
HEIL HITLER.
<ONLY A FEW ARE HERE. THE REST ARE FURTHER IN, UNDER GUARD.>
<VERY GOOD.>
<I WILL SPEAK WITH THEM. SEE THAT WE ARE NOT DISTURBED.>
<SHOULDN'T YOU BE ON GUARD DUTY?>
<YES, SIR, I-->
<IF MORE OF THESE MEN LAND, **WHO** WILL SEE THEM?>
<**WHO** WILL STOP THEM?>
<**GO!**>

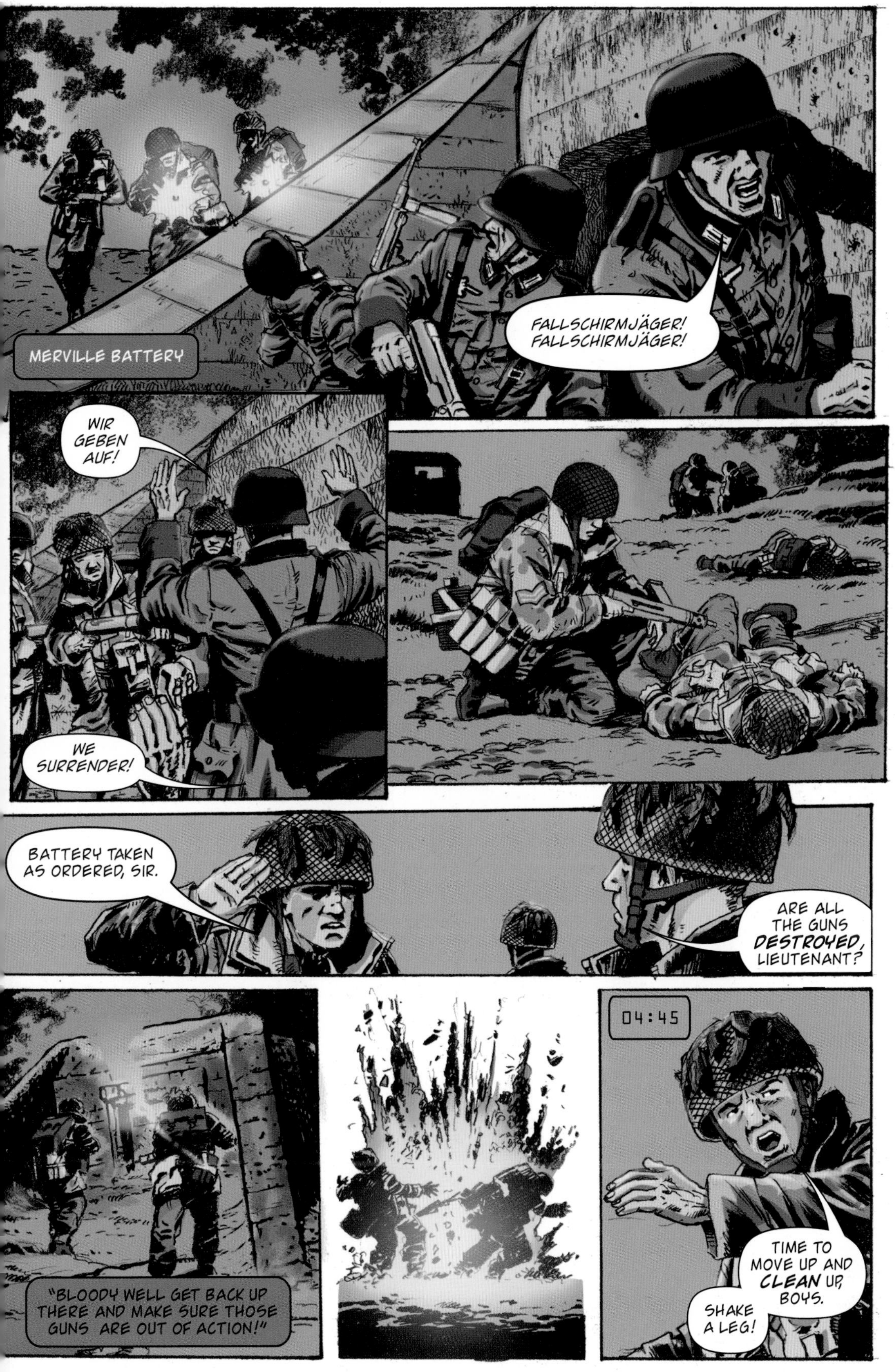
MERVILLE BATTERY
FALLSCHIRMJÄGER! FALLSCHIRMJÄGER!
WIR GEBEN AUF!
WE SURRENDER!
BATTERY TAKEN AS ORDERED, SIR.
ARE ALL THE GUNS DESTROYED, LIEUTENANT?
"BLOODY WELL GET BACK UP THERE AND MAKE SURE THOSE GUNS ARE OUT OF ACTION!"
04:45
TIME TO MOVE UP AND CLEAN UP, BOYS.
SHAKE A LEG!

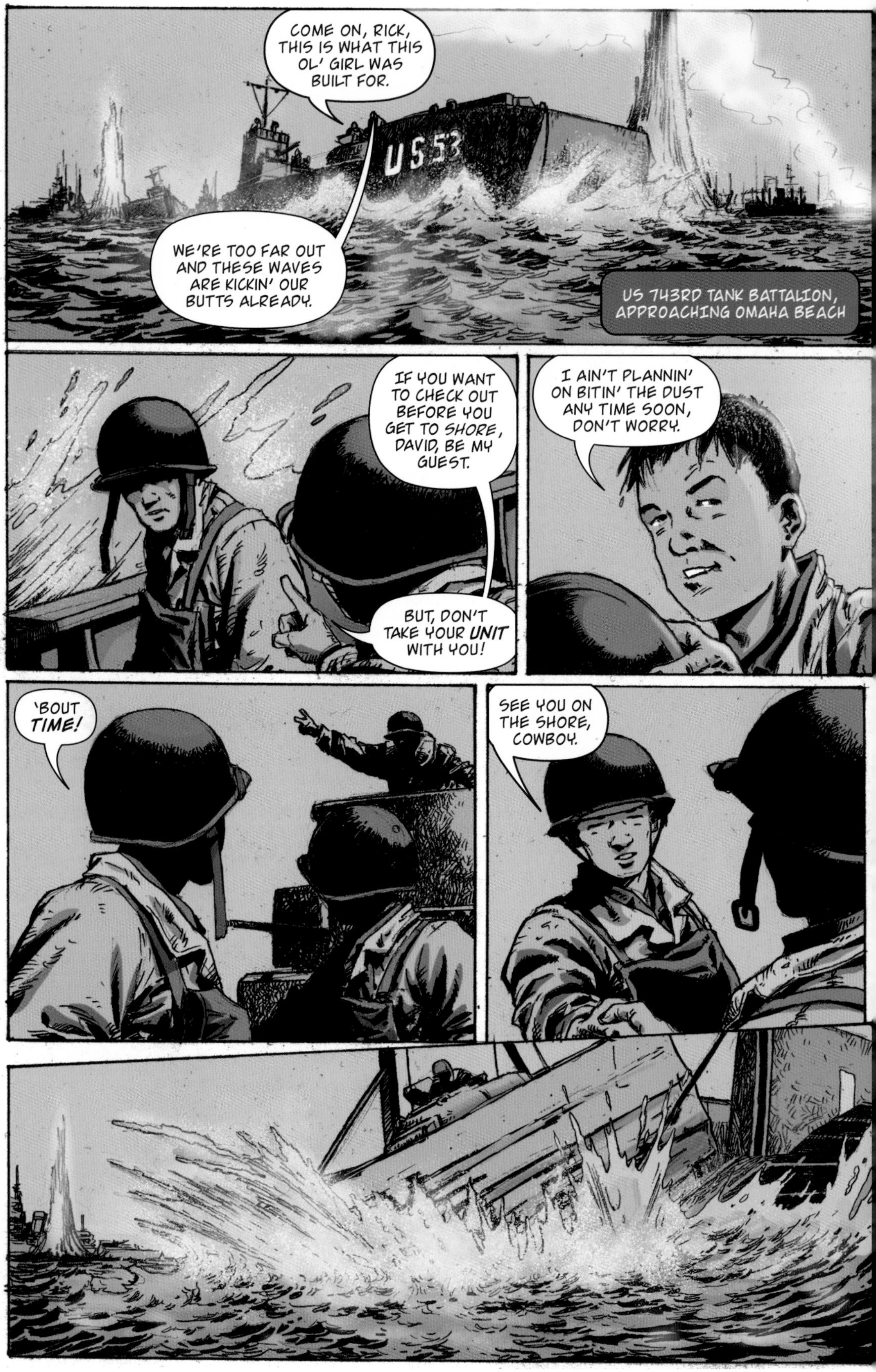
COME ON, RICK, THIS IS WHAT THIS OL' GIRL WAS BUILT FOR.
WE'RE TOO FAR OUT AND THESE WAVES ARE KICKIN' OUR BUTTS ALREADY.
US 53
US 743RD TANK BATTALION, APPROACHING OMAHA BEACH
IF YOU WANT TO CHECK OUT BEFORE YOU GET TO SHORE, DAVID, BE MY GUEST.
BUT, DON'T TAKE YOUR UNIT WITH YOU!
I AIN'T PLANNIN' ON BITIN' THE DUST ANY TIME SOON, DON'T WORRY.
'BOUT TIME!
SEE YOU ON THE SHORE, COWBOY.

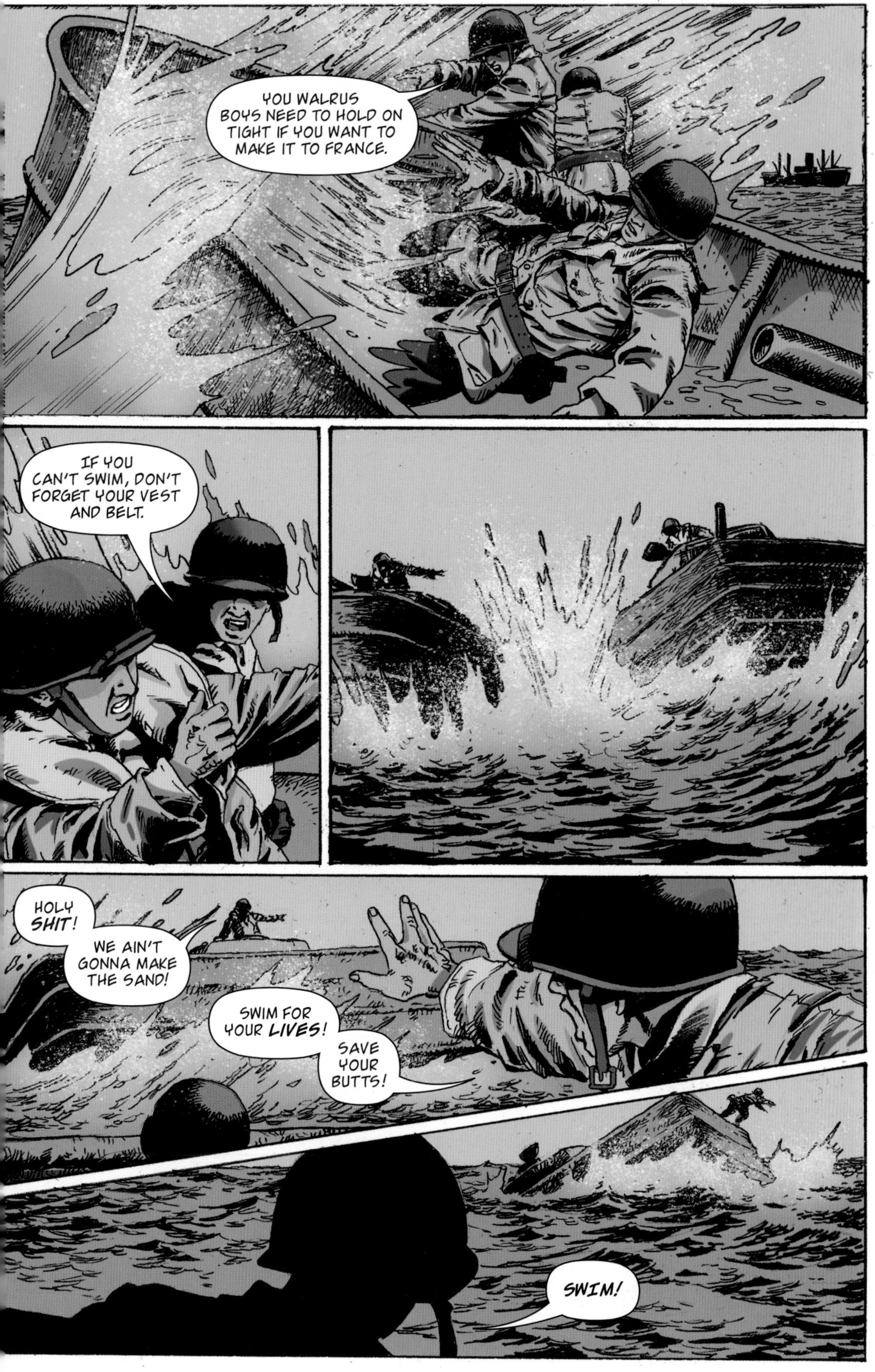
YOU WALRUS BOYS NEED TO HOLD ON TIGHT IF YOU WANT TO MAKE IT TO FRANCE.
IF YOU CAN'T SWIM, DON'T FORGET YOUR VEST AND BELT.
HOLY SHIT!
WE AIN'T GONNA MAKE THE SAND!
SWIM FOR YOUR LIVES!
SAVE YOUR BUTTS!
SWIM!

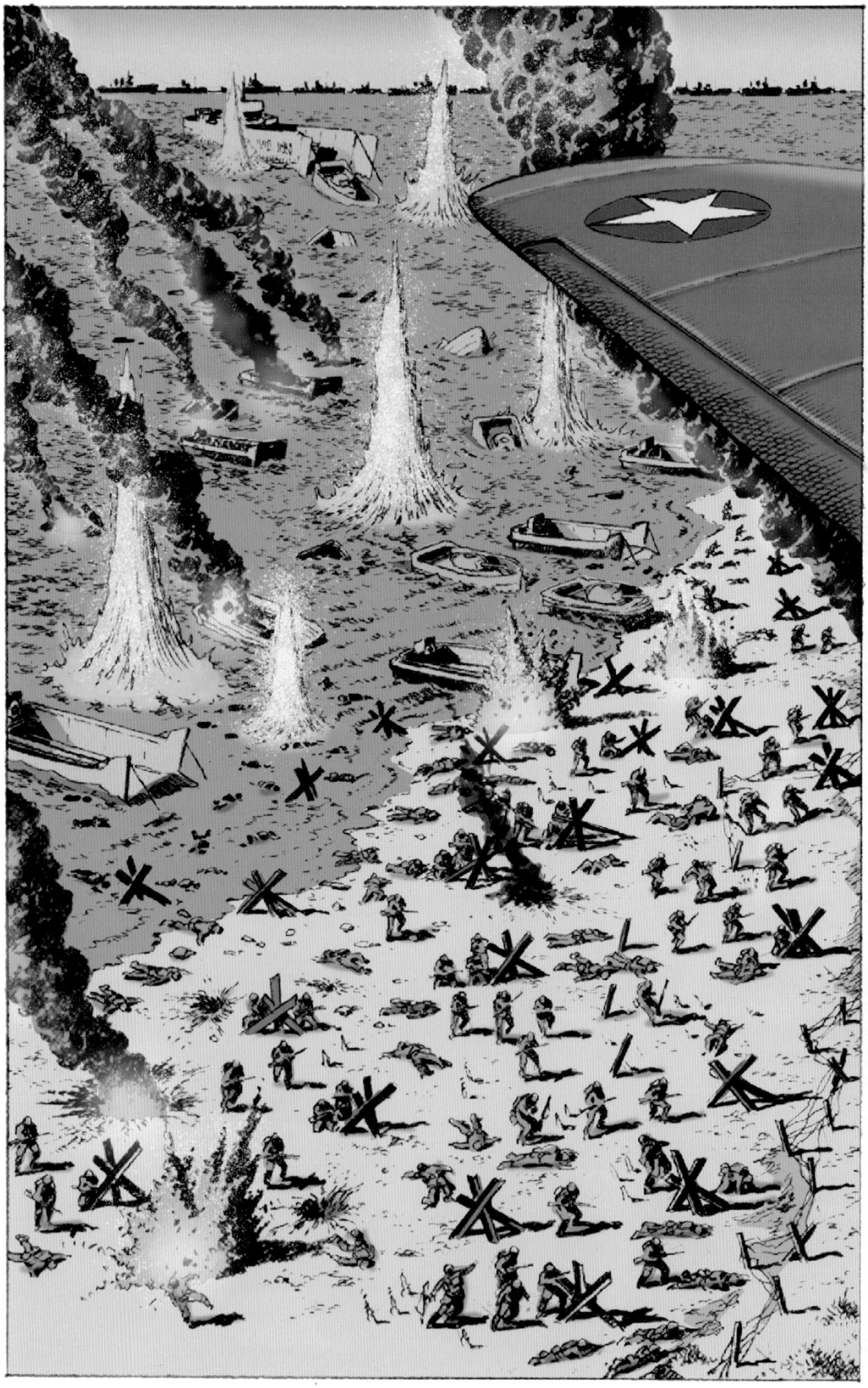

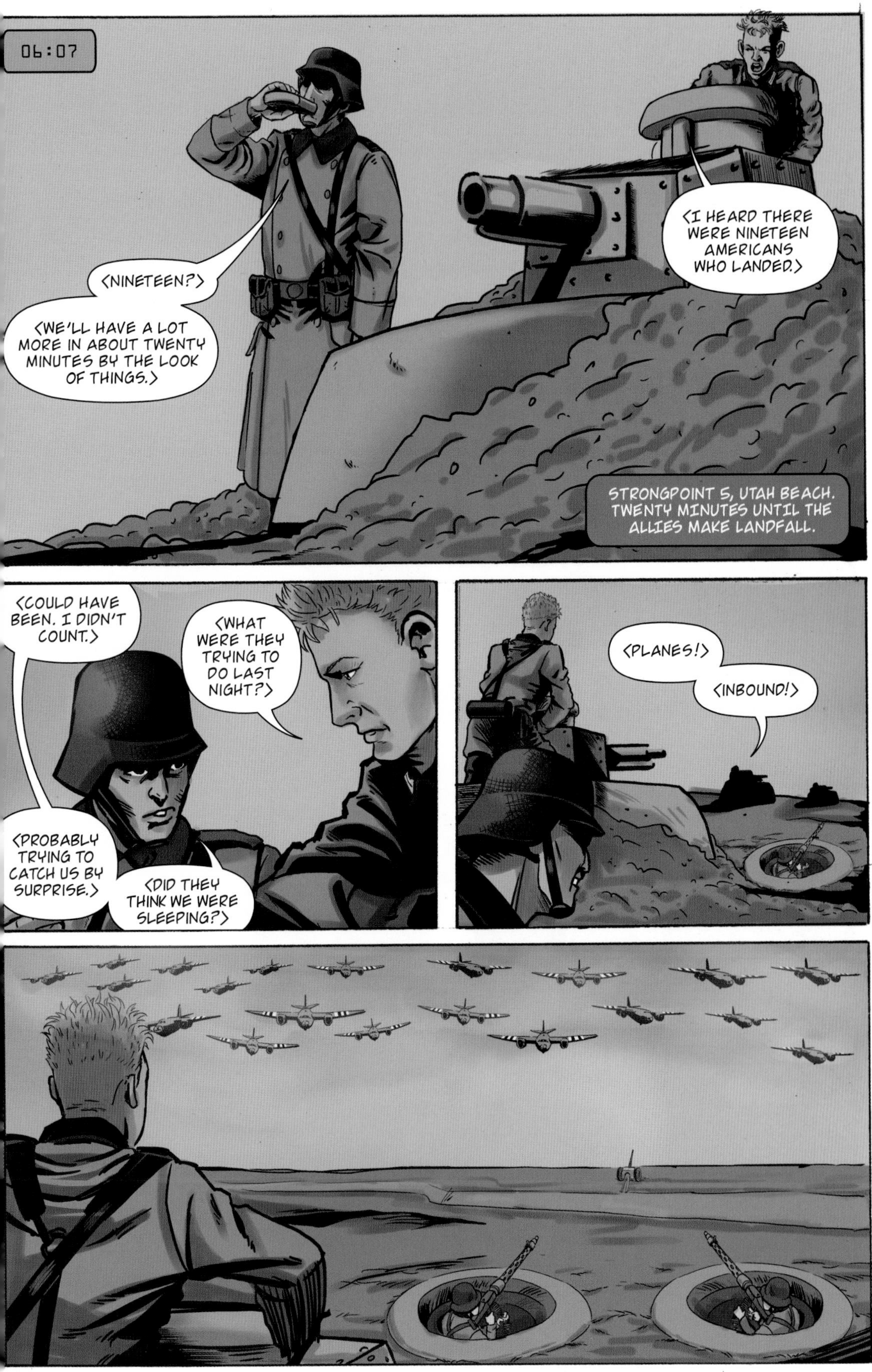
06:07
<I HEARD THERE WERE NINETEEN AMERICANS WHO LANDED.>
<NINETEEN?>
<WE'LL HAVE A LOT MORE IN ABOUT TWENTY MINUTES BY THE LOOK OF THINGS.>
STRONGPOINT 5, UTAH BEACH. TWENTY MINUTES UNTIL THE ALLIES MAKE LANDFALL.
<COULD HAVE BEEN. I DIDN'T COUNT.>
<WHAT WERE THEY TRYING TO DO LAST NIGHT?>
<PROBABLY TRYING TO CATCH US BY SURPRISE.>
<DID THEY THINK WE WERE SLEEPING?>
<PLANES!>
<INBOUND!>

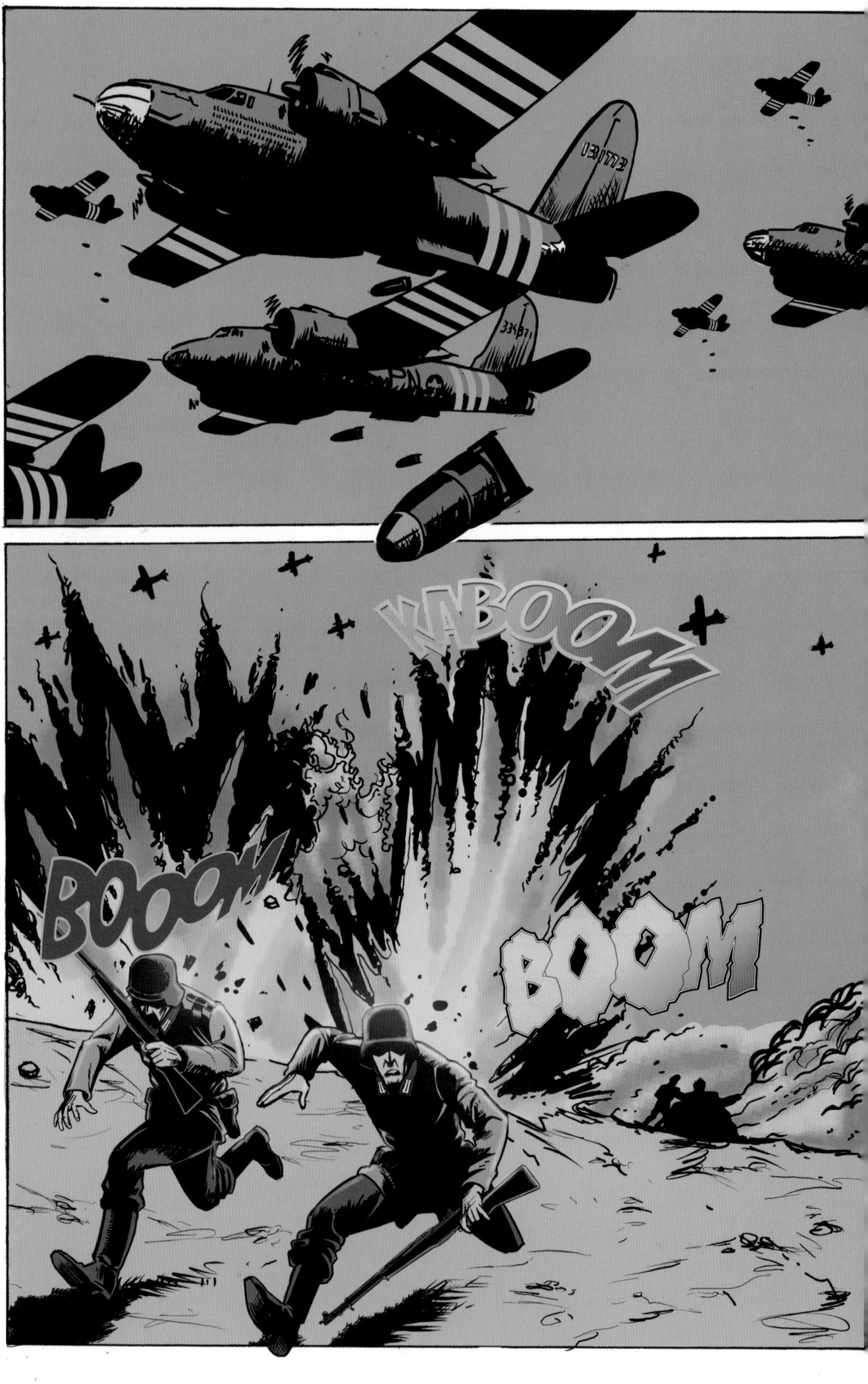
KABOOM
BOOOM
BOOM

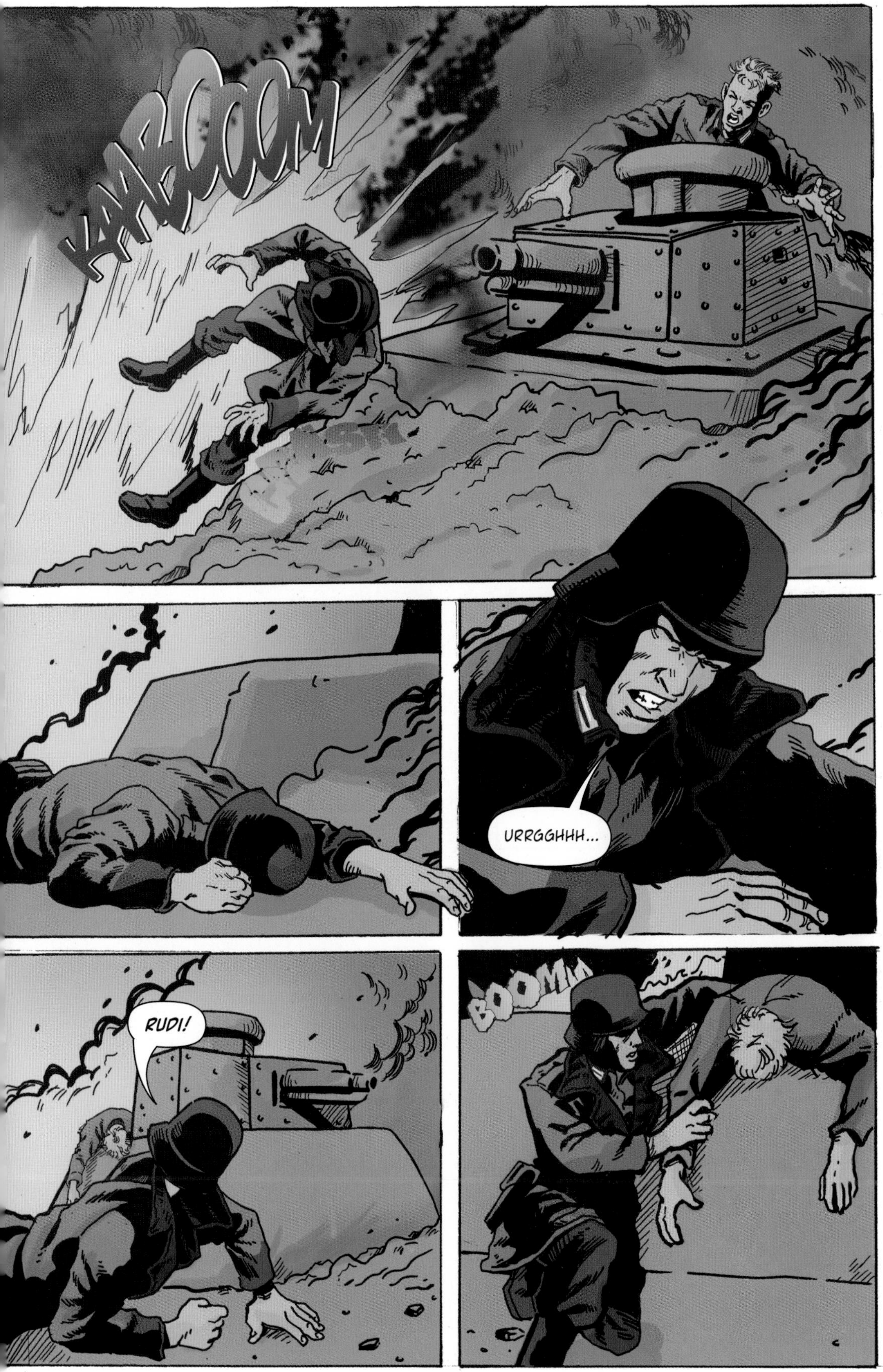
URRGGHHH...
RUDI!

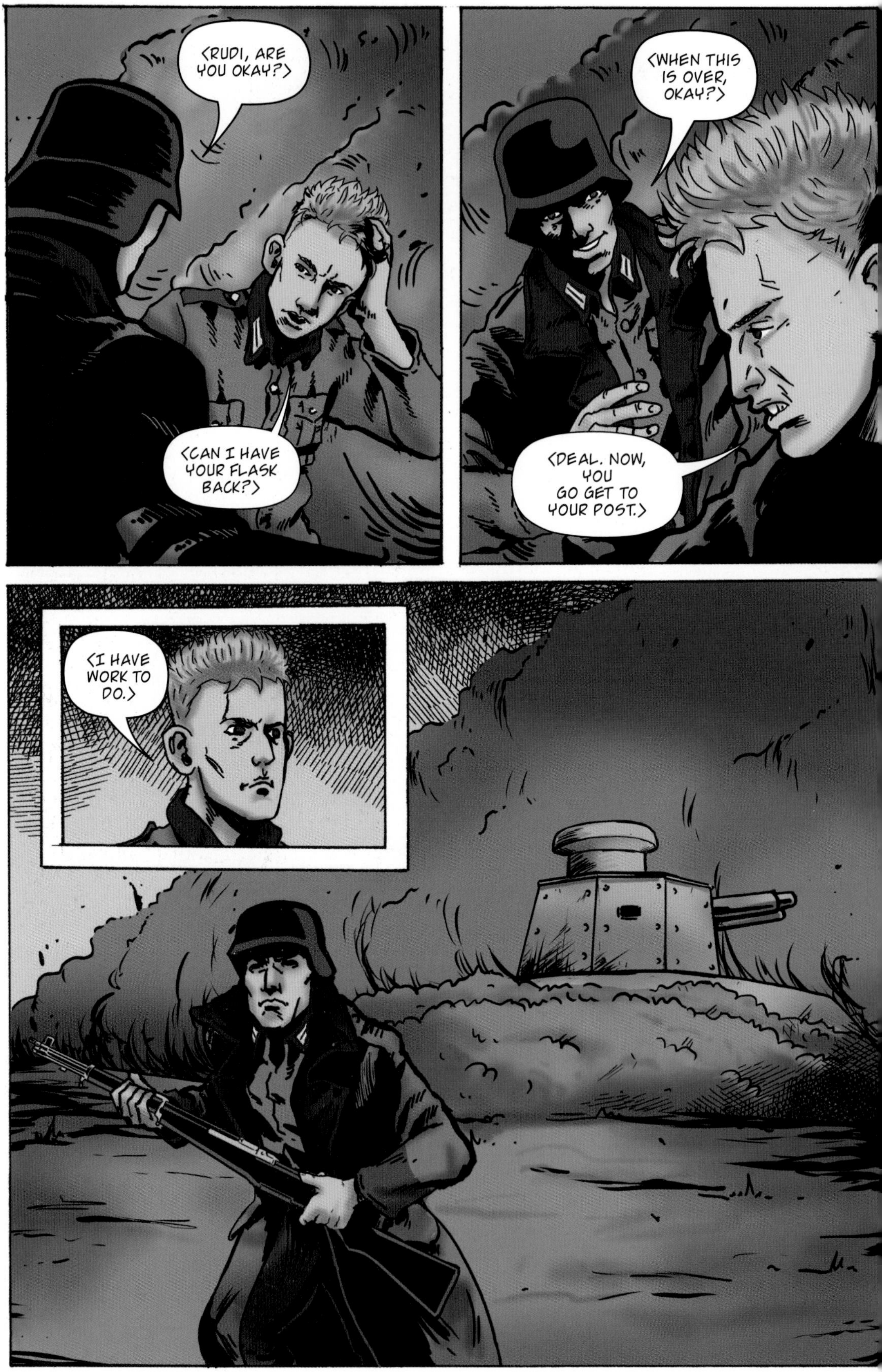
<RUDI, ARE YOU OKAY?>
<CAN I HAVE YOUR FLASK BACK?>
<WHEN THIS IS OVER, OKAY?>
<DEAL. NOW, YOU GO GET TO YOUR POST.>
<I HAVE WORK TO DO.>

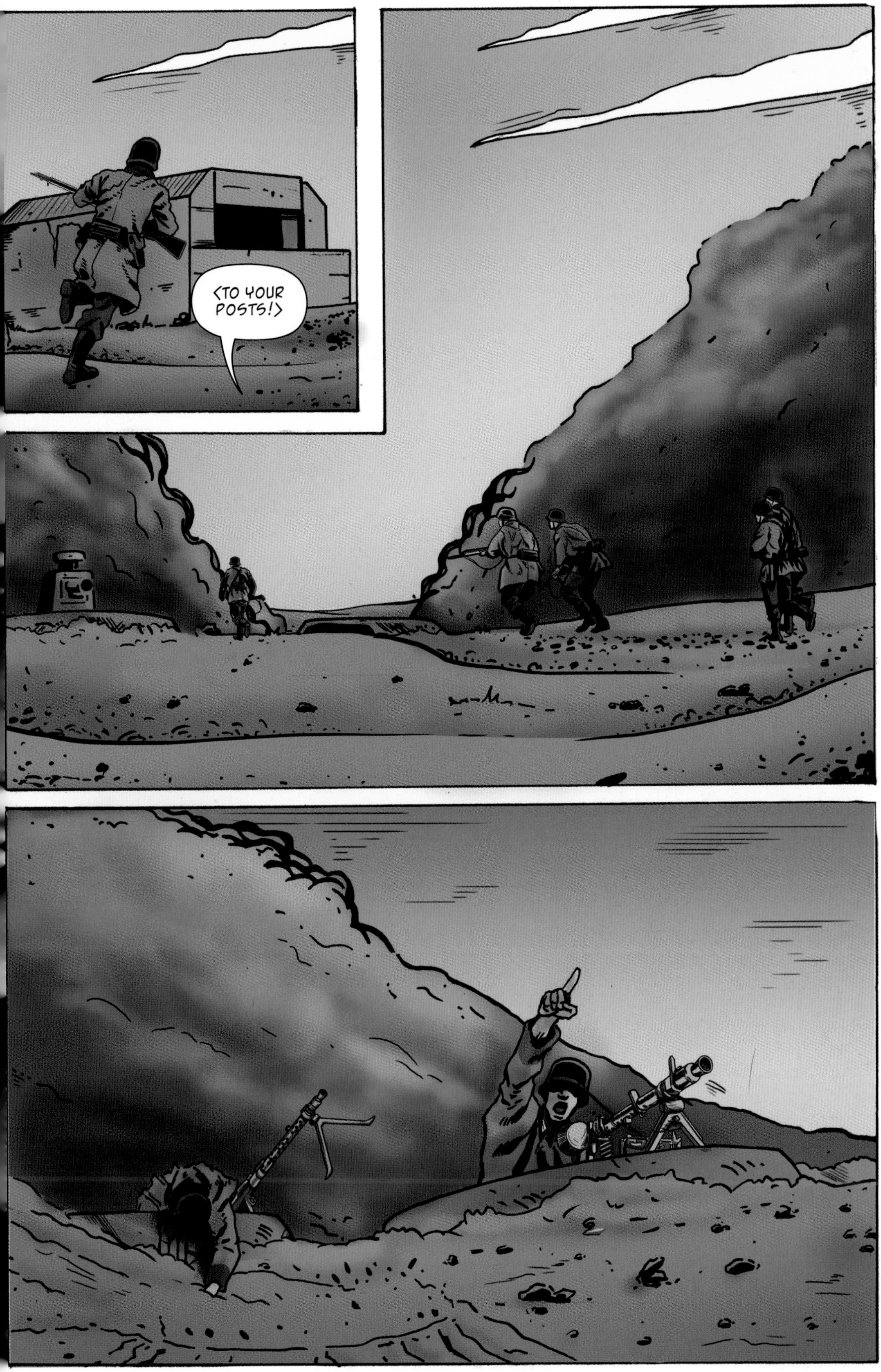
<TO YOUR POSTS!>

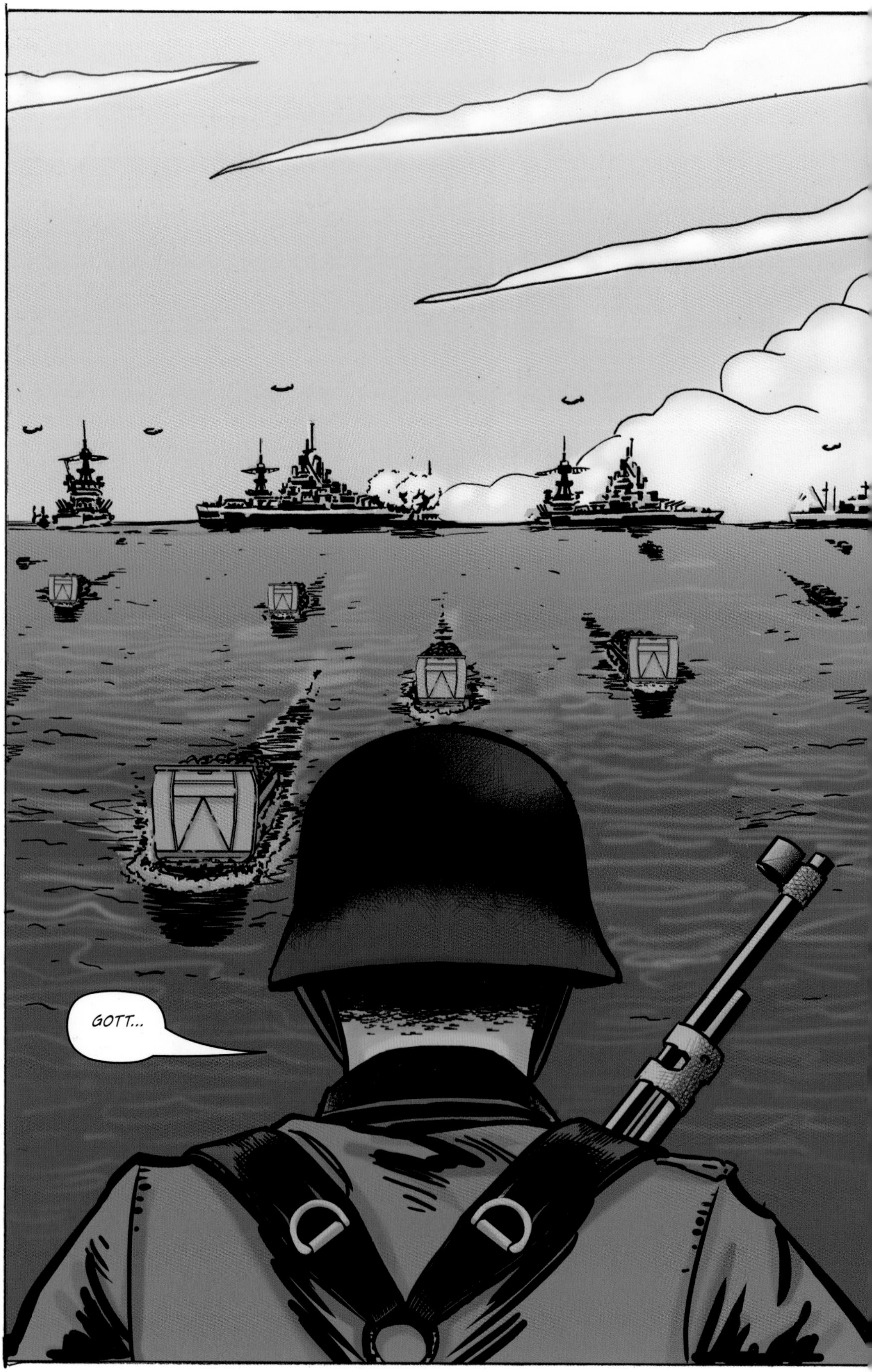
GOTT...

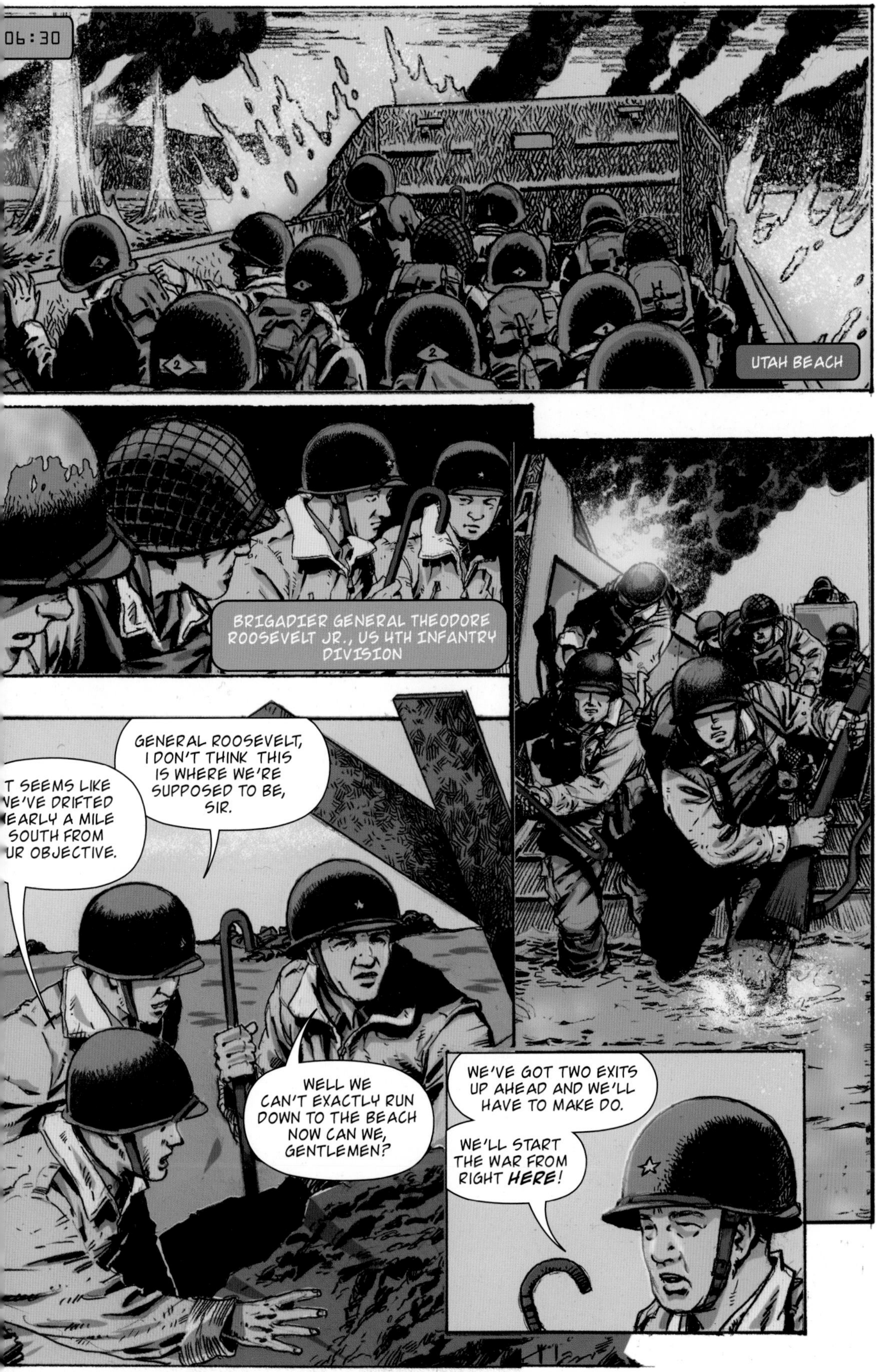

06:30
UTAH BEACH
BRIGADIER GENERAL THEODORE ROOSEVELT JR., US 4TH INFANTRY DIVISION
T SEEMS LIKE VE'VE DRIFTED EARLY A MILE SOUTH FROM UR OBJECTIVE.
GENERAL ROOSEVELT, I DON'T THINK THIS IS WHERE WE'RE SUPPOSED TO BE, SIR.
WELL WE CAN'T EXACTLY RUN DOWN TO THE BEACH NOW CAN WE, GENTLEMEN?
WE'VE GOT TWO EXITS UP AHEAD AND WE'LL HAVE TO MAKE DO.
WE'LL START THE WAR FROM RIGHT *HERE*!

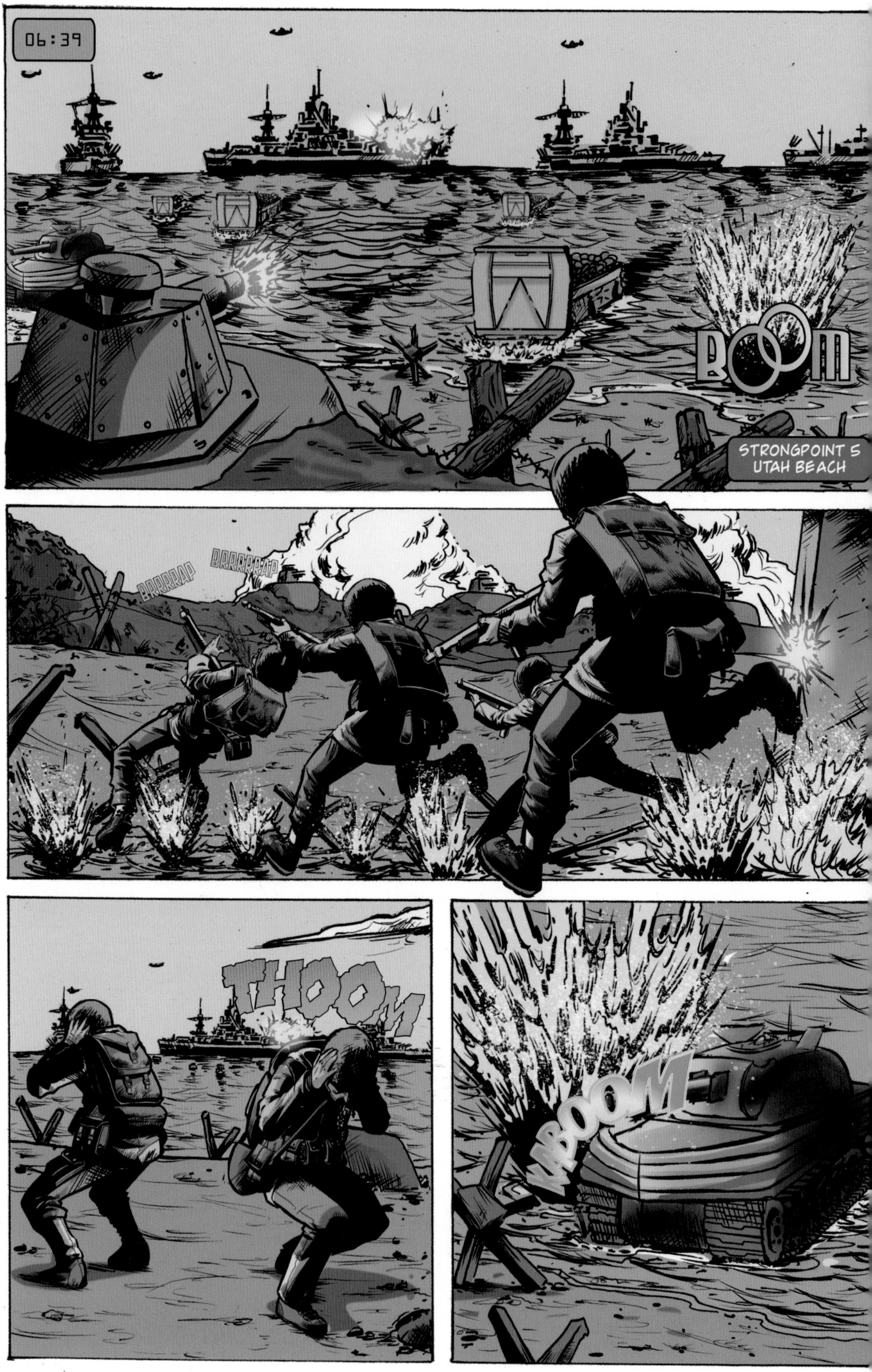
06:39
BOOM
STRONGPOINT 5
UTAH BEACH
BRRRRRAP
BRRRRAP
THOOM
WBOOM

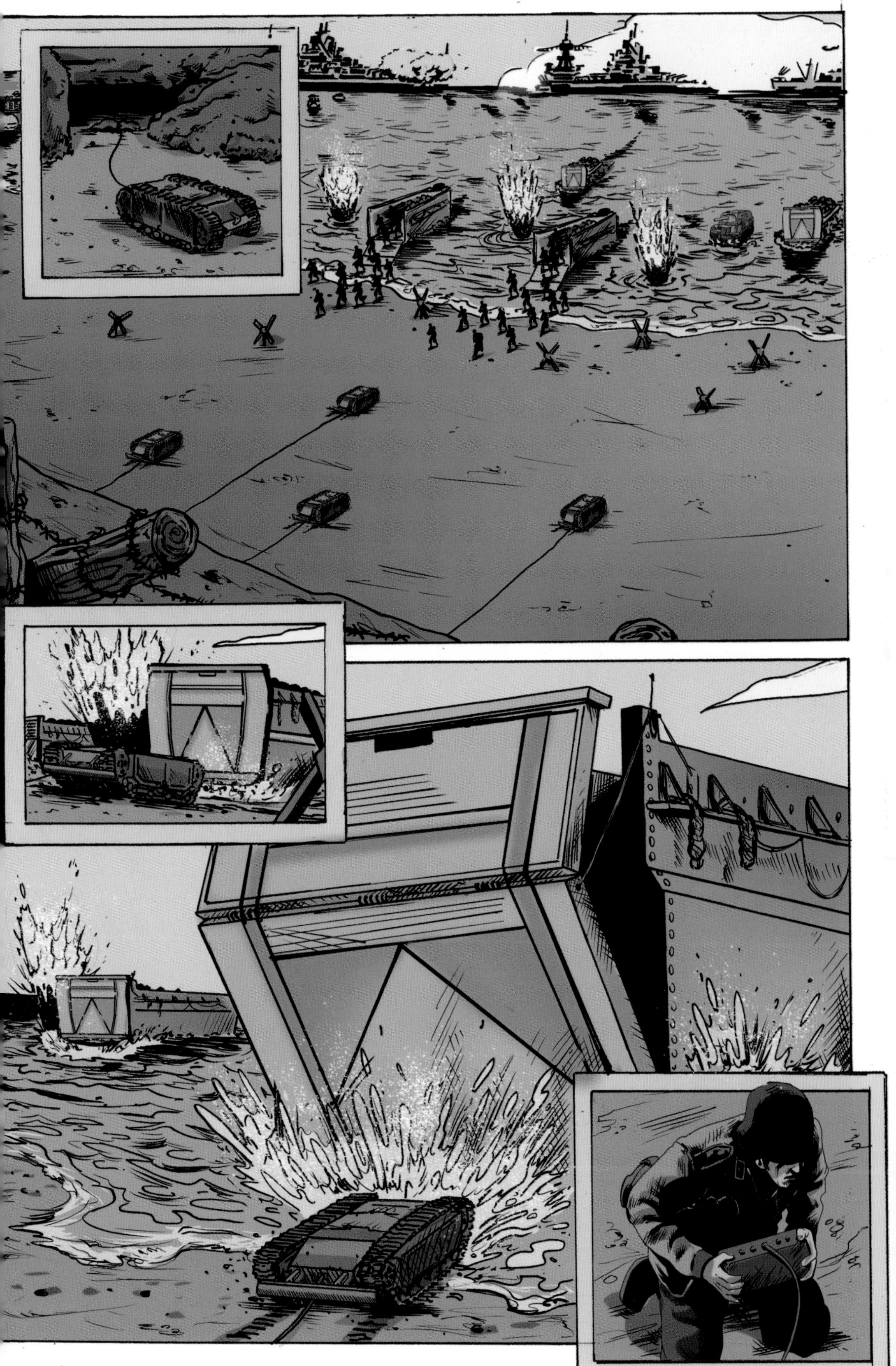

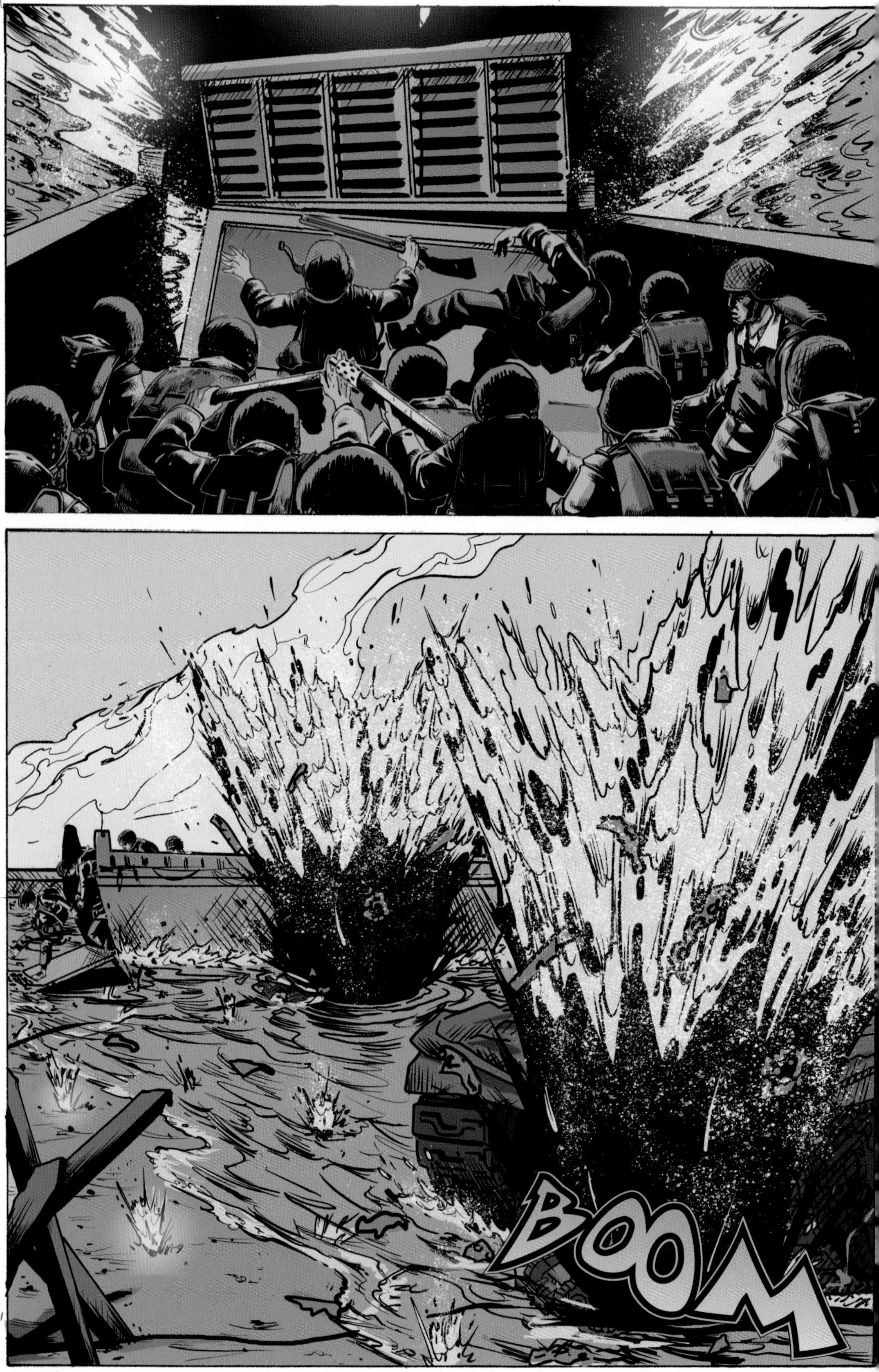
BOOM

KA-BOOOOM
POINT FIVE WEST.
MARK.
FIRE.
BOOM

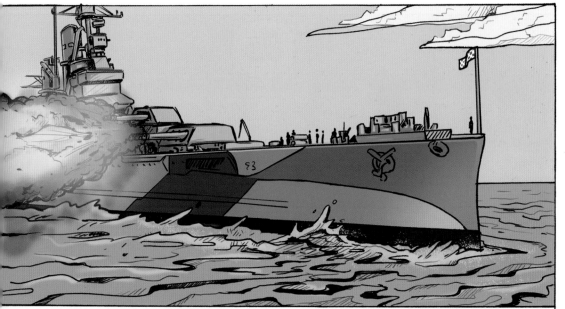

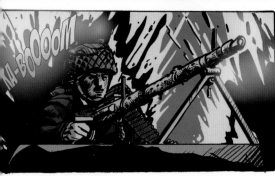

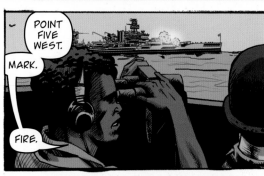

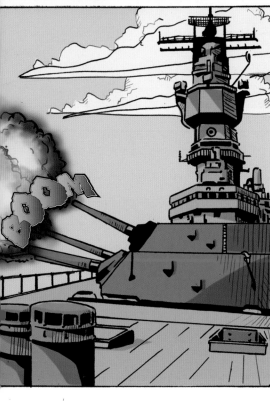

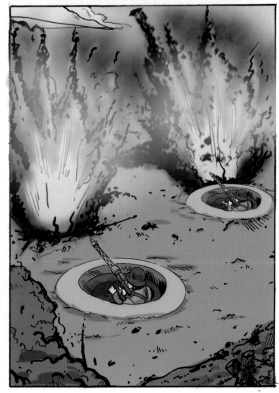

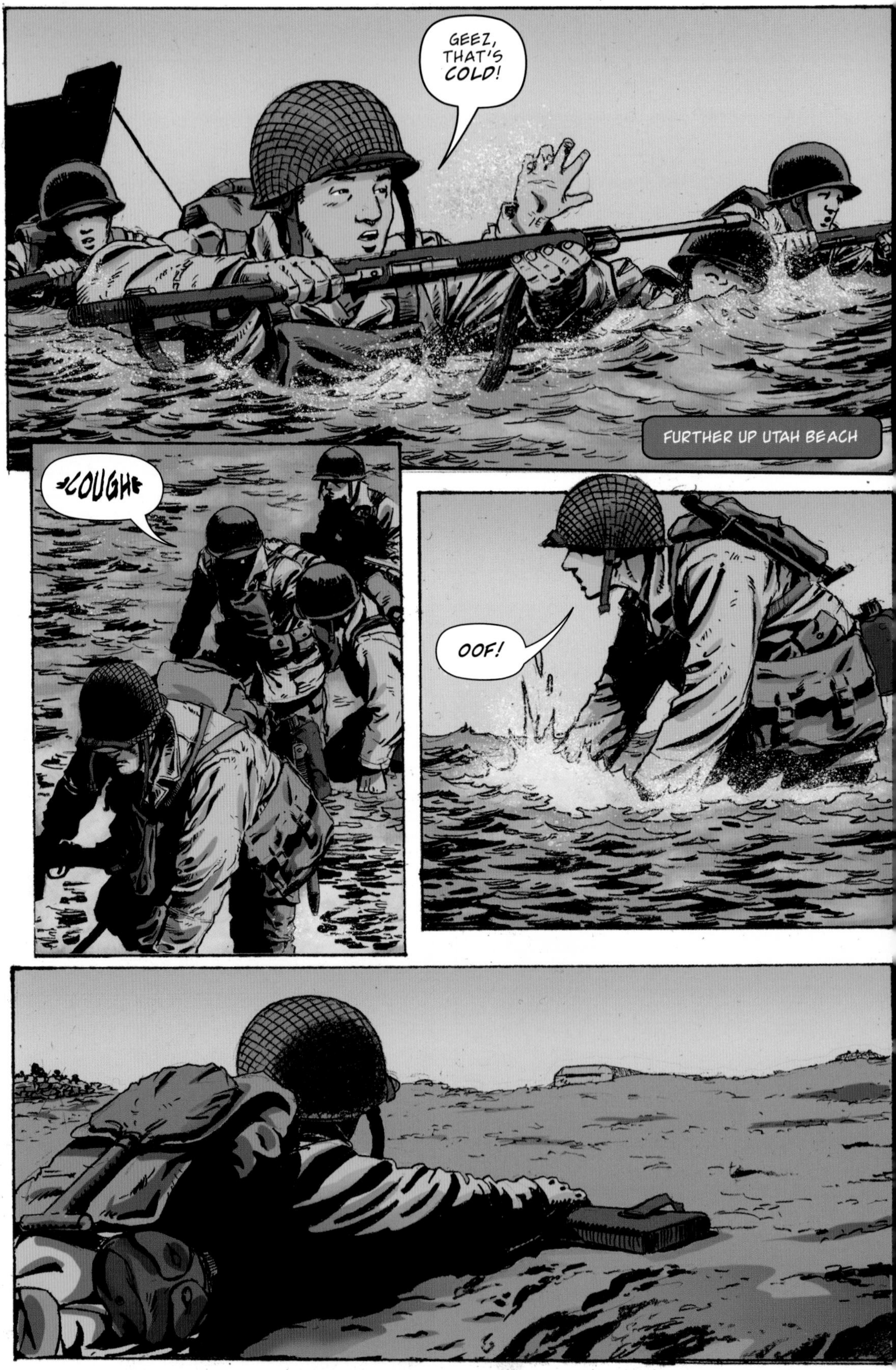
GEEZ, THAT'S COLD!
FURTHER UP UTAH BEACH
COUGH
OOF!

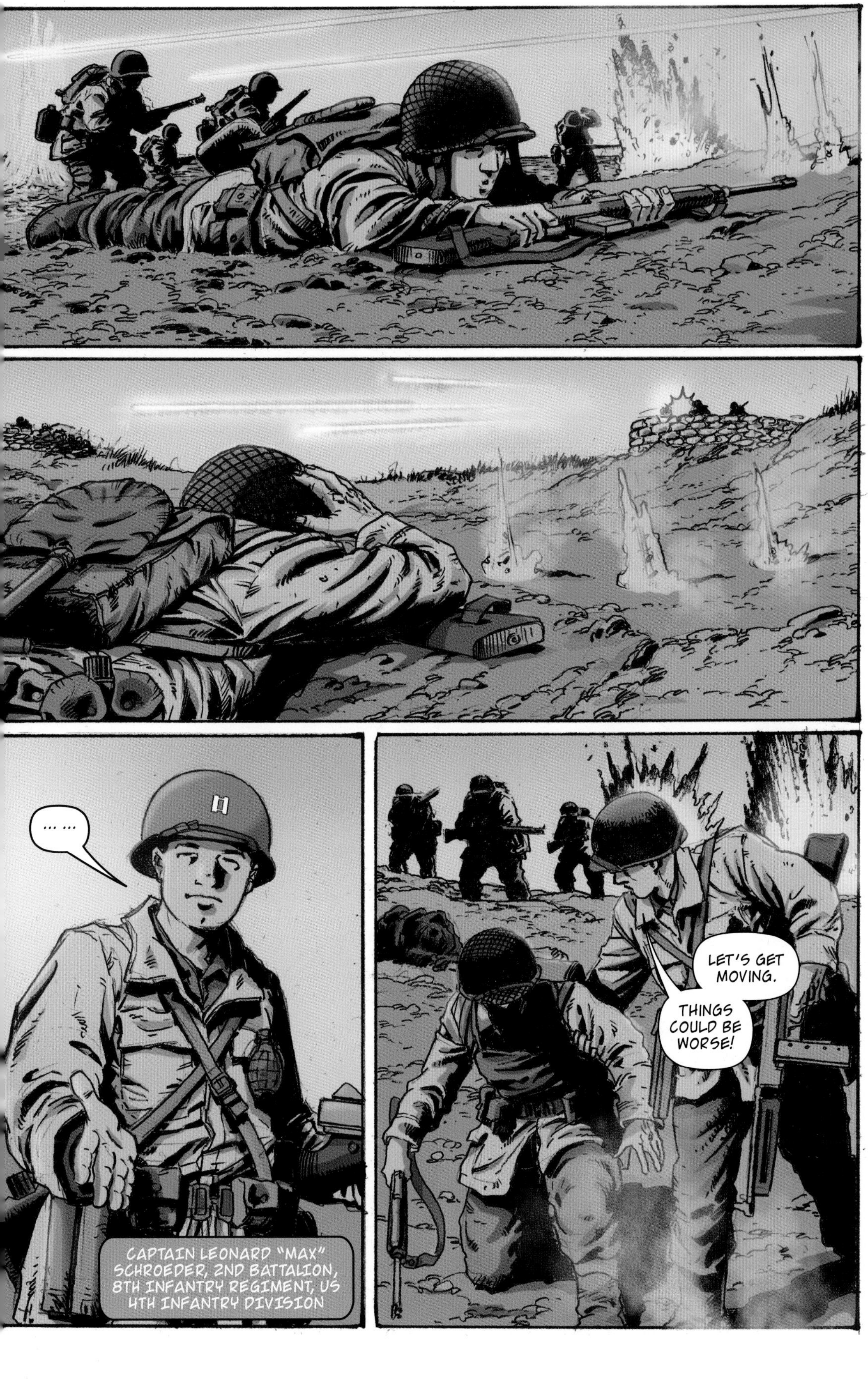
... ...
CAPTAIN LEONARD "MAX" SCHROEDER, 2ND BATTALION, 8TH INFANTRY REGIMENT, US 4TH INFANTRY DIVISION
LET'S GET MOVING.
THINGS COULD BE WORSE!

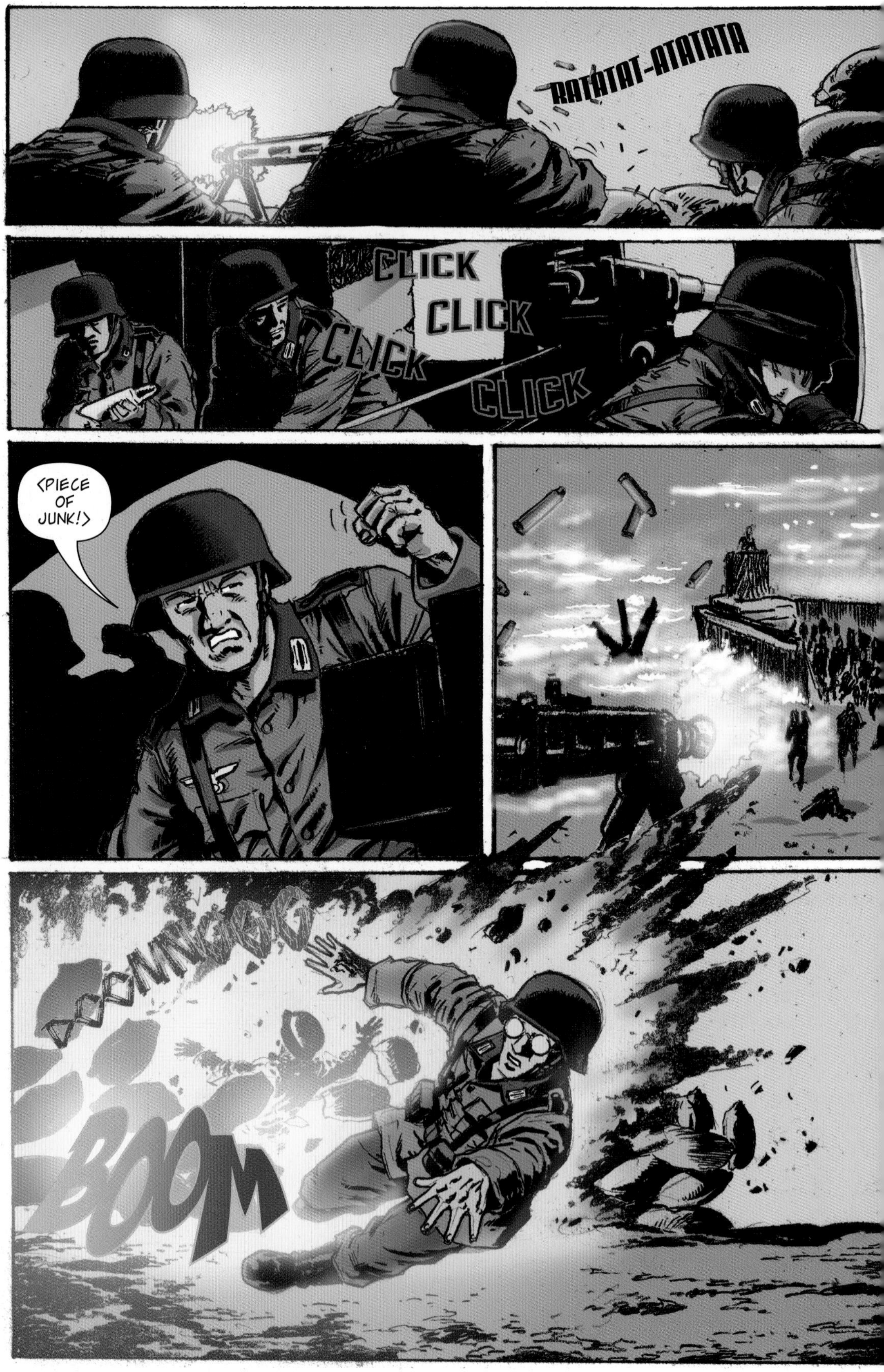
RATATAT-ATATATA
CLICK
CLICK
CLICK
CLICK
<PIECE OF JUNK!>
BOOM

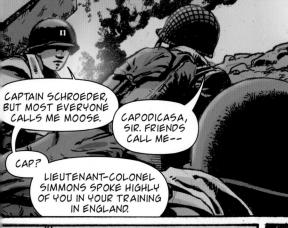

CAPTAIN SCHROEDER, BUT MOST EVERYONE CALLS ME MOOSE.

CAPODICASA, SIR. FRIENDS CALL ME--

CAP?

LIEUTENANT-COLONEL SIMMONS SPOKE HIGHLY OF YOU IN YOUR TRAINING IN ENGLAND.

HEY PAL, ARE YOU--

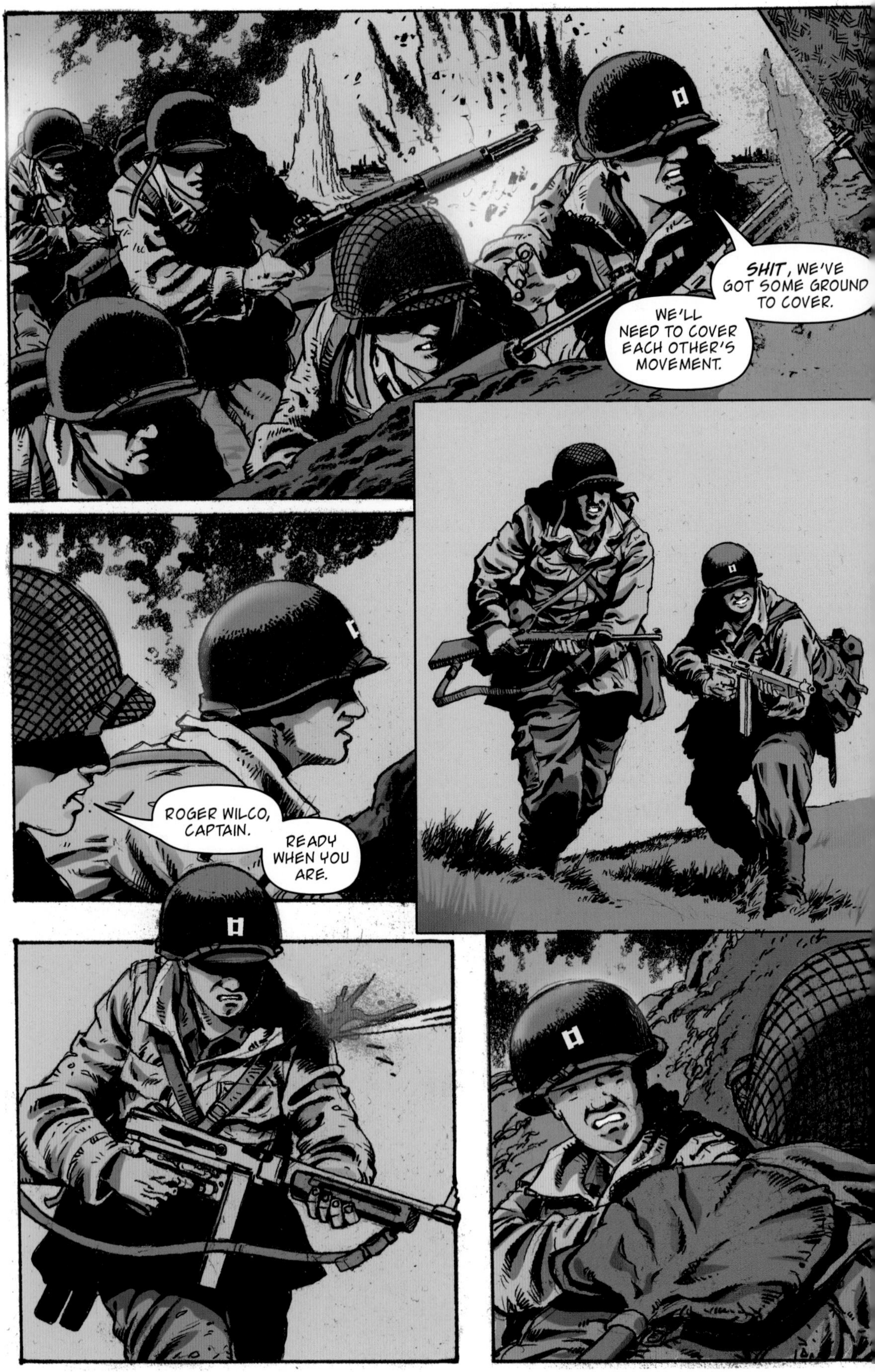
SHIT, WE'VE GOT SOME GROUND TO COVER.
WE'LL NEED TO COVER EACH OTHER'S MOVEMENT.
ROGER WILCO, CAPTAIN.
READY WHEN YOU ARE.

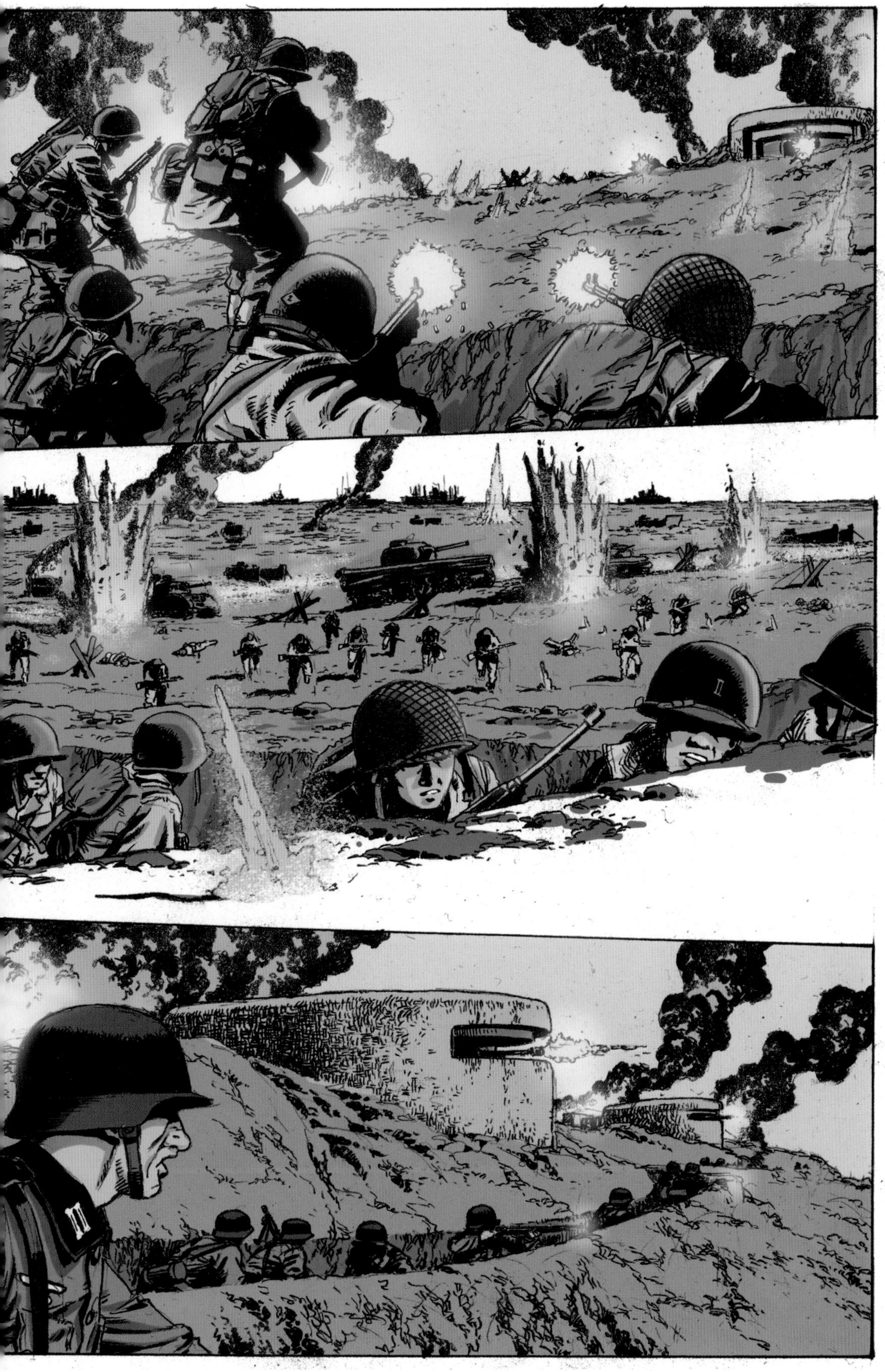

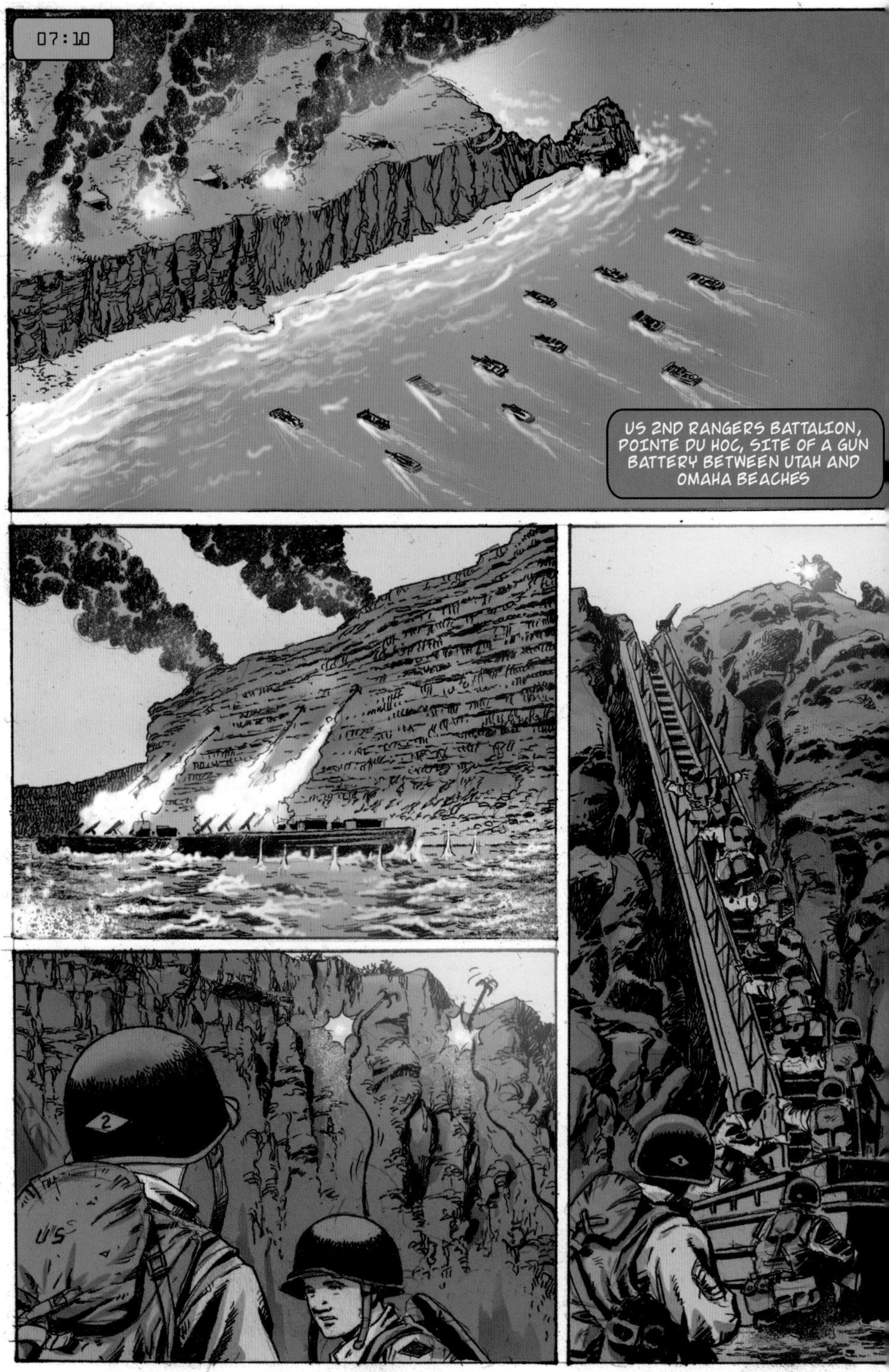
07:10
US 2ND RANGERS BATTALION, POINTE DU HOC, SITE OF A GUN BATTERY BETWEEN UTAH AND OMAHA BEACHES

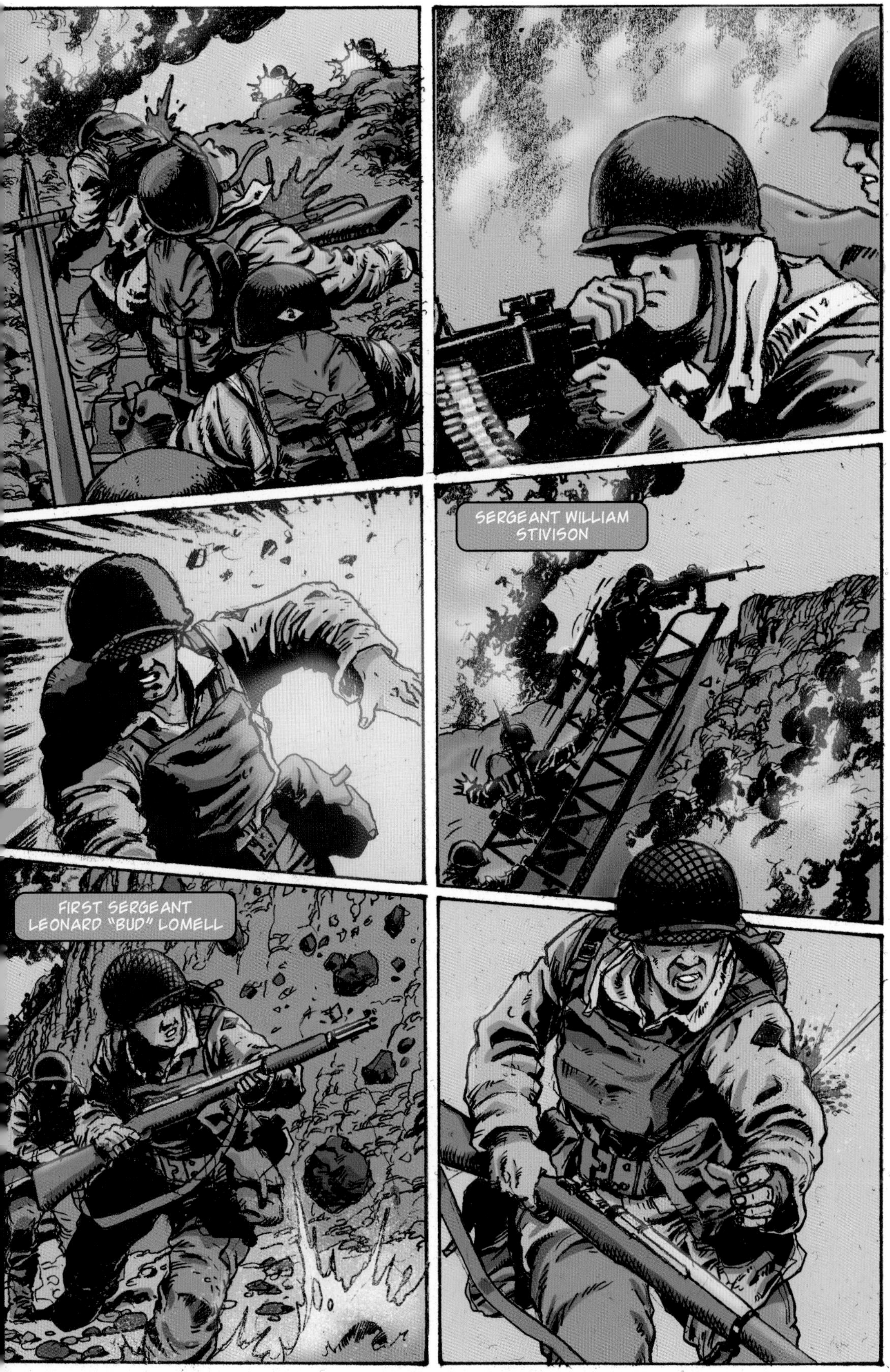
SERGEANT WILLIAM STIVISON
FIRST SERGEANT LEONARD "BUD" LOMELL

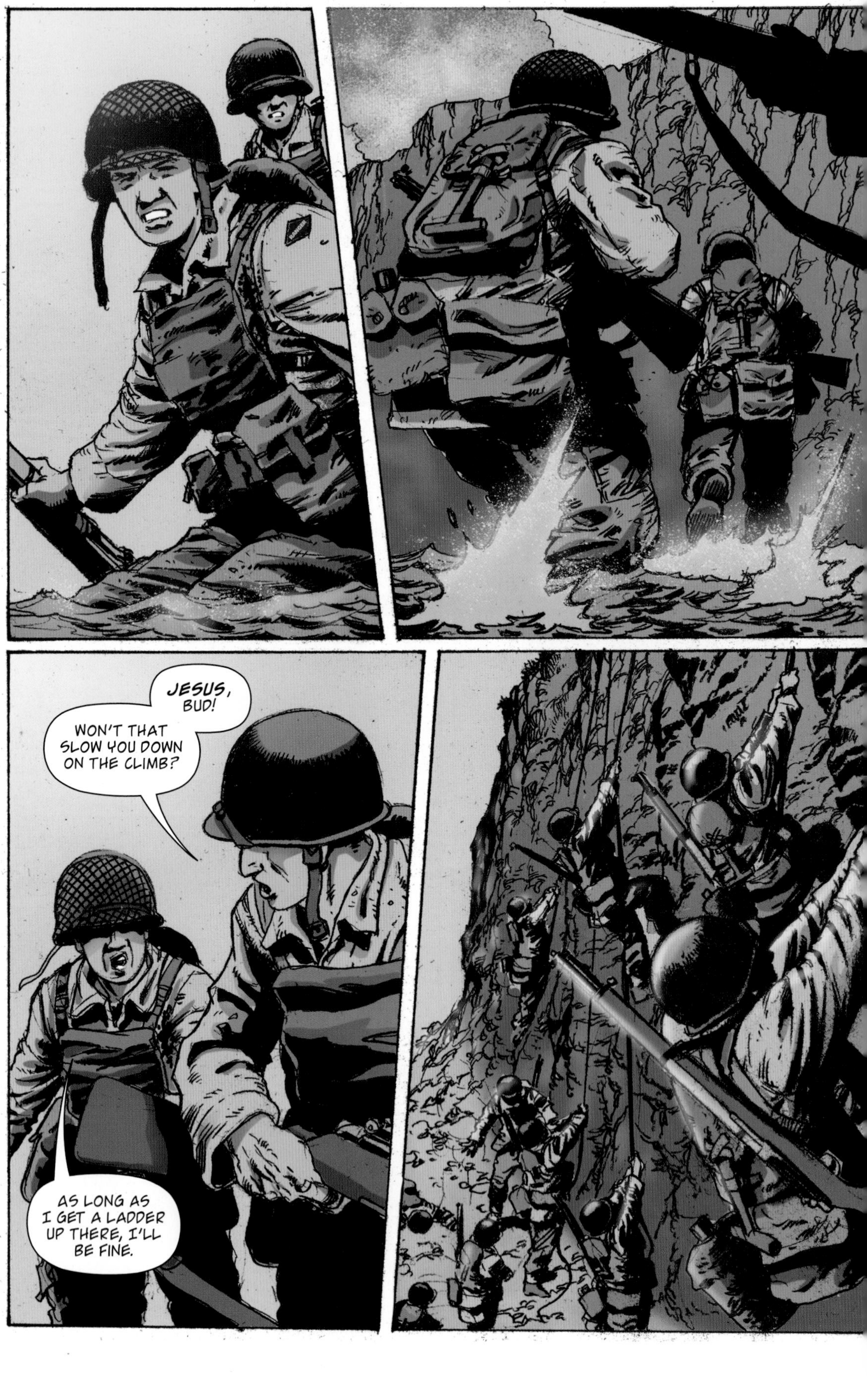

JESUS, BUD!
WON'T THAT SLOW YOU DOWN ON THE CLIMB?
AS LONG AS I GET A LADDER UP THERE, I'LL BE FINE.

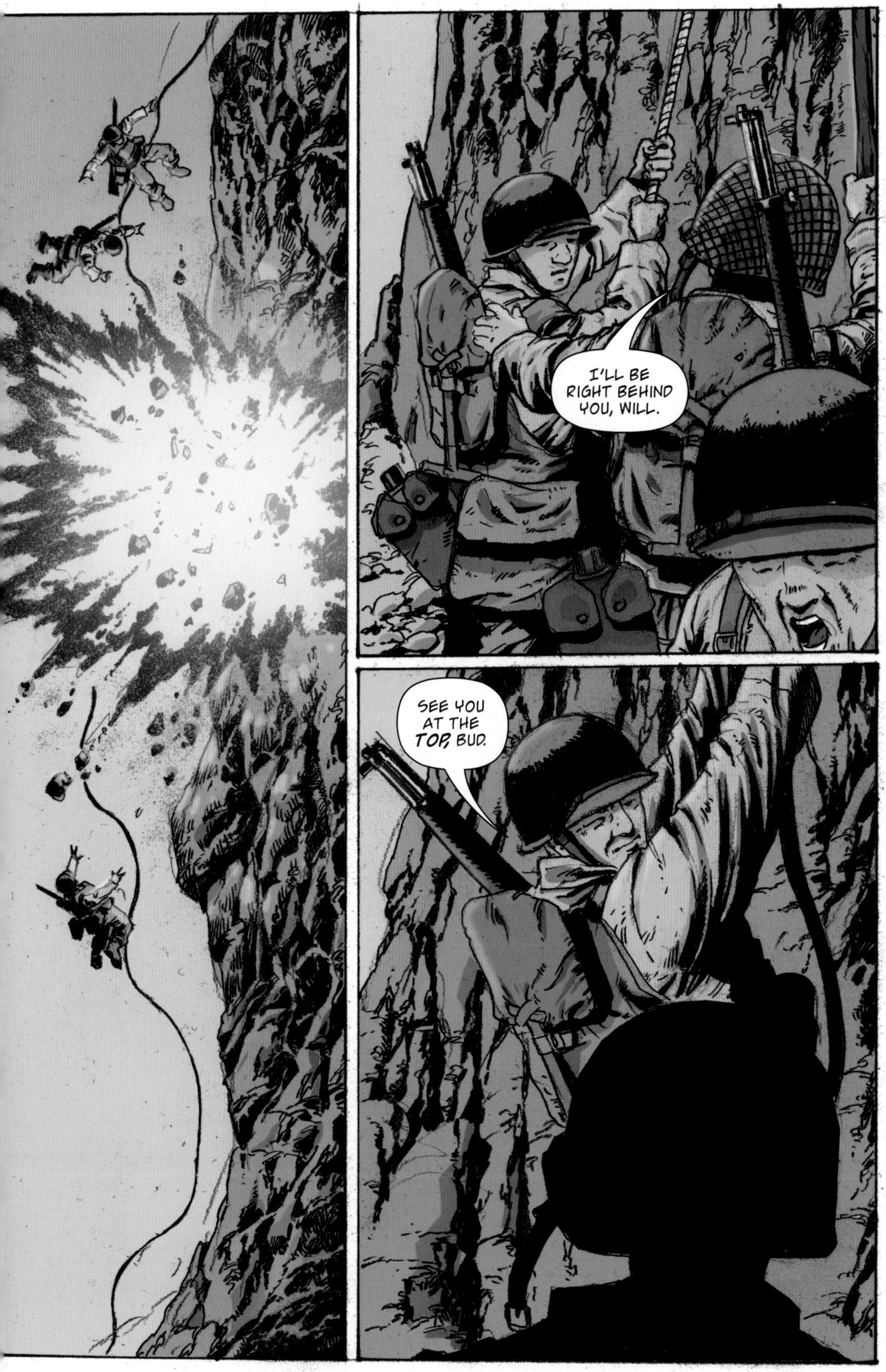
I'LL BE RIGHT BEHIND YOU, WILL.
SEE YOU AT THE *TOP*, BUD.

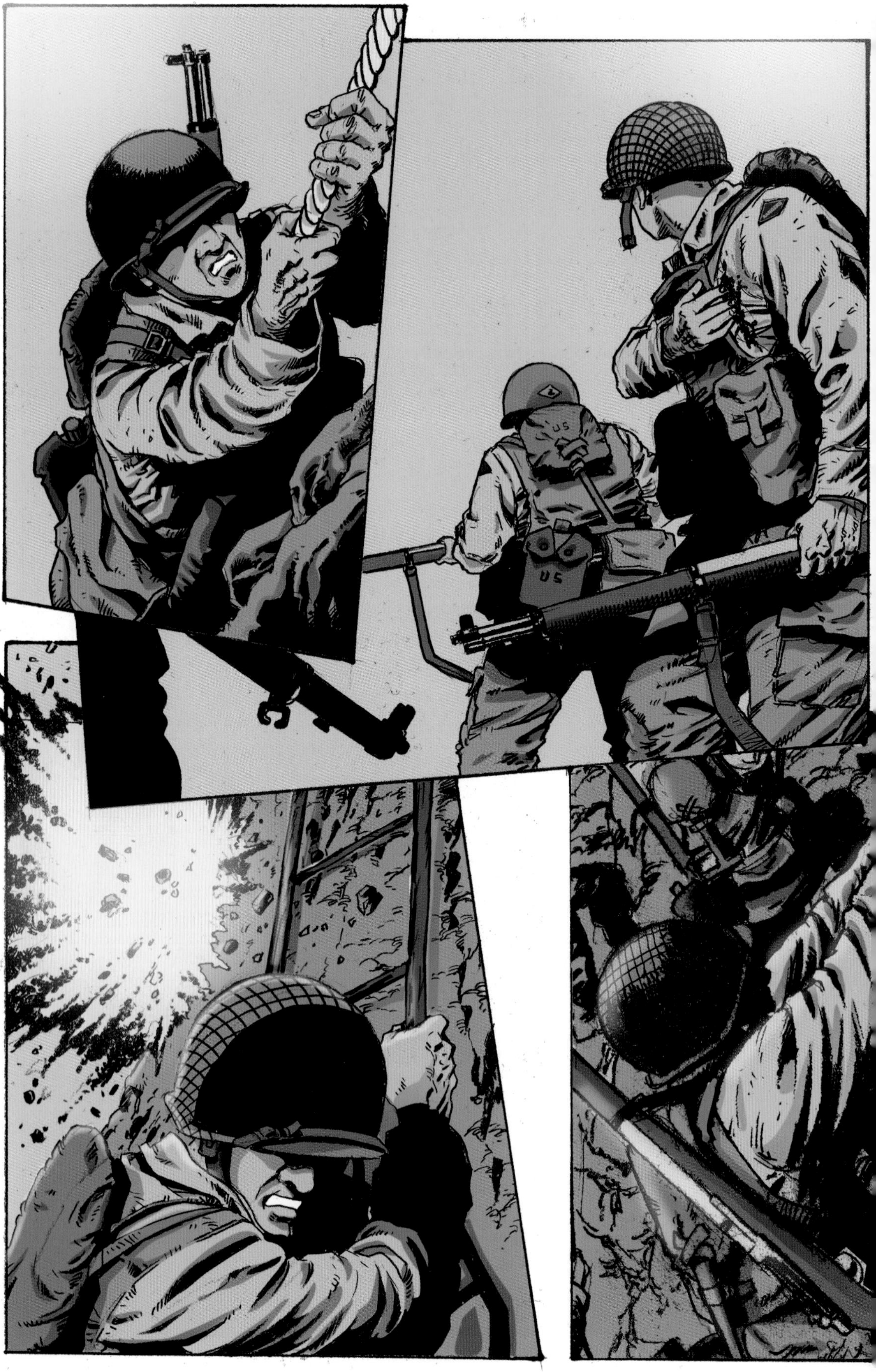
US
US

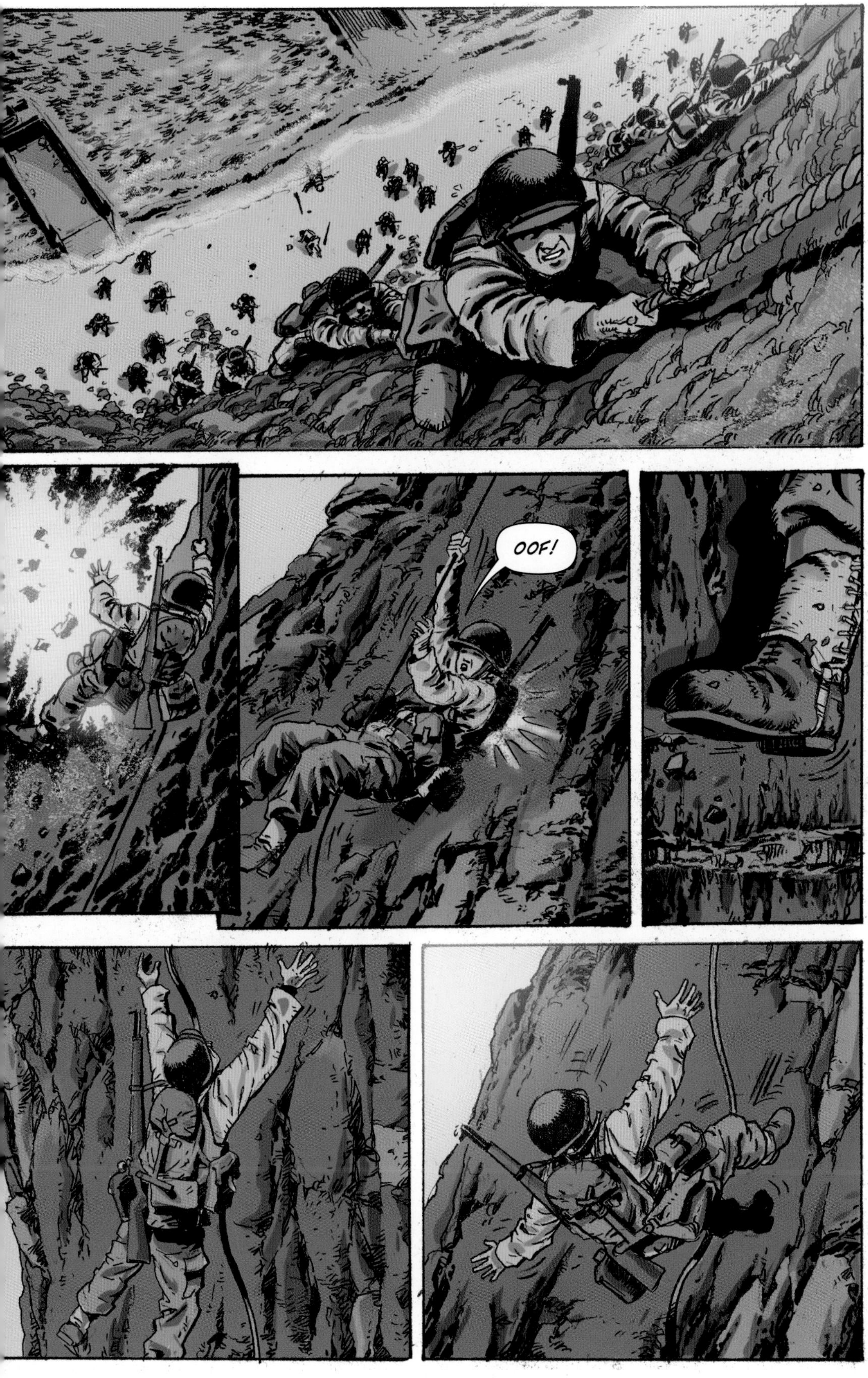
OOF!

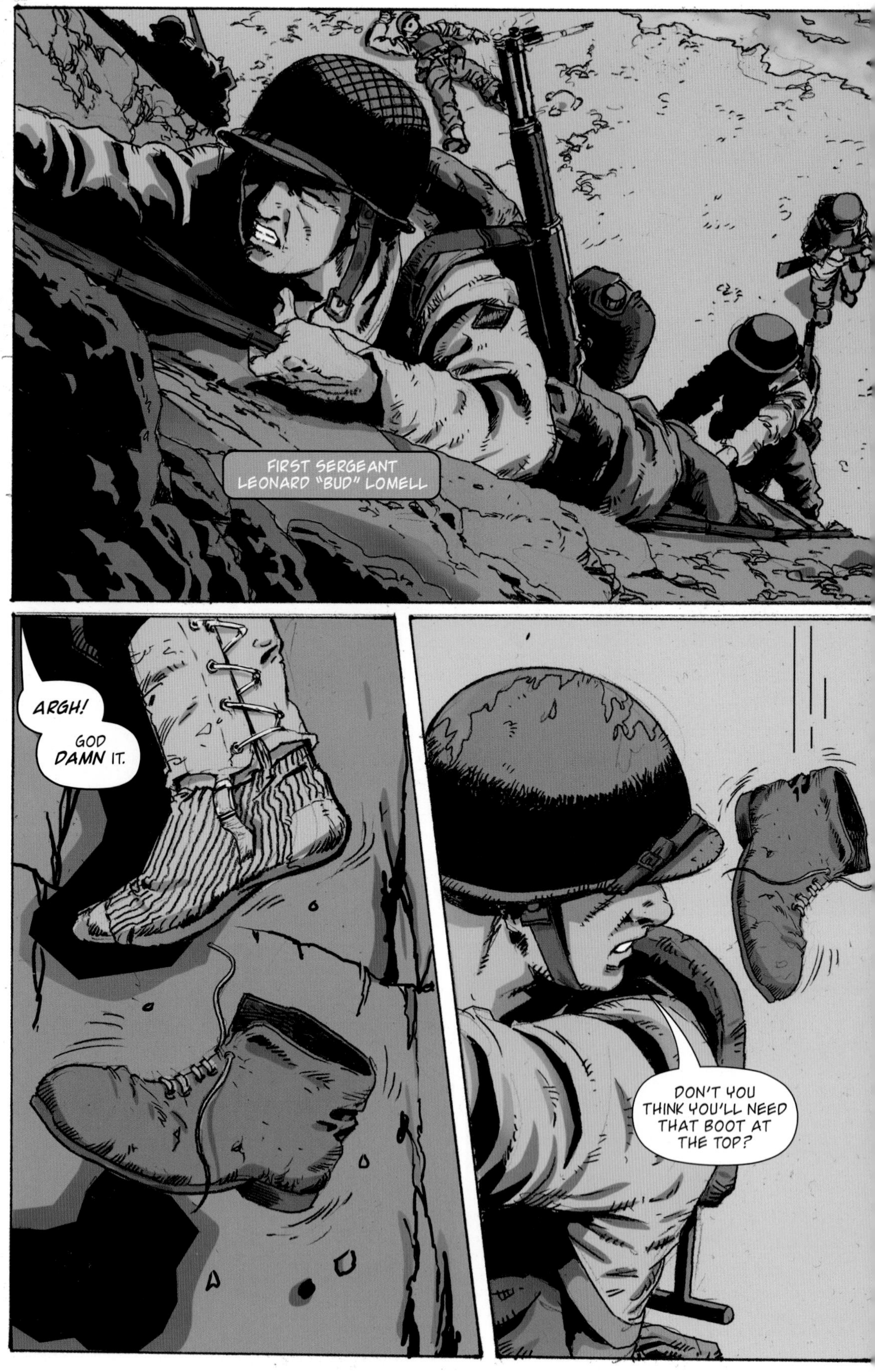
FIRST SERGEANT LEONARD "BUD" LOMELL
ARGH!
GOD DAMN IT.
DON'T YOU THINK YOU'LL NEED THAT BOOT AT THE TOP?

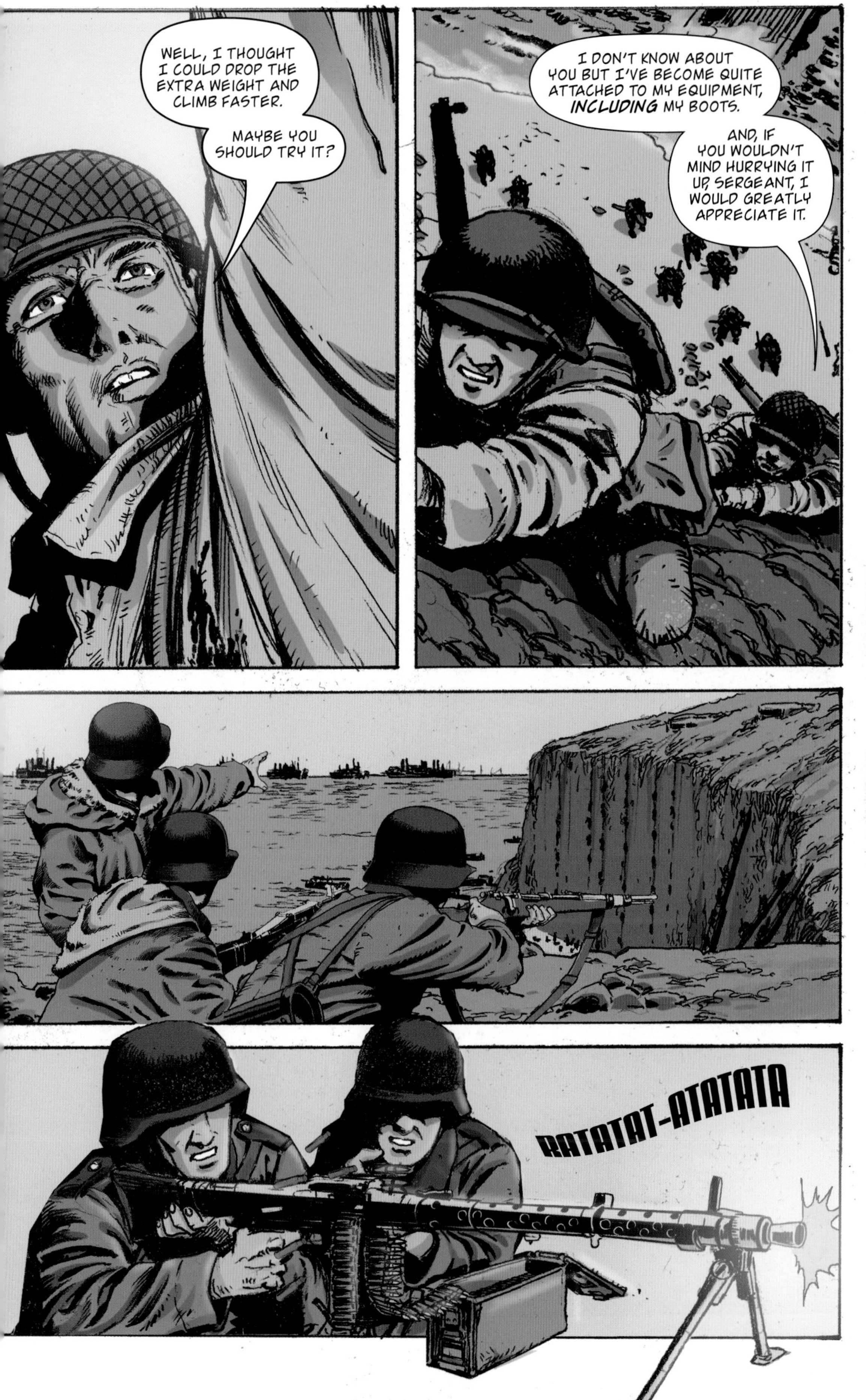
WELL, I THOUGHT I COULD DROP THE EXTRA WEIGHT AND CLIMB FASTER.
MAYBE YOU SHOULD TRY IT?
I DON'T KNOW ABOUT YOU BUT I'VE BECOME QUITE ATTACHED TO MY EQUIPMENT, *INCLUDING* MY BOOTS.
AND, IF YOU WOULDN'T MIND HURRYING IT UP, SERGEANT, I WOULD GREATLY APPRECIATE IT.
RATATAT-ATATATA

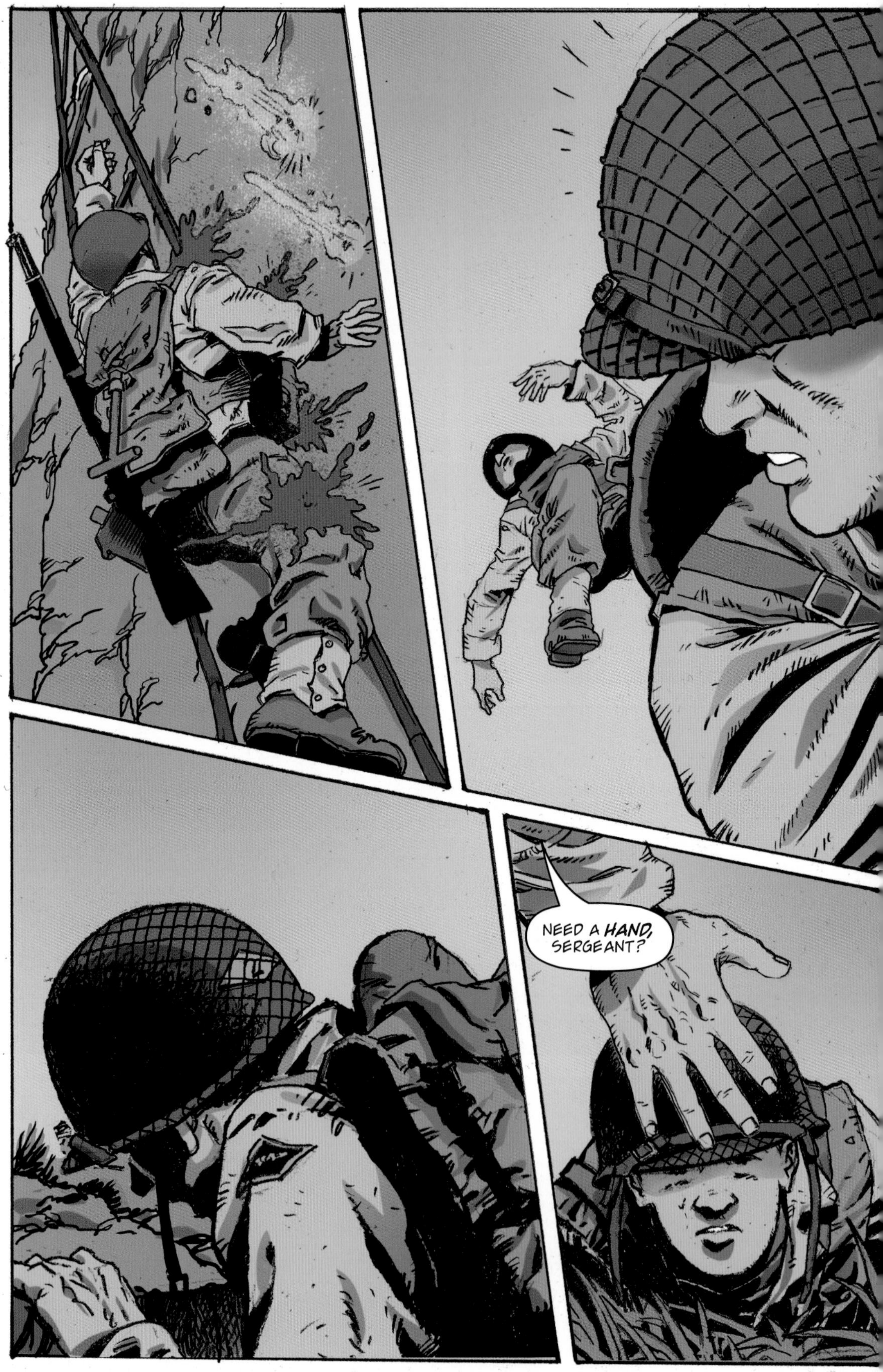
NEED A HAND, SERGEANT?

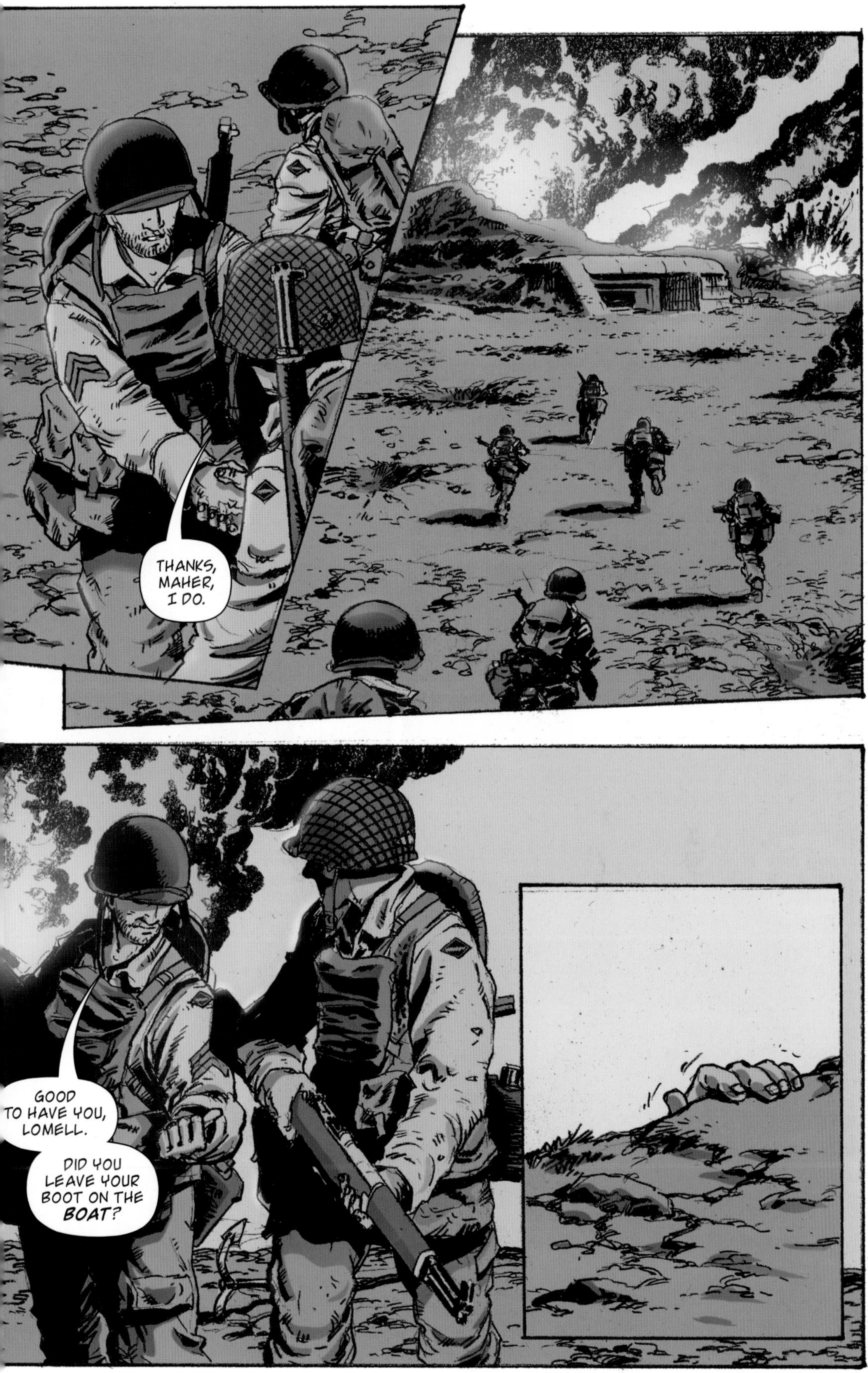
THANKS, MAHER, I DO.
GOOD TO HAVE YOU, LOMELL.
DID YOU LEAVE YOUR BOOT ON THE BOAT?

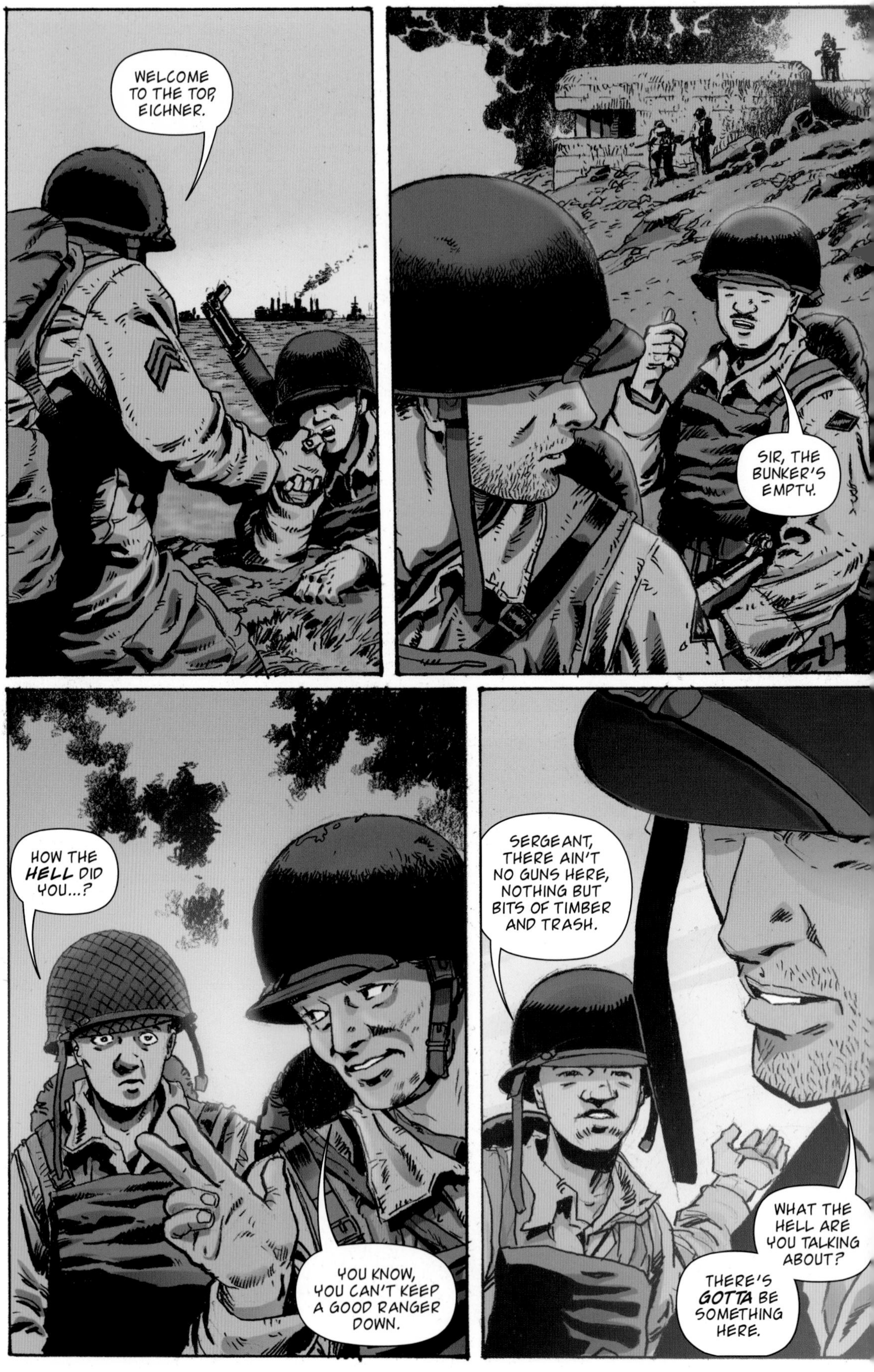
WELCOME TO THE TOP, EICHNER.
SIR, THE BUNKER'S EMPTY.
HOW THE HELL DID YOU...?
YOU KNOW, YOU CAN'T KEEP A GOOD RANGER DOWN.
SERGEANT, THERE AIN'T NO GUNS HERE, NOTHING BUT BITS OF TIMBER AND TRASH.
WHAT THE HELL ARE YOU TALKING ABOUT?
THERE'S GOTTA BE SOMETHING HERE.

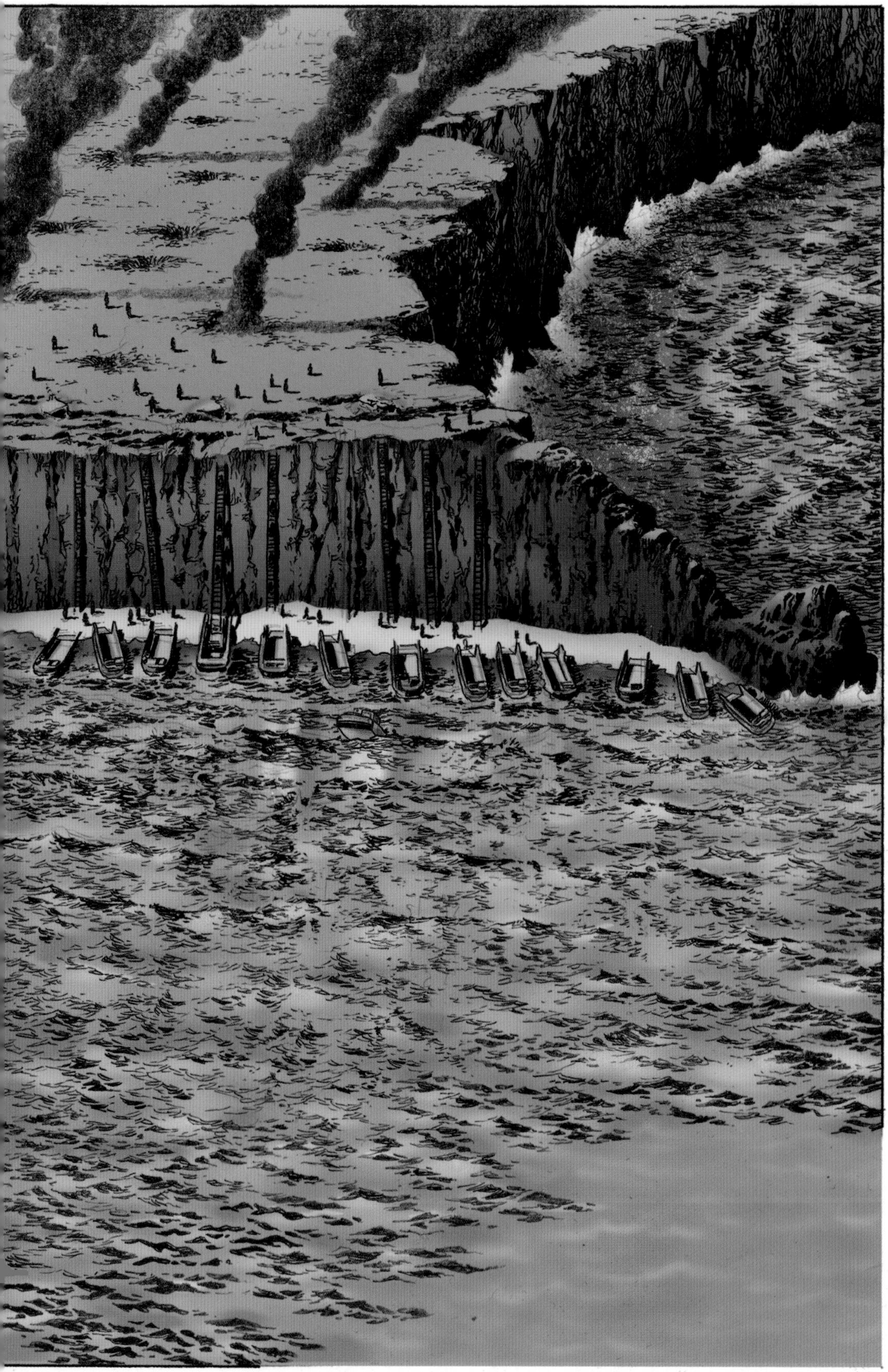

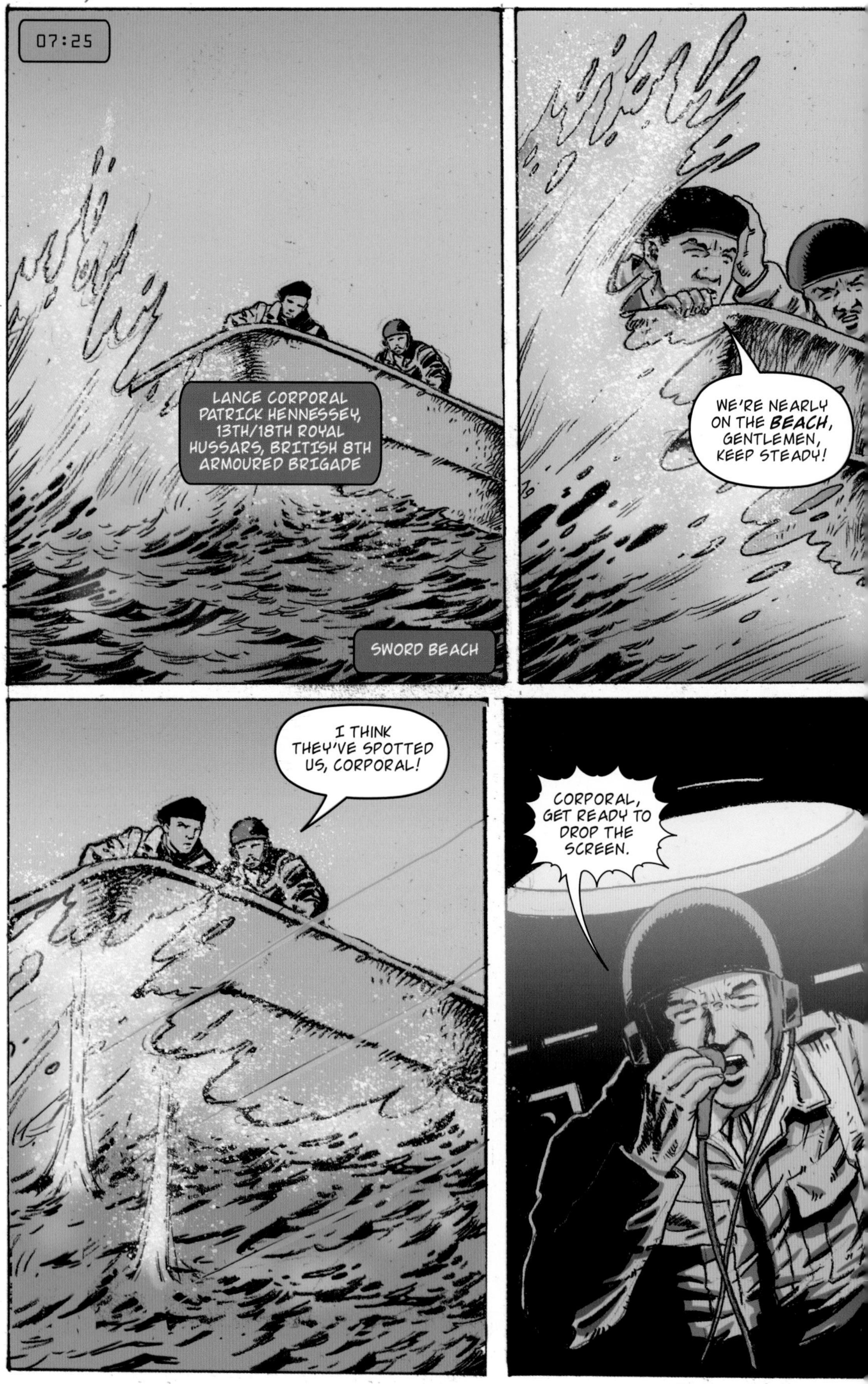
07:25
LANCE CORPORAL PATRICK HENNESSEY, 13TH/18TH ROYAL HUSSARS, BRITISH 8TH ARMOURED BRIGADE
SWORD BEACH
WE'RE NEARLY ON THE BEACH, GENTLEMEN, KEEP STEADY!
I THINK THEY'VE SPOTTED US, CORPORAL!
CORPORAL, GET READY TO DROP THE SCREEN.

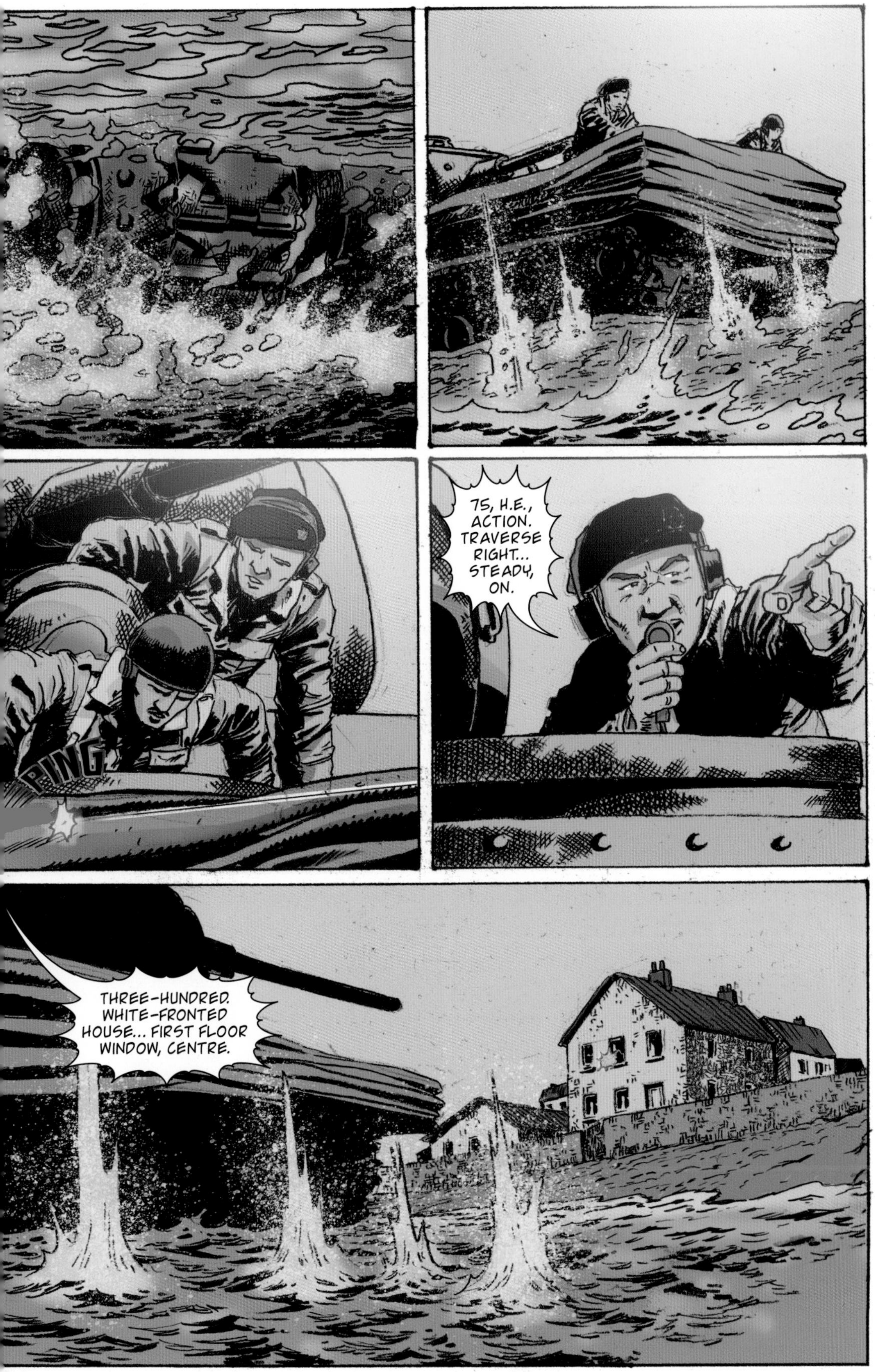
PING
75, H.E., ACTION. TRAVERSE RIGHT... STEADY, ON.
THREE-HUNDRED. WHITE-FRONTED HOUSE... FIRST FLOOR WINDOW, CENTRE.

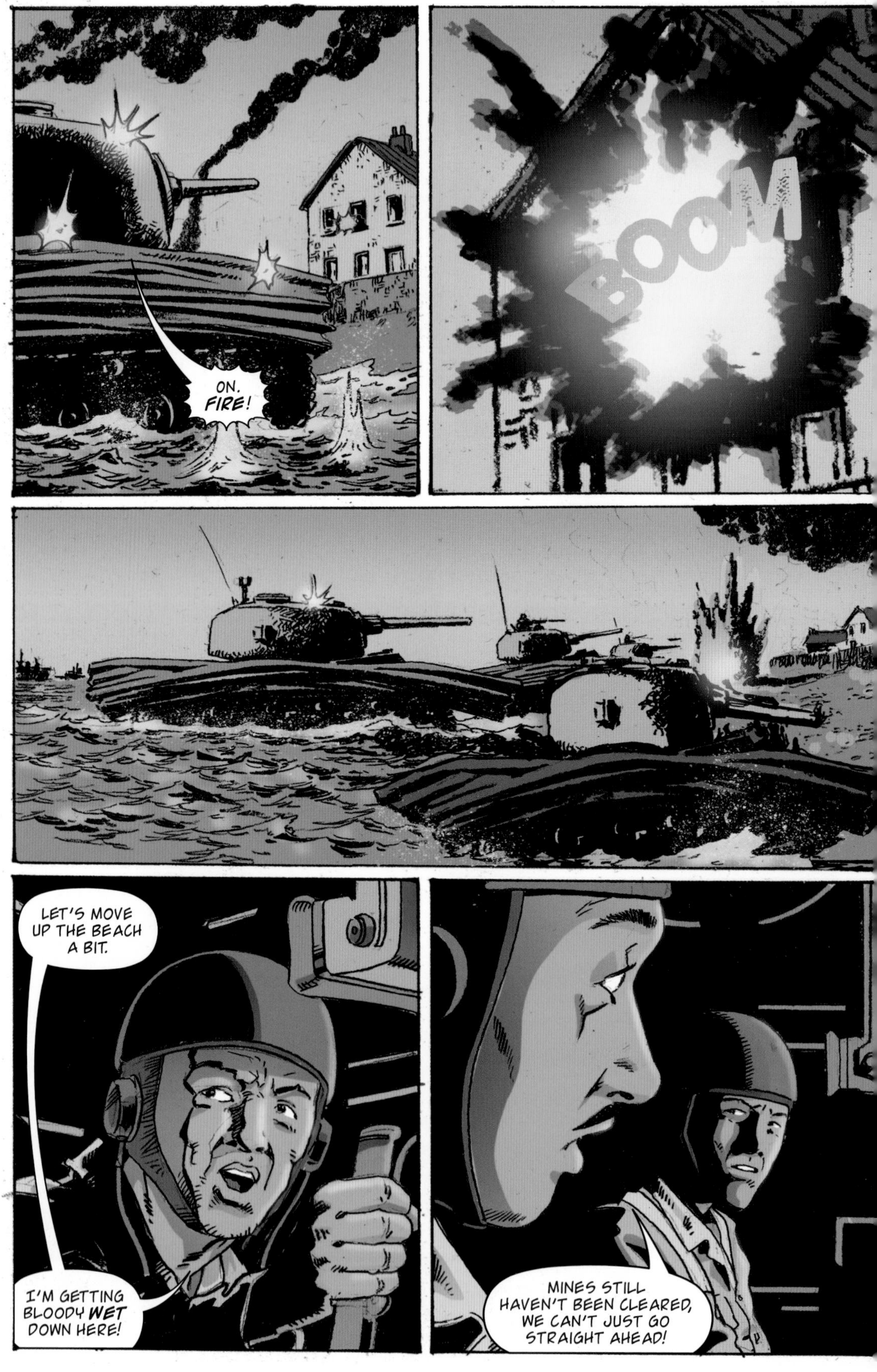
ON. FIRE!
BOOM
LET'S MOVE UP THE BEACH A BIT.
I'M GETTING BLOODY WET DOWN HERE!
MINES STILL HAVEN'T BEEN CLEARED, WE CAN'T JUST GO STRAIGHT AHEAD!

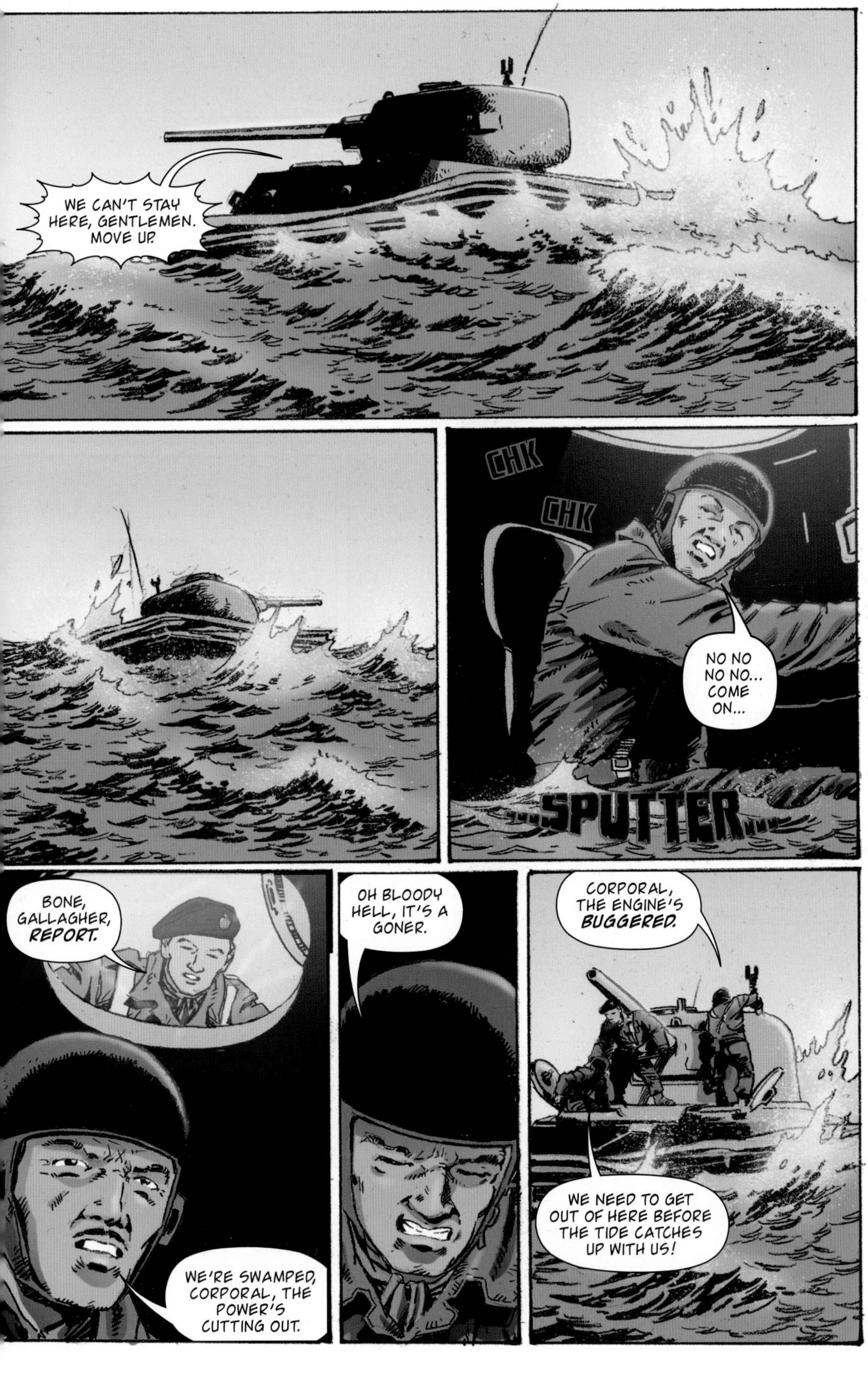
WE CAN'T STAY HERE, GENTLEMEN. MOVE UP.
CHK
CHK
NO NO NO NO... COME ON...
...SPUTTER...
BONE, GALLAGHER, *REPORT.*
WE'RE SWAMPED, CORPORAL, THE POWER'S CUTTING OUT.
OH BLOODY HELL, IT'S A GONER.
CORPORAL, THE ENGINE'S *BUGGERED.*
WE NEED TO GET OUT OF HERE BEFORE THE TIDE CATCHES UP WITH US!

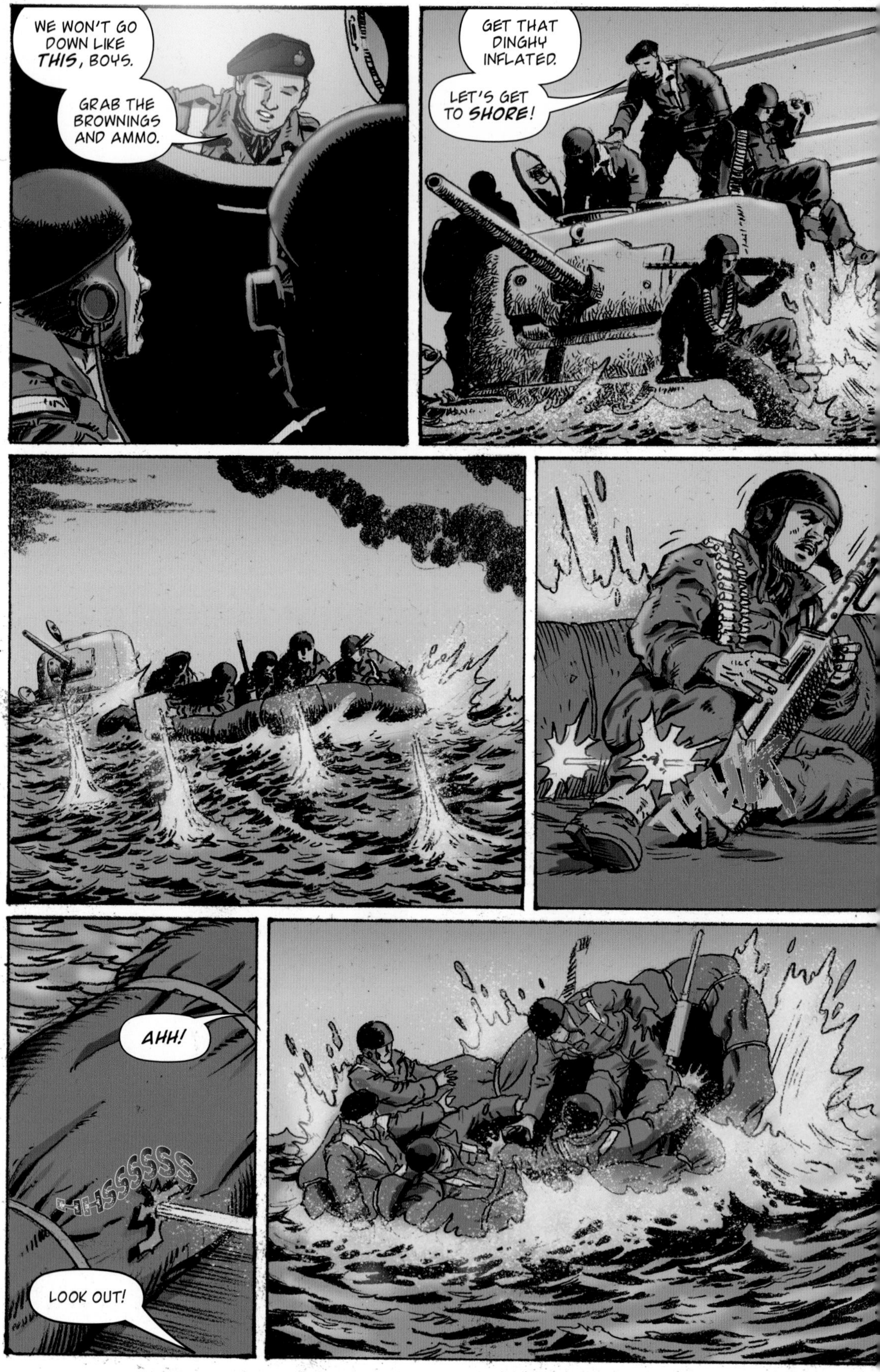

WE WON'T GO DOWN LIKE THIS, BOYS.
GRAB THE BROWNINGS AND AMMO.
GET THAT DINGHY INFLATED.
LET'S GET TO SHORE!
THUK
AHH!
HISSSSSS
LOOK OUT!

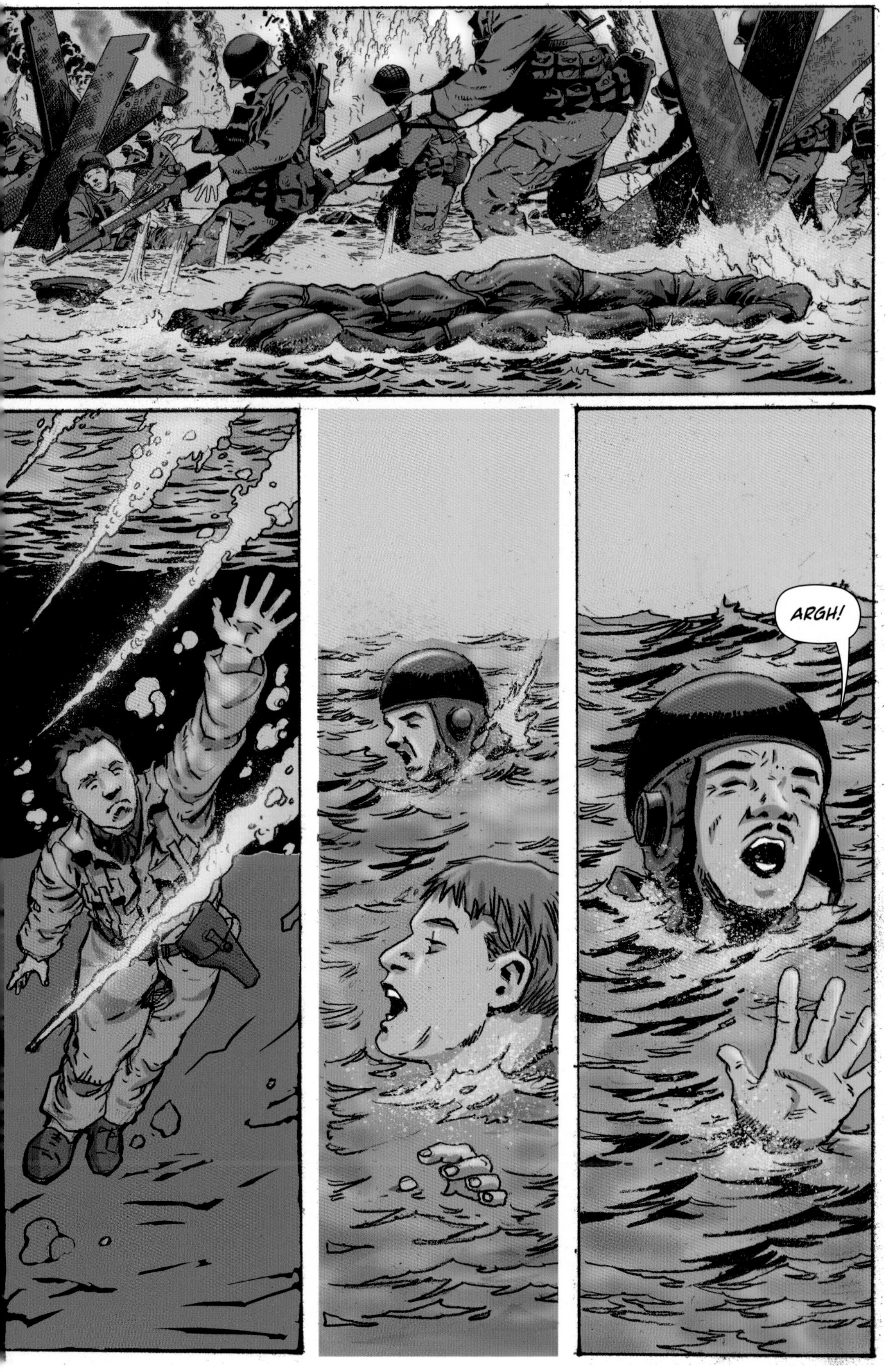
ARGH!

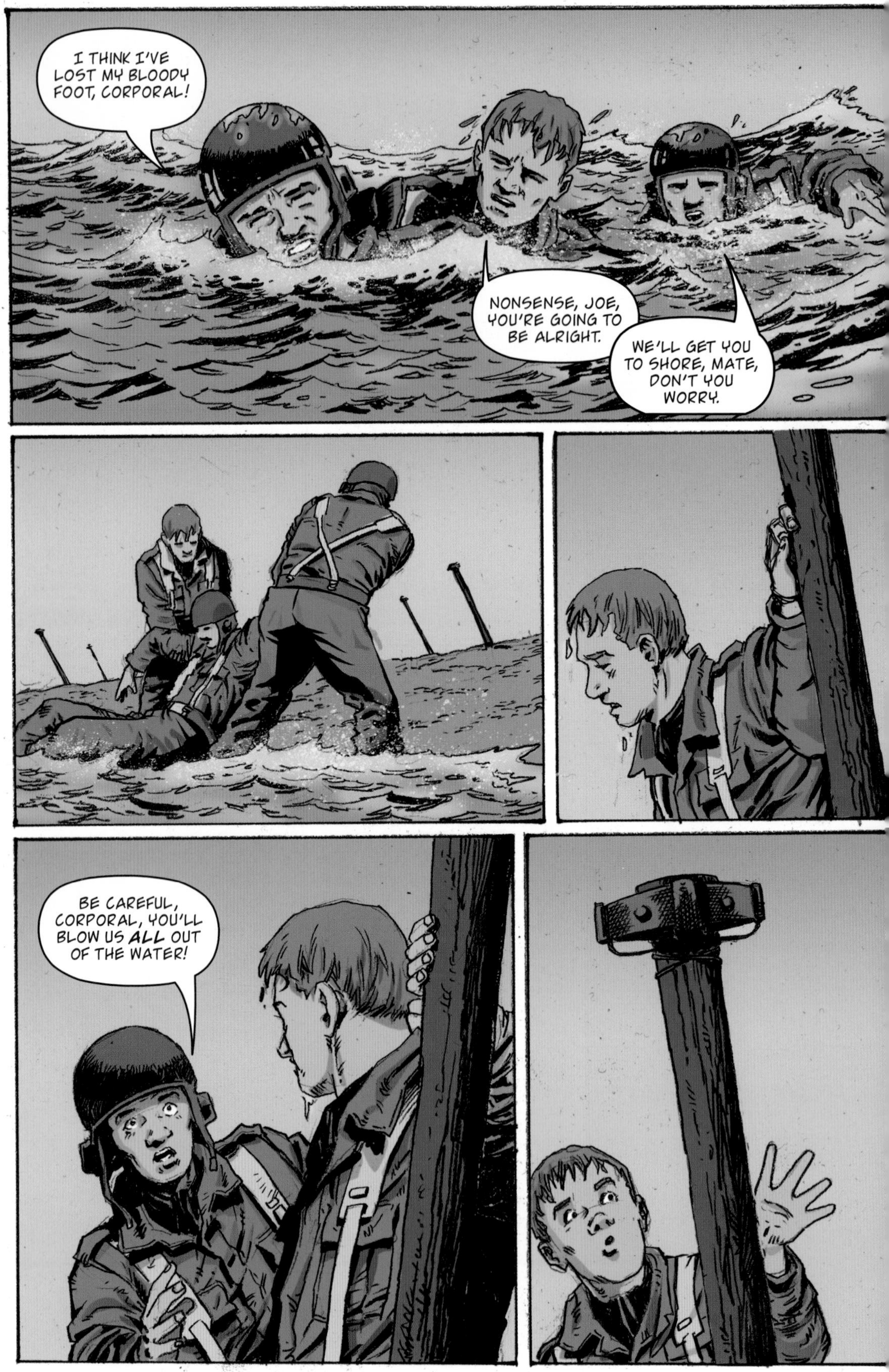
I THINK I'VE LOST MY BLOODY FOOT, CORPORAL!
NONSENSE, JOE, YOU'RE GOING TO BE ALRIGHT.
WE'LL GET YOU TO SHORE, MATE, DON'T YOU WORRY.
BE CAREFUL, CORPORAL, YOU'LL BLOW US ALL OUT OF THE WATER!

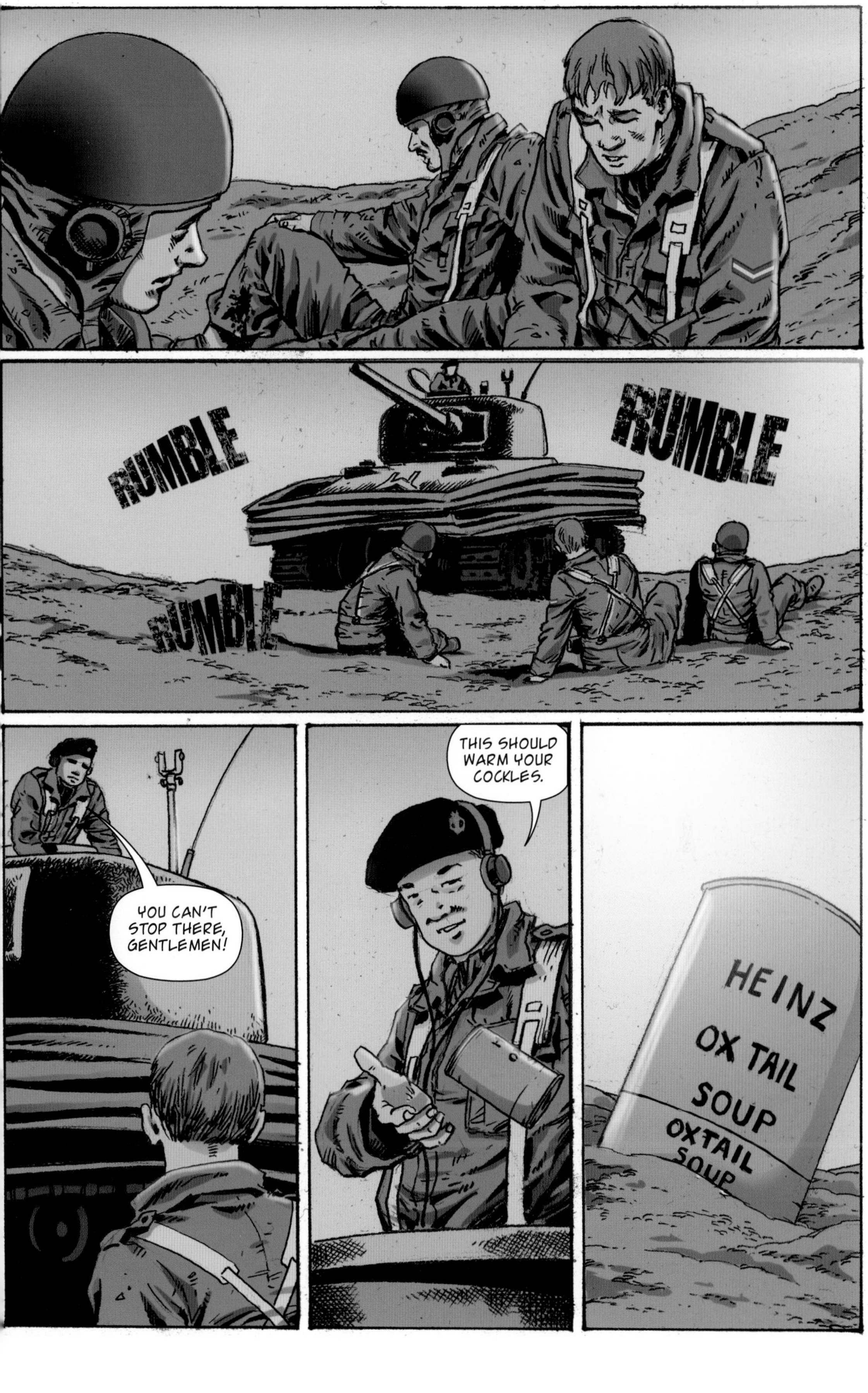
RUMBLE
RUMBLE
RUMBLE
YOU CAN'T STOP THERE, GENTLEMEN!
THIS SHOULD WARM YOUR COCKLES.
HEINZ
OX TAIL
SOUP
OXTAIL
SOUP

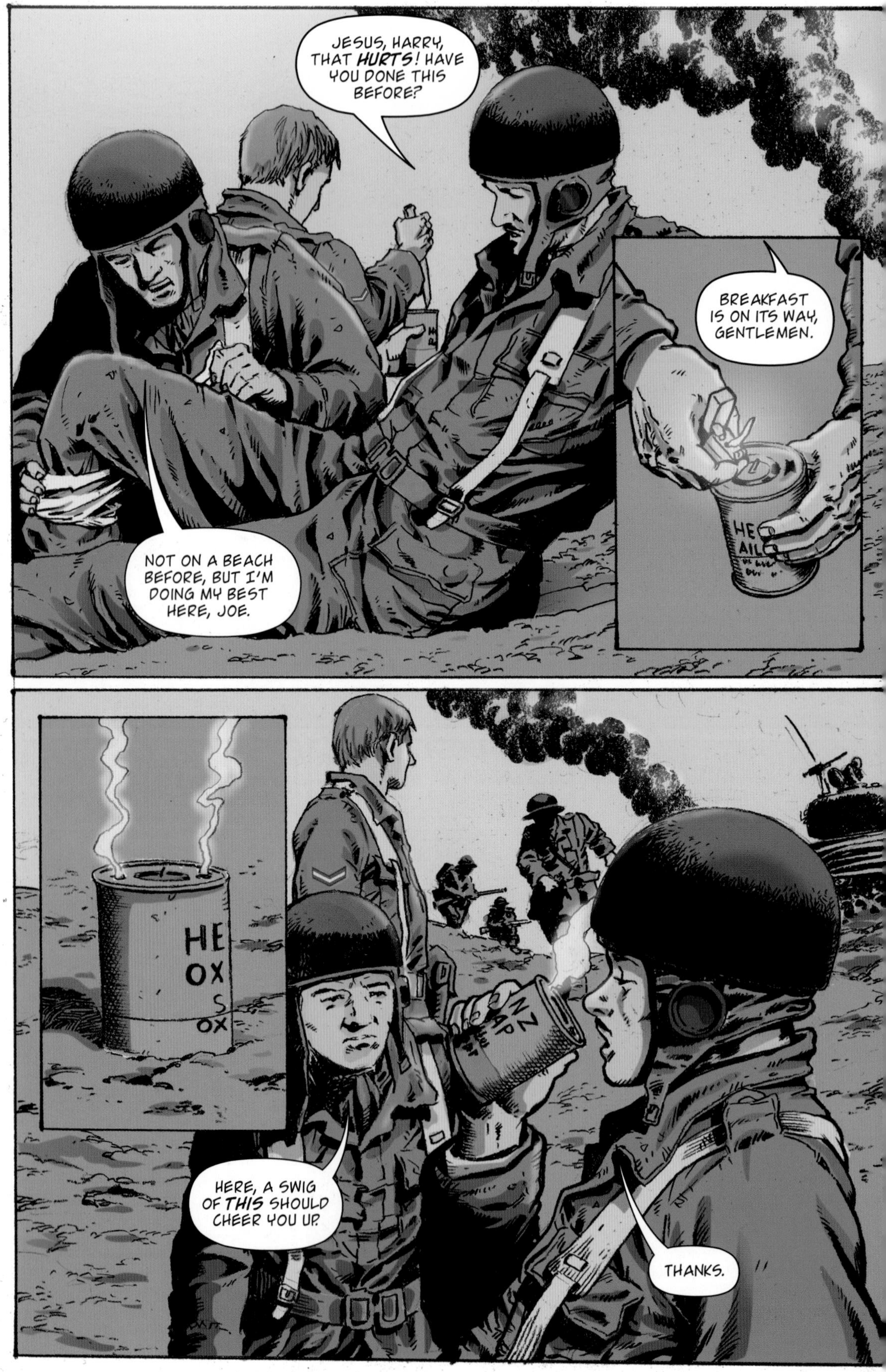
JESUS, HARRY, THAT HURTS! HAVE YOU DONE THIS BEFORE?
NOT ON A BEACH BEFORE, BUT I'M DOING MY BEST HERE, JOE.
BREAKFAST IS ON ITS WAY, GENTLEMEN.
HE OX S OX
HERE, A SWIG OF THIS SHOULD CHEER YOU UP.
THANKS.

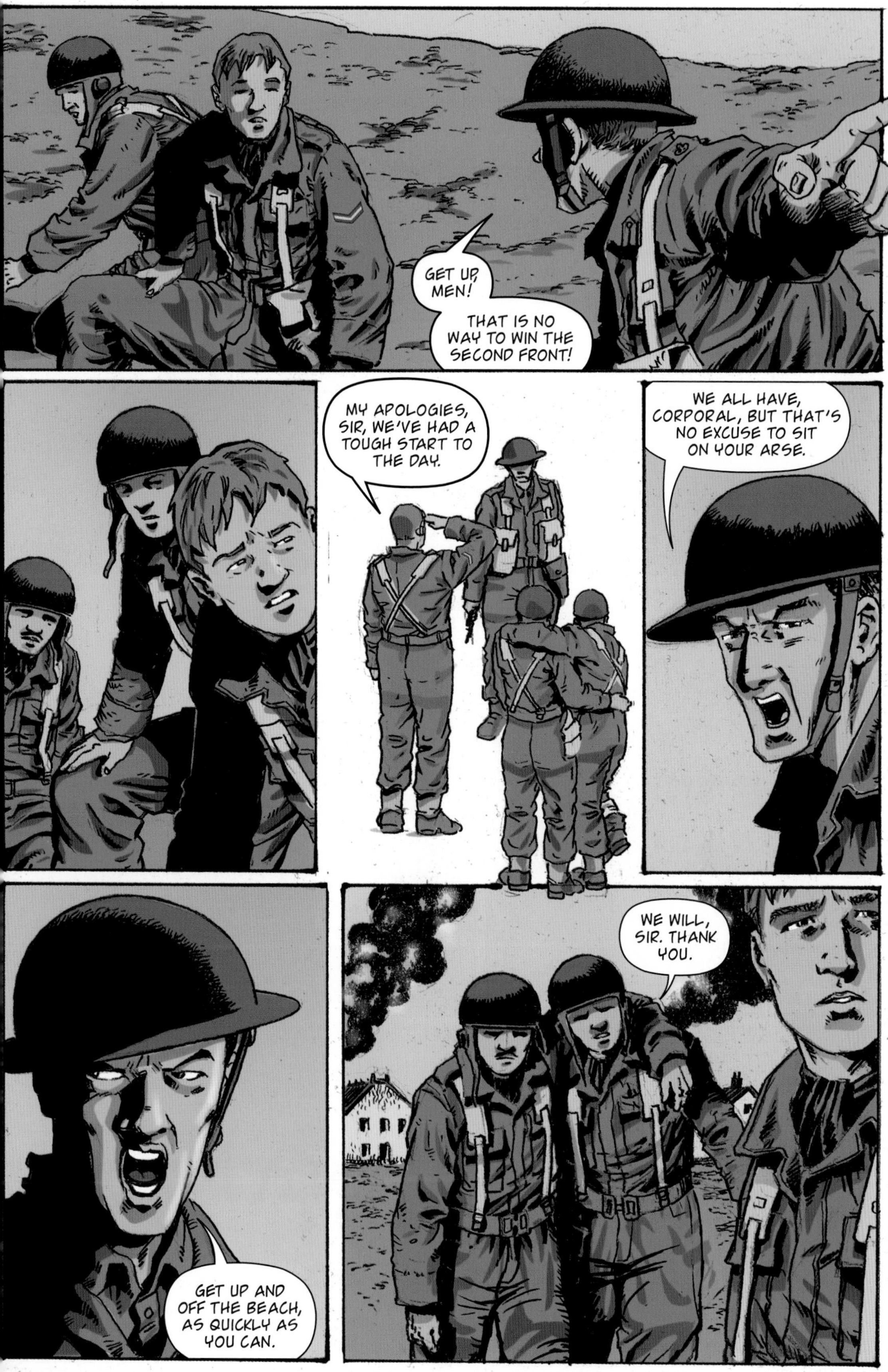
GET UP, MEN!
THAT IS NO WAY TO WIN THE SECOND FRONT!
MY APOLOGIES, SIR, WE'VE HAD A TOUGH START TO THE DAY.
WE ALL HAVE, CORPORAL, BUT THAT'S NO EXCUSE TO SIT ON YOUR ARSE.
GET UP AND OFF THE BEACH, AS QUICKLY AS YOU CAN.
WE WILL, SIR. THANK YOU.

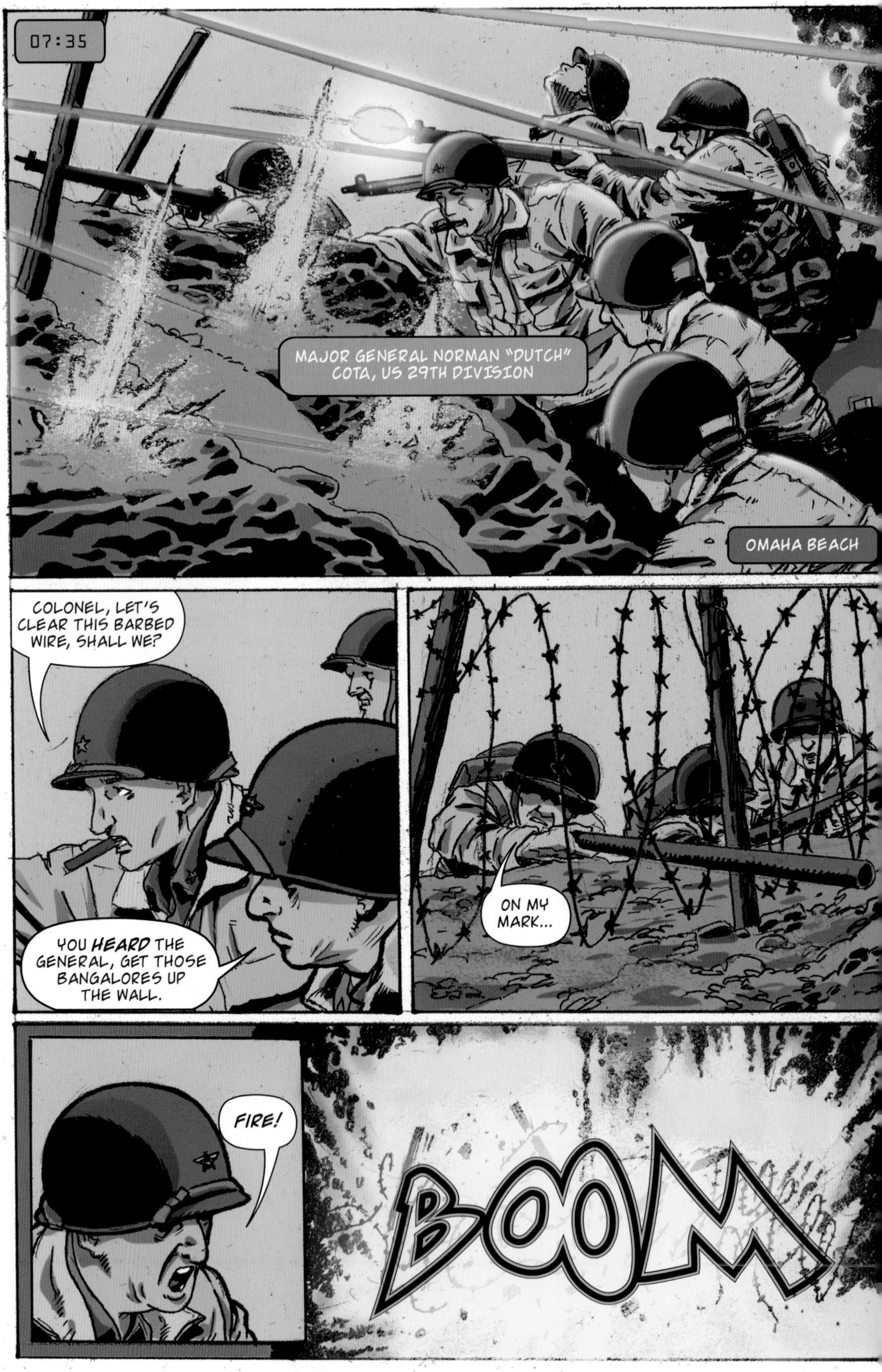
07:35
MAJOR GENERAL NORMAN "DUTCH" COTA, US 29TH DIVISION
OMAHA BEACH
COLONEL, LET'S CLEAR THIS BARBED WIRE, SHALL WE?
YOU **HEARD** THE GENERAL, GET THOSE BANGALORES UP THE WALL.
ON MY MARK...
FIRE!
BOOM

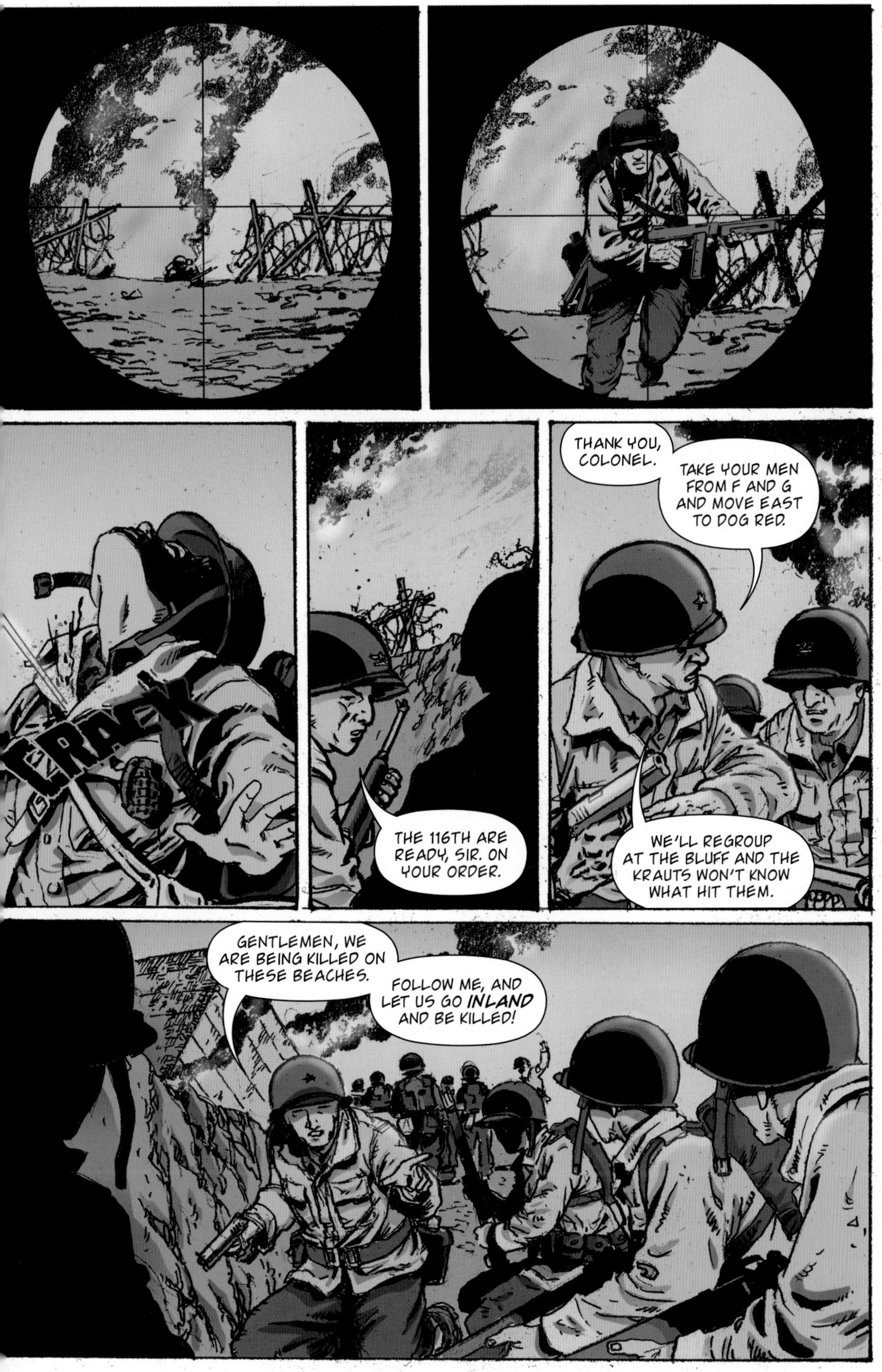
KRACK
THE 116TH ARE READY, SIR. ON YOUR ORDER.
THANK YOU, COLONEL.
TAKE YOUR MEN FROM F AND G AND MOVE EAST TO DOG RED.
WE'LL REGROUP AT THE BLUFF AND THE KRAUTS WON'T KNOW WHAT HIT THEM.
GENTLEMEN, WE ARE BEING KILLED ON THESE BEACHES.
FOLLOW ME, AND LET US GO *INLAND* AND BE KILLED!

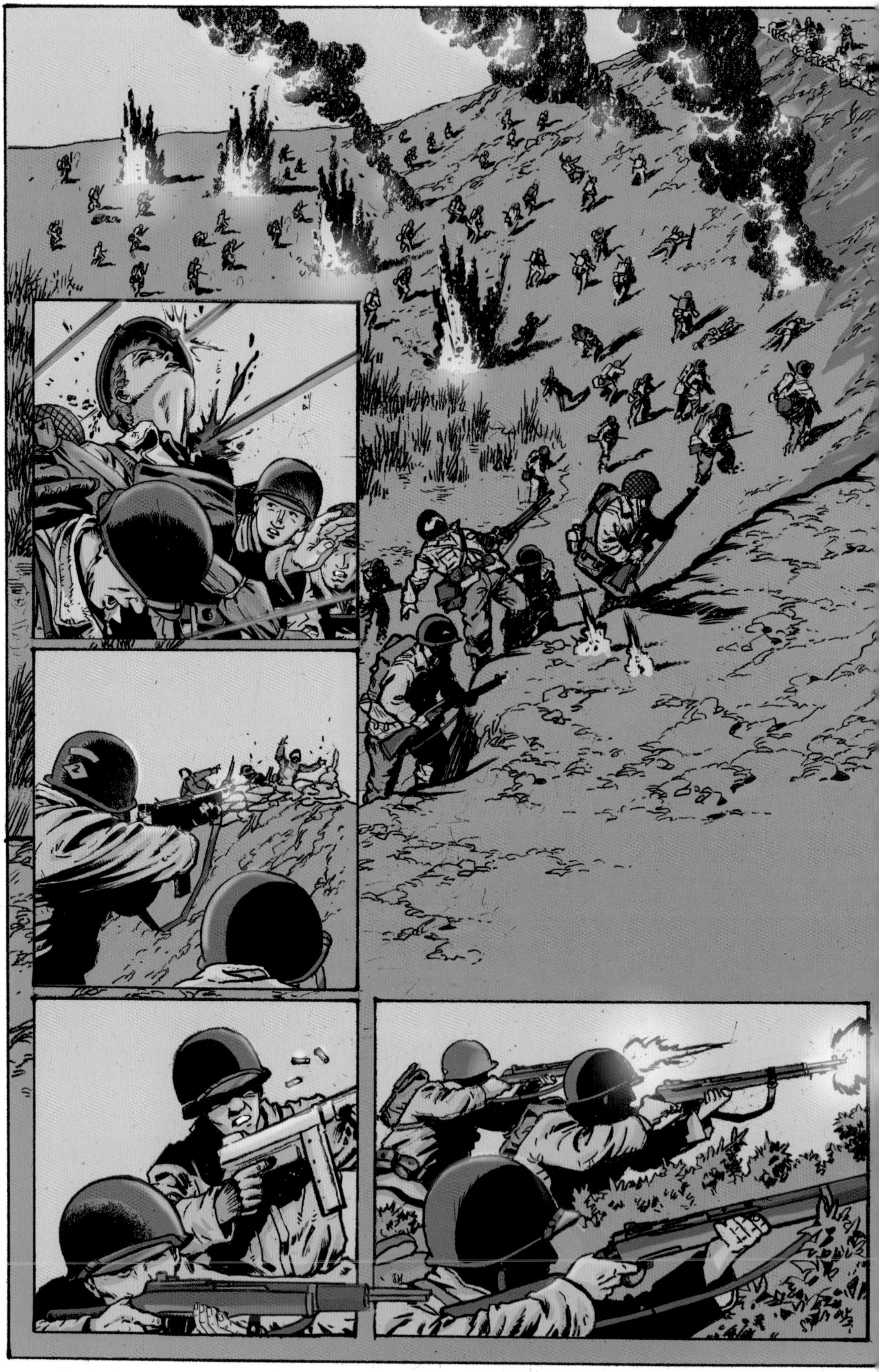

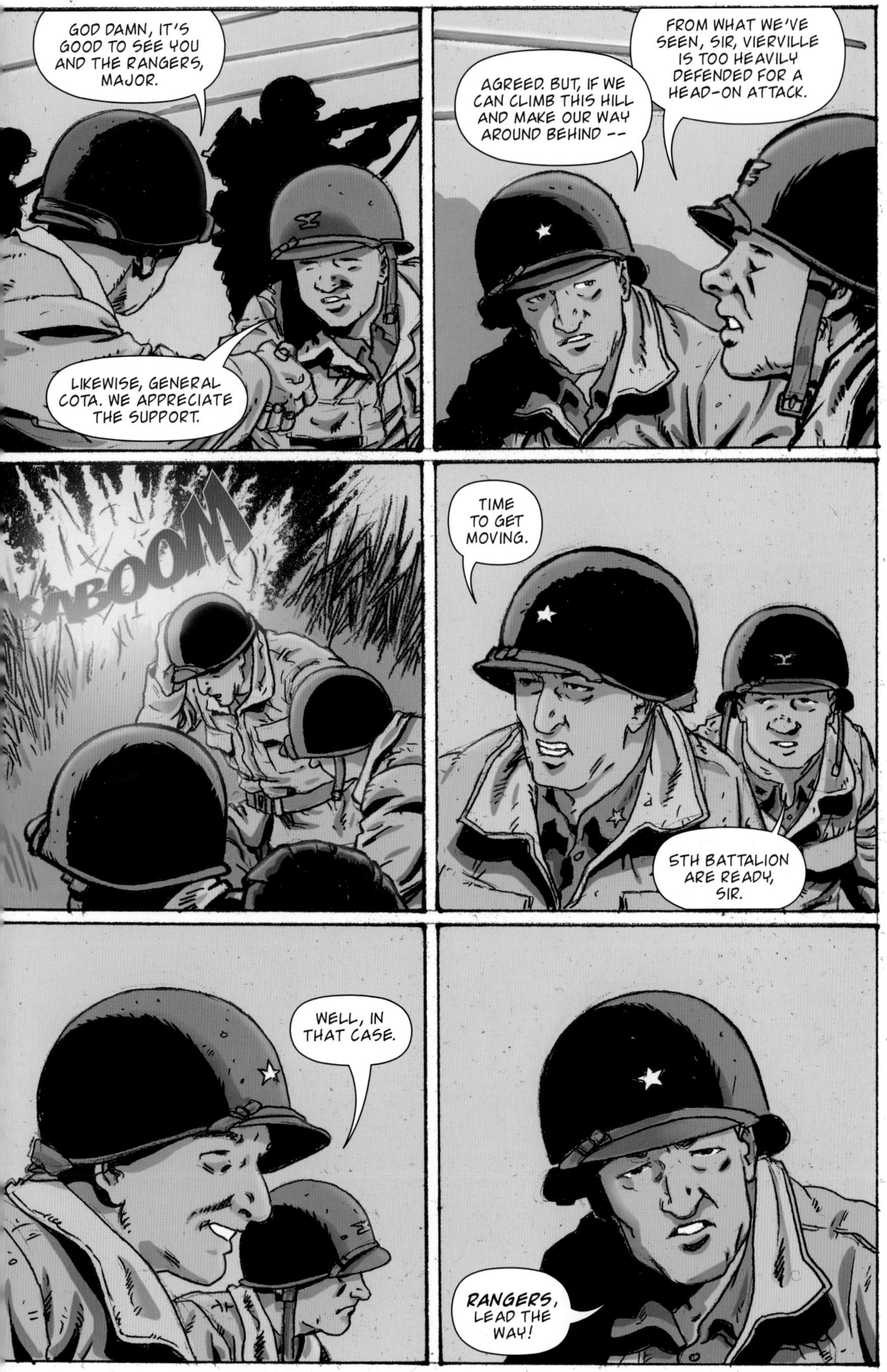
GOD DAMN, IT'S GOOD TO SEE YOU AND THE RANGERS, MAJOR.
LIKEWISE, GENERAL COTA. WE APPRECIATE THE SUPPORT.
FROM WHAT WE'VE SEEN, SIR, VIERVILLE IS TOO HEAVILY DEFENDED FOR A HEAD-ON ATTACK.
AGREED. BUT, IF WE CAN CLIMB THIS HILL AND MAKE OUR WAY AROUND BEHIND --
KABOOM
TIME TO GET MOVING.
5TH BATTALION ARE READY, SIR.
WELL, IN THAT CASE.
RANGERS, LEAD THE WAY!

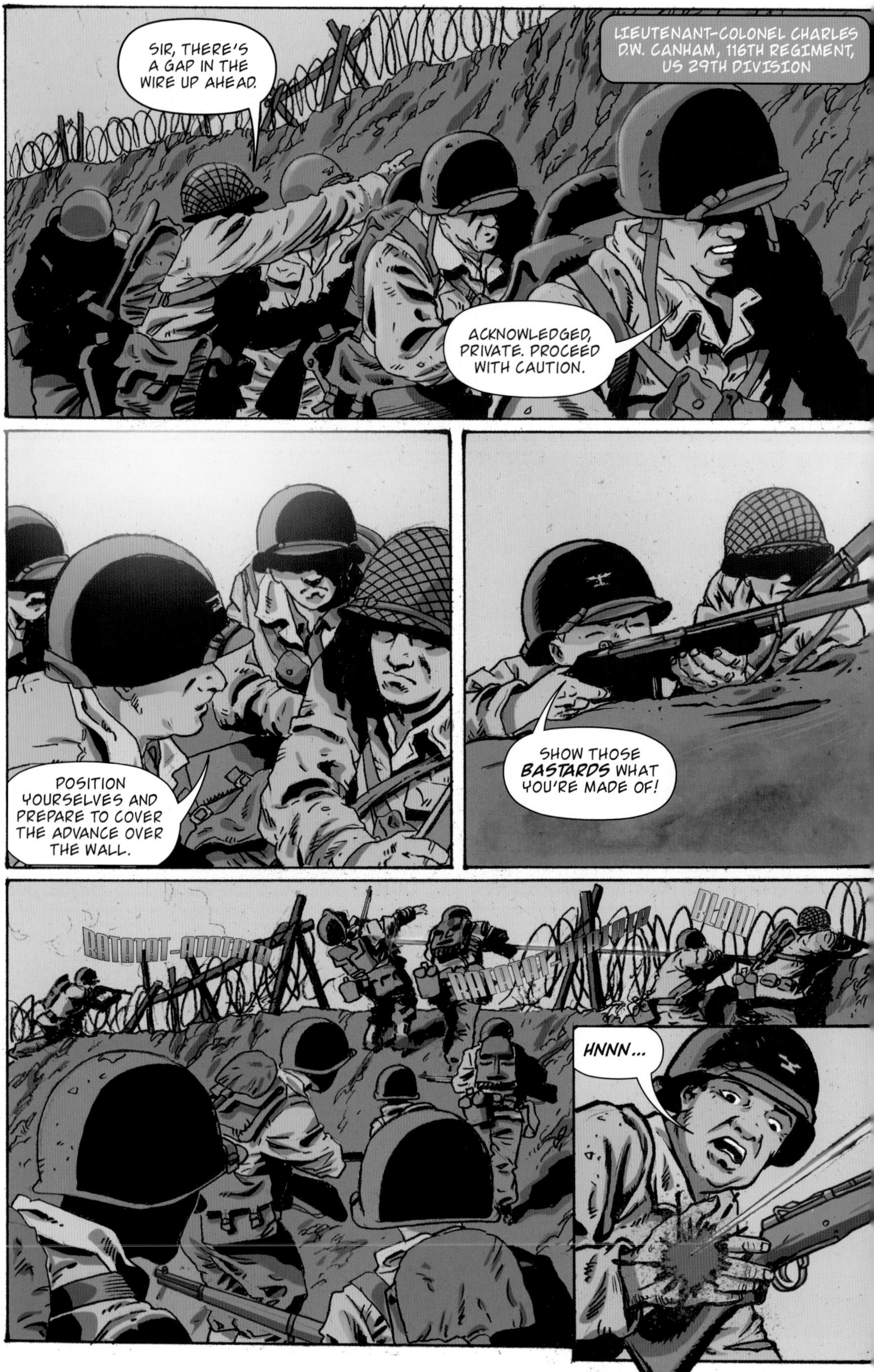
LIEUTENANT-COLONEL CHARLES D.W. CANHAM, 116TH REGIMENT, US 29TH DIVISION
SIR, THERE'S A GAP IN THE WIRE UP AHEAD.
ACKNOWLEDGED, PRIVATE. PROCEED WITH CAUTION.
POSITION YOURSELVES AND PREPARE TO COVER THE ADVANCE OVER THE WALL.
SHOW THOSE ***BASTARDS*** WHAT YOU'RE MADE OF!
RATATAT-ATATATA
RATATAT-ATATATA
BLAM
HNNN...

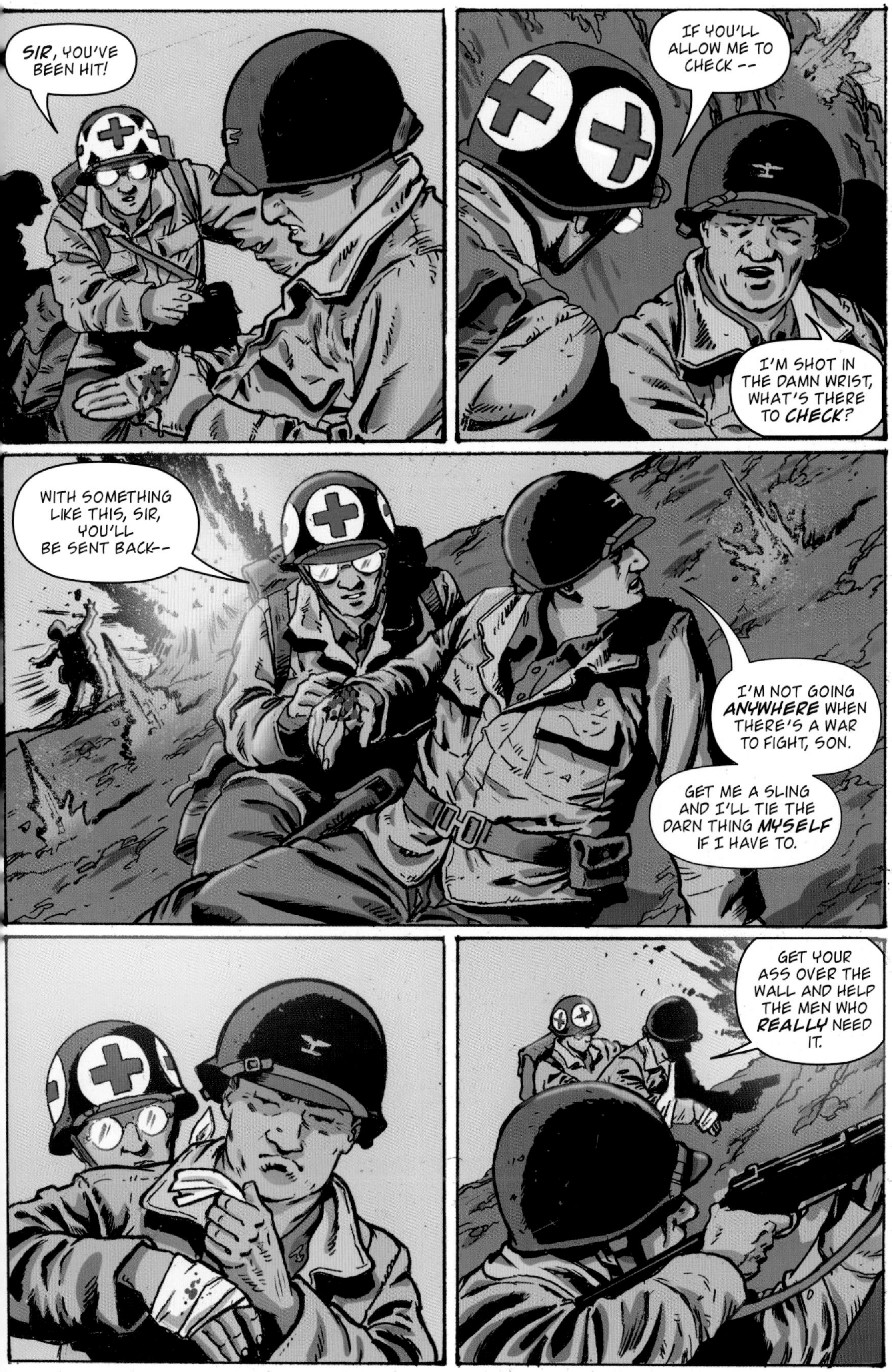
SIR, YOU'VE BEEN HIT!
IF YOU'LL ALLOW ME TO CHECK --
I'M SHOT IN THE DAMN WRIST, WHAT'S THERE TO CHECK?
WITH SOMETHING LIKE THIS, SIR, YOU'LL BE SENT BACK--
I'M NOT GOING ANYWHERE WHEN THERE'S A WAR TO FIGHT, SON.
GET ME A SLING AND I'LL TIE THE DARN THING MYSELF IF I HAVE TO.
GET YOUR ASS OVER THE WALL AND HELP THE MEN WHO REALLY NEED IT.

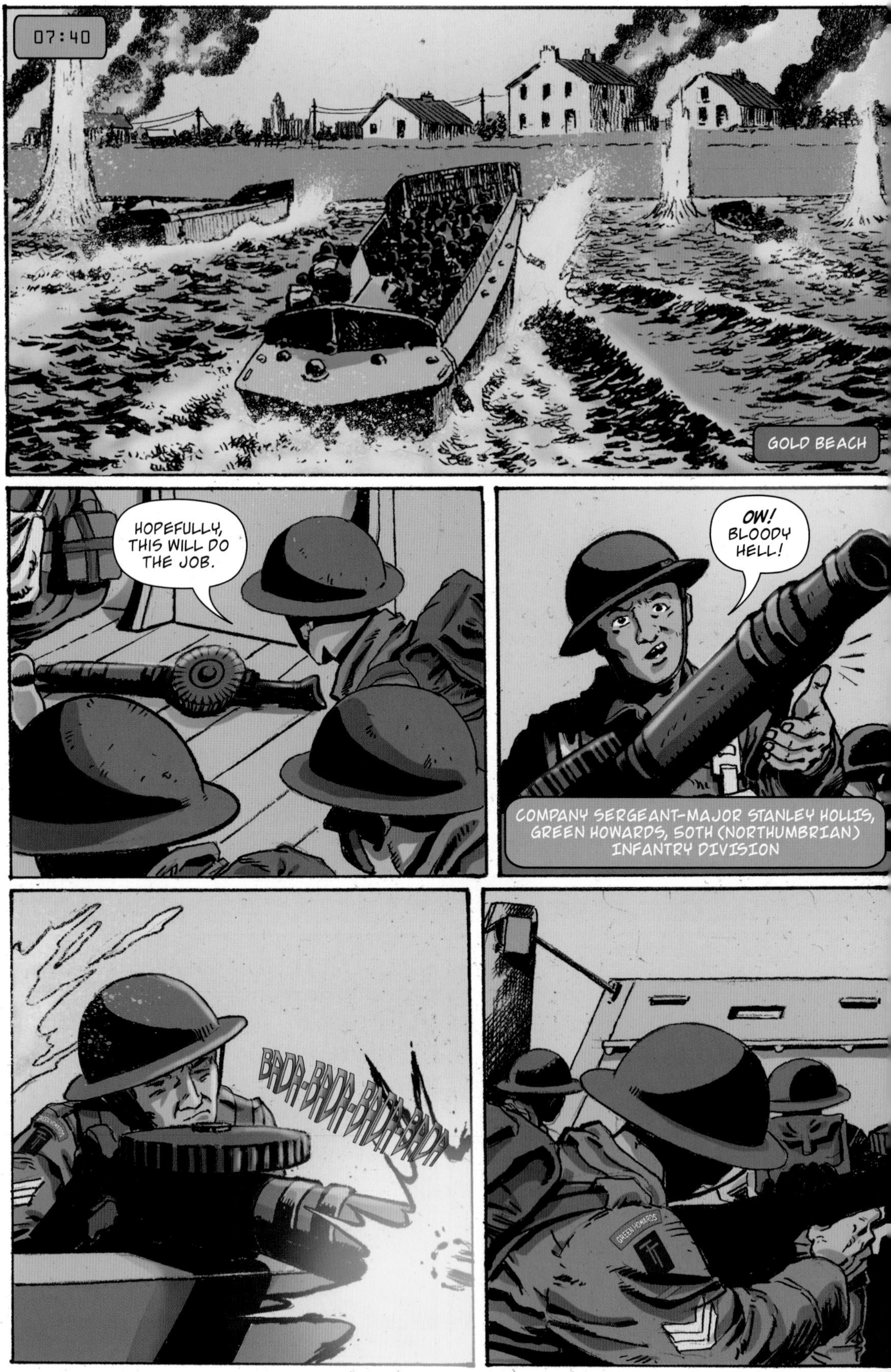
07:40
GOLD BEACH
HOPEFULLY, THIS WILL DO THE JOB.
OW! BLOODY HELL!
COMPANY SERGEANT-MAJOR STANLEY HOLLIS, GREEN HOWARDS, 50TH (NORTHUMBRIAN) INFANTRY DIVISION
BADA-BADA-BADA-BADA-BADA

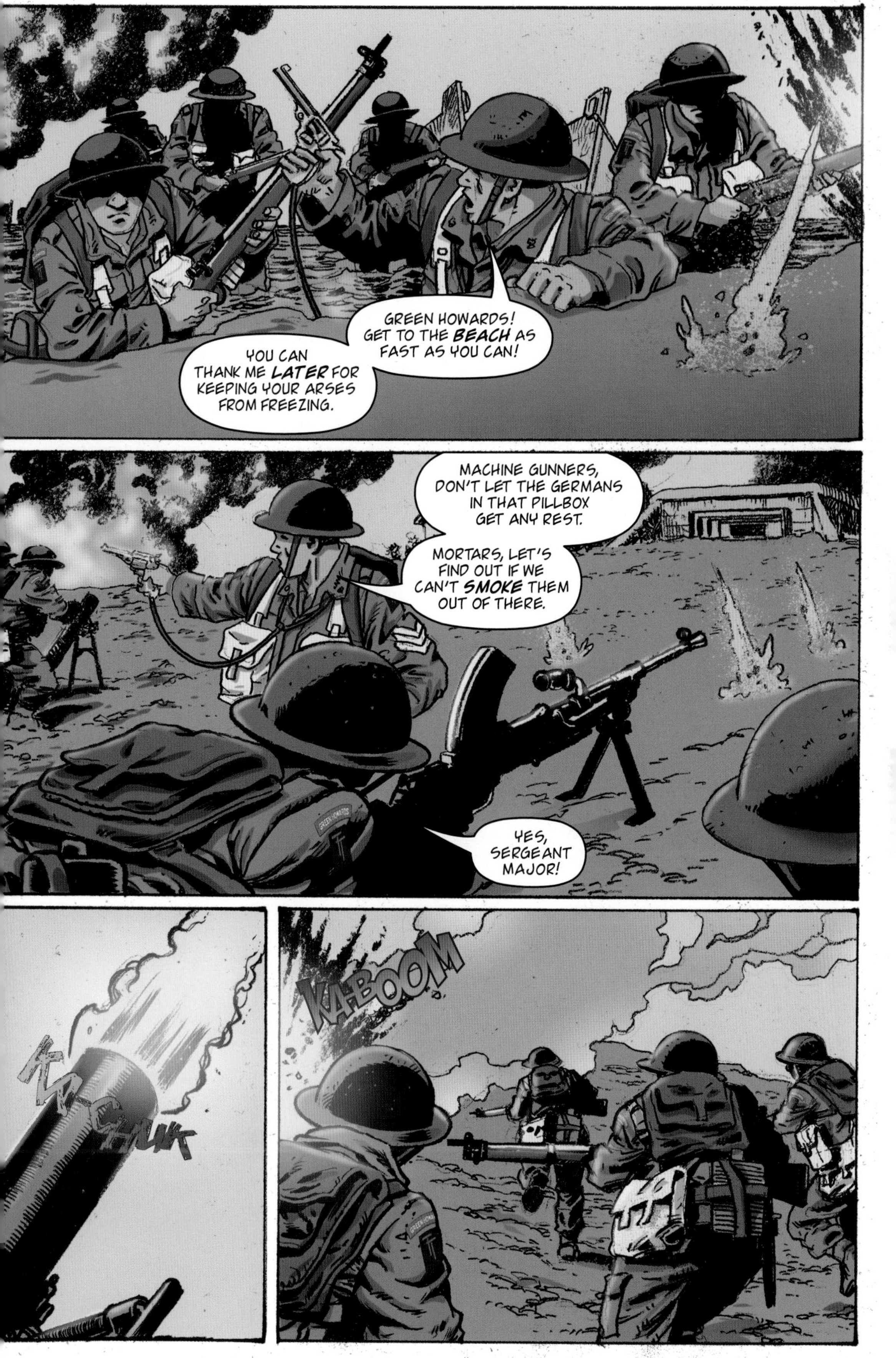
GREEN HOWARDS! GET TO THE **BEACH** AS FAST AS YOU CAN!
YOU CAN THANK ME **LATER** FOR KEEPING YOUR ARSES FROM FREEZING.
MACHINE GUNNERS, DON'T LET THE GERMANS IN THAT PILLBOX GET ANY REST.
MORTARS, LET'S FIND OUT IF WE CAN'T **SMOKE** THEM OUT OF THERE.
YES, SERGEANT MAJOR!
KA-CHUK
KA-BOOM

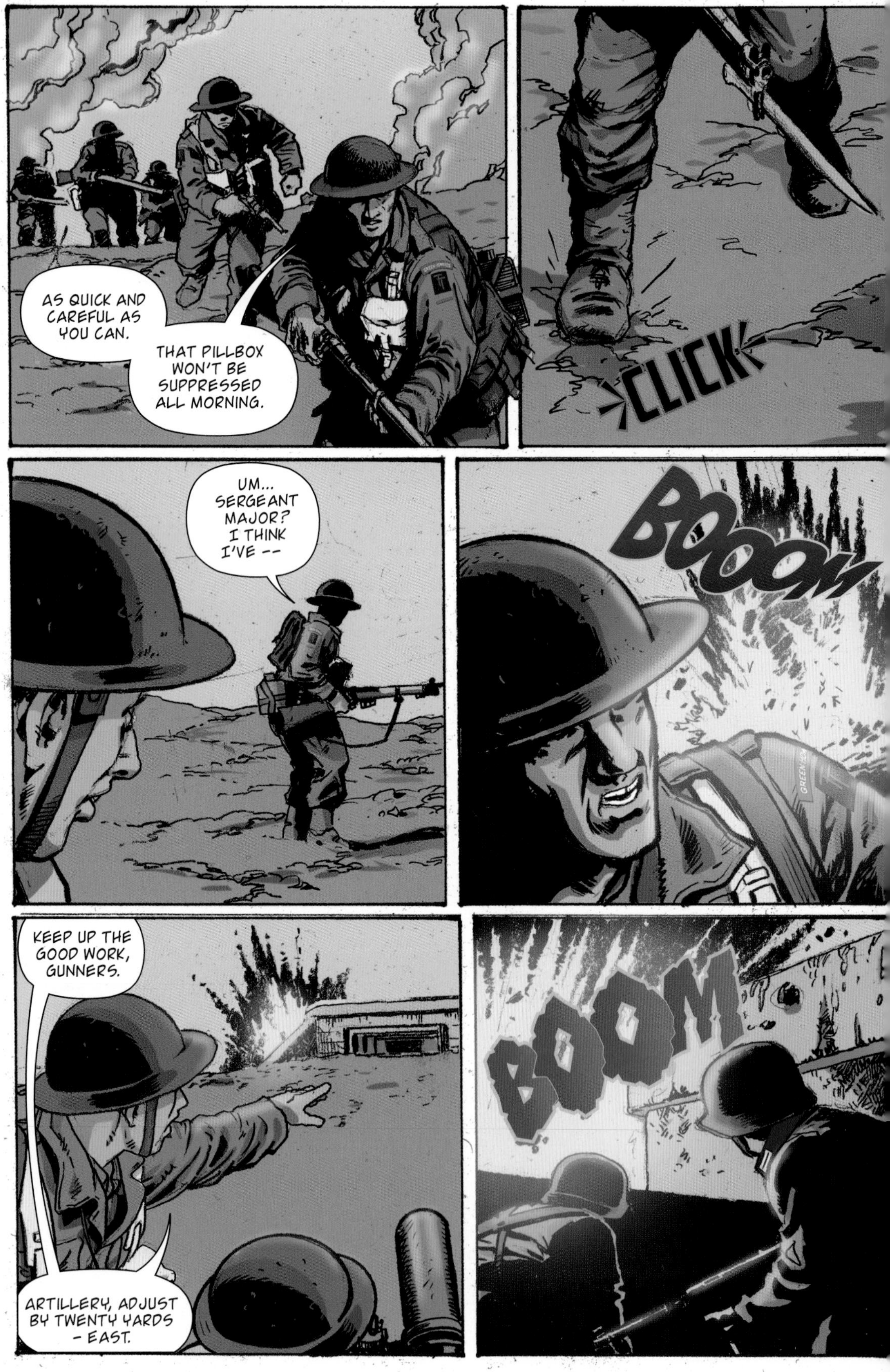
AS QUICK AND CAREFUL AS YOU CAN.
THAT PILLBOX WON'T BE SUPPRESSED ALL MORNING.
CLICK
UM... SERGEANT MAJOR? I THINK I'VE --
BOOOM
KEEP UP THE GOOD WORK, GUNNERS.
ARTILLERY, ADJUST BY TWENTY YARDS - EAST.
BOOM

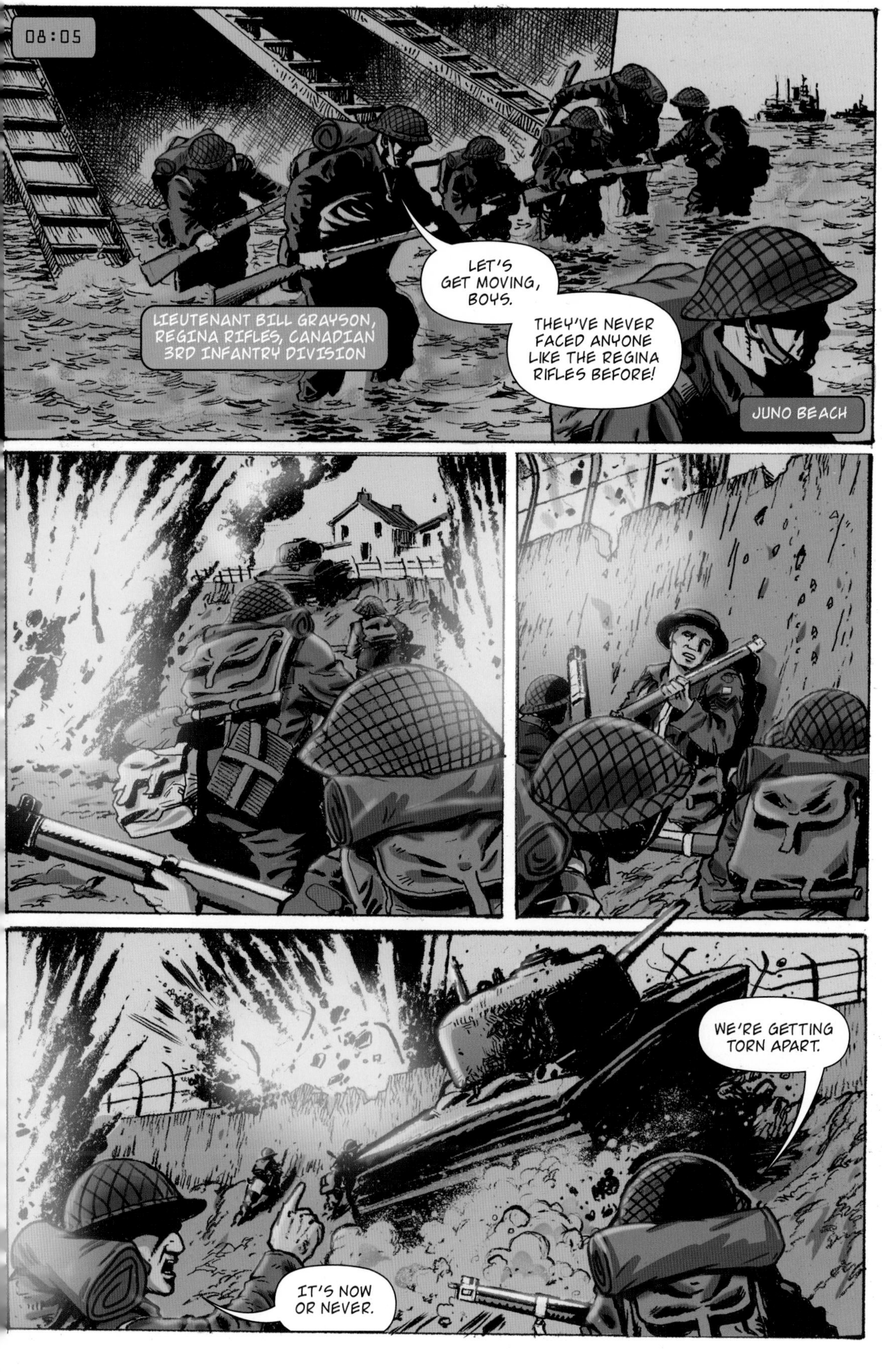
08:05
LIEUTENANT BILL GRAYSON, REGINA RIFLES, CANADIAN 3RD INFANTRY DIVISION
LET'S GET MOVING, BOYS.
THEY'VE NEVER FACED ANYONE LIKE THE REGINA RIFLES BEFORE!
JUNO BEACH
WE'RE GETTING TORN APART.
IT'S NOW OR NEVER.

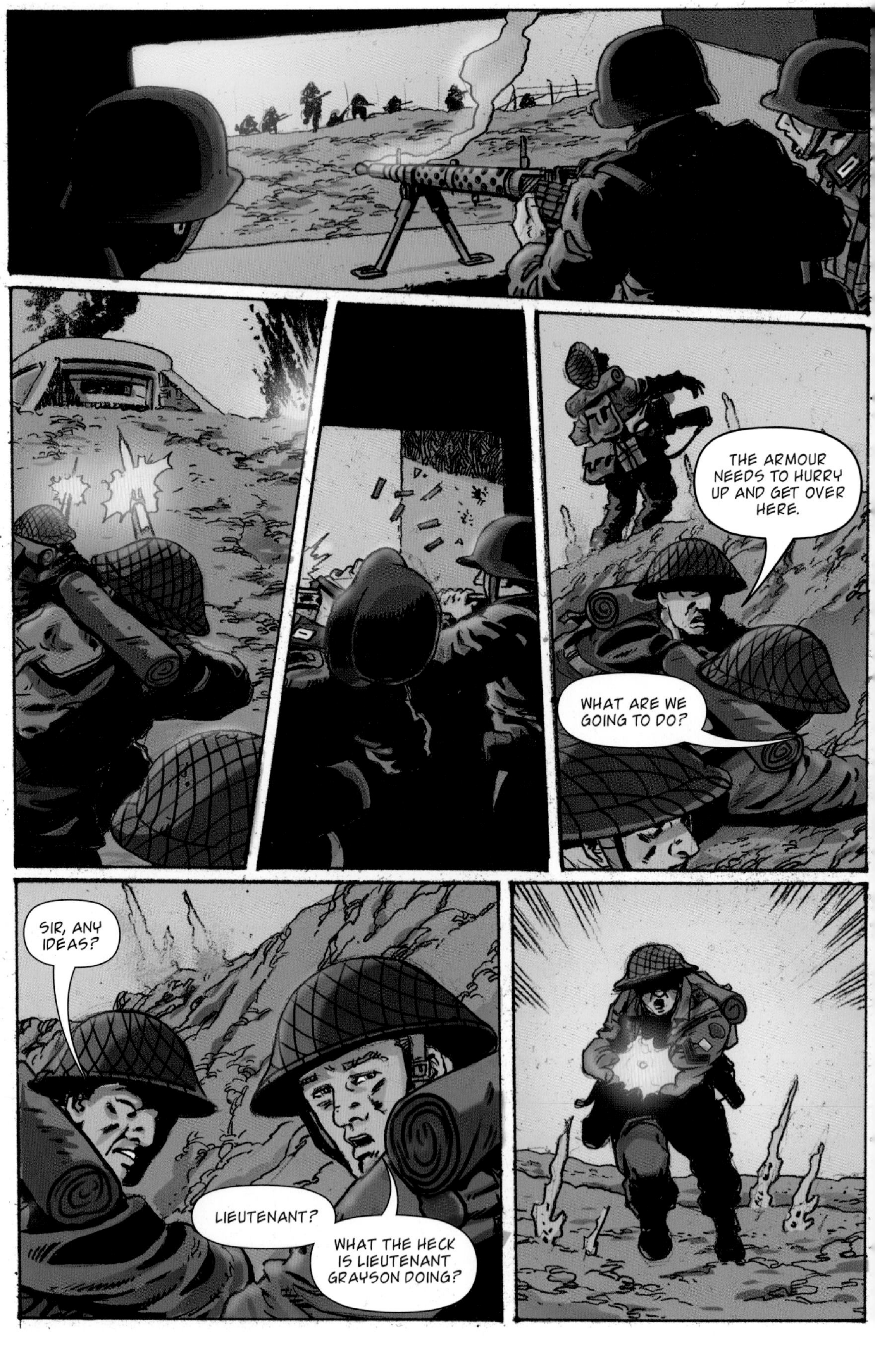
THE ARMOUR NEEDS TO HURRY UP AND GET OVER HERE.
WHAT ARE WE GOING TO DO?
SIR, ANY IDEAS?
LIEUTENANT?
WHAT THE HECK IS LIEUTENANT GRAYSON DOING?

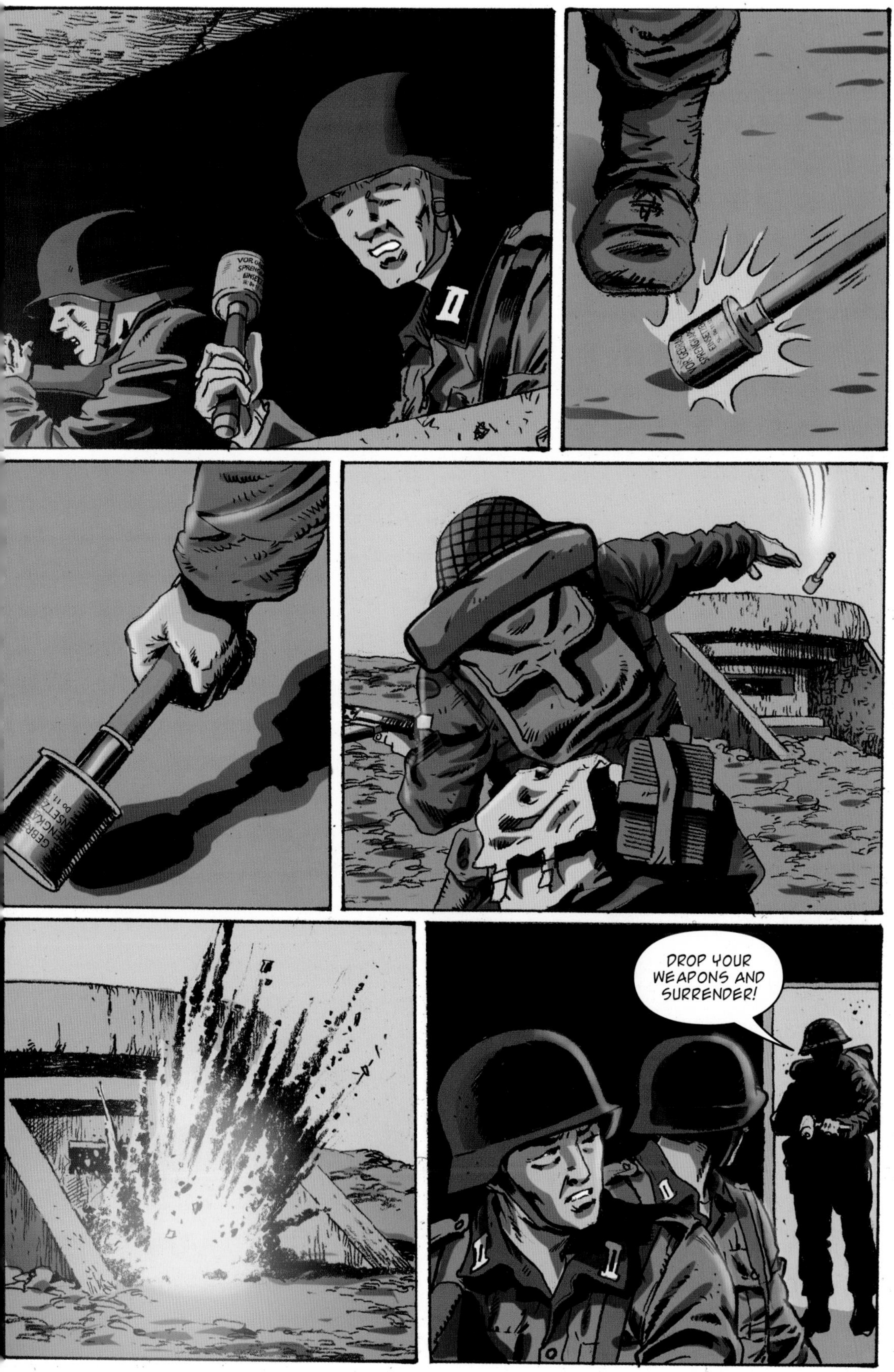
DROP YOUR WEAPONS AND SURRENDER!

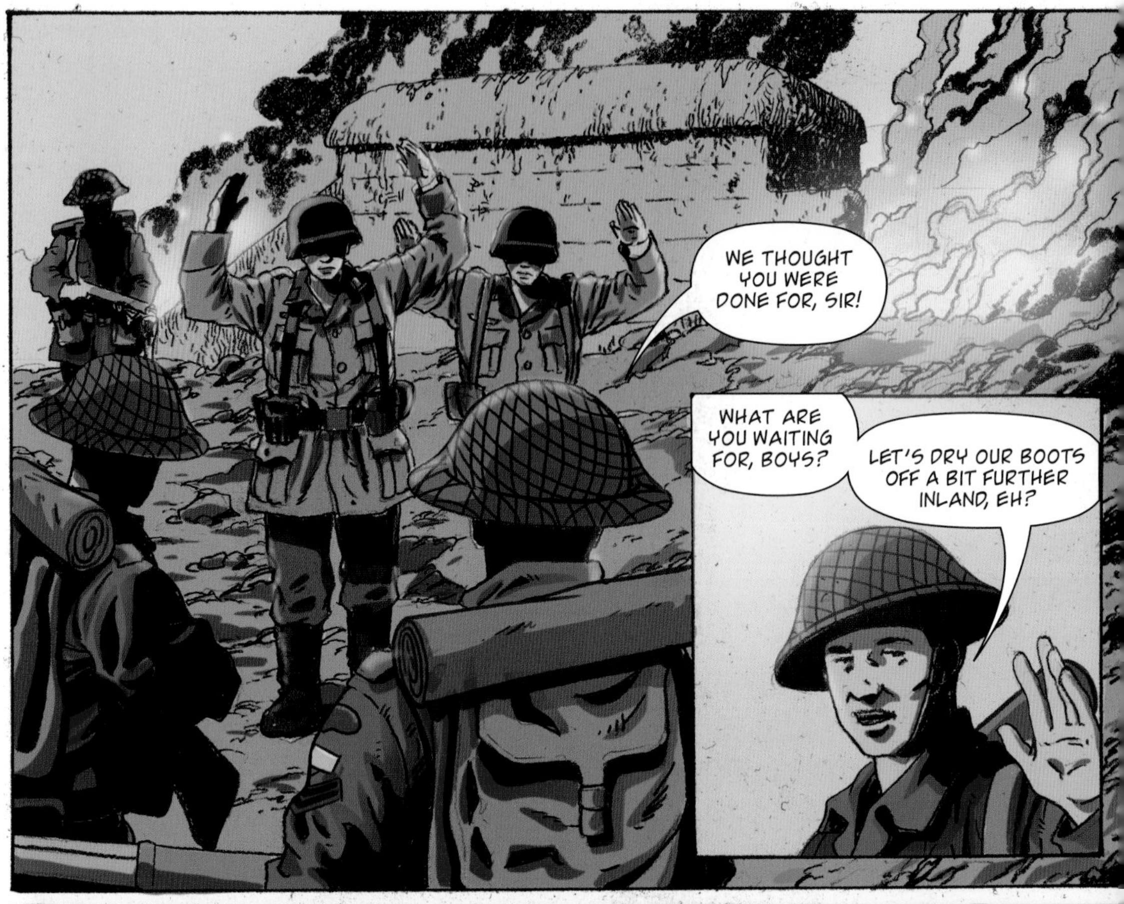
WE THOUGHT YOU WERE DONE FOR, SIR!
WHAT ARE YOU WAITING FOR, BOYS?
LET'S DRY OUR BOOTS OFF A BIT FURTHER INLAND, EH?

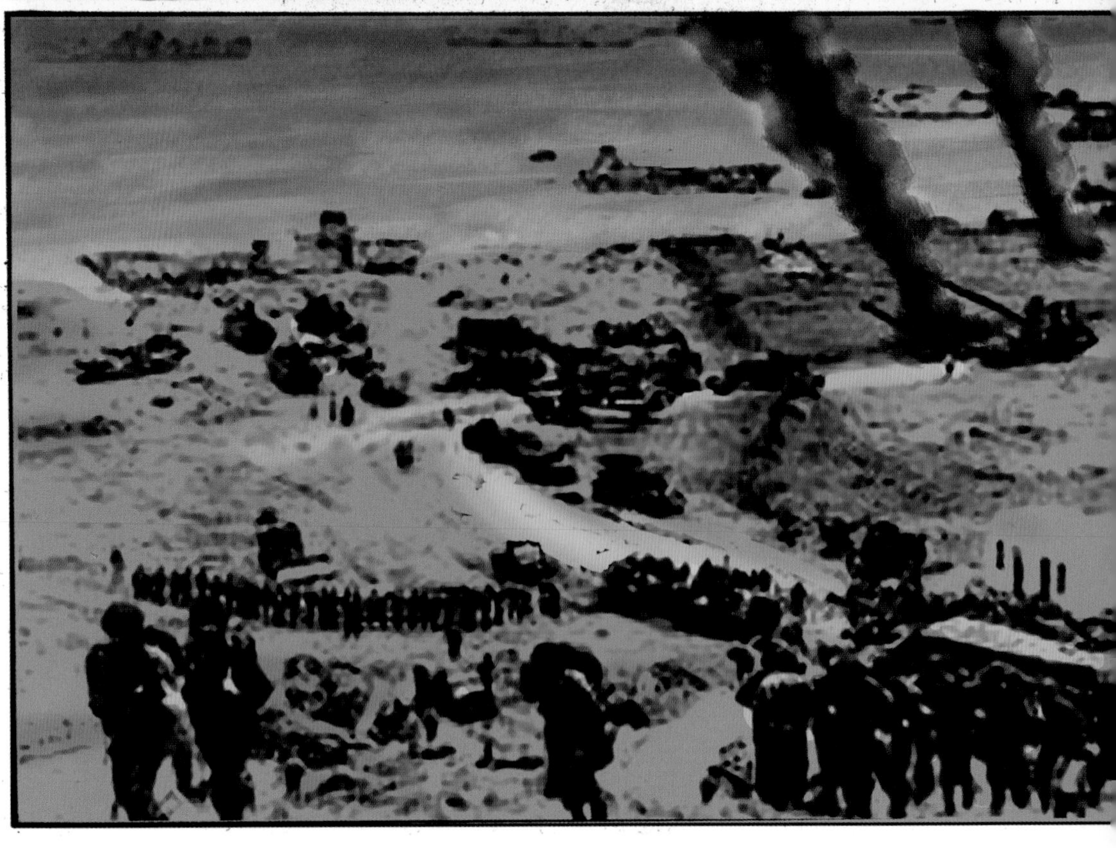

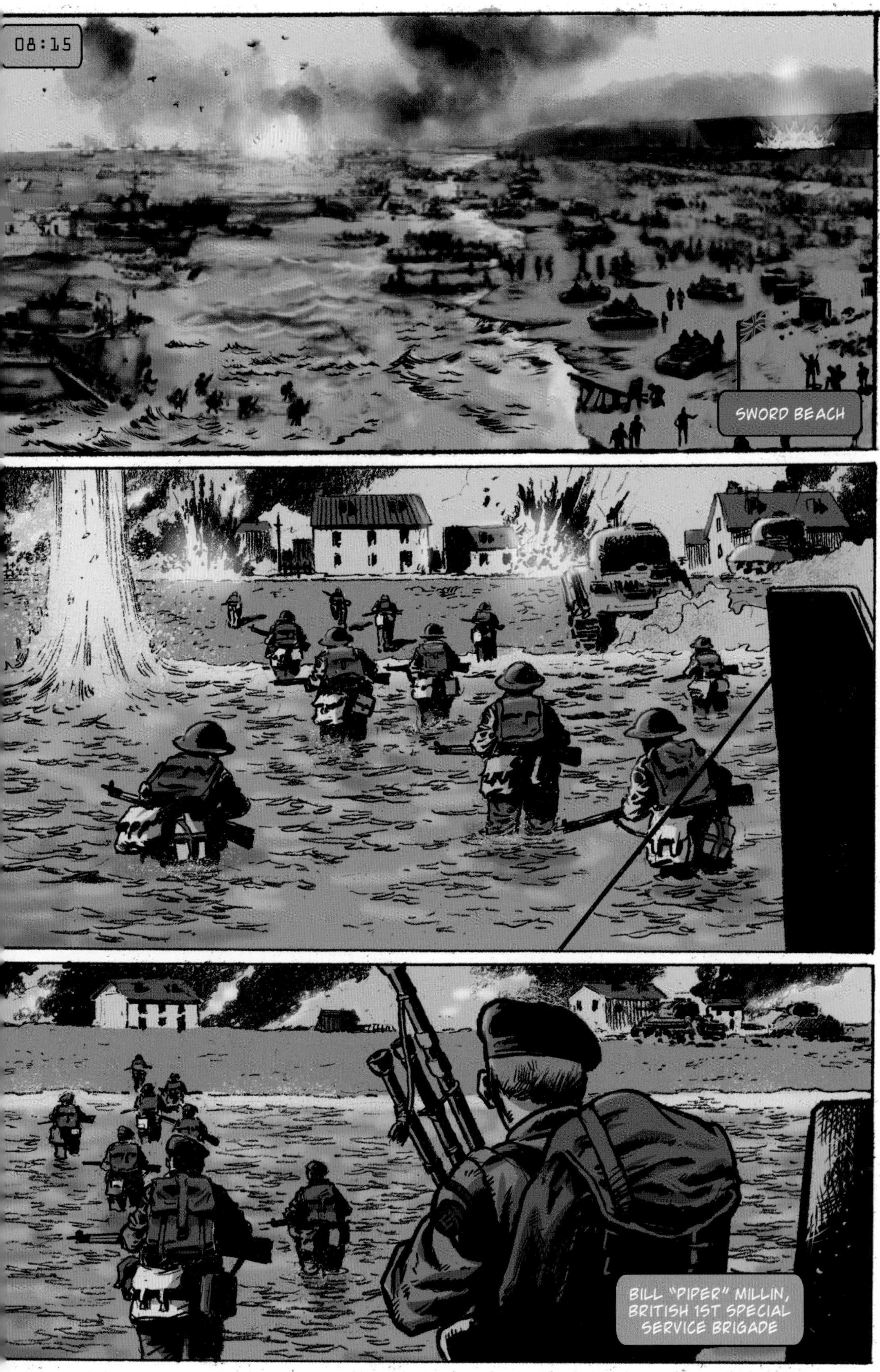
08:15
SWORD BEACH
BILL "PIPER" MILLIN,
BRITISH 1ST SPECIAL
SERVICE BRIGADE

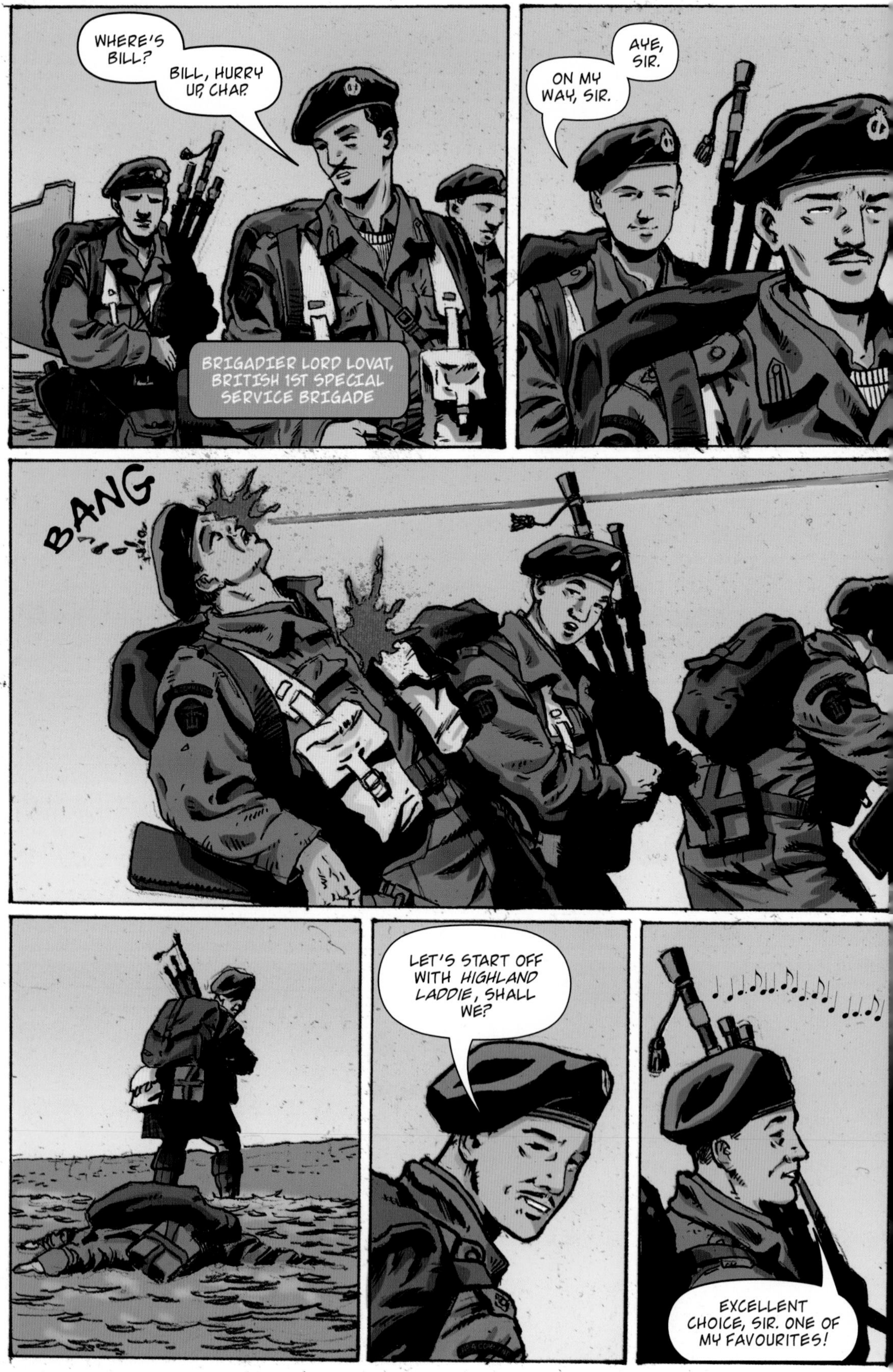
WHERE'S BILL?
BILL, HURRY UP, CHAP.
BRIGADIER LORD LOVAT, BRITISH 1ST SPECIAL SERVICE BRIGADE
AYE, SIR.
ON MY WAY, SIR.
BANG
LET'S START OFF WITH *HIGHLAND LADDIE*, SHALL WE?
EXCELLENT CHOICE, SIR. ONE OF MY FAVOURITES!

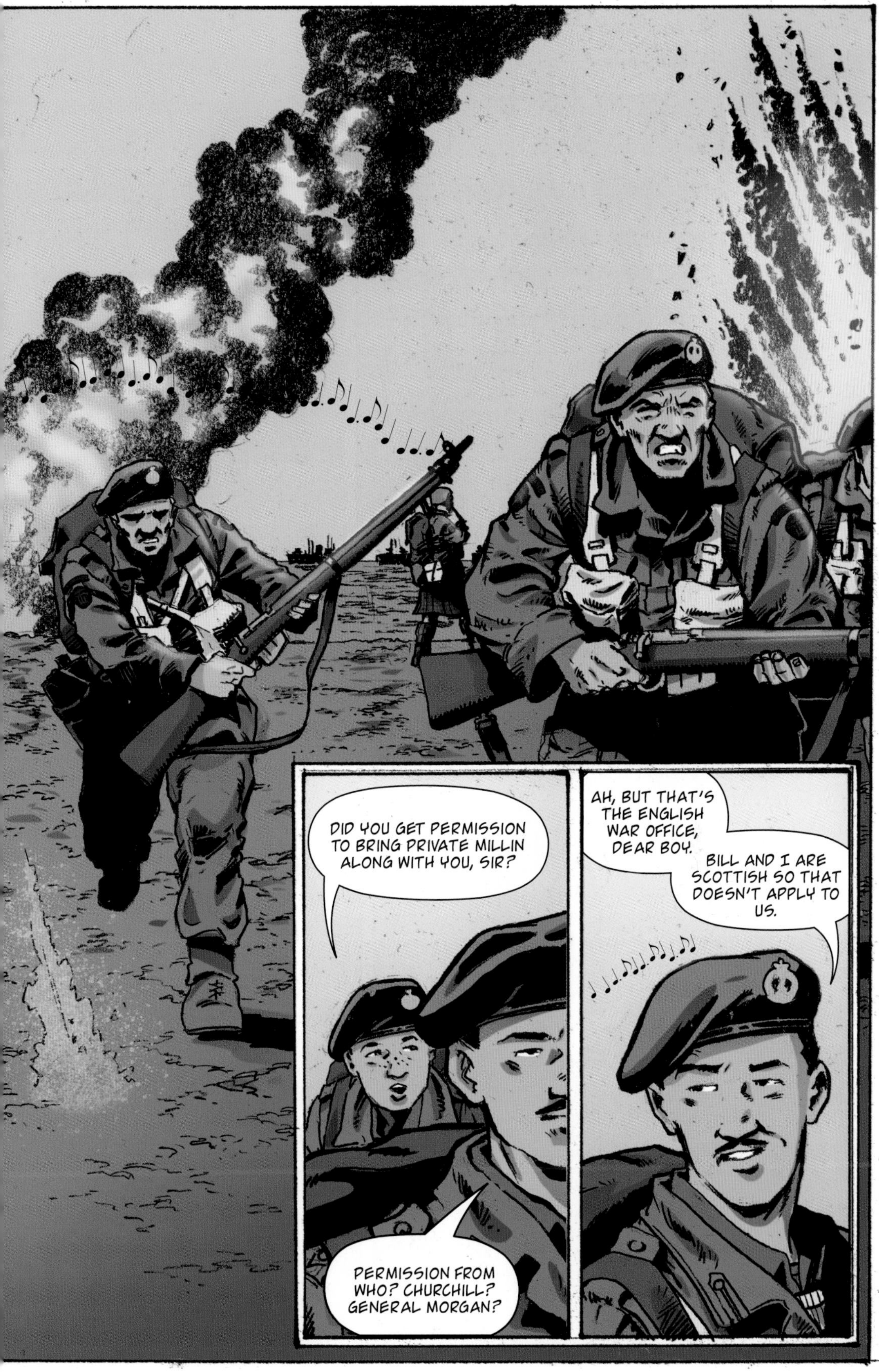
DID YOU GET PERMISSION TO BRING PRIVATE MILLIN ALONG WITH YOU, SIR?
PERMISSION FROM WHO? CHURCHILL? GENERAL MORGAN?
AH, BUT THAT'S THE ENGLISH WAR OFFICE, DEAR BOY.
BILL AND I ARE SCOTTISH SO THAT DOESN'T APPLY TO US.

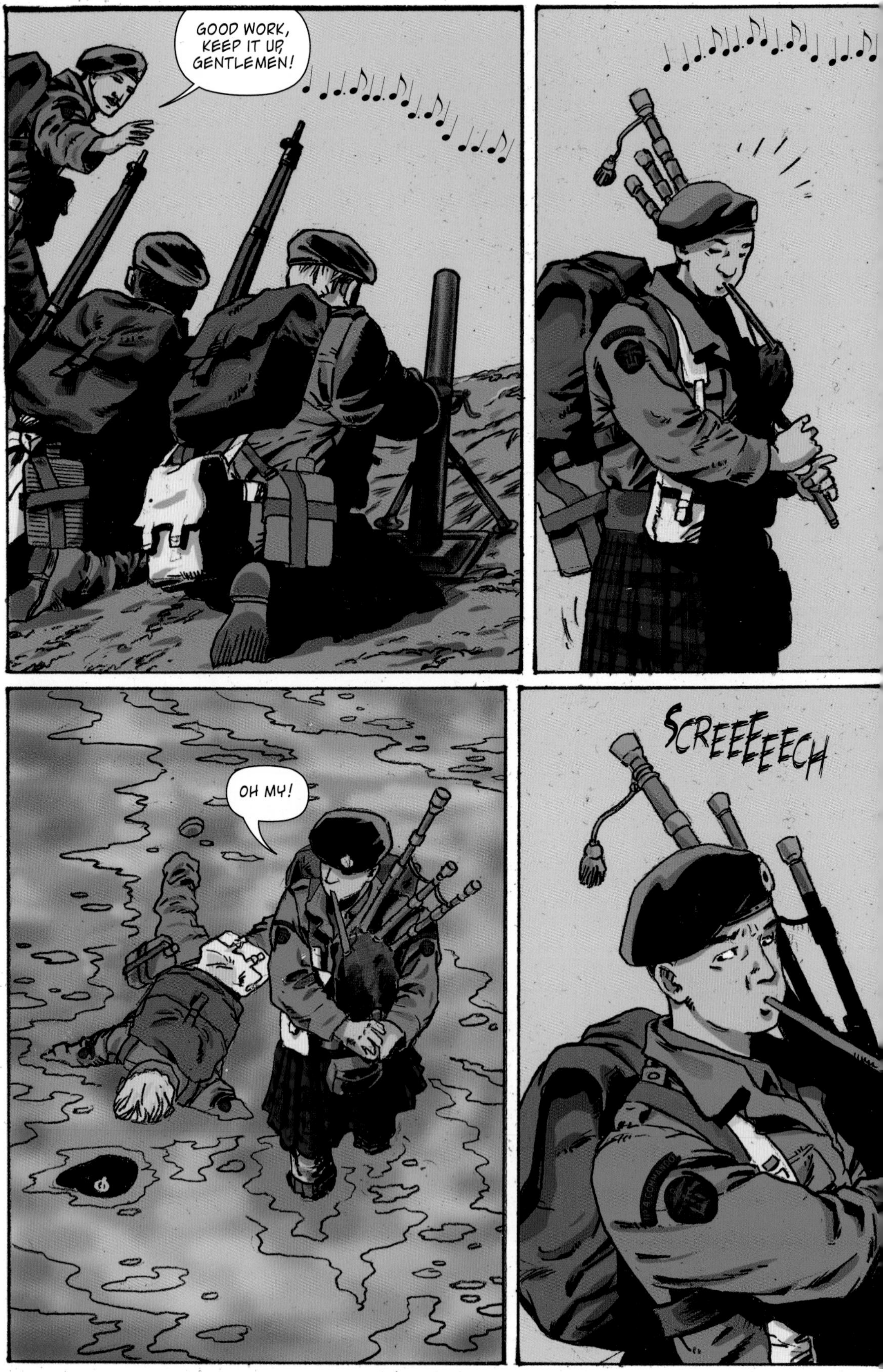
GOOD WORK, KEEP IT UP, GENTLEMEN!
OH MY!
SCREEEEECH

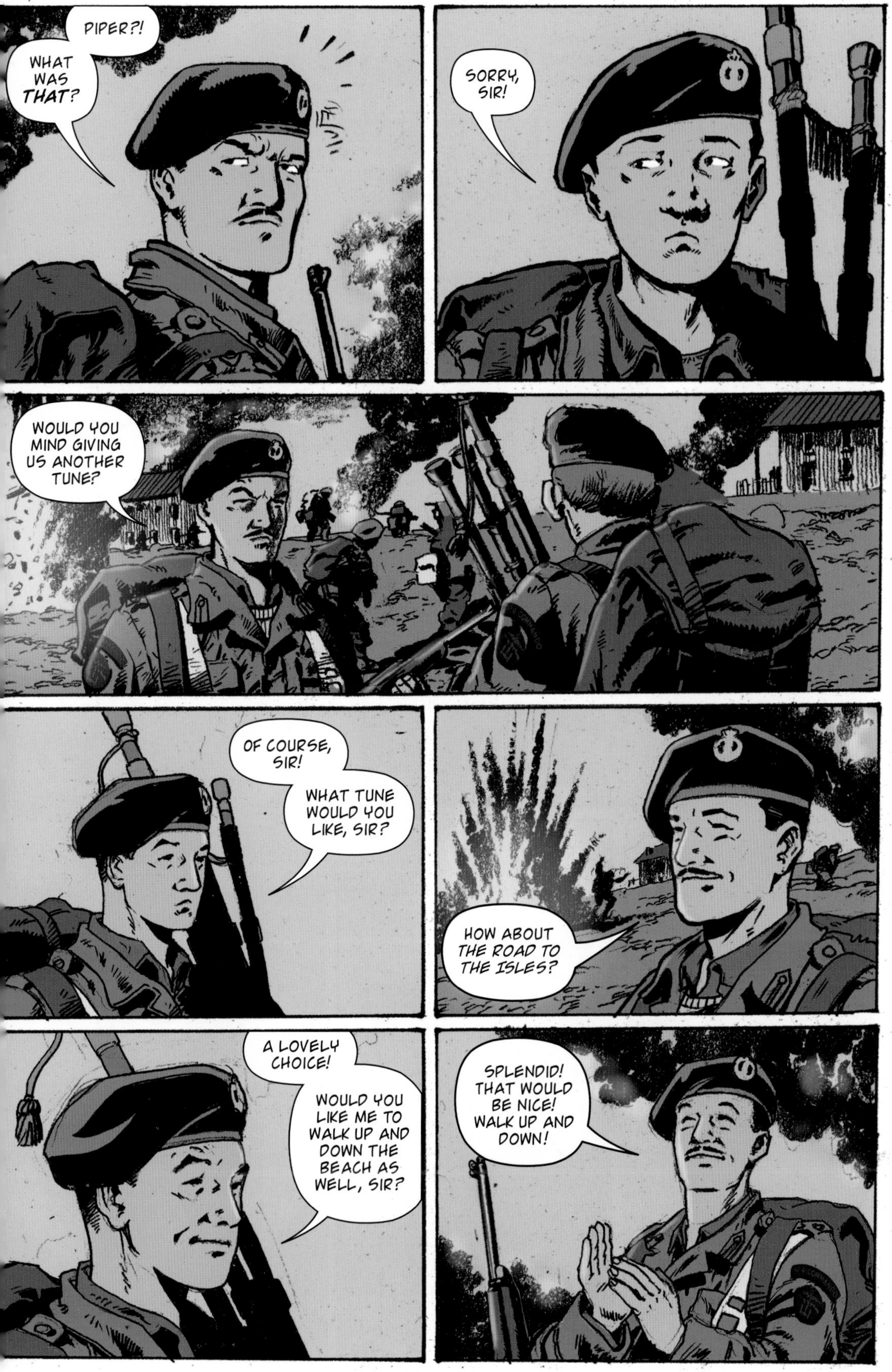
PIPER?!
WHAT WAS THAT?
SORRY, SIR!
WOULD YOU MIND GIVING US ANOTHER TUNE?
OF COURSE, SIR!
WHAT TUNE WOULD YOU LIKE, SIR?
HOW ABOUT THE ROAD TO THE ISLES?
A LOVELY CHOICE!
WOULD YOU LIKE ME TO WALK UP AND DOWN THE BEACH AS WELL, SIR?
SPLENDID! THAT WOULD BE NICE! WALK UP AND DOWN!

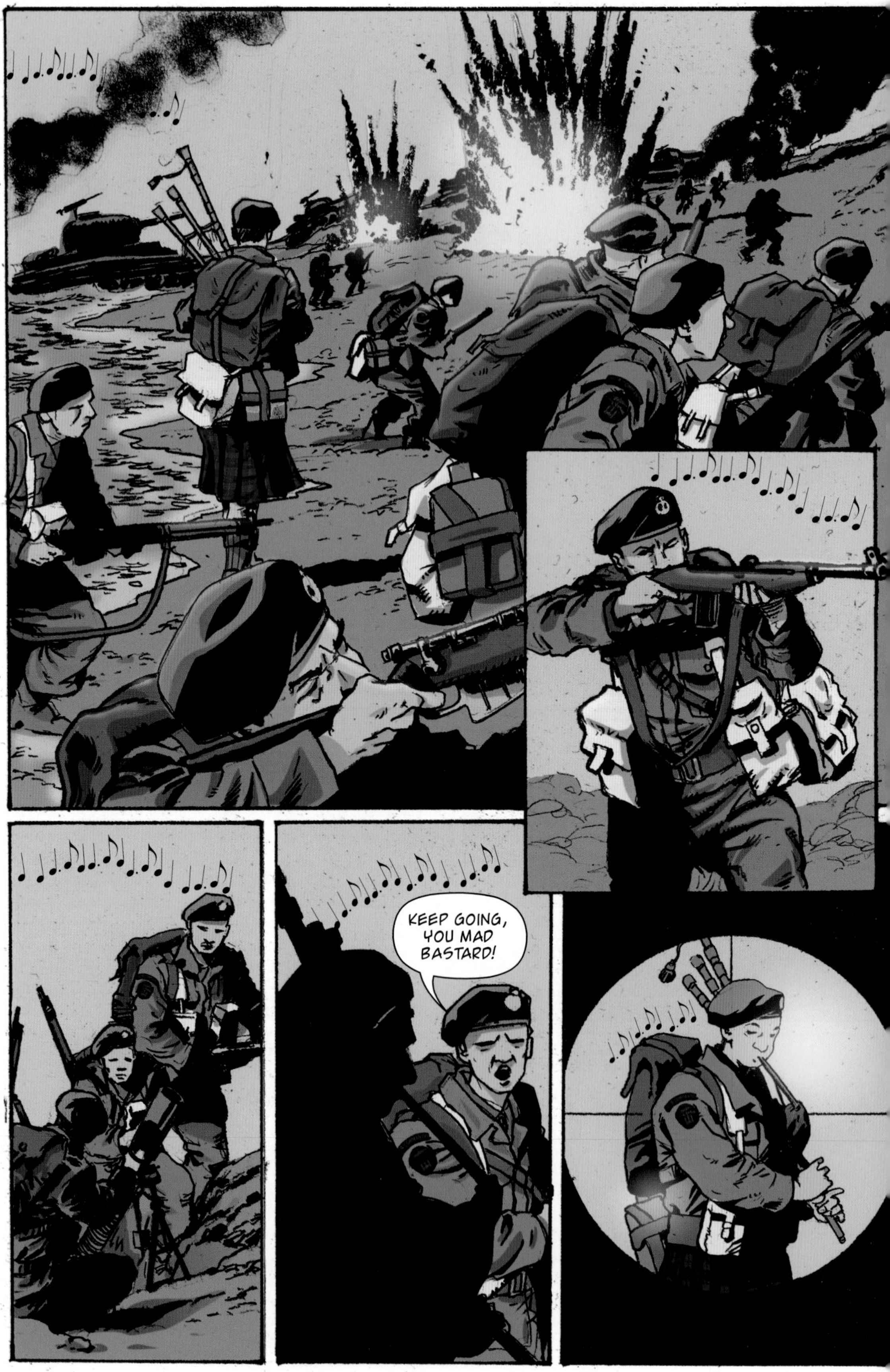
KEEP GOING, YOU MAD BASTARD!

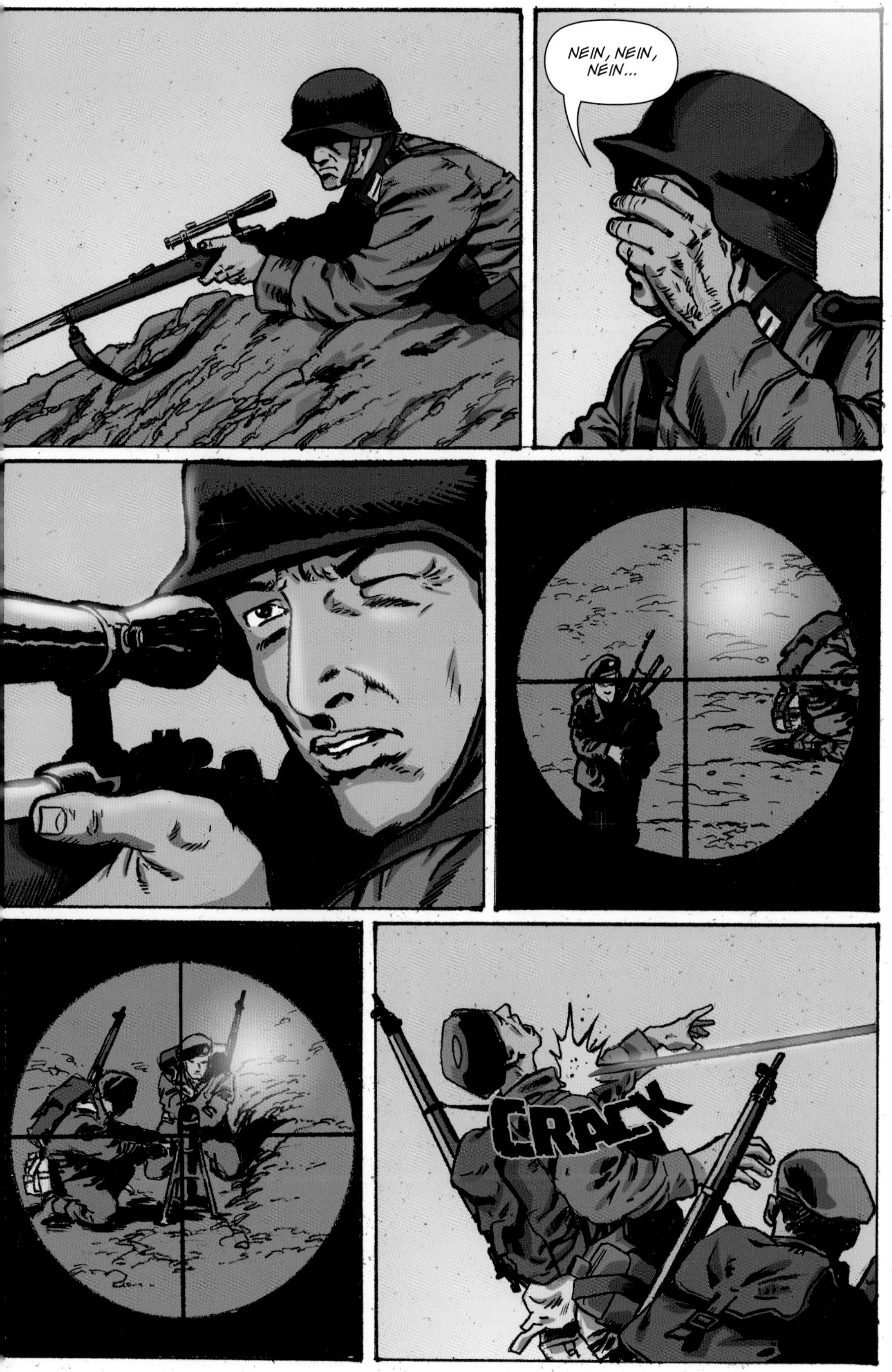
NEIN, NEIN, NEIN...
CRACK

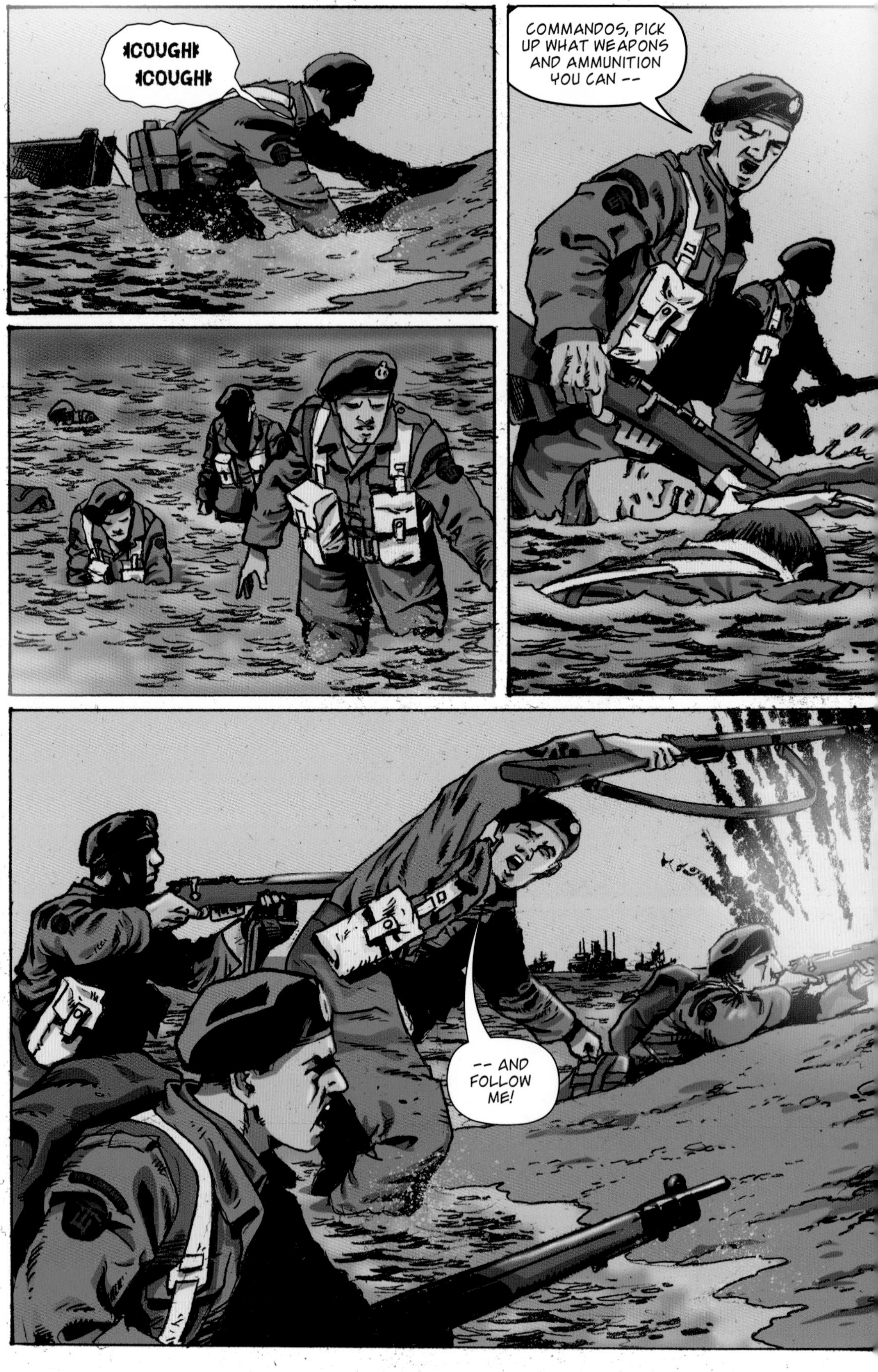

COUGH
COUGH
COMMANDOS, PICK UP WHAT WEAPONS AND AMMUNITION YOU CAN --
-- AND FOLLOW ME!

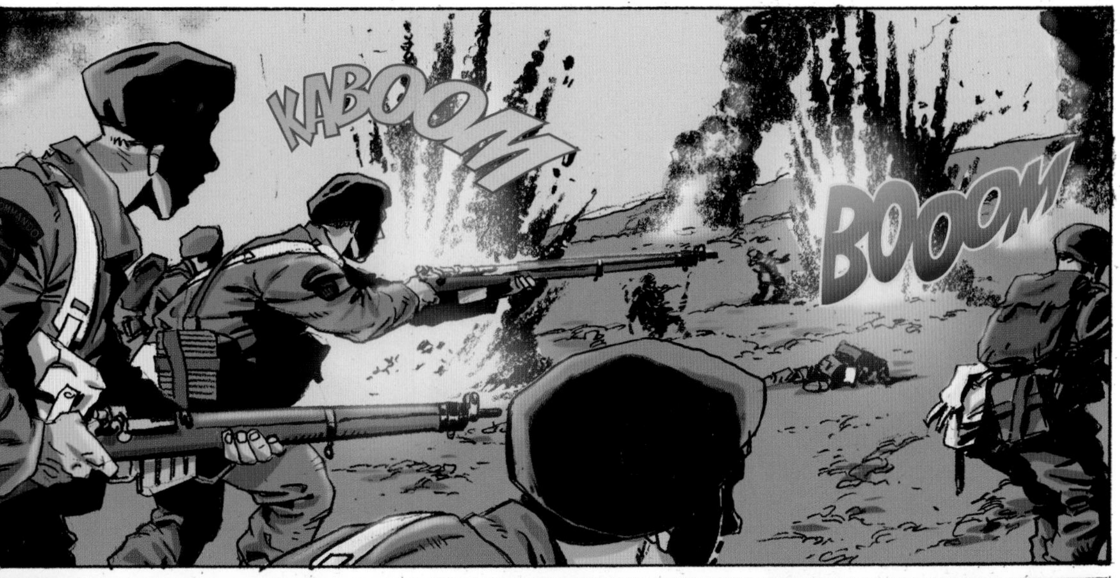
KABOOM
BOOOM

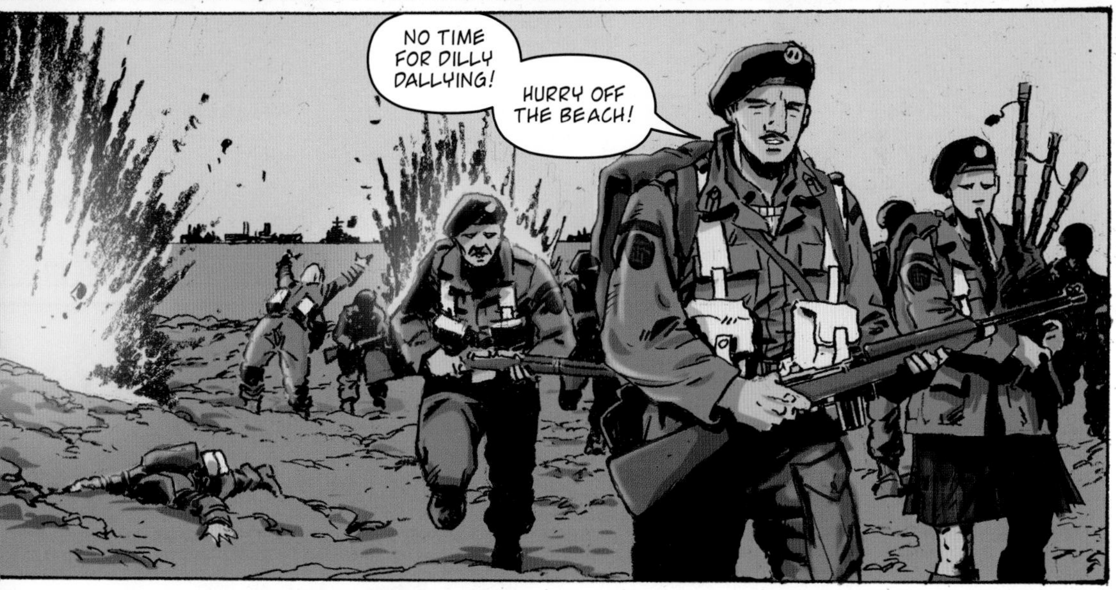
NO TIME FOR DILLY DALLYING!
HURRY OFF THE BEACH!

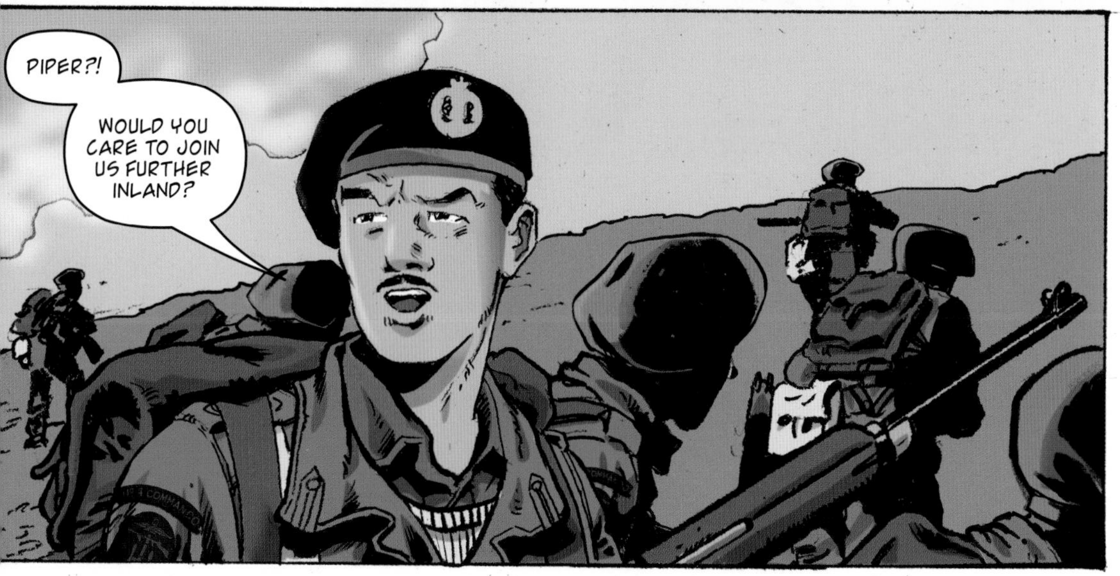
PIPER?!
WOULD YOU CARE TO JOIN US FURTHER INLAND?

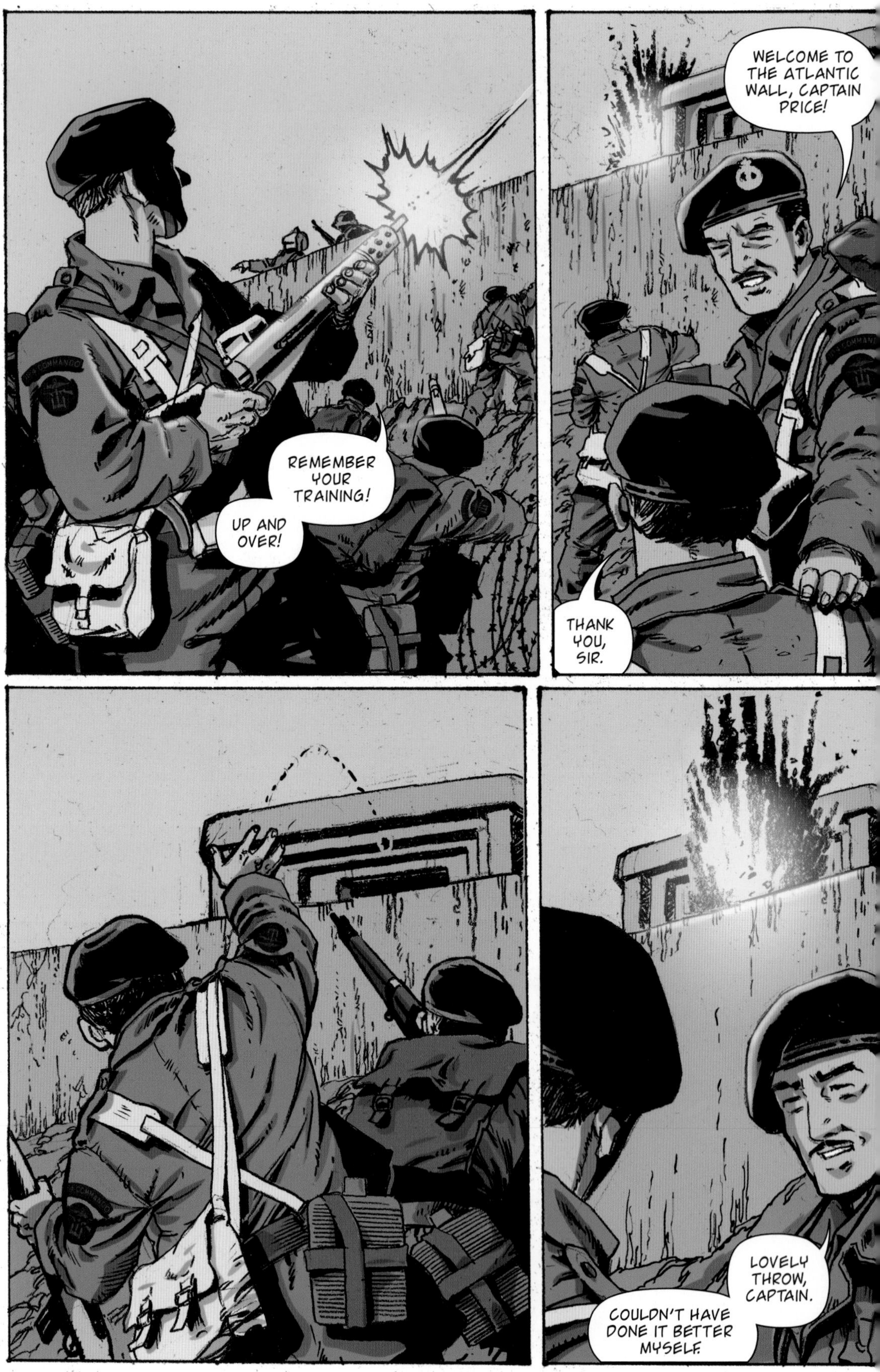
REMEMBER YOUR TRAINING!
UP AND OVER!
WELCOME TO THE ATLANTIC WALL, CAPTAIN PRICE!
THANK YOU, SIR.
LOVELY THROW, CAPTAIN.
COULDN'T HAVE DONE IT BETTER MYSELF.

TUBBY! IT'S NICE TO SEE YOU SO EARLY IN THE MORNING. HOW WAS YOUR JOURNEY?

GENERAL ROOSEVELT, I NEVER THOUGHT I'D SEE YOU AGAIN AND HERE YOU ARE, WORKING THE TRAFFIC BEAT.

IT'S A NICE DRIVE UP THE BEACH ACTUALLY, YOU SHOULD TRY IT.

MAJOR GENERAL RAYMOND "TUBBY" BARTON, US 4TH INFANTRY DIVISION

UTAH BEACH

I'LL KEEP MY BOOTS ON THE SAND FOR NOW, THANKS.

"THIS IS LONDON. LONDON CALLING IN THE HOME, OVERSEAS AND EUROPEAN SERVICES OF THE BBC AND THROUGH UNITED NATIONS MEDITERRANEAN, AND THIS IS JOHN SNAGGE SPEAKING."

WELL, YOU CERTAINLY GIVE A HELL OF A WELCOME, TED.

THANK YOU, I DO TRY TO MAKE EVERYONE FEEL AT HOME.

"SUPREME HEADQUARTERS ALLIED EXPEDITIONARY FORCE HAVE JUST ISSUED COMMUNIQU NO 1."

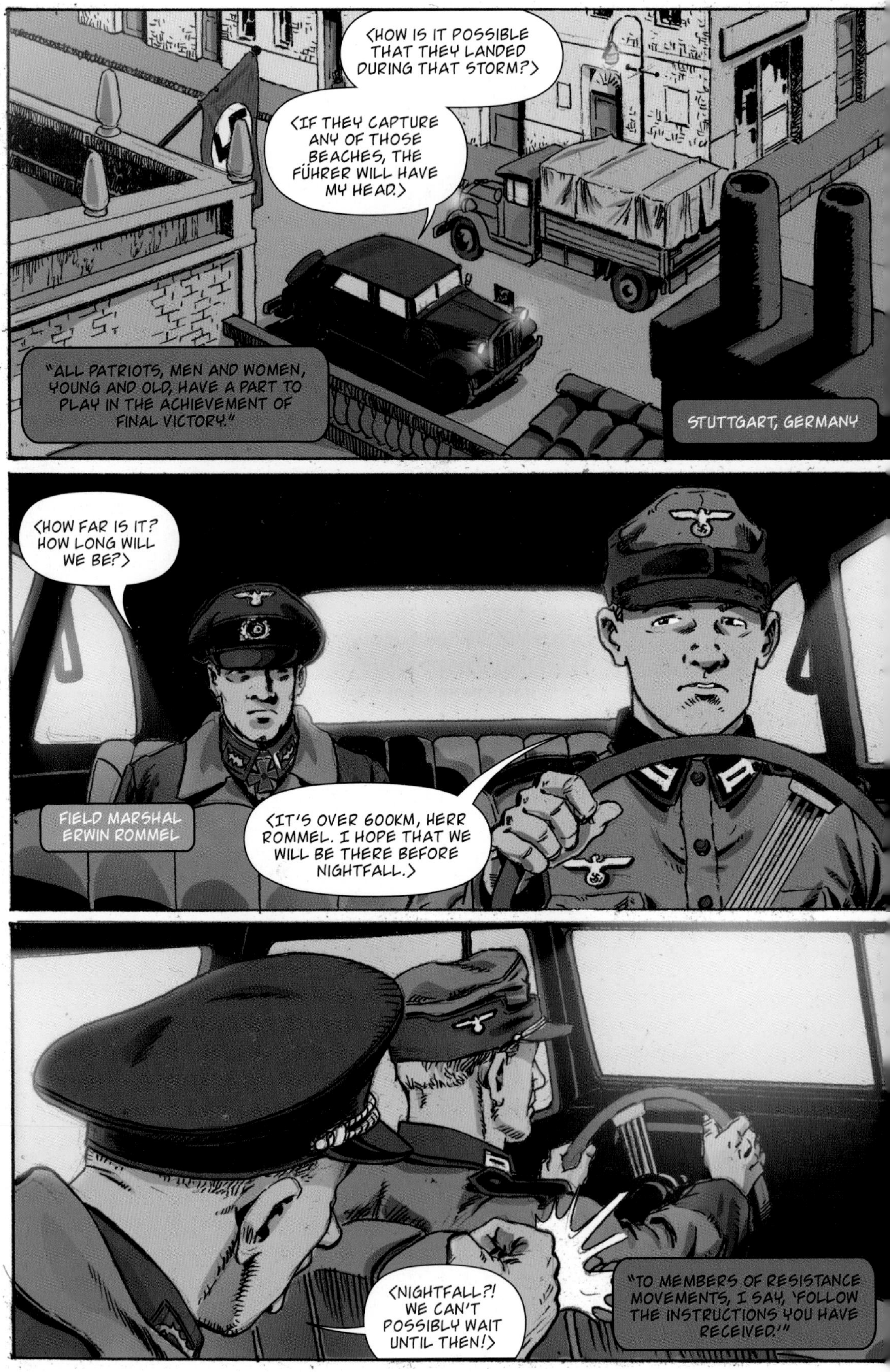

<HOW IS IT POSSIBLE THAT THEY LANDED DURING THAT STORM?>
<IF THEY CAPTURE ANY OF THOSE BEACHES, THE FÜHRER WILL HAVE MY HEAD.>
"ALL PATRIOTS, MEN AND WOMEN, YOUNG AND OLD, HAVE A PART TO PLAY IN THE ACHIEVEMENT OF FINAL VICTORY."
STUTTGART, GERMANY
<HOW FAR IS IT? HOW LONG WILL WE BE?>
FIELD MARSHAL ERWIN ROMMEL
<IT'S OVER 600KM, HERR ROMMEL. I HOPE THAT WE WILL BE THERE BEFORE NIGHTFALL.>
<NIGHTFALL?! WE CAN'T POSSIBLY WAIT UNTIL THEN!>
"TO MEMBERS OF RESISTANCE MOVEMENTS, I SAY, 'FOLLOW THE INSTRUCTIONS YOU HAVE RECEIVED.'"

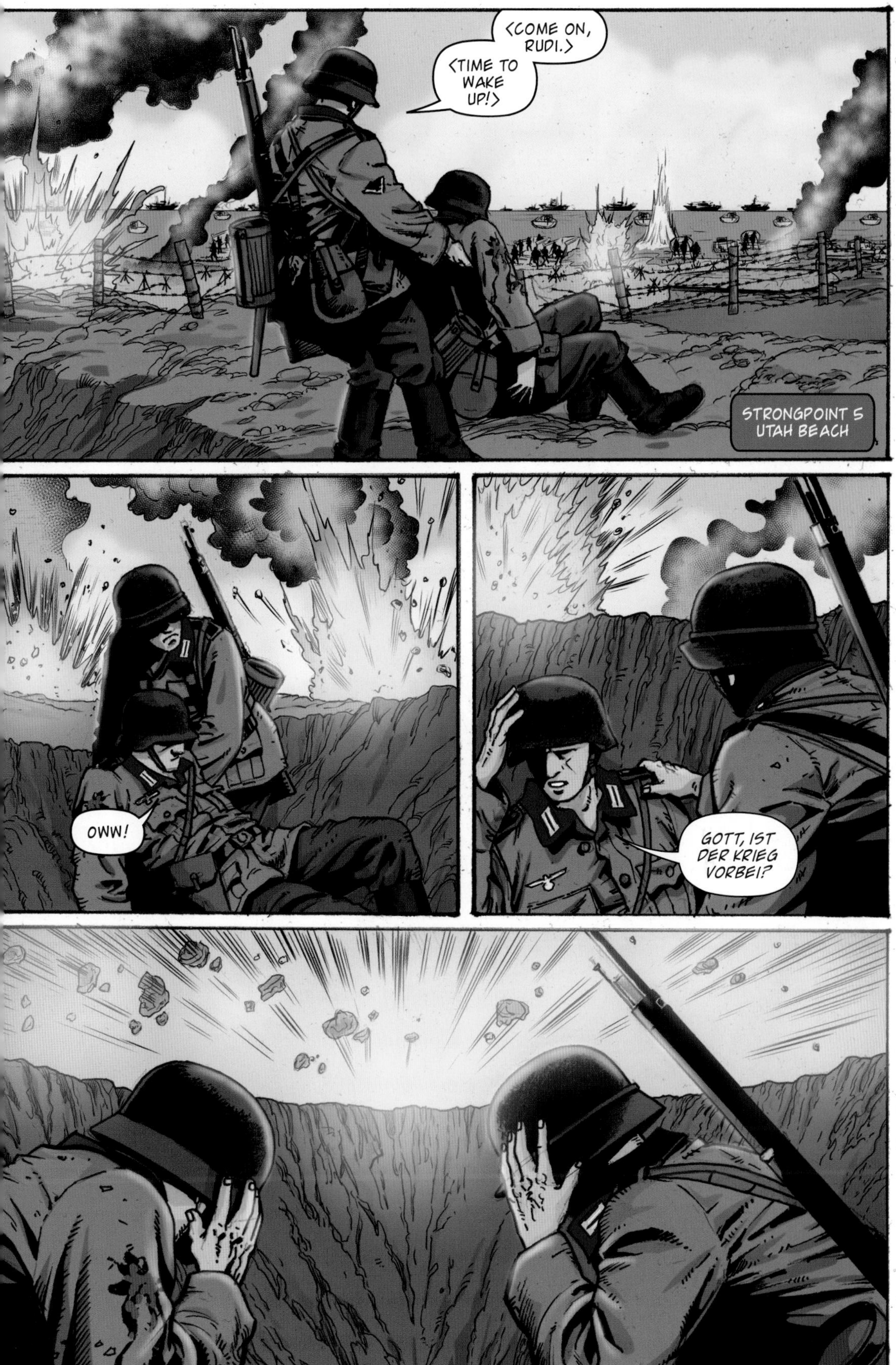
<COME ON, RUDI.>
<TIME TO WAKE UP!>
STRONGPOINT 5 UTAH BEACH
OWW!
GOTT, IST DER KRIEG VORBEI?

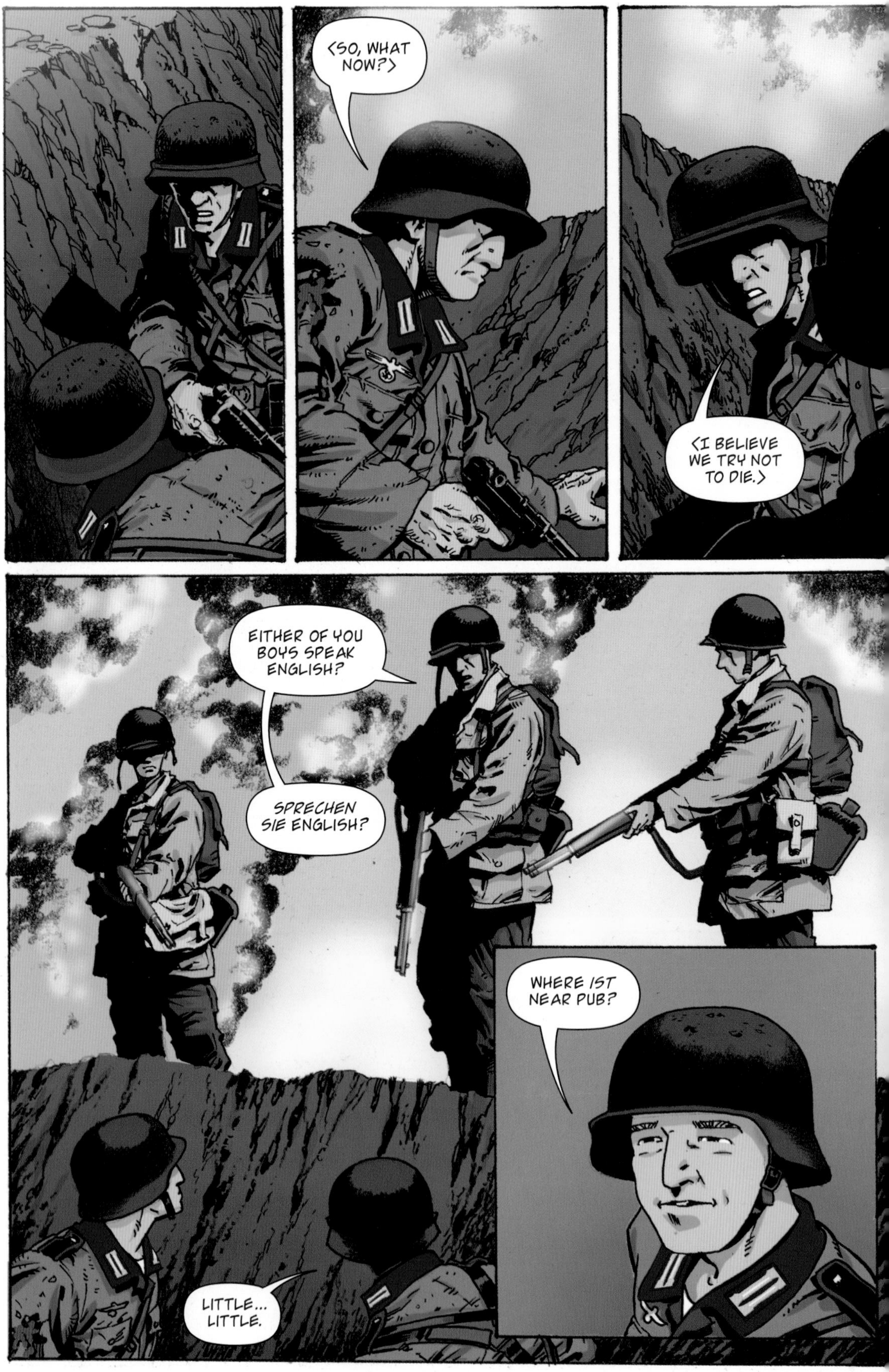

<SO, WHAT NOW?>
<I BELIEVE WE TRY NOT TO DIE.>
EITHER OF YOU BOYS SPEAK ENGLISH?
SPRECHEN SIE ENGLISH?
LITTLE... LITTLE.
WHERE IST NEAR PUB?

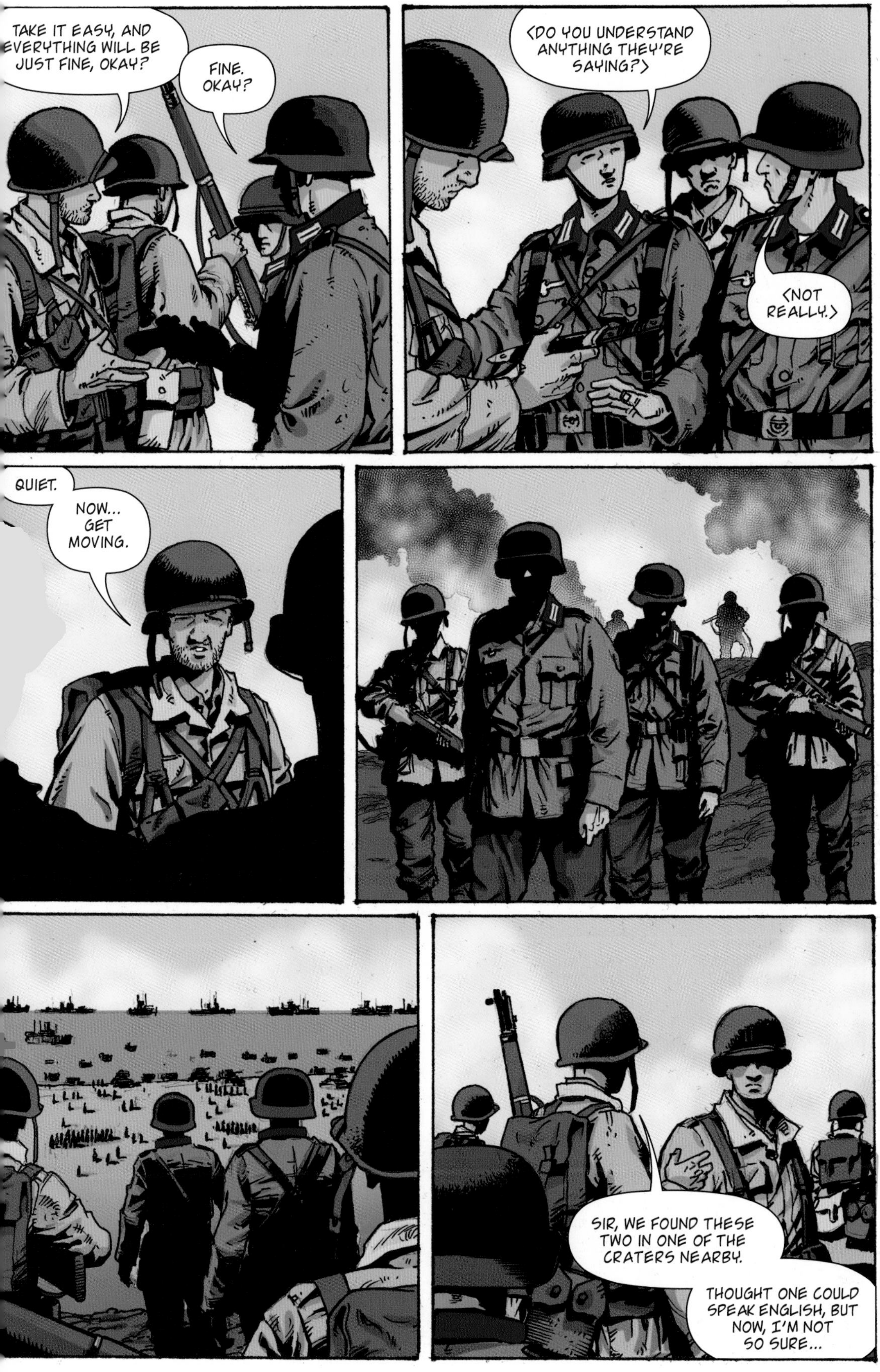
TAKE IT EASY, AND EVERYTHING WILL BE JUST FINE, OKAY?
FINE. OKAY?
<DO YOU UNDERSTAND ANYTHING THEY'RE SAYING?>
<NOT REALLY.>
QUIET.
NOW... GET MOVING.
SIR, WE FOUND THESE TWO IN ONE OF THE CRATERS NEARBY.
THOUGHT ONE COULD SPEAK ENGLISH, BUT NOW, I'M NOT SO SURE...

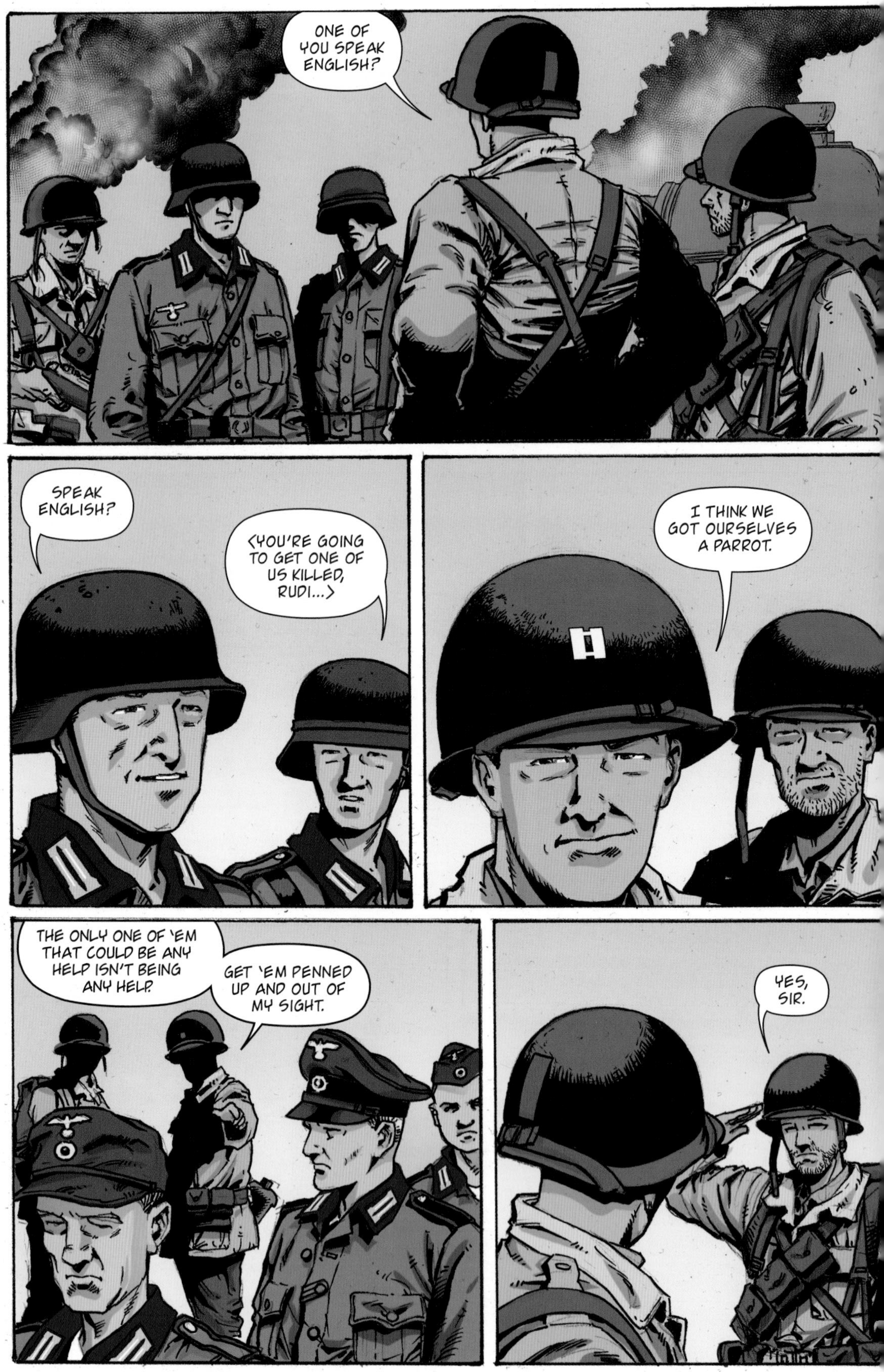
ONE OF YOU SPEAK ENGLISH?
SPEAK ENGLISH?
<YOU'RE GOING TO GET ONE OF US KILLED, RUDI...>
I THINK WE GOT OURSELVES A PARROT.
THE ONLY ONE OF 'EM THAT COULD BE ANY HELP ISN'T BEING ANY HELP.
GET 'EM PENNED UP AND OUT OF MY SIGHT.
YES, SIR.

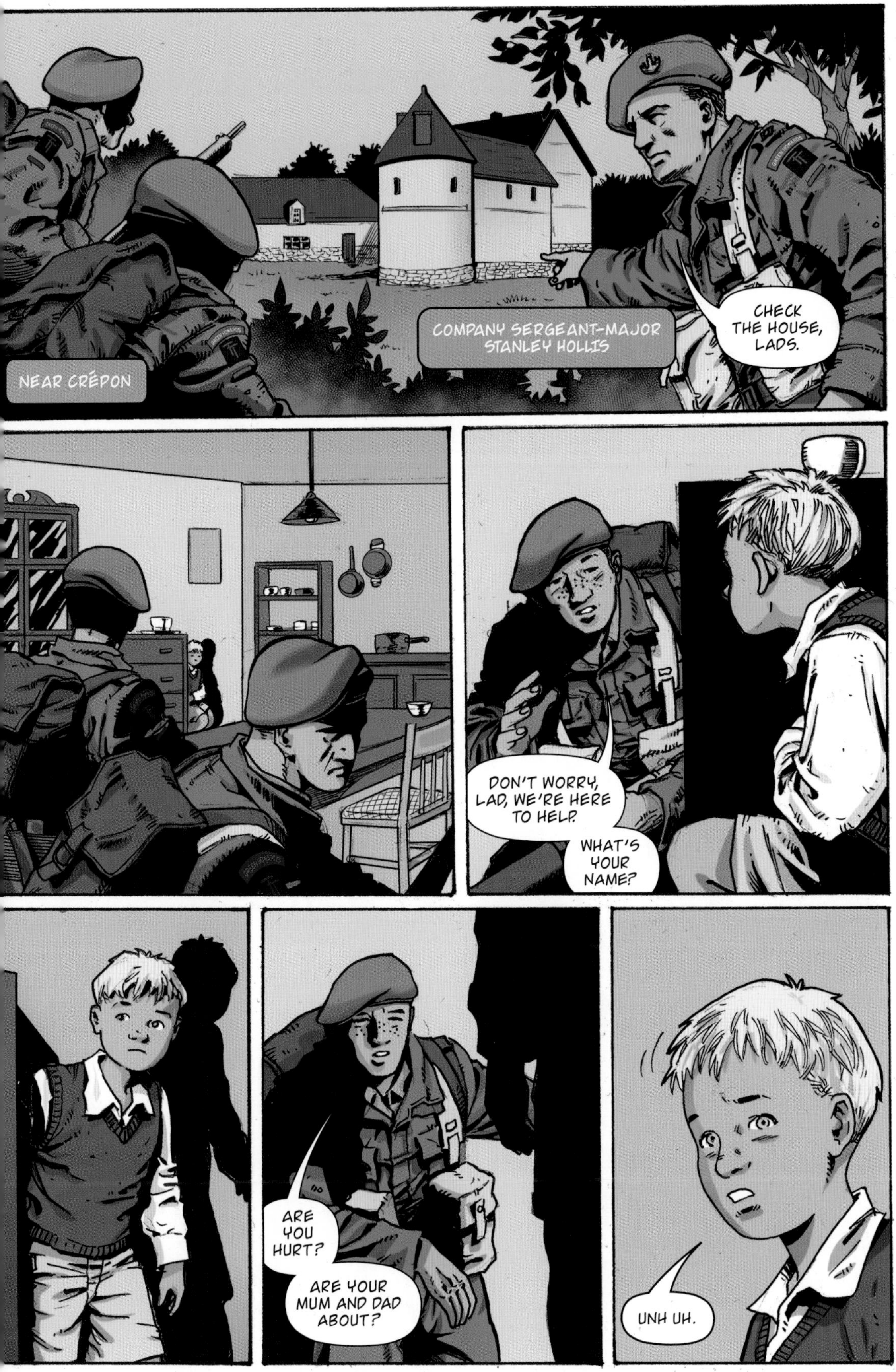

NEAR CRÉPON
COMPANY SERGEANT-MAJOR STANLEY HOLLIS
CHECK THE HOUSE, LADS.
DON'T WORRY, LAD, WE'RE HERE TO HELP.
WHAT'S YOUR NAME?
ARE YOU HURT?
ARE YOUR MUM AND DAD ABOUT?
UNH UH.

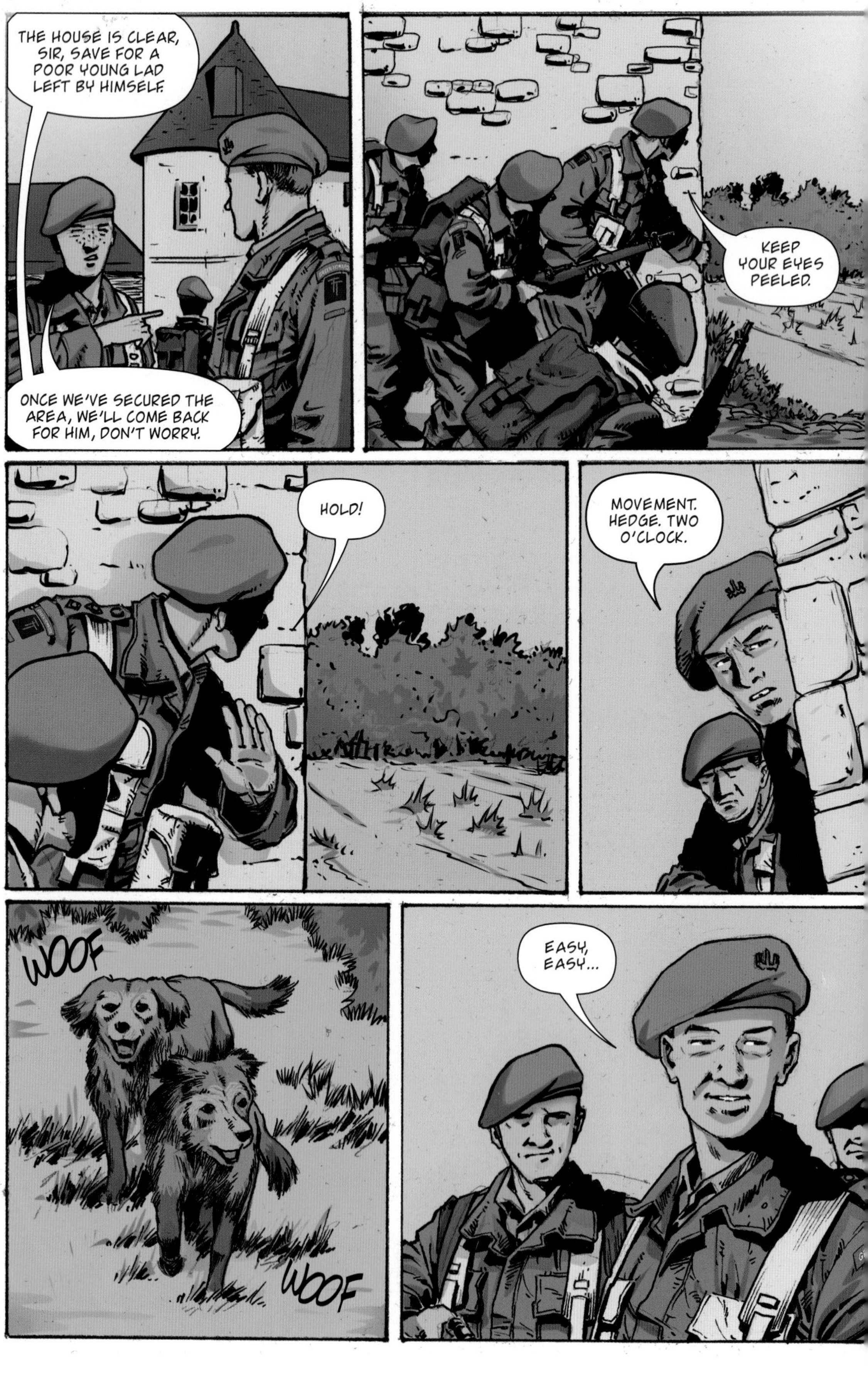
THE HOUSE IS CLEAR, SIR, SAVE FOR A POOR YOUNG LAD LEFT BY HIMSELF.
ONCE WE'VE SECURED THE AREA, WE'LL COME BACK FOR HIM, DON'T WORRY.
KEEP YOUR EYES PEELED.
HOLD!
MOVEMENT. HEDGE. TWO O'CLOCK.
WOOF
WOOF
EASY, EASY...

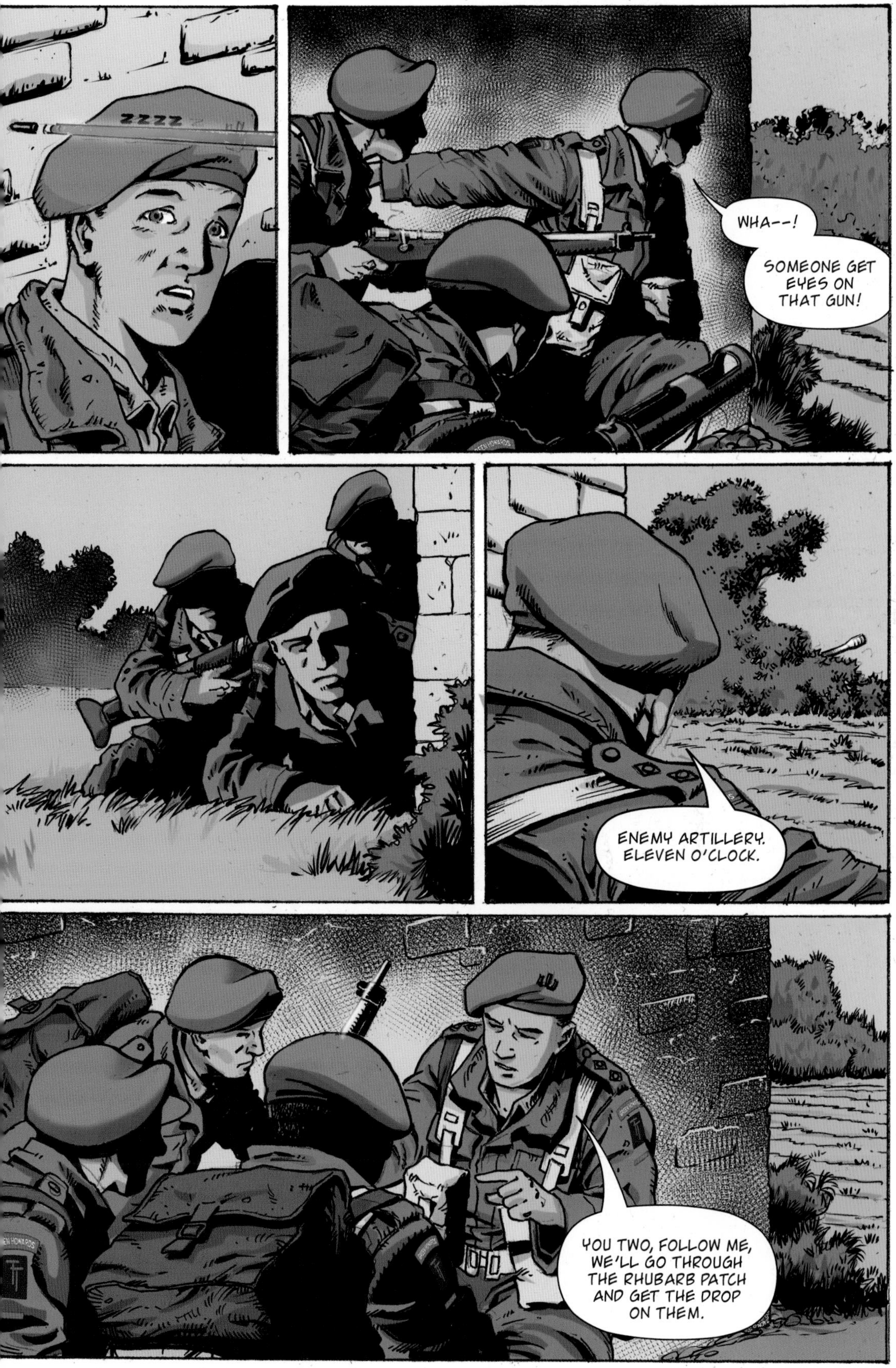
ZZZZ
WHA--!
SOMEONE GET EYES ON THAT GUN!
ENEMY ARTILLERY. ELEVEN O'CLOCK.
YOU TWO, FOLLOW ME, WE'LL GO THROUGH THE RHUBARB PATCH AND GET THE DROP ON THEM.

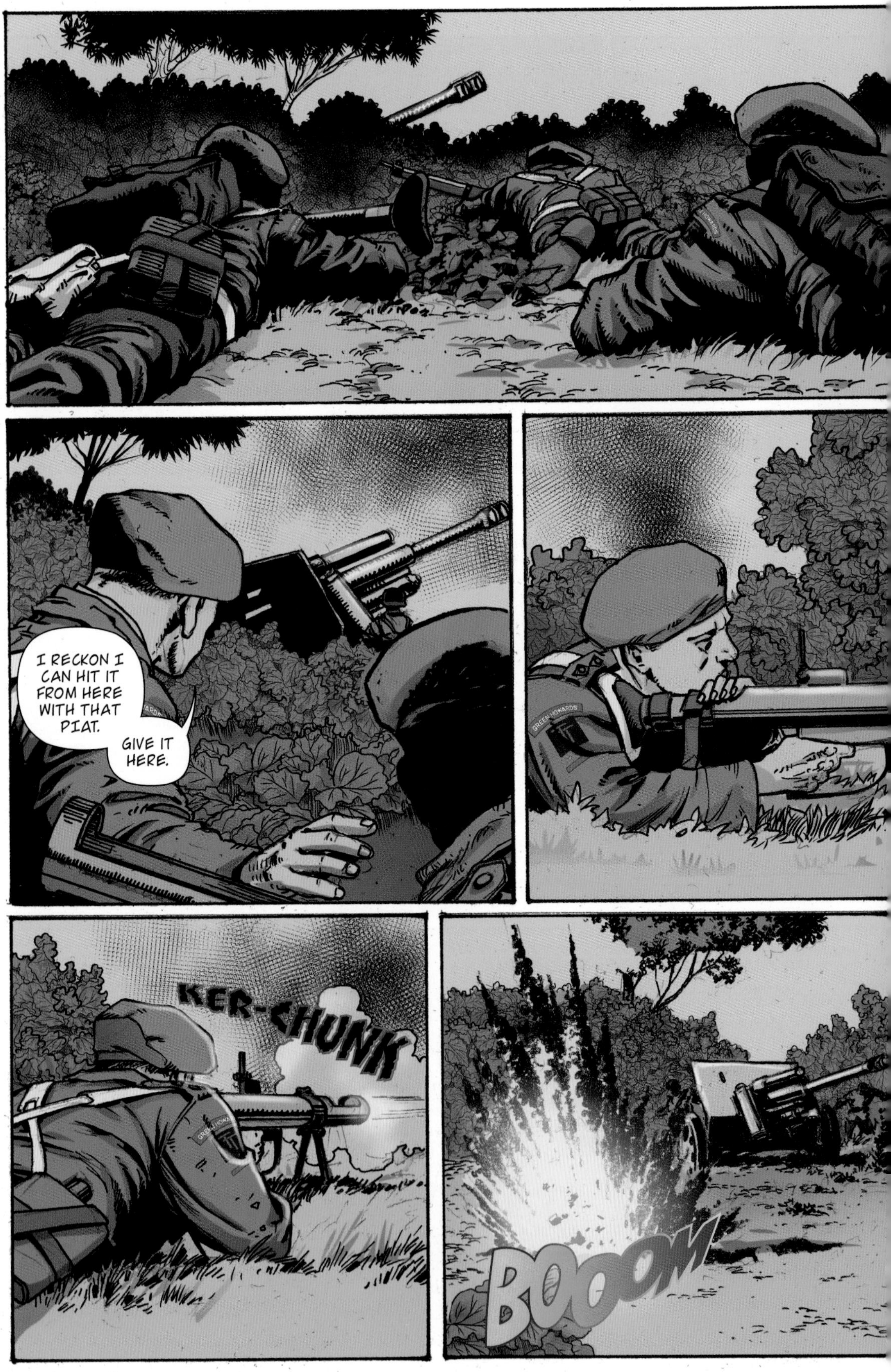
I RECKON I CAN HIT IT FROM HERE WITH THAT PIAT.
GIVE IT HERE.
KER-CHUNK
BOOOM

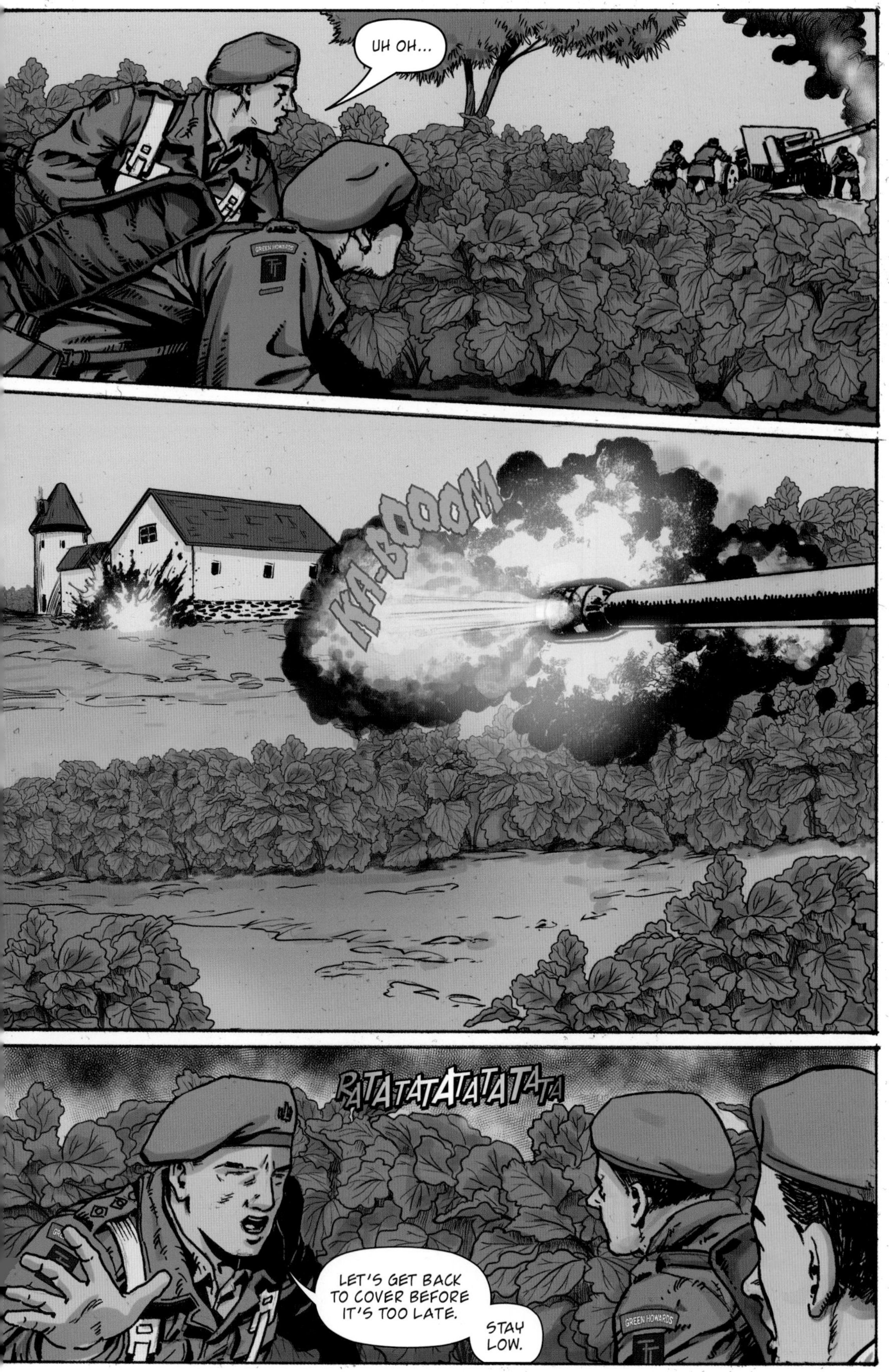
UH OH...
GREEN HOWARDS
KA-BOOOM
RATATATATATATATATA
LET'S GET BACK TO COVER BEFORE IT'S TOO LATE.
STAY LOW.
GREEN HOWARDS

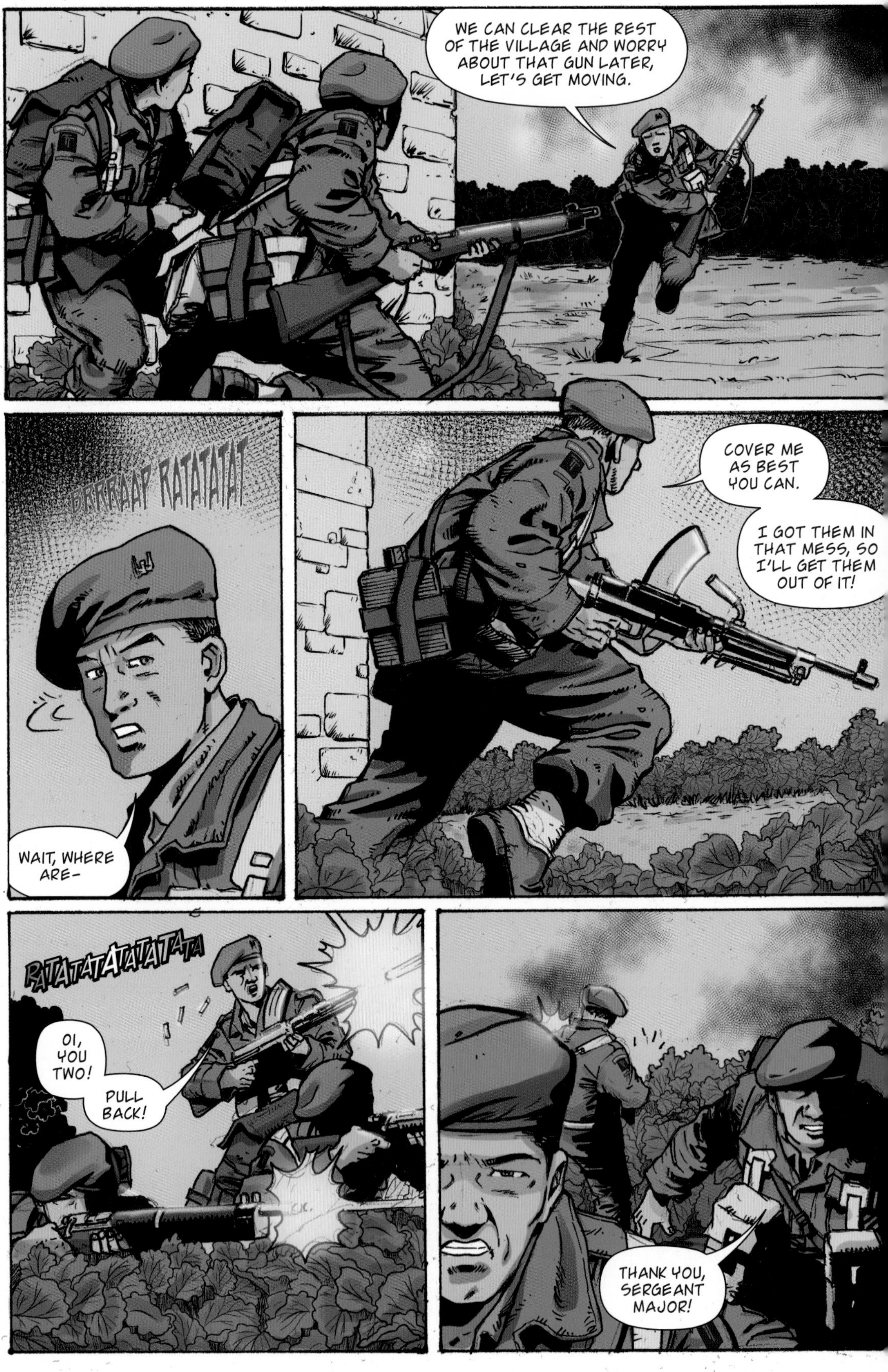
WE CAN CLEAR THE REST OF THE VILLAGE AND WORRY ABOUT THAT GUN LATER, LET'S GET MOVING.
BRRRAAP RATATATAT
WAIT, WHERE ARE-
COVER ME AS BEST YOU CAN.
I GOT THEM IN THAT MESS, SO I'LL GET THEM OUT OF IT!
RATATATATATATATA
OI, YOU TWO!
PULL BACK!
THANK YOU, SERGEANT MAJOR!

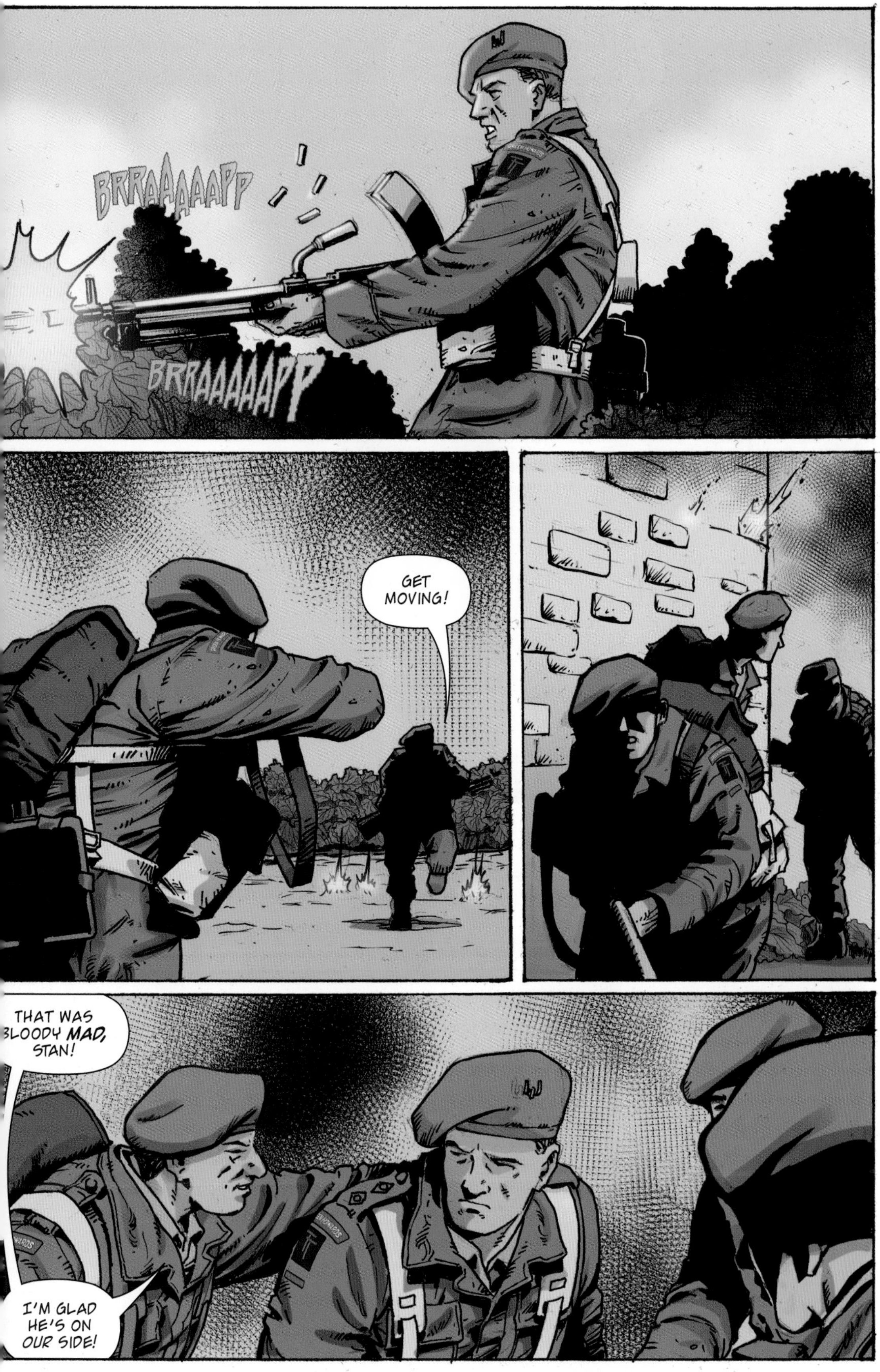

BRRAAAAAPP
BRRAAAAAPP
GET MOVING!
THAT WAS BLOODY *MAD*, STAN!
I'M GLAD HE'S ON *OUR SIDE!*

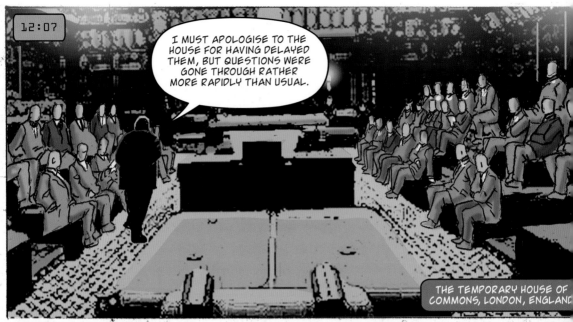

12:07

I MUST APOLOGISE TO THE HOUSE FOR HAVING DELAYED THEM, BUT QUESTIONS WERE GONE THROUGH RATHER MORE RAPIDLY THAN USUAL.

THE TEMPORARY HOUSE OF COMMONS, LONDON, ENGLAND

THIS IS A MEMORABLE AND GLORIOUS EVENT, WHICH REWARDS THE INTENSE FIGHTING OF THE LAST FIVE MONTHS IN ITALY.

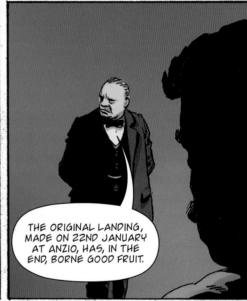

THE ORIGINAL LANDING, MADE ON 22ND JANUARY AT ANZIO, HAS, IN THE END, BORNE GOOD FRUIT.

PRIME MINISTER WINSTON CHURCHILL

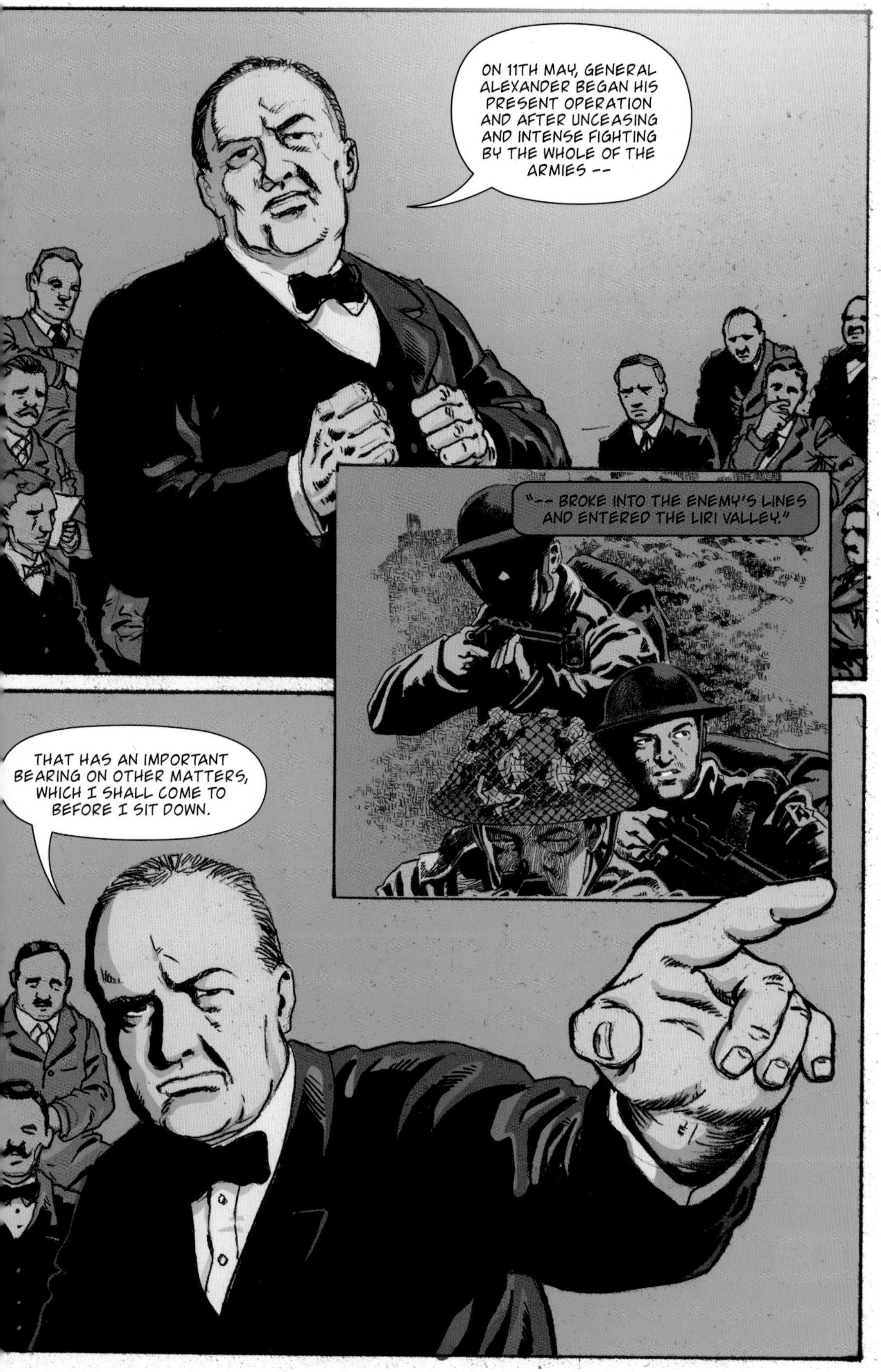
ON 11TH MAY, GENERAL ALEXANDER BEGAN HIS PRESENT OPERATION AND AFTER UNCEASING AND INTENSE FIGHTING BY THE WHOLE OF THE ARMIES --
"-- BROKE INTO THE ENEMY'S LINES AND ENTERED THE LIRI VALLEY."
THAT HAS AN IMPORTANT BEARING ON OTHER MATTERS, WHICH I SHALL COME TO BEFORE I SIT DOWN.

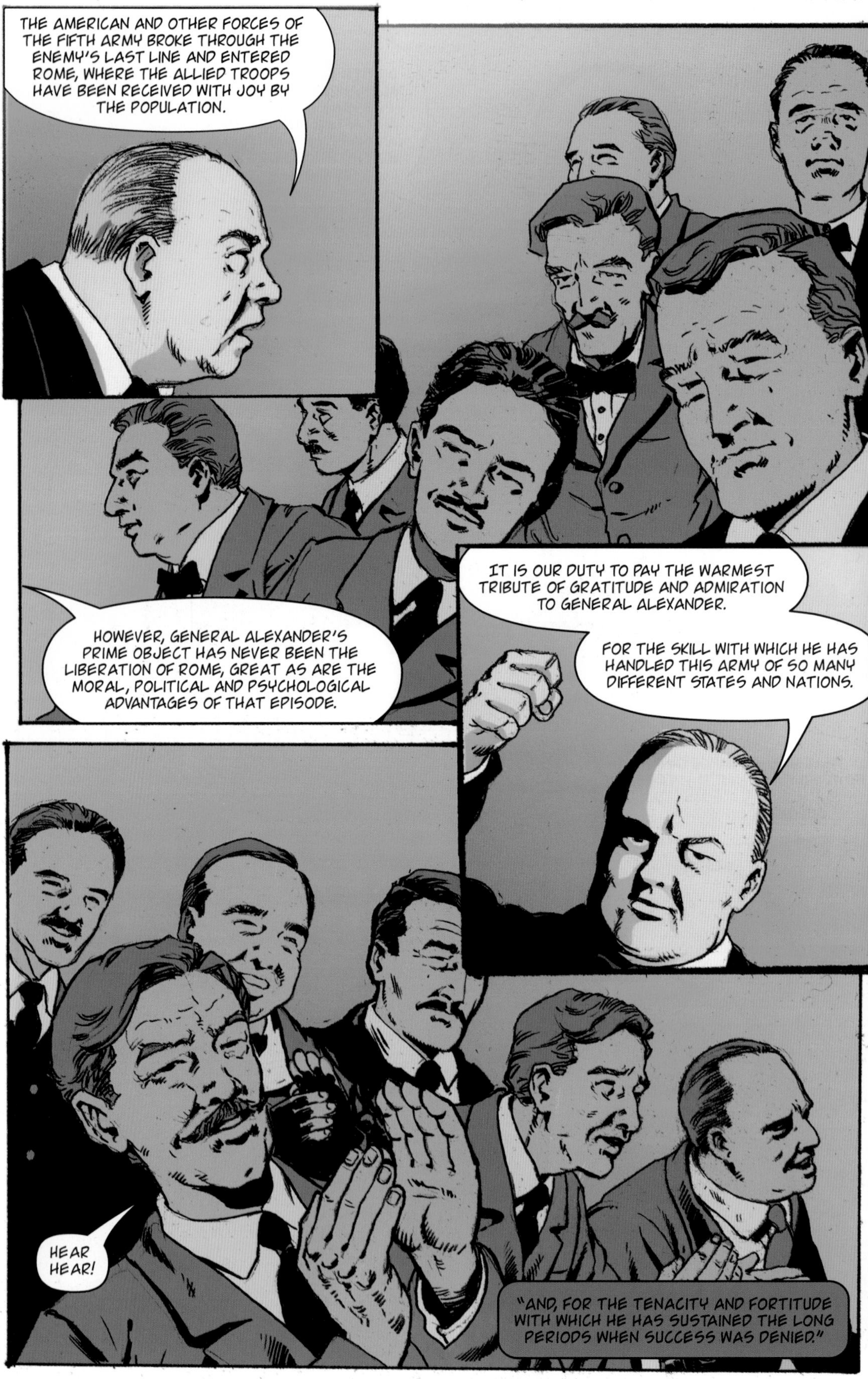
THE AMERICAN AND OTHER FORCES OF THE FIFTH ARMY BROKE THROUGH THE ENEMY'S LAST LINE AND ENTERED ROME, WHERE THE ALLIED TROOPS HAVE BEEN RECEIVED WITH JOY BY THE POPULATION.
HOWEVER, GENERAL ALEXANDER'S PRIME OBJECT HAS NEVER BEEN THE LIBERATION OF ROME, GREAT AS ARE THE MORAL, POLITICAL AND PSYCHOLOGICAL ADVANTAGES OF THAT EPISODE.
IT IS OUR DUTY TO PAY THE WARMEST TRIBUTE OF GRATITUDE AND ADMIRATION TO GENERAL ALEXANDER.
FOR THE SKILL WITH WHICH HE HAS HANDLED THIS ARMY OF SO MANY DIFFERENT STATES AND NATIONS.
HEAR HEAR!
"AND, FOR THE TENACITY AND FORTITUDE WITH WHICH HE HAS SUSTAINED THE LONG PERIODS WHEN SUCCESS WAS DENIED."

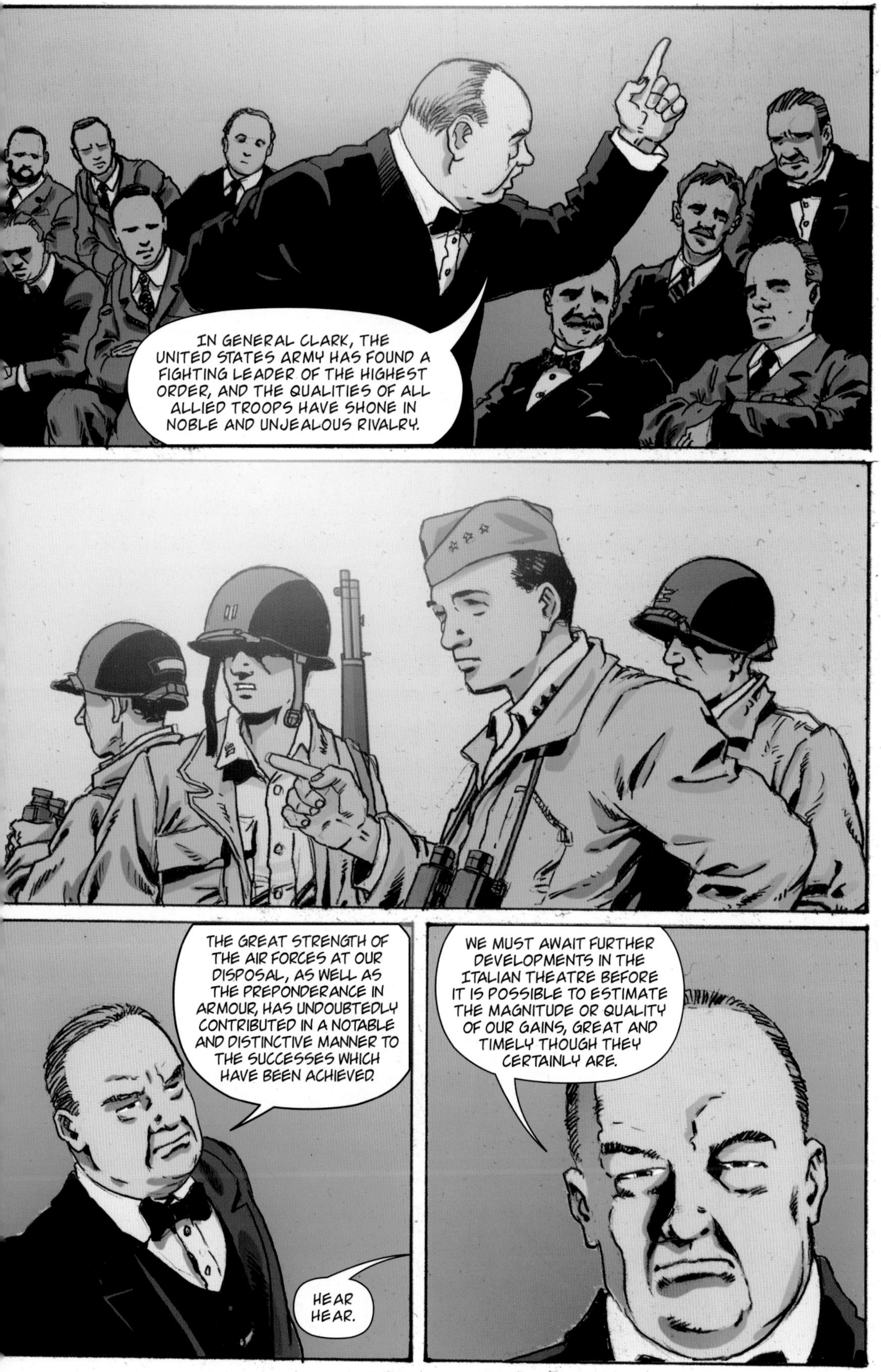
IN GENERAL CLARK, THE UNITED STATES ARMY HAS FOUND A FIGHTING LEADER OF THE HIGHEST ORDER, AND THE QUALITIES OF ALL ALLIED TROOPS HAVE SHONE IN NOBLE AND UNJEALOUS RIVALRY.
THE GREAT STRENGTH OF THE AIR FORCES AT OUR DISPOSAL, AS WELL AS THE PREPONDERANCE IN ARMOUR, HAS UNDOUBTEDLY CONTRIBUTED IN A NOTABLE AND DISTINCTIVE MANNER TO THE SUCCESSES WHICH HAVE BEEN ACHIEVED.
HEAR HEAR.
WE MUST AWAIT FURTHER DEVELOPMENTS IN THE ITALIAN THEATRE BEFORE IT IS POSSIBLE TO ESTIMATE THE MAGNITUDE OR QUALITY OF OUR GAINS, GREAT AND TIMELY THOUGH THEY CERTAINLY ARE.

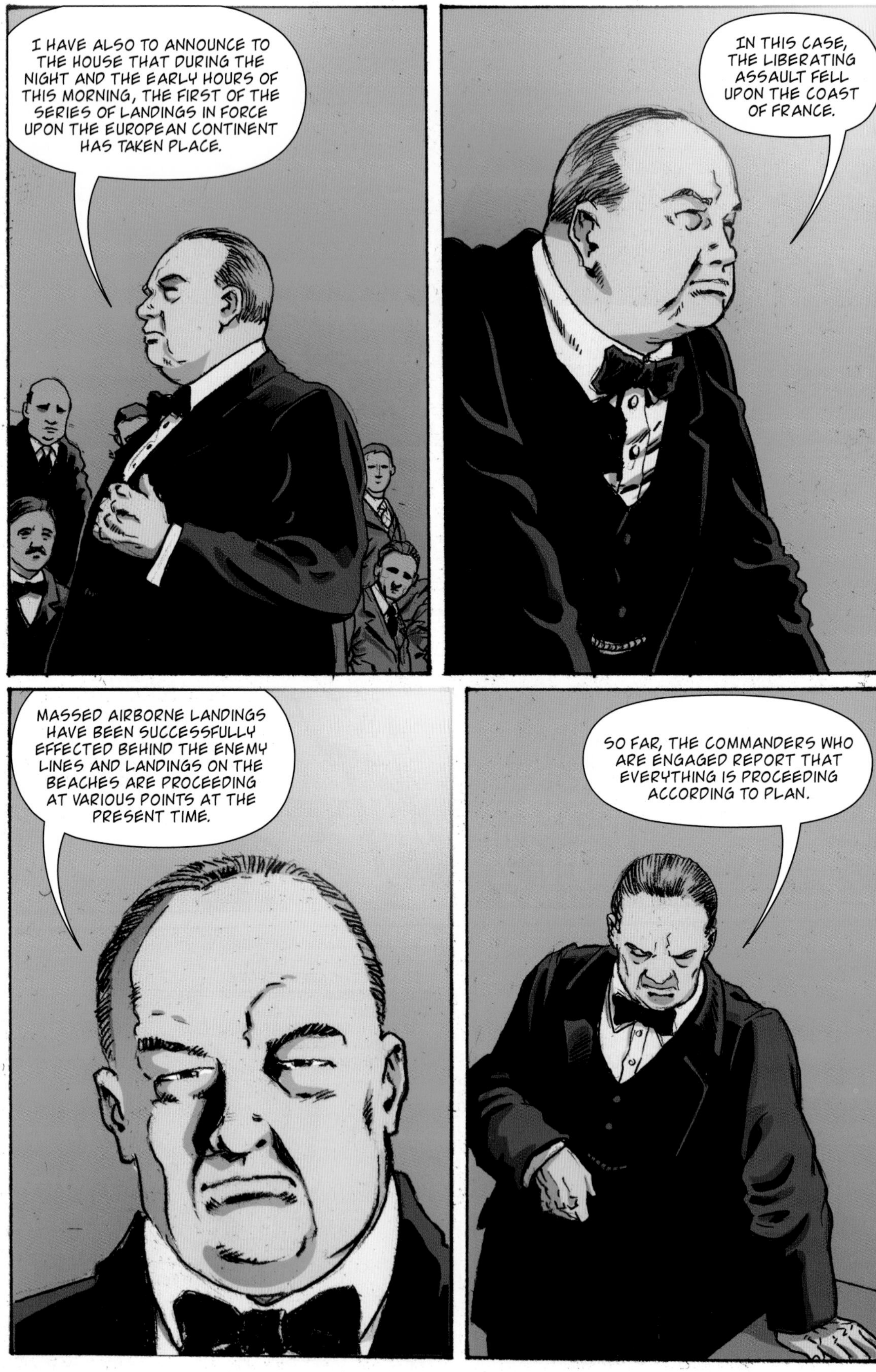
I HAVE ALSO TO ANNOUNCE TO THE HOUSE THAT DURING THE NIGHT AND THE EARLY HOURS OF THIS MORNING, THE FIRST OF THE SERIES OF LANDINGS IN FORCE UPON THE EUROPEAN CONTINENT HAS TAKEN PLACE.
IN THIS CASE, THE LIBERATING ASSAULT FELL UPON THE COAST OF FRANCE.
MASSED AIRBORNE LANDINGS HAVE BEEN SUCCESSFULLY EFFECTED BEHIND THE ENEMY LINES AND LANDINGS ON THE BEACHES ARE PROCEEDING AT VARIOUS POINTS AT THE PRESENT TIME.
SO FAR, THE COMMANDERS WHO ARE ENGAGED REPORT THAT EVERYTHING IS PROCEEDING ACCORDING TO PLAN.

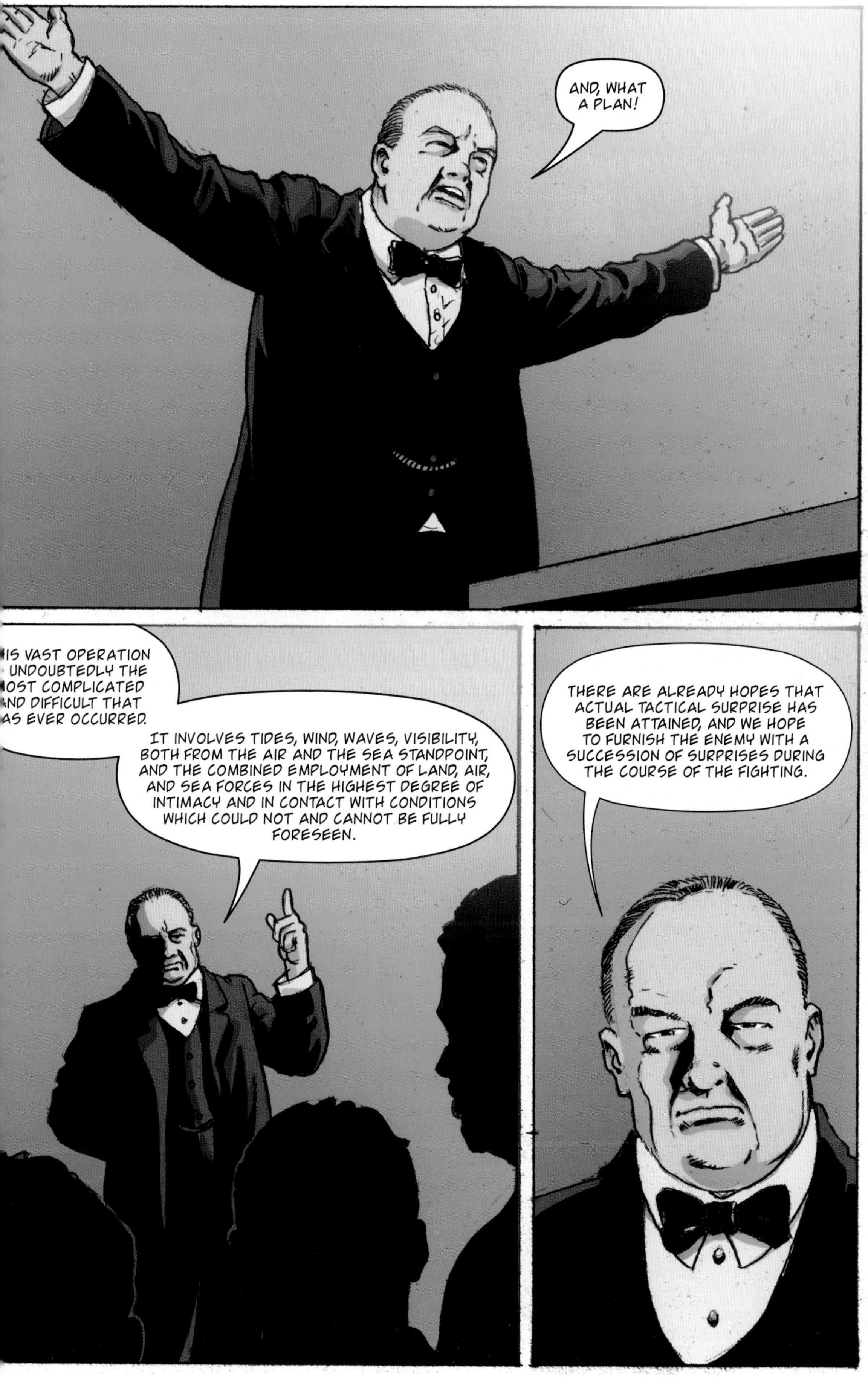
AND, WHAT A PLAN!
IS VAST OPERATION UNDOUBTEDLY THE OST COMPLICATED ND DIFFICULT THAT AS EVER OCCURRED.
IT INVOLVES TIDES, WIND, WAVES, VISIBILITY, BOTH FROM THE AIR AND THE SEA STANDPOINT, AND THE COMBINED EMPLOYMENT OF LAND, AIR, AND SEA FORCES IN THE HIGHEST DEGREE OF INTIMACY AND IN CONTACT WITH CONDITIONS WHICH COULD NOT AND CANNOT BE FULLY FORESEEN.
THERE ARE ALREADY HOPES THAT ACTUAL TACTICAL SURPRISE HAS BEEN ATTAINED, AND WE HOPE TO FURNISH THE ENEMY WITH A SUCCESSION OF SURPRISES DURING THE COURSE OF THE FIGHTING.

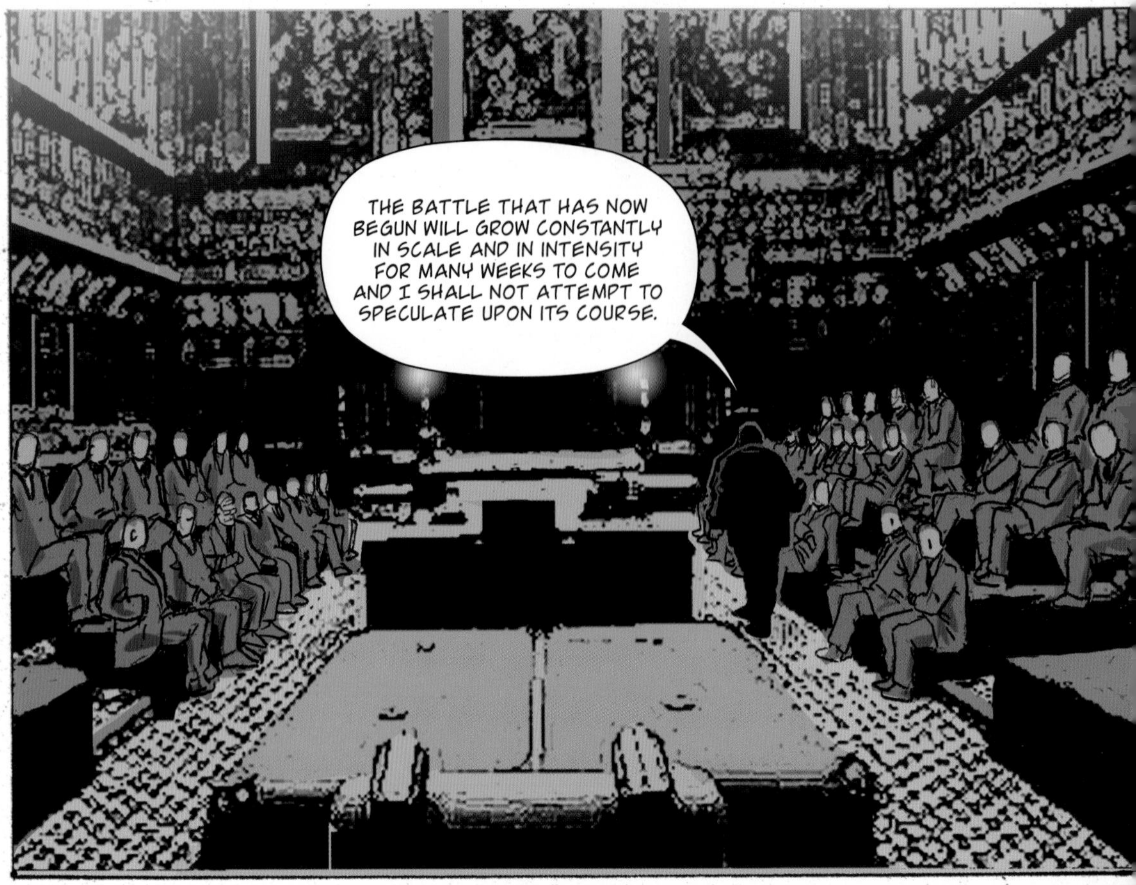
THE BATTLE THAT HAS NOW BEGUN WILL GROW CONSTANTLY IN SCALE AND IN INTENSITY FOR MANY WEEKS TO COME AND I SHALL NOT ATTEMPT TO SPECULATE UPON ITS COURSE.

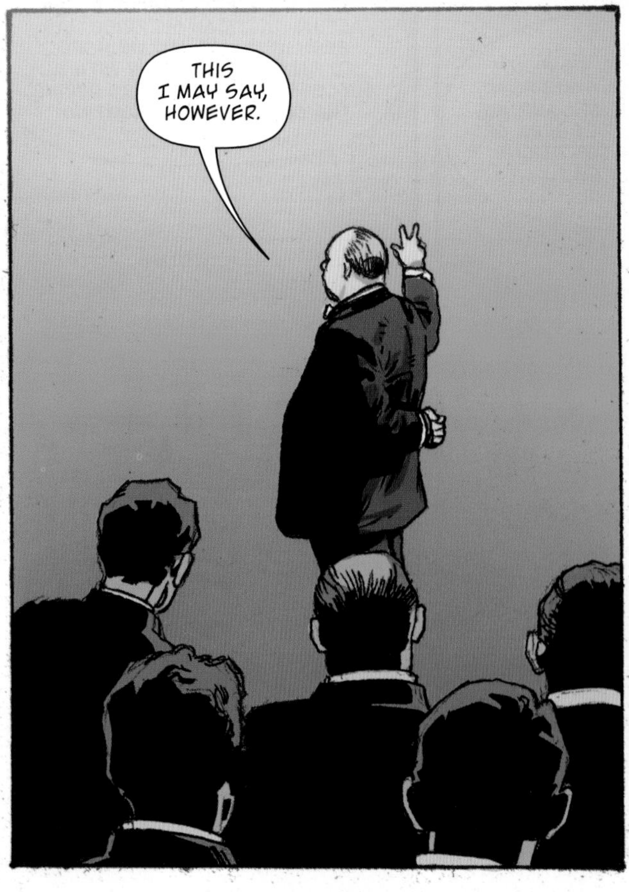
THIS I MAY SAY, HOWEVER.

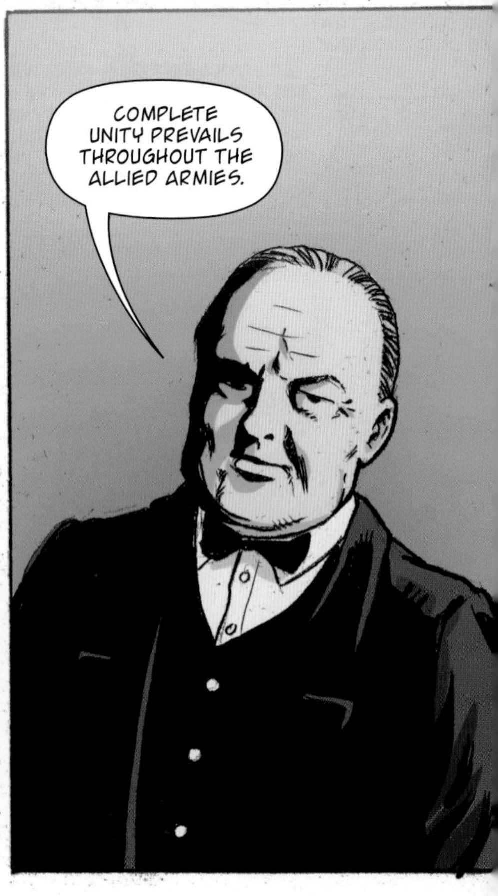
COMPLETE UNITY PREVAILS THROUGHOUT THE ALLIED ARMIES.

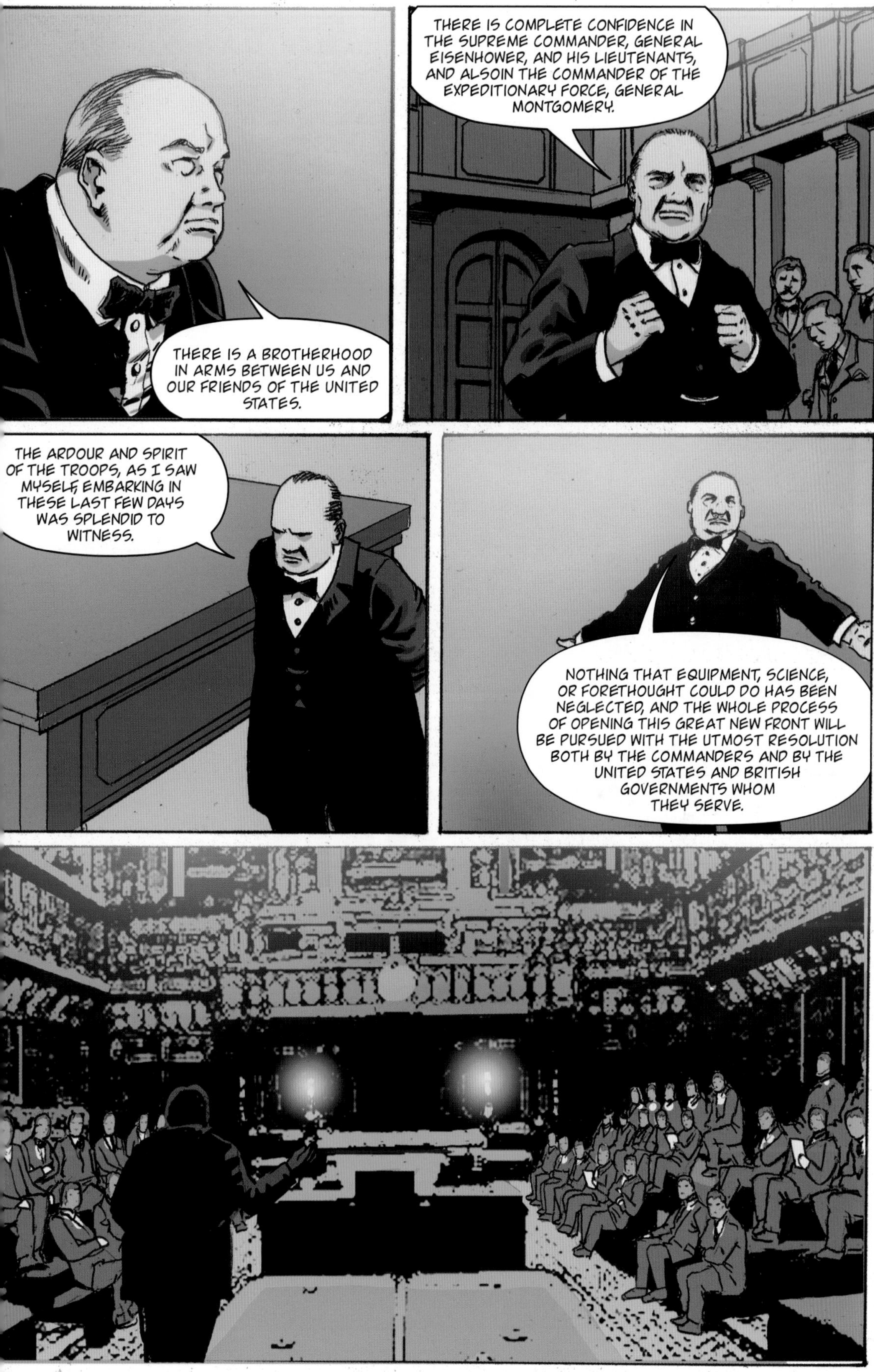
THERE IS A BROTHERHOOD IN ARMS BETWEEN US AND OUR FRIENDS OF THE UNITED STATES.
THERE IS COMPLETE CONFIDENCE IN THE SUPREME COMMANDER, GENERAL EISENHOWER, AND HIS LIEUTENANTS, AND ALSOIN THE COMMANDER OF THE EXPEDITIONARY FORCE, GENERAL MONTGOMERY.
THE ARDOUR AND SPIRIT OF THE TROOPS, AS I SAW MYSELF, EMBARKING IN THESE LAST FEW DAYS WAS SPLENDID TO WITNESS.
NOTHING THAT EQUIPMENT, SCIENCE, OR FORETHOUGHT COULD DO HAS BEEN NEGLECTED, AND THE WHOLE PROCESS OF OPENING THIS GREAT NEW FRONT WILL BE PURSUED WITH THE UTMOST RESOLUTION BOTH BY THE COMMANDERS AND BY THE UNITED STATES AND BRITISH GOVERNMENTS WHOM THEY SERVE.

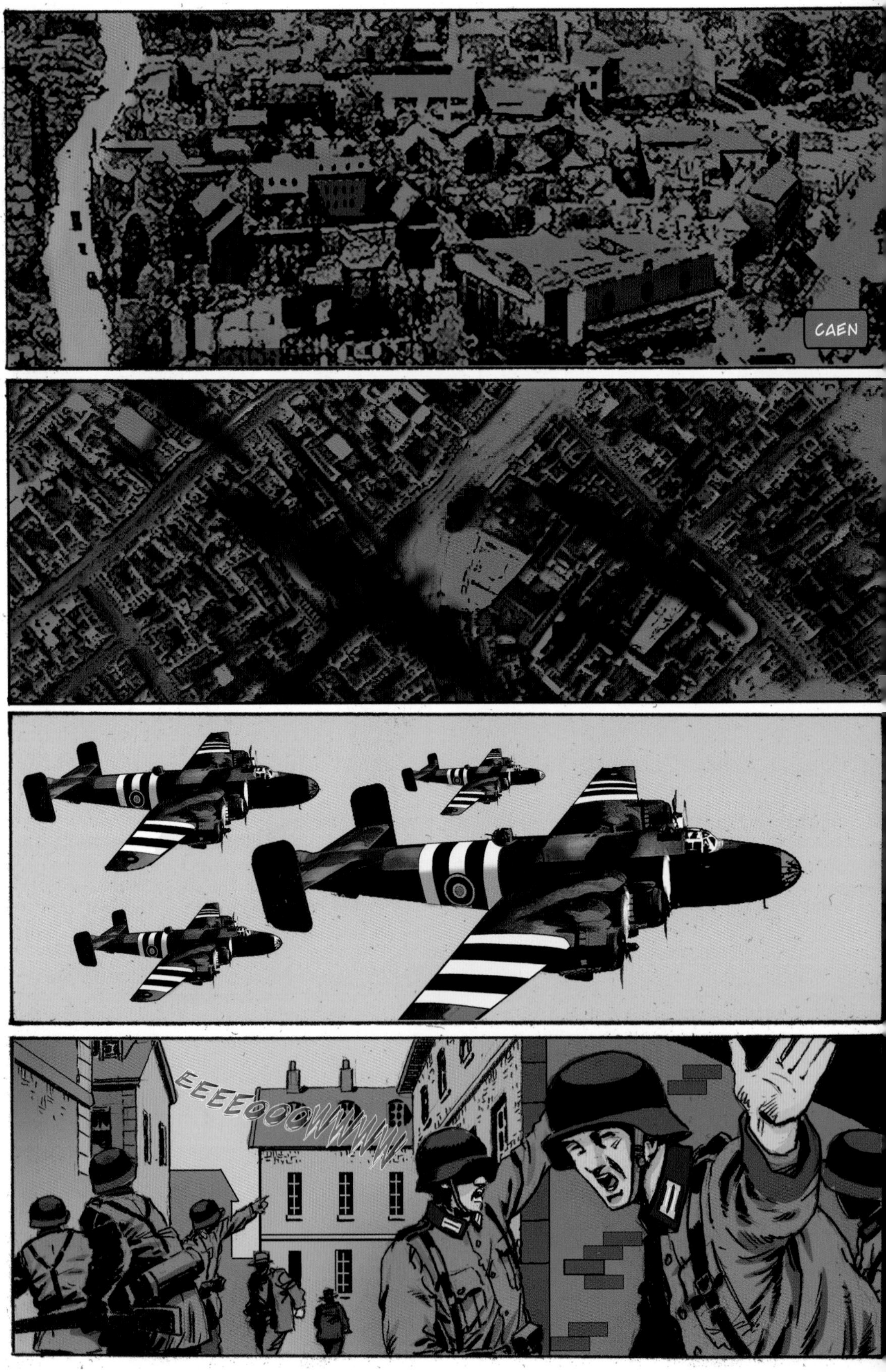
CAEN
EEEEOOOOWWWWW

EEEEOOOWWWWW

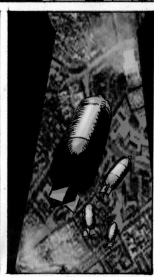

KABOOM

BOOOM

BOOM

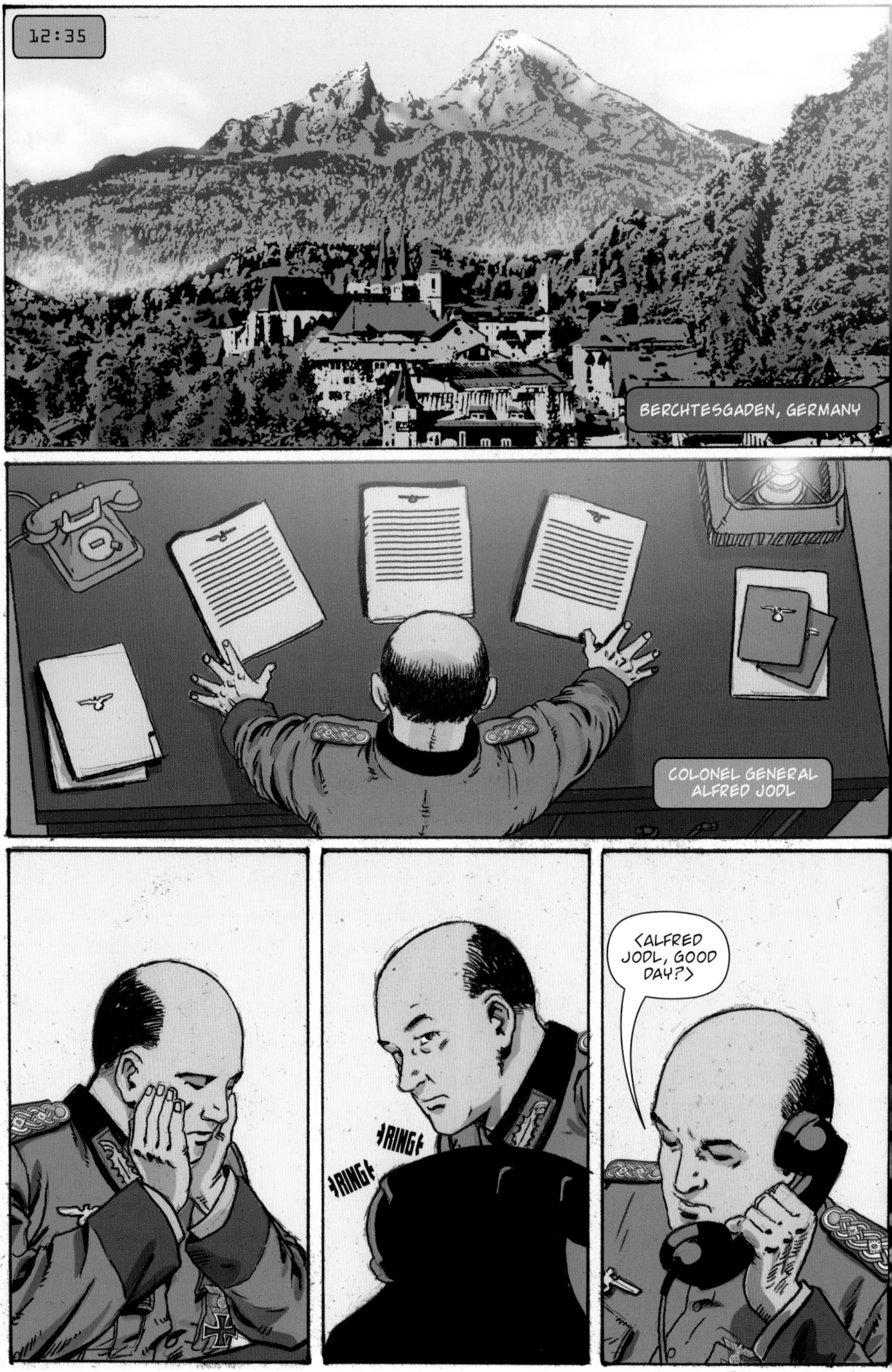
12:35
BERCHTESGADEN, GERMANY
COLONEL GENERAL ALFRED JODL
RING
RING
<ALFRED JODL, GOOD DAY?>

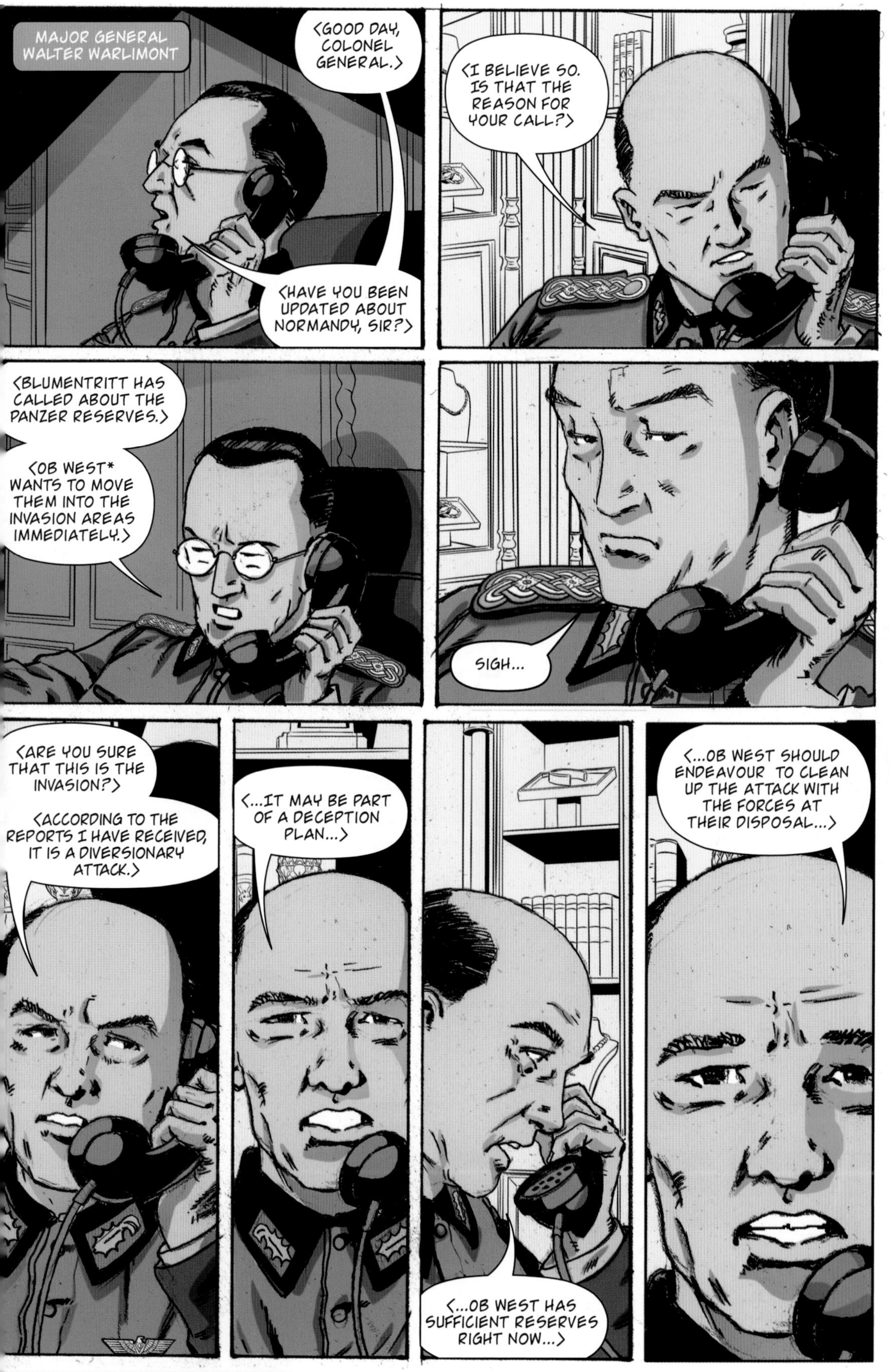
MAJOR GENERAL WALTER WARLIMONT
<GOOD DAY, COLONEL GENERAL.>
<HAVE YOU BEEN UPDATED ABOUT NORMANDY, SIR?>
<I BELIEVE SO. IS THAT THE REASON FOR YOUR CALL?>
<BLUMENTRITT HAS CALLED ABOUT THE PANZER RESERVES.>
<OB WEST* WANTS TO MOVE THEM INTO THE INVASION AREAS IMMEDIATELY.>
SIGH...
<ARE YOU SURE THAT THIS IS THE INVASION?>
<ACCORDING TO THE REPORTS I HAVE RECEIVED, IT IS A DIVERSIONARY ATTACK.>
<...IT MAY BE PART OF A DECEPTION PLAN...>
<...OB WEST HAS SUFFICIENT RESERVES RIGHT NOW...>
<...OB WEST SHOULD ENDEAVOUR TO CLEAN UP THE ATTACK WITH THE FORCES AT THEIR DISPOSAL...>

*OBERBEFEHLSHABER WEST OR GERMAN ARMY COMMAND IN THE WEST.

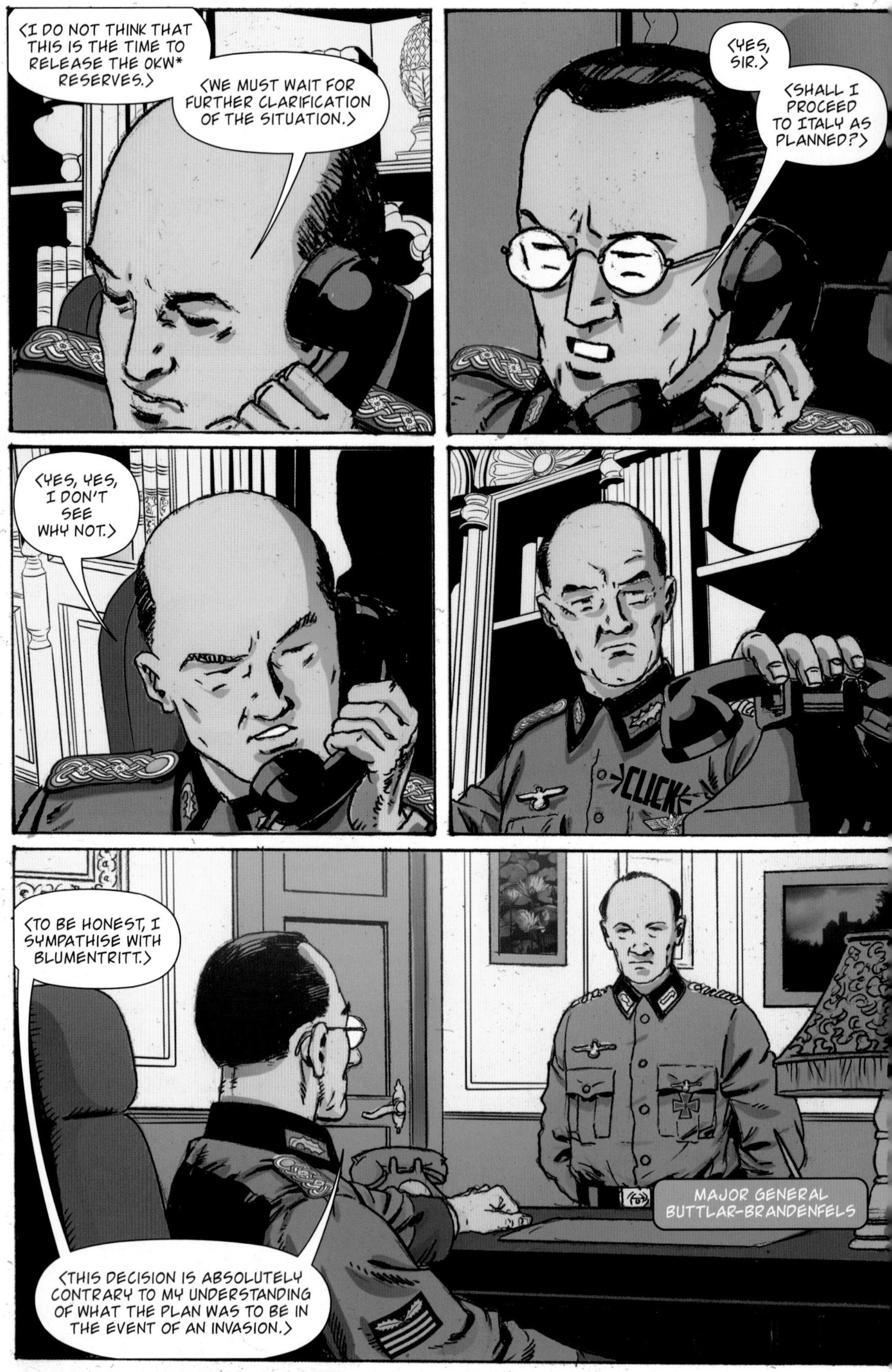
<I DO NOT THINK THAT THIS IS THE TIME TO RELEASE THE OKW* RESERVES.>
<WE MUST WAIT FOR FURTHER CLARIFICATION OF THE SITUATION.>
<YES, SIR.>
<SHALL I PROCEED TO ITALY AS PLANNED?>
<YES, YES, I DON'T SEE WHY NOT.>
CLICK
<TO BE HONEST, I SYMPATHISE WITH BLUMENTRITT.>
MAJOR GENERAL BUTTLAR-BRANDENFELS
<THIS DECISION IS ABSOLUTELY CONTRARY TO MY UNDERSTANDING OF WHAT THE PLAN WAS TO BE IN THE EVENT OF AN INVASION.>

*OBERKOMMANDO DER WEHRMACHT OR WEHRMACHT SUPREME HEADQUARTERS.

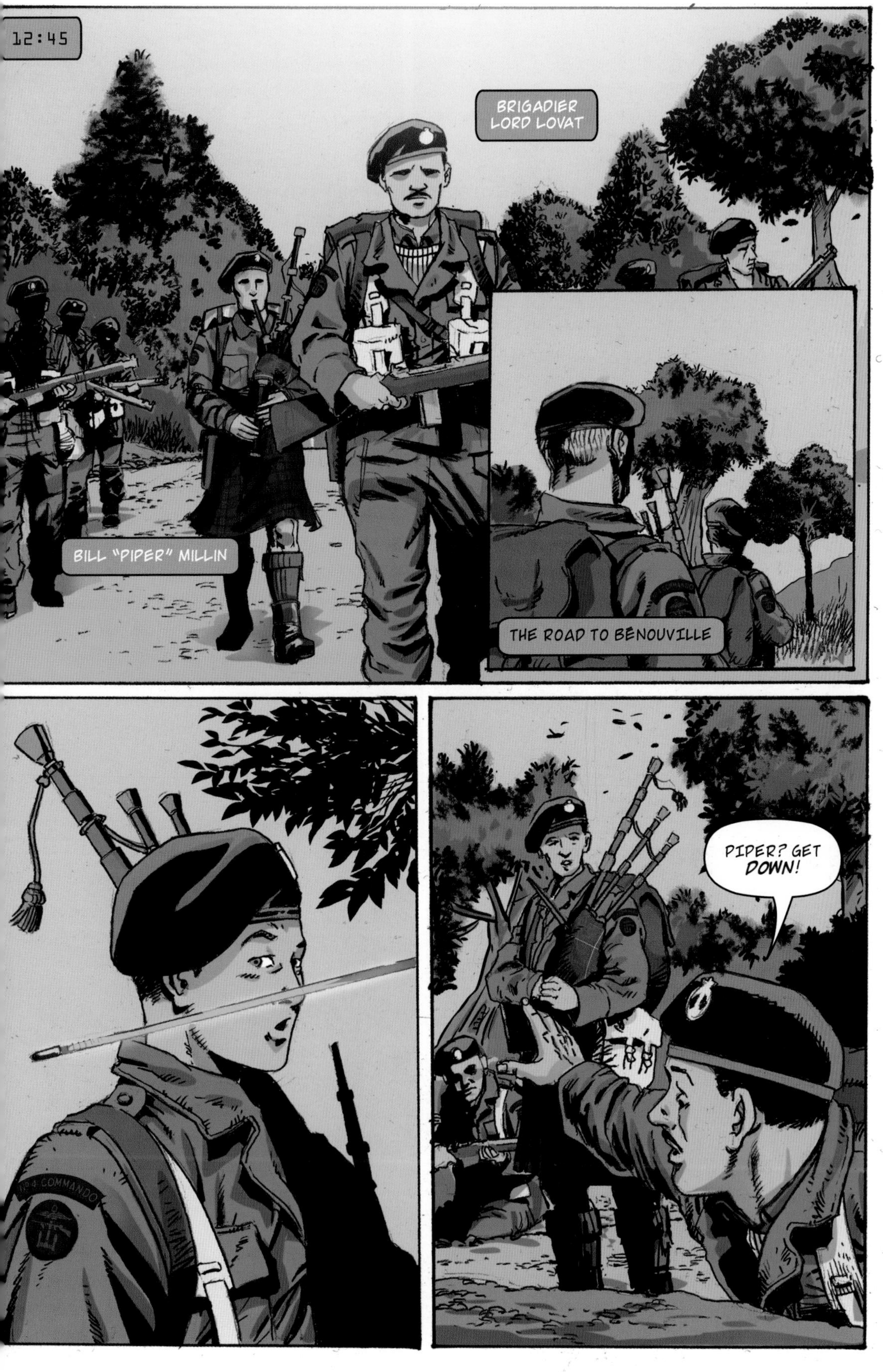
12:45
BRIGADIER LORD LOVAT
BILL "PIPER" MILLIN
THE ROAD TO BÉNOUVILLE
PIPER? GET DOWN!

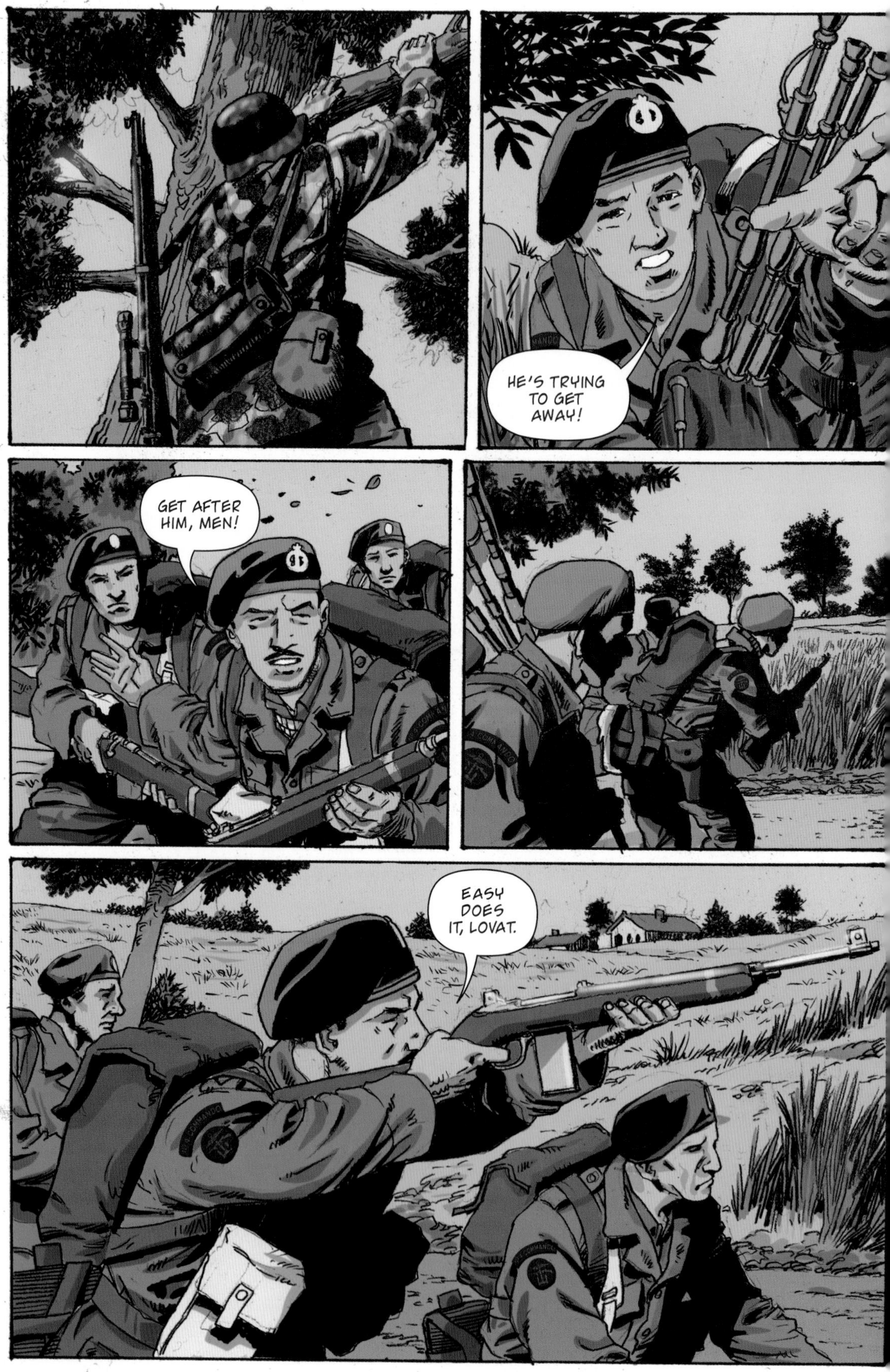
HE'S TRYING TO GET AWAY!
GET AFTER HIM, MEN!
EASY DOES IT, LOVAT.

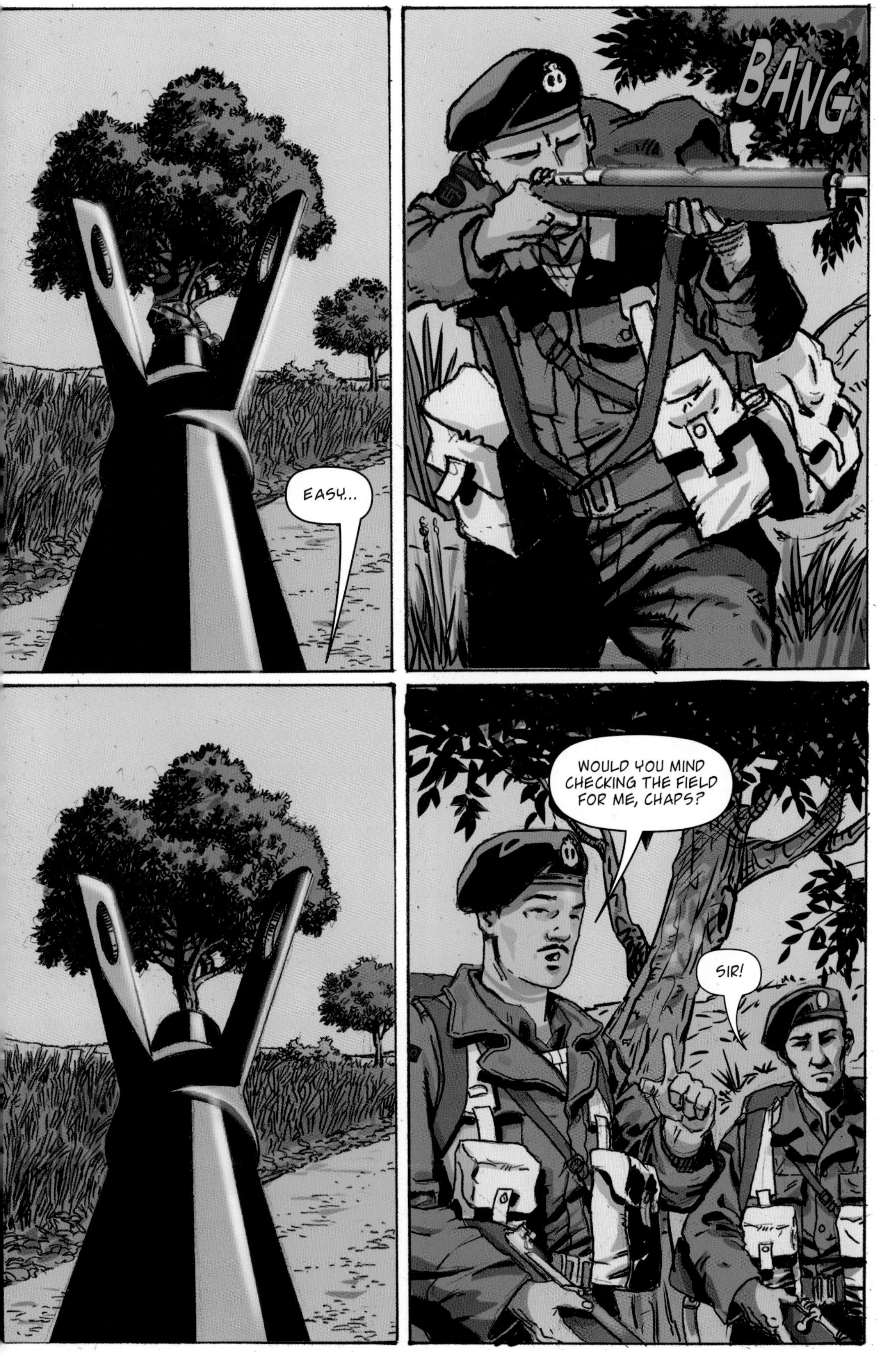
EASY...
BANG
WOULD YOU MIND CHECKING THE FIELD FOR ME, CHAPS?
SIR!

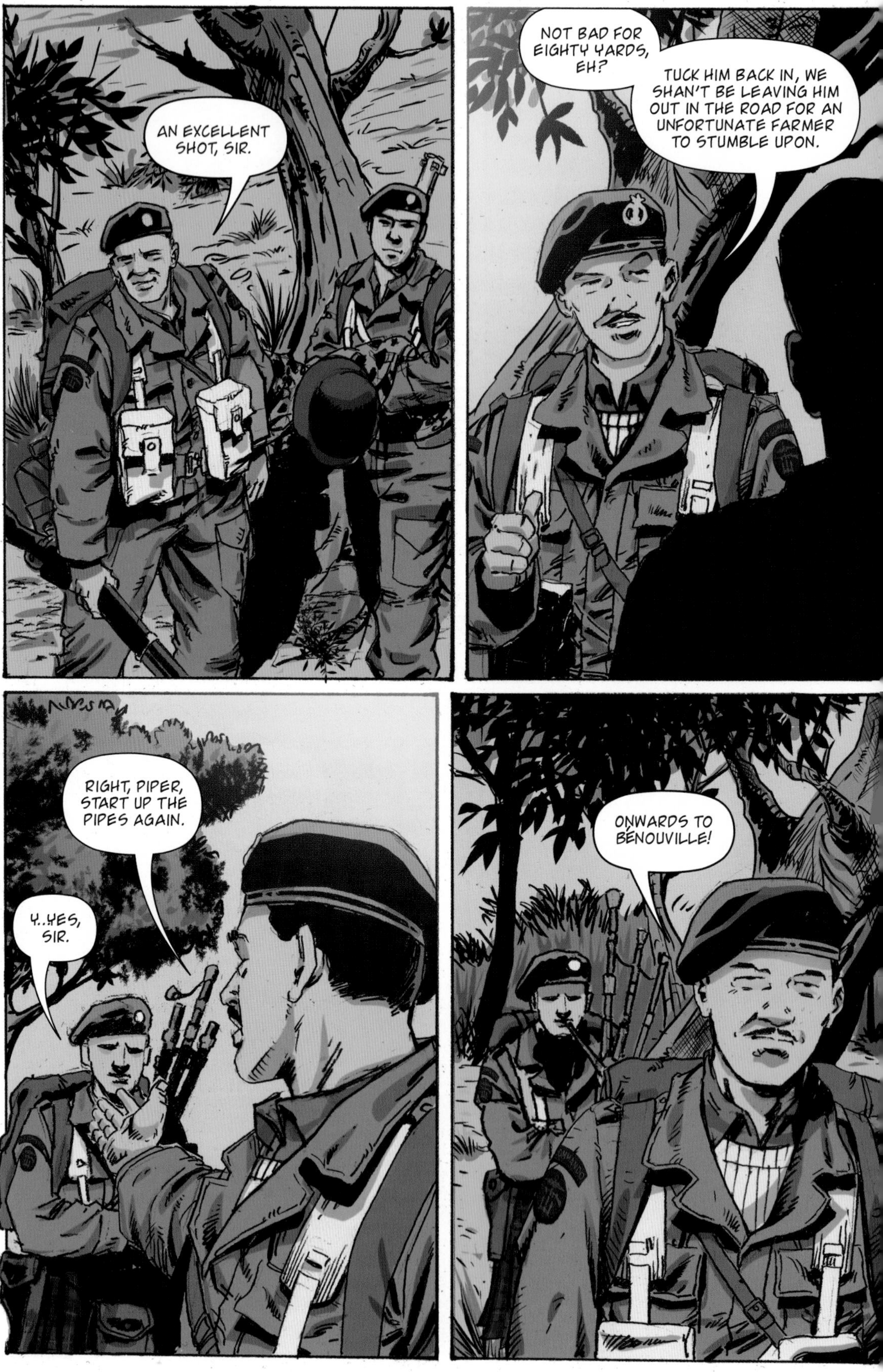
AN EXCELLENT SHOT, SIR.
NOT BAD FOR EIGHTY YARDS, EH?
TUCK HIM BACK IN, WE SHAN'T BE LEAVING HIM OUT IN THE ROAD FOR AN UNFORTUNATE FARMER TO STUMBLE UPON.
RIGHT, PIPER, START UP THE PIPES AGAIN.
Y..YES, SIR.
ONWARDS TO BÉNOUVILLE!

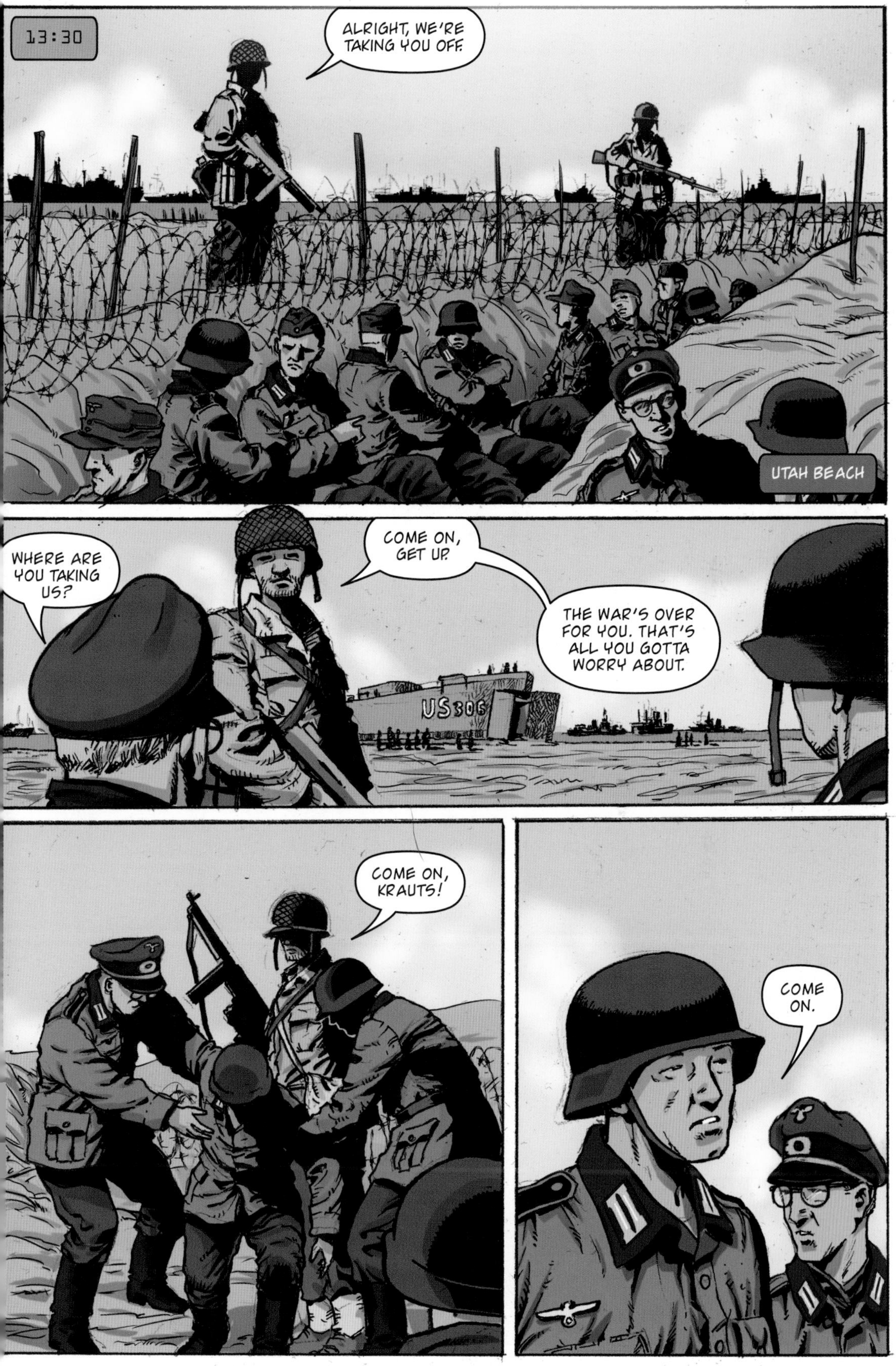
13:30
ALRIGHT, WE'RE TAKING YOU OFF.
UTAH BEACH
WHERE ARE YOU TAKING US?
COME ON, GET UP.
THE WAR'S OVER FOR YOU. THAT'S ALL YOU GOTTA WORRY ABOUT.
US306
COME ON, KRAUTS!
COME ON.

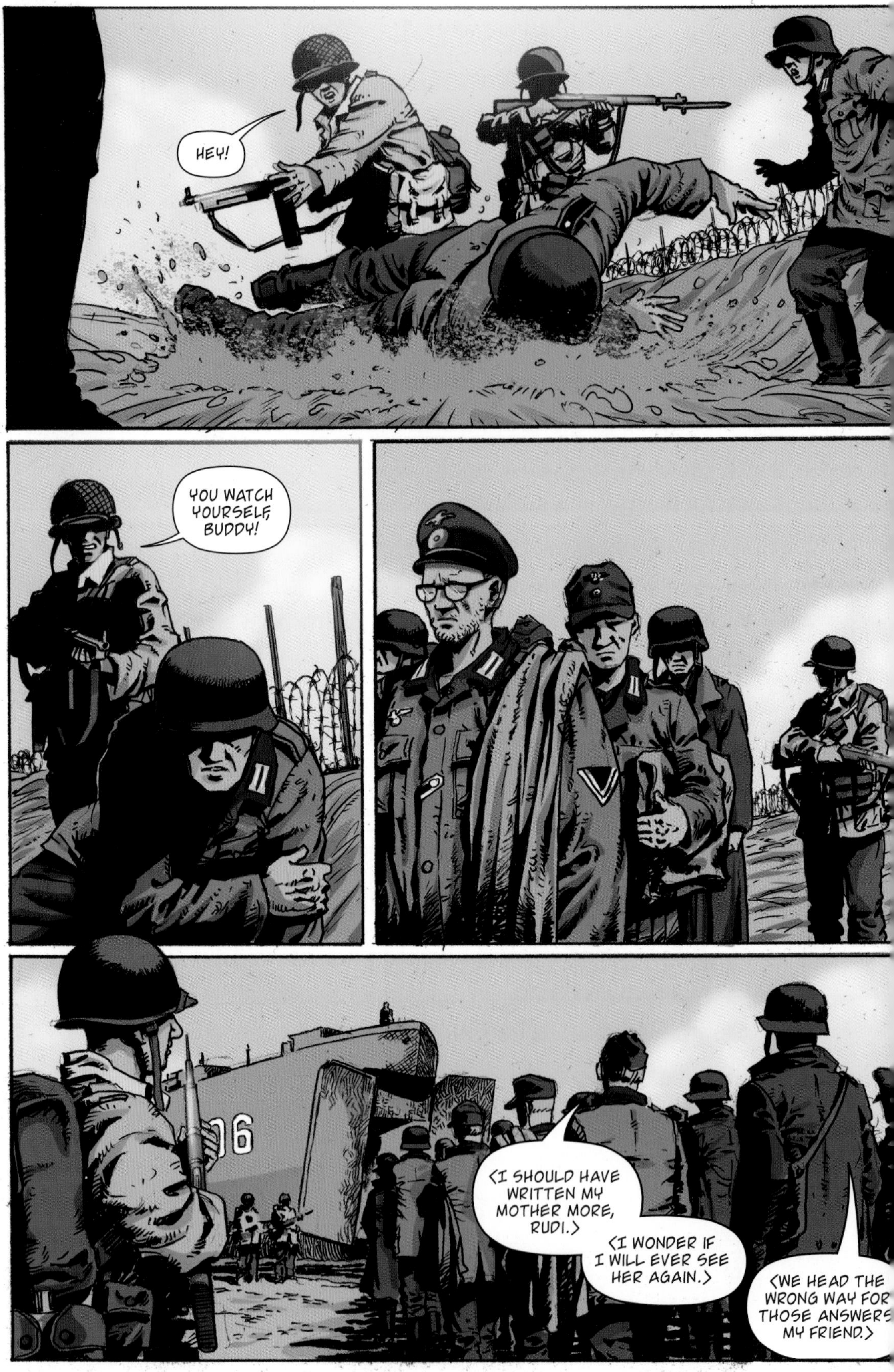
HEY!
YOU WATCH YOURSELF, BUDDY!
<I SHOULD HAVE WRITTEN MY MOTHER MORE, RUDI.>
<I WONDER IF I WILL EVER SEE HER AGAIN.>
<WE HEAD THE WRONG WAY FOR THOSE ANSWERS MY FRIEND.>

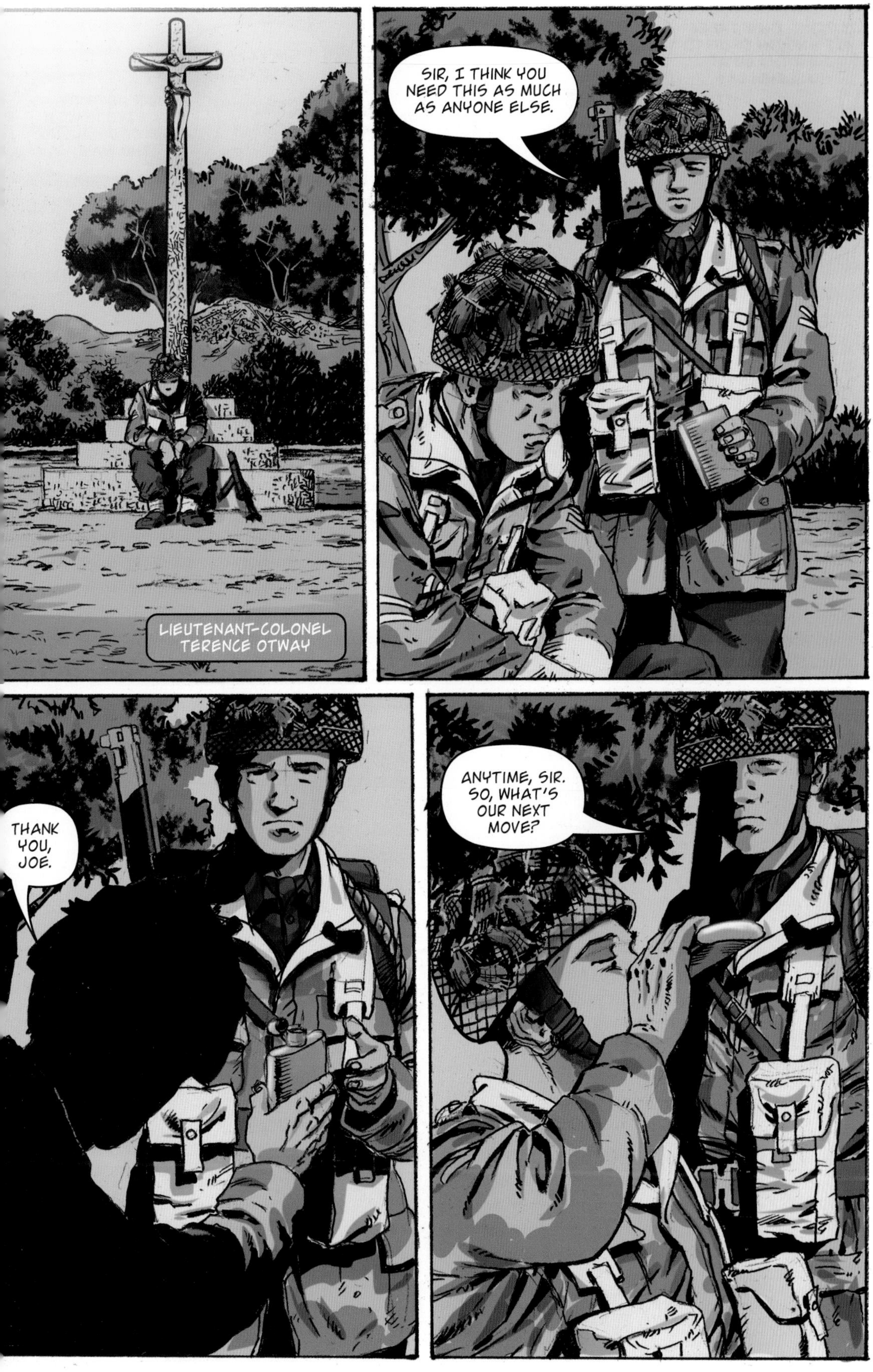
LIEUTENANT-COLONEL TERENCE OTWAY
SIR, I THINK YOU NEED THIS AS MUCH AS ANYONE ELSE.
THANK YOU, JOE.
ANYTIME, SIR. SO, WHAT'S OUR NEXT MOVE?

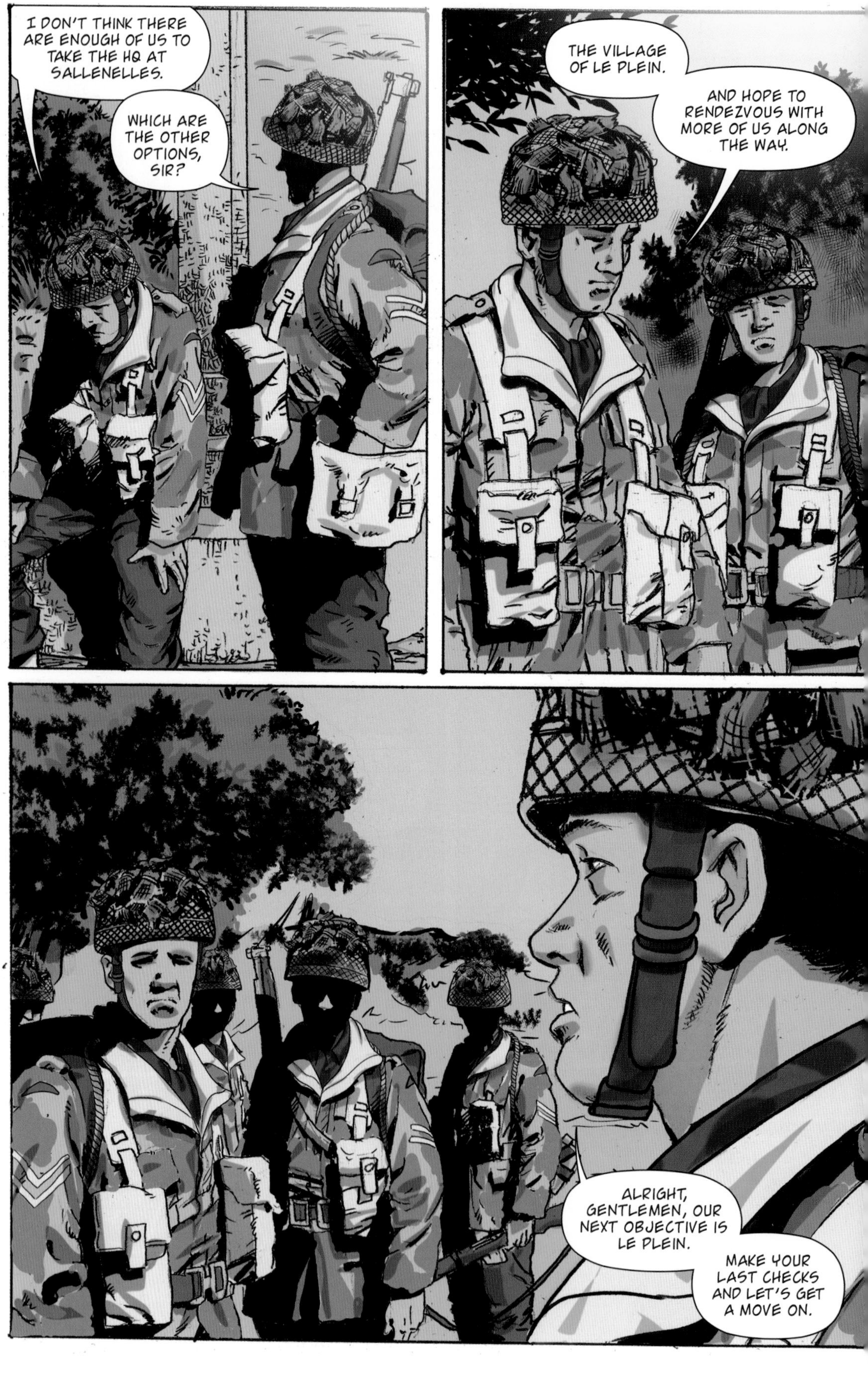
I DON'T THINK THERE ARE ENOUGH OF US TO TAKE THE HQ AT SALLENELLES.
WHICH ARE THE OTHER OPTIONS, SIR?
THE VILLAGE OF LE PLEIN.
AND HOPE TO RENDEZVOUS WITH MORE OF US ALONG THE WAY.
ALRIGHT, GENTLEMEN, OUR NEXT OBJECTIVE IS LE PLEIN.
MAKE YOUR LAST CHECKS AND LET'S GET A MOVE ON.

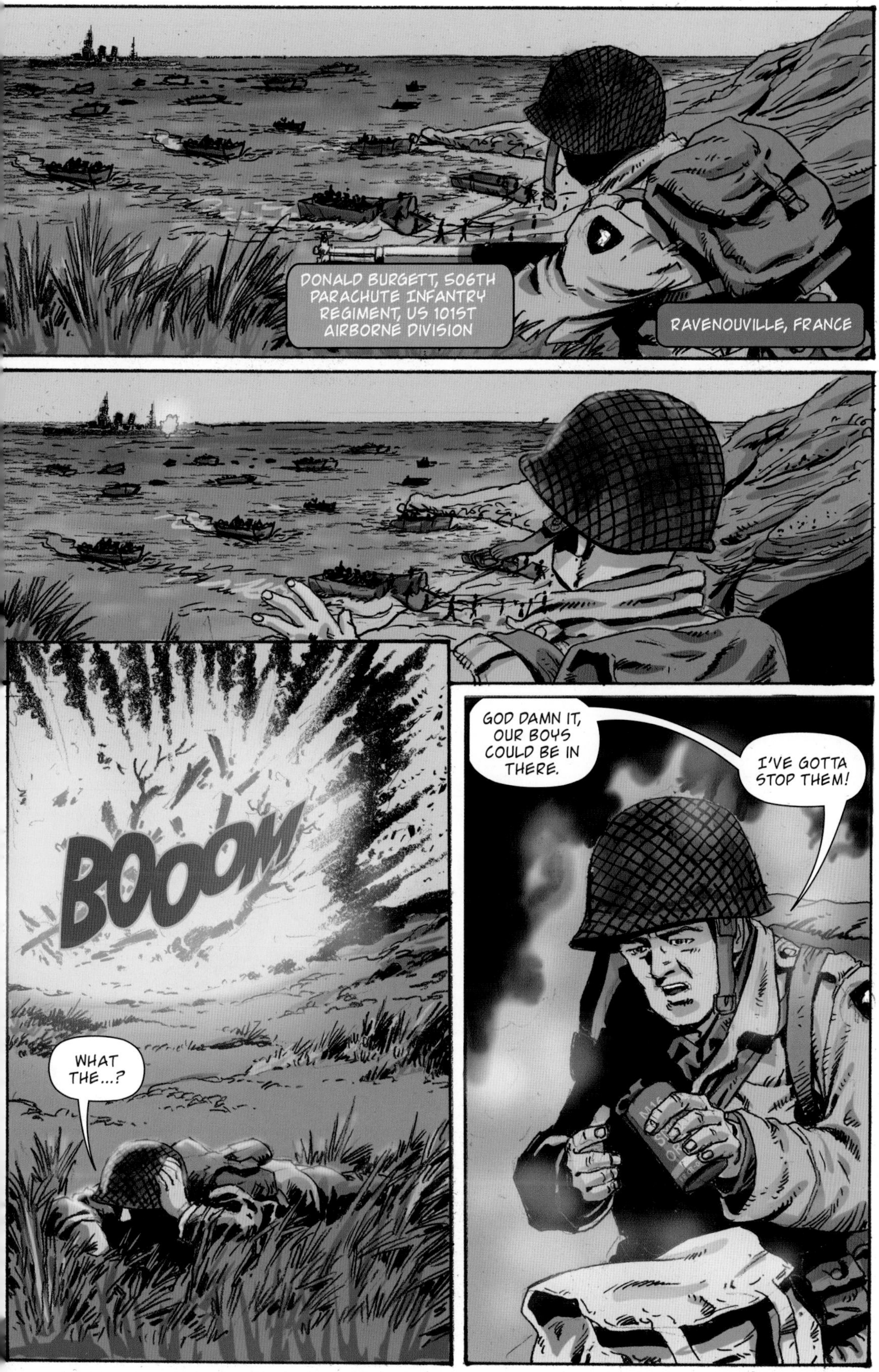

DONALD BURGETT, 506TH PARACHUTE INFANTRY REGIMENT, US 101ST AIRBORNE DIVISION
RAVENOUVILLE, FRANCE
BOOOM
WHAT THE...?
GOD DAMN IT, OUR BOYS COULD BE IN THERE.
I'VE GOTTA STOP THEM!

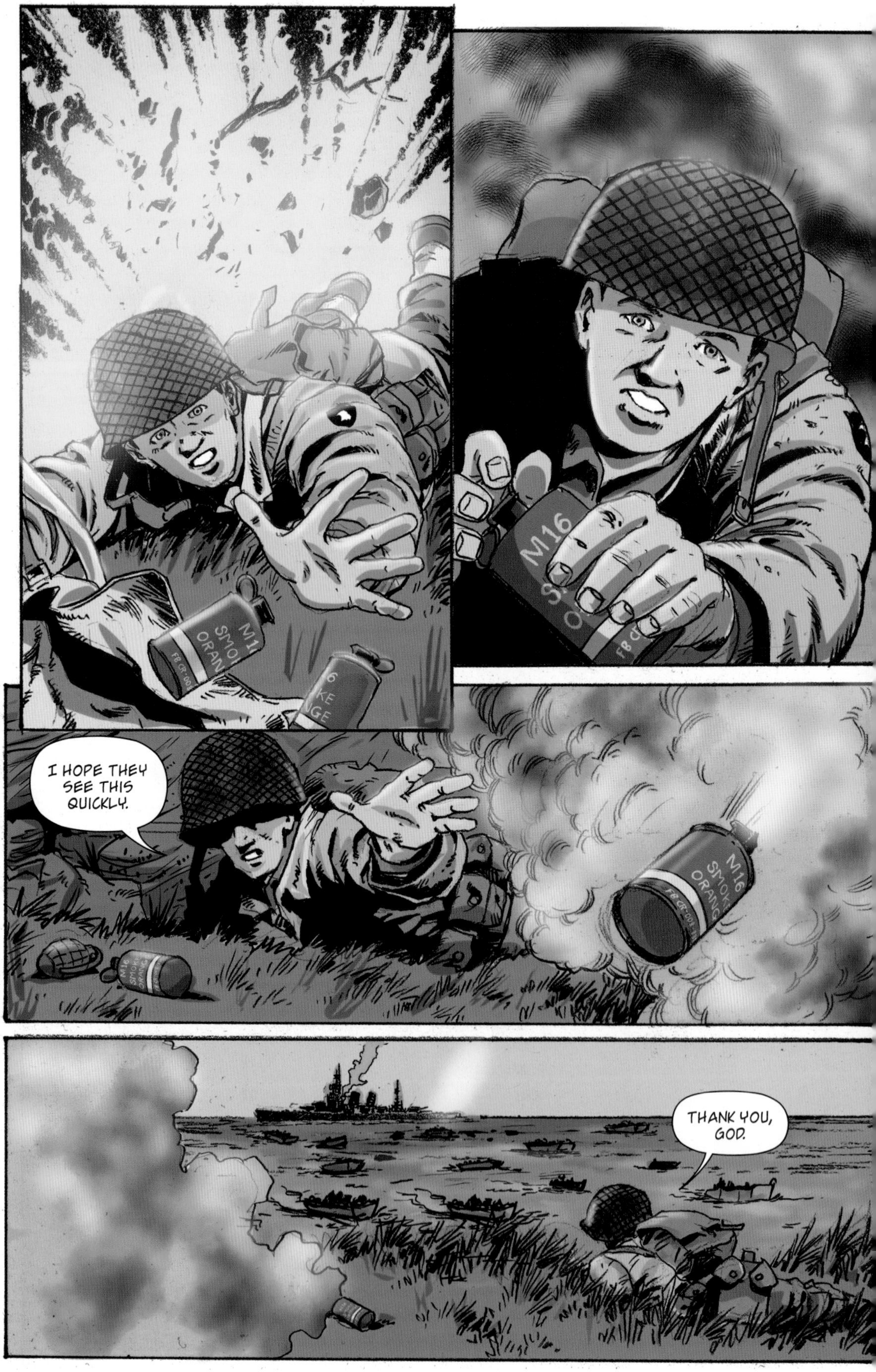
I HOPE THEY SEE THIS QUICKLY.
THANK YOU, GOD.

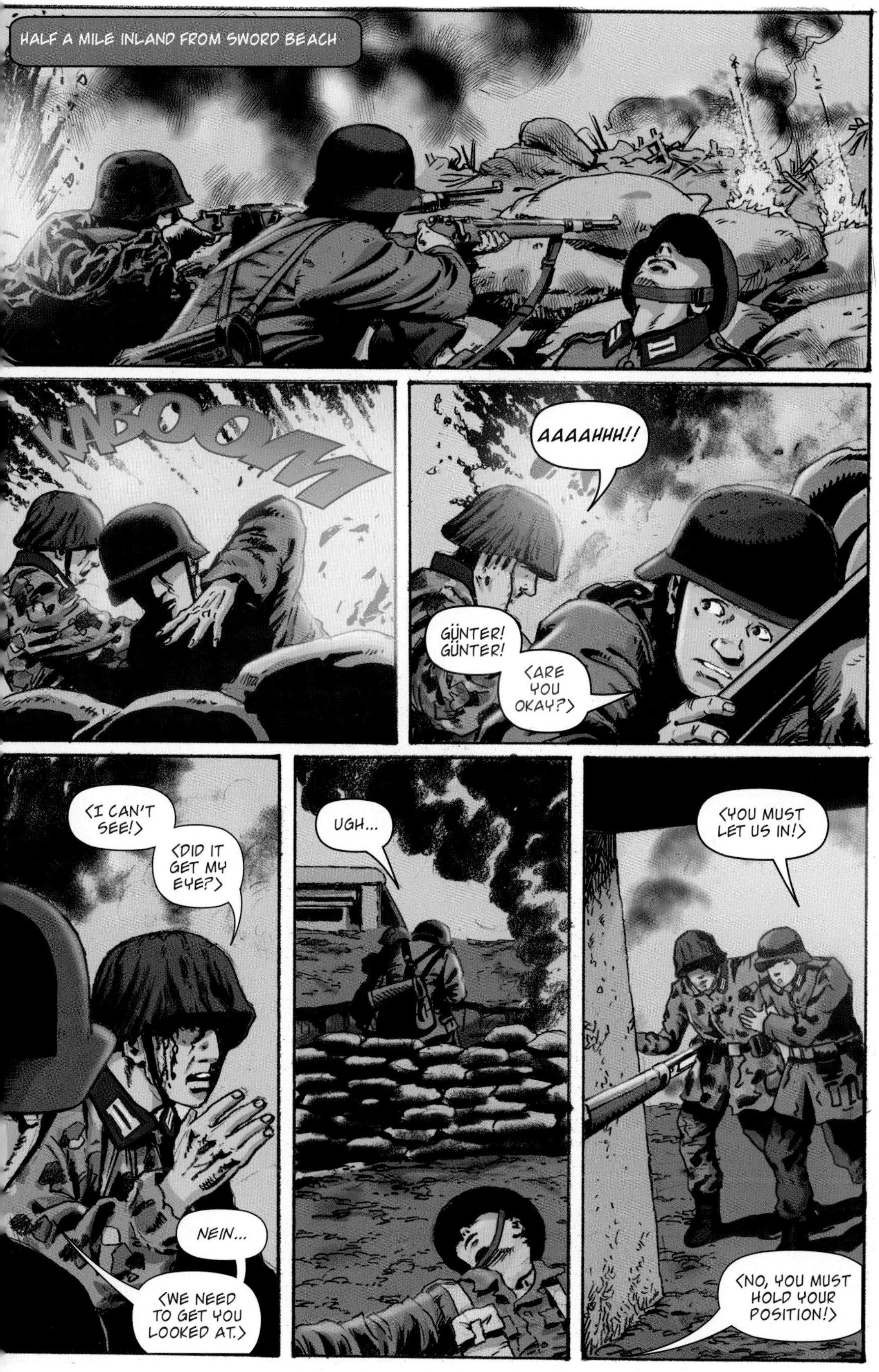
HALF A MILE INLAND FROM SWORD BEACH
KABOOM
AAAAHHH!!
GÜNTER! GÜNTER!
<ARE YOU OKAY?>
<I CAN'T SEE!>
<DID IT GET MY EYE?>
NEIN...
<WE NEED TO GET YOU LOOKED AT.>
UGH...
<YOU MUST LET US IN!>
<NO, YOU MUST HOLD YOUR POSITION!>

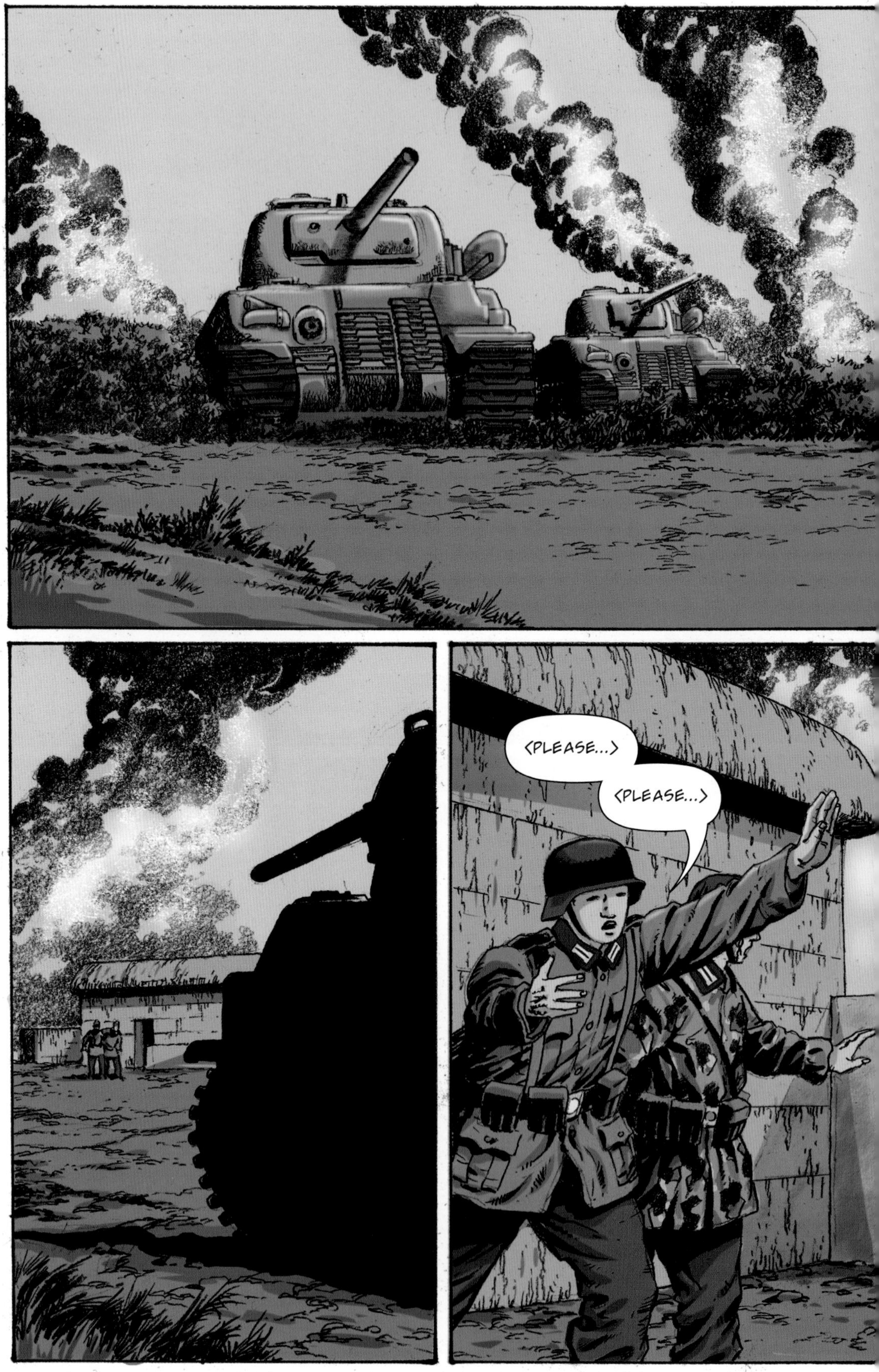
<PLEASE...>
<PLEASE...>

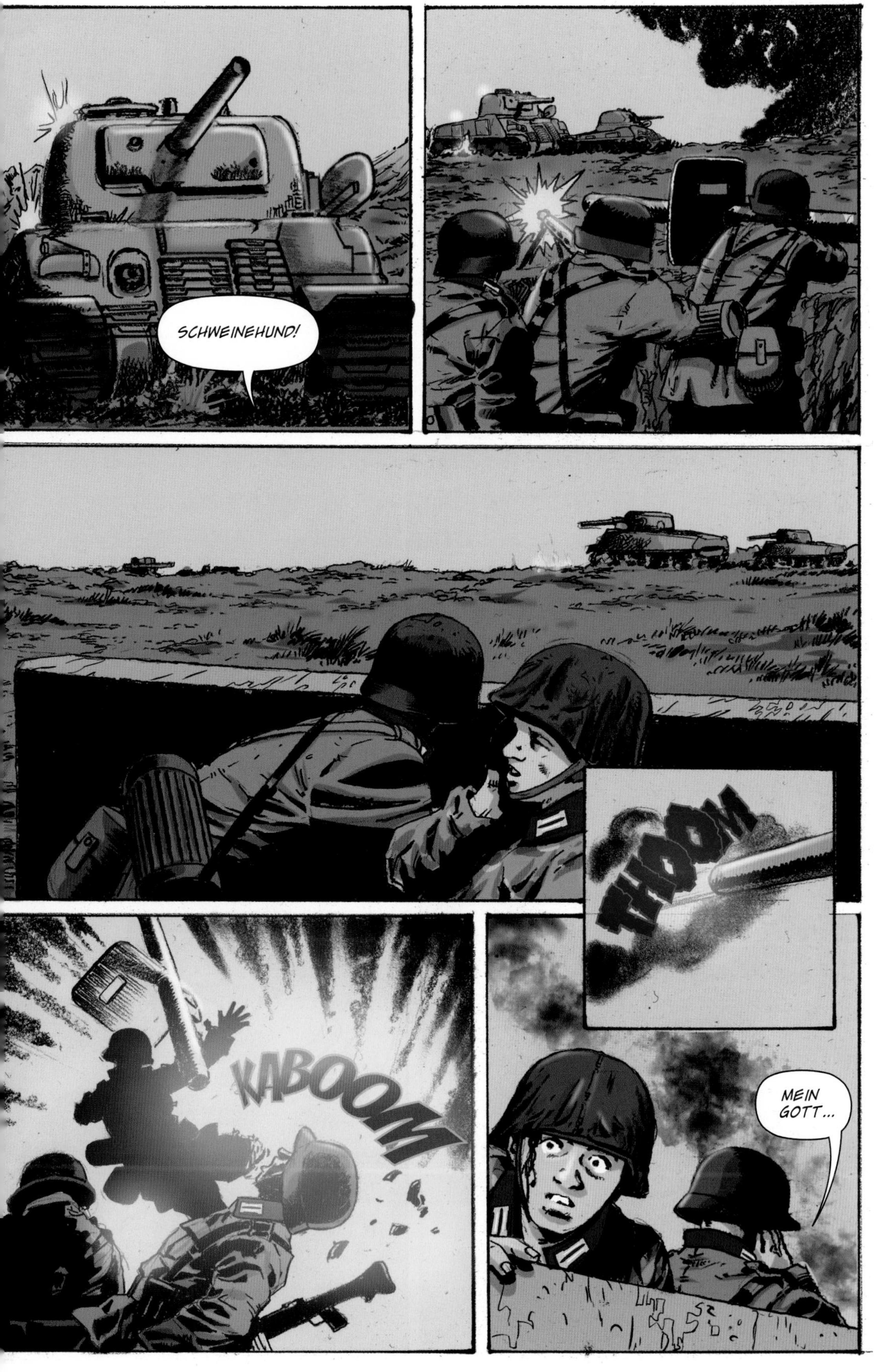
SCHWEINEHUND!
THOOM
KABOOM
MEIN GOTT...

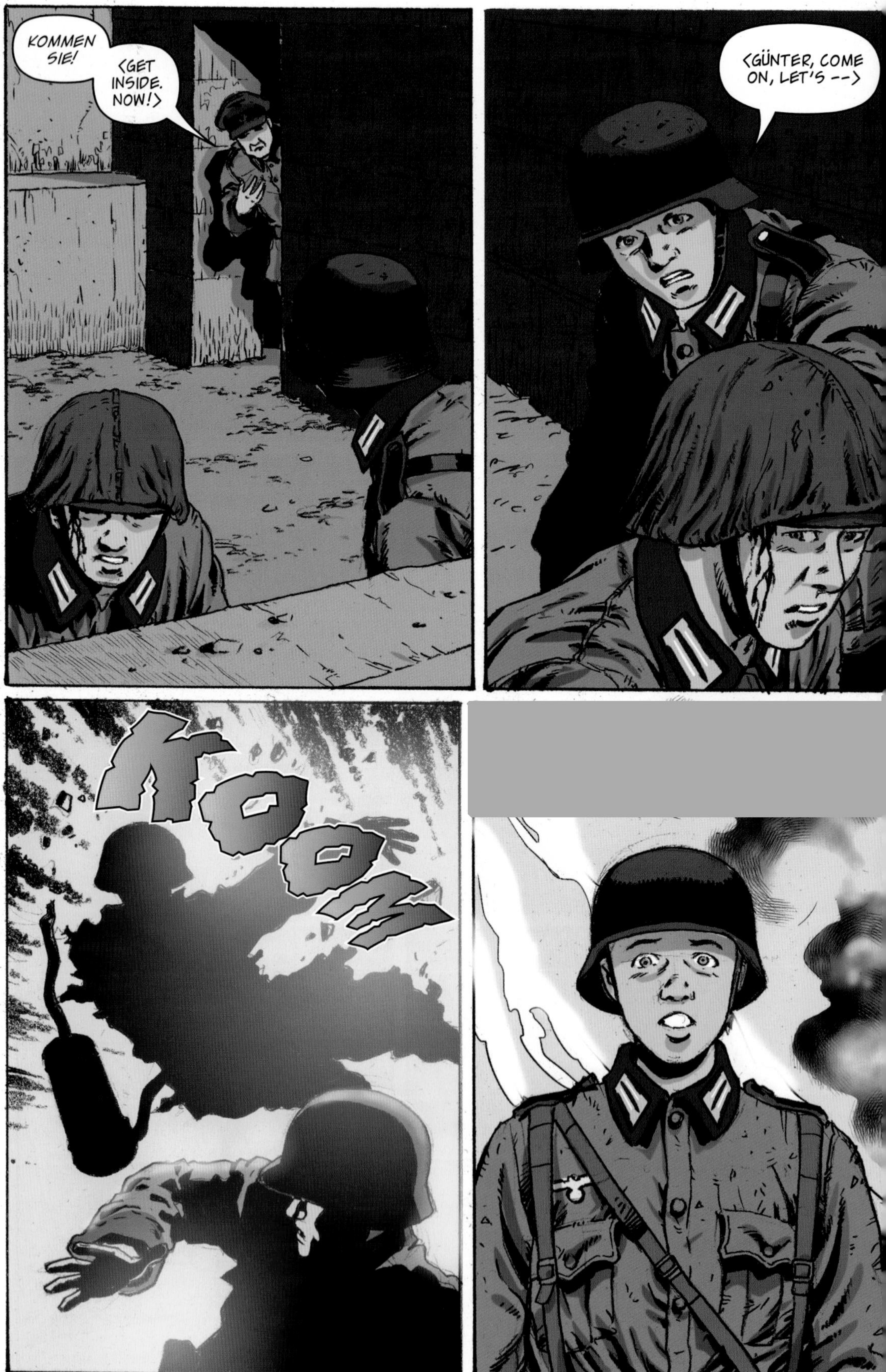
KOMMEN SIE!
<GET INSIDE. NOW!>
<GÜNTER, COME ON, LET'S -->
KRUMM

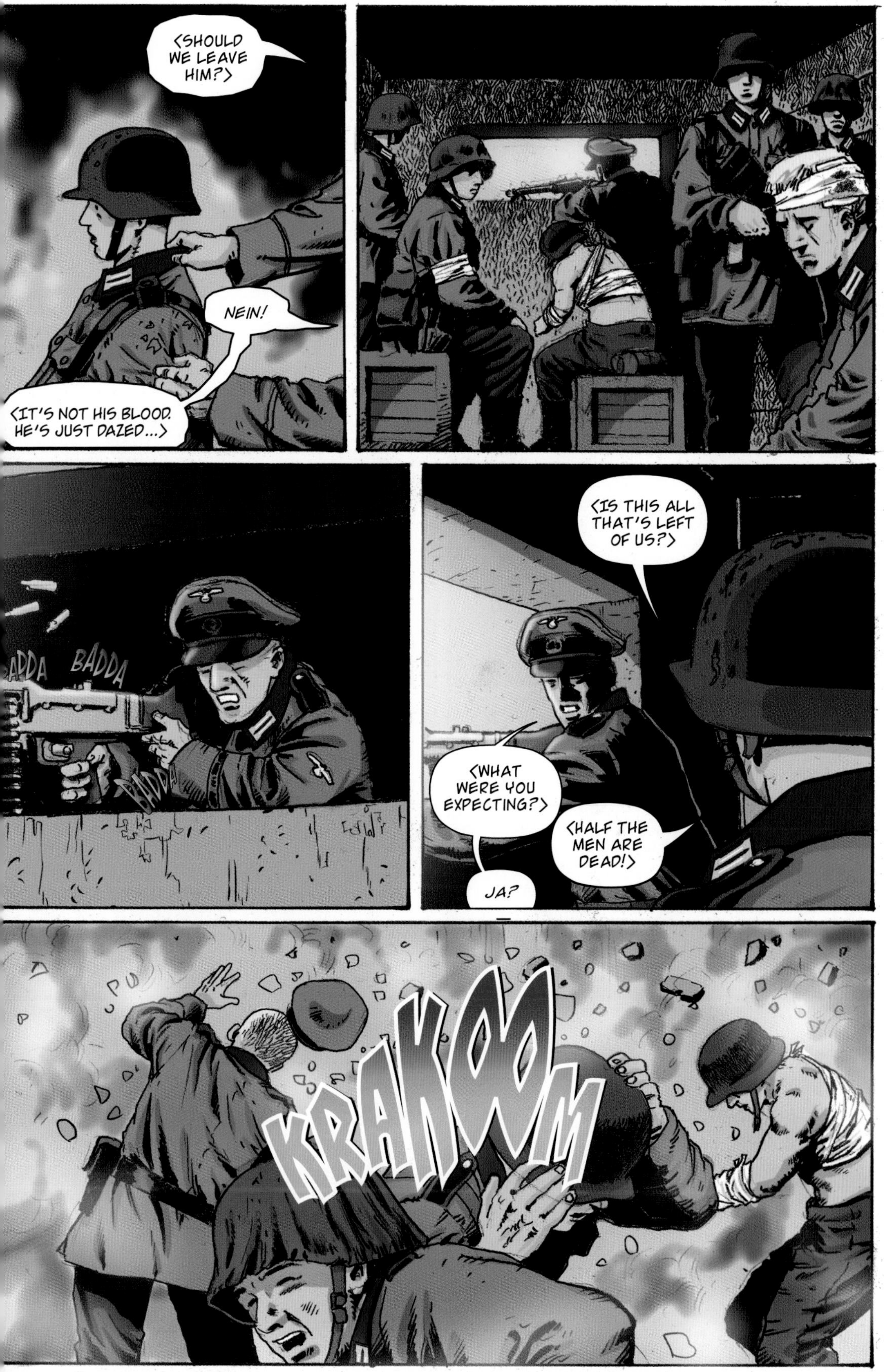
<SHOULD WE LEAVE HIM?>
NEIN!
<IT'S NOT HIS BLOOD. HE'S JUST DAZED...>
BADDA BADDA
BADDA
<IS THIS ALL THAT'S LEFT OF US?>
<WHAT WERE YOU EXPECTING?>
JA?
<HALF THE MEN ARE DEAD!>
KRAKOOM

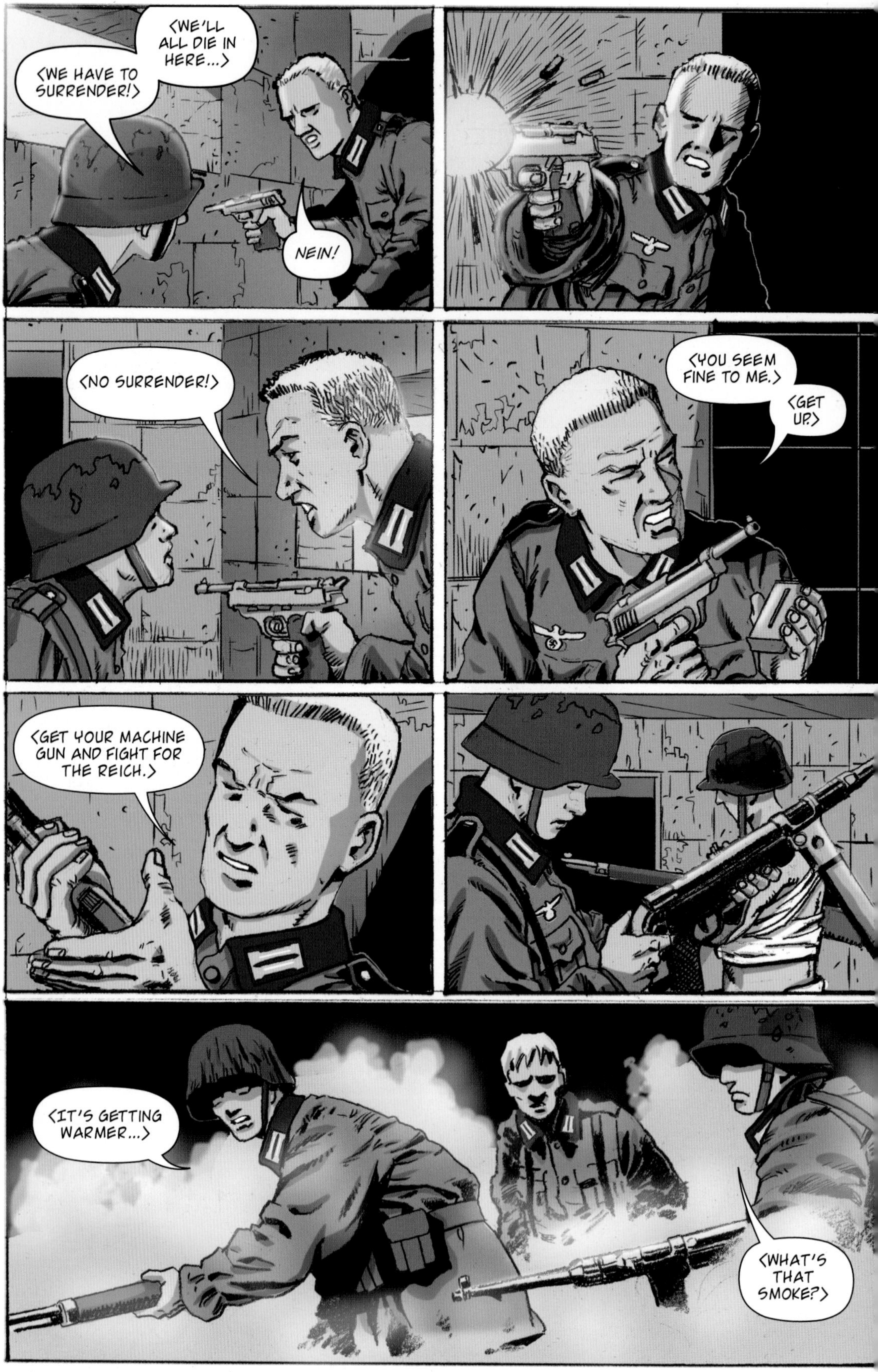
<WE HAVE TO SURRENDER!>
<WE'LL ALL DIE IN HERE...>
NEIN!
<NO SURRENDER!>
<YOU SEEM FINE TO ME.>
<GET UP.>
<GET YOUR MACHINE GUN AND FIGHT FOR THE REICH.>
<IT'S GETTING WARMER...>
<WHAT'S THAT SMOKE?>

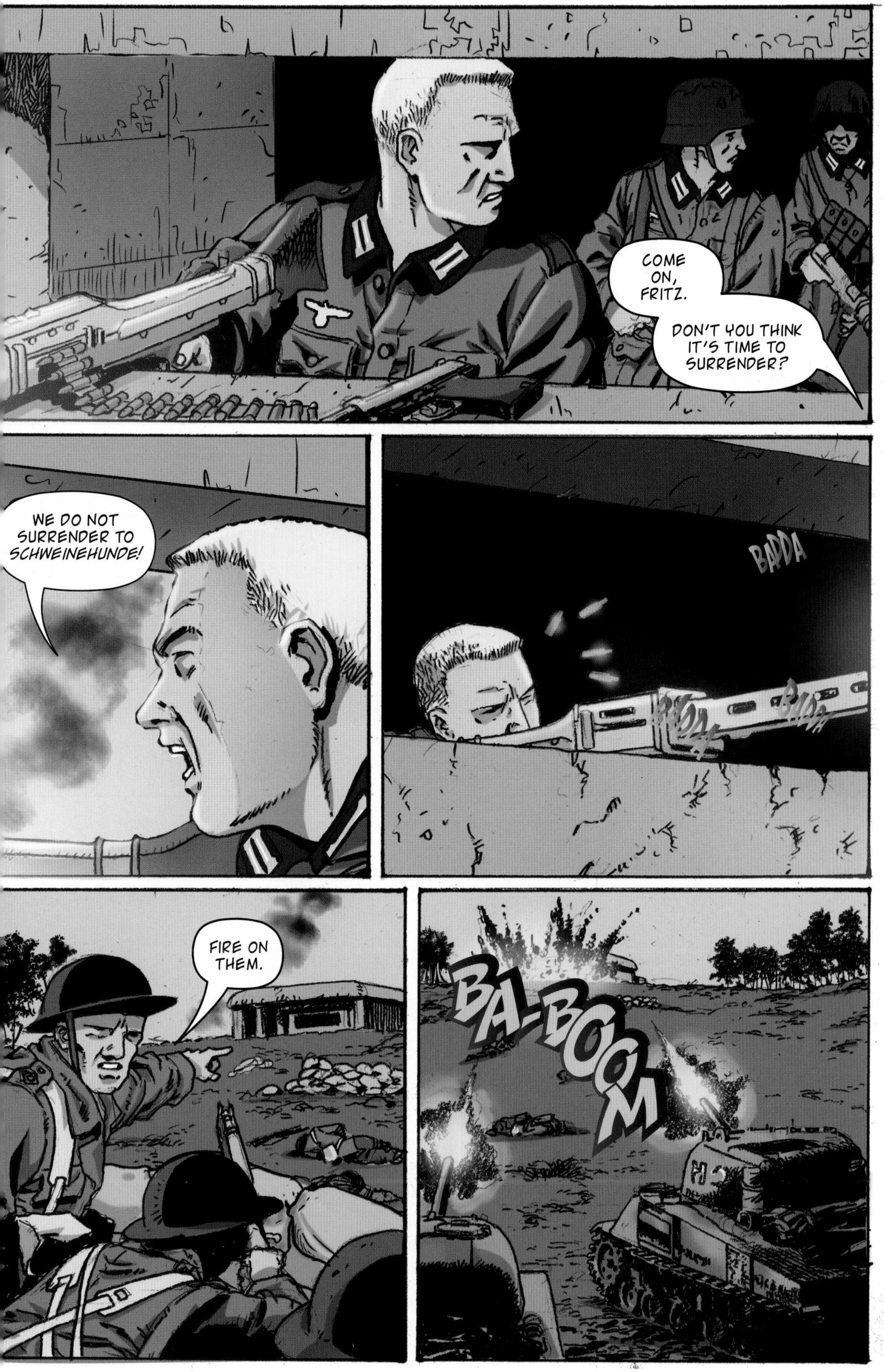

COME ON, FRITZ.
DON'T YOU THINK IT'S TIME TO SURRENDER?
WE DO NOT SURRENDER TO SCHWEINEHUNDE!
BADDA
BADDA
BADDA
FIRE ON THEM.
BA-BOOM

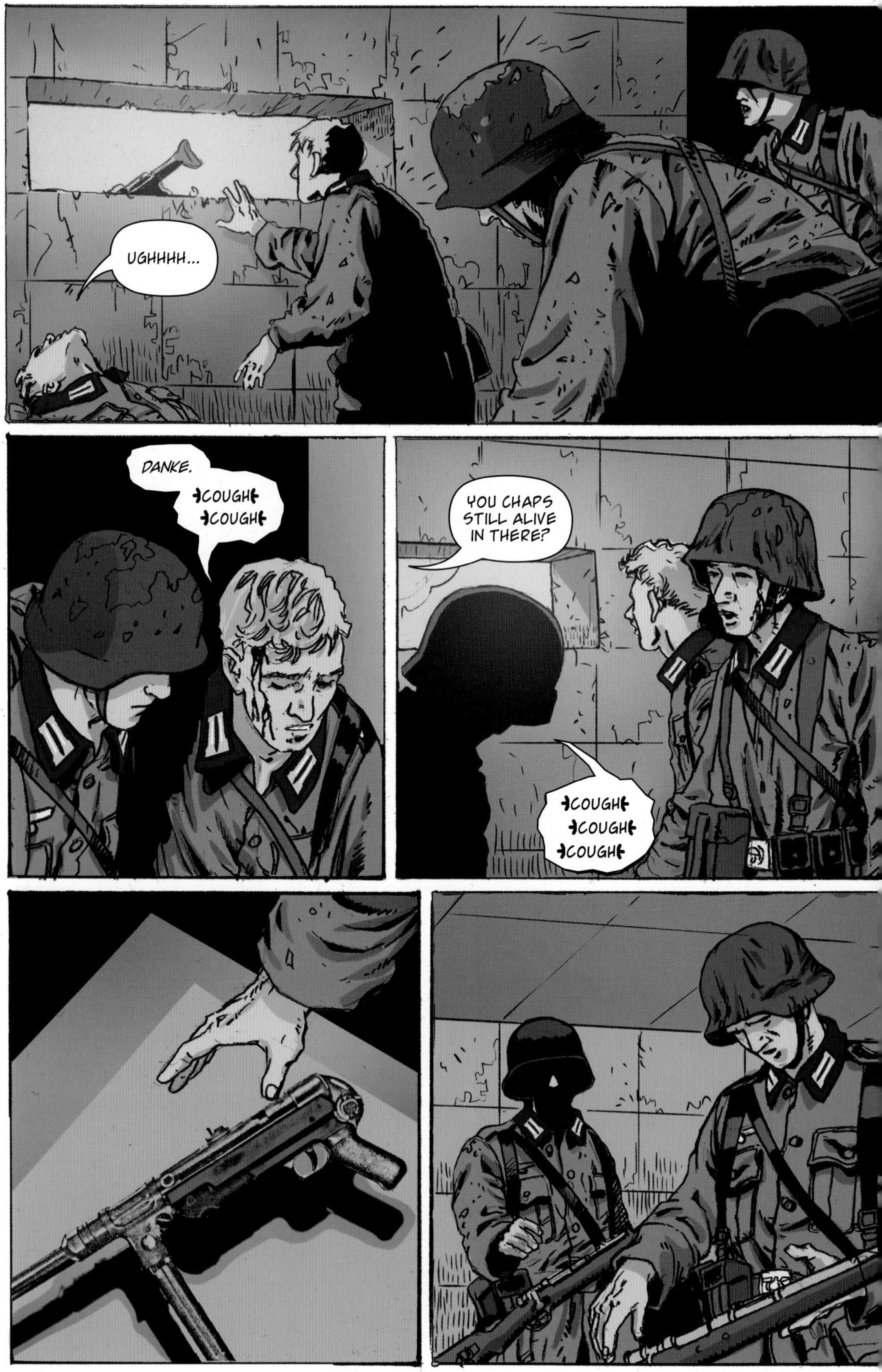
UGHHHH...
DANKE. *COUGH* *COUGH*
YOU CHAPS STILL ALIVE IN THERE?
COUGH *COUGH* *COUGH*

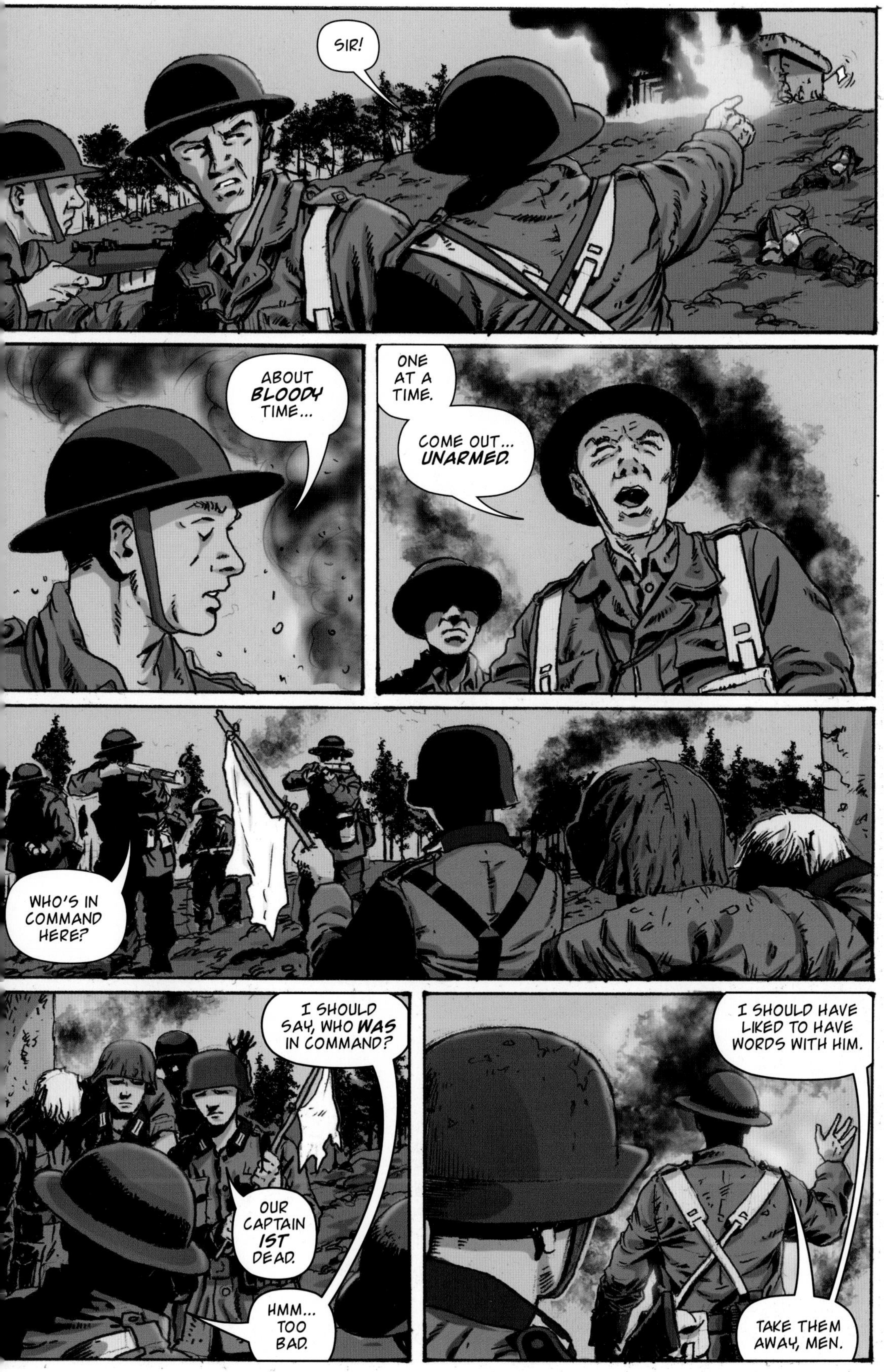
SIR!
ABOUT BLOODY TIME...
ONE AT A TIME.
COME OUT... UNARMED.
WHO'S IN COMMAND HERE?
I SHOULD SAY, WHO WAS IN COMMAND?
OUR CAPTAIN IST DEAD.
HMM... TOO BAD.
I SHOULD HAVE LIKED TO HAVE WORDS WITH HIM.
TAKE THEM AWAY, MEN.

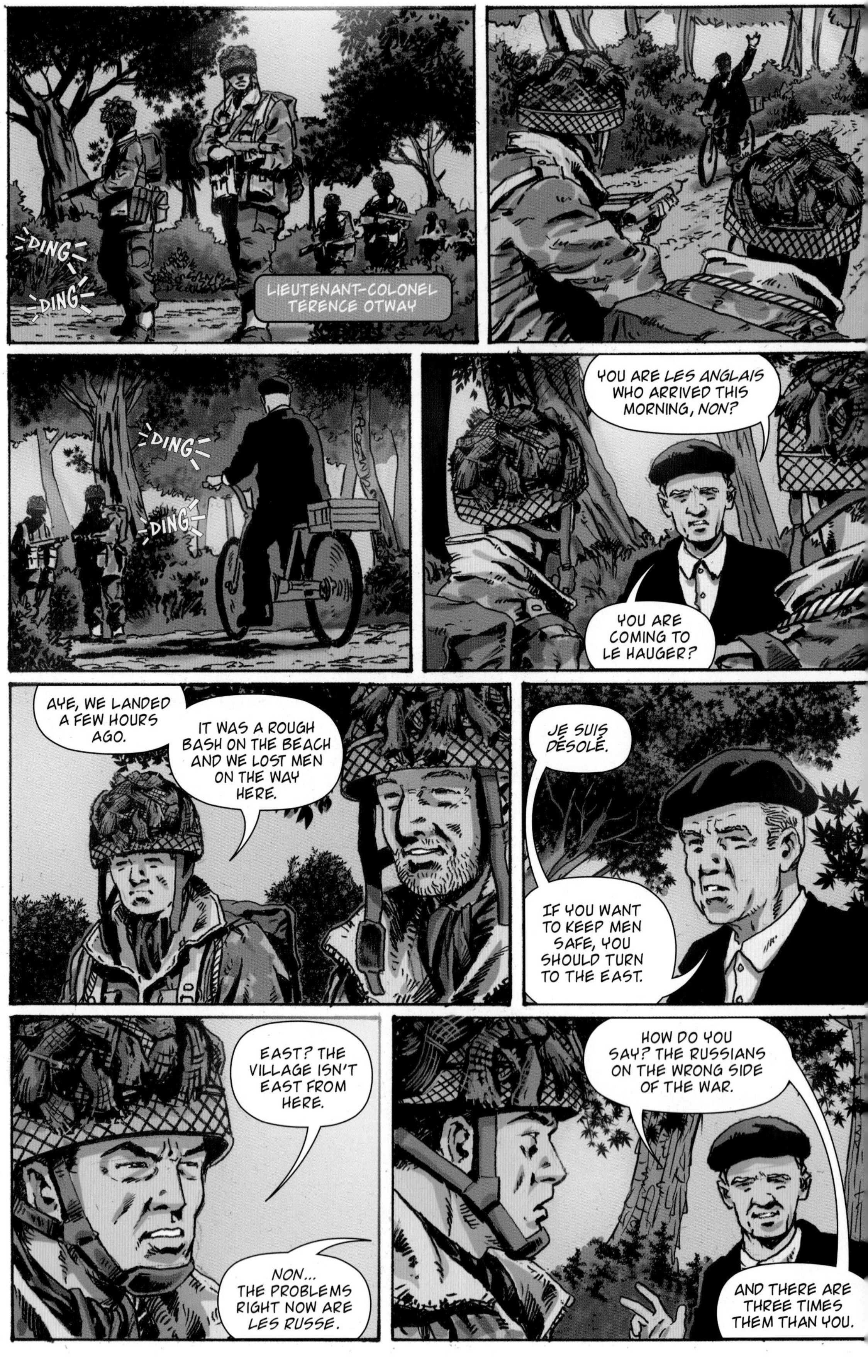
DING
DING
LIEUTENANT-COLONEL TERENCE OTWAY
DING
DING
YOU ARE *LES ANGLAIS* WHO ARRIVED THIS MORNING, *NON?*
YOU ARE COMING TO LE HAUGER?
AYE, WE LANDED A FEW HOURS AGO.
IT WAS A ROUGH BASH ON THE BEACH AND WE LOST MEN ON THE WAY HERE.
JE SUIS DÉSOLÉ.
IF YOU WANT TO KEEP MEN SAFE, YOU SHOULD TURN TO THE EAST.
EAST? THE VILLAGE ISN'T EAST FROM HERE.
NON... THE PROBLEMS RIGHT NOW ARE *LES RUSSE.*
HOW DO YOU SAY? THE RUSSIANS ON THE WRONG SIDE OF THE WAR.
AND THERE ARE THREE TIMES THEM THAN YOU.

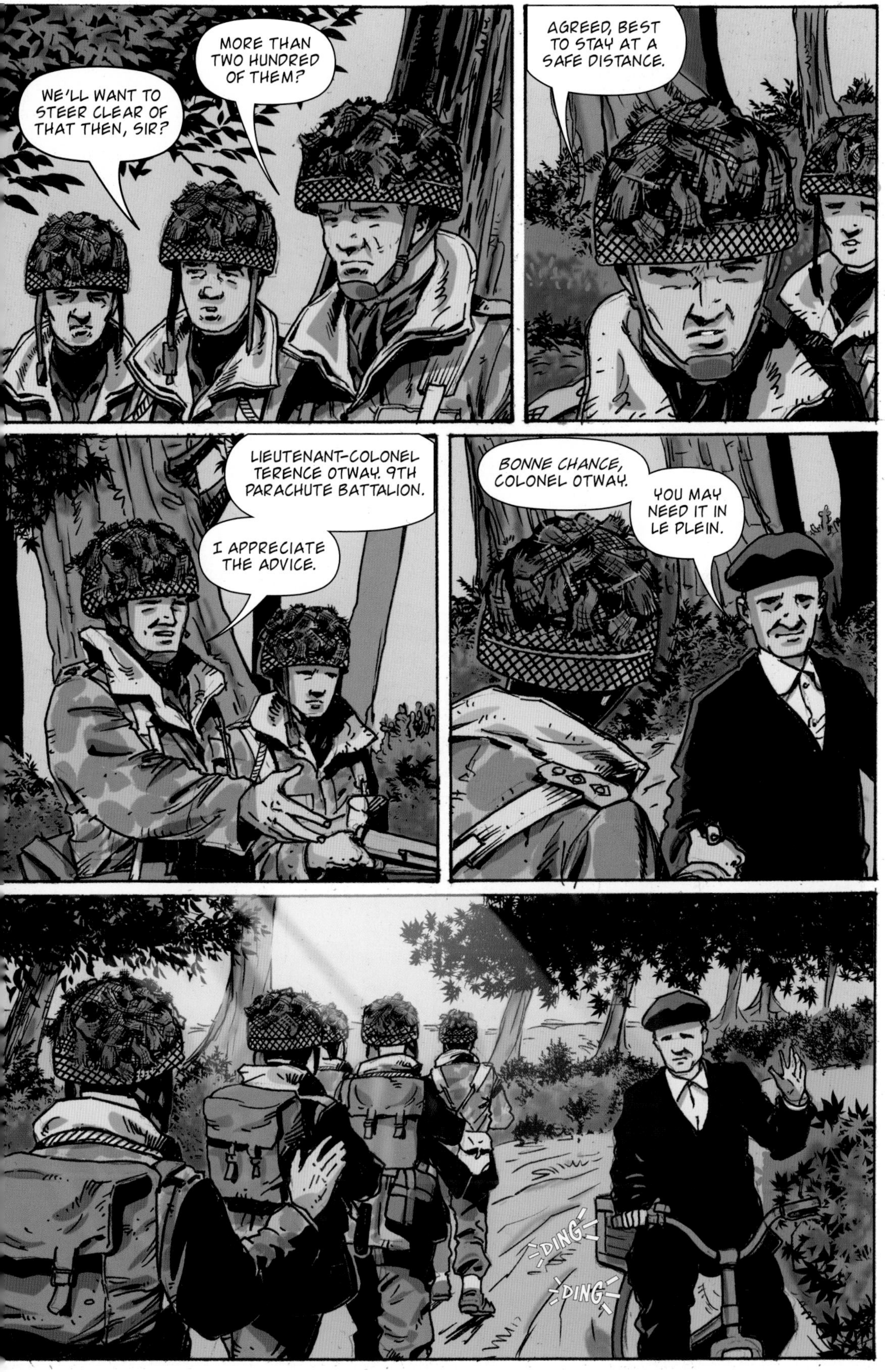
WE'LL WANT TO STEER CLEAR OF THAT THEN, SIR?
MORE THAN TWO HUNDRED OF THEM?
AGREED, BEST TO STAY AT A SAFE DISTANCE.
LIEUTENANT-COLONEL TERENCE OTWAY. 9TH PARACHUTE BATTALION.
I APPRECIATE THE ADVICE.
BONNE CHANCE, COLONEL OTWAY.
YOU MAY NEED IT IN LE PLEIN.
DING
DING

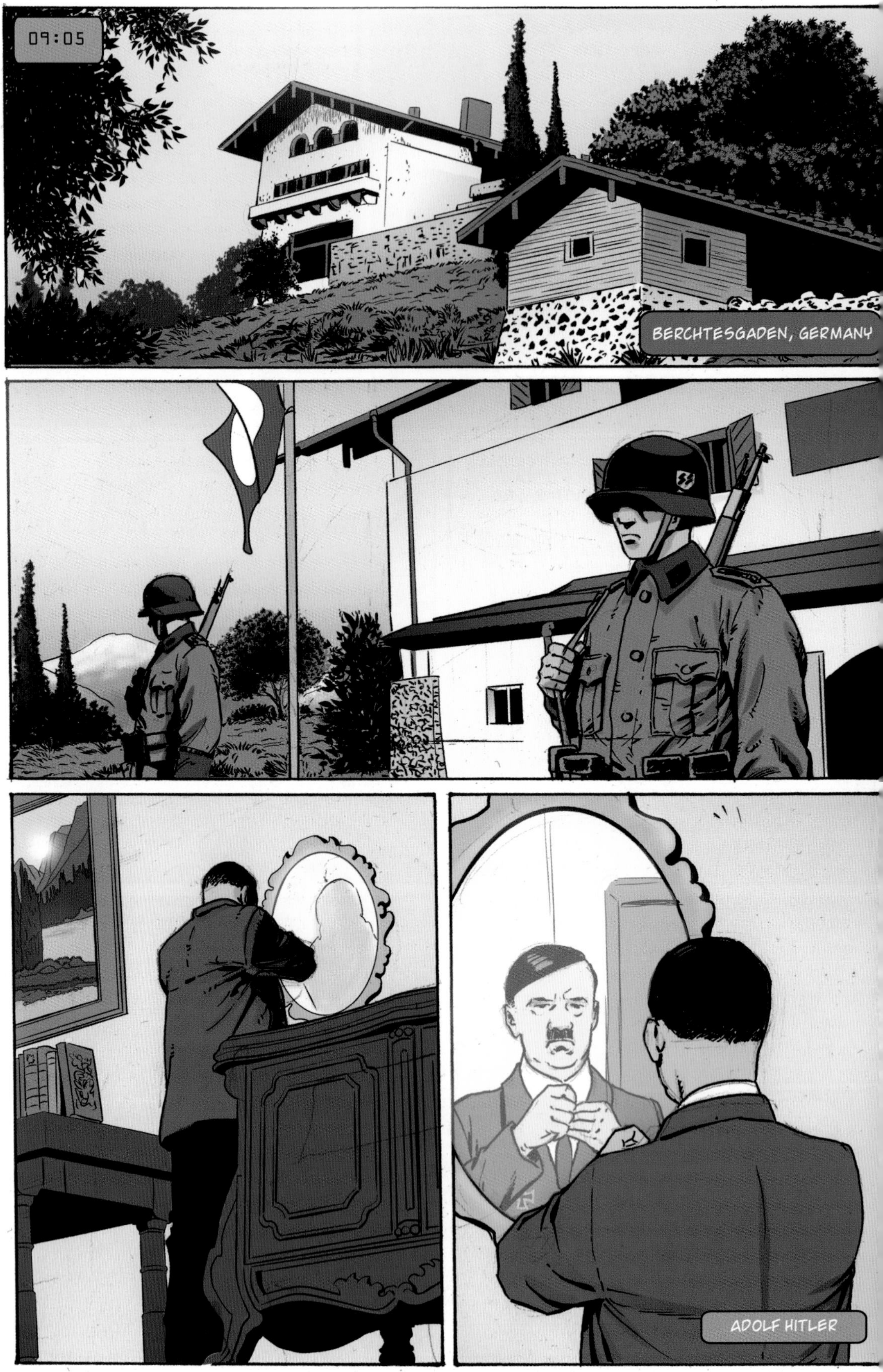
09:05
BERCHTESGADEN, GERMANY
ADOLF HITLER

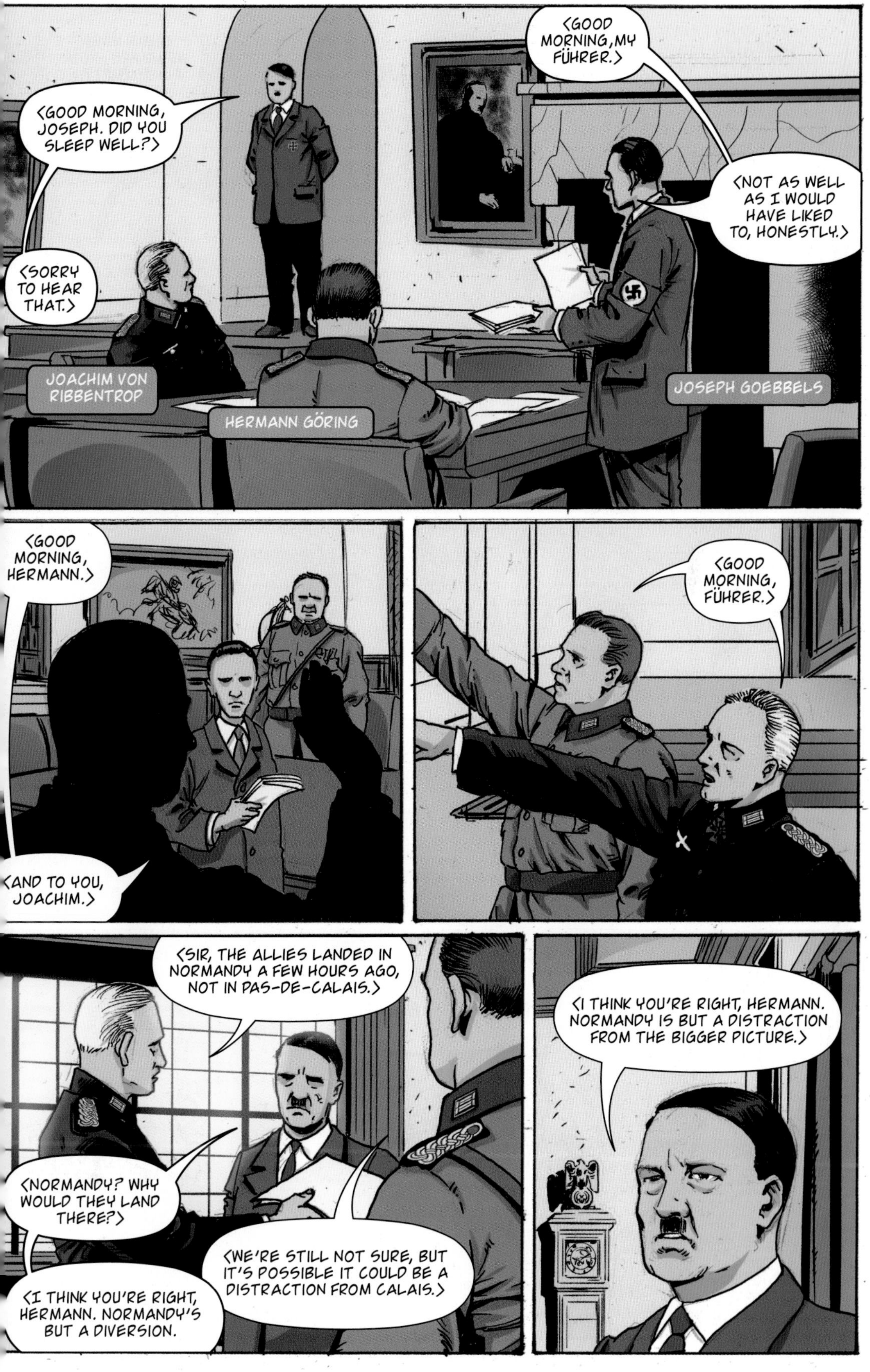
<GOOD MORNING, MY FÜHRER.>
<GOOD MORNING, JOSEPH. DID YOU SLEEP WELL?>
<NOT AS WELL AS I WOULD HAVE LIKED TO, HONESTLY.>
<SORRY TO HEAR THAT.>
JOACHIM VON RIBBENTROP
HERMANN GÖRING
JOSEPH GOEBBELS
<GOOD MORNING, HERMANN.>
<AND TO YOU, JOACHIM.>
<GOOD MORNING, FÜHRER.>
<SIR, THE ALLIES LANDED IN NORMANDY A FEW HOURS AGO, NOT IN PAS-DE-CALAIS.>
<NORMANDY? WHY WOULD THEY LAND THERE?>
<WE'RE STILL NOT SURE, BUT IT'S POSSIBLE IT COULD BE A DISTRACTION FROM CALAIS.>
<I THINK YOU'RE RIGHT, HERMANN. NORMANDY'S BUT A DIVERSION.
<I THINK YOU'RE RIGHT, HERMANN. NORMANDY IS BUT A DISTRACTION FROM THE BIGGER PICTURE.>

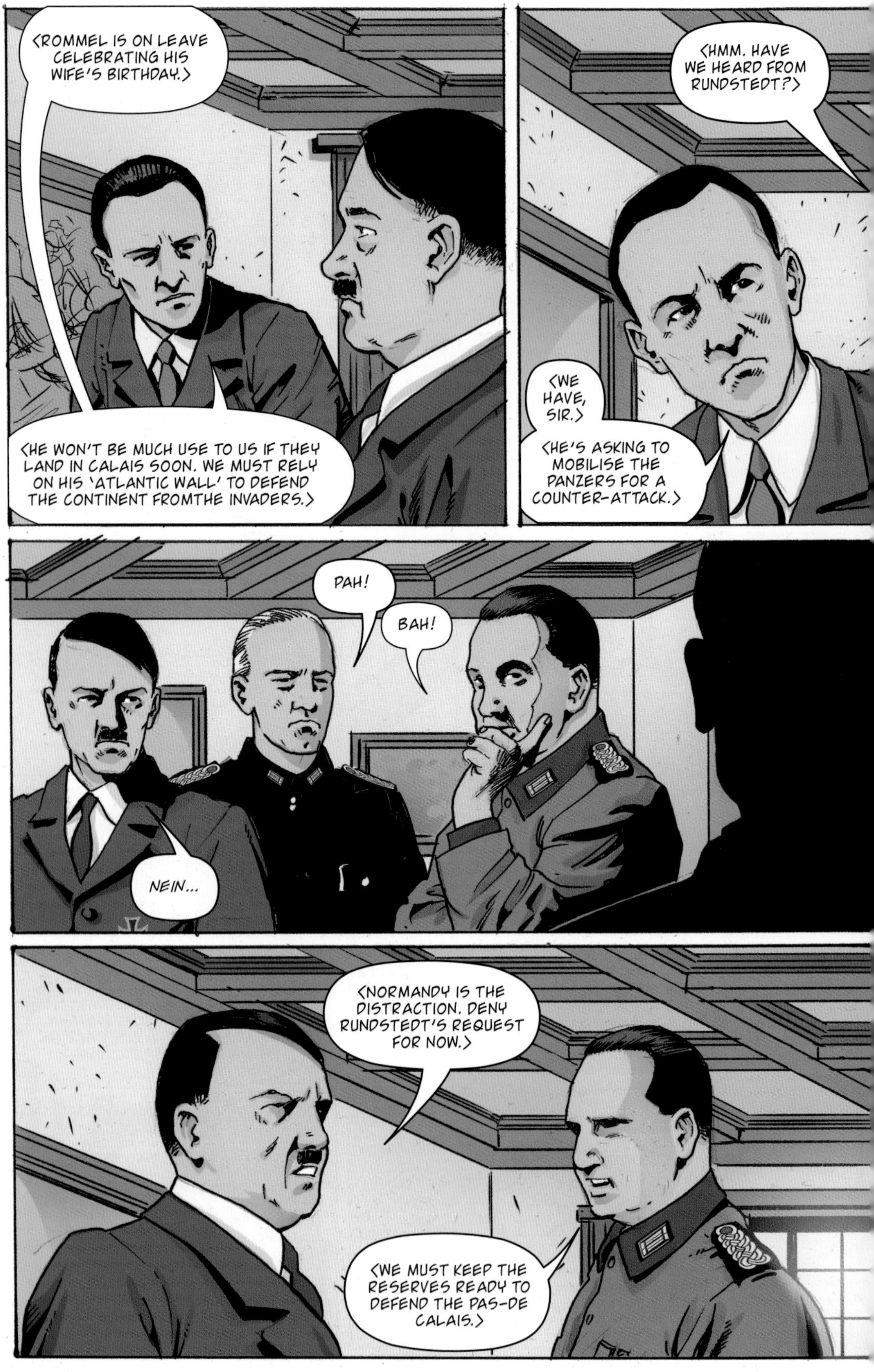
<ROMMEL IS ON LEAVE CELEBRATING HIS WIFE'S BIRTHDAY.>
<HE WON'T BE MUCH USE TO US IF THEY LAND IN CALAIS SOON. WE MUST RELY ON HIS 'ATLANTIC WALL' TO DEFEND THE CONTINENT FROMTHE INVADERS.>
<HMM. HAVE WE HEARD FROM RUNDSTEDT?>
<WE HAVE, SIR.>
<HE'S ASKING TO MOBILISE THE PANZERS FOR A COUNTER-ATTACK.>
PAH!
BAH!
NEIN...
<NORMANDY IS THE DISTRACTION. DENY RUNDSTEDT'S REQUEST FOR NOW.>
<WE MUST KEEP THE RESERVES READY TO DEFEND THE PAS-DE CALAIS.>

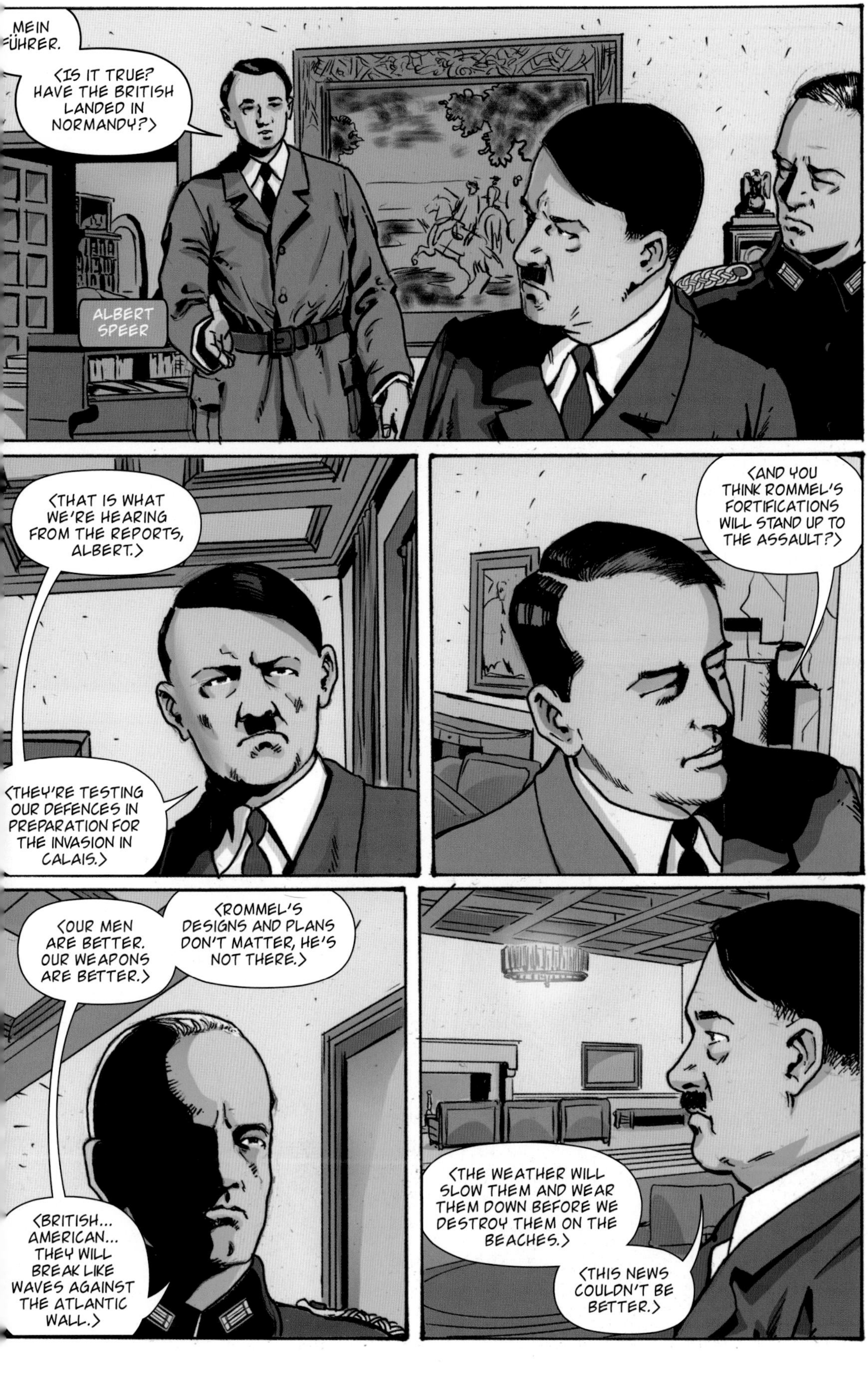

MEIN FÜHRER.
<IS IT TRUE? HAVE THE BRITISH LANDED IN NORMANDY?>
ALBERT SPEER
<THAT IS WHAT WE'RE HEARING FROM THE REPORTS, ALBERT.>
<THEY'RE TESTING OUR DEFENCES IN PREPARATION FOR THE INVASION IN CALAIS.>
<AND YOU THINK ROMMEL'S FORTIFICATIONS WILL STAND UP TO THE ASSAULT?>
<OUR MEN ARE BETTER. OUR WEAPONS ARE BETTER.>
<ROMMEL'S DESIGNS AND PLANS DON'T MATTER, HE'S NOT THERE.>
<BRITISH... AMERICAN... THEY WILL BREAK LIKE WAVES AGAINST THE ATLANTIC WALL.>
<THE WEATHER WILL SLOW THEM AND WEAR THEM DOWN BEFORE WE DESTROY THEM ON THE BEACHES.>
<THIS NEWS COULDN'T BE BETTER.>

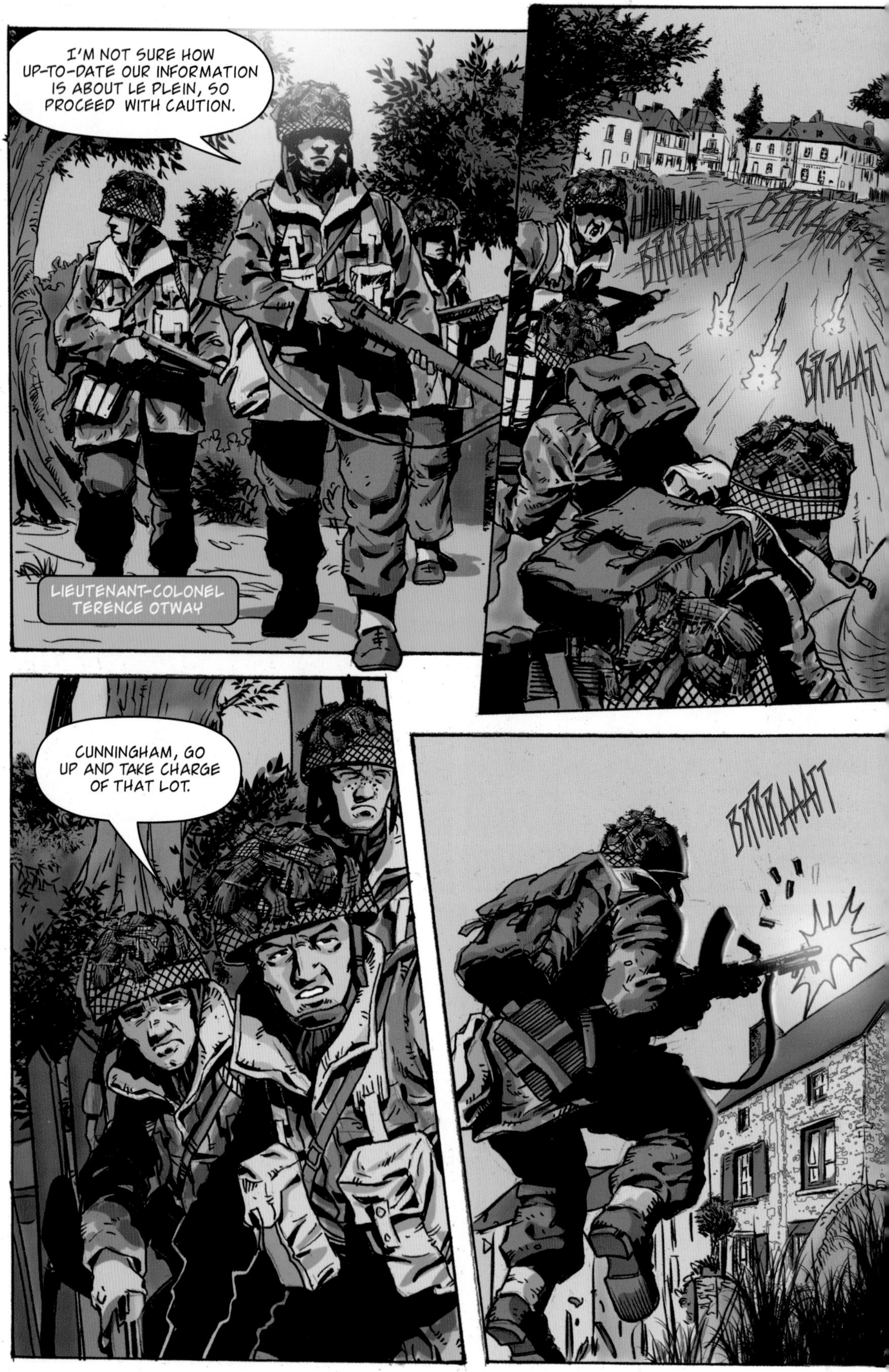
I'M NOT SURE HOW UP-TO-DATE OUR INFORMATION IS ABOUT LE PLEIN, SO PROCEED WITH CAUTION.
LIEUTENANT-COLONEL TERENCE OTWAY
BRRRAAAT
BRRRAAAT
BRRAAT
CUNNINGHAM, GO UP AND TAKE CHARGE OF THAT LOT.
BRRRAAAT

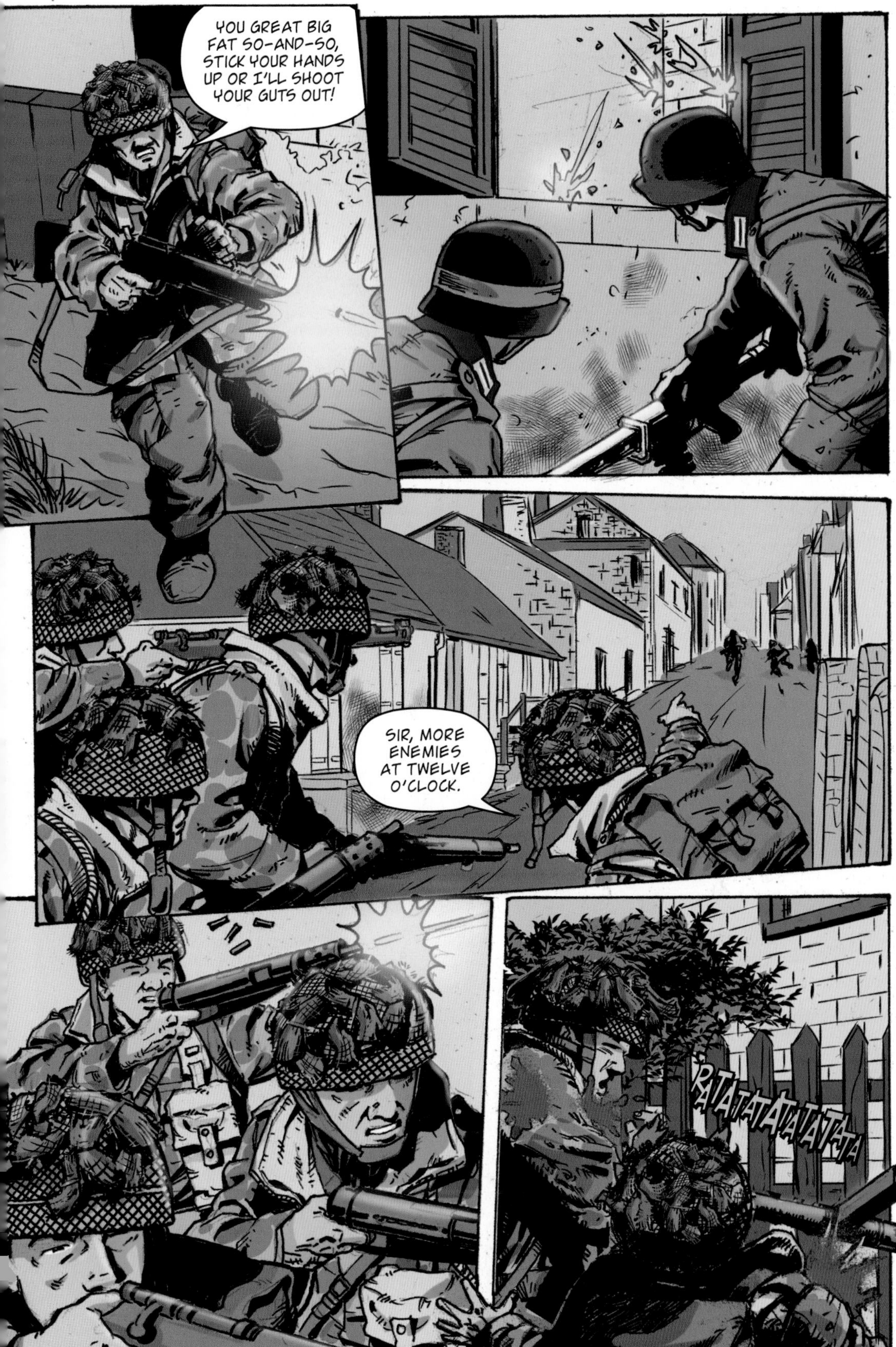
YOU GREAT BIG FAT SO-AND-SO, STICK YOUR HANDS UP OR I'LL SHOOT YOUR GUTS OUT!
SIR, MORE ENEMIES AT TWELVE O'CLOCK.
RATATATATATATATA

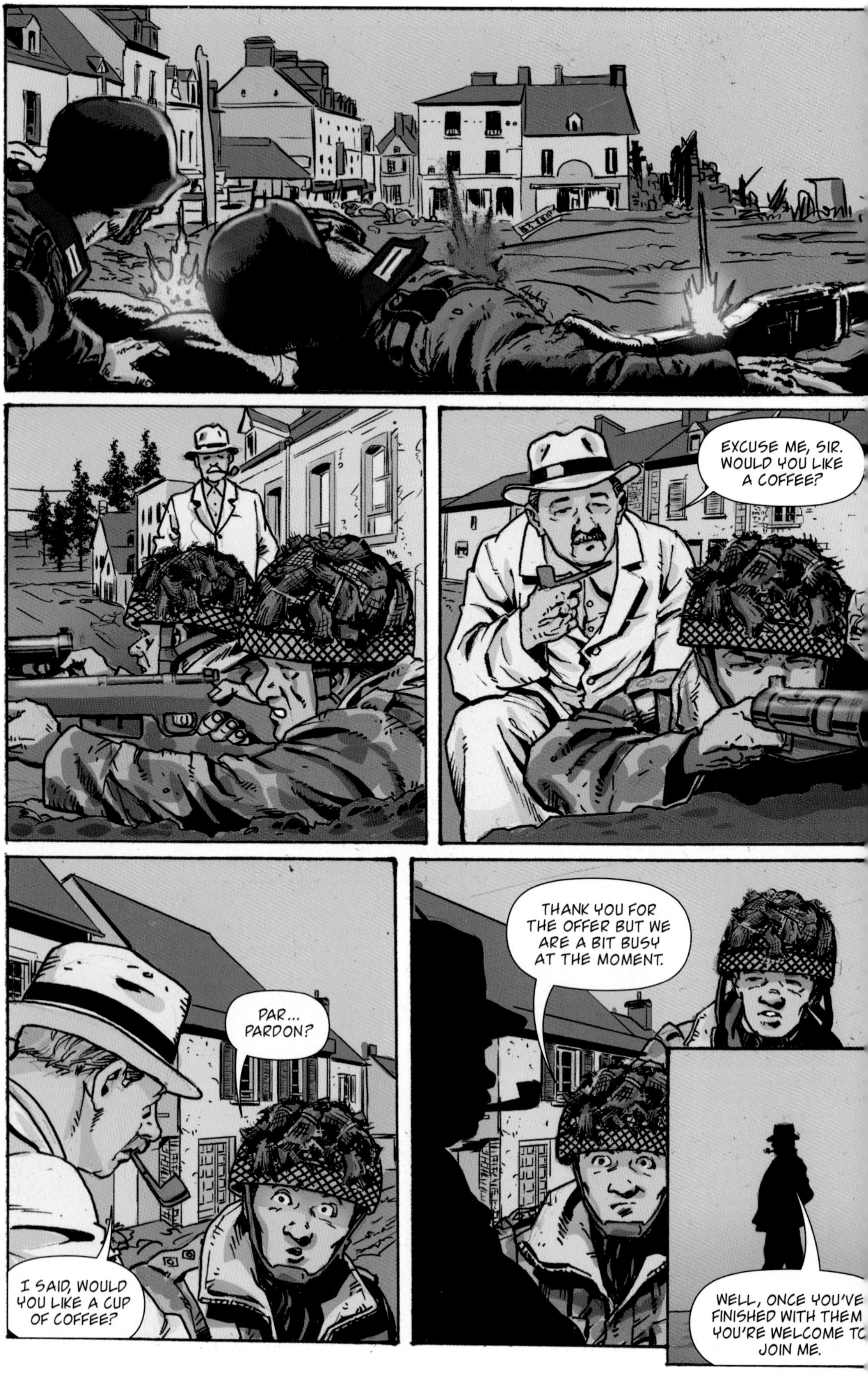
EXCUSE ME, SIR. WOULD YOU LIKE A COFFEE?
PAR... PARDON?
I SAID, WOULD YOU LIKE A CUP OF COFFEE?
THANK YOU FOR THE OFFER BUT WE ARE A BIT BUSY AT THE MOMENT.
WELL, ONCE YOU'VE FINISHED WITH THEM YOU'RE WELCOME TO JOIN ME.

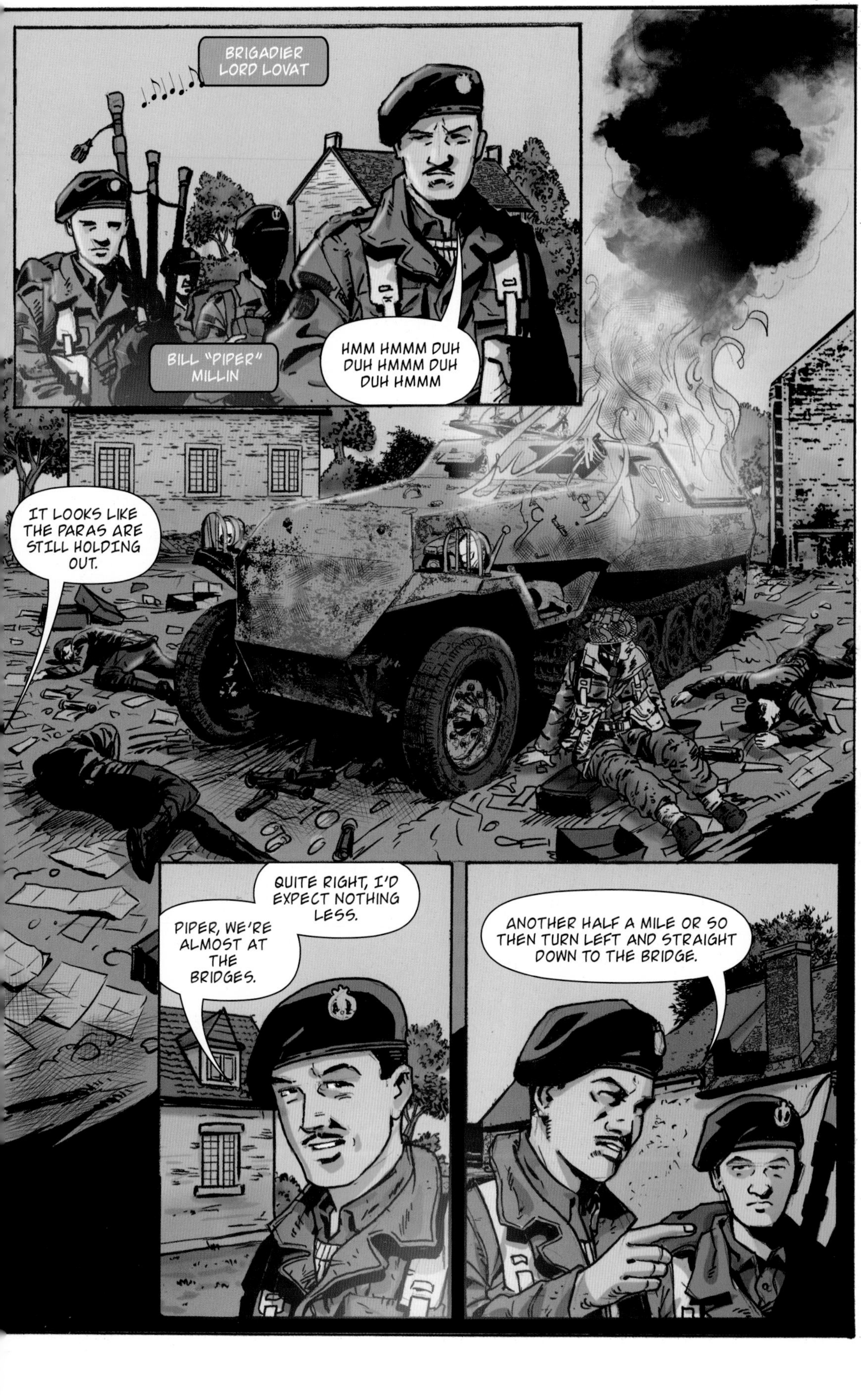
BRIGADIER
LORD LOVAT
BILL "PIPER"
MILLIN
HMM HMMM DUH
DUH HMMM DUH
DUH HMMM
IT LOOKS LIKE
THE PARAS ARE
STILL HOLDING
OUT.
PIPER, WE'RE
ALMOST AT
THE
BRIDGES.
QUITE RIGHT, I'D
EXPECT NOTHING
LESS.
ANOTHER HALF A MILE OR SO
THEN TURN LEFT AND STRAIGHT
DOWN TO THE BRIDGE.

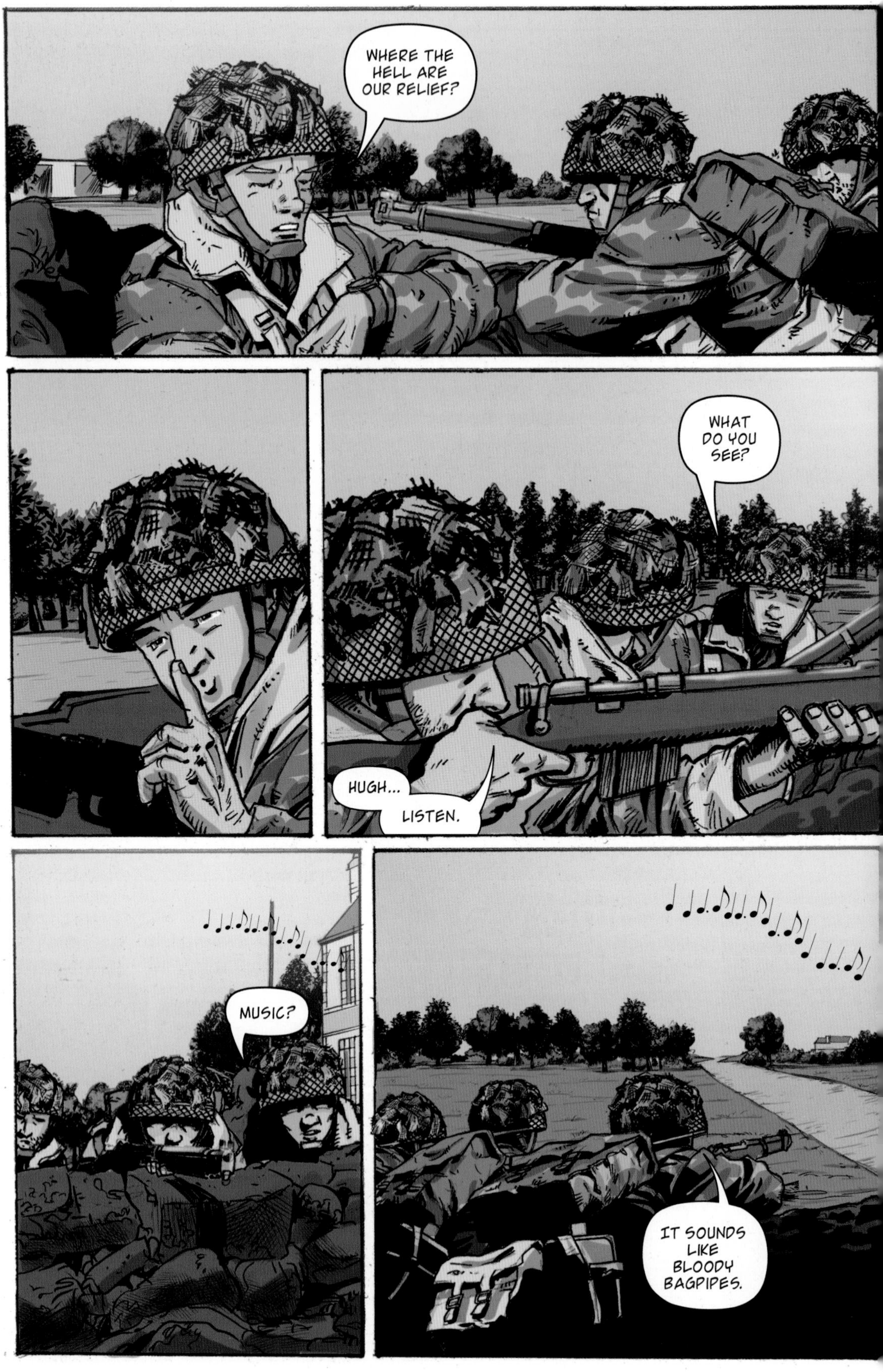
WHERE THE HELL ARE OUR RELIEF?
WHAT DO YOU SEE?
HUGH...
LISTEN.
MUSIC?
IT SOUNDS LIKE BLOODY BAGPIPES.

WE'RE NEARLY THERE, DON'T STOP NOW, DEAR BOY.
RIGHT YOU ARE, SORRY, SIR!

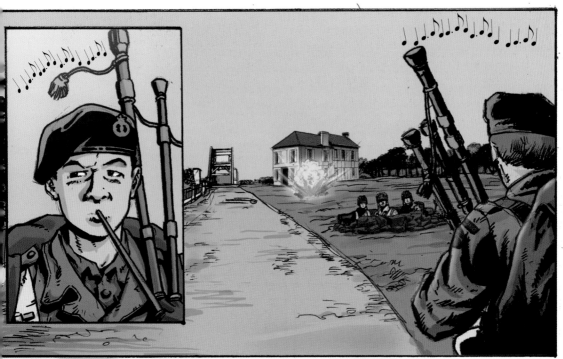

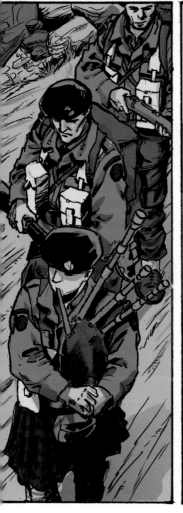

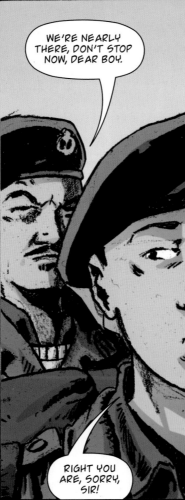

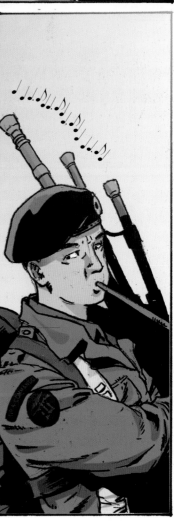

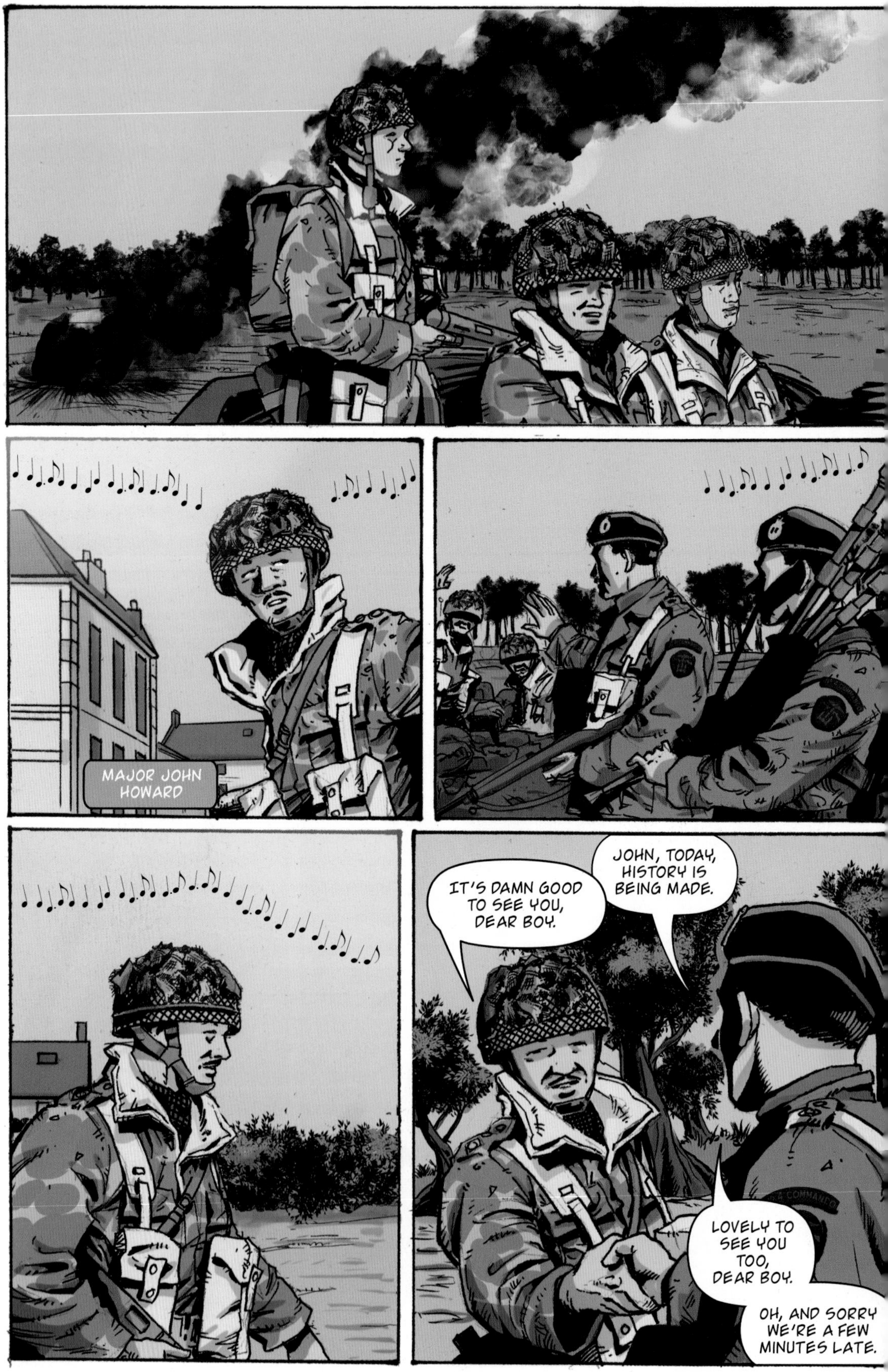
MAJOR JOHN HOWARD
IT'S DAMN GOOD TO SEE YOU, DEAR BOY.
JOHN, TODAY, HISTORY IS BEING MADE.
LOVELY TO SEE YOU TOO, DEAR BOY.
OH, AND SORRY WE'RE A FEW MINUTES LATE.

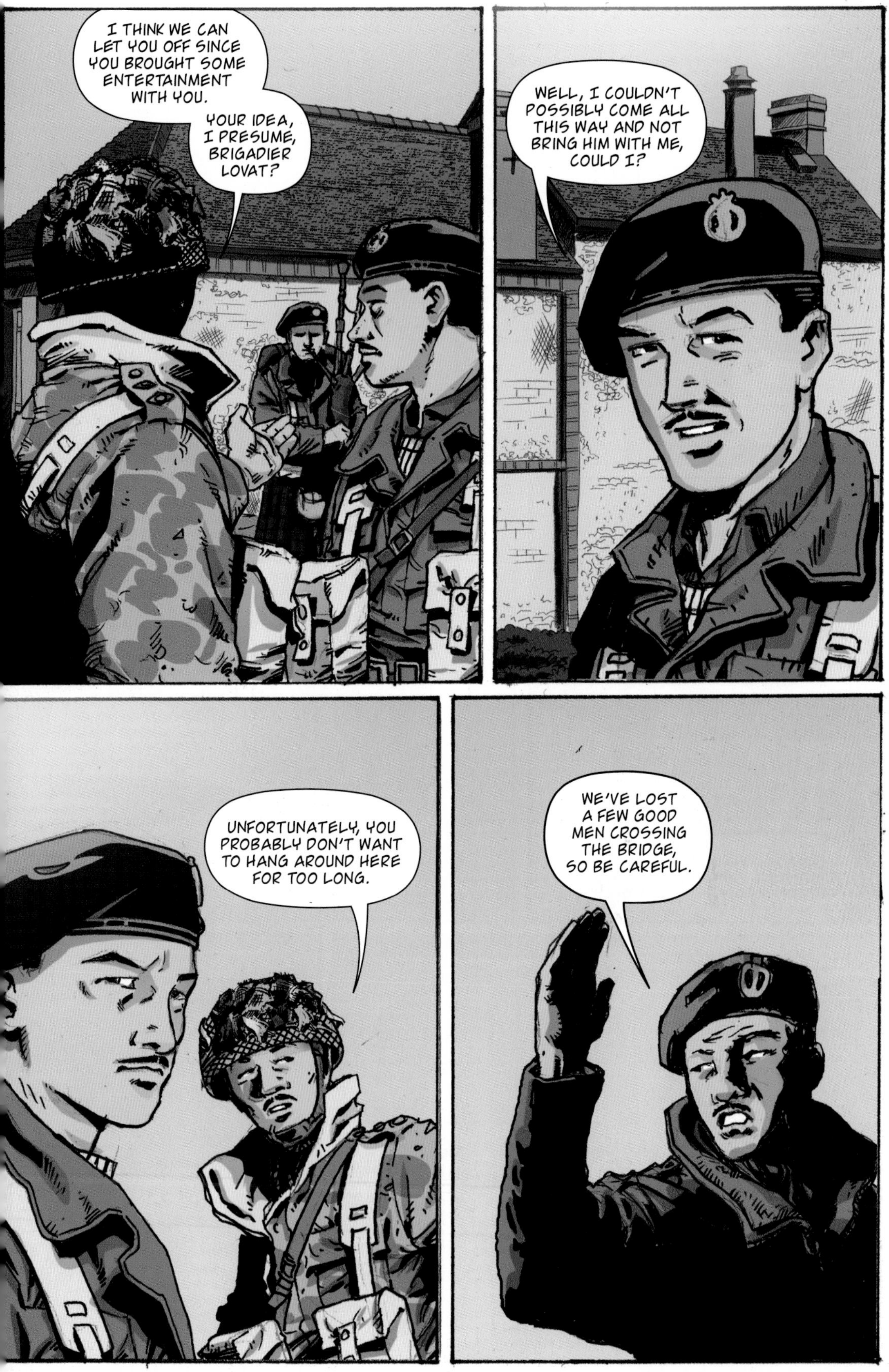
I THINK WE CAN LET YOU OFF SINCE YOU BROUGHT SOME ENTERTAINMENT WITH YOU.
YOUR IDEA, I PRESUME, BRIGADIER LOVAT?
WELL, I COULDN'T POSSIBLY COME ALL THIS WAY AND NOT BRING HIM WITH ME, COULD I?
UNFORTUNATELY, YOU PROBABLY DON'T WANT TO HANG AROUND HERE FOR TOO LONG.
WE'VE LOST A FEW GOOD MEN CROSSING THE BRIDGE, SO BE CAREFUL.

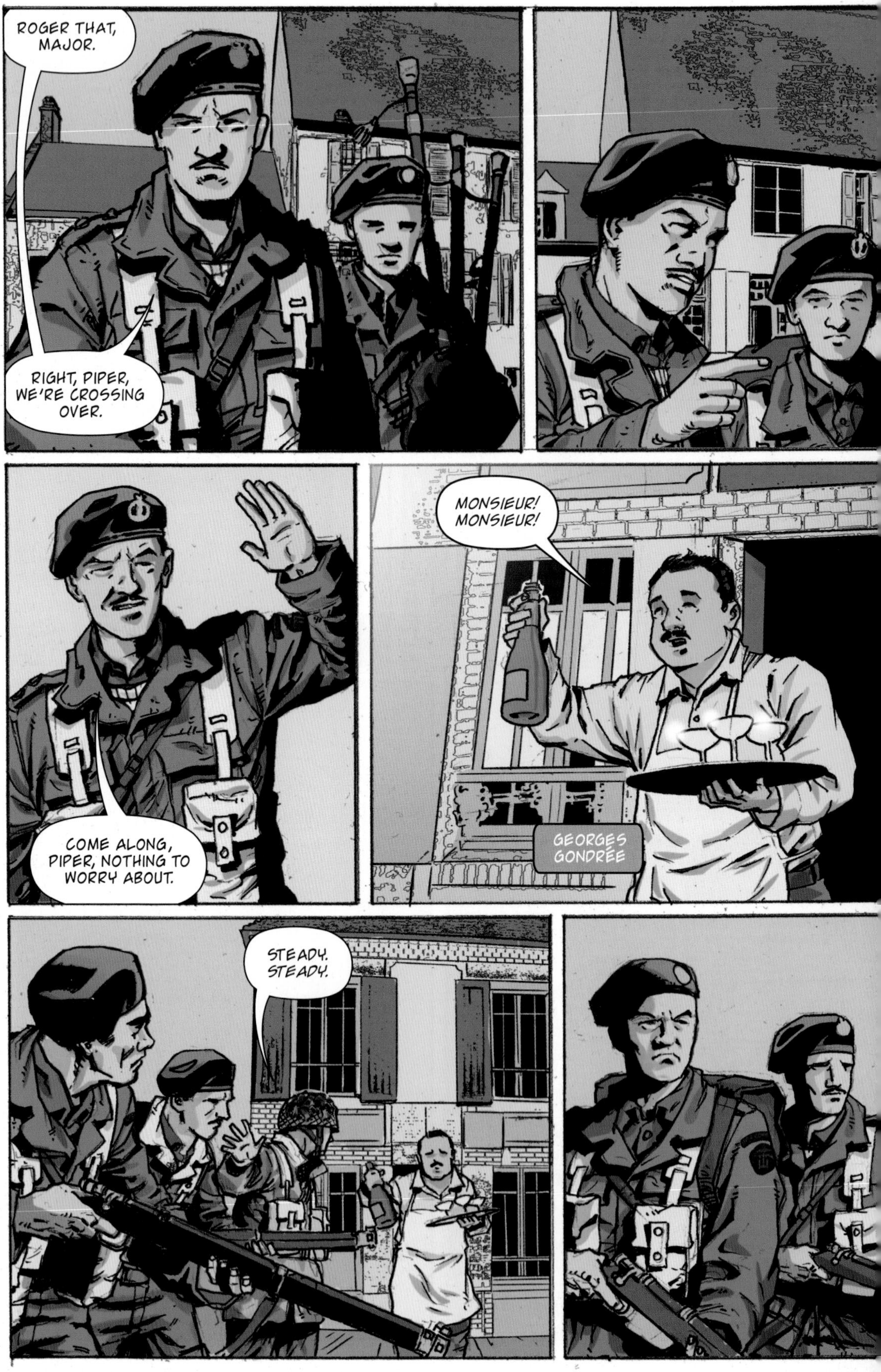
ROGER THAT, MAJOR.
RIGHT, PIPER, WE'RE CROSSING OVER.
COME ALONG, PIPER, NOTHING TO WORRY ABOUT.
MONSIEUR! MONSIEUR!
GEORGES GONDRÉE
STEADY. STEADY.

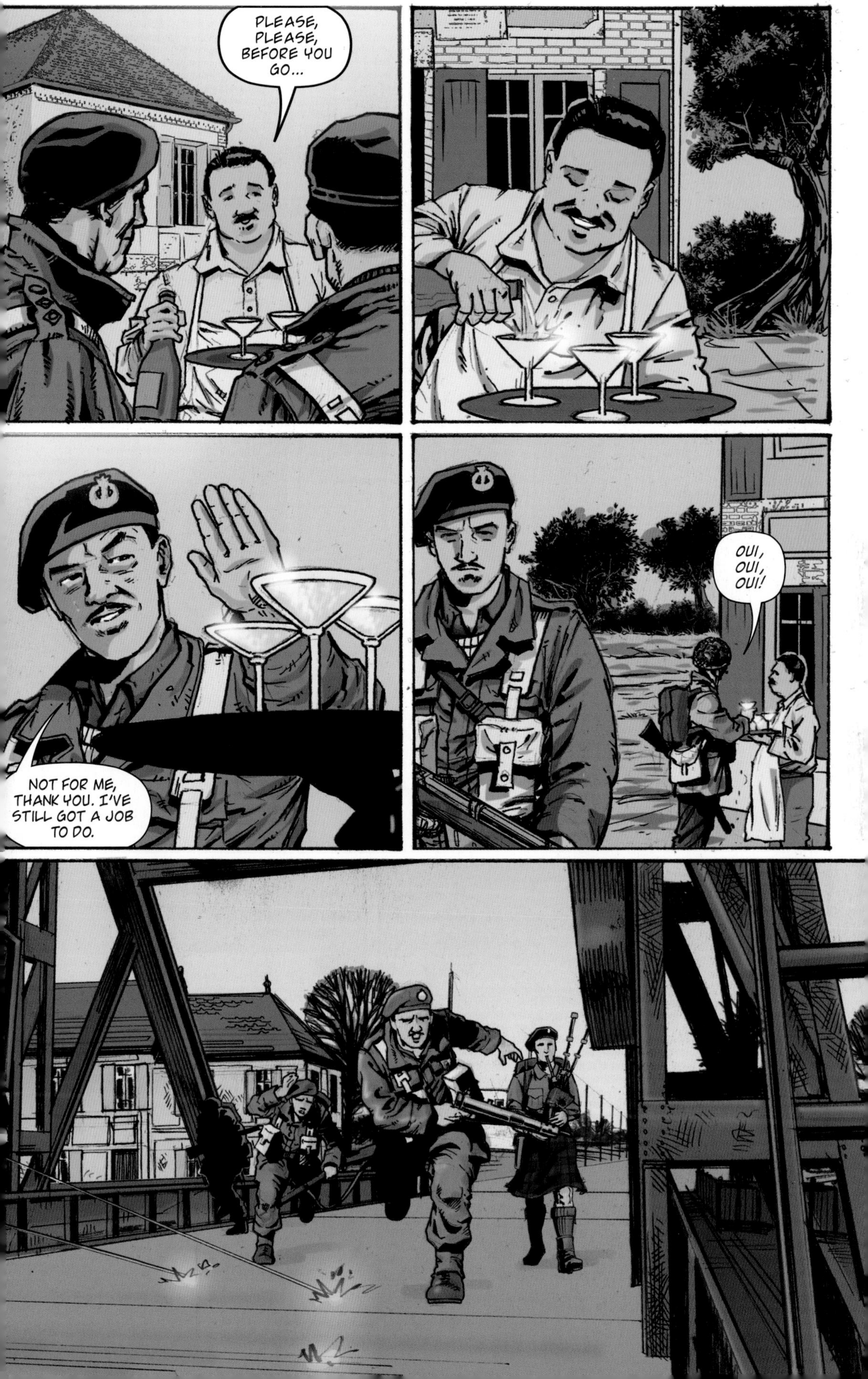
PLEASE, PLEASE, BEFORE YOU GO...
NOT FOR ME, THANK YOU. I'VE STILL GOT A JOB TO DO.
OUI, OUI, OUI!

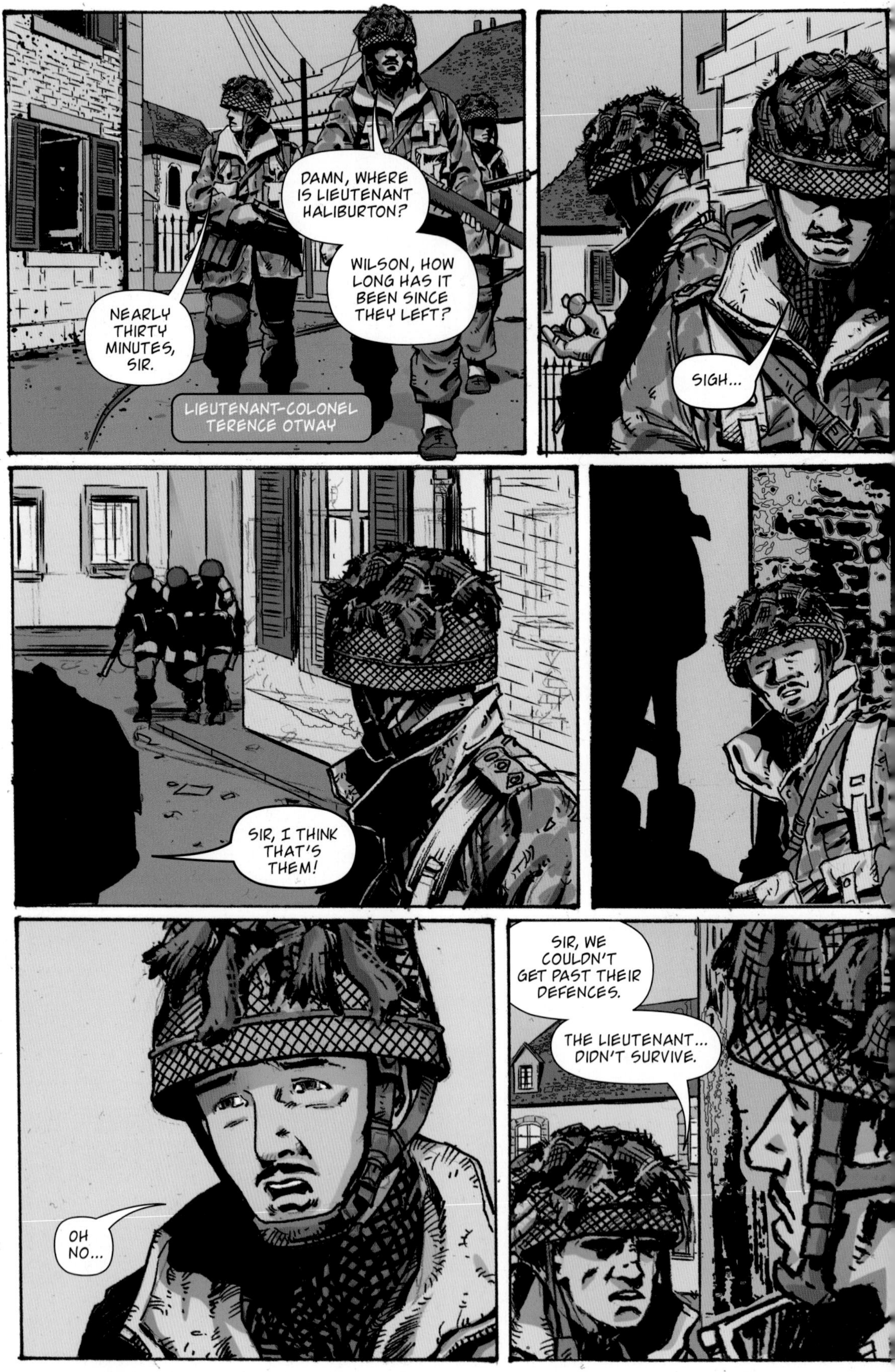
DAMN, WHERE IS LIEUTENANT HALIBURTON?
WILSON, HOW LONG HAS IT BEEN SINCE THEY LEFT?
NEARLY THIRTY MINUTES, SIR.
LIEUTENANT-COLONEL TERENCE OTWAY
SIGH...
SIR, I THINK THAT'S THEM!
SIR, WE COULDN'T GET PAST THEIR DEFENCES.
THE LIEUTENANT... DIDN'T SURVIVE.
OH NO...

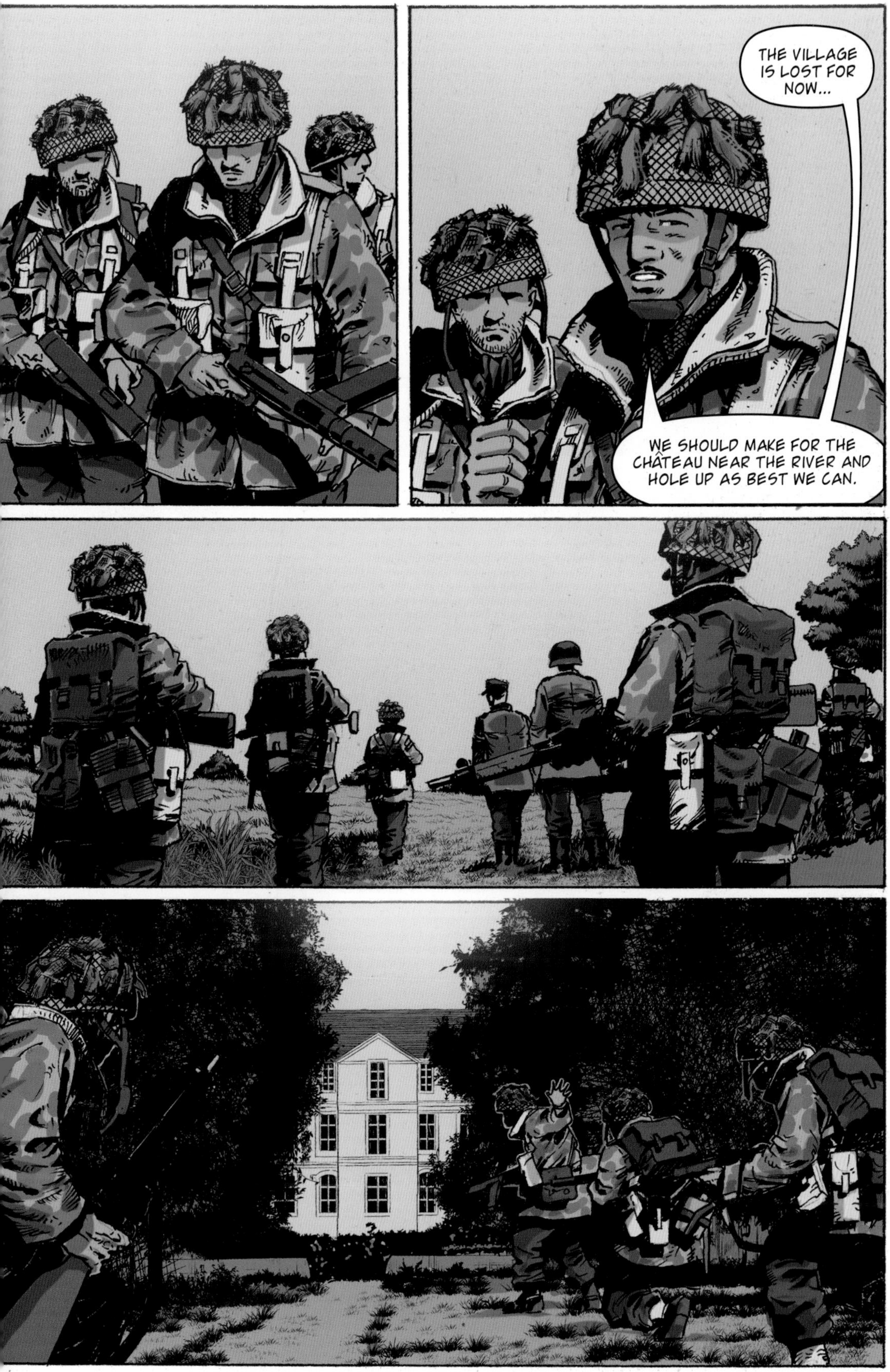
THE VILLAGE IS LOST FOR NOW...
WE SHOULD MAKE FOR THE CHÂTEAU NEAR THE RIVER AND HOLE UP AS BEST WE CAN.

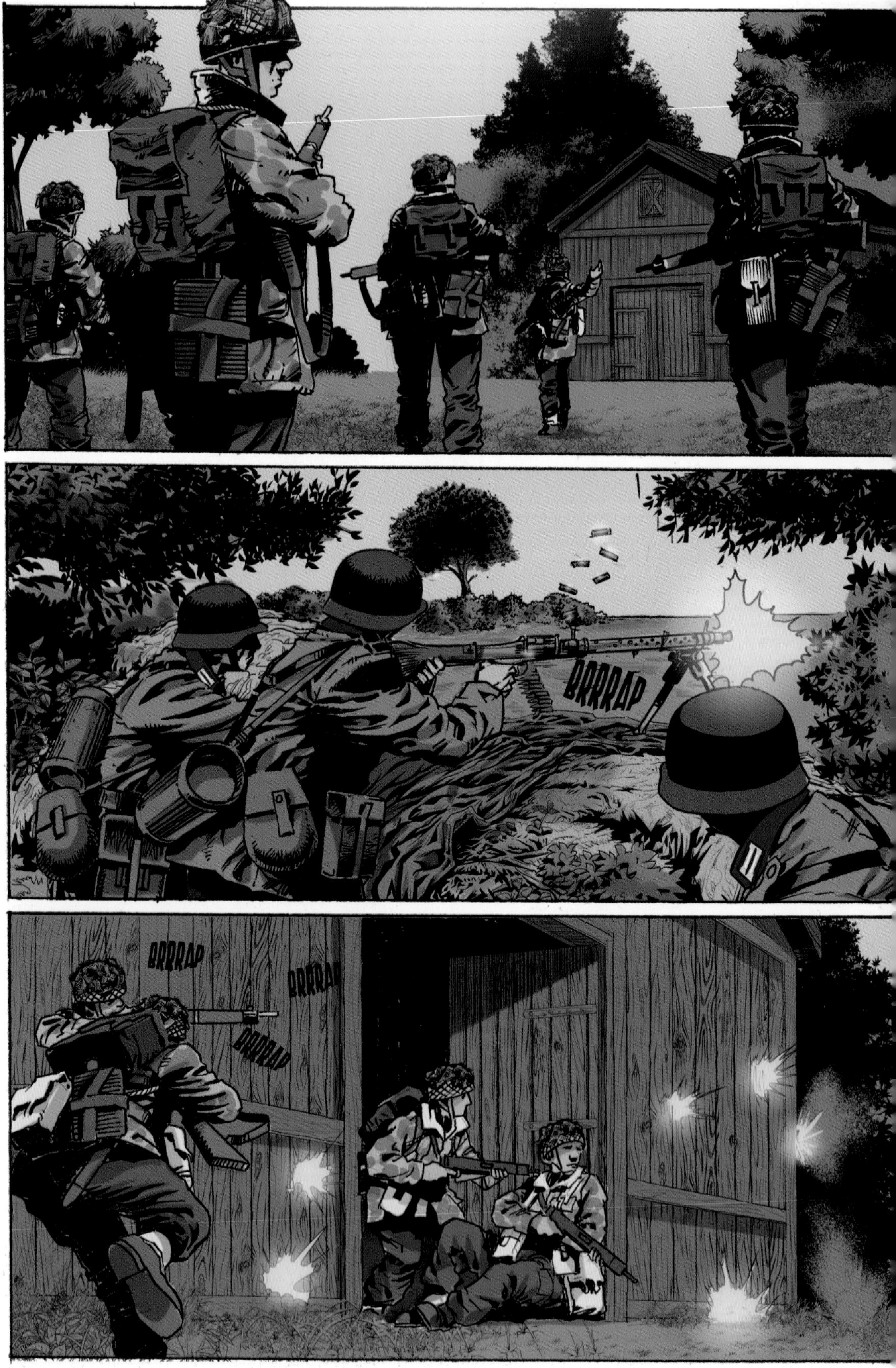
BRRRAP
BRRRAP
BRRRAP
BRRRAP

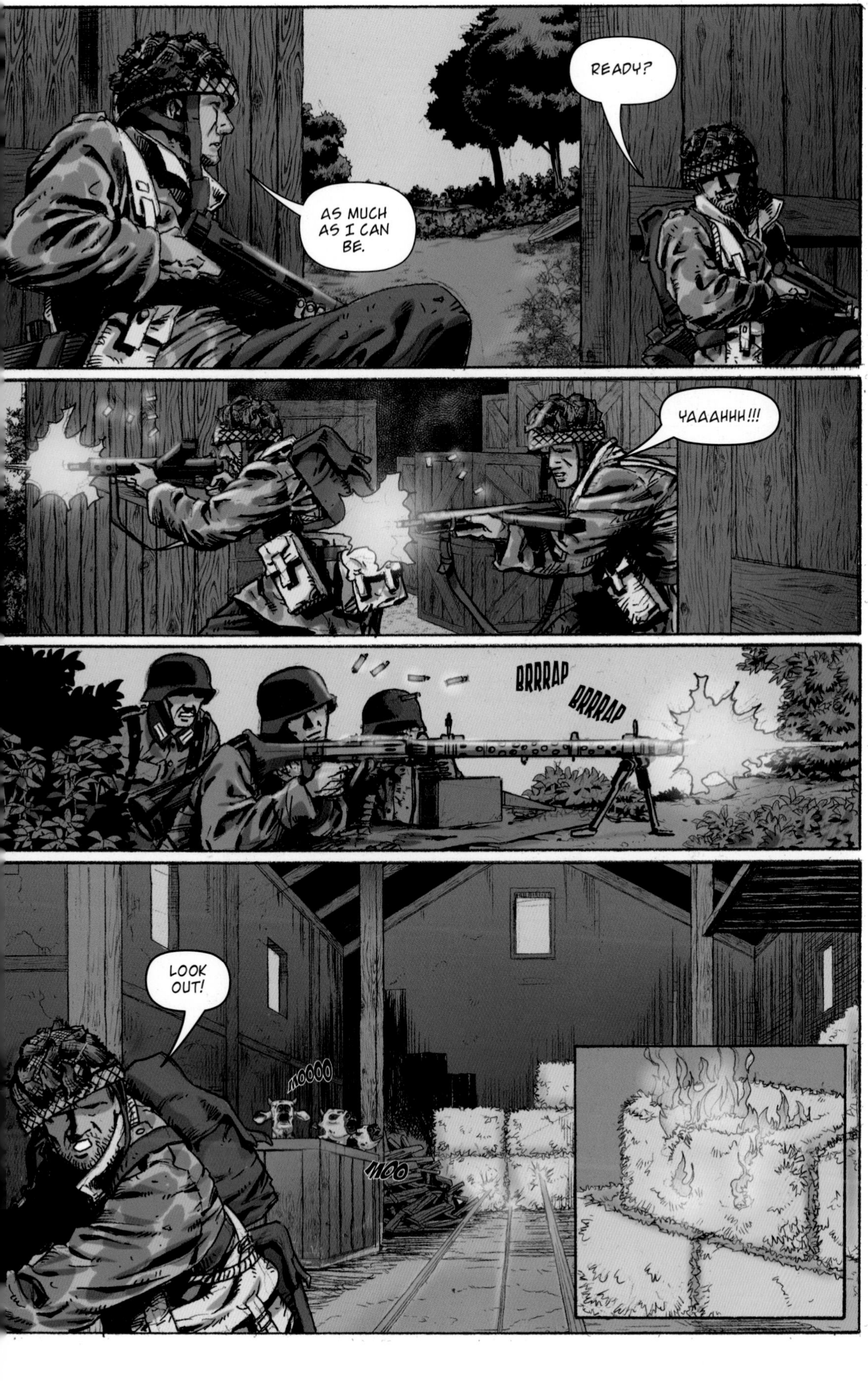
AS MUCH AS I CAN BE.
READY?
YAAAHHH!!!
BRRRAP
BRRRAP
LOOK OUT!
MOOOO
MOO

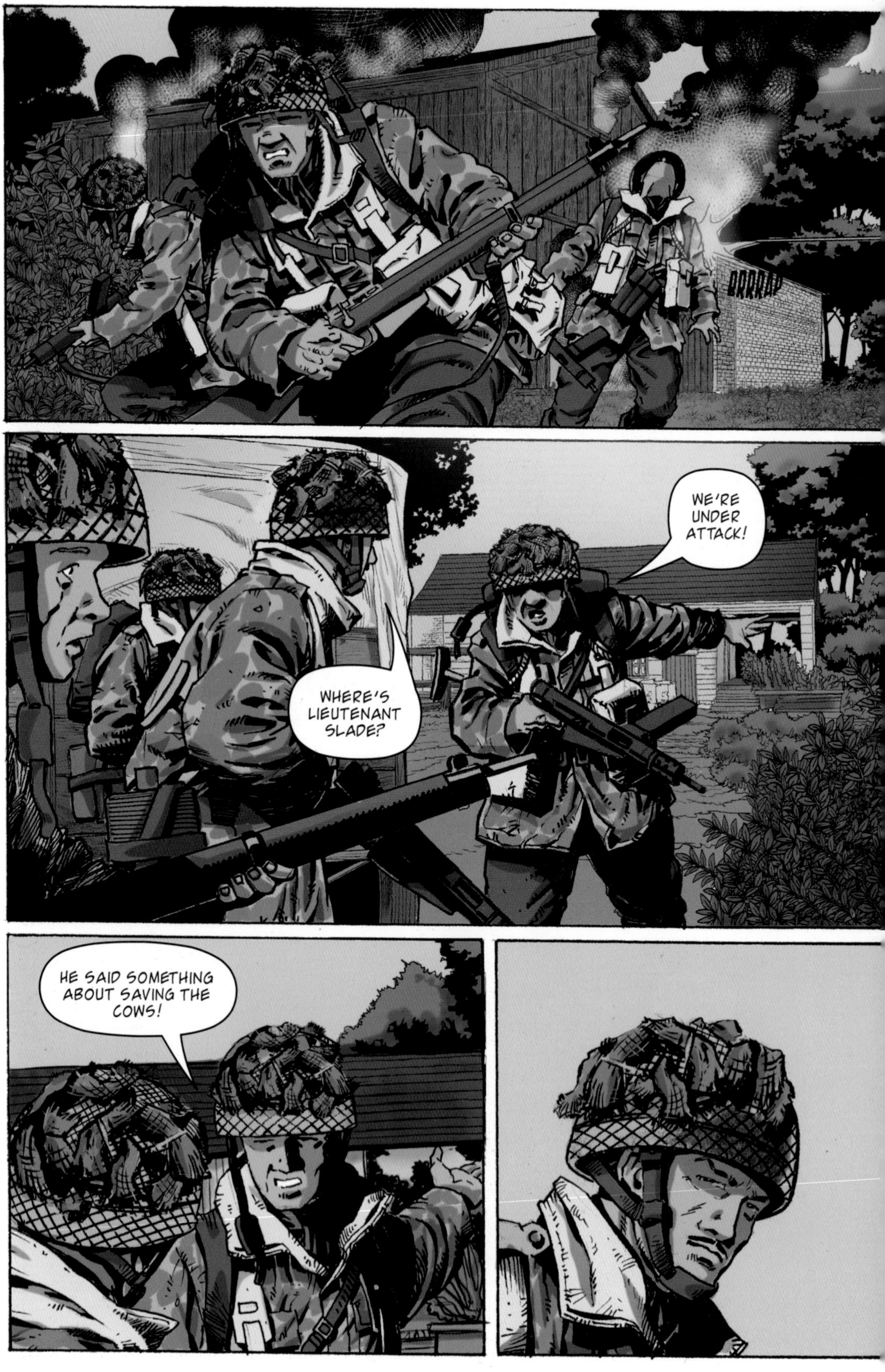
BRRRAP
WHERE'S LIEUTENANT SLADE?
WE'RE UNDER ATTACK!
HE SAID SOMETHING ABOUT SAVING THE COWS!

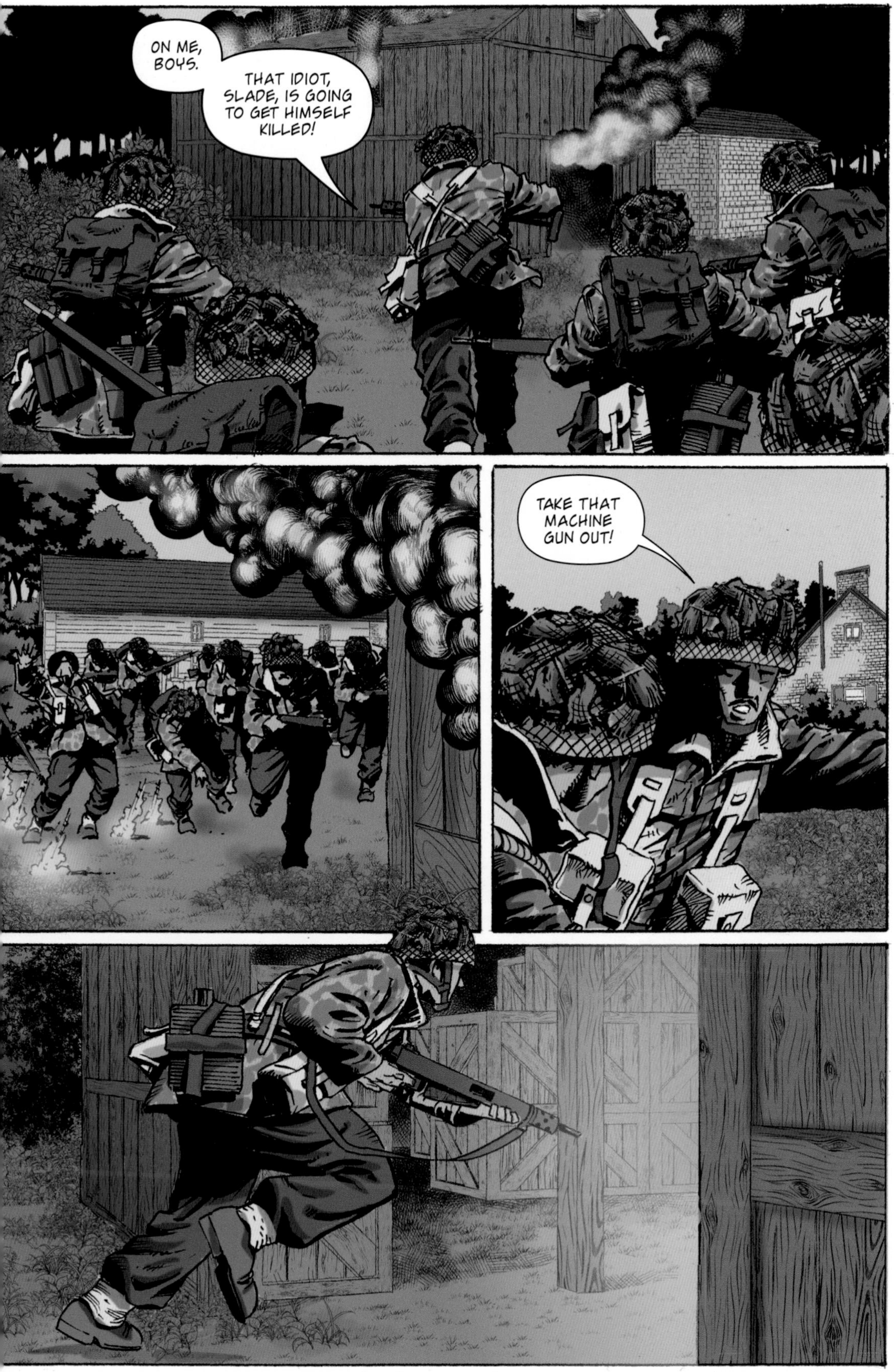
ON ME, BOYS.
THAT IDIOT, SLADE, IS GOING TO GET HIMSELF KILLED!
TAKE THAT MACHINE GUN OUT!

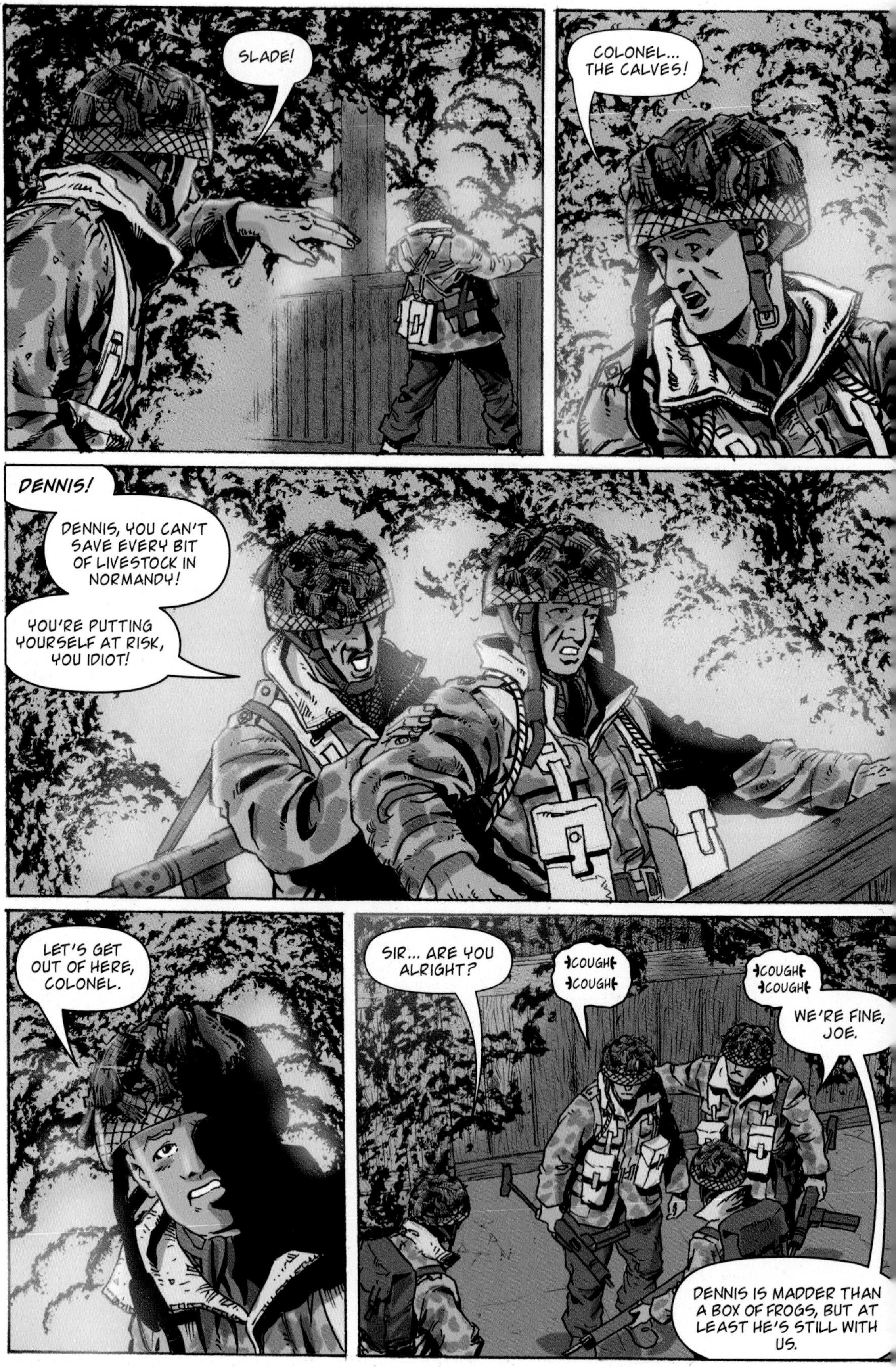
SLADE!
COLONEL... THE CALVES!
DENNIS!
DENNIS, YOU CAN'T SAVE EVERY BIT OF LIVESTOCK IN NORMANDY!
YOU'RE PUTTING YOURSELF AT RISK, YOU IDIOT!
LET'S GET OUT OF HERE, COLONEL.
SIR... ARE YOU ALRIGHT?
COUGH *COUGH*
COUGH *COUGH*
WE'RE FINE, JOE.
DENNIS IS MADDER THAN A BOX OF FROGS, BUT AT LEAST HE'S STILL WITH US.

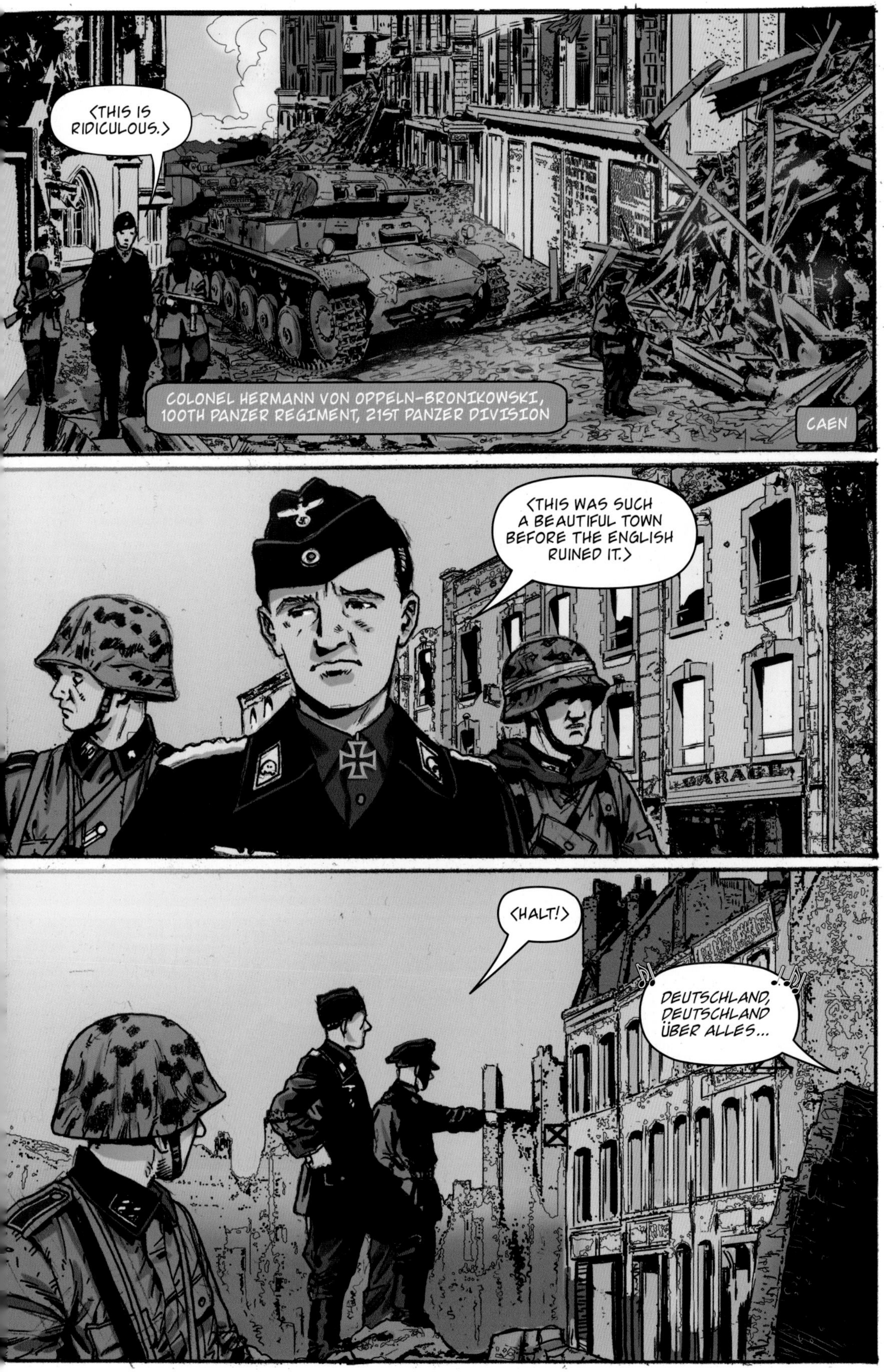

<THIS IS RIDICULOUS.>
COLONEL HERMANN VON OPPELN-BRONIKOWSKI, 100TH PANZER REGIMENT, 21ST PANZER DIVISION
CAEN
<THIS WAS SUCH A BEAUTIFUL TOWN BEFORE THE ENGLISH RUINED IT.>
GARAGE
<HALT!>
DEUTSCHLAND, DEUTSCHLAND ÜBER ALLES...

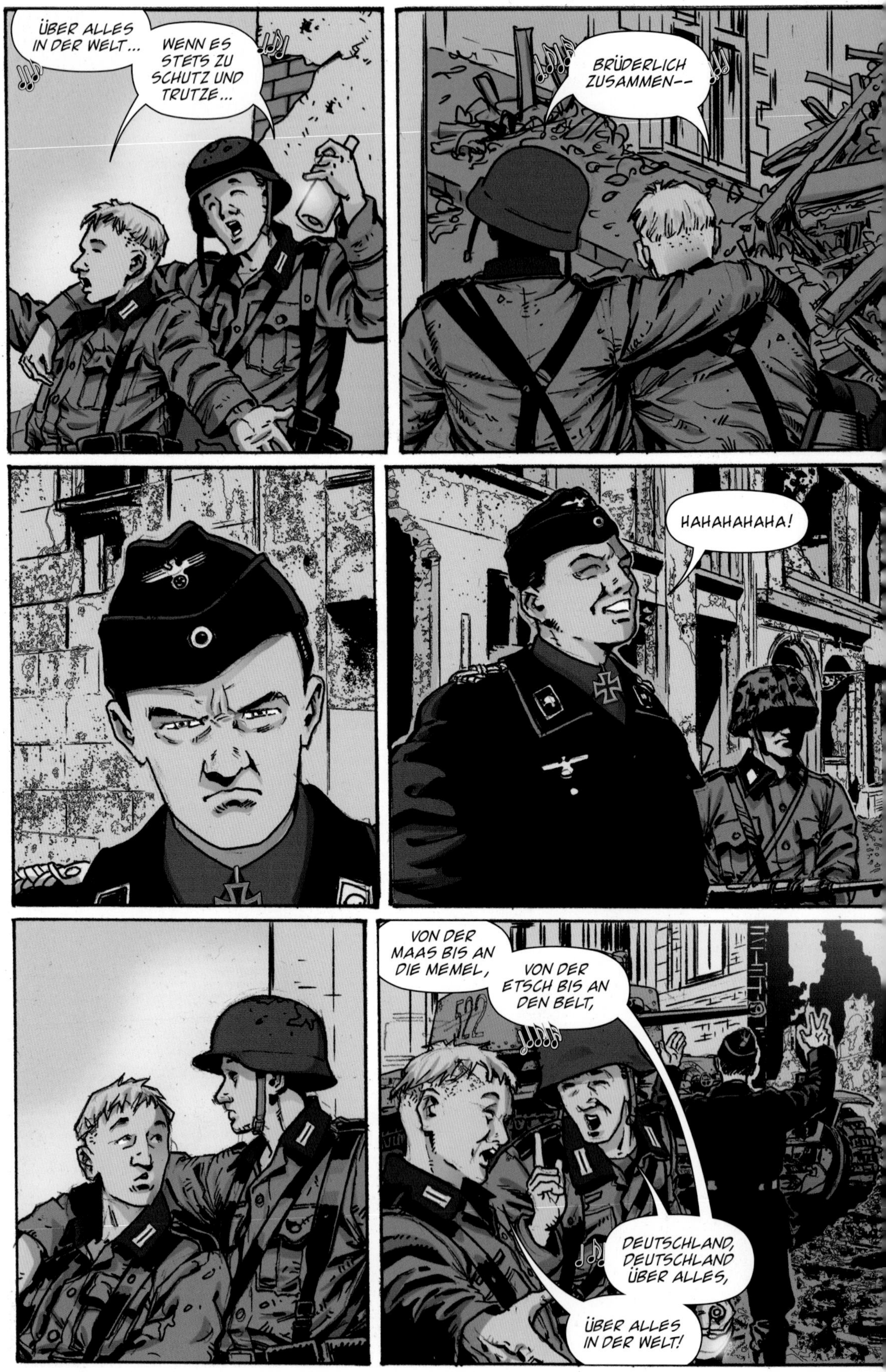
ÜBER ALLES IN DER WELT...
WENN ES STETS ZU SCHUTZ UND TRUTZE...
BRÜDERLICH ZUSAMMEN--
HAHAHAHAHA!
VON DER MAAS BIS AN DIE MEMEL,
VON DER ETSCH BIS AN DEN BELT,
DEUTSCHLAND, DEUTSCHLAND ÜBER ALLES,
ÜBER ALLES IN DER WELT!

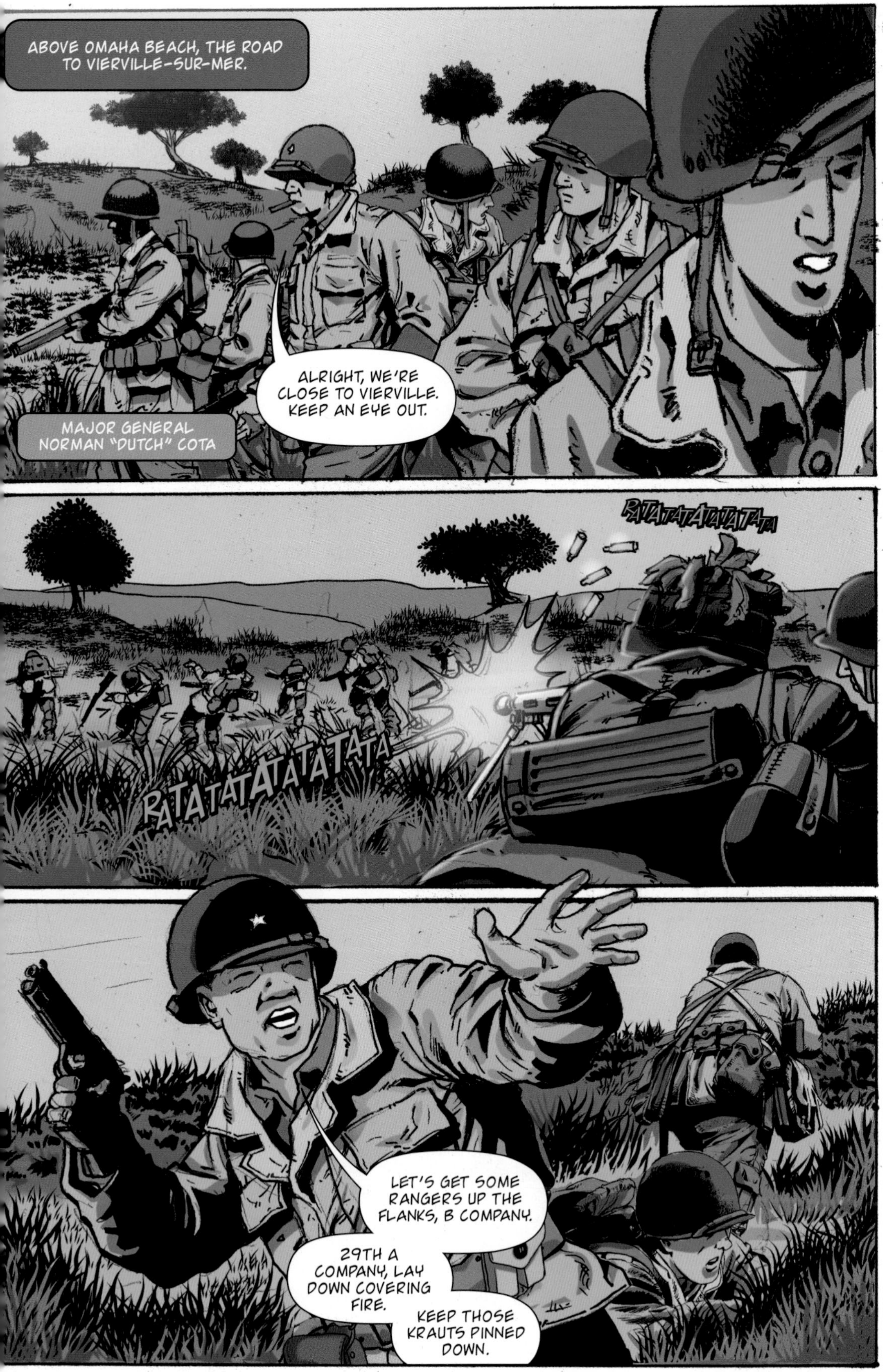
ABOVE OMAHA BEACH, THE ROAD TO VIERVILLE-SUR-MER.
ALRIGHT, WE'RE CLOSE TO VIERVILLE. KEEP AN EYE OUT.
MAJOR GENERAL NORMAN "DUTCH" COTA
RATATATATATATATATA
RATATATATATATATATA
LET'S GET SOME RANGERS UP THE FLANKS, B COMPANY.
29TH A COMPANY, LAY DOWN COVERING FIRE.
KEEP THOSE KRAUTS PINNED DOWN.

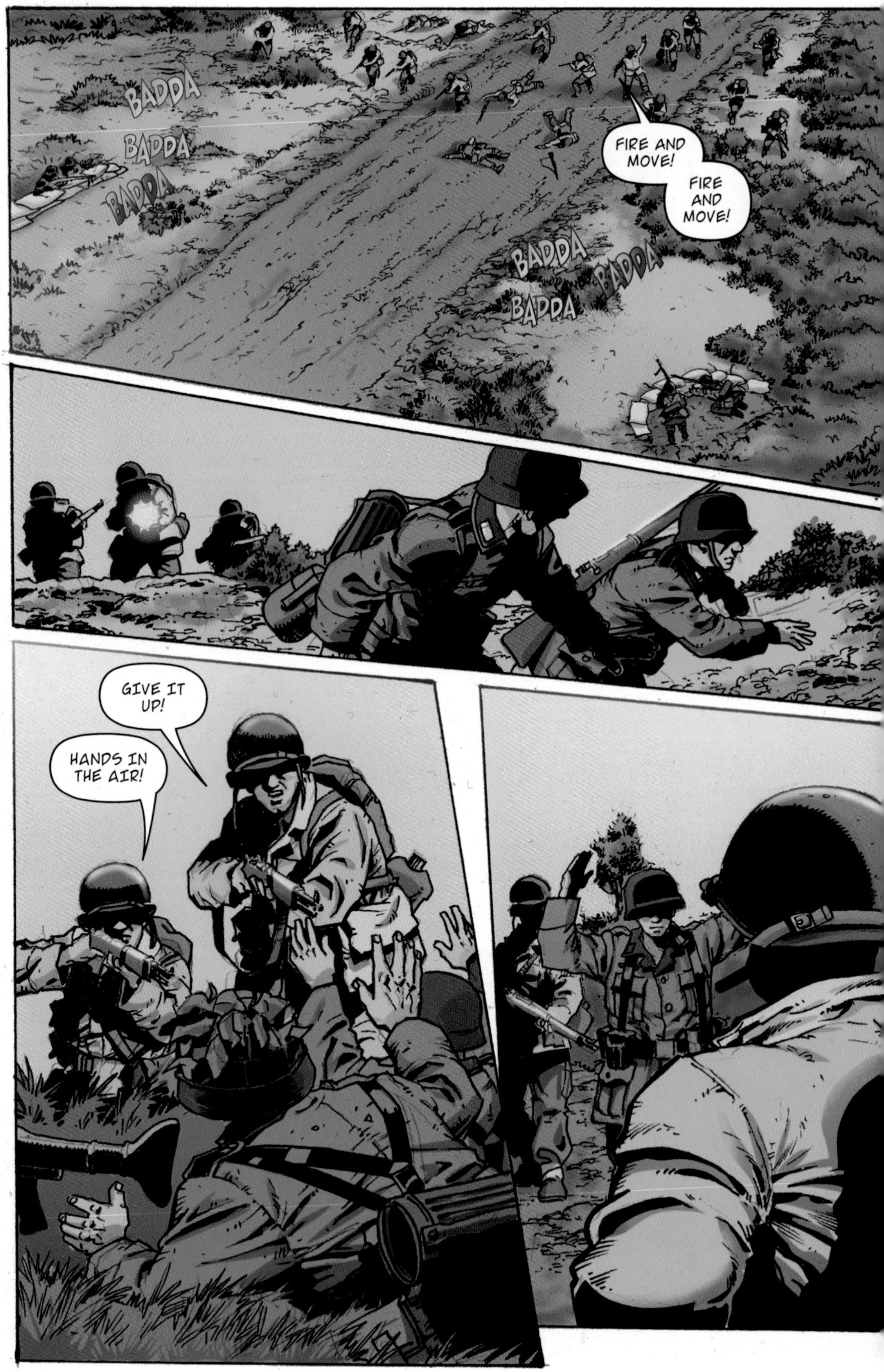
BADDA
BADDA
BADDA
FIRE AND MOVE!
FIRE AND MOVE!
BADDA
BADDA
BADDA
GIVE IT UP!
HANDS IN THE AIR!

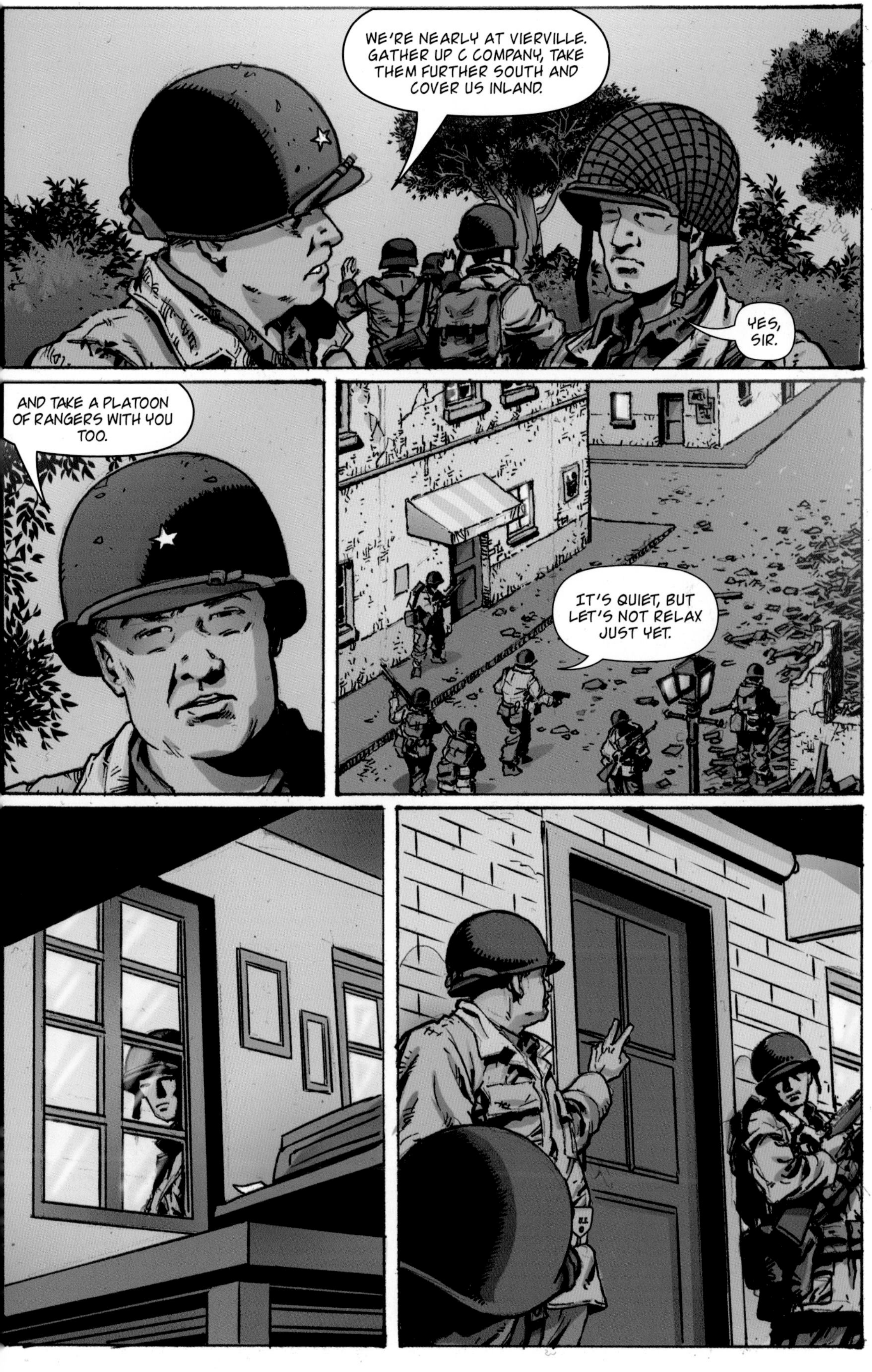
WE'RE NEARLY AT VIERVILLE. GATHER UP C COMPANY, TAKE THEM FURTHER SOUTH AND COVER US INLAND.
YES, SIR.
AND TAKE A PLATOON OF RANGERS WITH YOU TOO.
IT'S QUIET, BUT LET'S NOT RELAX JUST YET.

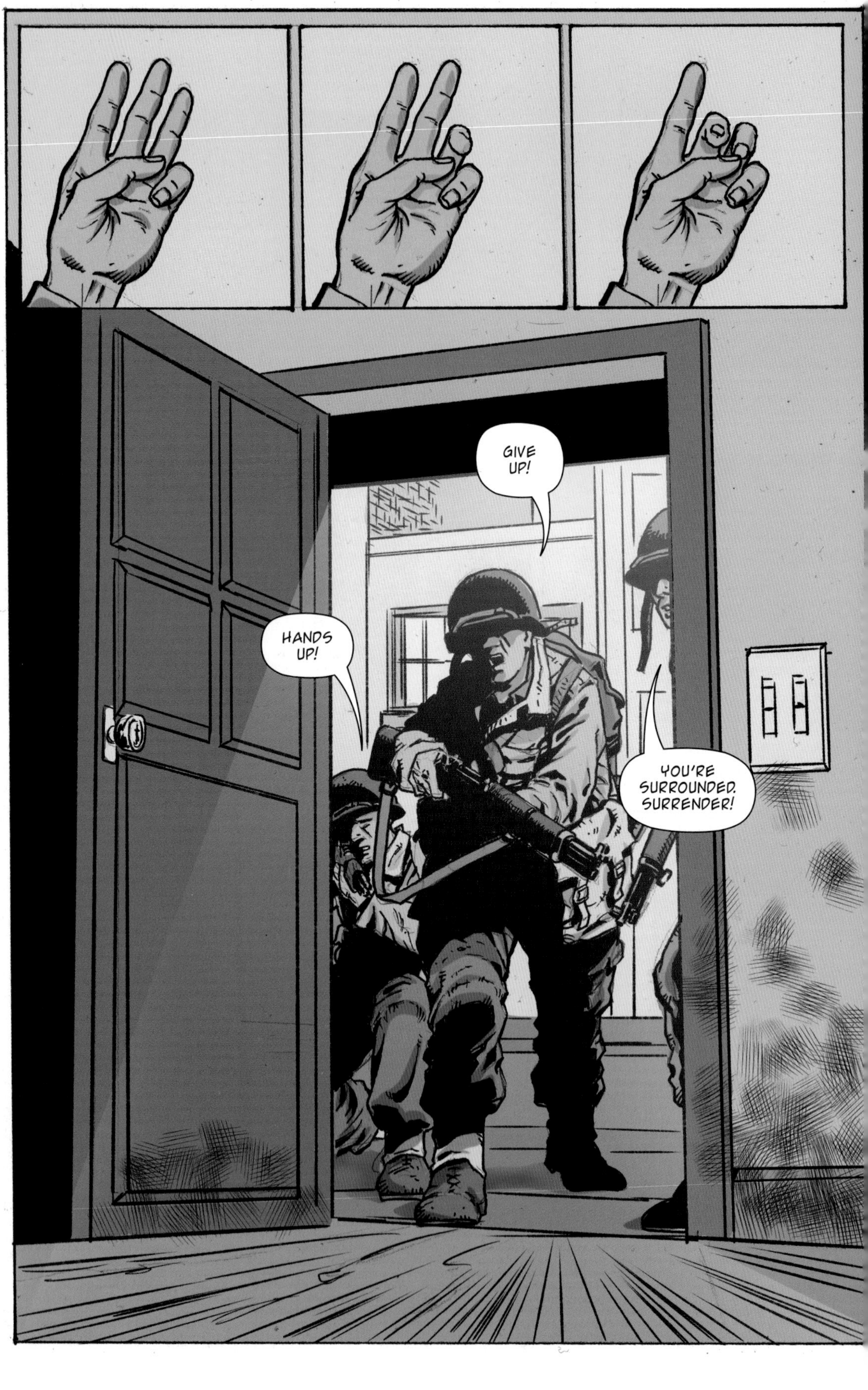
GIVE UP!
HANDS UP!
YOU'RE SURROUNDED. SURRENDER!

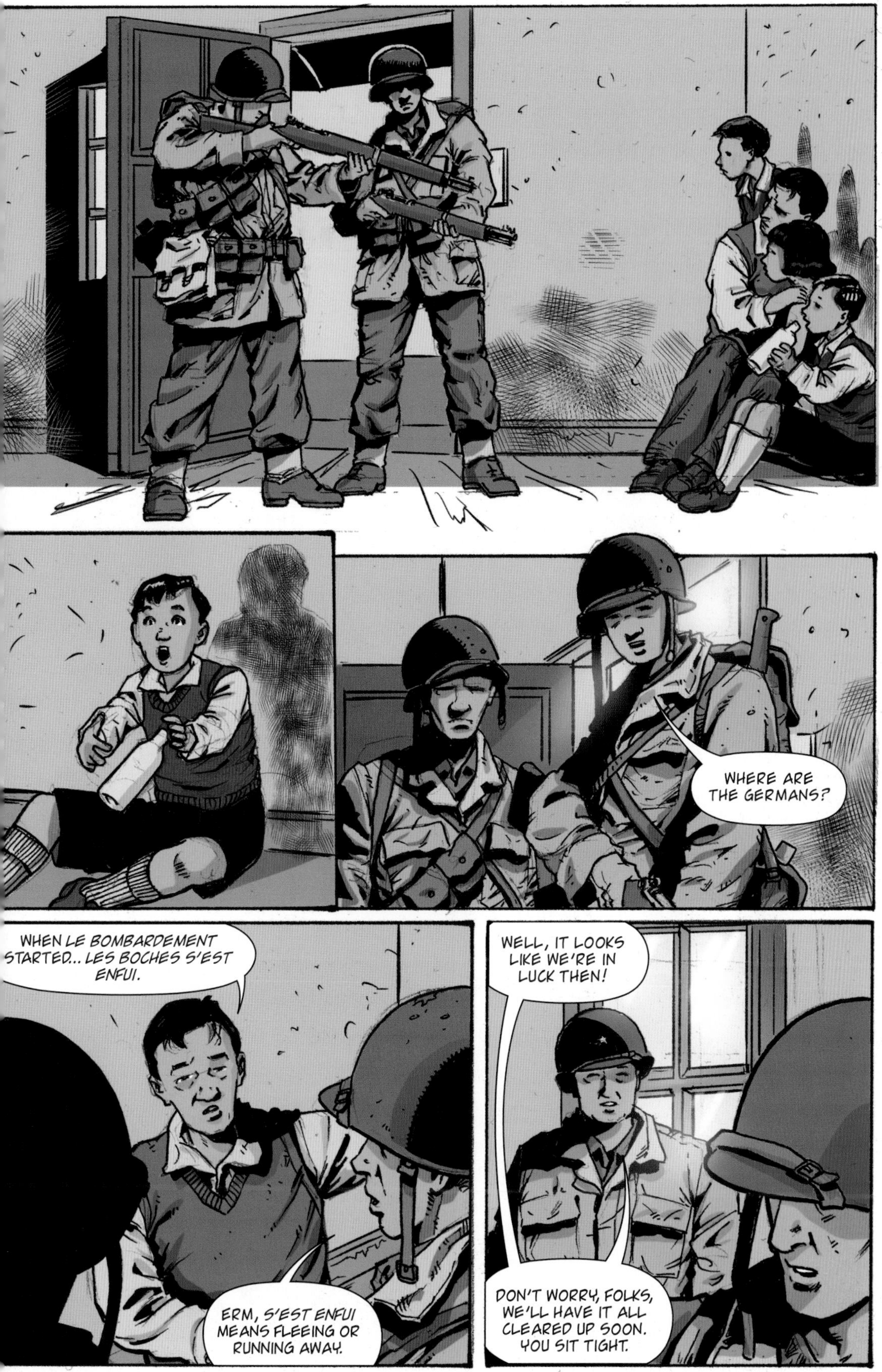
WHERE ARE THE GERMANS?
WHEN LE BOMBARDEMENT STARTED... LES BOCHES S'EST ENFUI.
ERM, S'EST ENFUI MEANS FLEEING OR RUNNING AWAY.
WELL, IT LOOKS LIKE WE'RE IN LUCK THEN!
DON'T WORRY, FOLKS, WE'LL HAVE IT ALL CLEARED UP SOON. YOU SIT TIGHT.

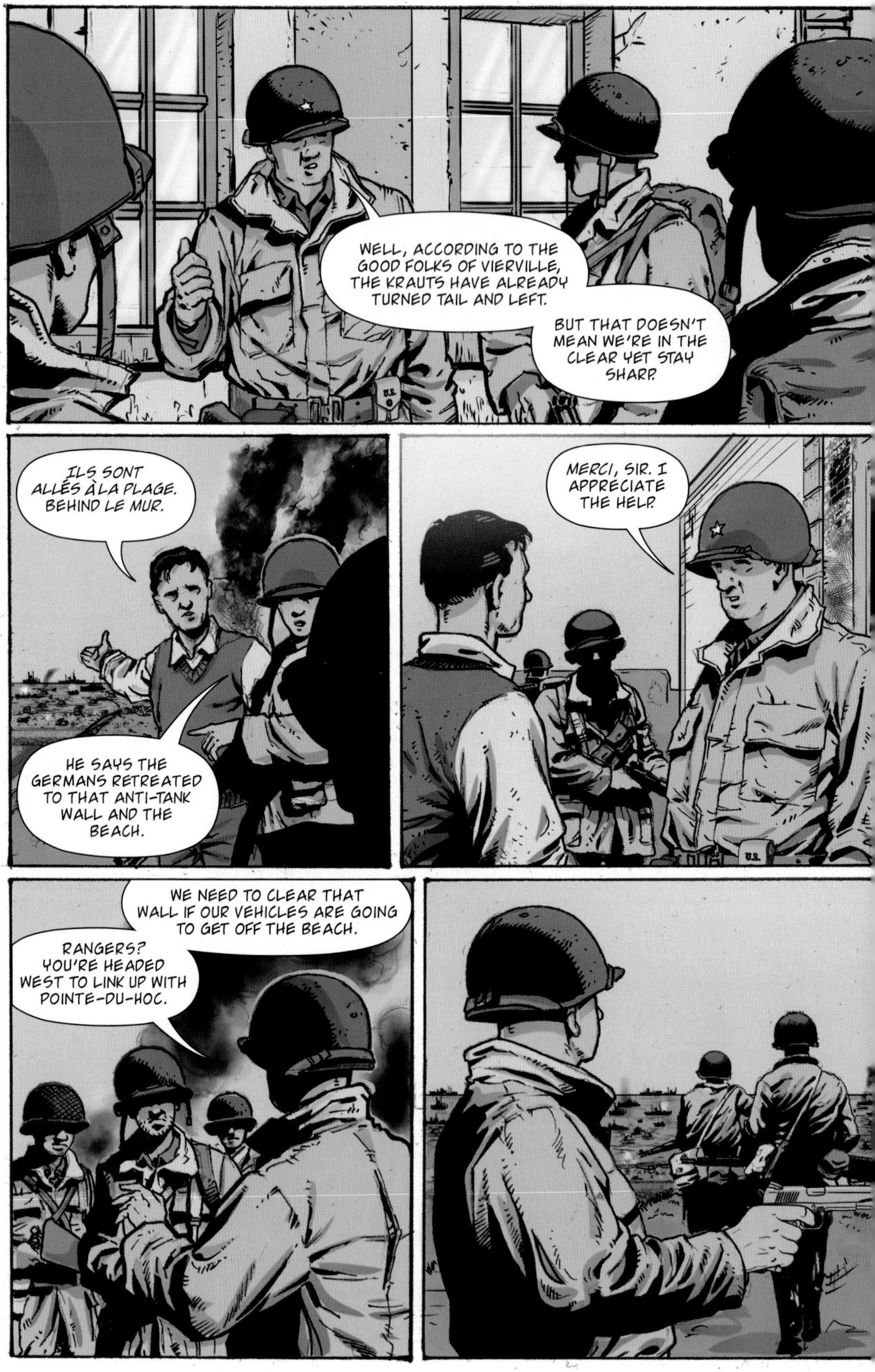
WELL, ACCORDING TO THE GOOD FOLKS OF VIERVILLE, THE KRAUTS HAVE ALREADY TURNED TAIL AND LEFT.
BUT THAT DOESN'T MEAN WE'RE IN THE CLEAR YET STAY SHARP.
ILS SONT ALLÉS À LA PLAGE. BEHIND LE MUR.
HE SAYS THE GERMANS RETREATED TO THAT ANTI-TANK WALL AND THE BEACH.
MERCI, SIR. I APPRECIATE THE HELP.
WE NEED TO CLEAR THAT WALL IF OUR VEHICLES ARE GOING TO GET OFF THE BEACH.
RANGERS? YOU'RE HEADED WEST TO LINK UP WITH POINTE-DU-HOC.

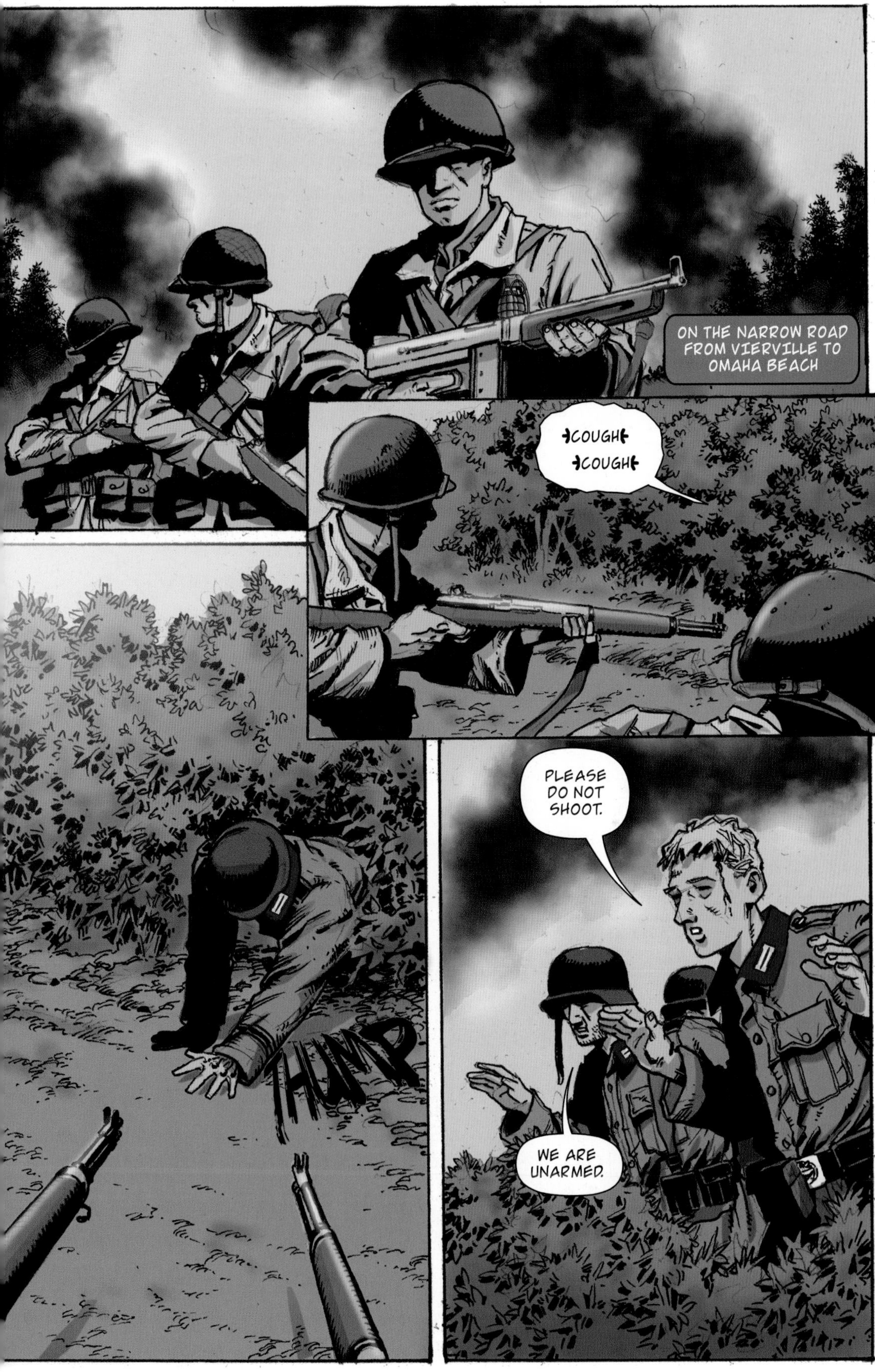
ON THE NARROW ROAD FROM VIERVILLE TO OMAHA BEACH
COUGH COUGH
THUMP
PLEASE DO NOT SHOOT.
WE ARE UNARMED.

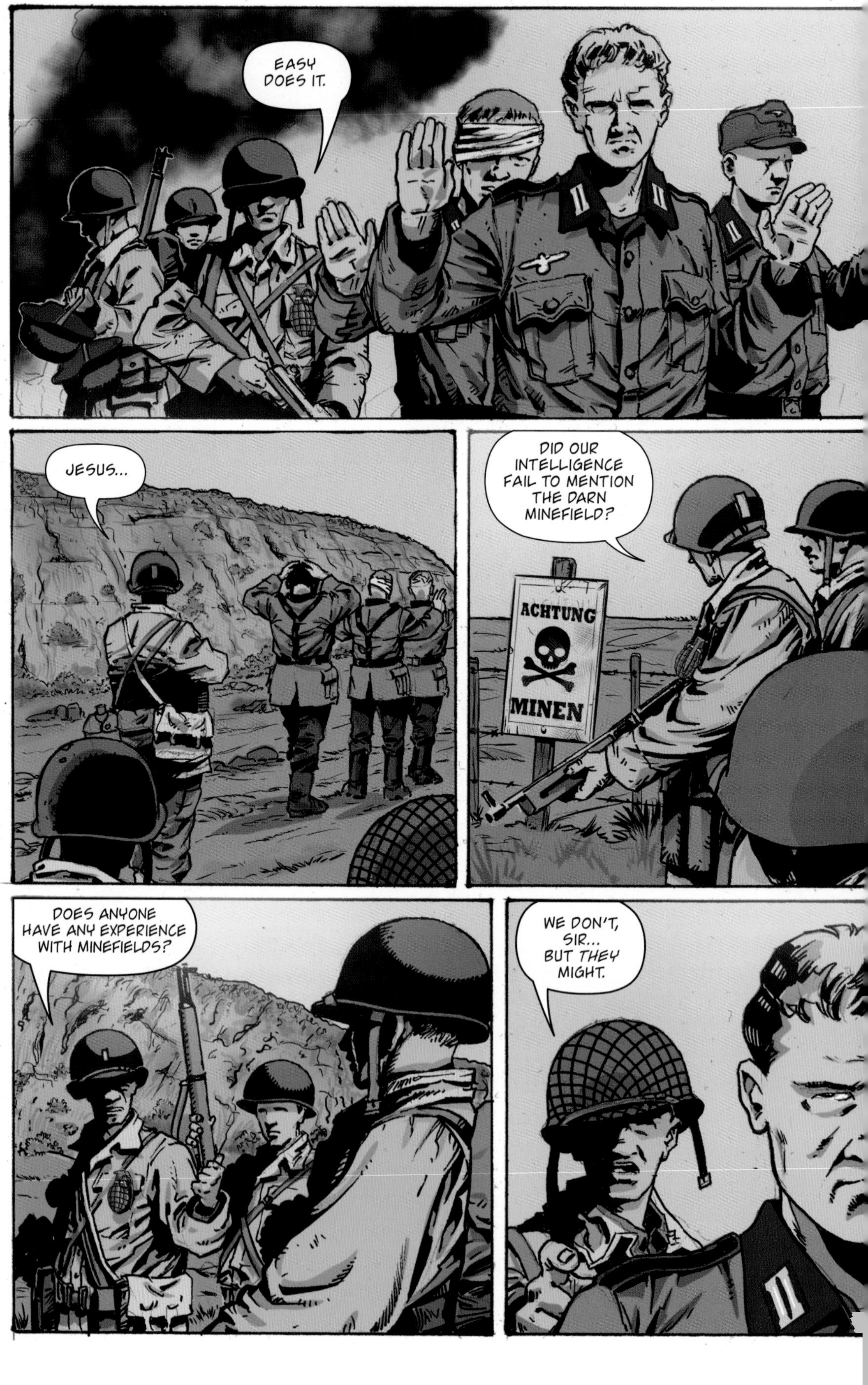

EASY DOES IT.
JESUS...
DID OUR INTELLIGENCE FAIL TO MENTION THE DARN MINEFIELD?
ACHTUNG
MINEN
DOES ANYONE HAVE ANY EXPERIENCE WITH MINEFIELDS?
WE DON'T, SIR... BUT *THEY* MIGHT.

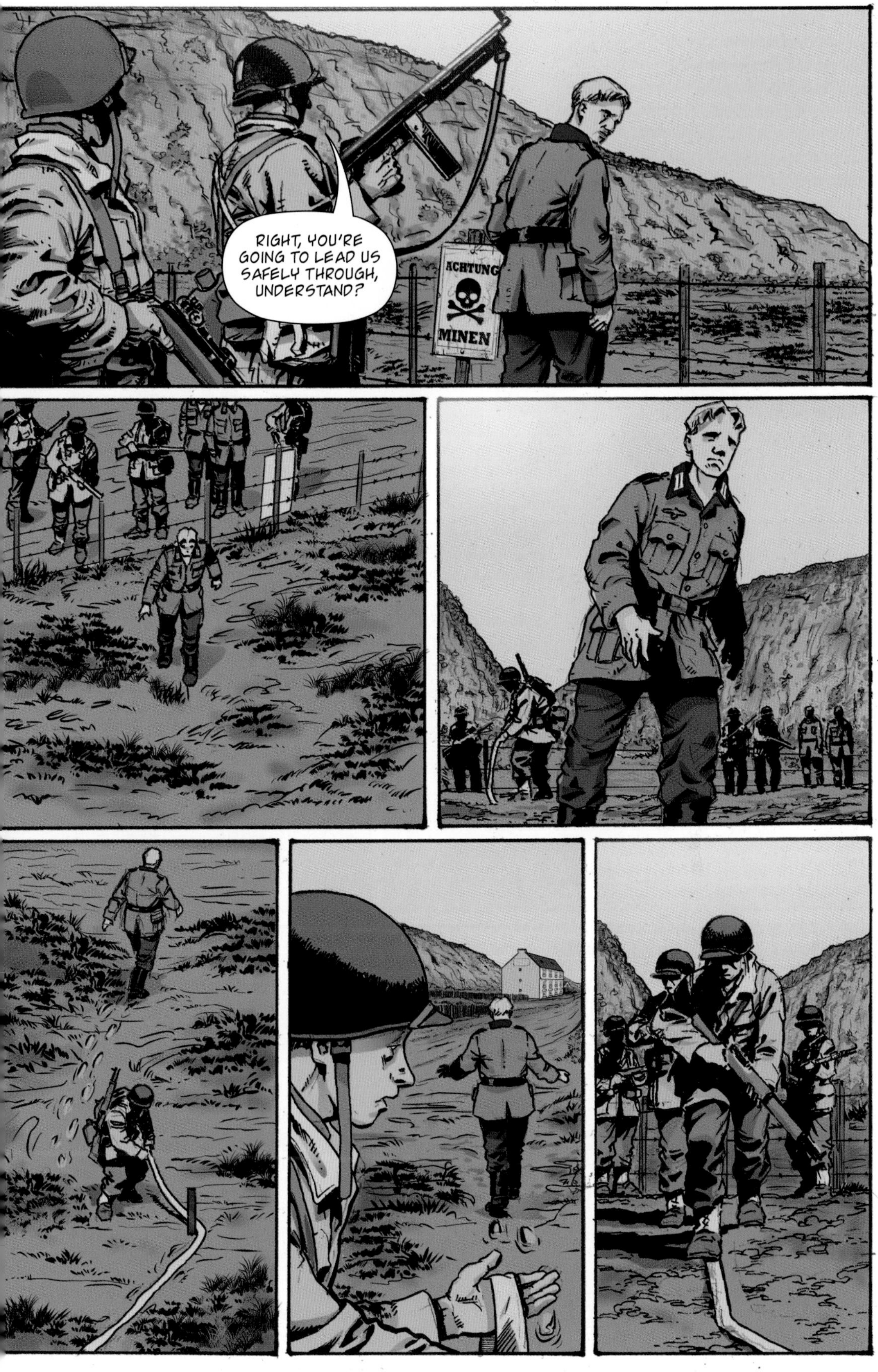
RIGHT, YOU'RE GOING TO LEAD US SAFELY THROUGH, UNDERSTAND?
ACHTUNG
MINEN

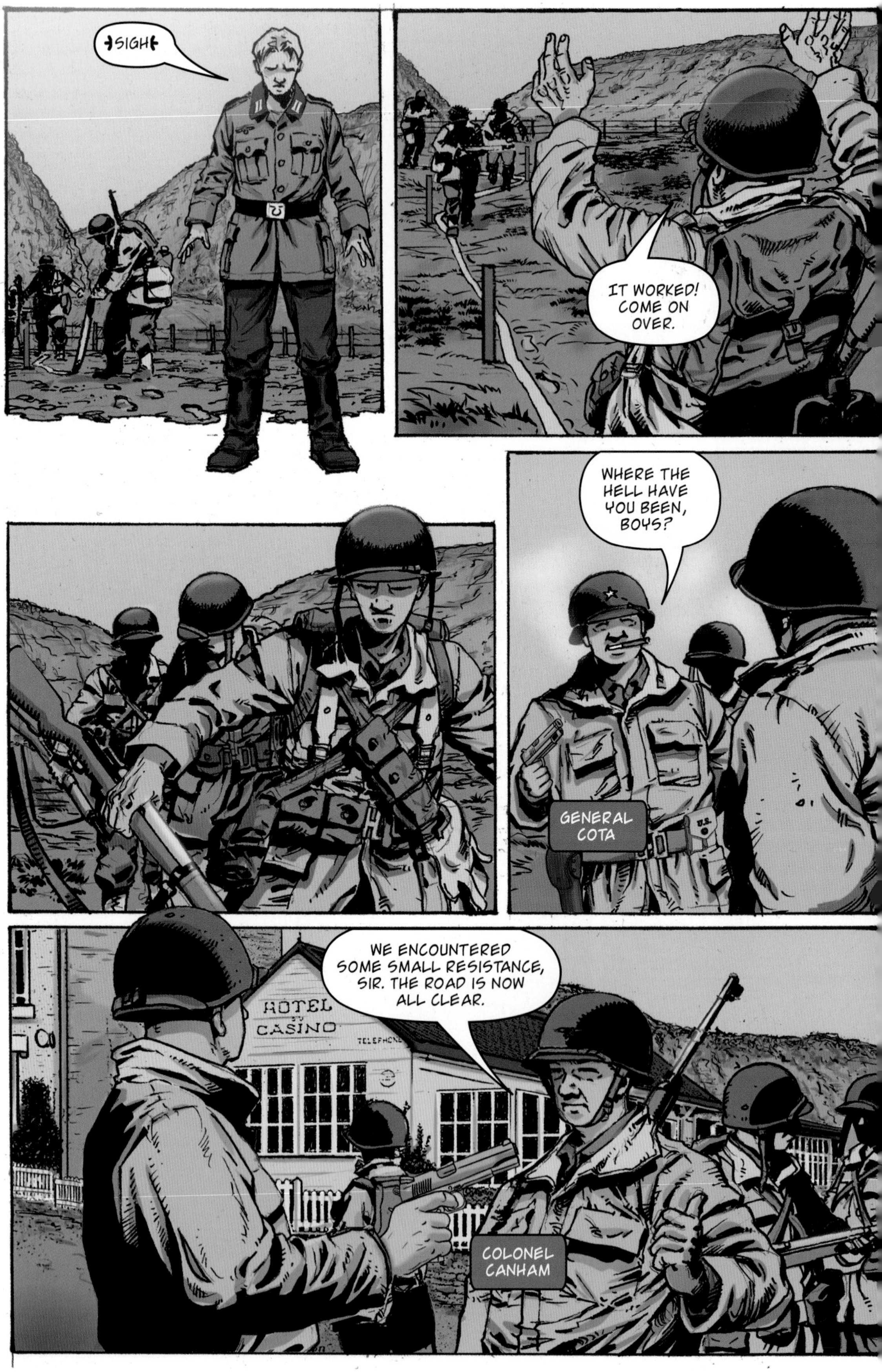
SIGH
IT WORKED! COME ON OVER.
WHERE THE HELL HAVE YOU BEEN, BOYS?
GENERAL COTA
WE ENCOUNTERED SOME SMALL RESISTANCE, SIR. THE ROAD IS NOW ALL CLEAR.
HOTEL CASINO
TELEPHONE
COLONEL CANHAM

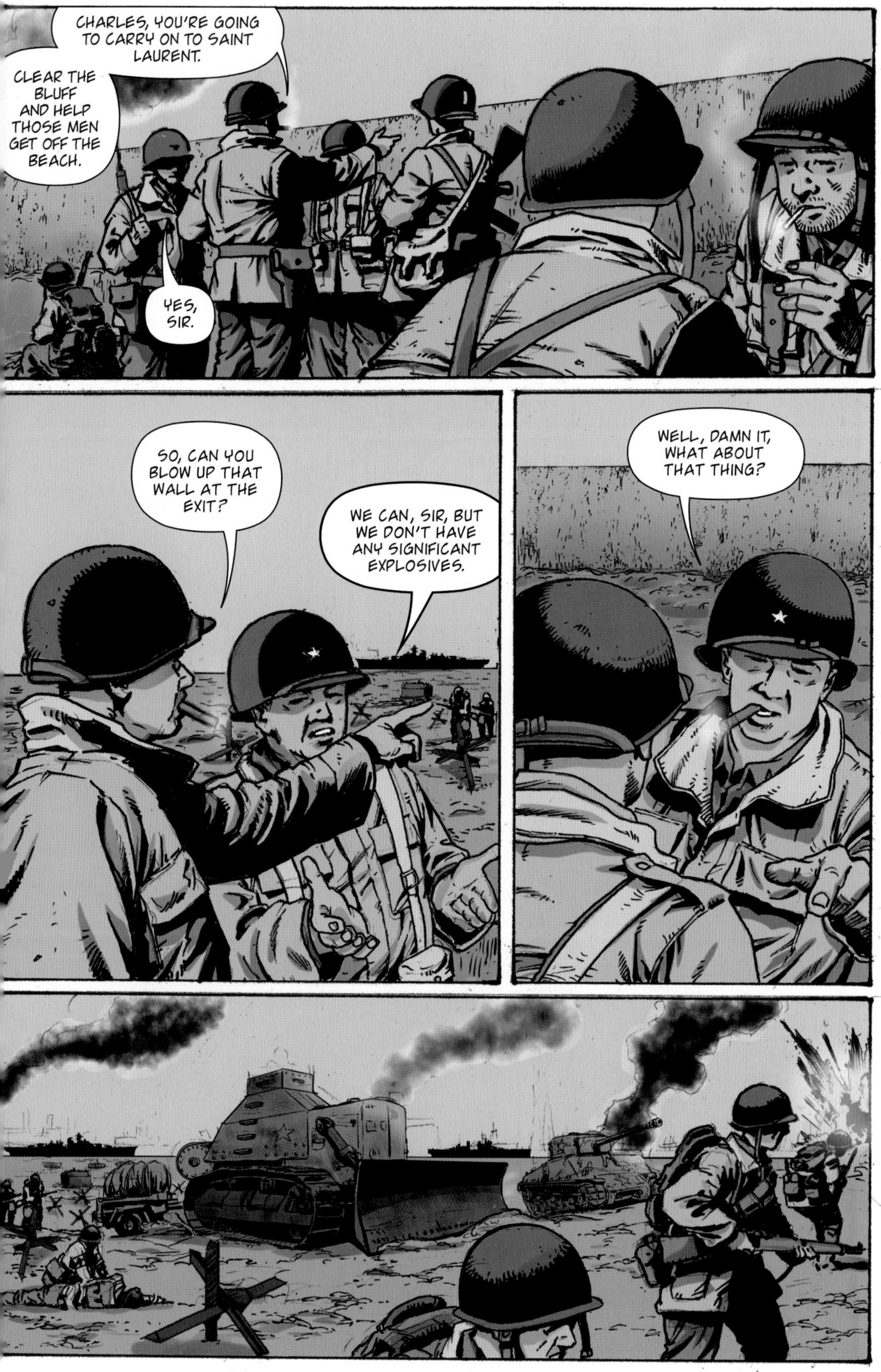
CHARLES, YOU'RE GOING TO CARRY ON TO SAINT LAURENT.
CLEAR THE BLUFF AND HELP THOSE MEN GET OFF THE BEACH.
YES, SIR.
SO, CAN YOU BLOW UP THAT WALL AT THE EXIT?
WE CAN, SIR, BUT WE DON'T HAVE ANY SIGNIFICANT EXPLOSIVES.
WELL, DAMN IT, WHAT ABOUT THAT THING?

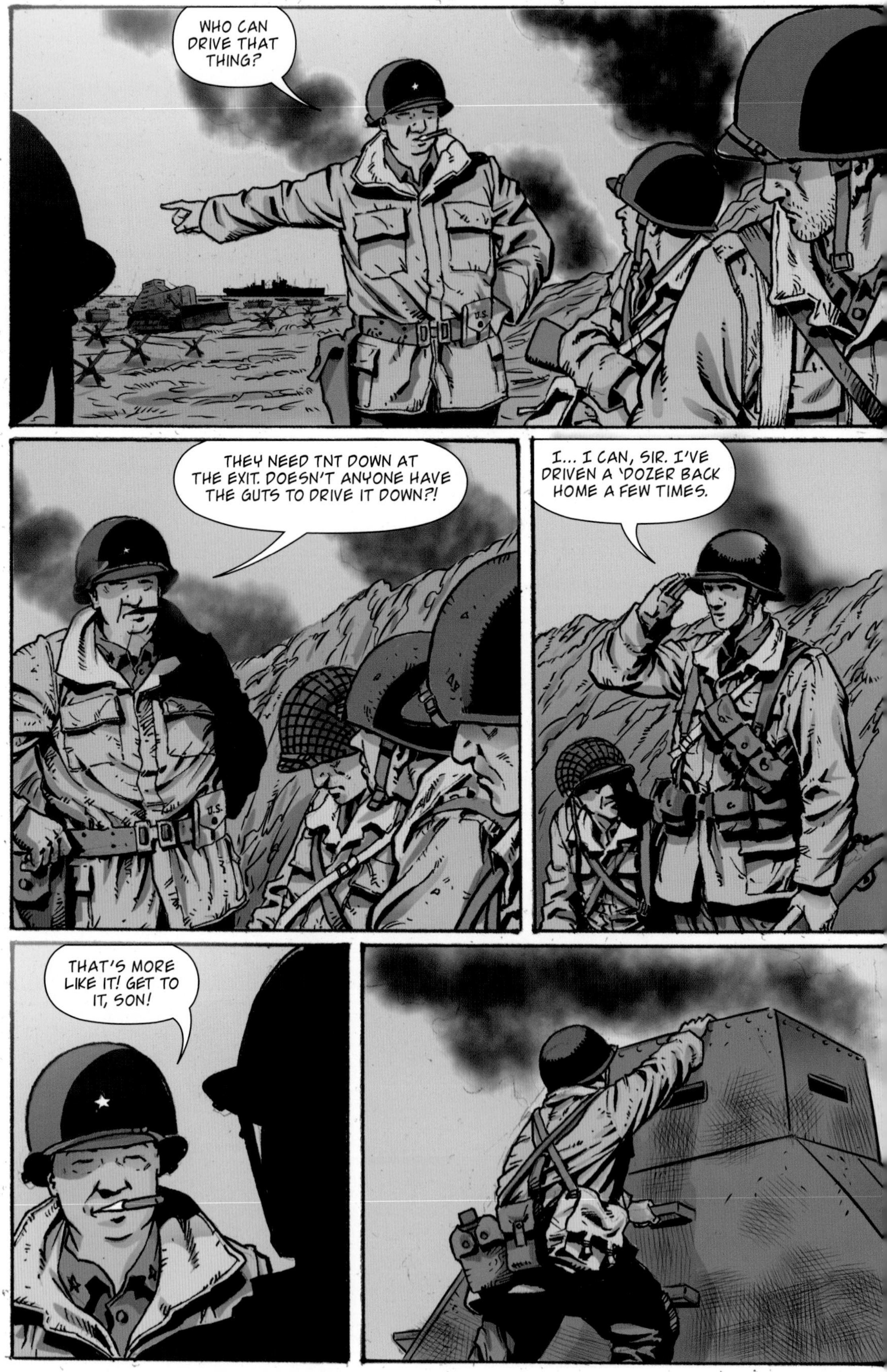
WHO CAN DRIVE THAT THING?
THEY NEED TNT DOWN AT THE EXIT. DOESN'T ANYONE HAVE THE GUTS TO DRIVE IT DOWN?!
I... I CAN, SIR. I'VE DRIVEN A 'DOZER BACK HOME A FEW TIMES.
THAT'S MORE LIKE IT! GET TO IT, SON!

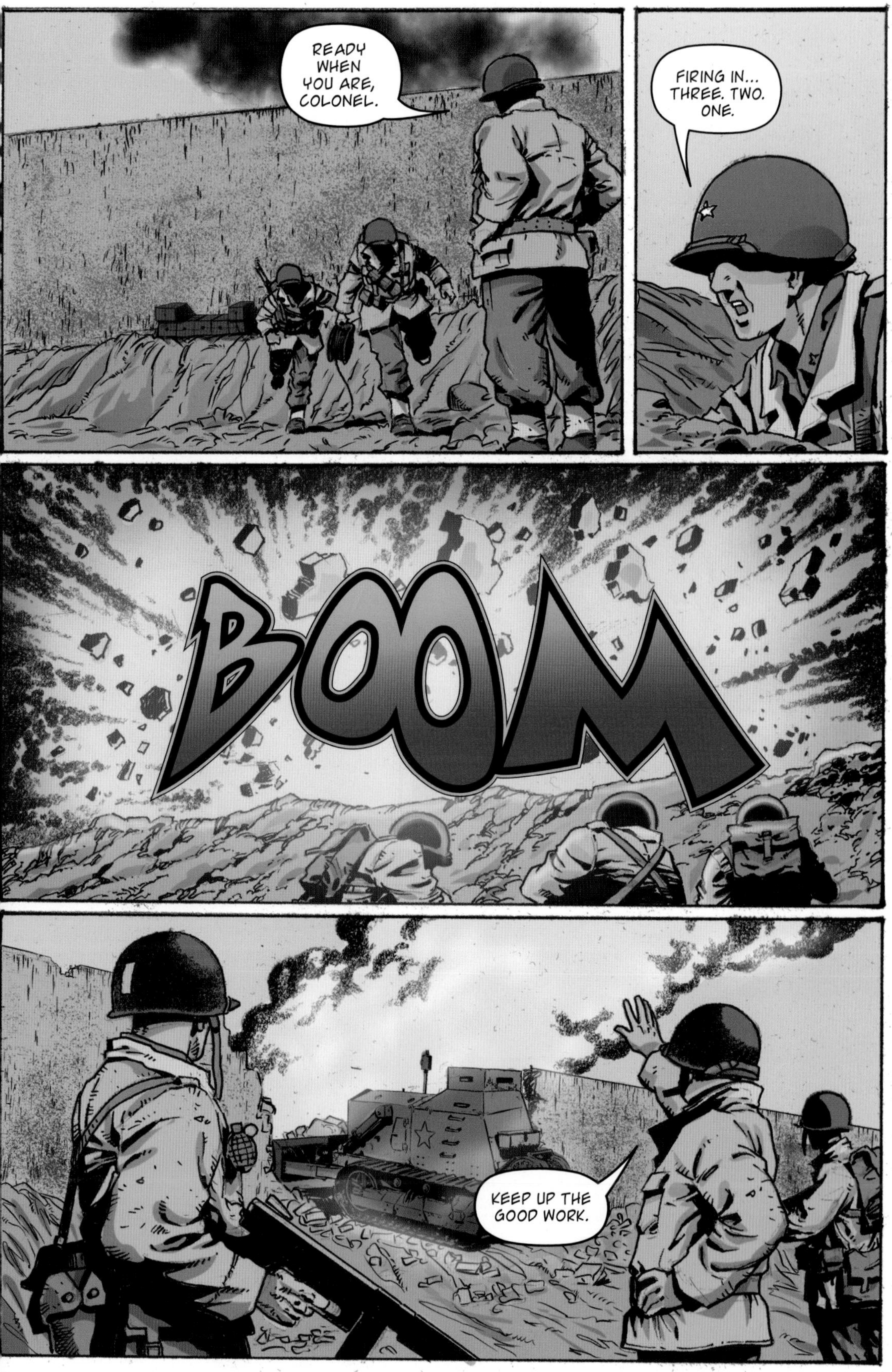
READY WHEN YOU ARE, COLONEL.
FIRING IN... THREE. TWO. ONE.
BOOM
KEEP UP THE GOOD WORK.

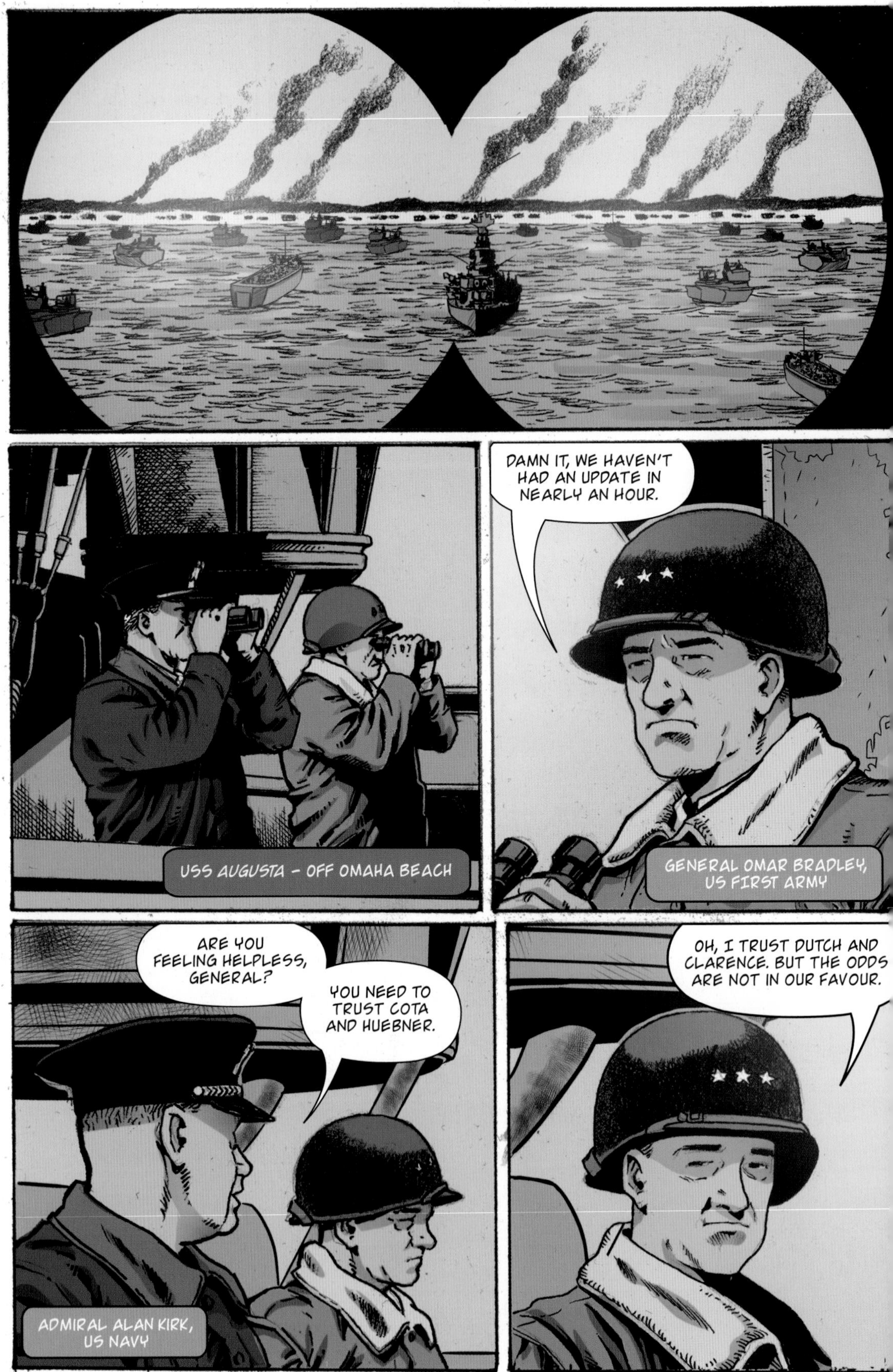

USS AUGUSTA – OFF OMAHA BEACH
DAMN IT, WE HAVEN'T HAD AN UPDATE IN NEARLY AN HOUR.
GENERAL OMAR BRADLEY, US FIRST ARMY
ARE YOU FEELING HELPLESS, GENERAL?
YOU NEED TO TRUST COTA AND HUEBNER.
ADMIRAL ALAN KIRK, US NAVY
OH, I TRUST DUTCH AND CLARENCE. BUT THE ODDS ARE NOT IN OUR FAVOUR.

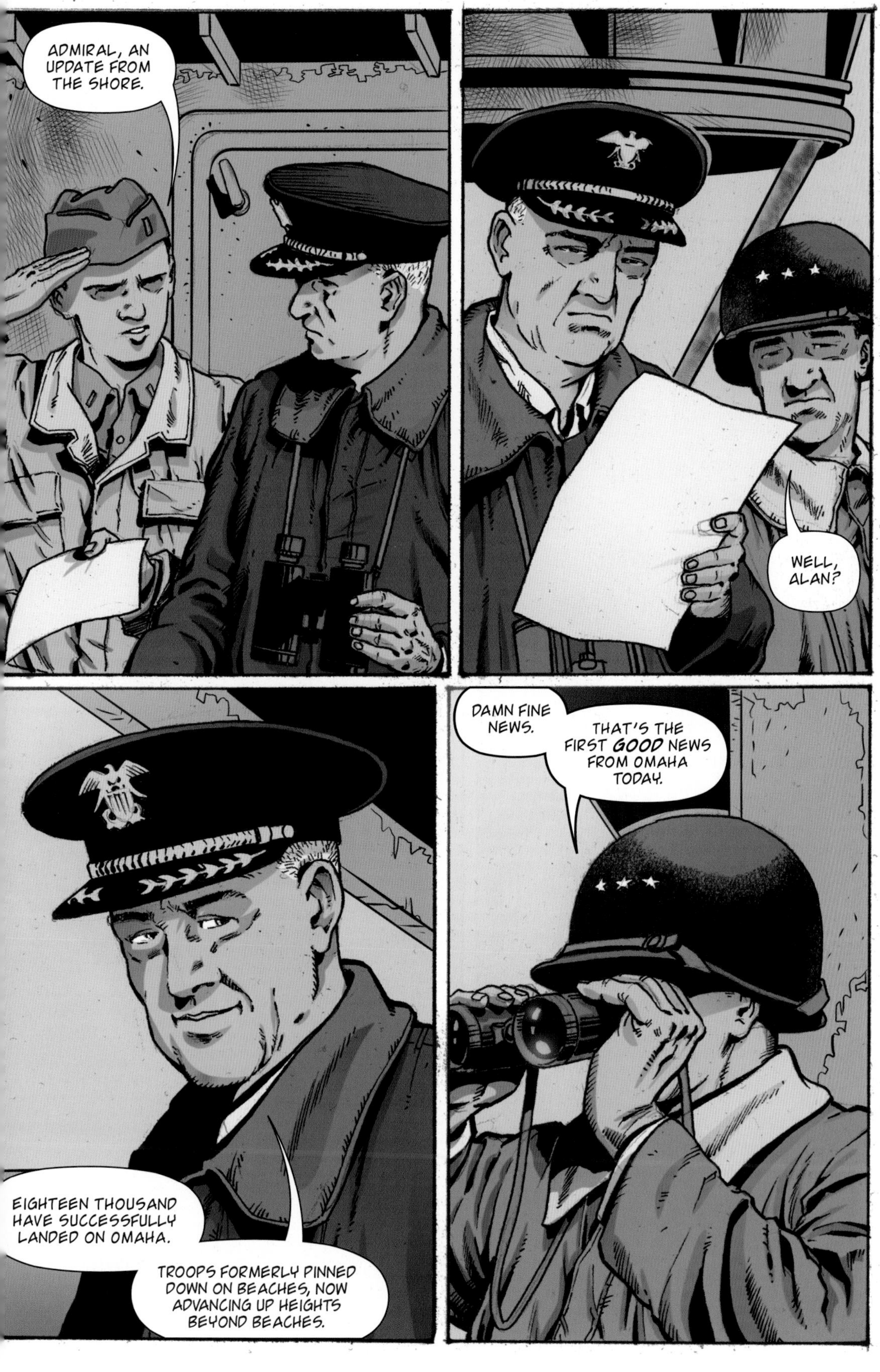
ADMIRAL, AN UPDATE FROM THE SHORE.
WELL, ALAN?
EIGHTEEN THOUSAND HAVE SUCCESSFULLY LANDED ON OMAHA.
TROOPS FORMERLY PINNED DOWN ON BEACHES, NOW ADVANCING UP HEIGHTS BEYOND BEACHES.
DAMN FINE NEWS.
THAT'S THE FIRST GOOD NEWS FROM OMAHA TODAY.

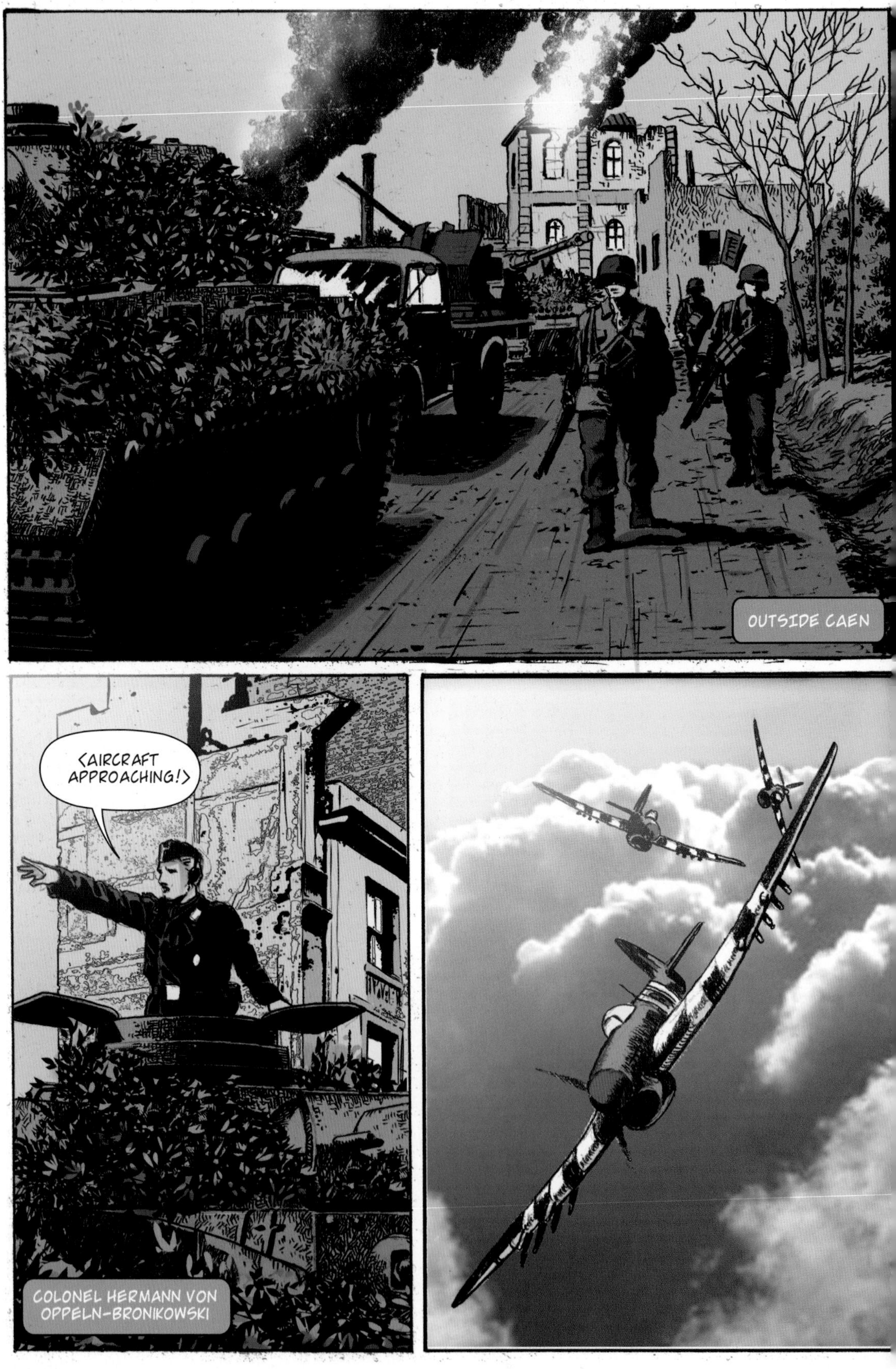
OUTSIDE CAEN
<AIRCRAFT APPROACHING!>
COLONEL HERMANN VON OPPELN-BRONIKOWSKI

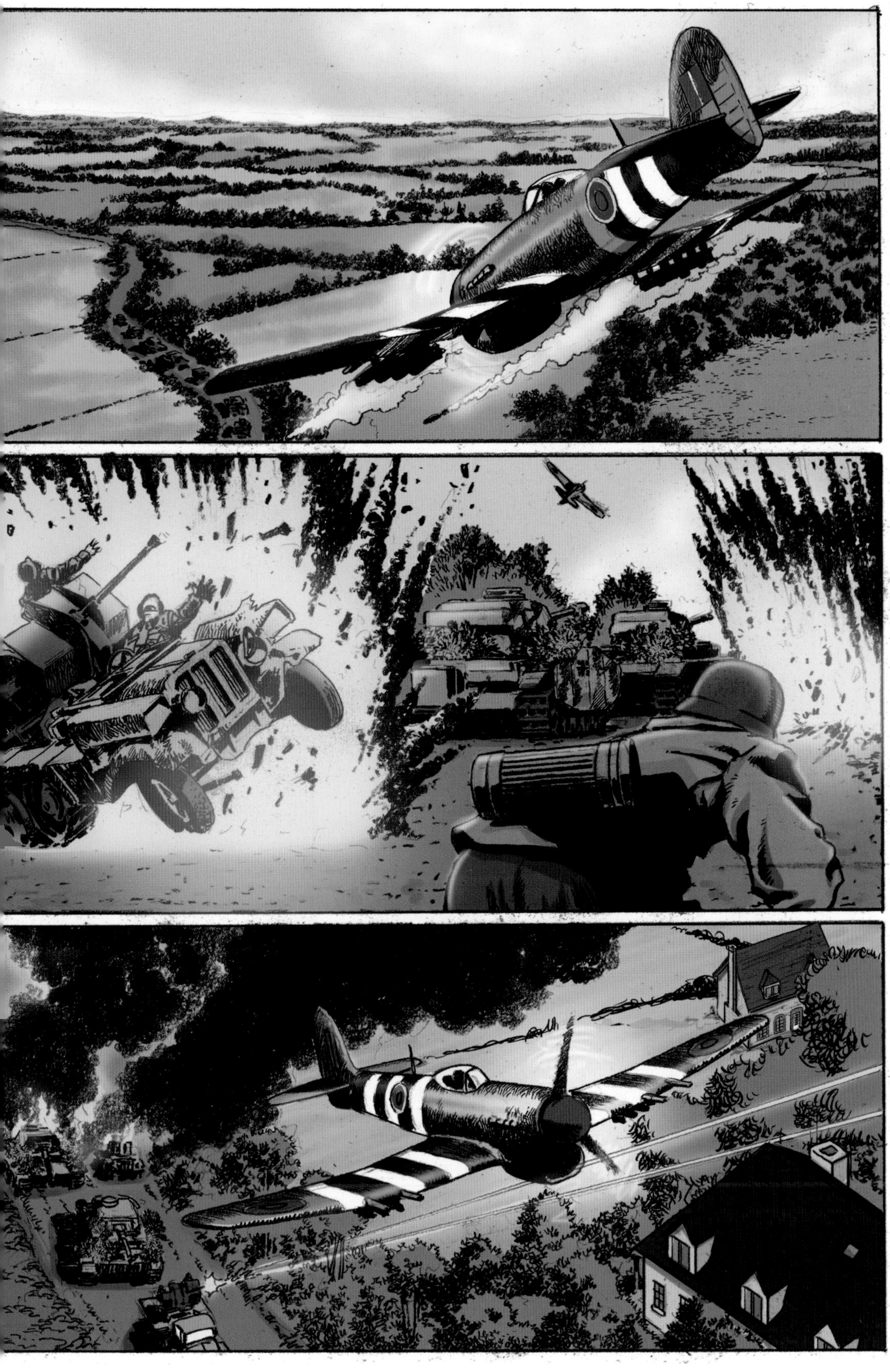

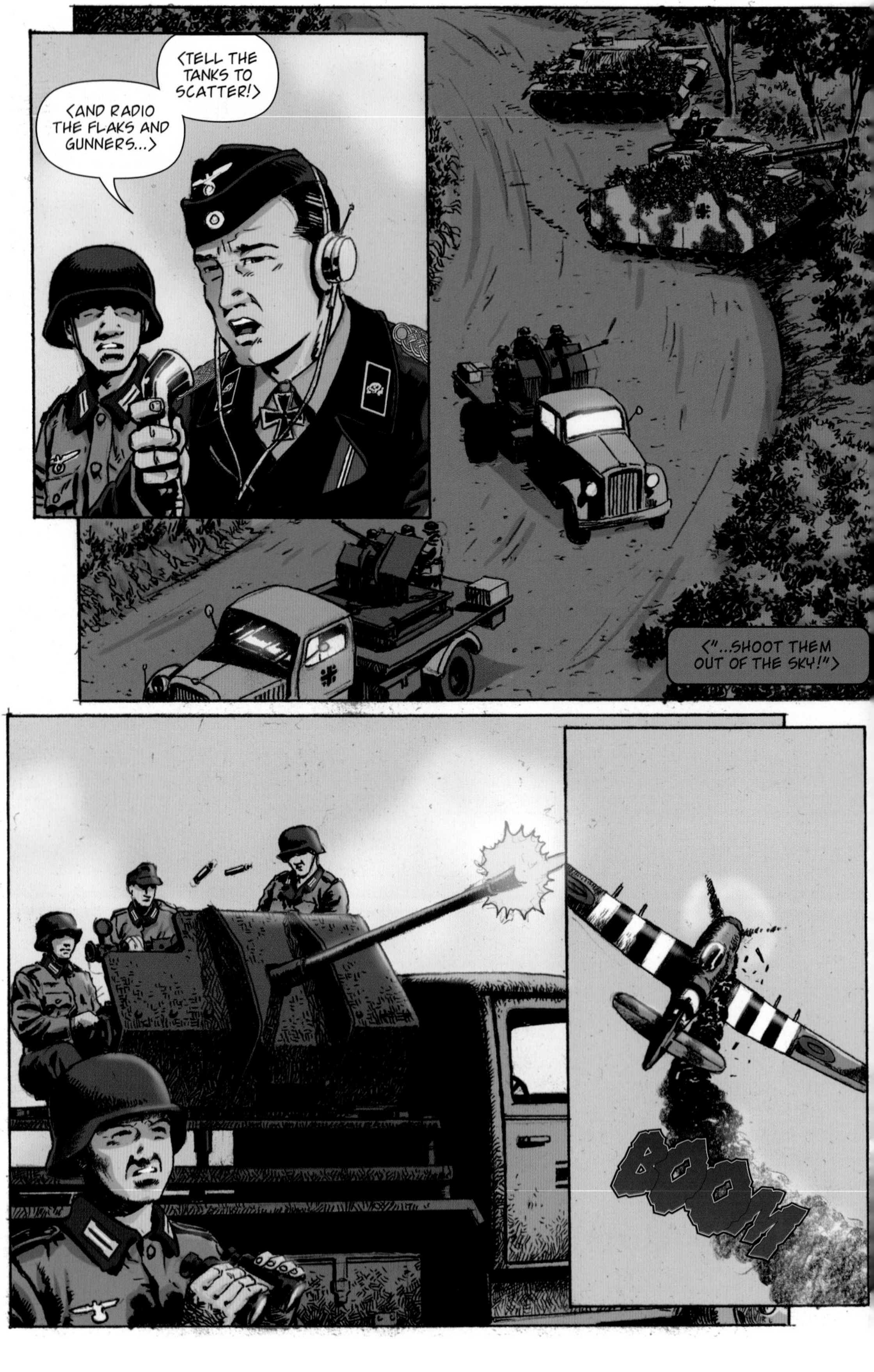
<TELL THE TANKS TO SCATTER!>
<AND RADIO THE FLAKS AND GUNNERS...>
<"...SHOOT THEM OUT OF THE SKY!">
BOOM

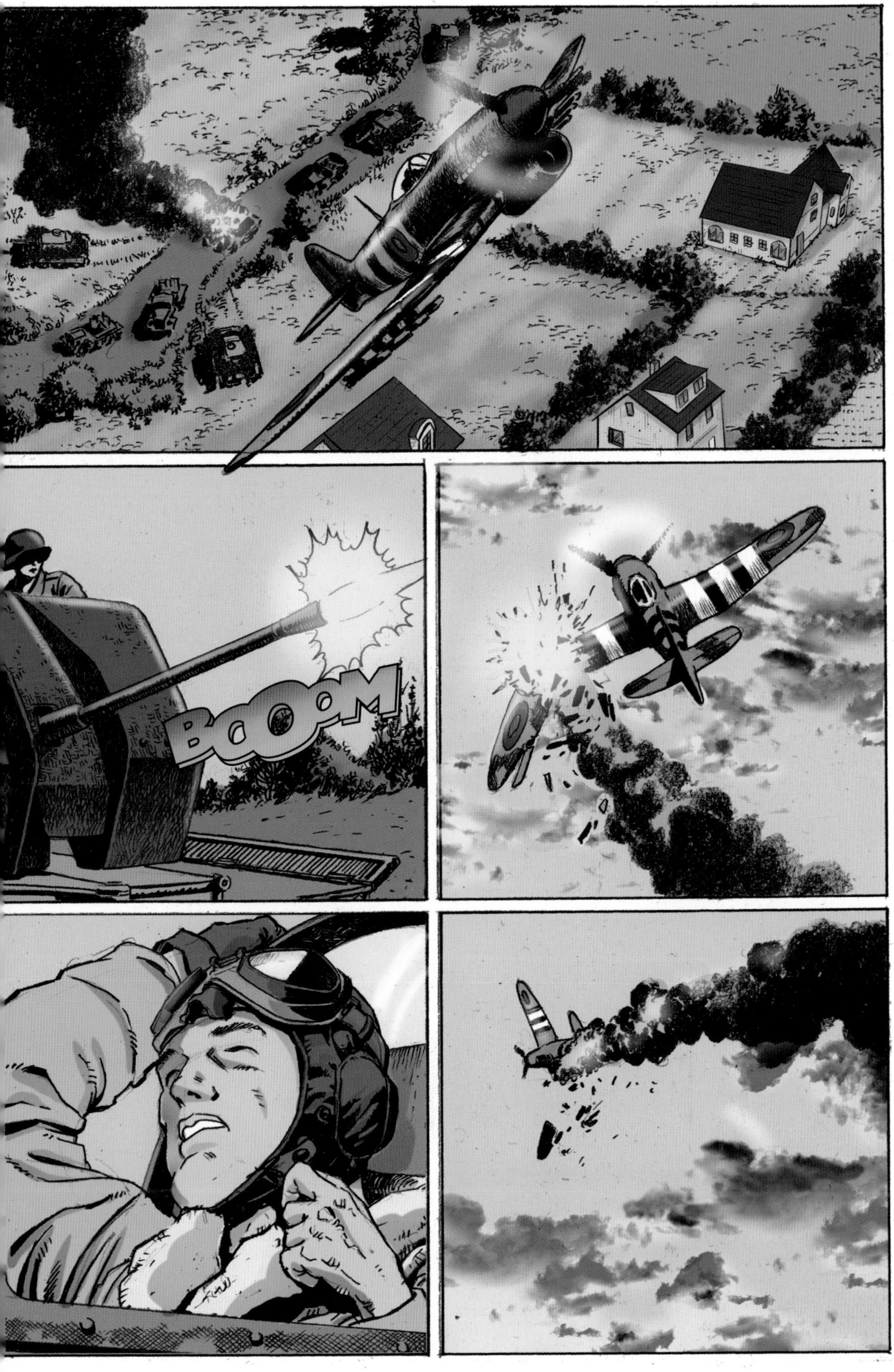
BOOOM

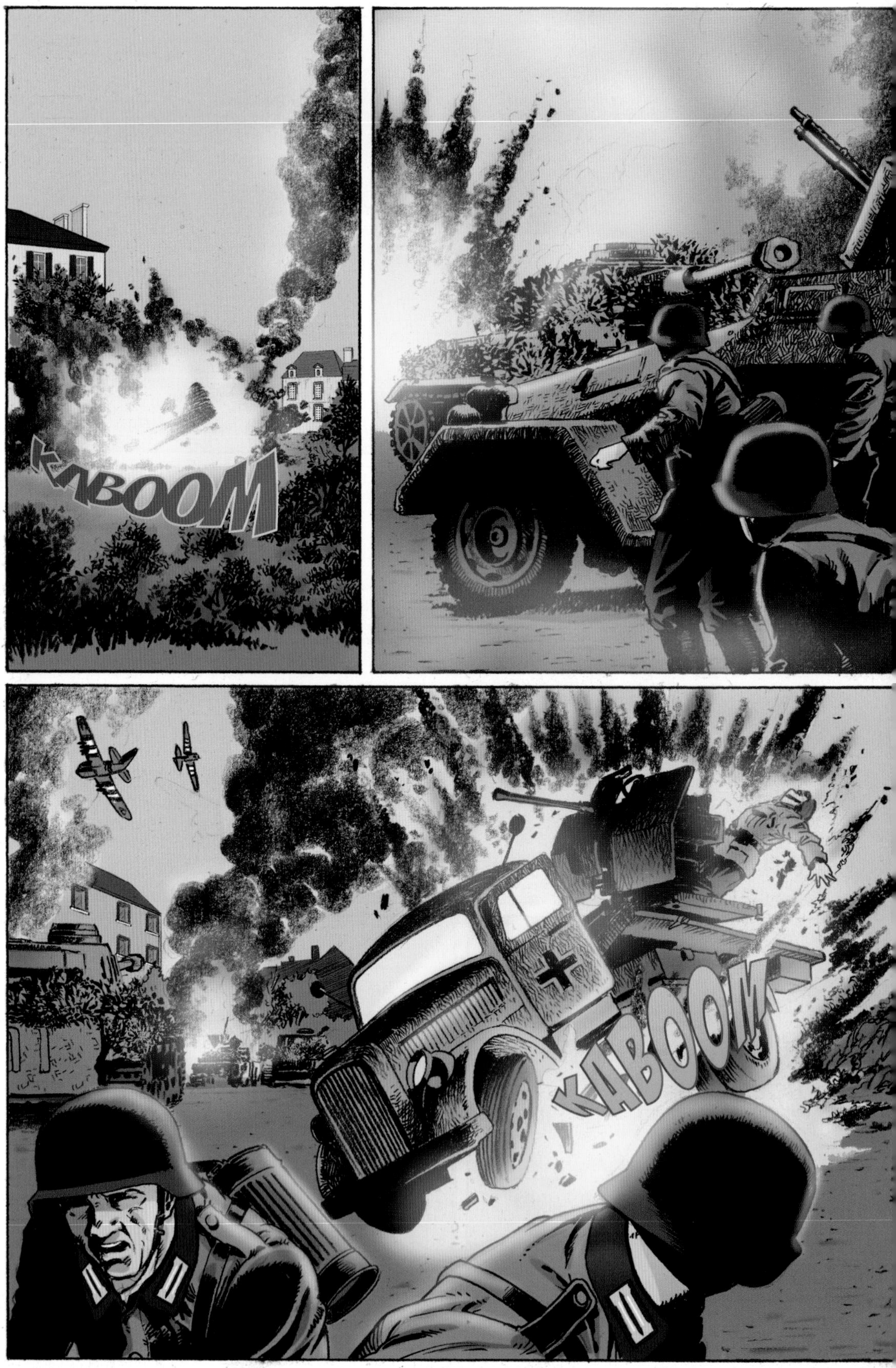
KABOOM
KABOOM

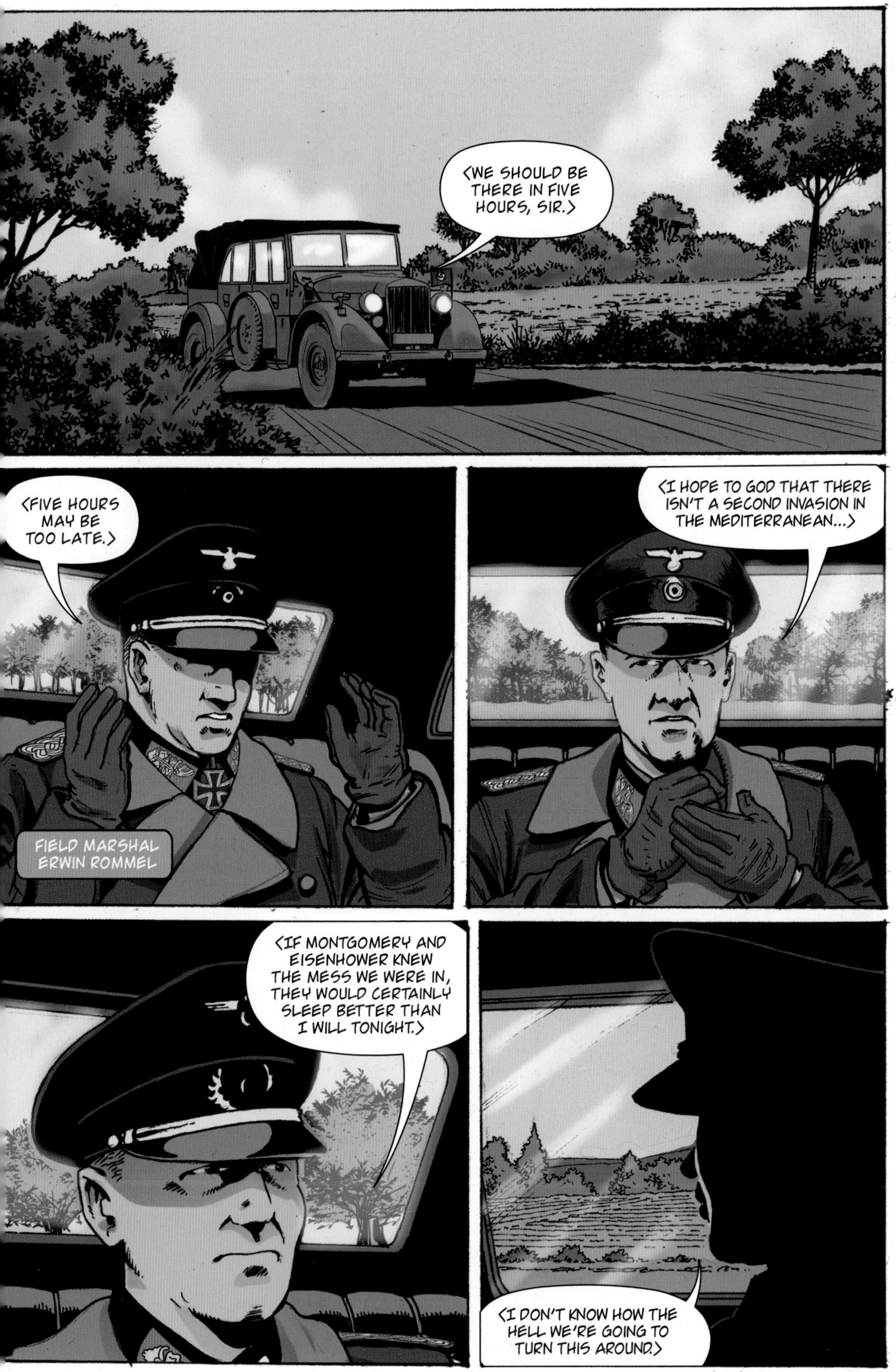

<WE SHOULD BE THERE IN FIVE HOURS, SIR.>
<FIVE HOURS MAY BE TOO LATE.>
FIELD MARSHAL ERWIN ROMMEL
<I HOPE TO GOD THAT THERE ISN'T A SECOND INVASION IN THE MEDITERRANEAN...>
<IF MONTGOMERY AND EISENHOWER KNEW THE MESS WE WERE IN, THEY WOULD CERTAINLY SLEEP BETTER THAN I WILL TONIGHT.>
<I DON'T KNOW HOW THE HELL WE'RE GOING TO TURN THIS AROUND.>

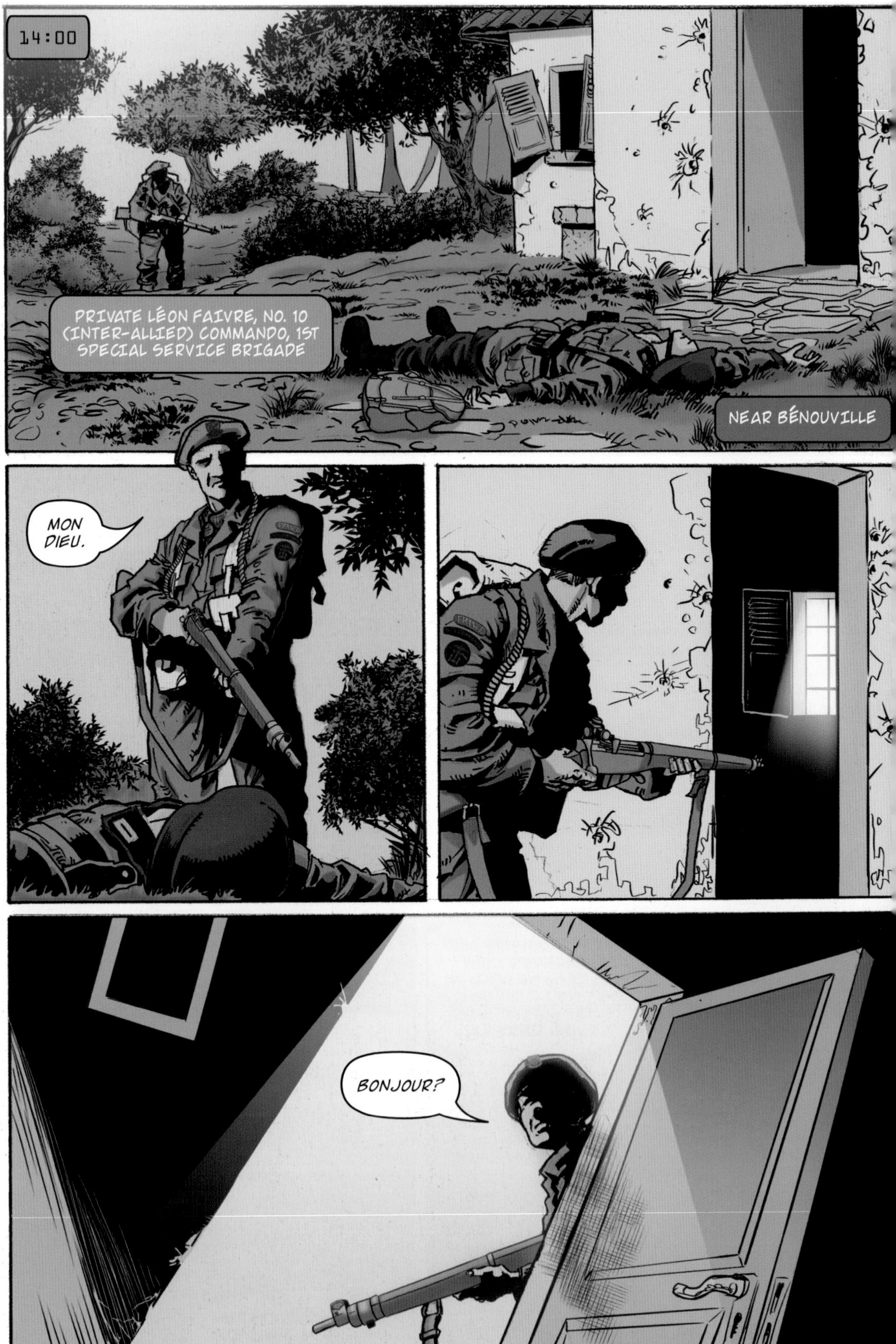
14:00
PRIVATE LÉON FAIVRE, NO. 10 (INTER-ALLIED) COMMANDO, 1ST SPECIAL SERVICE BRIGADE
NEAR BÉNOUVILLE
MON DIEU.
BONJOUR?

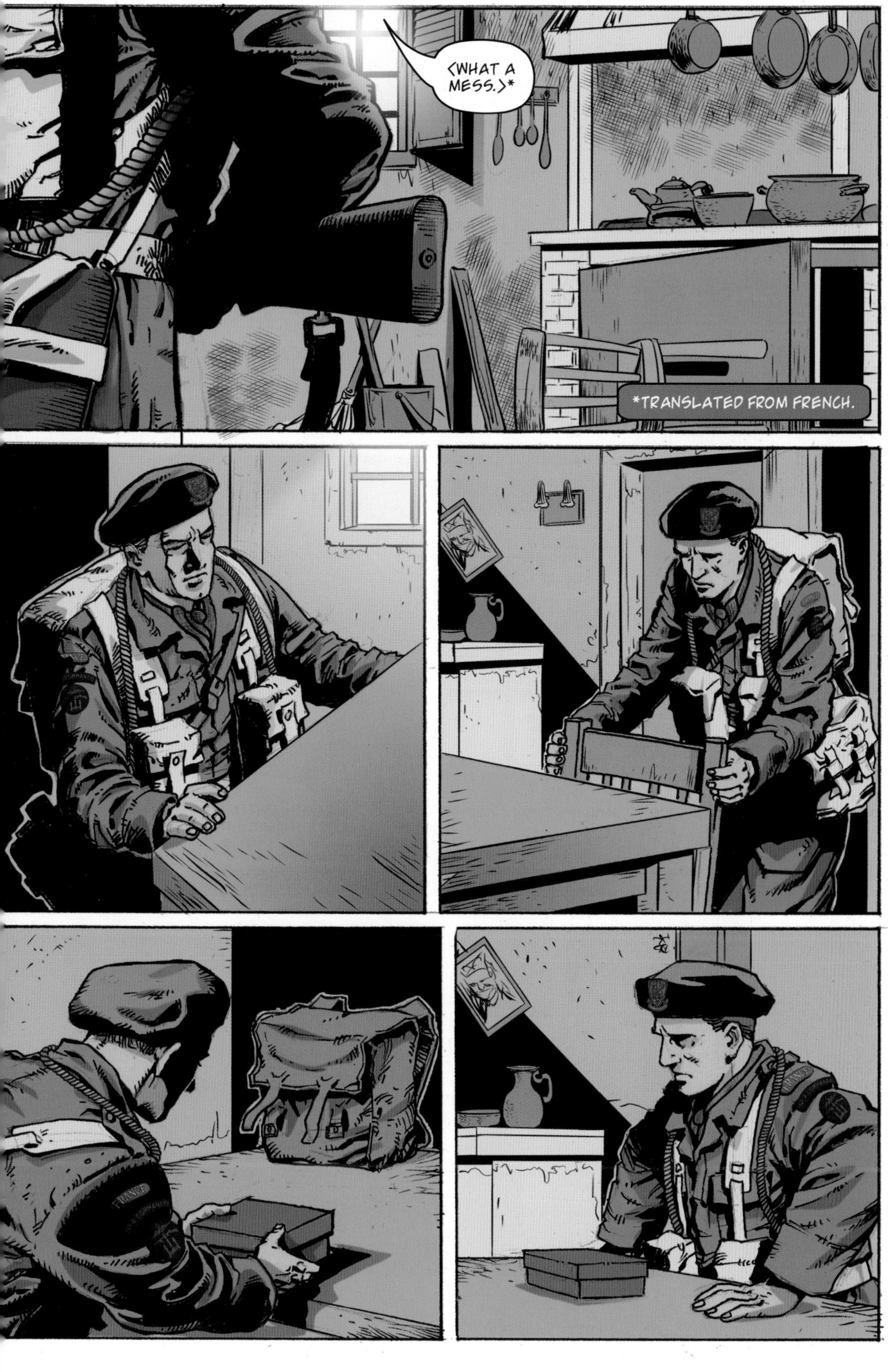

<WHAT A MESS.>*
*TRANSLATED FROM FRENCH.

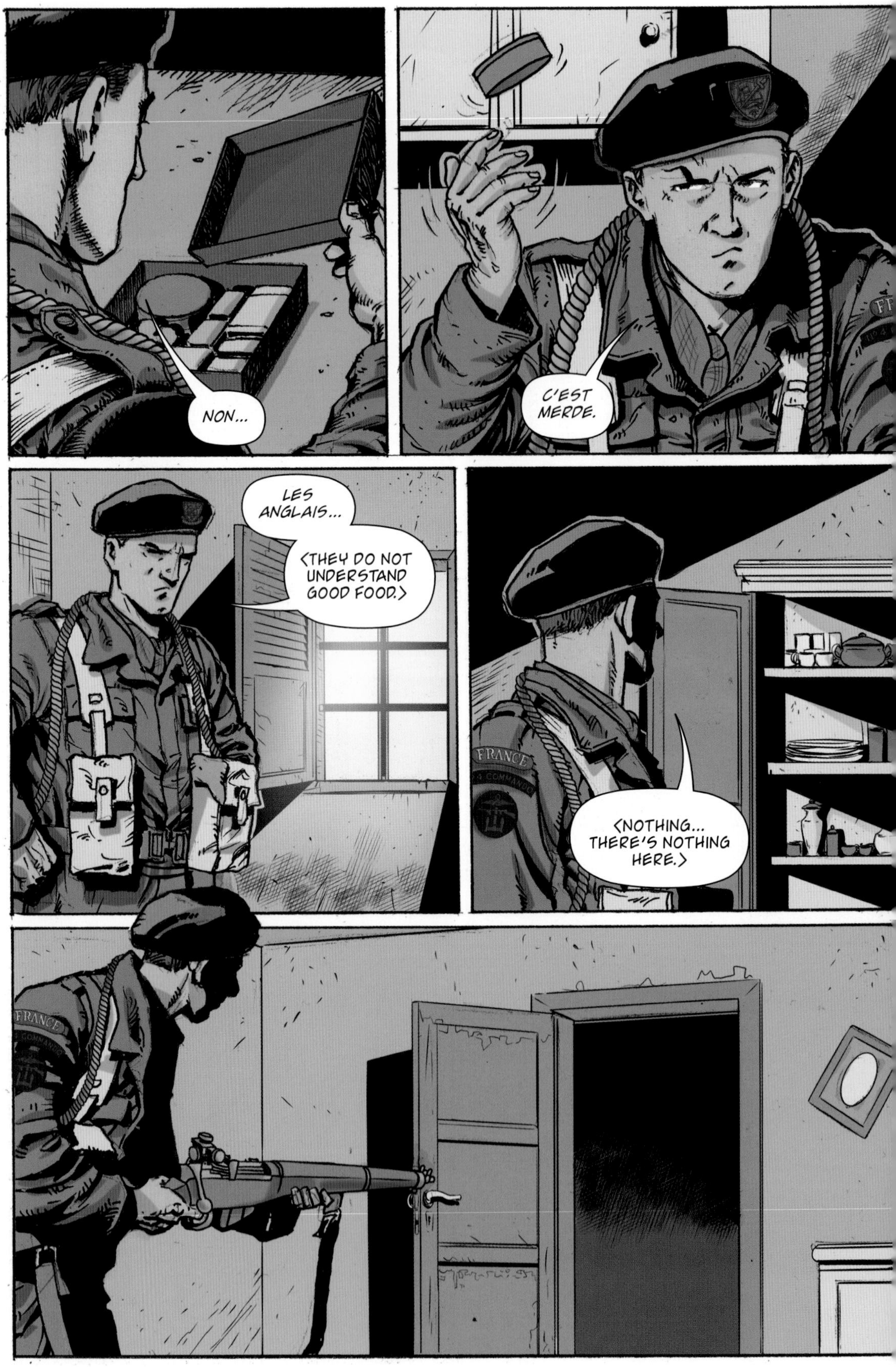
NON...
C'EST MERDE.
LES ANGLAIS...
<THEY DO NOT UNDERSTAND GOOD FOOD.>
FRANCE
<NOTHING... THERE'S NOTHING HERE.>
FRANCE

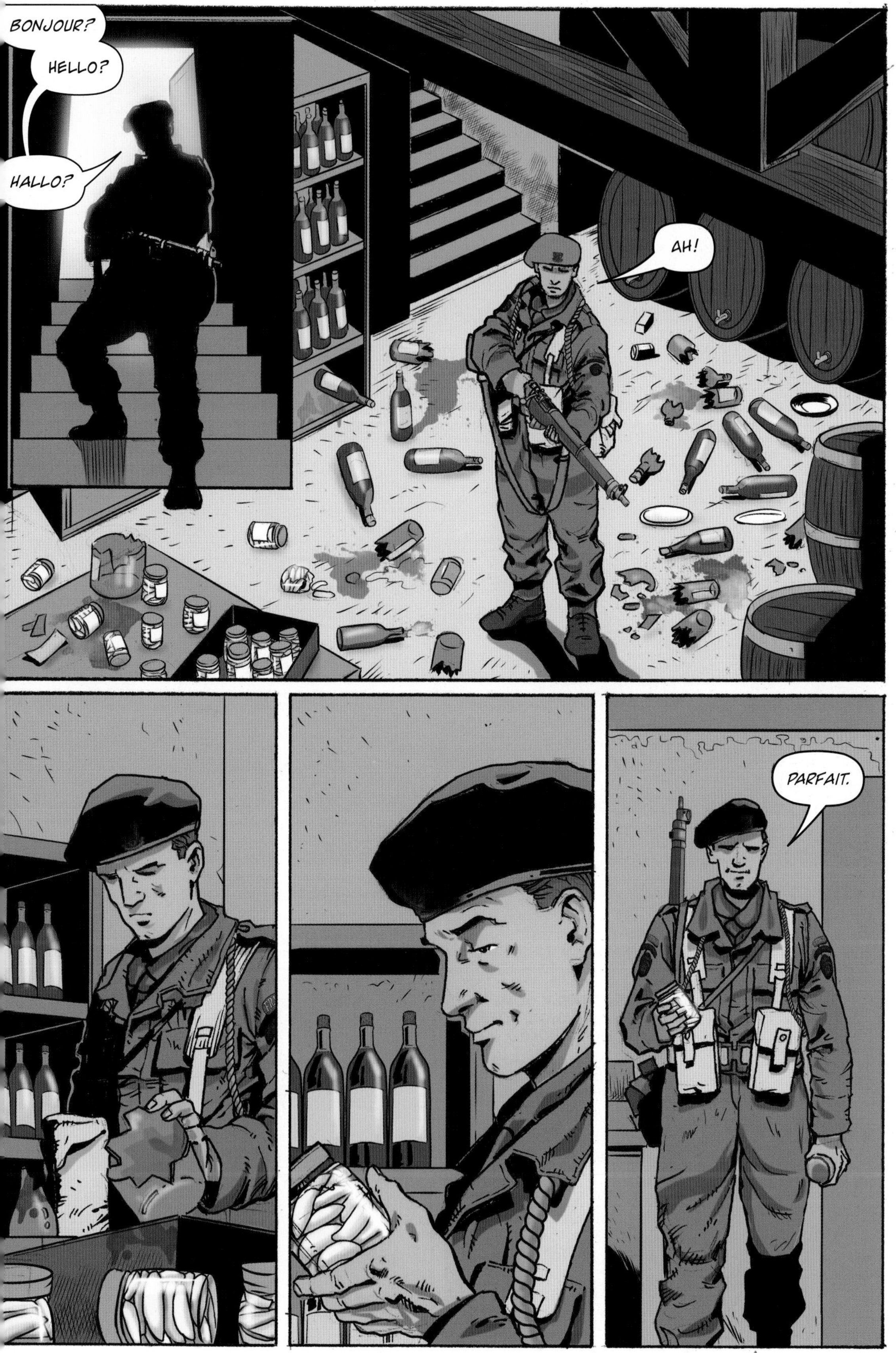
BONJOUR?
HELLO?
HALLO?
AH!
PARFAIT.

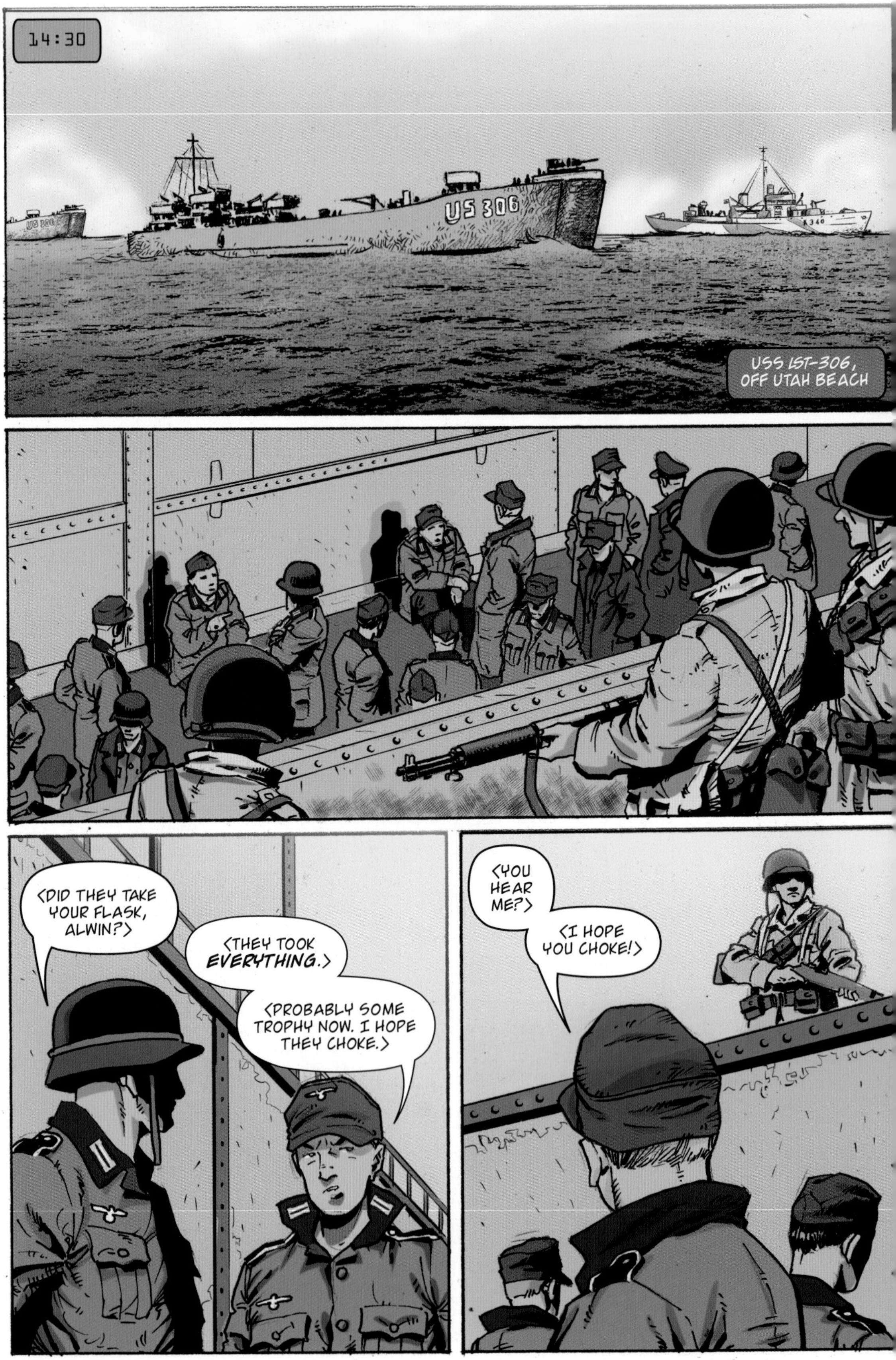

14:30
USS LST-306, OFF UTAH BEACH
<DID THEY TAKE YOUR FLASK, ALWIN?>
<THEY TOOK EVERYTHING.>
<PROBABLY SOME TROPHY NOW. I HOPE THEY CHOKE.>
<YOU HEAR ME?>
<I HOPE YOU CHOKE!>

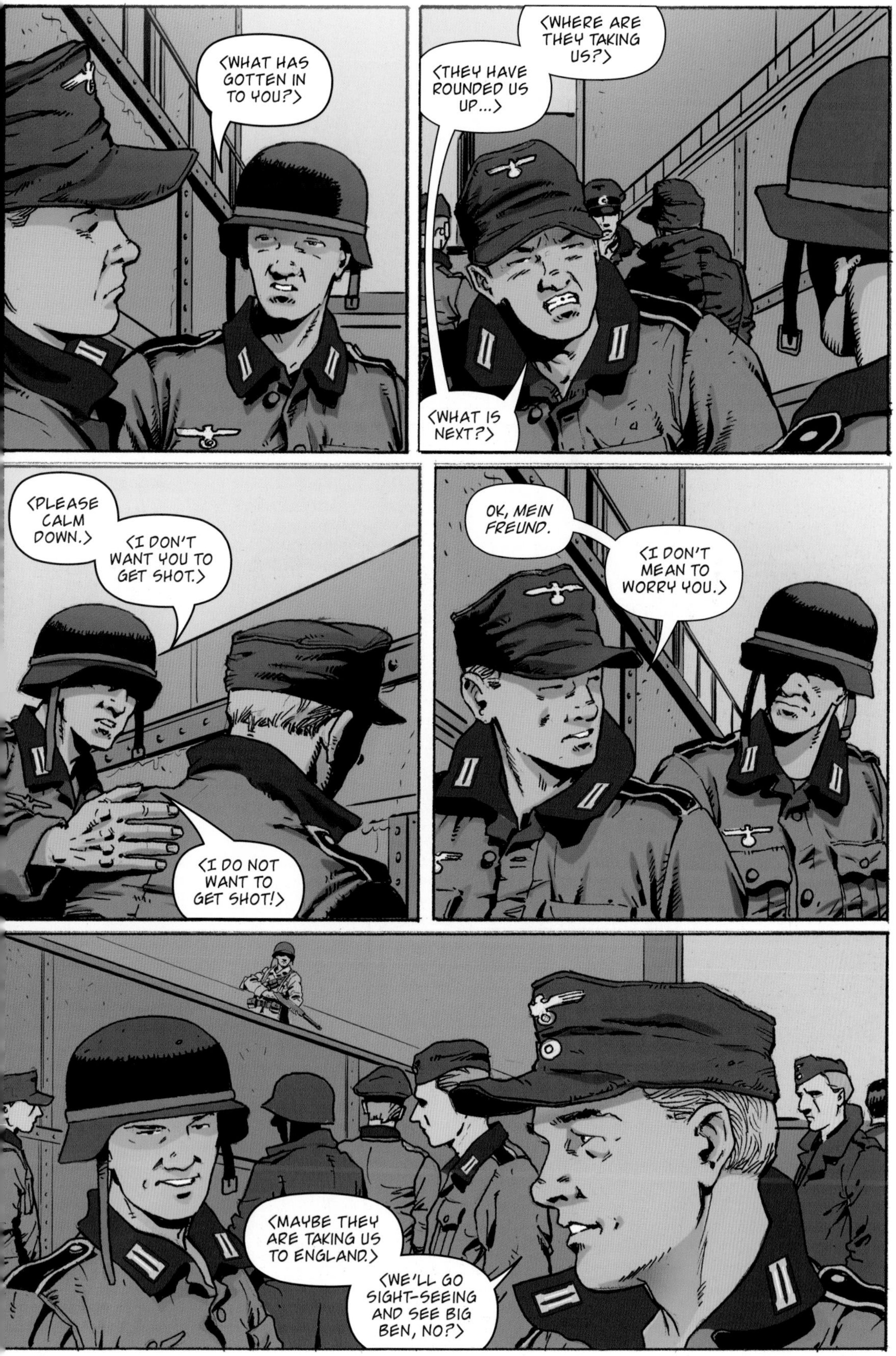

<WHAT HAS GOTTEN IN TO YOU?>
<THEY HAVE ROUNDED US UP...>
<WHERE ARE THEY TAKING US?>
<WHAT IS NEXT?>
<PLEASE CALM DOWN.>
<I DON'T WANT YOU TO GET SHOT.>
<I DO NOT WANT TO GET SHOT!>
OK, MEIN FREUND.
<I DON'T MEAN TO WORRY YOU.>
<MAYBE THEY ARE TAKING US TO ENGLAND.>
<WE'LL GO SIGHT-SEEING AND SEE BIG BEN, NO?>

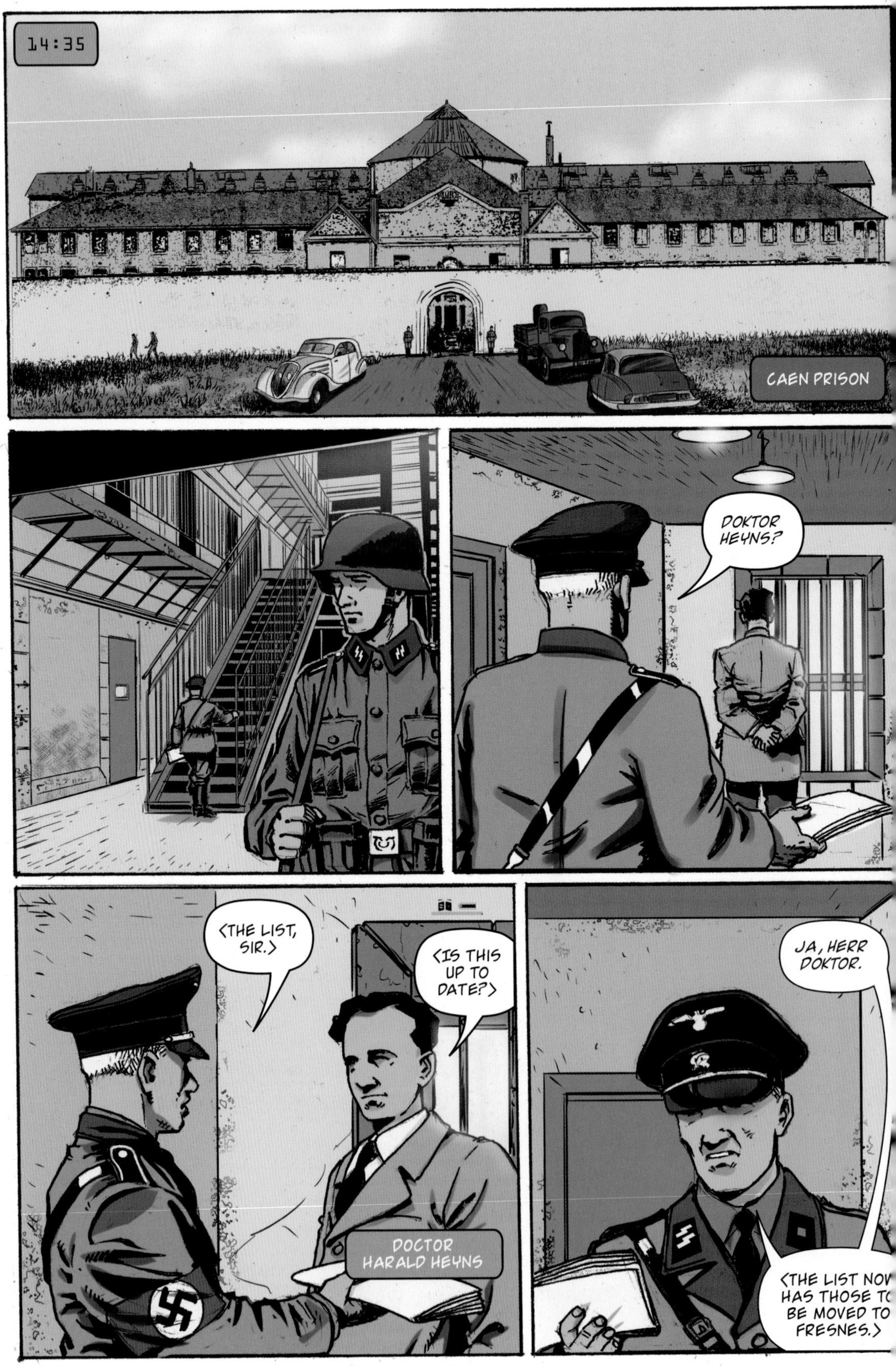
14:35
CAEN PRISON
DOKTOR HEYNS?
<THE LIST, SIR.>
<IS THIS UP TO DATE?>
DOCTOR HARALD HEYNS
JA, HERR DOKTOR.
<THE LIST NOW HAS THOSE TO BE MOVED TO FRESNES.>

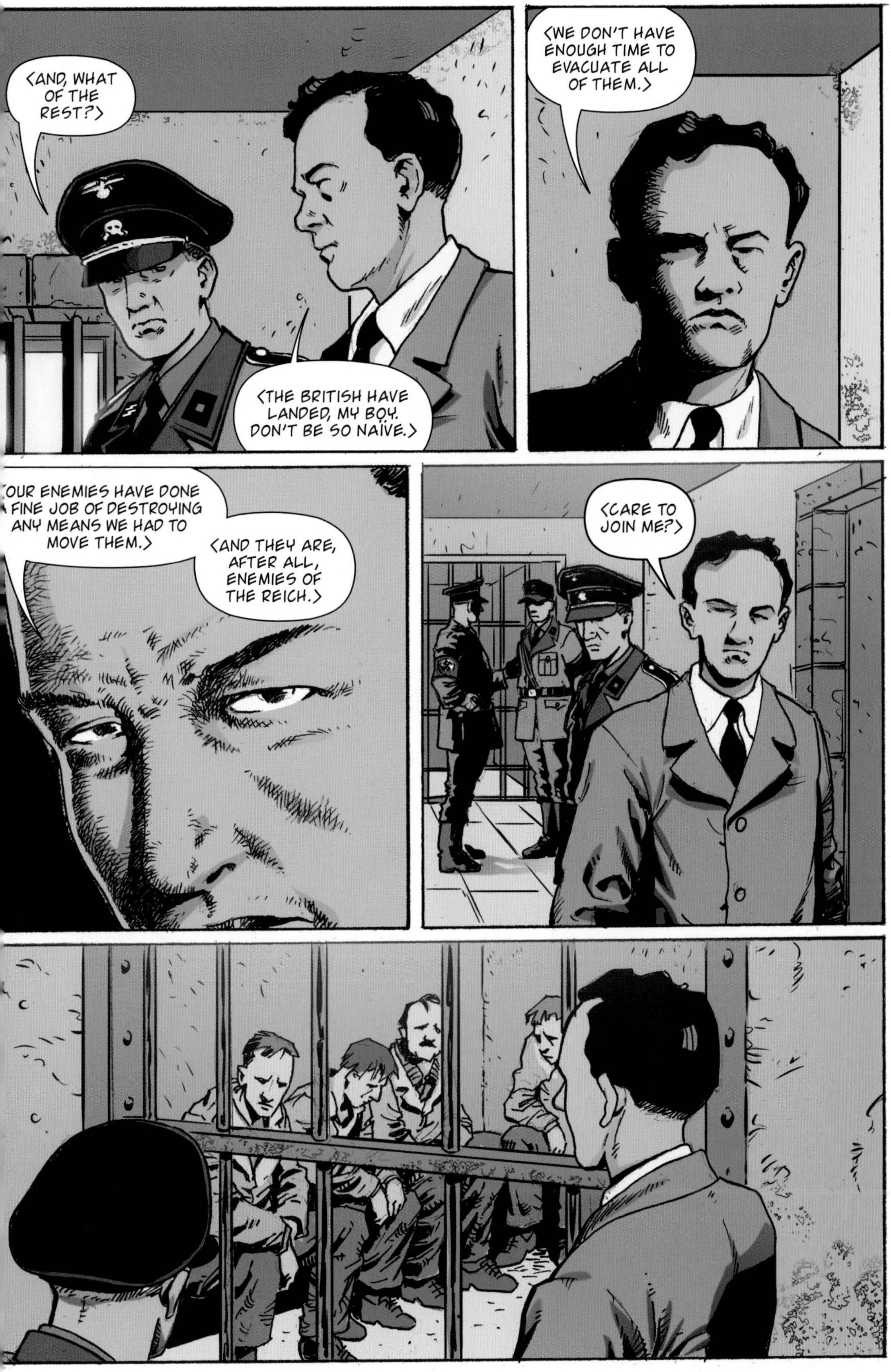

<AND, WHAT OF THE REST?>
<THE BRITISH HAVE LANDED, MY BOY. DON'T BE SO NAÏVE.>
<WE DON'T HAVE ENOUGH TIME TO EVACUATE ALL OF THEM.>
<OUR ENEMIES HAVE DONE A FINE JOB OF DESTROYING ANY MEANS WE HAD TO MOVE THEM.>
<AND THEY ARE, AFTER ALL, ENEMIES OF THE REICH.>
<CARE TO JOIN ME?>

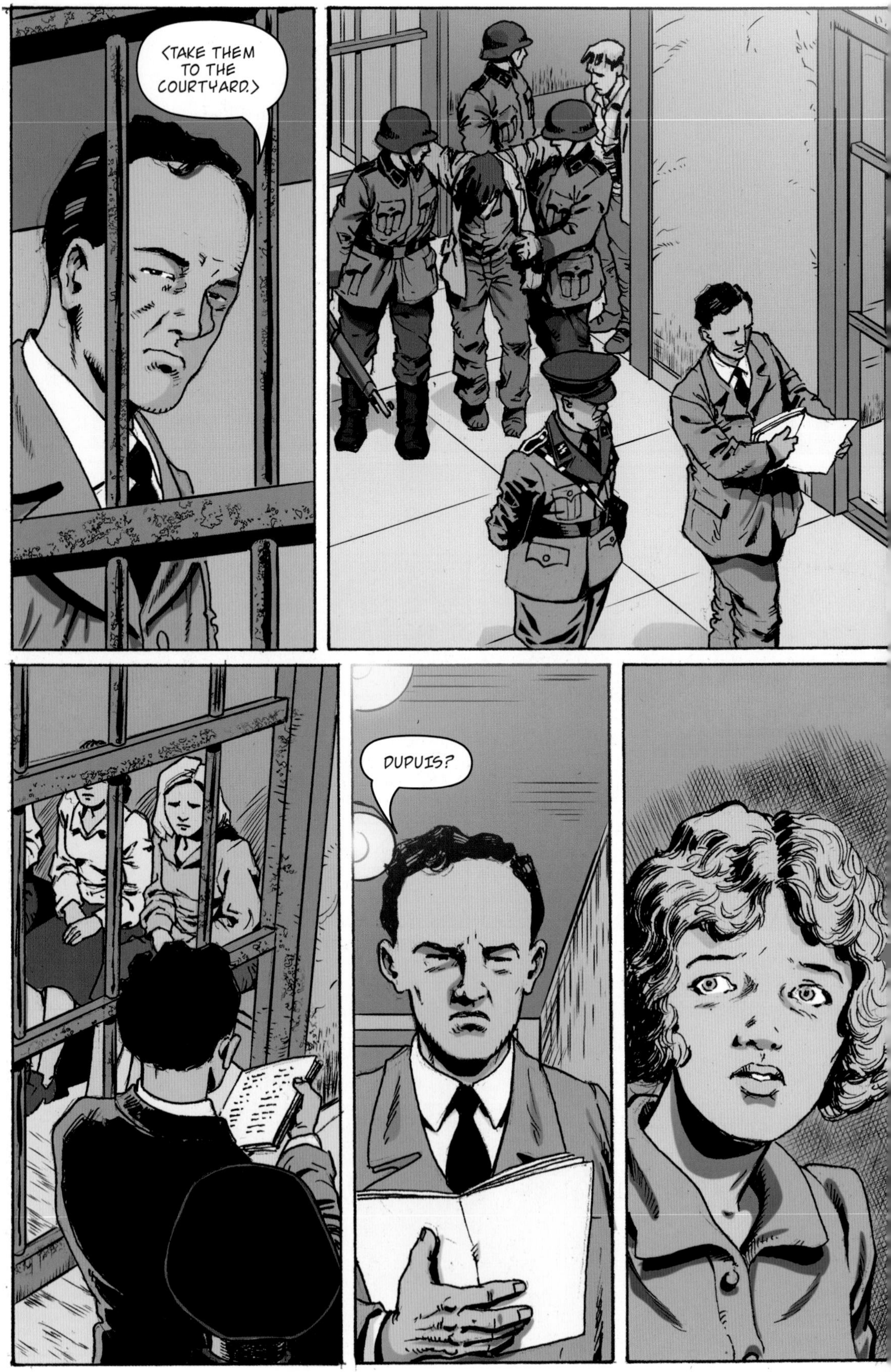
<TAKE THEM TO THE COURTYARD.>
DUPUIS?

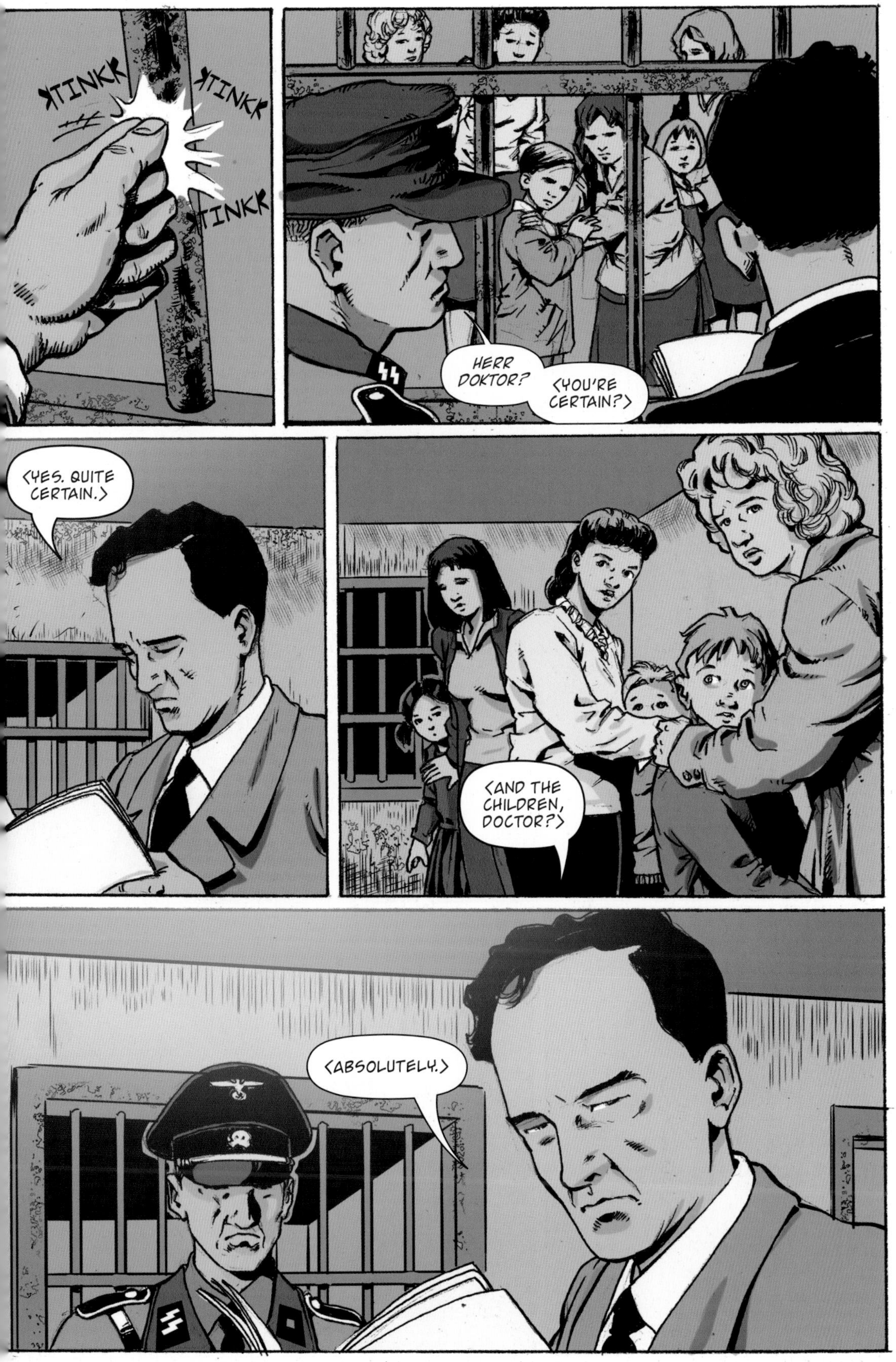
TINKK
TINKK
TINKK
HERR DOKTOR?
<YOU'RE CERTAIN?>
<YES. QUITE CERTAIN.>
<AND THE CHILDREN, DOCTOR?>
<ABSOLUTELY.>

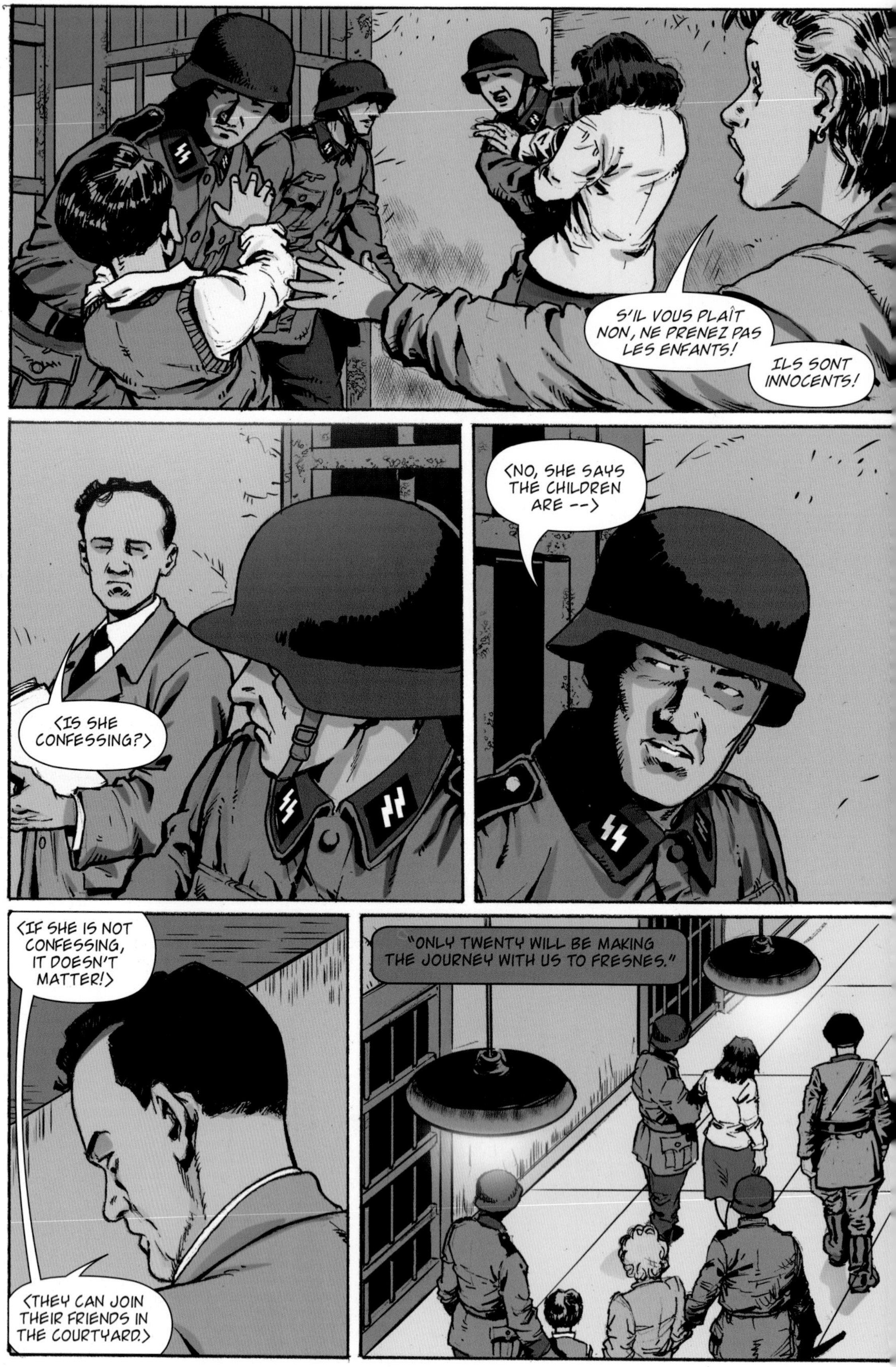
S'IL VOUS PLAÎT NON, NE PRENEZ PAS LES ENFANTS!
ILS SONT INNOCENTS!
<IS SHE CONFESSING?>
<NO, SHE SAYS THE CHILDREN ARE -->
<IF SHE IS NOT CONFESSING, IT DOESN'T MATTER!>
<THEY CAN JOIN THEIR FRIENDS IN THE COURTYARD.>
"ONLY TWENTY WILL BE MAKING THE JOURNEY WITH US TO FRESNES."

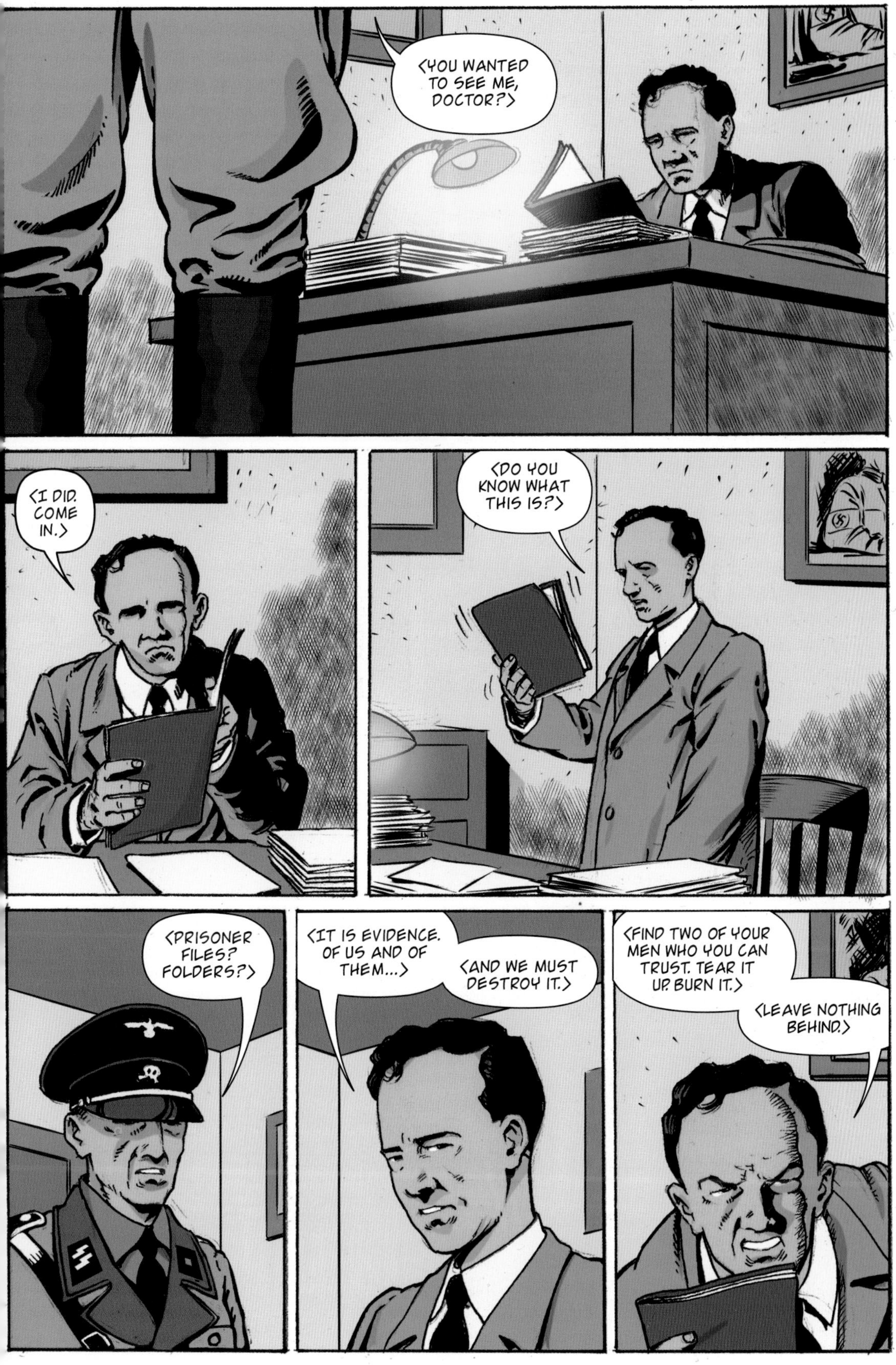
<YOU WANTED TO SEE ME, DOCTOR?>
<I DID. COME IN.>
<DO YOU KNOW WHAT THIS IS?>
<PRISONER FILES? FOLDERS?>
<IT IS EVIDENCE. OF US AND OF THEM...>
<AND WE MUST DESTROY IT.>
<FIND TWO OF YOUR MEN WHO YOU CAN TRUST. TEAR IT UP. BURN IT.>
<LEAVE NOTHING BEHIND.>

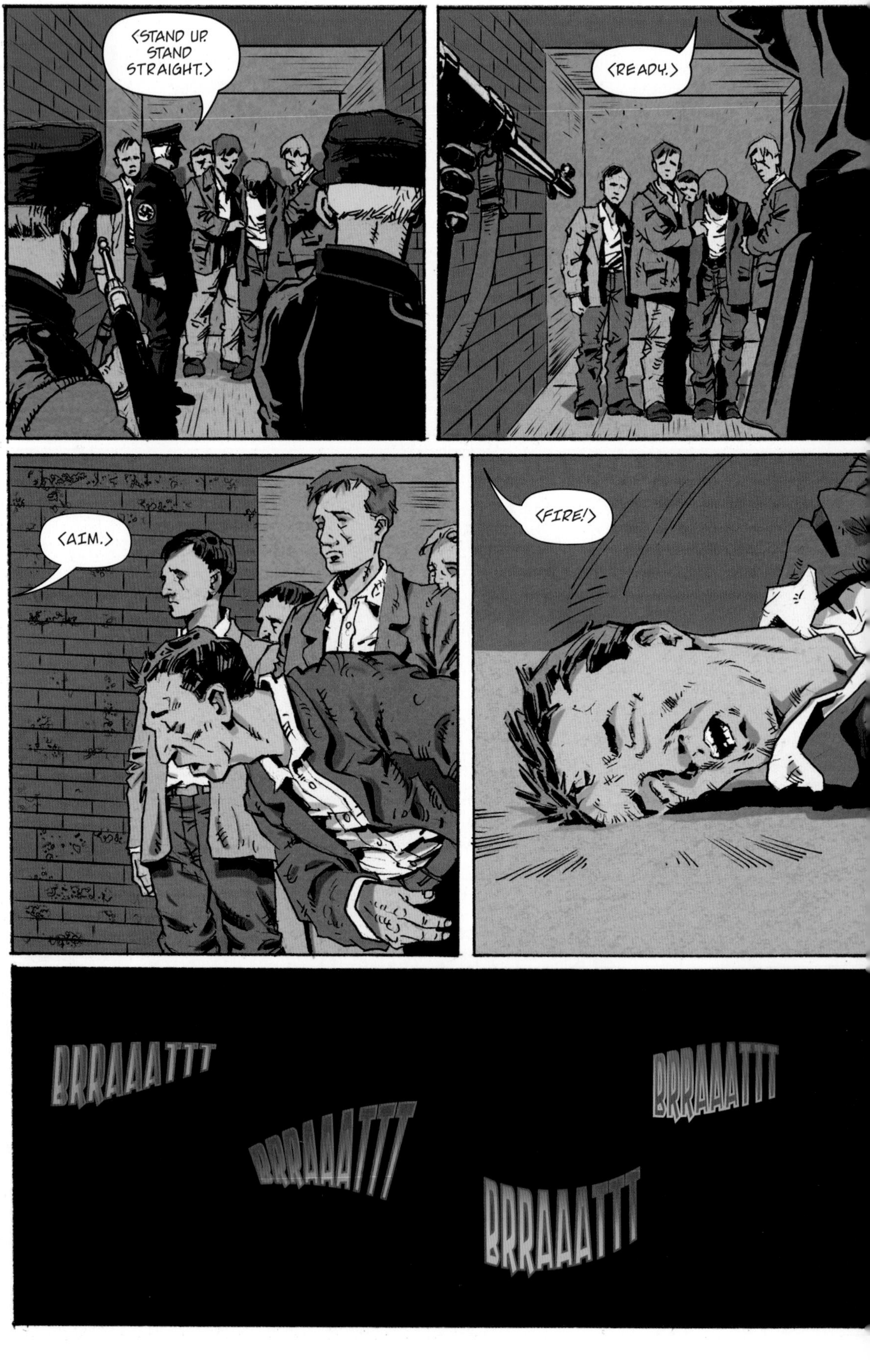
<STAND UP. STAND STRAIGHT.>
<READY.>
<AIM.>
<FIRE!>
BRRAAATTT
BRRAAATTT
BRRAAATTT
BRRAAATTT

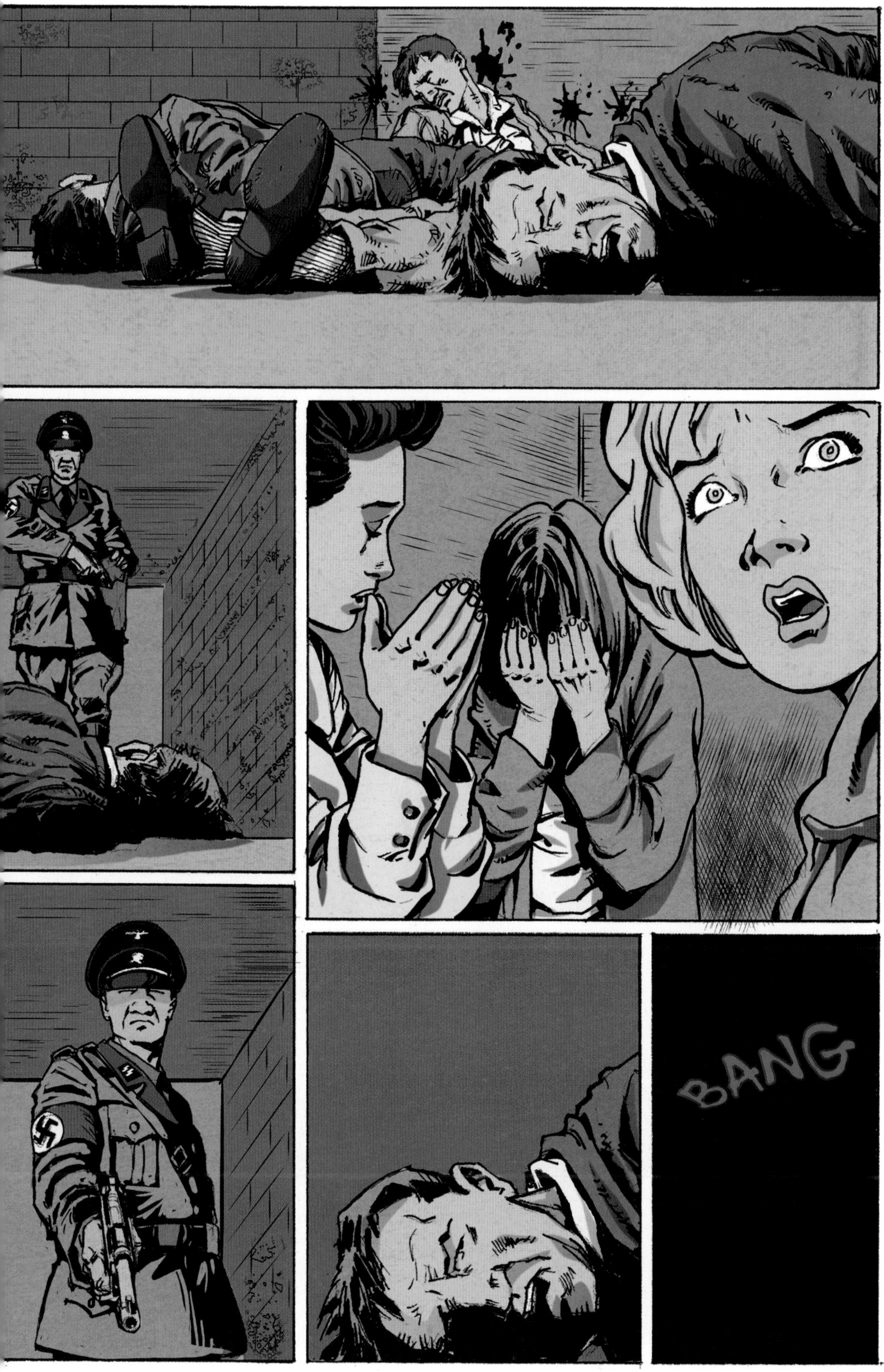
BANG

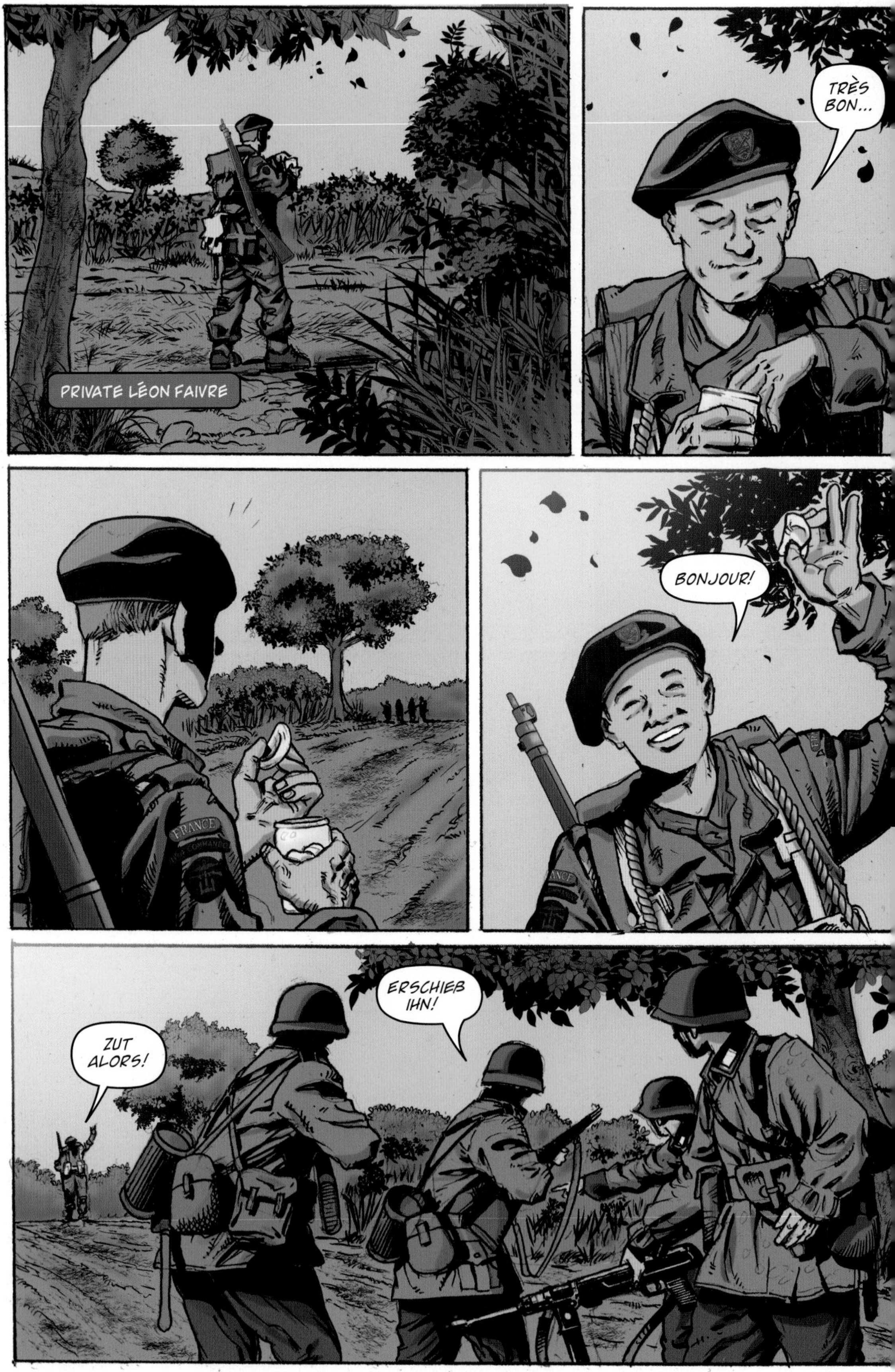
PRIVATE LÉON FAIVRE
TRÈS BON...
BONJOUR!
ZUT ALORS!
ERSCHIEB IHN!

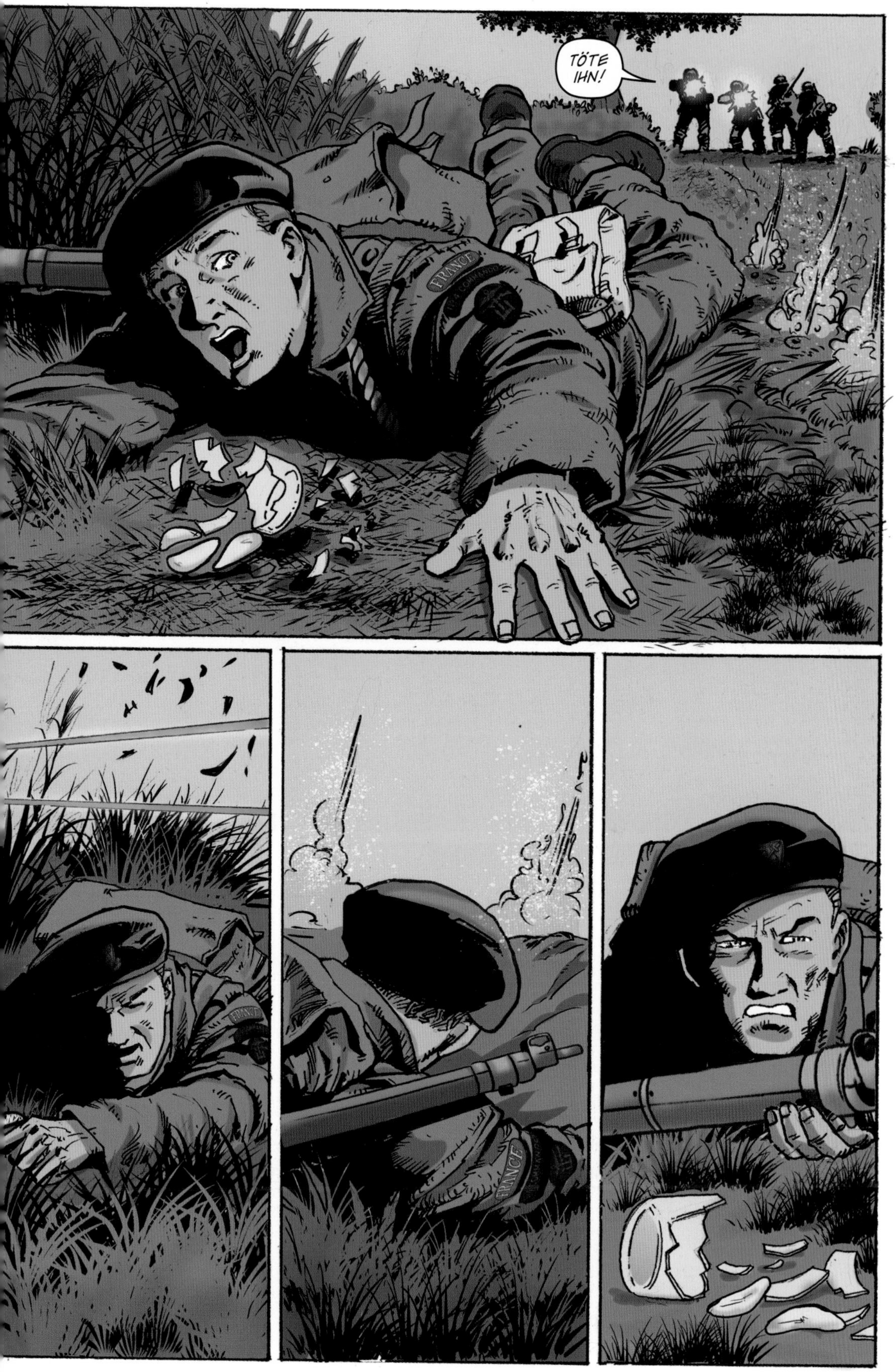
TÖTE IHN!

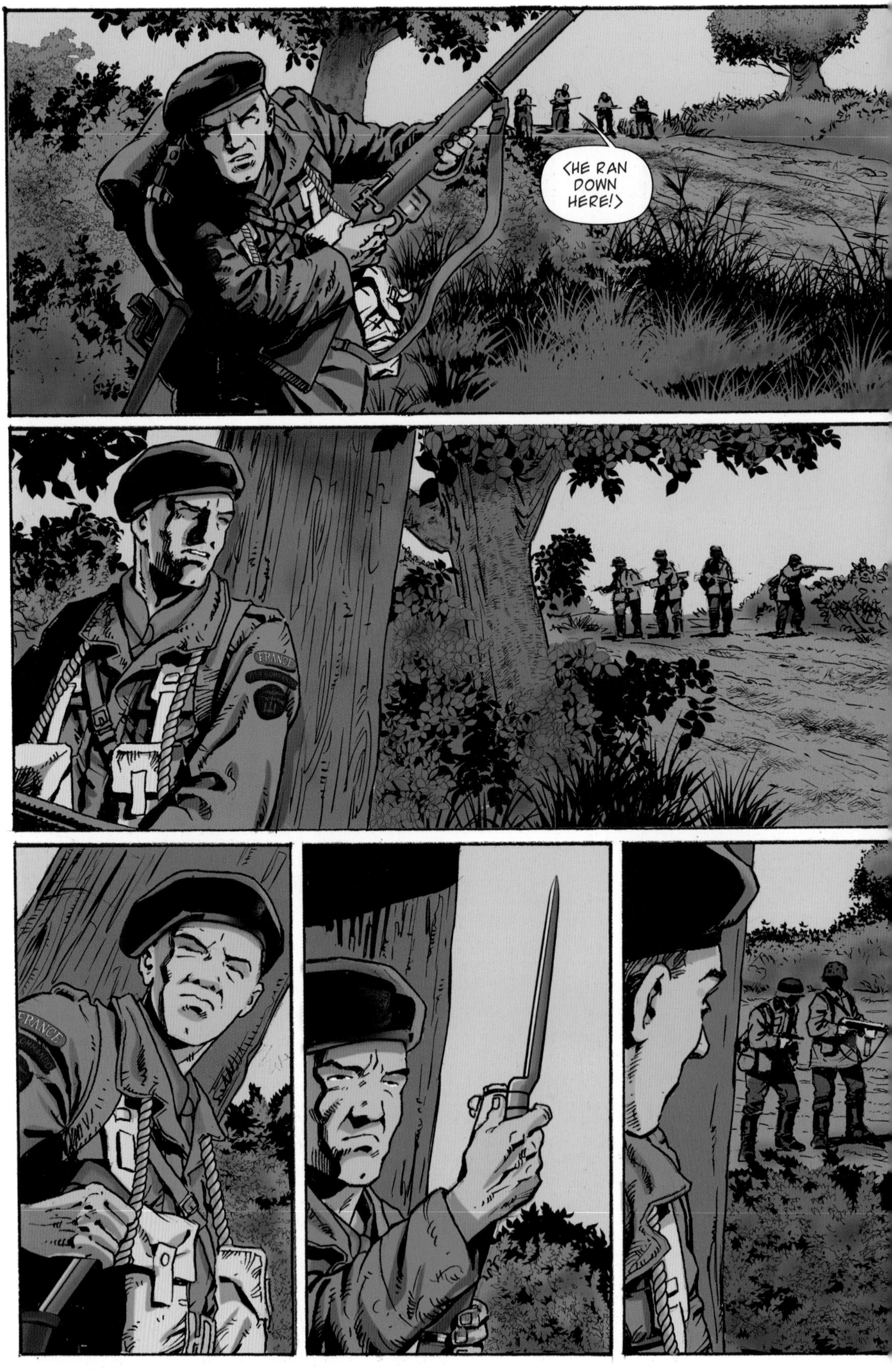
<HE RAN DOWN HERE!>
FRANCE

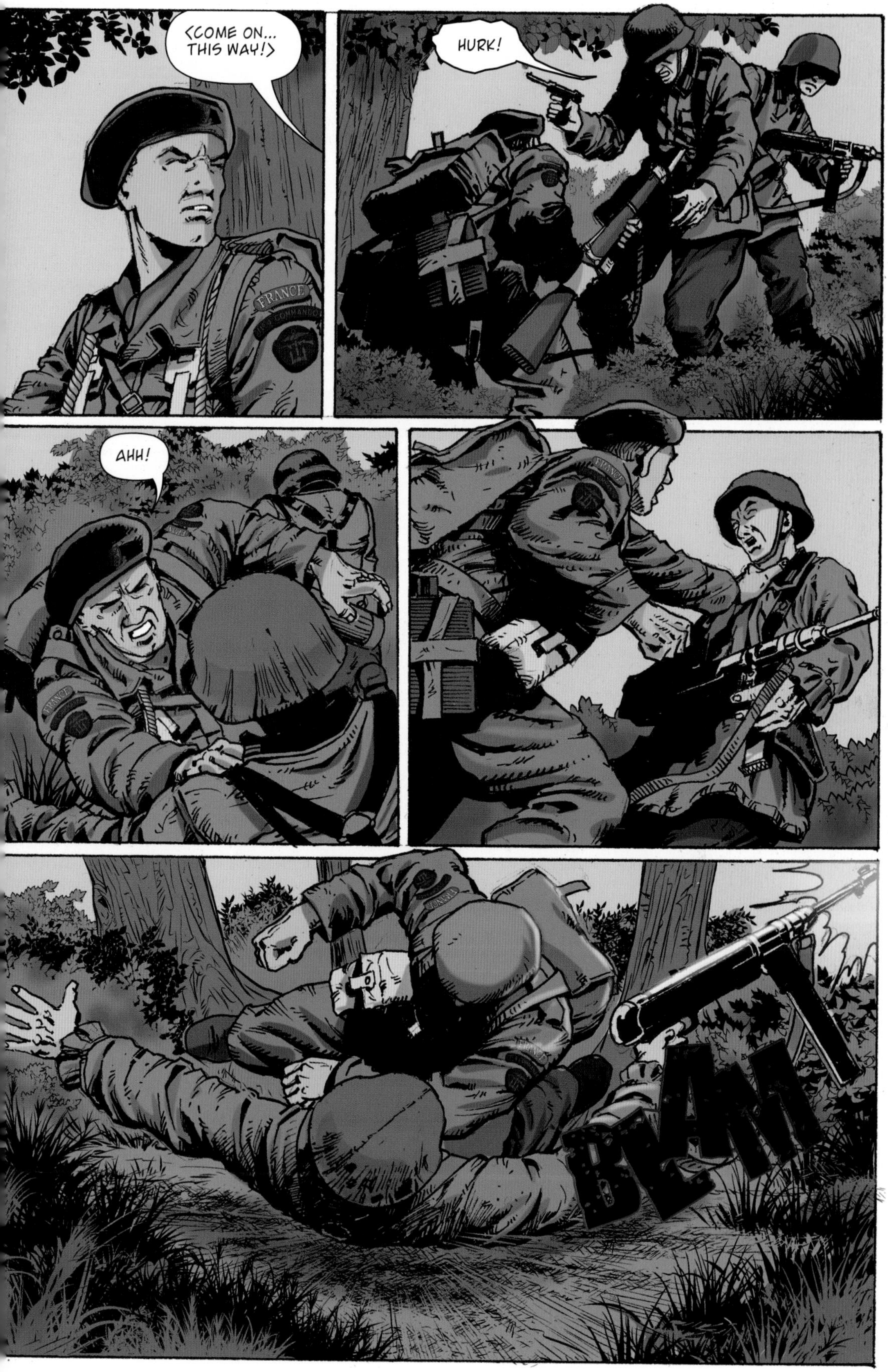
<COME ON... THIS WAY!>
FRANCE
HURK!
AHH!
BLAM

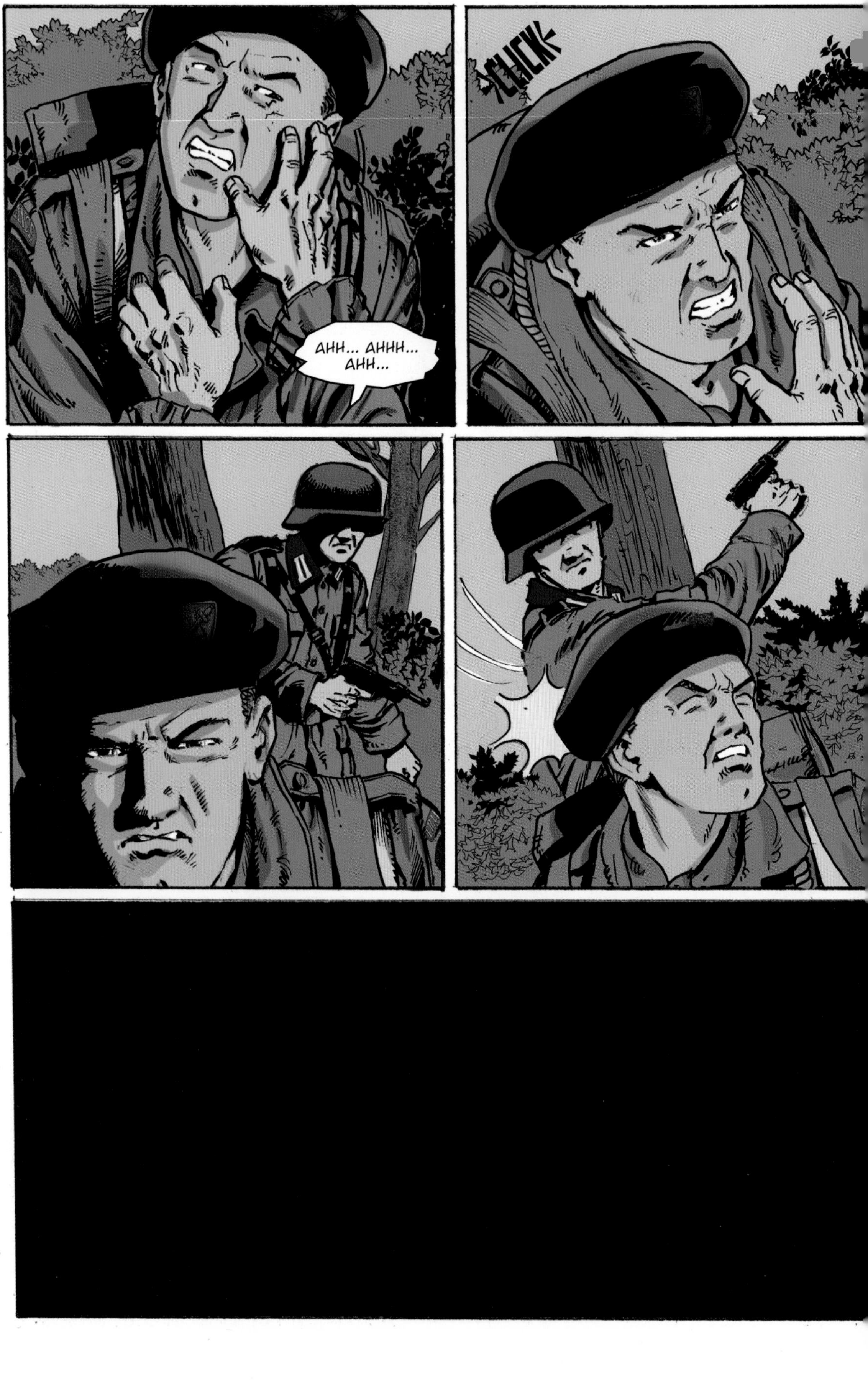
AHH... AHHH... AHH...
CLICK

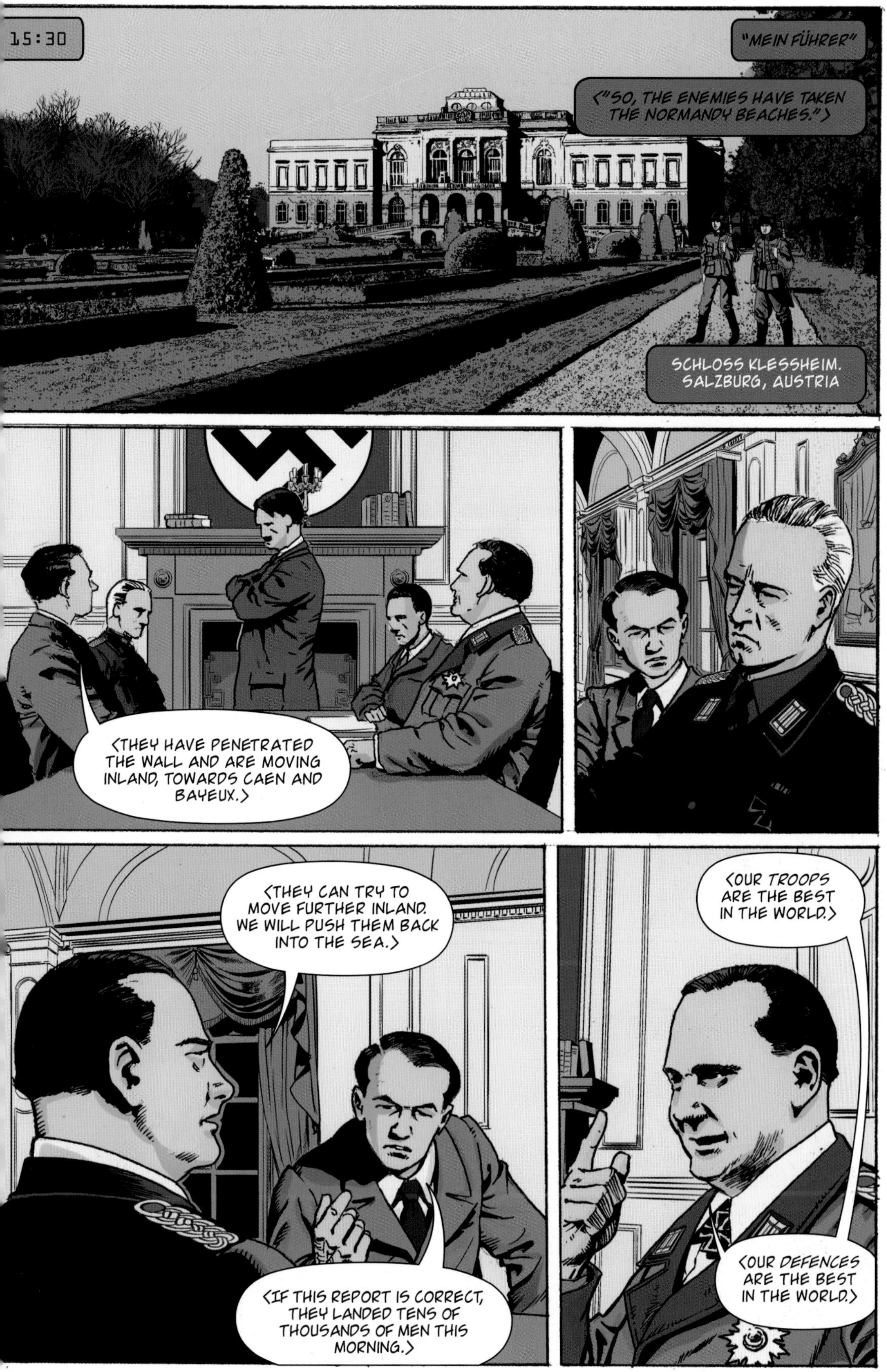
15:30
"MEIN FÜHRER"
<"SO, THE ENEMIES HAVE TAKEN THE NORMANDY BEACHES.">
SCHLOSS KLESSHEIM. SALZBURG, AUSTRIA
<THEY HAVE PENETRATED THE WALL AND ARE MOVING INLAND, TOWARDS CAEN AND BAYEUX.>
<THEY CAN TRY TO MOVE FURTHER INLAND. WE WILL PUSH THEM BACK INTO THE SEA.>
<IF THIS REPORT IS CORRECT, THEY LANDED TENS OF THOUSANDS OF MEN THIS MORNING.>
<OUR *TROOPS* ARE THE BEST IN THE WORLD.>
<OUR *DEFENCES* ARE THE BEST IN THE WORLD.>

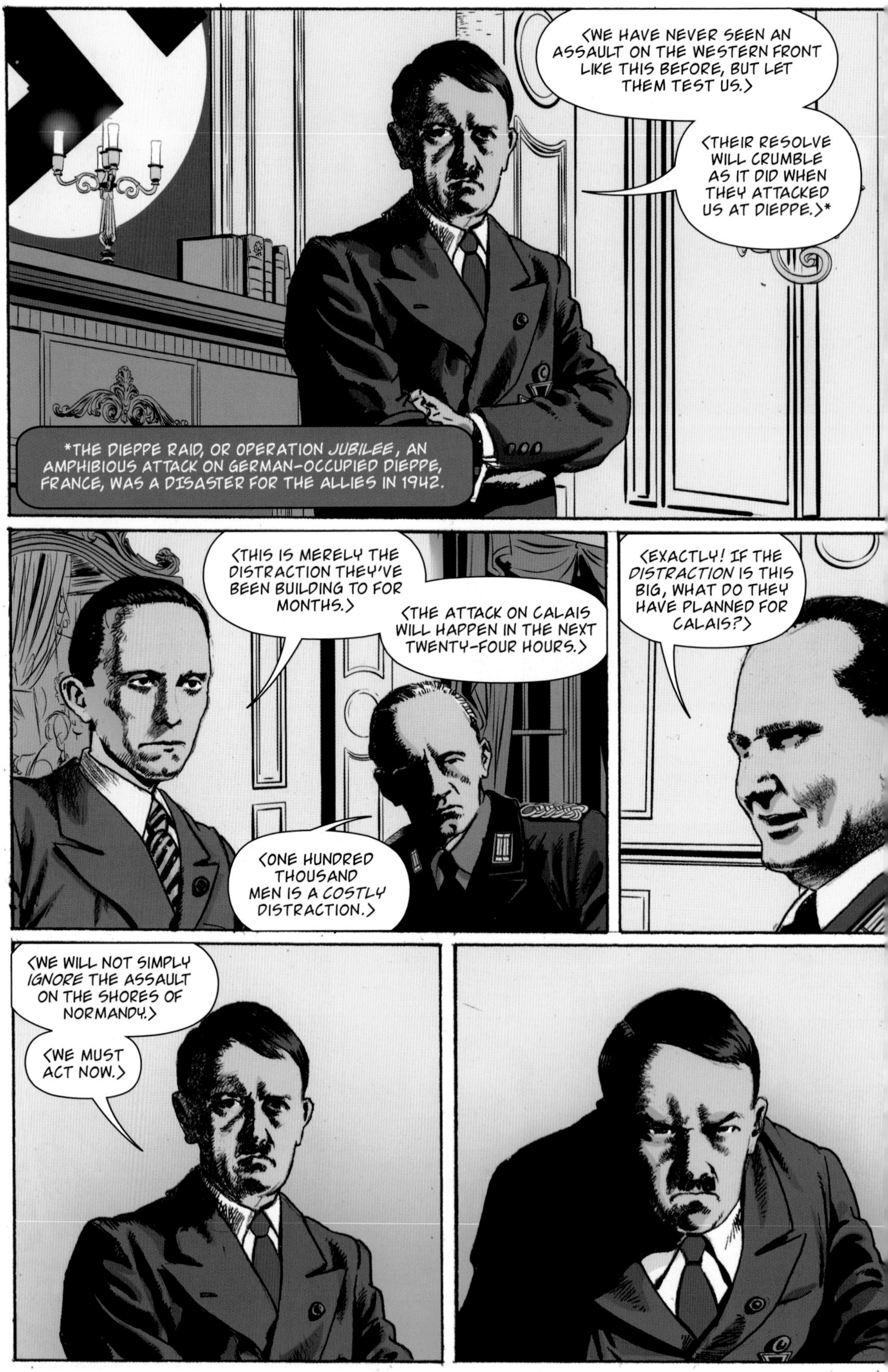
<WE HAVE NEVER SEEN AN ASSAULT ON THE WESTERN FRONT LIKE THIS BEFORE, BUT LET THEM TEST US.>
<THEIR RESOLVE WILL CRUMBLE AS IT DID WHEN THEY ATTACKED US AT DIEPPE.>*
*THE DIEPPE RAID, OR OPERATION *JUBILEE*, AN AMPHIBIOUS ATTACK ON GERMAN-OCCUPIED DIEPPE, FRANCE, WAS A DISASTER FOR THE ALLIES IN 1942.
<THIS IS MERELY THE DISTRACTION THEY'VE BEEN BUILDING TO FOR MONTHS.>
<THE ATTACK ON CALAIS WILL HAPPEN IN THE NEXT TWENTY-FOUR HOURS.>
<ONE HUNDRED THOUSAND MEN IS A *COSTLY* DISTRACTION.>
<EXACTLY! IF THE *DISTRACTION* IS THIS BIG, WHAT DO THEY HAVE PLANNED FOR CALAIS?>
<WE WILL NOT SIMPLY *IGNORE* THE ASSAULT ON THE SHORES OF NORMANDY.>
<WE MUST ACT NOW.>

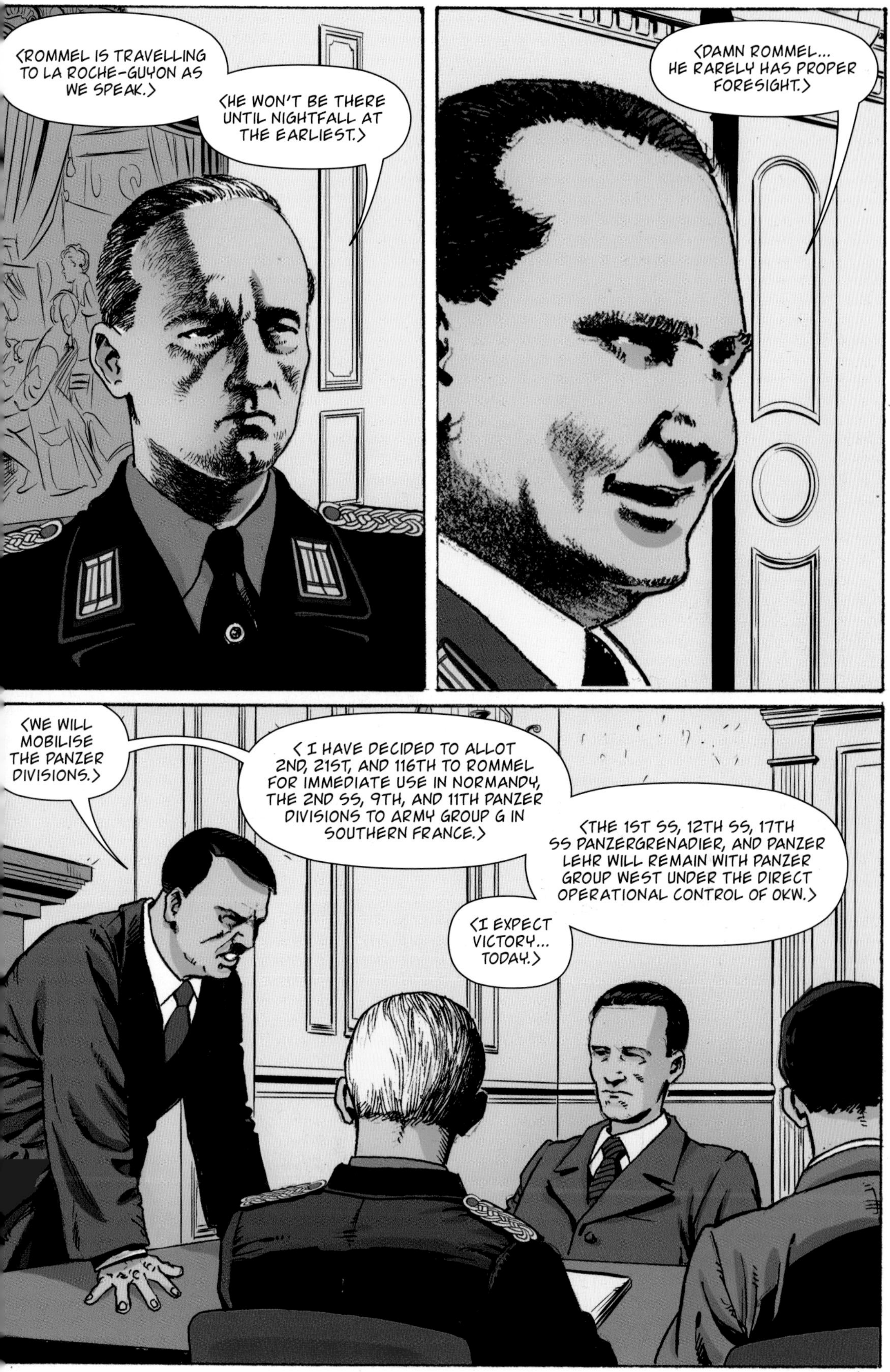
<ROMMEL IS TRAVELLING TO LA ROCHE-GUYON AS WE SPEAK.>
<HE WON'T BE THERE UNTIL NIGHTFALL AT THE EARLIEST.>
<DAMN ROMMEL... HE RARELY HAS PROPER FORESIGHT.>
<WE WILL MOBILISE THE PANZER DIVISIONS.>
< I HAVE DECIDED TO ALLOT 2ND, 21ST, AND 116TH TO ROMMEL FOR IMMEDIATE USE IN NORMANDY, THE 2ND SS, 9TH, AND 11TH PANZER DIVISIONS TO ARMY GROUP G IN SOUTHERN FRANCE.>
<THE 1ST SS, 12TH SS, 17TH SS PANZERGRENADIER, AND PANZER LEHR WILL REMAIN WITH PANZER GROUP WEST UNDER THE DIRECT OPERATIONAL CONTROL OF OKW.>
<I EXPECT VICTORY... TODAY.>

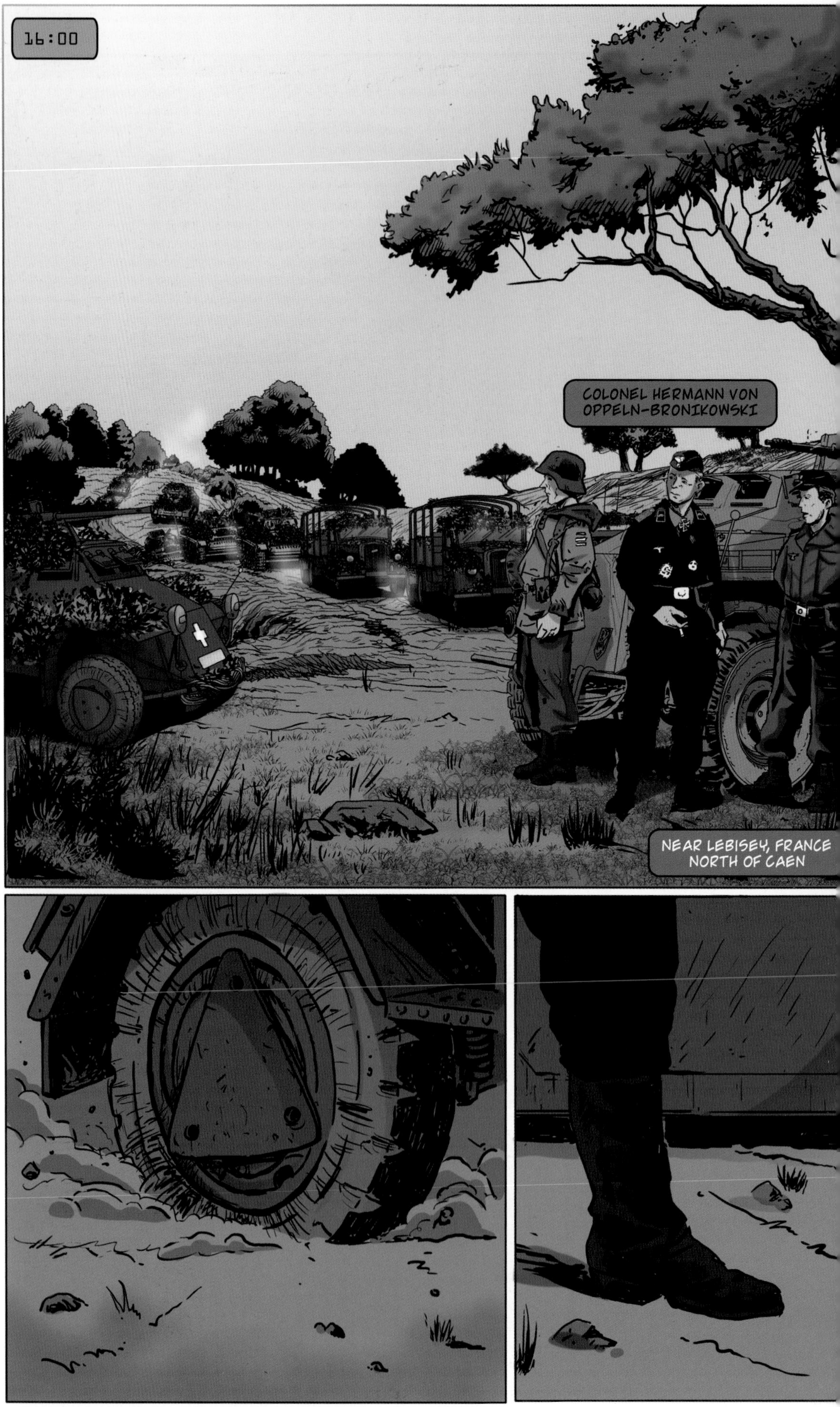
16:00
COLONEL HERMANN VON OPPELN-BRONIKOWSKI
NEAR LEBISEY, FRANCE NORTH OF CAEN

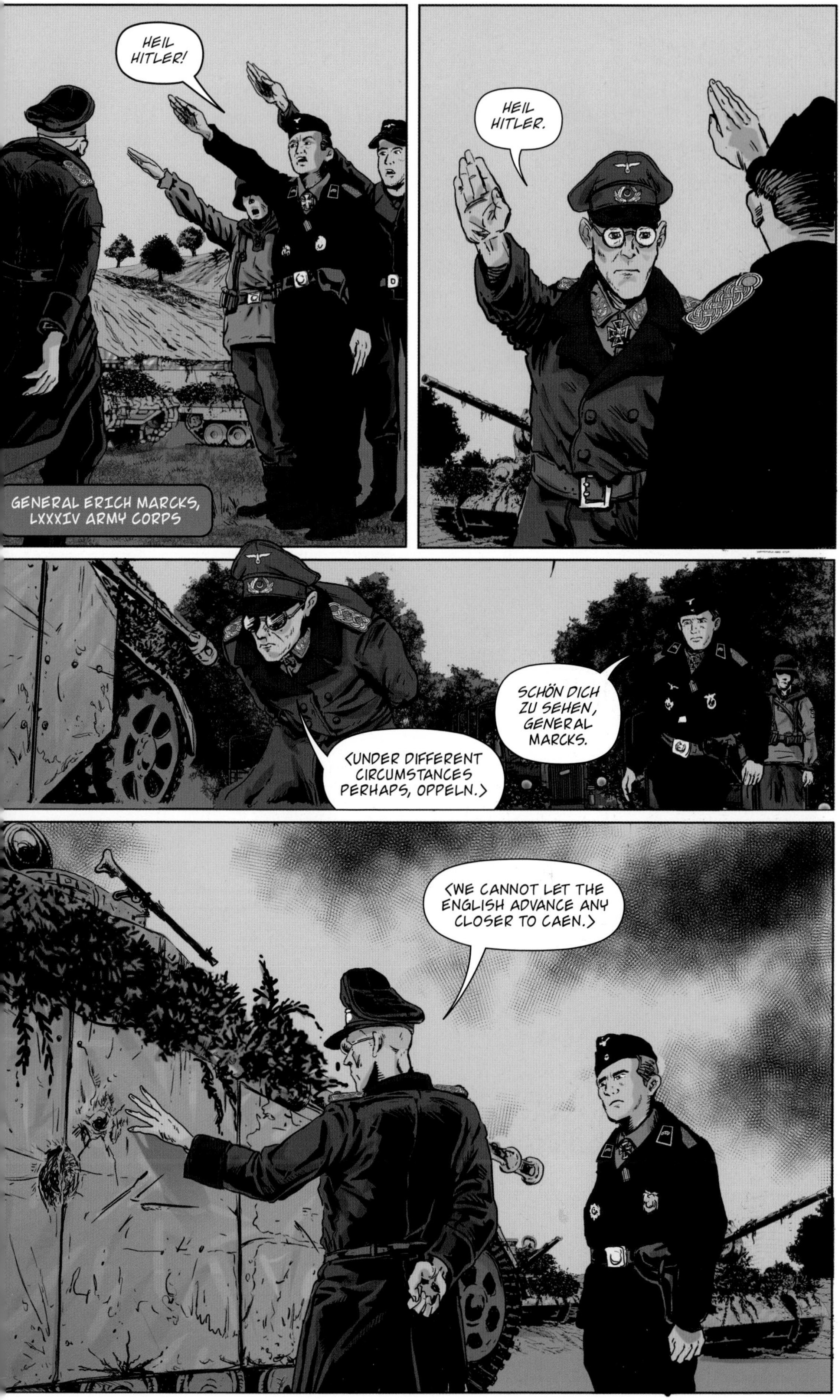
HEIL HITLER!
GENERAL ERICH MARCKS, LXXXIV ARMY CORPS
HEIL HITLER.
SCHÖN DICH ZU SEHEN, GENERAL MARCKS.
<UNDER DIFFERENT CIRCUMSTANCES PERHAPS, OPPELN.>
<WE CANNOT LET THE ENGLISH ADVANCE ANY CLOSER TO CAEN.>

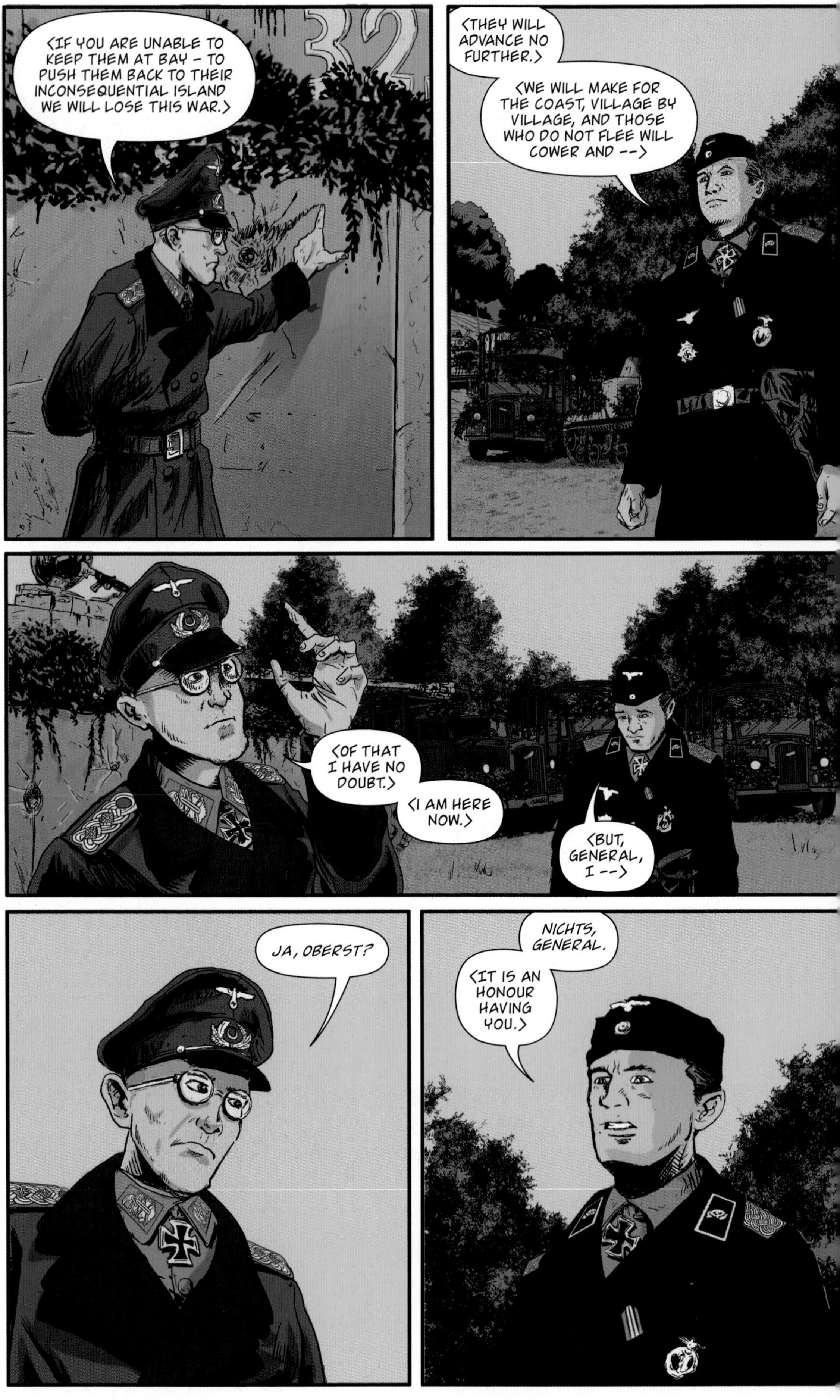
<IF YOU ARE UNABLE TO KEEP THEM AT BAY – TO PUSH THEM BACK TO THEIR INCONSEQUENTIAL ISLAND WE WILL LOSE THIS WAR.>
<THEY WILL ADVANCE NO FURTHER.>
<WE WILL MAKE FOR THE COAST, VILLAGE BY VILLAGE, AND THOSE WHO DO NOT FLEE WILL COWER AND -->
<OF THAT I HAVE NO DOUBT.>
<I AM HERE NOW.>
<BUT, GENERAL, I -->
JA, OBERST?
NICHTS, GENERAL.
<IT IS AN HONOUR HAVING YOU.>

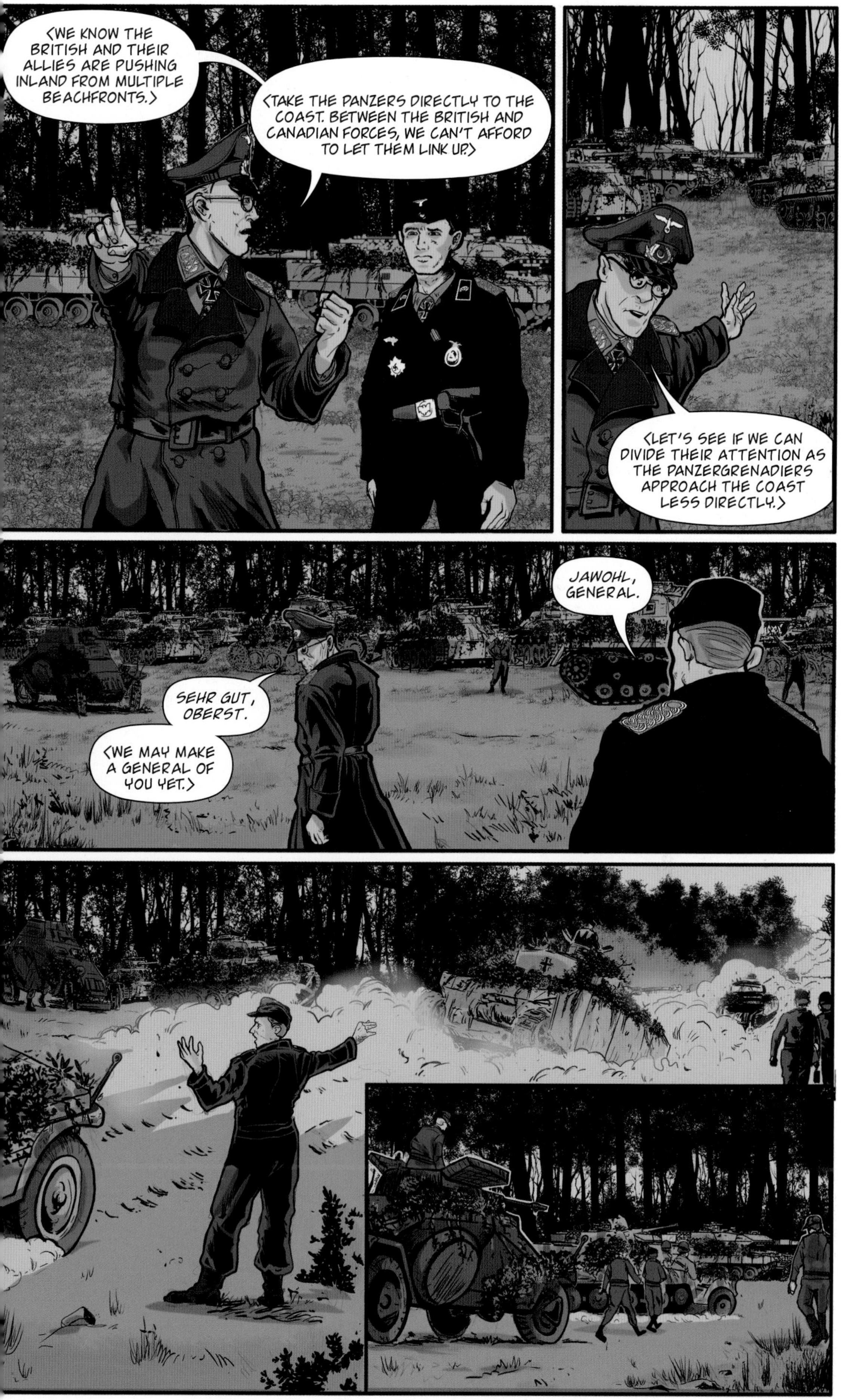
<WE KNOW THE BRITISH AND THEIR ALLIES ARE PUSHING INLAND FROM MULTIPLE BEACHFRONTS.>
<TAKE THE PANZERS DIRECTLY TO THE COAST. BETWEEN THE BRITISH AND CANADIAN FORCES, WE CAN'T AFFORD TO LET THEM LINK UP.>
<LET'S SEE IF WE CAN DIVIDE THEIR ATTENTION AS THE PANZERGRENADIERS APPROACH THE COAST LESS DIRECTLY.>
JAWOHL, GENERAL.
SEHR GUT, OBERST.
<WE MAY MAKE A GENERAL OF YOU YET.>

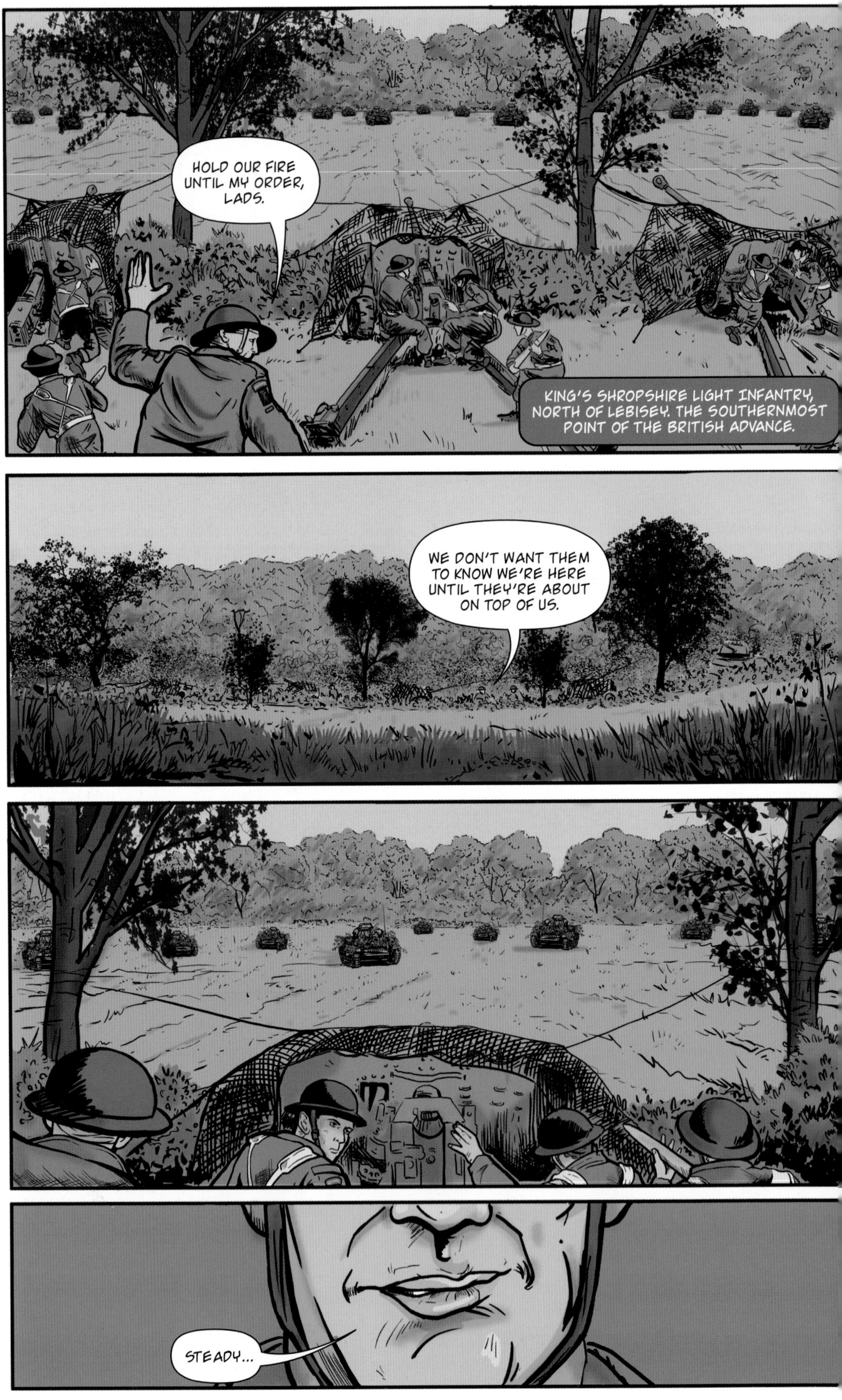
HOLD OUR FIRE UNTIL MY ORDER, LADS.
KING'S SHROPSHIRE LIGHT INFANTRY, NORTH OF LEBISEY. THE SOUTHERNMOST POINT OF THE BRITISH ADVANCE.
WE DON'T WANT THEM TO KNOW WE'RE HERE UNTIL THEY'RE ABOUT ON TOP OF US.
STEADY...

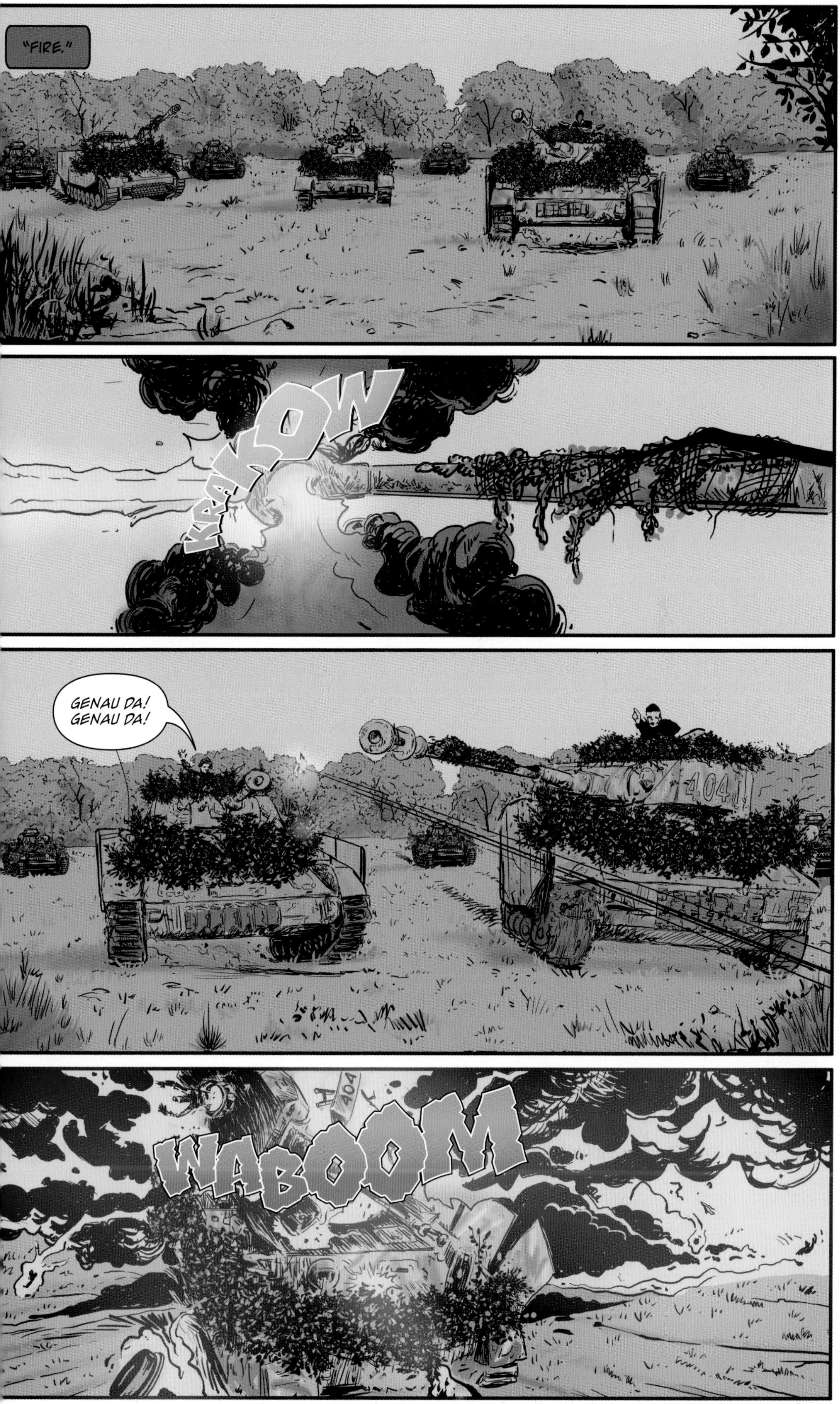
"FIRE."
KRAKOW
GENAU DA! GENAU DA!
404
WABOOM

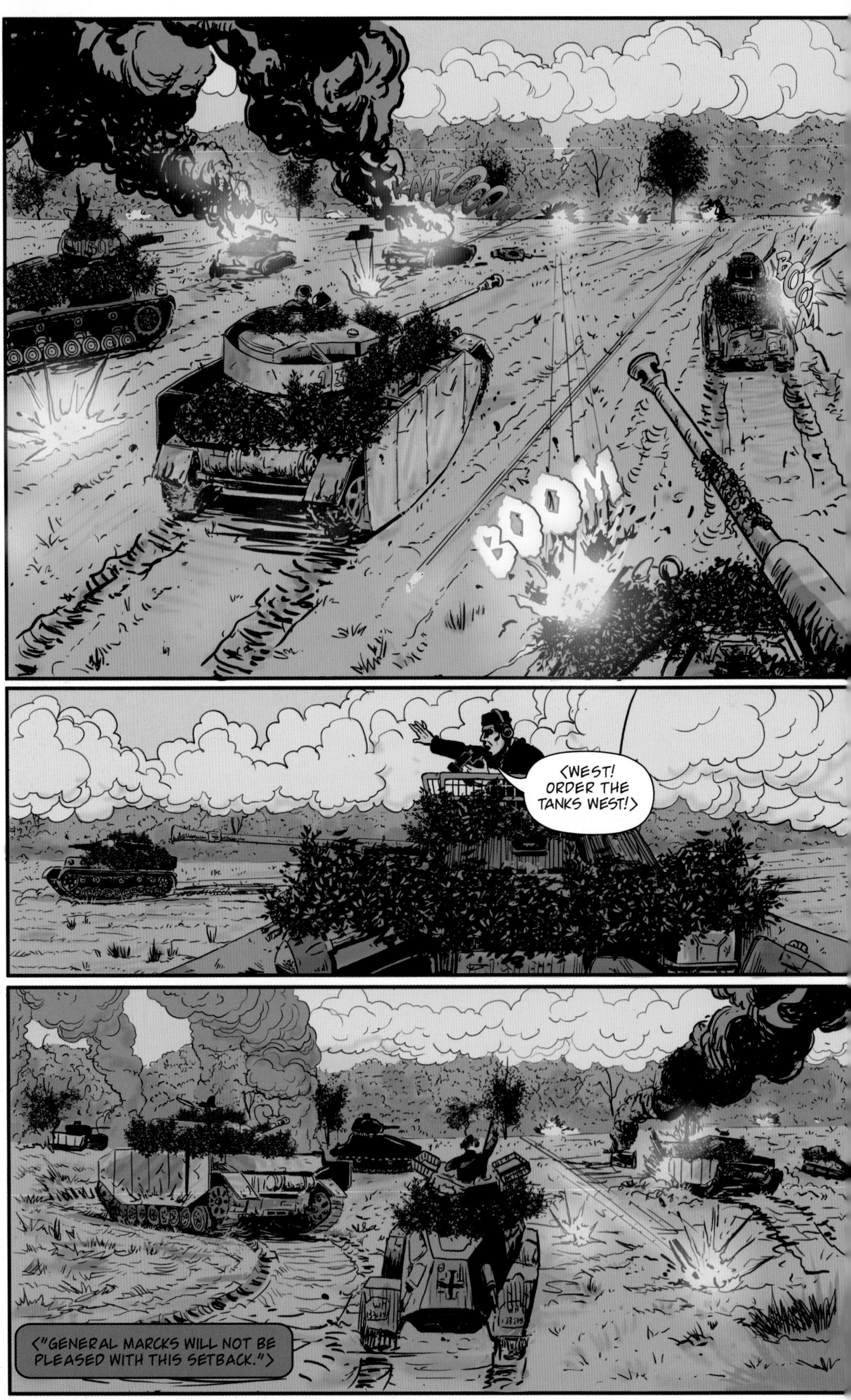
KAABOOOM
BOOM
BOOM
<WEST! ORDER THE TANKS WEST!>
<"GENERAL MARCKS WILL NOT BE PLEASED WITH THIS SETBACK.">

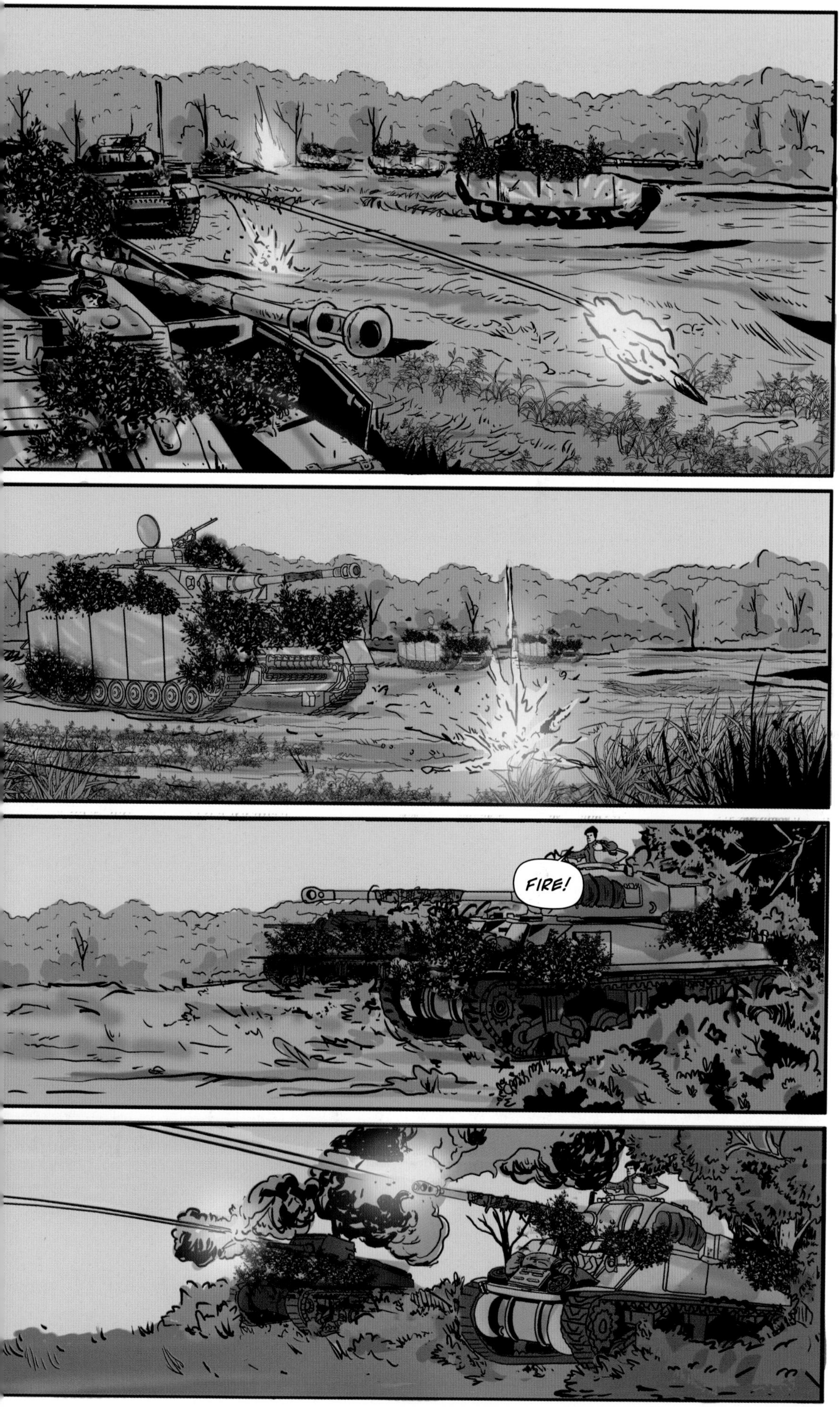
FIRE!

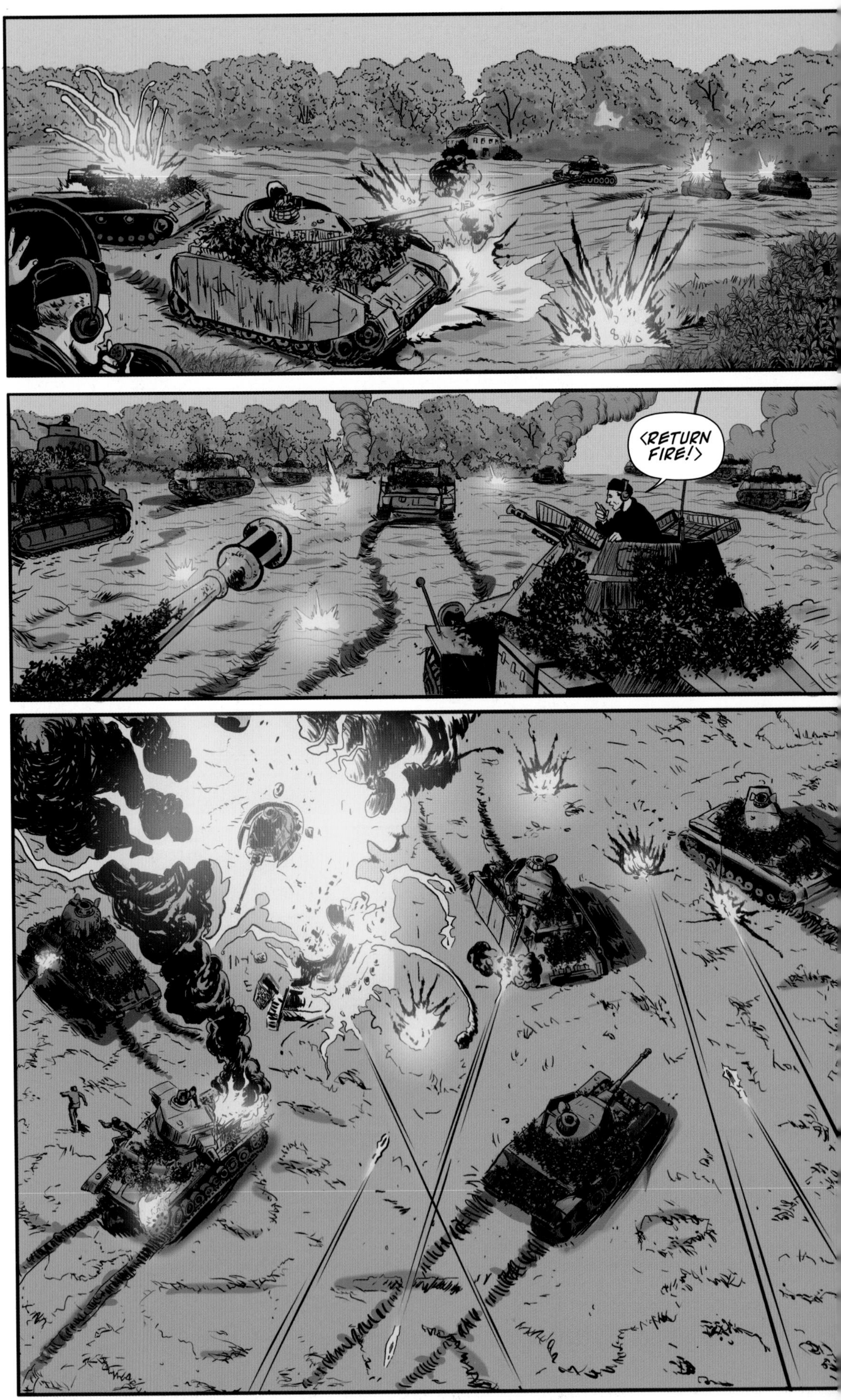
<RETURN FIRE!>

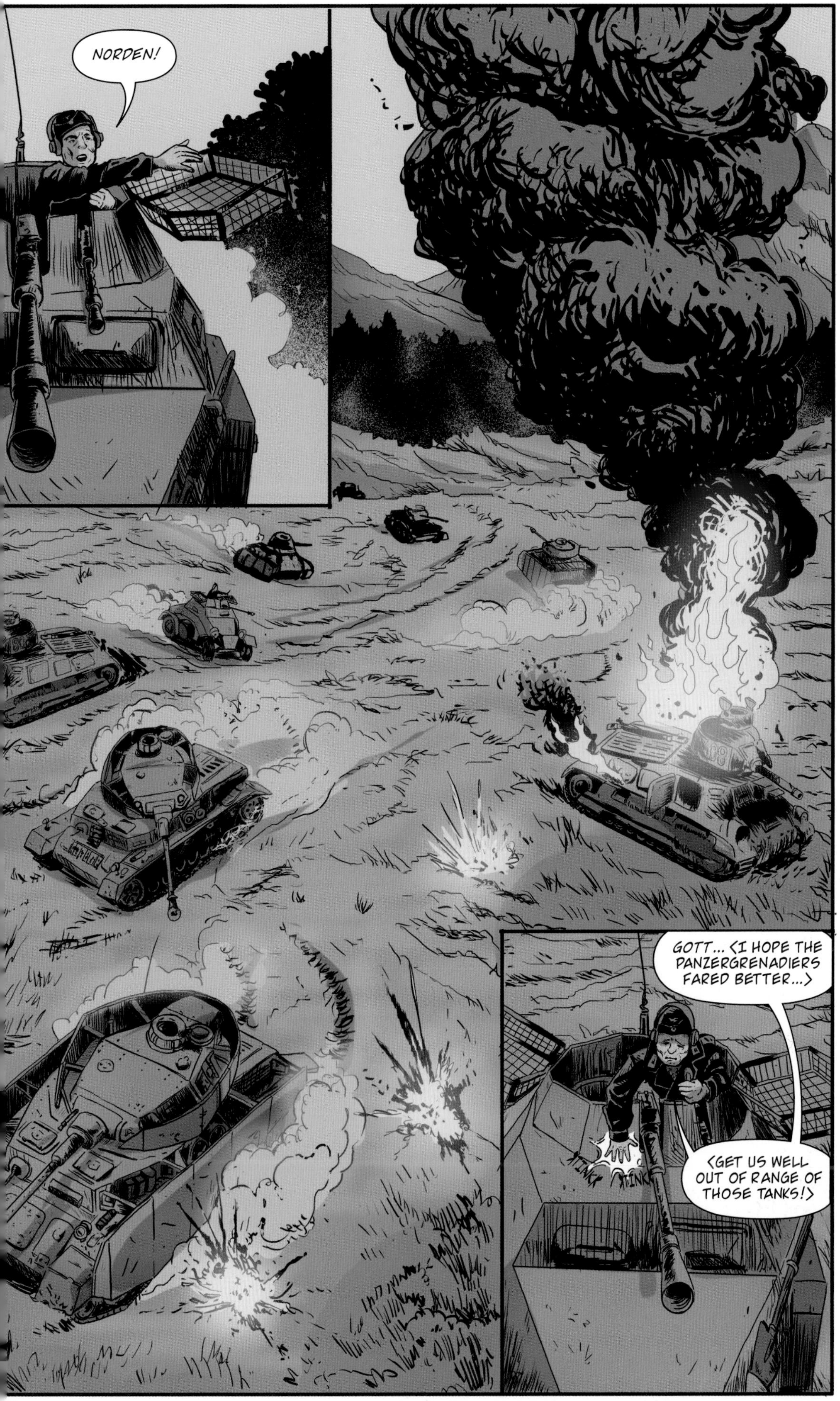
NORDEN!
GOTT... <I HOPE THE PANZERGRENADIERS FARED BETTER...>
<GET US WELL OUT OF RANGE OF THOSE TANKS!>

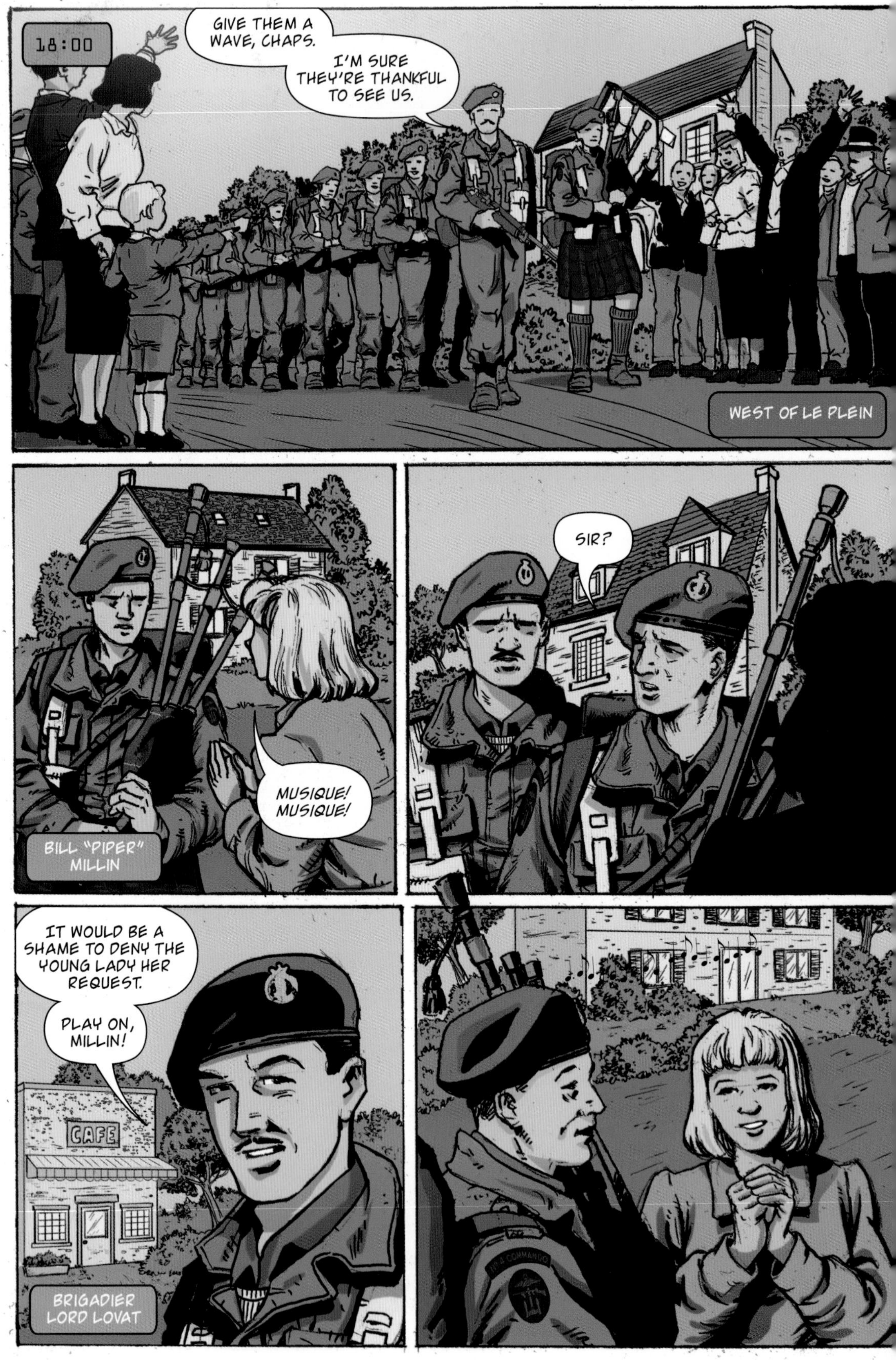
18:00
GIVE THEM A WAVE, CHAPS.
I'M SURE THEY'RE THANKFUL TO SEE US.
WEST OF LE PLEIN
BILL "PIPER" MILLIN
MUSIQUE! MUSIQUE!
SIR?
BRIGADIER LORD LOVAT
IT WOULD BE A SHAME TO DENY THE YOUNG LADY HER REQUEST.
PLAY ON, MILLIN!
CAFE

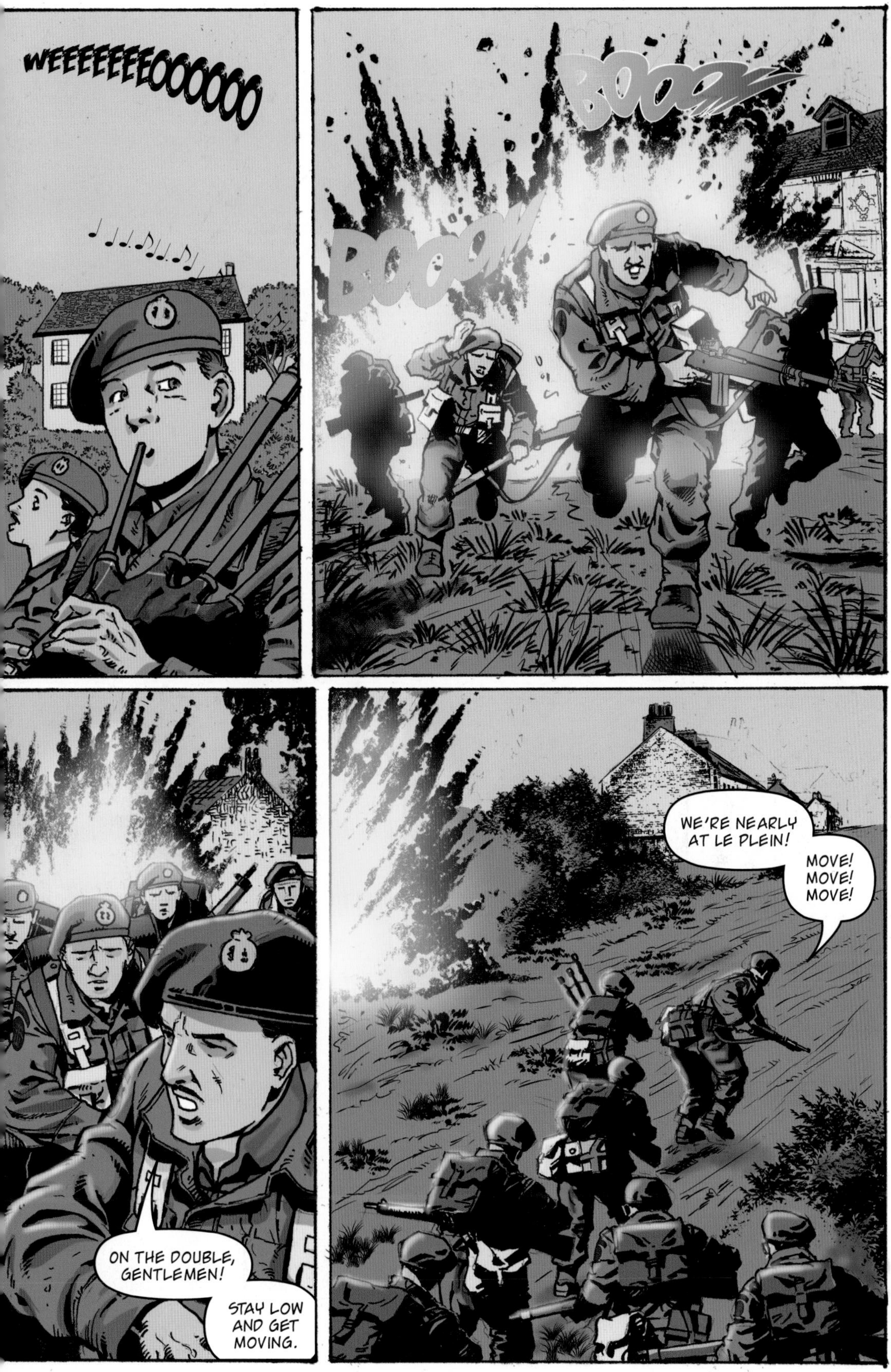
WEEEEEEEOOOOOO
BOOOM
BOOOM
ON THE DOUBLE, GENTLEMEN!
STAY LOW AND GET MOVING.
WE'RE NEARLY AT LE PLEIN!
MOVE! MOVE! MOVE!

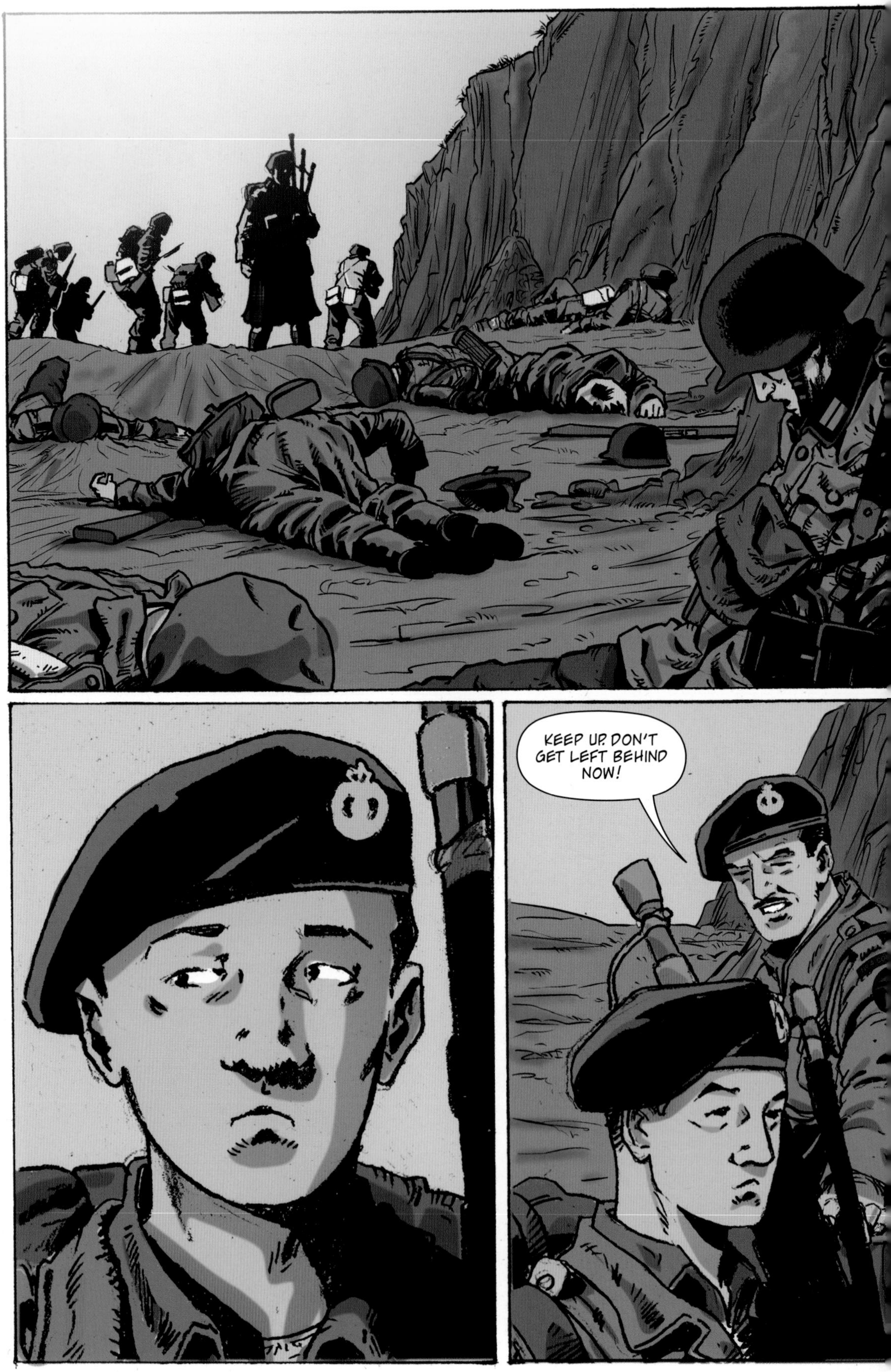
KEEP UP. DON'T GET LEFT BEHIND NOW!

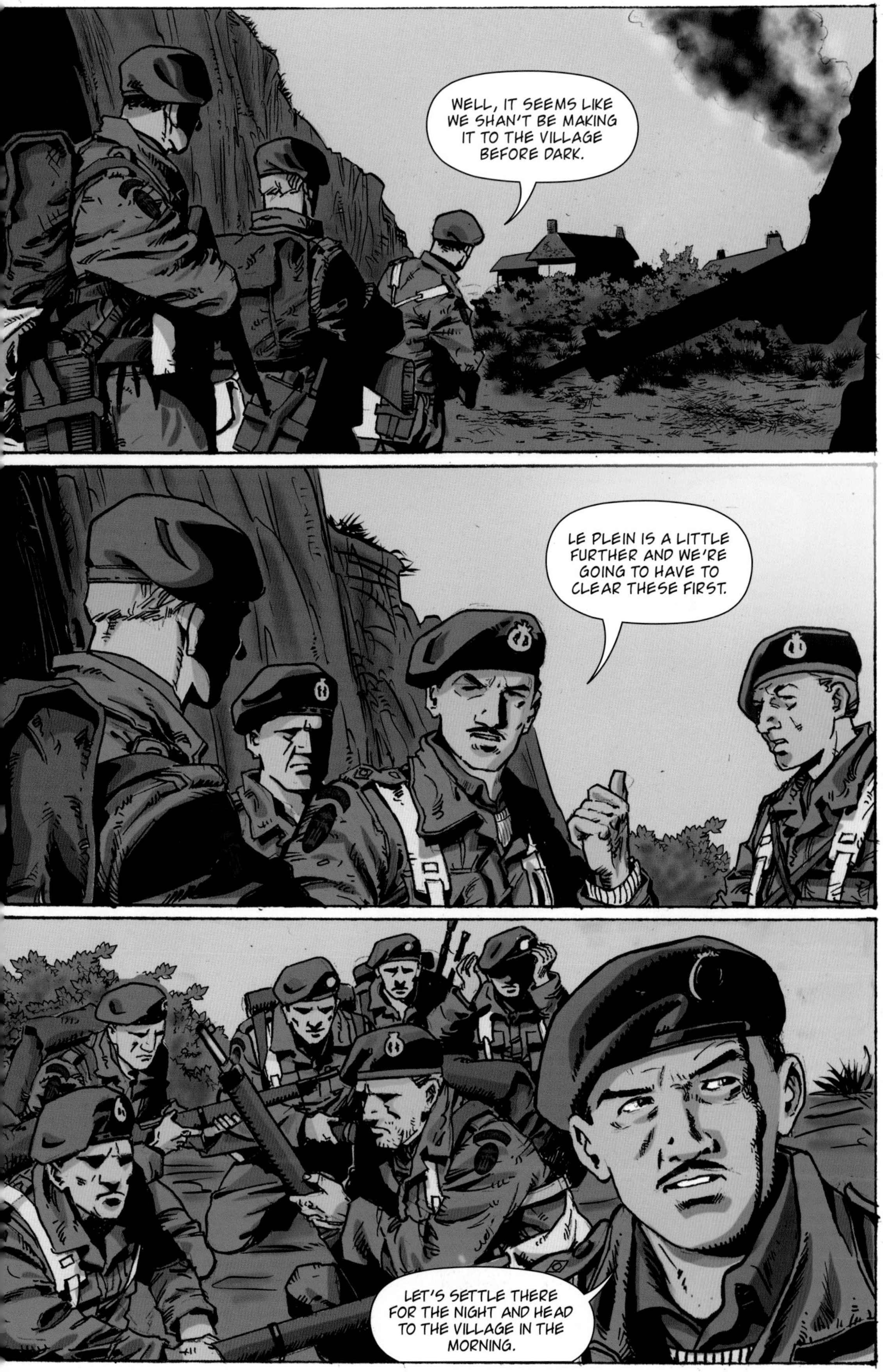
WELL, IT SEEMS LIKE WE SHAN'T BE MAKING IT TO THE VILLAGE BEFORE DARK.
LE PLEIN IS A LITTLE FURTHER AND WE'RE GOING TO HAVE TO CLEAR THESE FIRST.
LET'S SETTLE THERE FOR THE NIGHT AND HEAD TO THE VILLAGE IN THE MORNING.

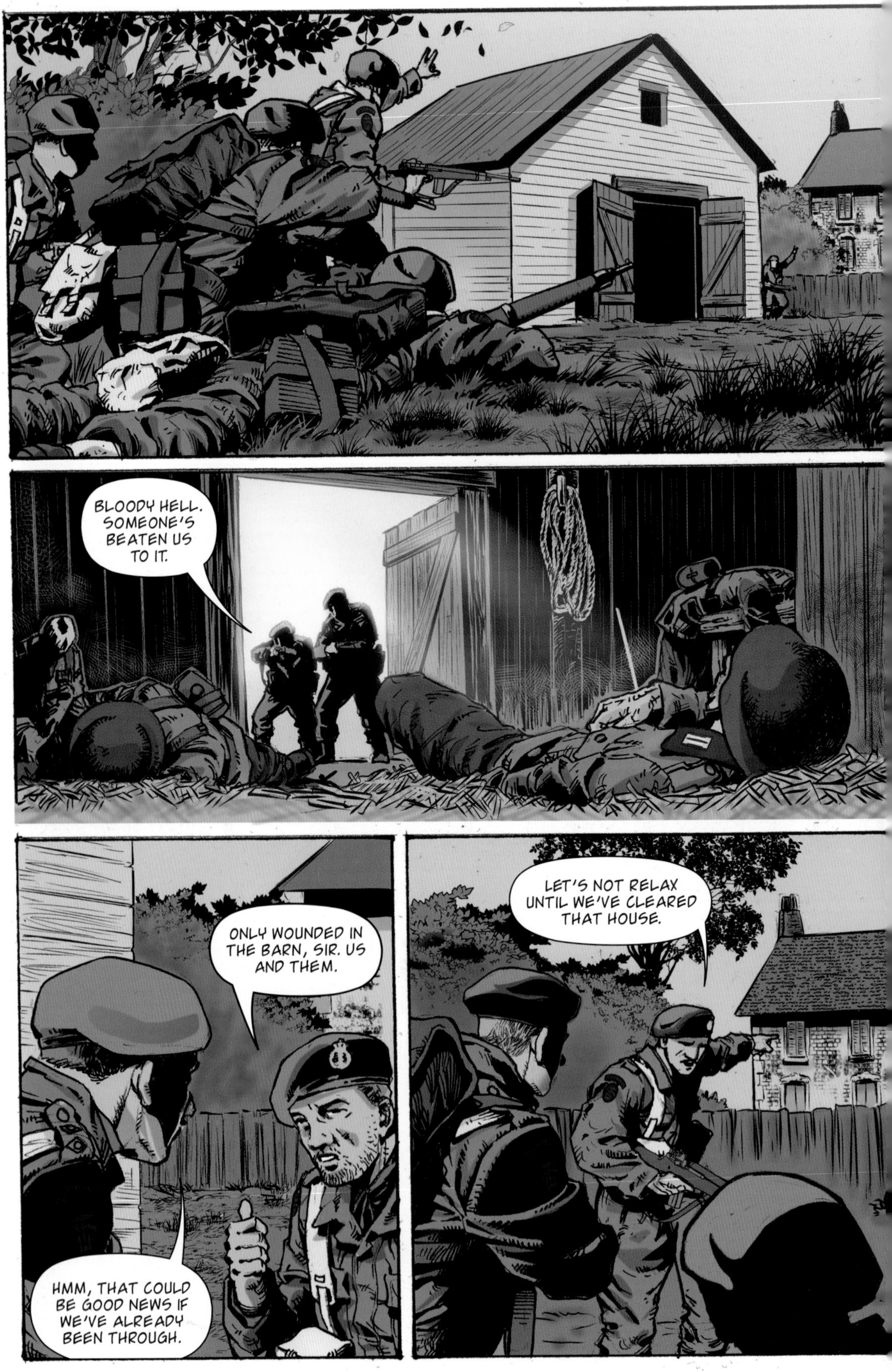
BLOODY HELL. SOMEONE'S BEATEN US TO IT.
ONLY WOUNDED IN THE BARN, SIR. US AND THEM.
HMM, THAT COULD BE GOOD NEWS IF WE'VE ALREADY BEEN THROUGH.
LET'S NOT RELAX UNTIL WE'VE CLEARED THAT HOUSE.

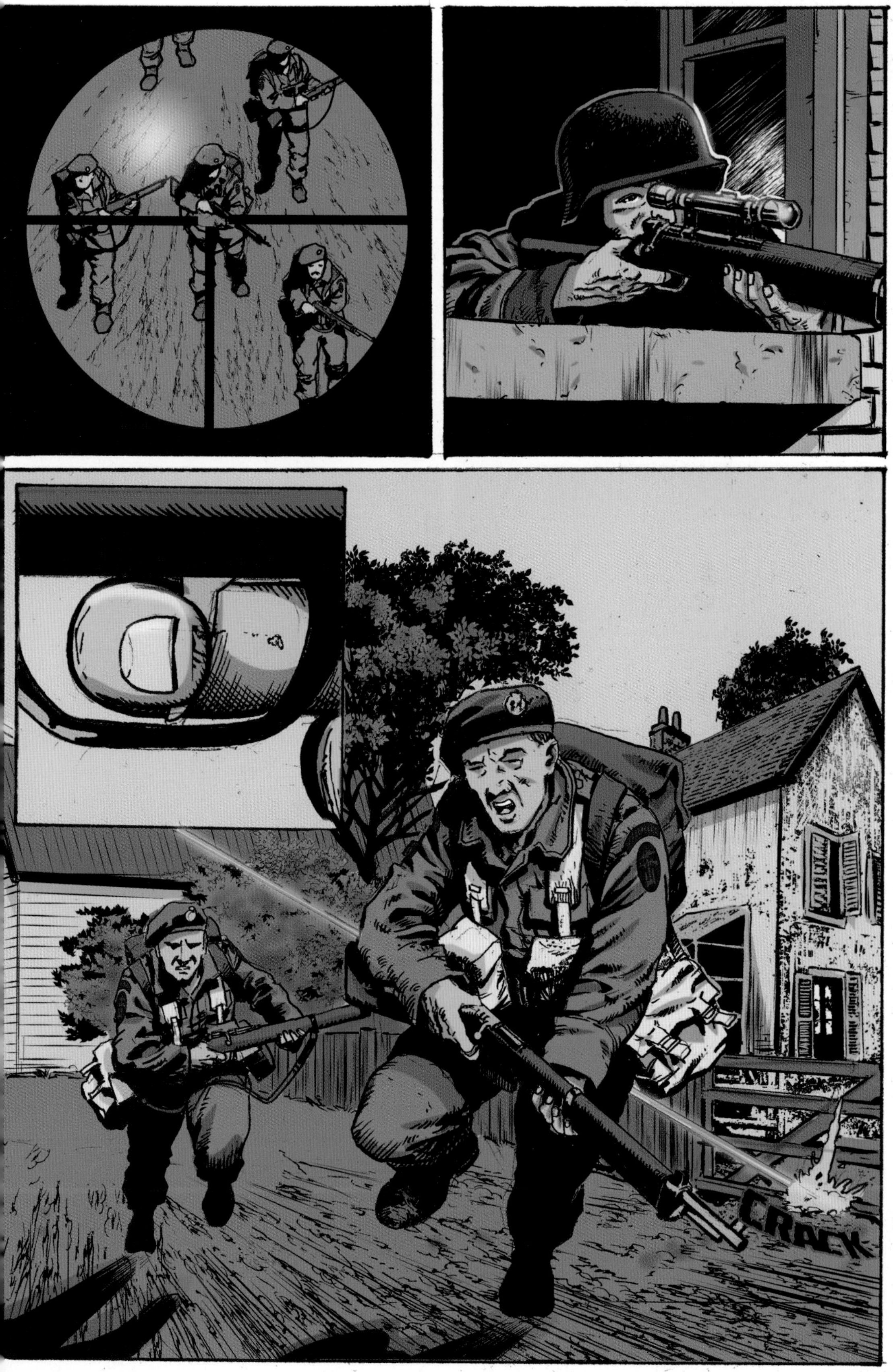
CRACK

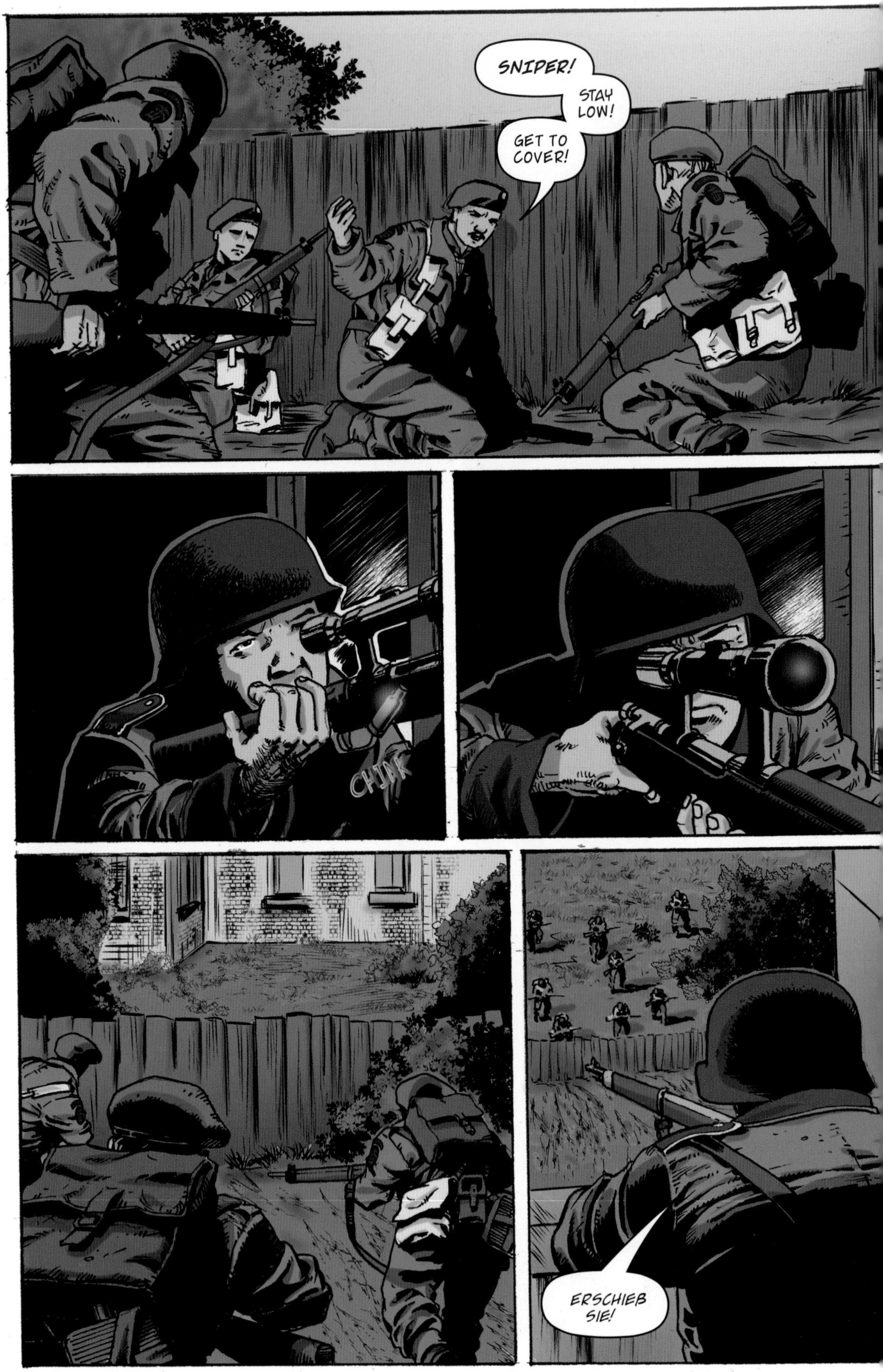
SNIPER!
STAY LOW!
GET TO COVER!
CHINK
ERSCHIEB SIE!

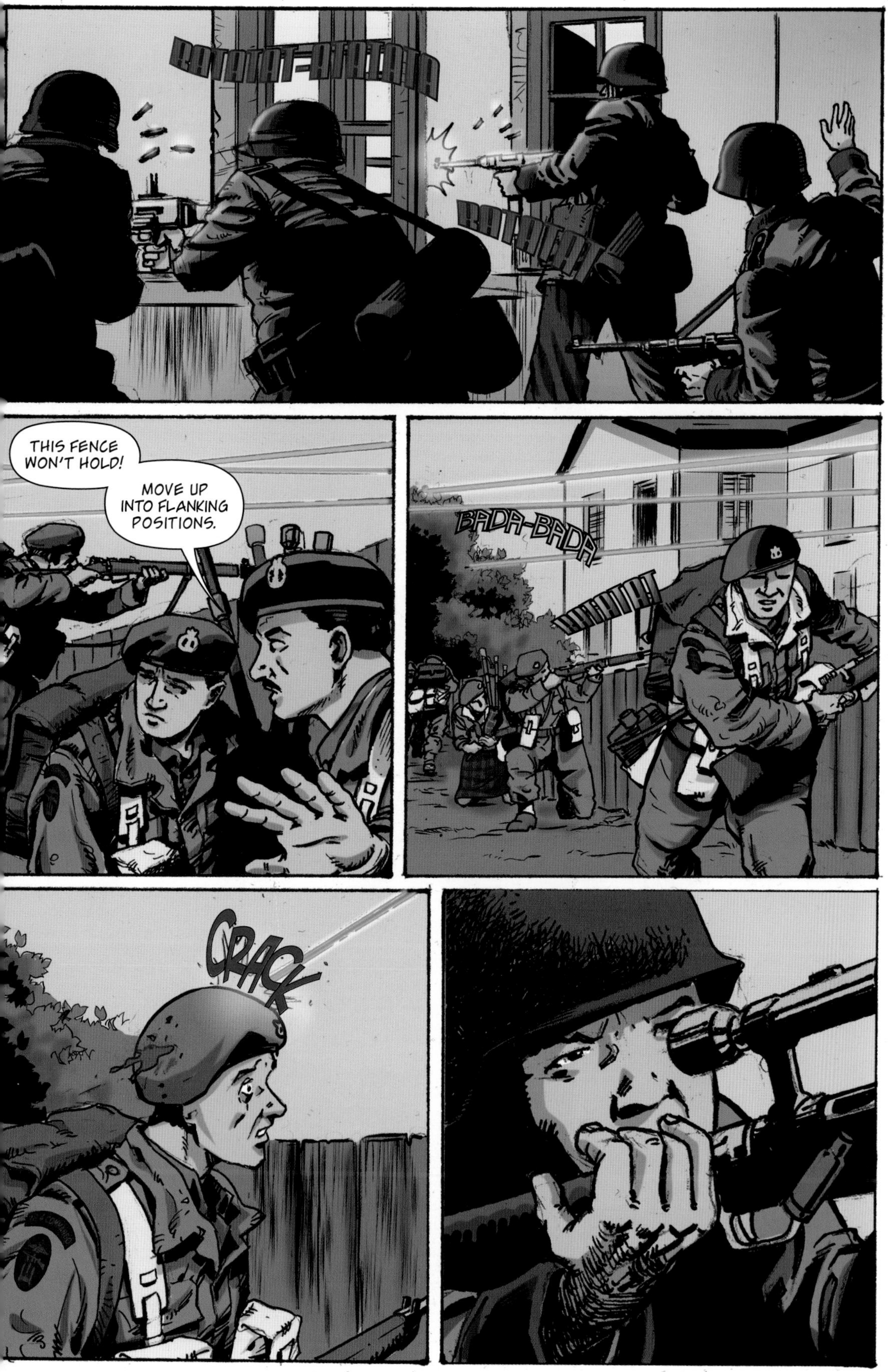
RATATAT-ATATATA
RATATAT
THIS FENCE WON'T HOLD!
MOVE UP INTO FLANKING POSITIONS.
BADA-BADA
CRACK

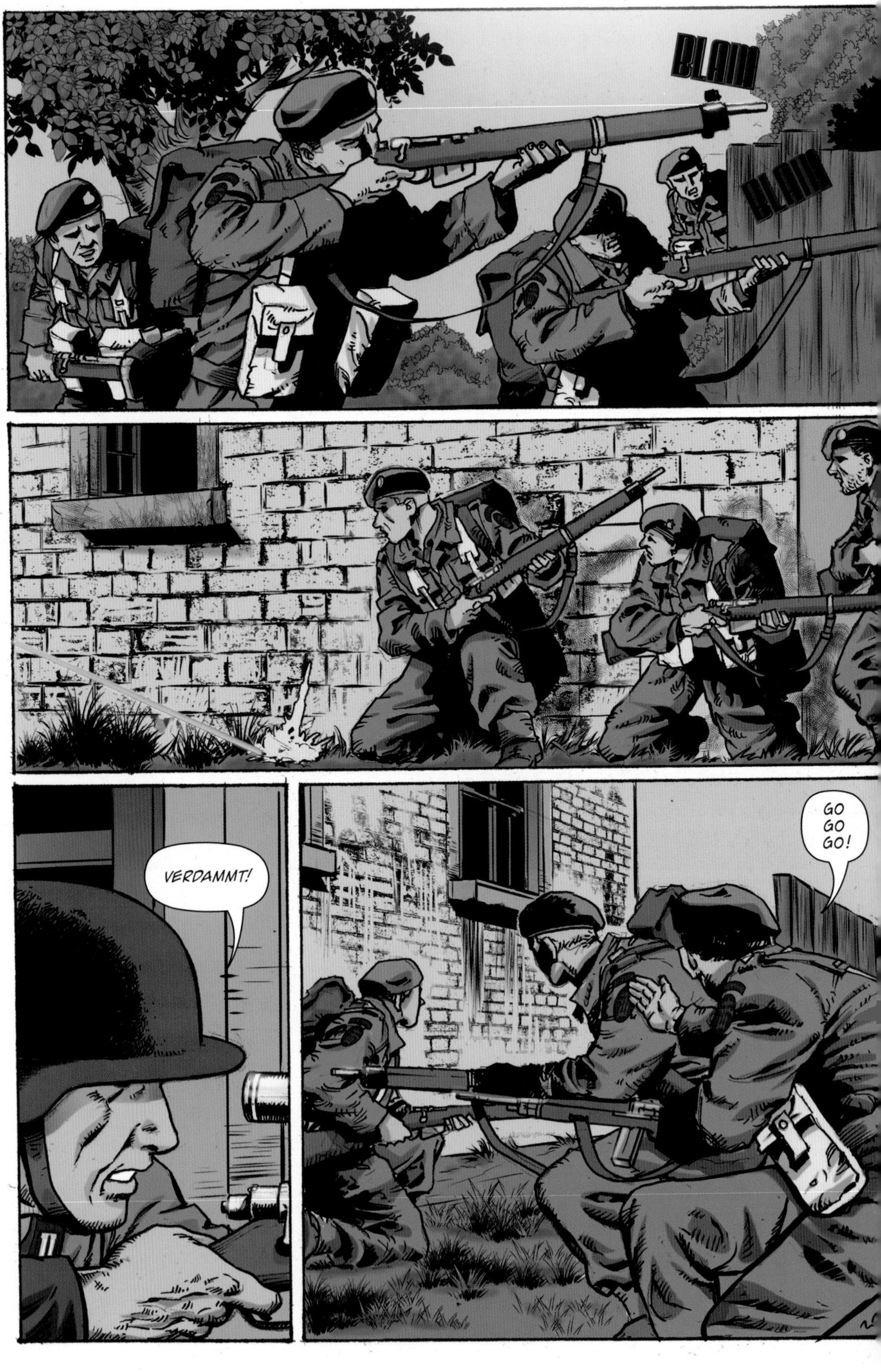
BLAM
BLAM
VERDAMMT!
GO GO GO!

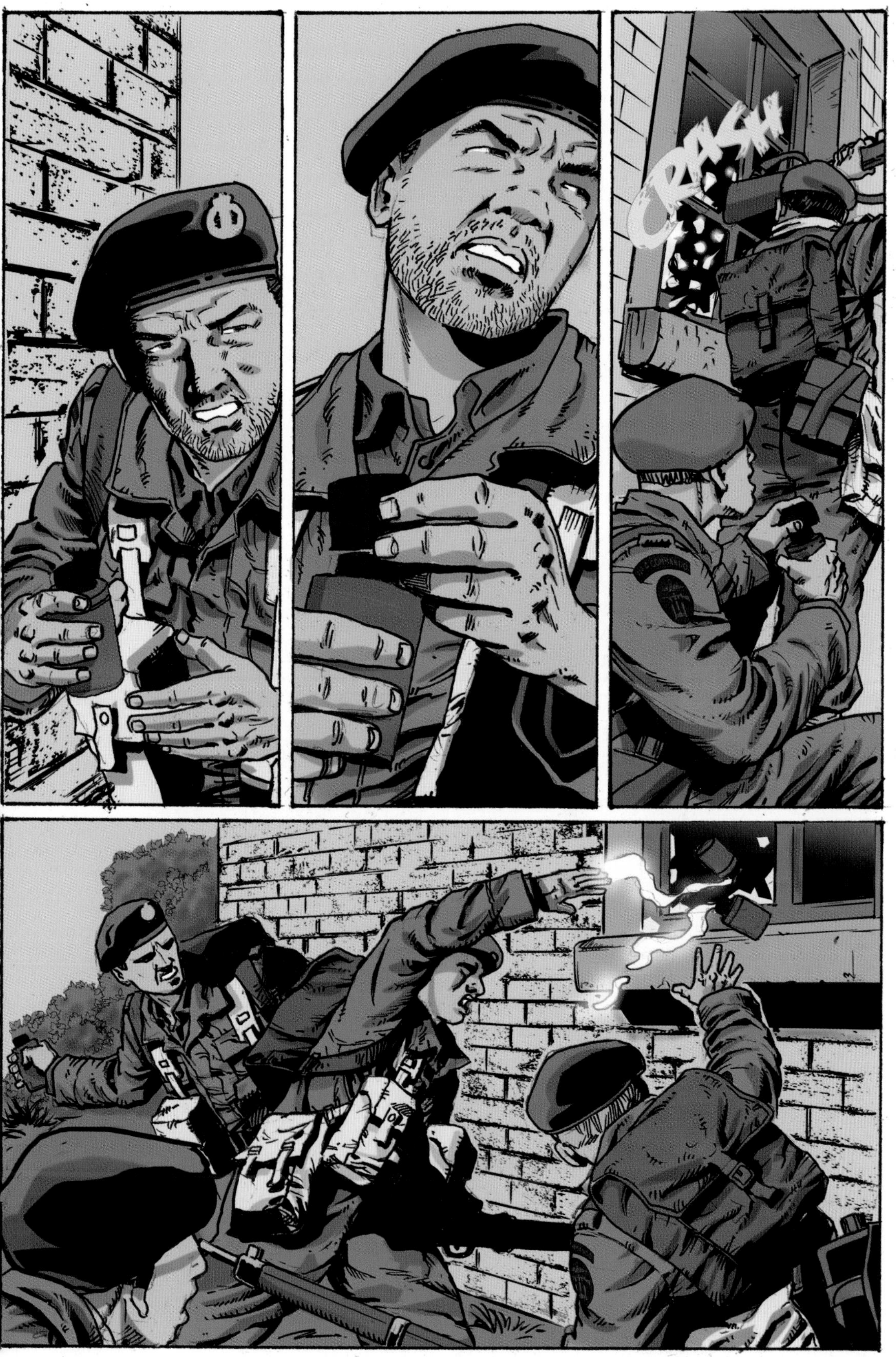
CRASH

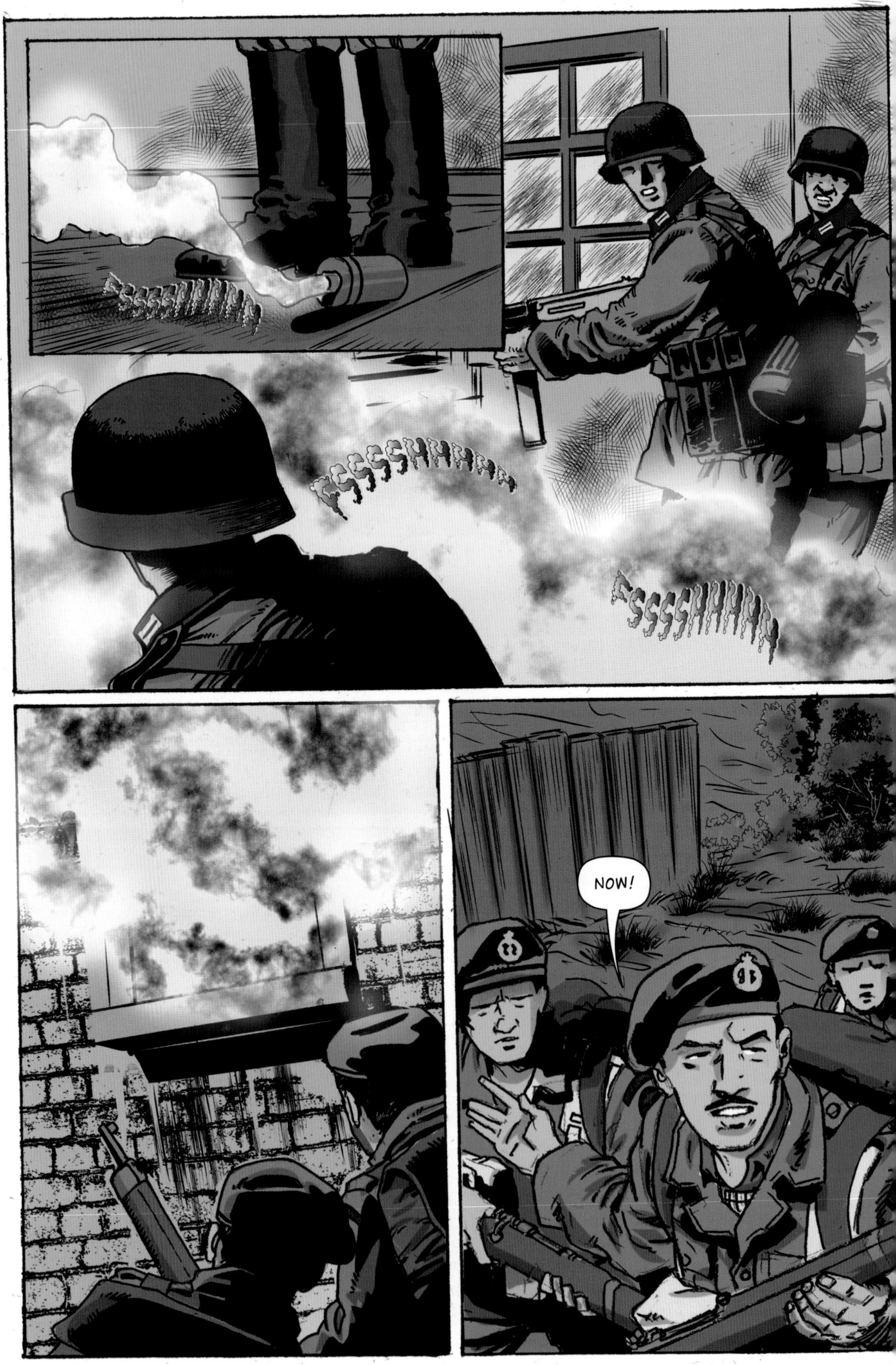

FSSSSHHHHH
FSSSSHHHHH
FSSSSHHHHH
NOW!

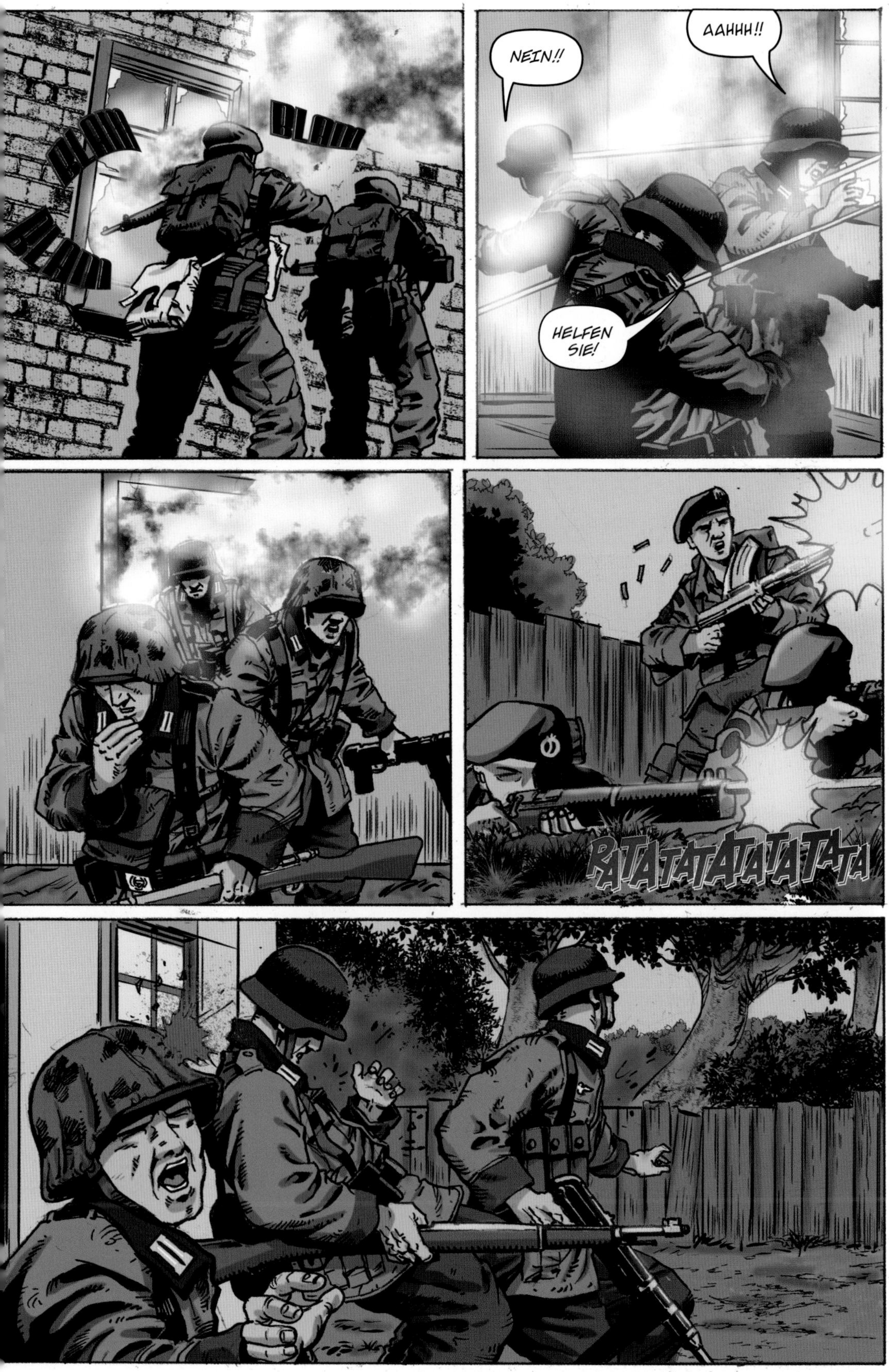
BLAM
BLAM
BLAM
NEIN!!
AAHHH!!
HELFEN SIE!
RATATATATATATATA

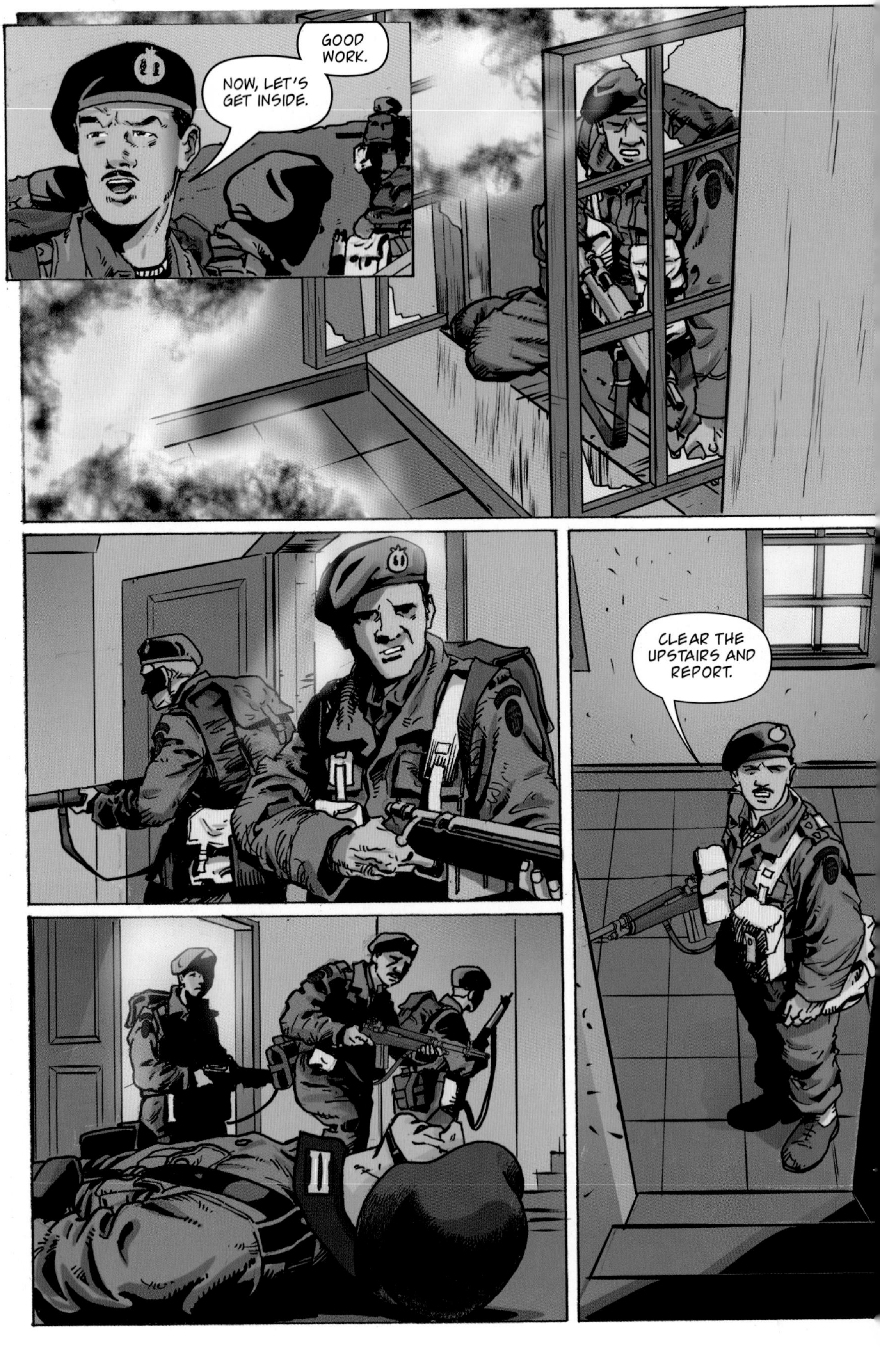
GOOD WORK.
NOW, LET'S GET INSIDE.
CLEAR THE UPSTAIRS AND REPORT.

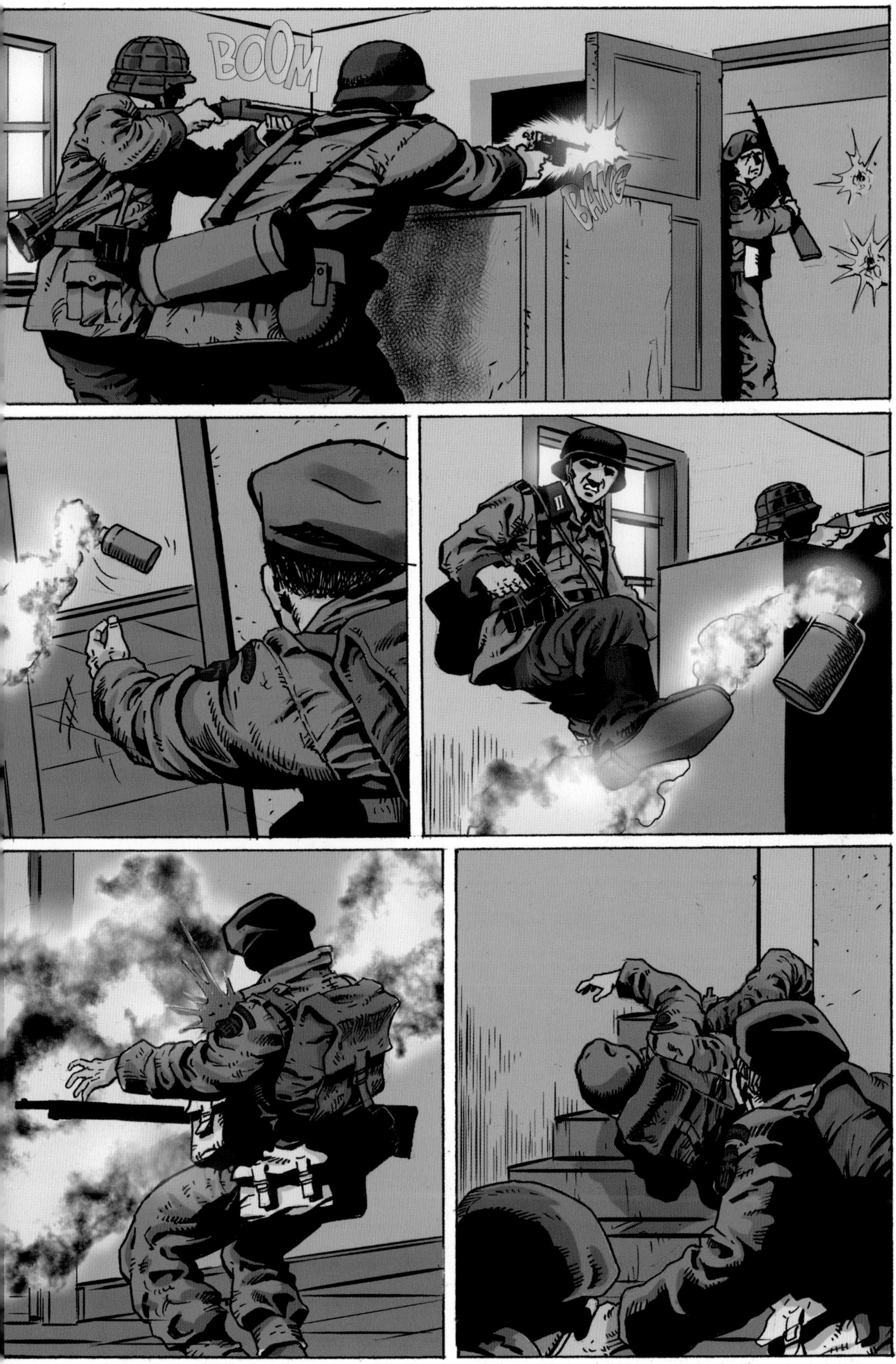
BOOM
BANG

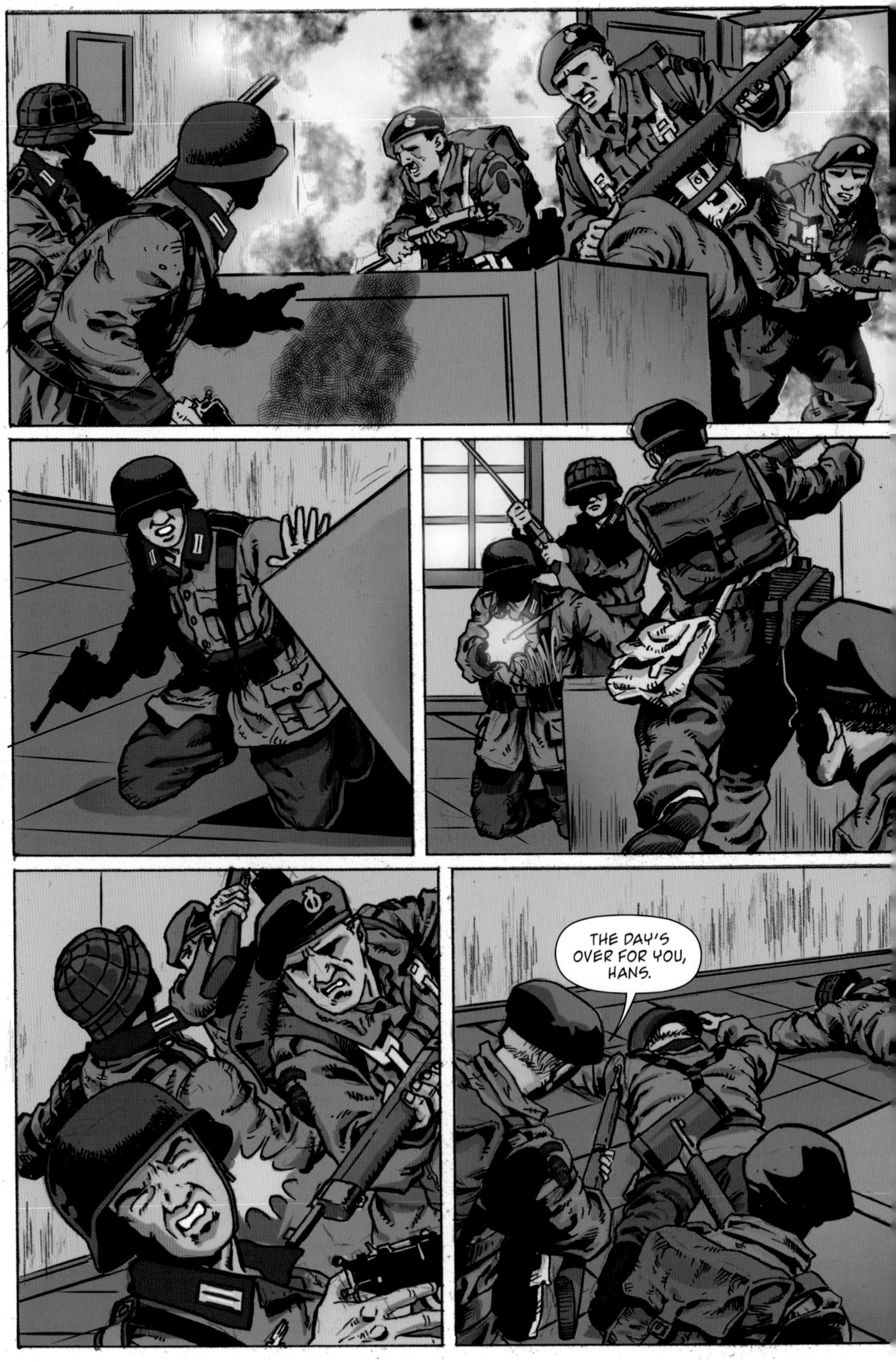
BANG
THE DAY'S OVER FOR YOU, HANS.

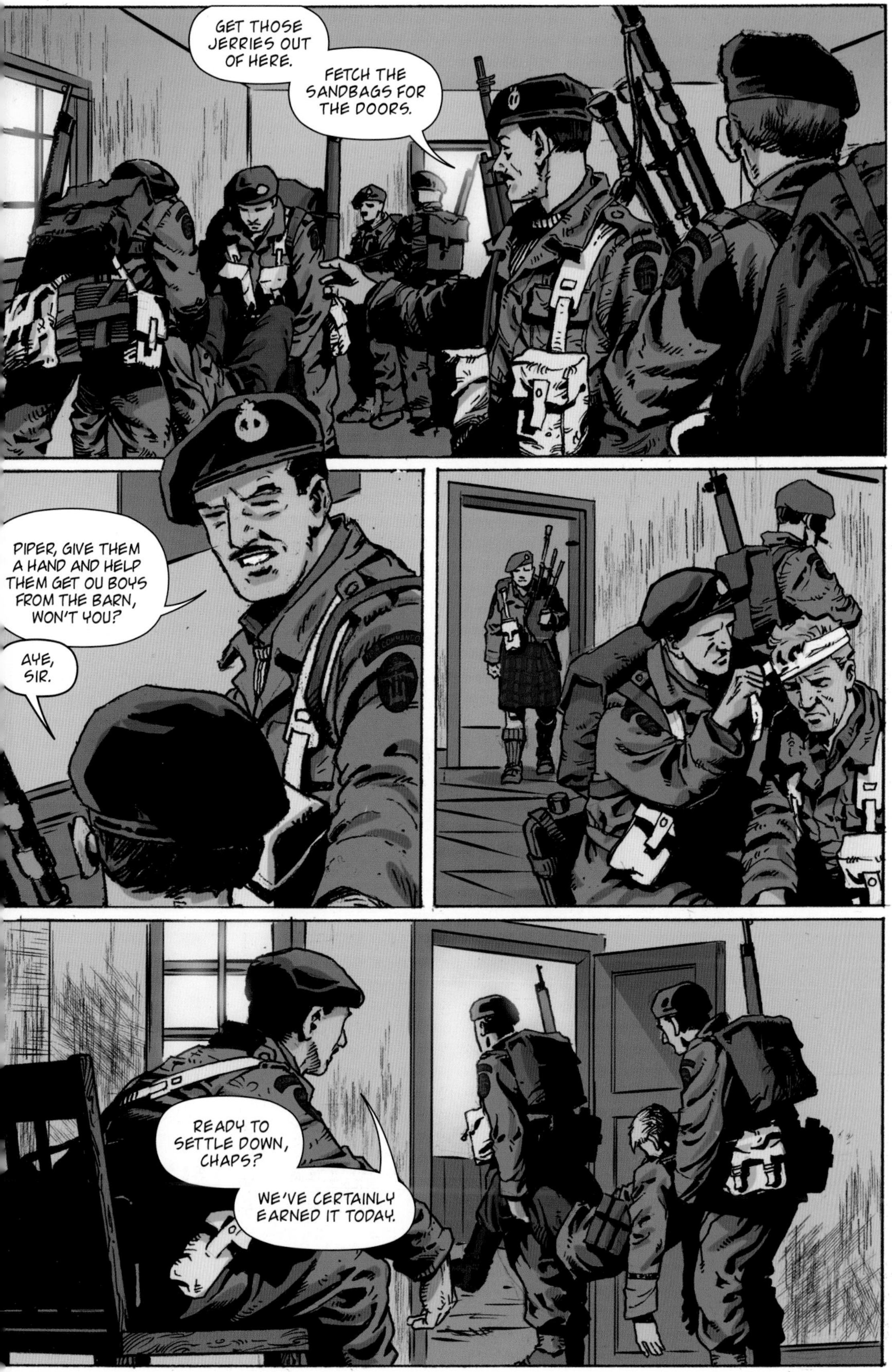
GET THOSE JERRIES OUT OF HERE.
FETCH THE SANDBAGS FOR THE DOORS.
PIPER, GIVE THEM A HAND AND HELP THEM GET OU BOYS FROM THE BARN, WON'T YOU?
AYE, SIR.
READY TO SETTLE DOWN, CHAPS?
WE'VE CERTAINLY EARNED IT TODAY.

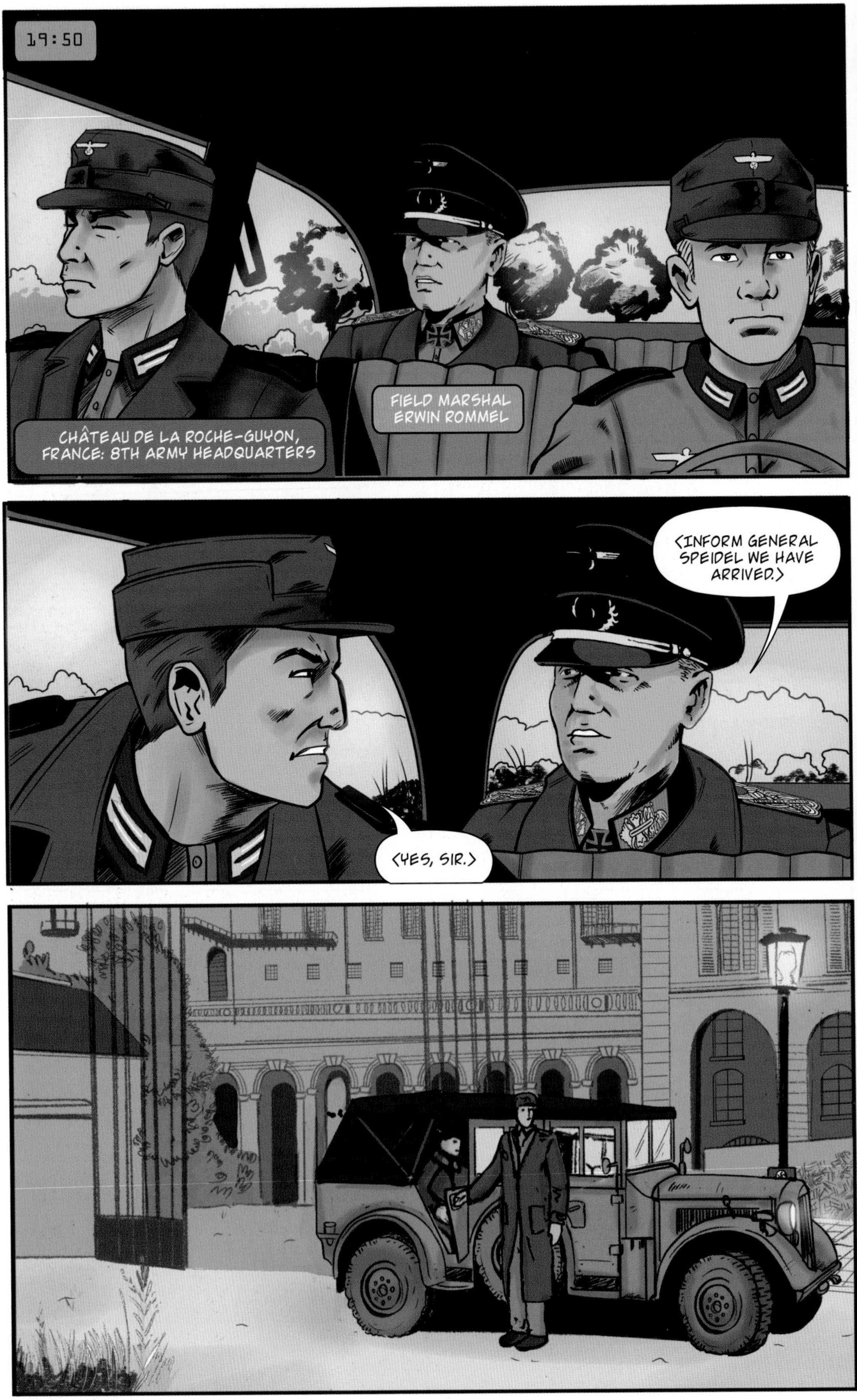
19:50
CHÂTEAU DE LA ROCHE-GUYON, FRANCE: 8TH ARMY HEADQUARTERS
FIELD MARSHAL ERWIN ROMMEL
<INFORM GENERAL SPEIDEL WE HAVE ARRIVED.>
<YES, SIR.>

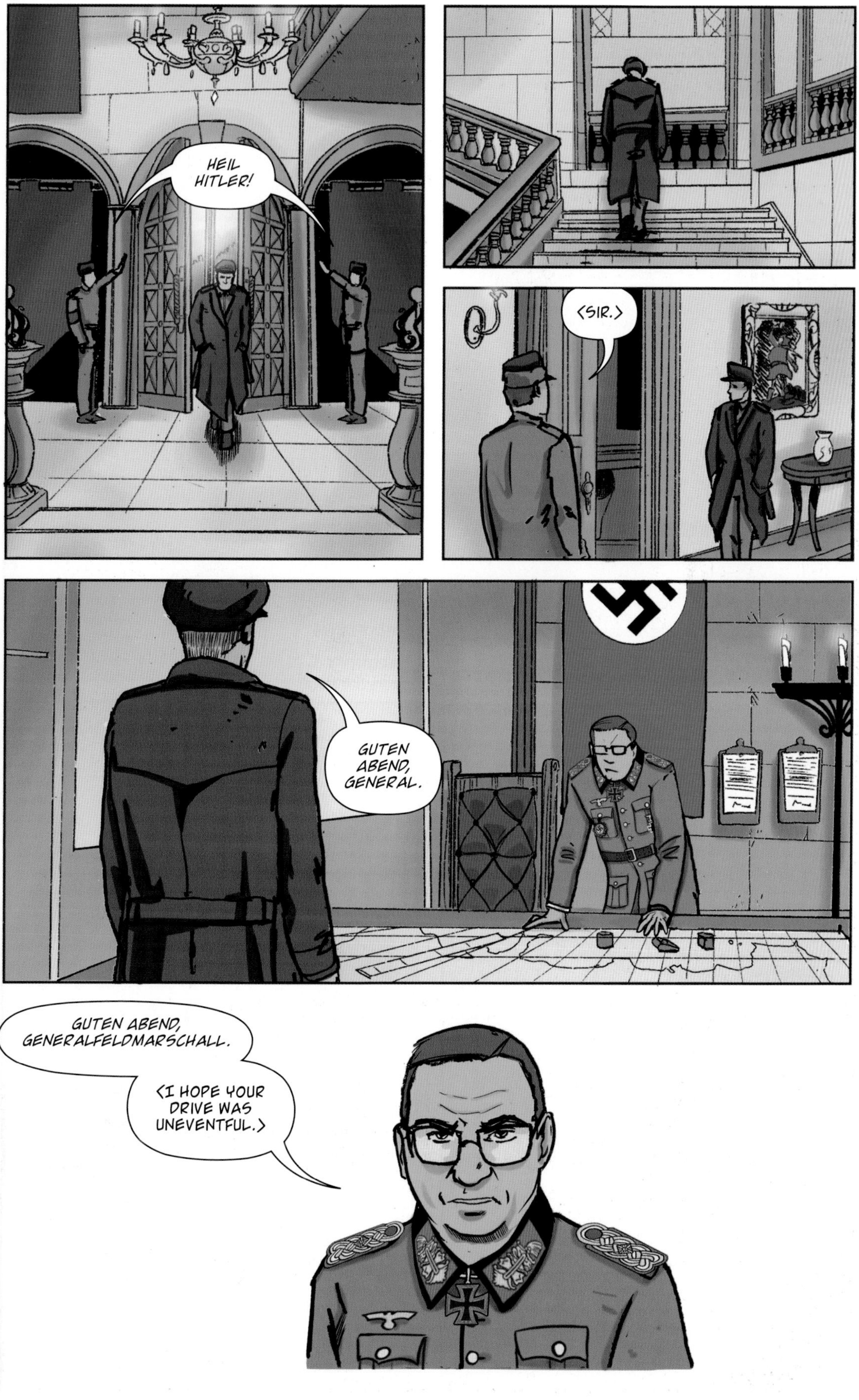
HEIL HITLER!
<SIR.>
GUTEN ABEND, GENERAL.
GUTEN ABEND, GENERALFELDMARSCHALL.
<I HOPE YOUR DRIVE WAS UNEVENTFUL.>

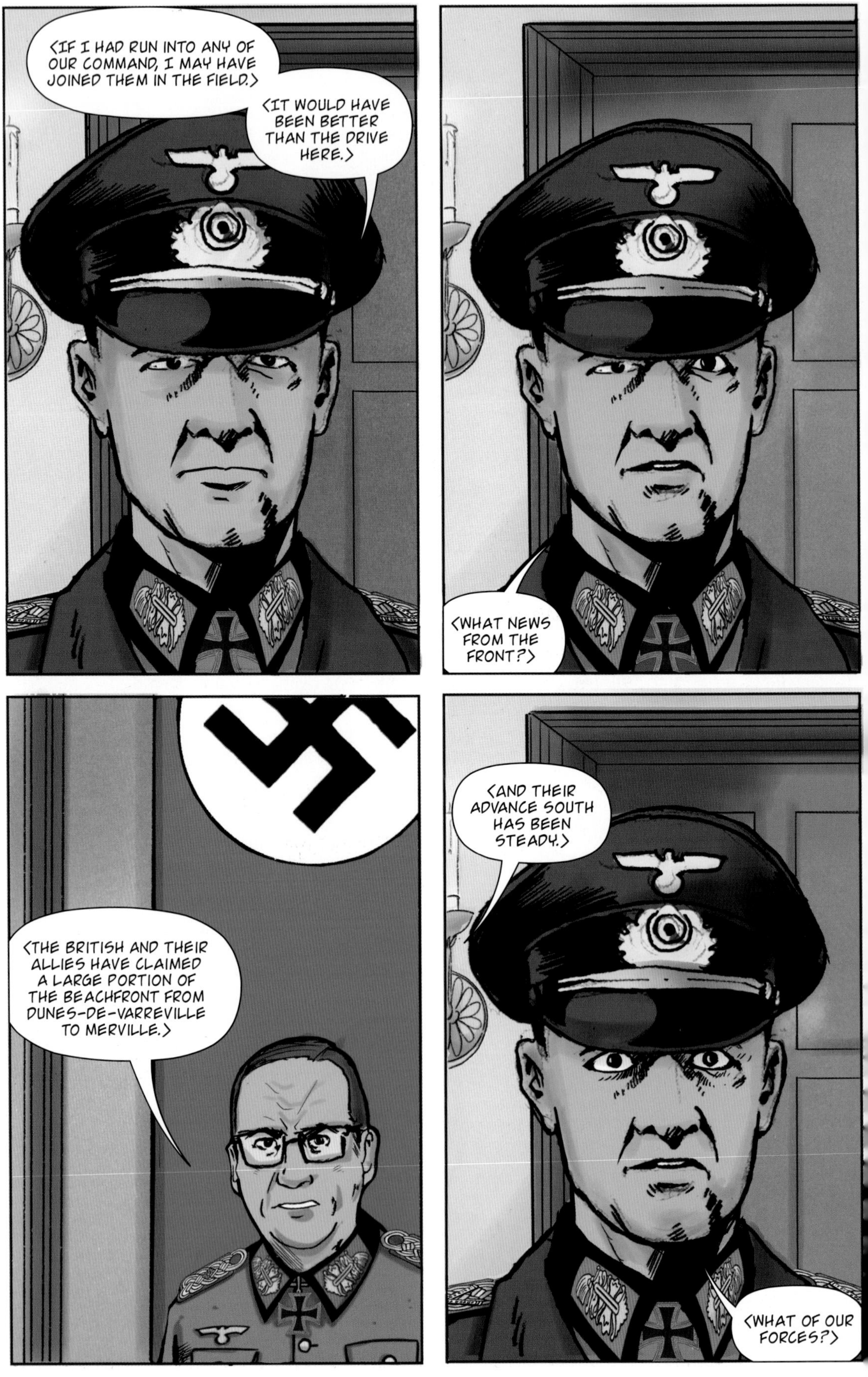
<IF I HAD RUN INTO ANY OF OUR COMMAND, I MAY HAVE JOINED THEM IN THE FIELD.>
<IT WOULD HAVE BEEN BETTER THAN THE DRIVE HERE.>
<WHAT NEWS FROM THE FRONT?>
<THE BRITISH AND THEIR ALLIES HAVE CLAIMED A LARGE PORTION OF THE BEACHFRONT FROM DUNES-DE-VARREVILLE TO MERVILLE.>
<AND THEIR ADVANCE SOUTH HAS BEEN STEADY.>
<WHAT OF OUR FORCES?>

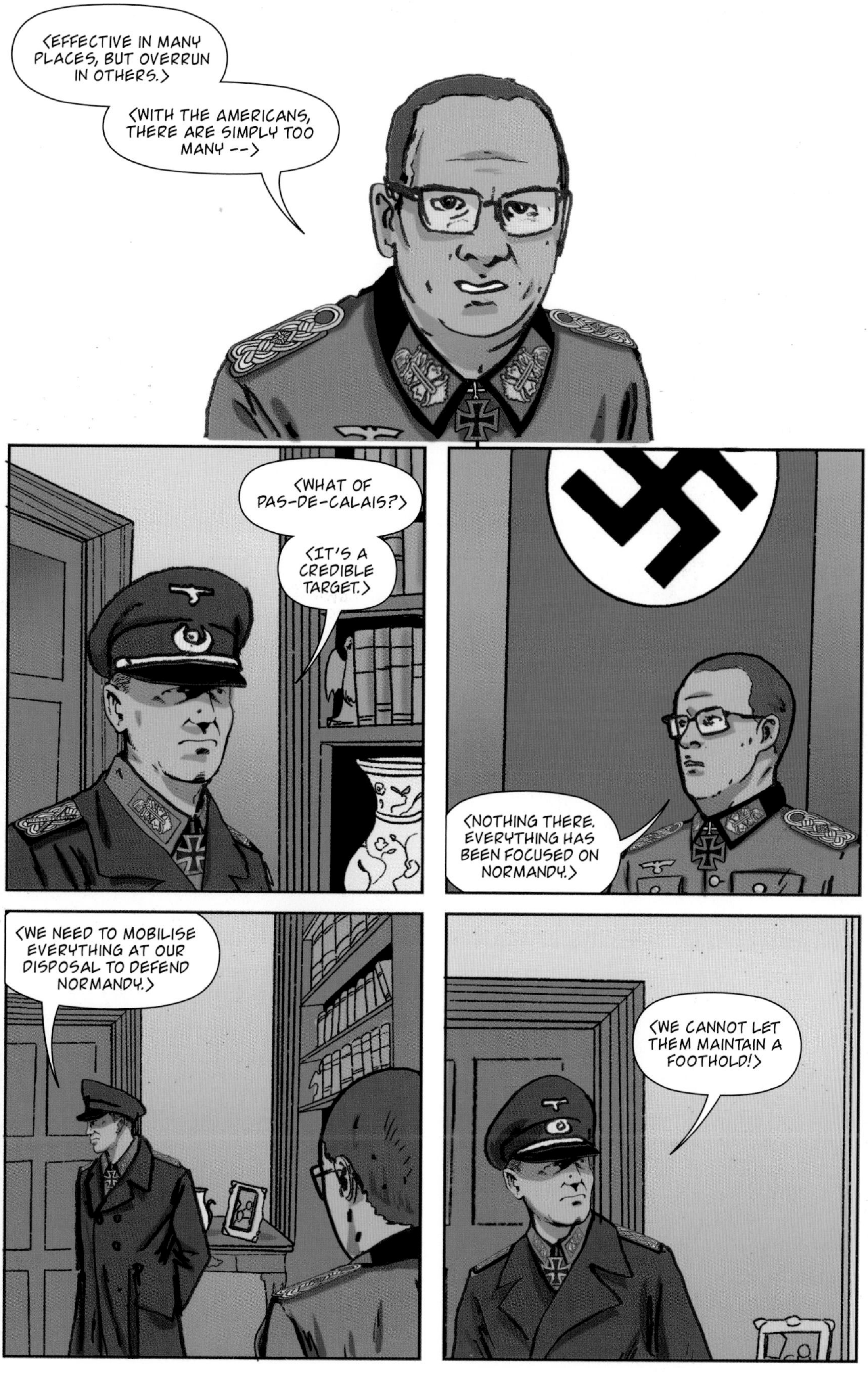
<EFFECTIVE IN MANY PLACES, BUT OVERRUN IN OTHERS.>
<WITH THE AMERICANS, THERE ARE SIMPLY TOO MANY -->
<WHAT OF PAS-DE-CALAIS?>
<IT'S A CREDIBLE TARGET.>
<NOTHING THERE. EVERYTHING HAS BEEN FOCUSED ON NORMANDY.>
<WE NEED TO MOBILISE EVERYTHING AT OUR DISPOSAL TO DEFEND NORMANDY.>
<WE CANNOT LET THEM MAINTAIN A FOOTHOLD!>

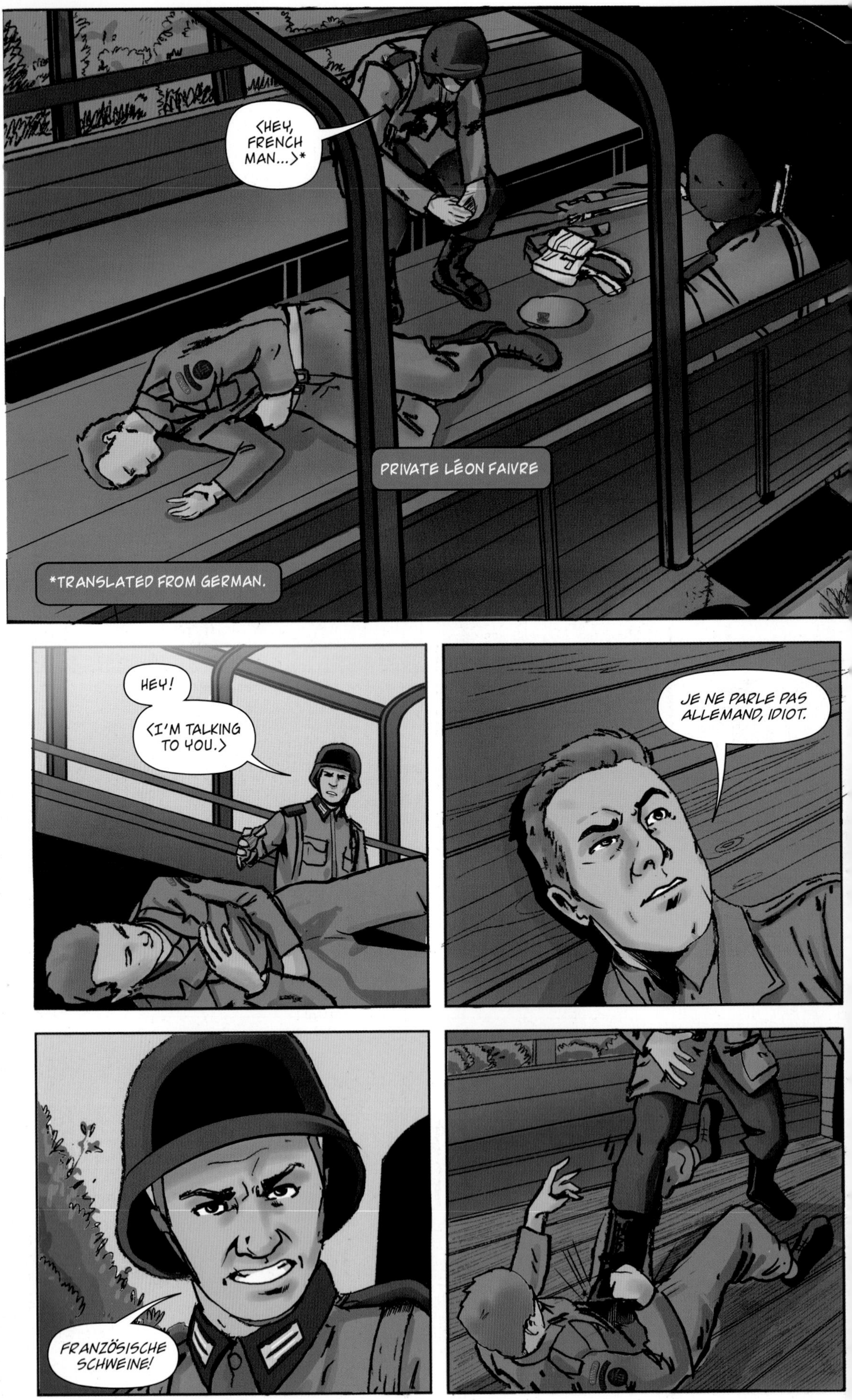

<HEY, FRENCH MAN...>*
PRIVATE LÉON FAIVRE
*TRANSLATED FROM GERMAN.
HEY!
<I'M TALKING TO YOU.>
JE NE PARLE PAS ALLEMAND, IDIOT.
FRANZÖSISCHE SCHWEINE!

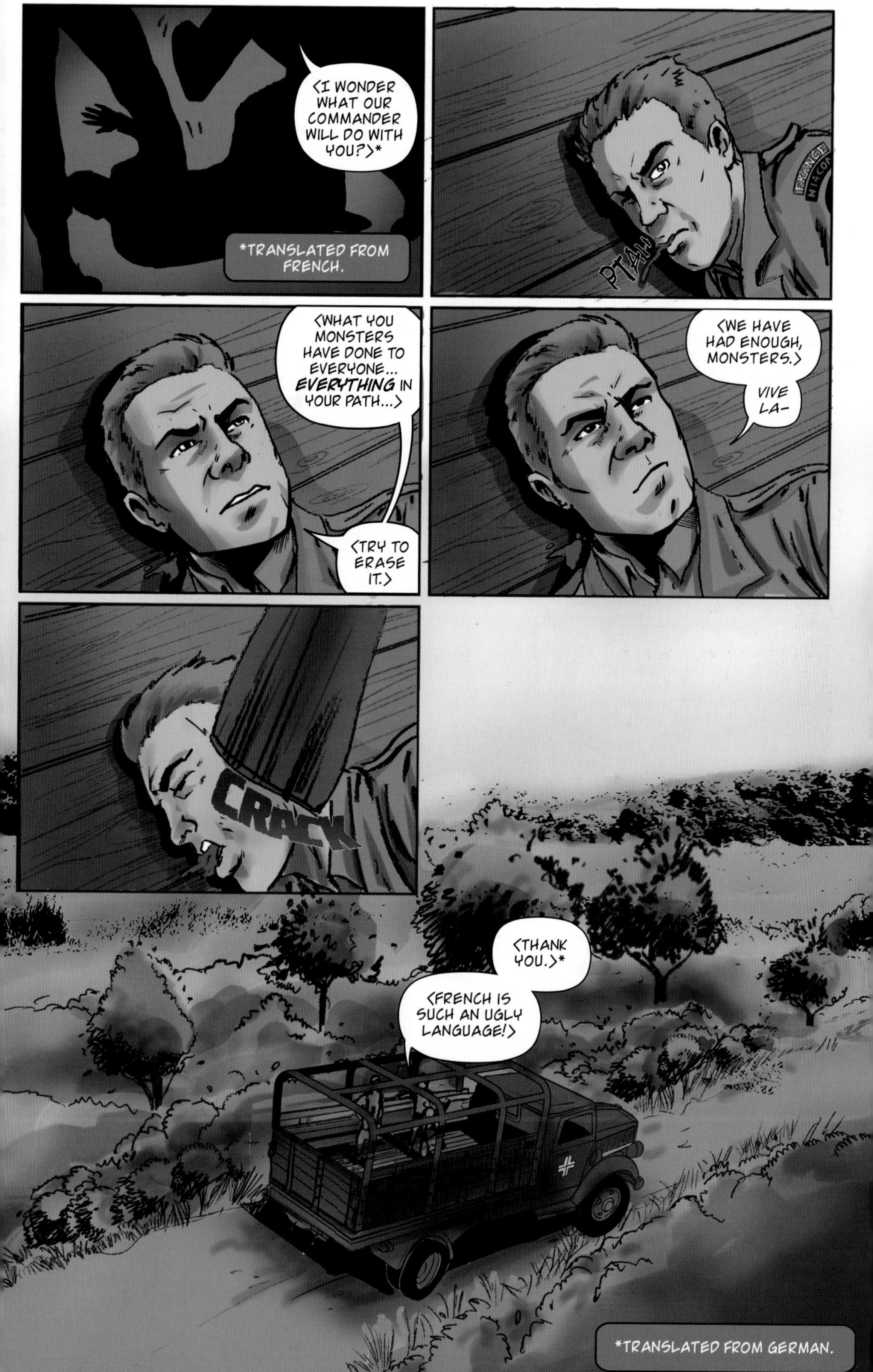

<I WONDER WHAT OUR COMMANDER WILL DO WITH YOU?>*
*TRANSLATED FROM FRENCH.
FRANCE
PTAH
<WHAT YOU MONSTERS HAVE DONE TO EVERYONE... EVERYTHING IN YOUR PATH...>
<TRY TO ERASE IT.>
<WE HAVE HAD ENOUGH, MONSTERS.>
VIVE LA-
CRACK
<THANK YOU.>*
<FRENCH IS SUCH AN UGLY LANGUAGE!>
*TRANSLATED FROM GERMAN.

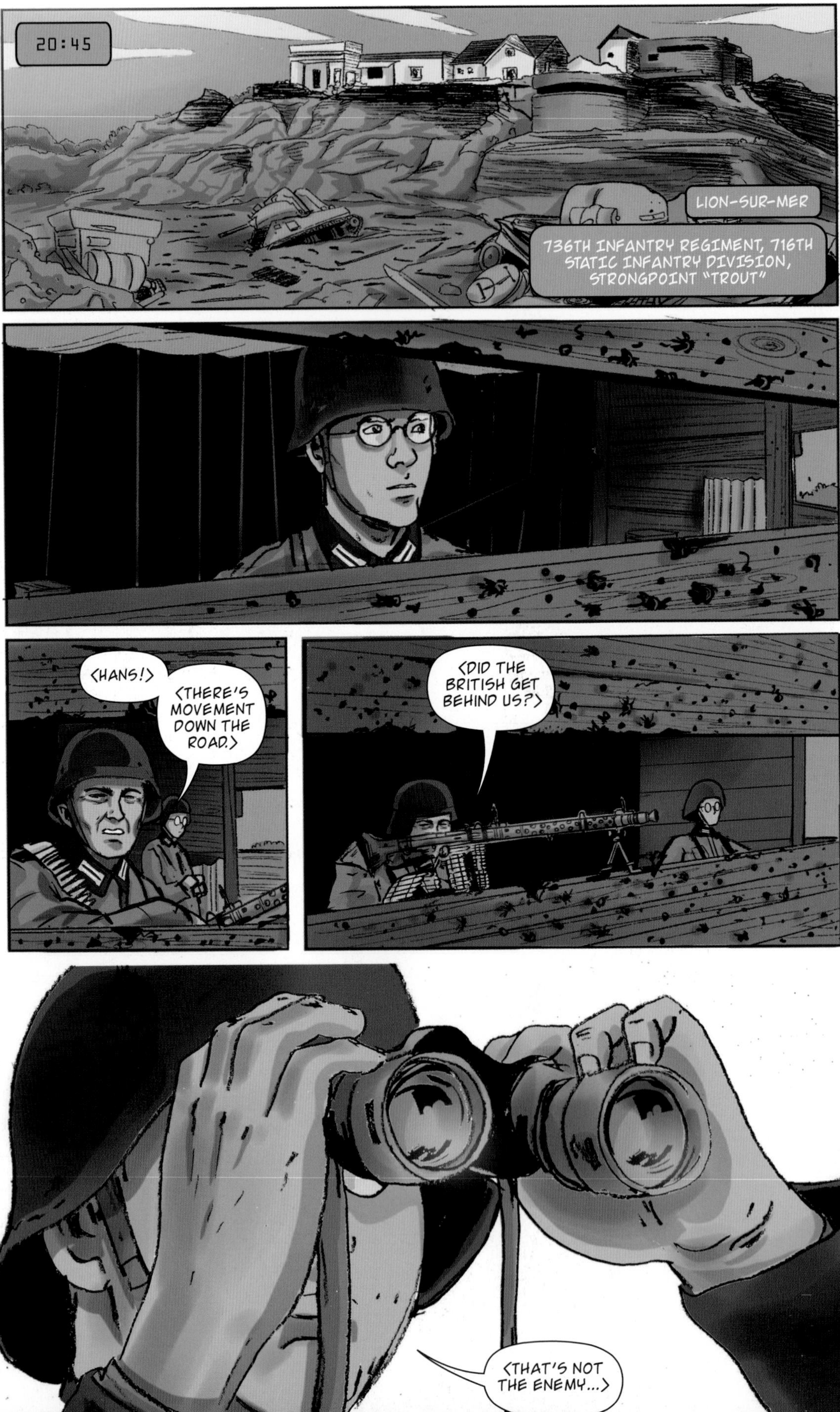
20:45
LION-SUR-MER
736TH INFANTRY REGIMENT, 716TH STATIC INFANTRY DIVISION, STRONGPOINT "TROUT"
<HANS!>
<THERE'S MOVEMENT DOWN THE ROAD.>
<DID THE BRITISH GET BEHIND US?>
<THAT'S NOT THE ENEMY...>

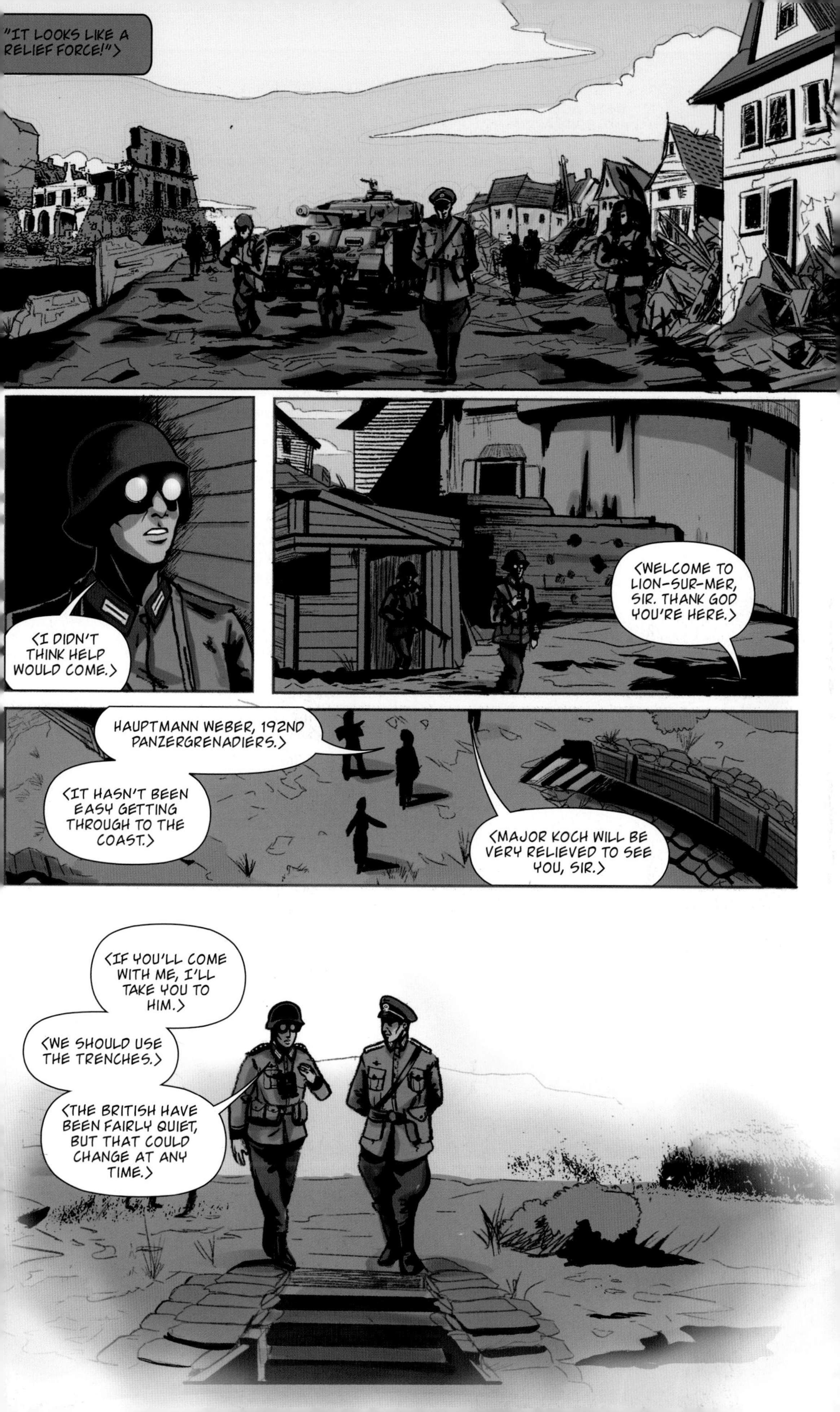
"IT LOOKS LIKE A RELIEF FORCE!">
<I DIDN'T THINK HELP WOULD COME.>
<WELCOME TO LION-SUR-MER, SIR. THANK GOD YOU'RE HERE.>
HAUPTMANN WEBER, 192ND PANZERGRENADIERS.>
<IT HASN'T BEEN EASY GETTING THROUGH TO THE COAST.>
<MAJOR KOCH WILL BE VERY RELIEVED TO SEE YOU, SIR.>
<IF YOU'LL COME WITH ME, I'LL TAKE YOU TO HIM.>
<WE SHOULD USE THE TRENCHES.>
<THE BRITISH HAVE BEEN FAIRLY QUIET, BUT THAT COULD CHANGE AT ANY TIME.>

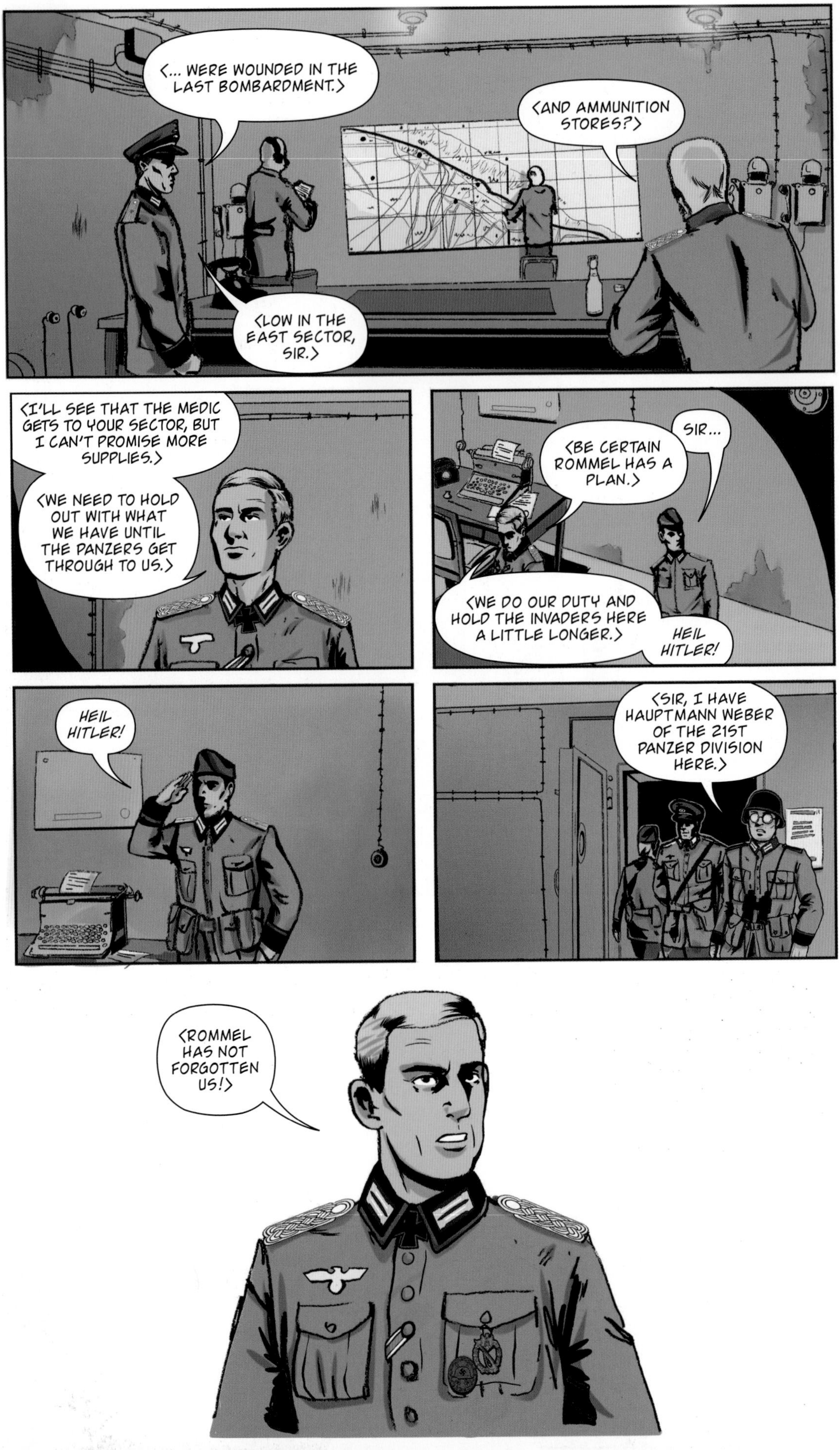

<... WERE WOUNDED IN THE LAST BOMBARDMENT.>
<AND AMMUNITION STORES?>
<LOW IN THE EAST SECTOR, SIR.>
<I'LL SEE THAT THE MEDIC GETS TO YOUR SECTOR, BUT I CAN'T PROMISE MORE SUPPLIES.>
<WE NEED TO HOLD OUT WITH WHAT WE HAVE UNTIL THE PANZERS GET THROUGH TO US.>
SIR...
<BE CERTAIN ROMMEL HAS A PLAN.>
<WE DO OUR DUTY AND HOLD THE INVADERS HERE A LITTLE LONGER.>
HEIL HITLER!
HEIL HITLER!
<SIR, I HAVE HAUPTMANN WEBER OF THE 21ST PANZER DIVISION HERE.>
<ROMMEL HAS NOT FORGOTTEN US!>

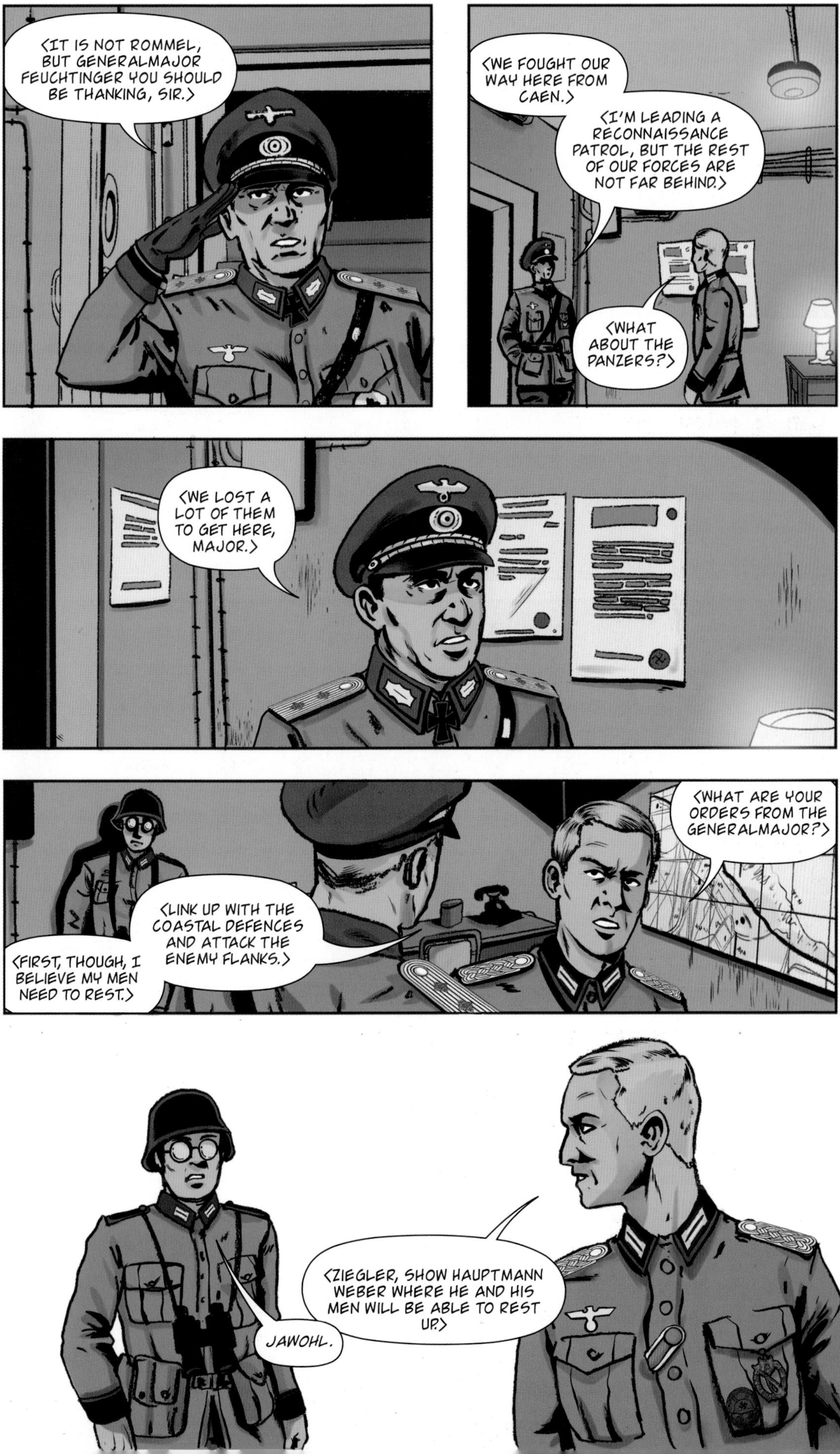

<IT IS NOT ROMMEL, BUT GENERALMAJOR FEUCHTINGER YOU SHOULD BE THANKING, SIR.>
<WE FOUGHT OUR WAY HERE FROM CAEN.>
<I'M LEADING A RECONNAISSANCE PATROL, BUT THE REST OF OUR FORCES ARE NOT FAR BEHIND.>
<WHAT ABOUT THE PANZERS?>
<WE LOST A LOT OF THEM TO GET HERE, MAJOR.>
<WHAT ARE YOUR ORDERS FROM THE GENERALMAJOR?>
<LINK UP WITH THE COASTAL DEFENCES AND ATTACK THE ENEMY FLANKS.>
<FIRST, THOUGH, I BELIEVE MY MEN NEED TO REST.>
<ZIEGLER, SHOW HAUPTMANN WEBER WHERE HE AND HIS MEN WILL BE ABLE TO REST UP.>
JAWOHL.

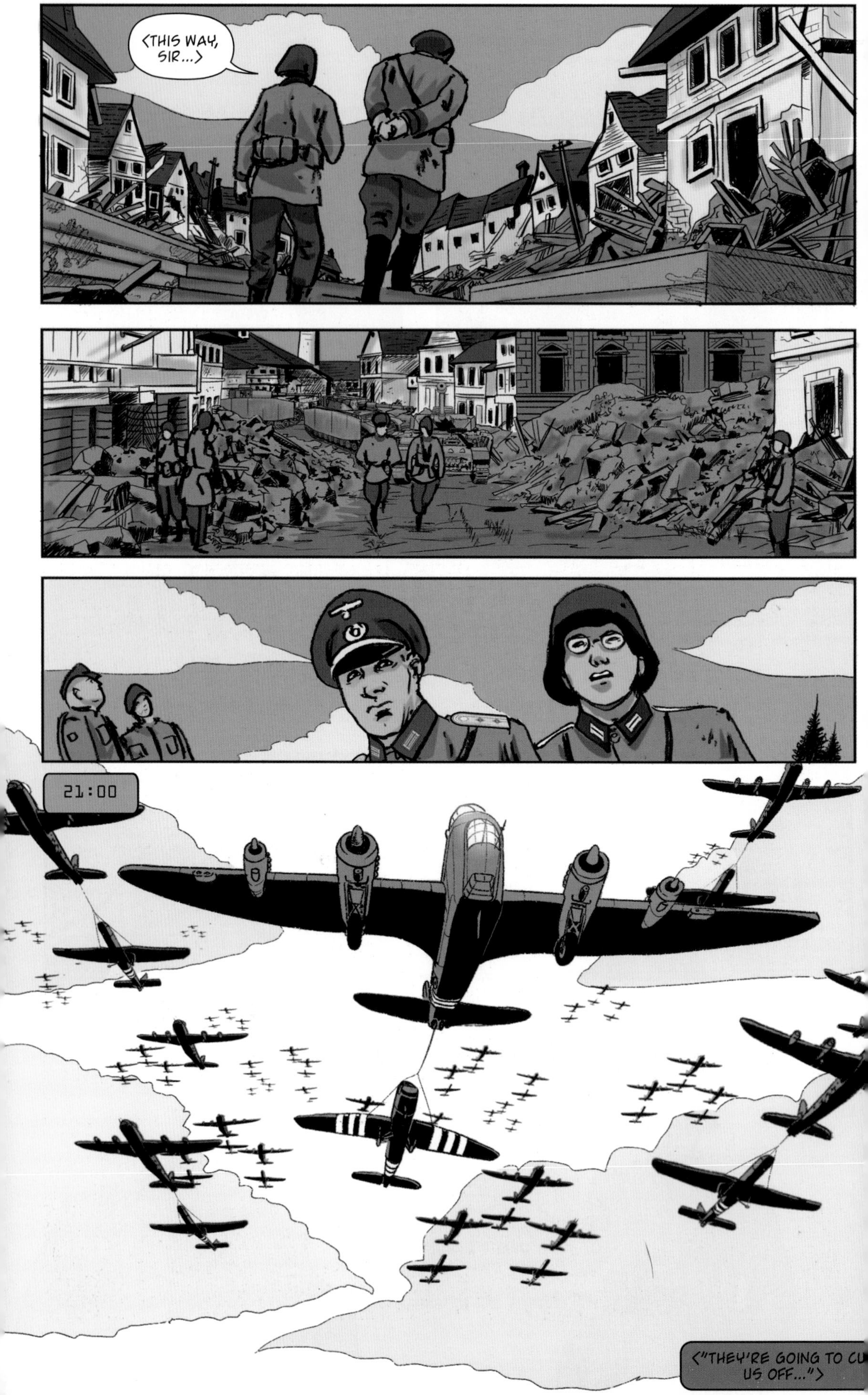
<THIS WAY, SIR...>
21:00
<"THEY'RE GOING TO CU
US OFF...">

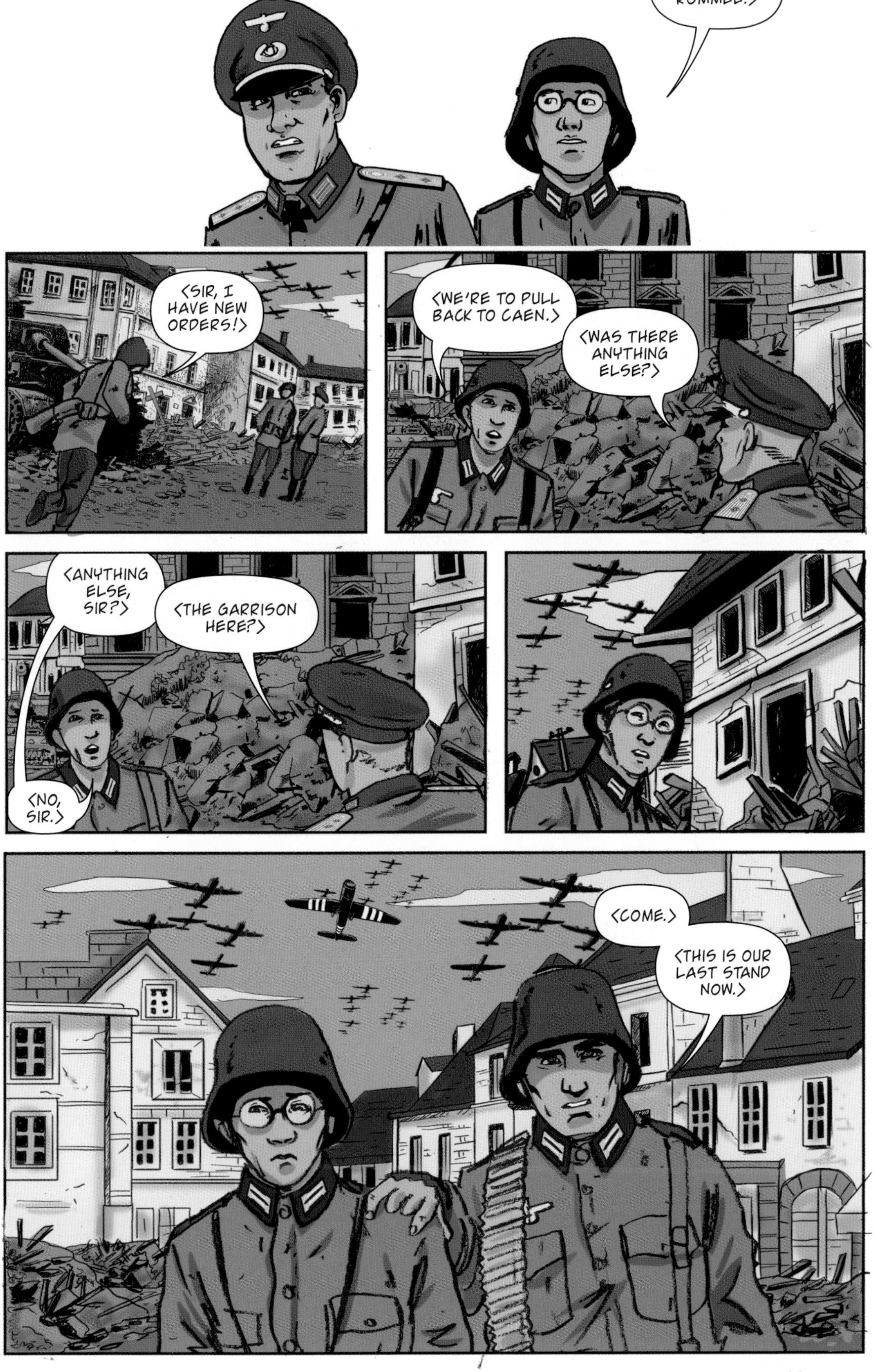
<BUT THE PANZERS... ROMMEL.>
<SIR, I HAVE NEW ORDERS!>
<WE'RE TO PULL BACK TO CAEN.>
<WAS THERE ANYTHING ELSE?>
<ANYTHING ELSE, SIR?>
<THE GARRISON HERE?>
<NO, SIR.>
<COME.>
<THIS IS OUR LAST STAND NOW.>

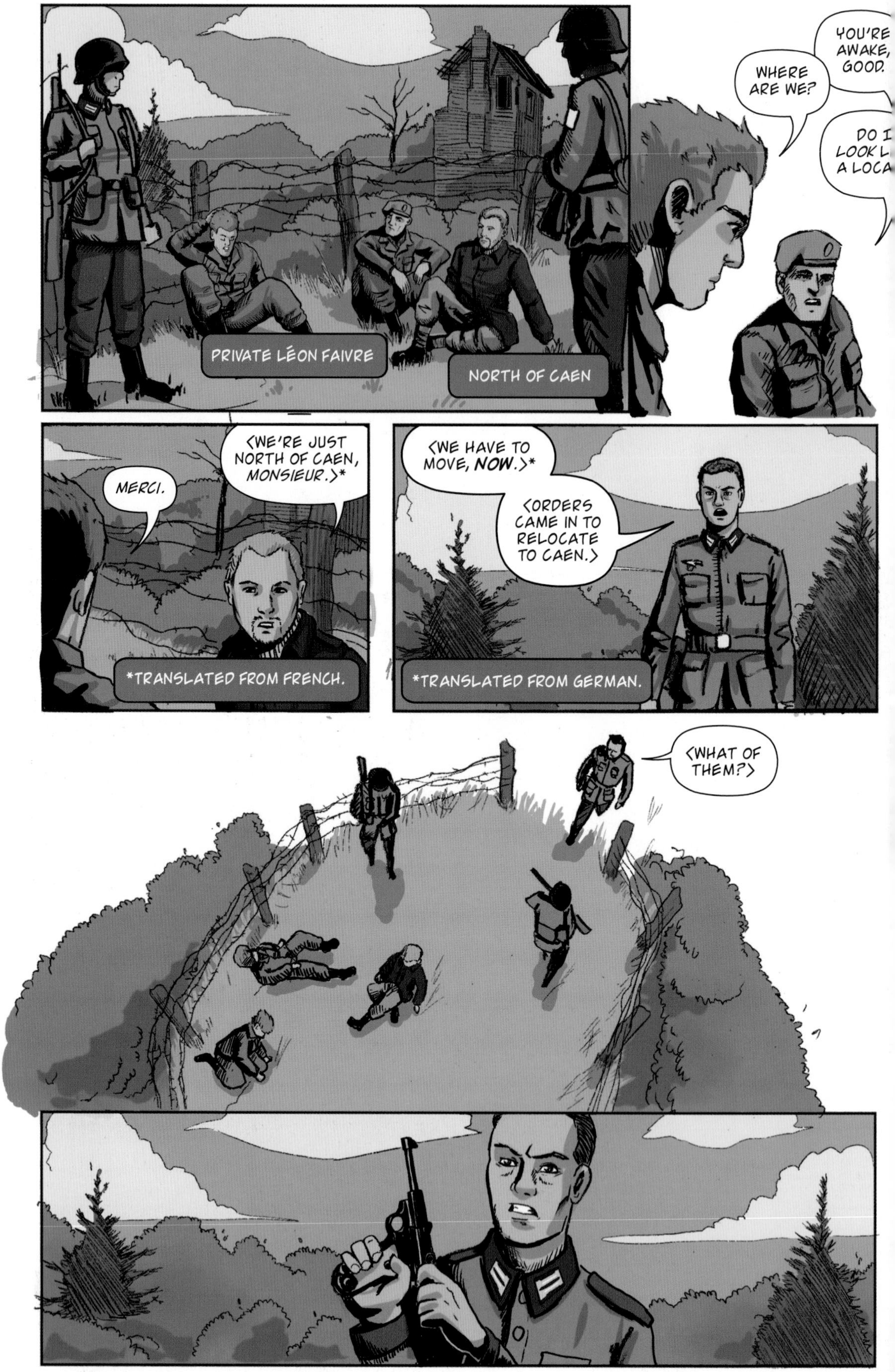
PRIVATE LÉON FAIVRE
NORTH OF CAEN
WHERE ARE WE?
YOU'RE AWAKE, GOOD.
DO I LOOK L A LOCA
<WE'RE JUST NORTH OF CAEN, MONSIEUR.>*
MERCI.
*TRANSLATED FROM FRENCH.
<WE HAVE TO MOVE, NOW.>*
<ORDERS CAME IN TO RELOCATE TO CAEN.>
*TRANSLATED FROM GERMAN.
<WHAT OF THEM?>

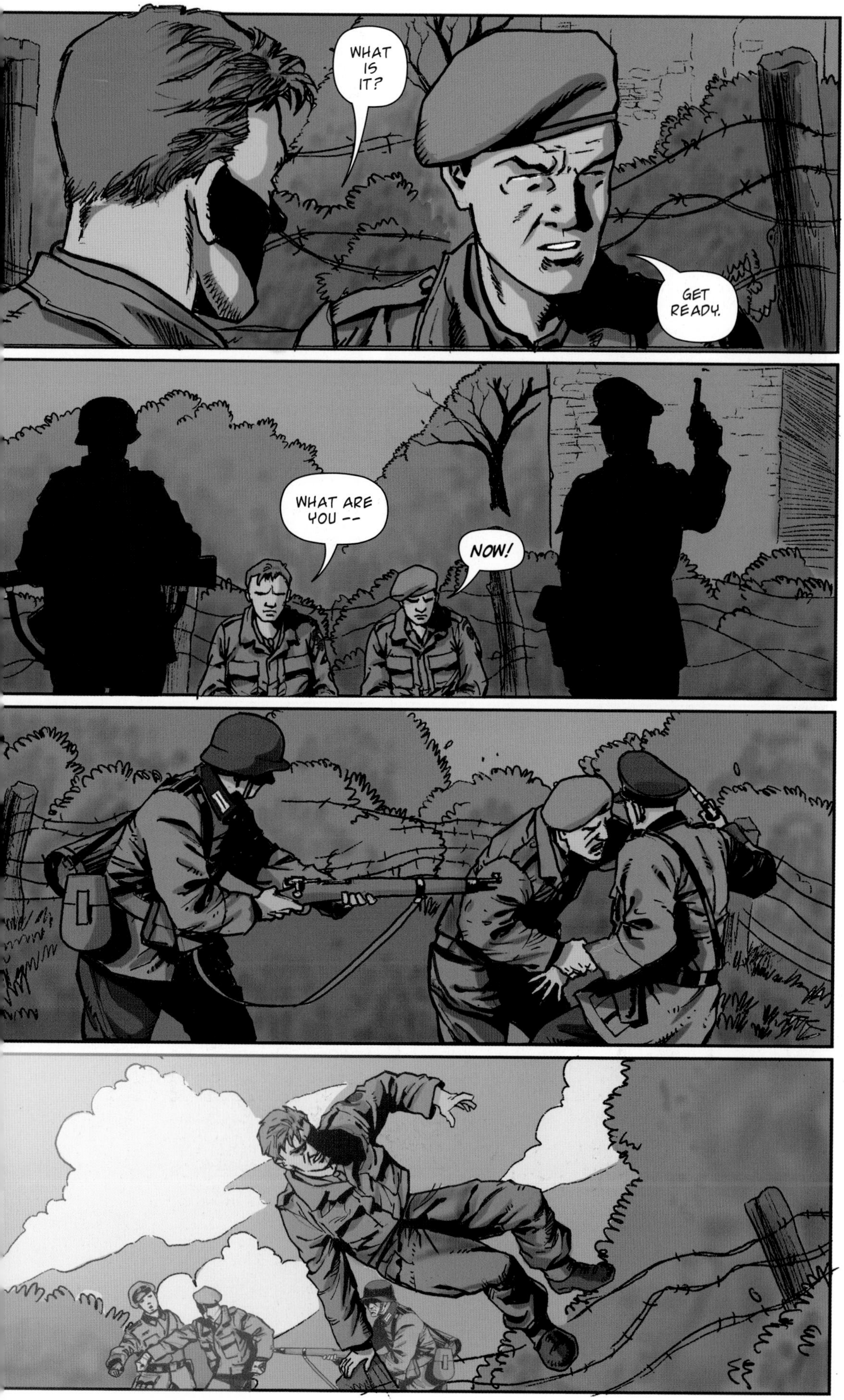
WHAT IS IT?
GET READY.
WHAT ARE YOU --
NOW!

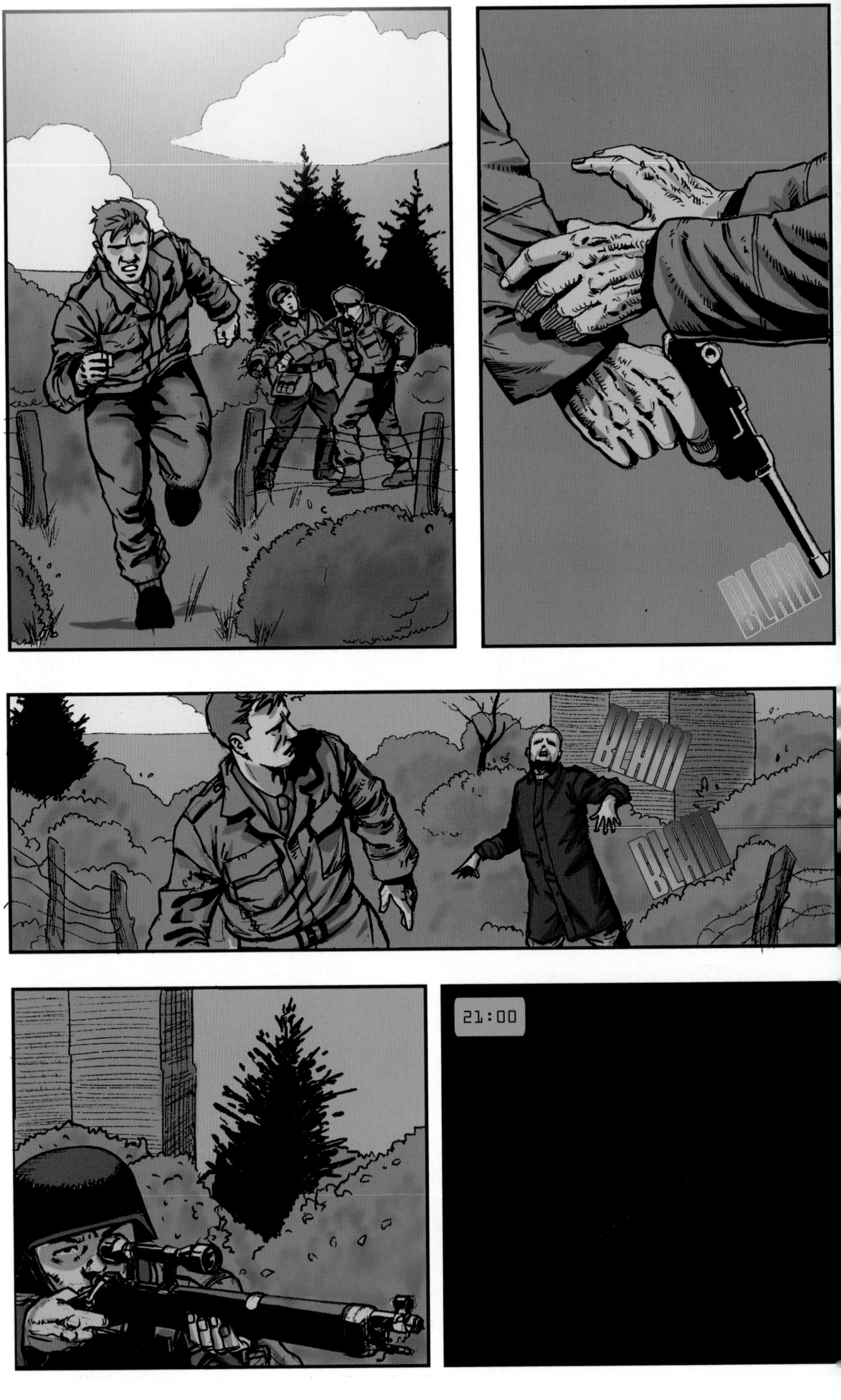
BLAM
BLAM
BLAM
21:00

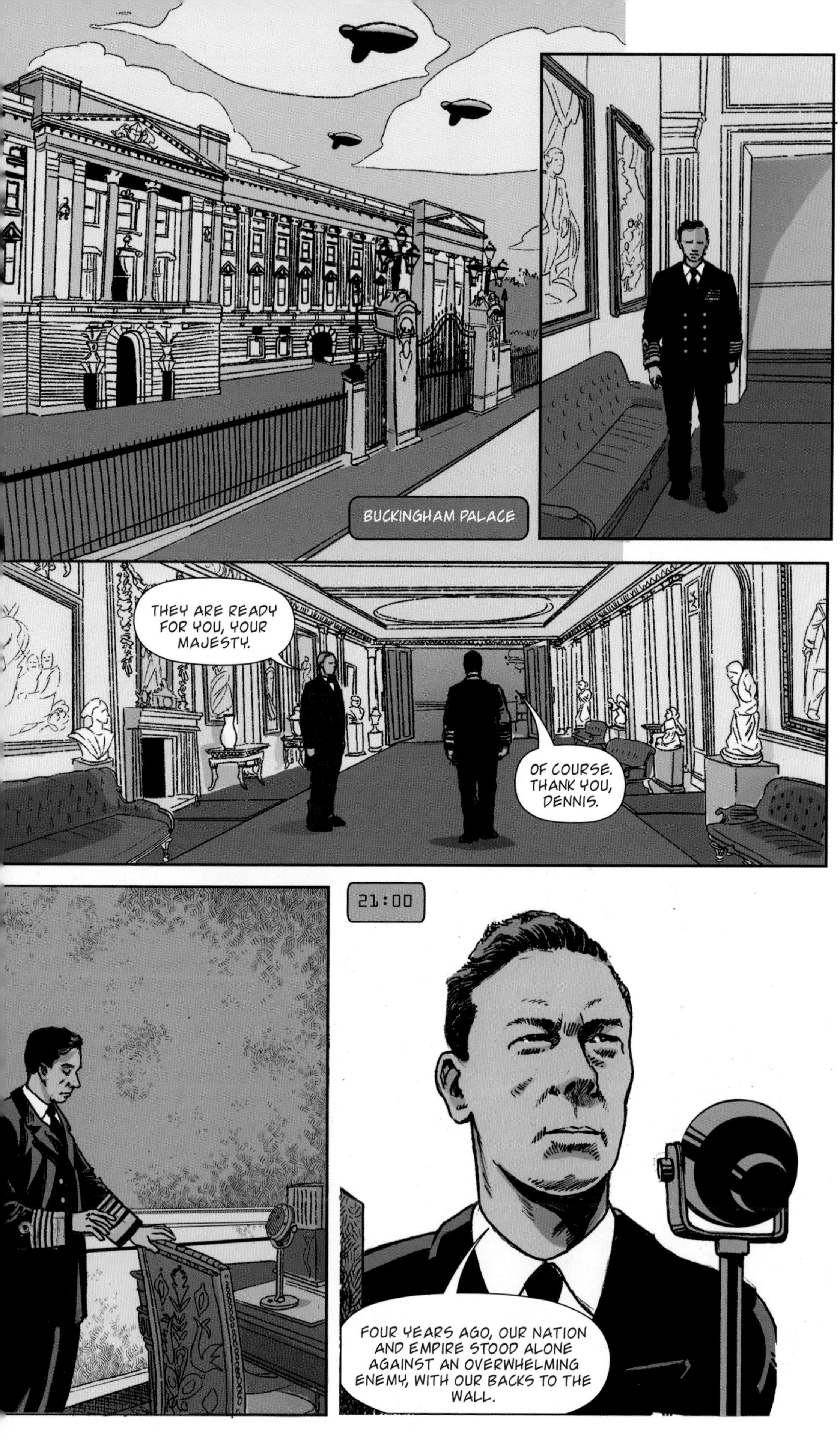
BUCKINGHAM PALACE
THEY ARE READY FOR YOU, YOUR MAJESTY.
OF COURSE. THANK YOU, DENNIS.
21:00
FOUR YEARS AGO, OUR NATION AND EMPIRE STOOD ALONE AGAINST AN OVERWHELMING ENEMY, WITH OUR BACKS TO THE WALL.

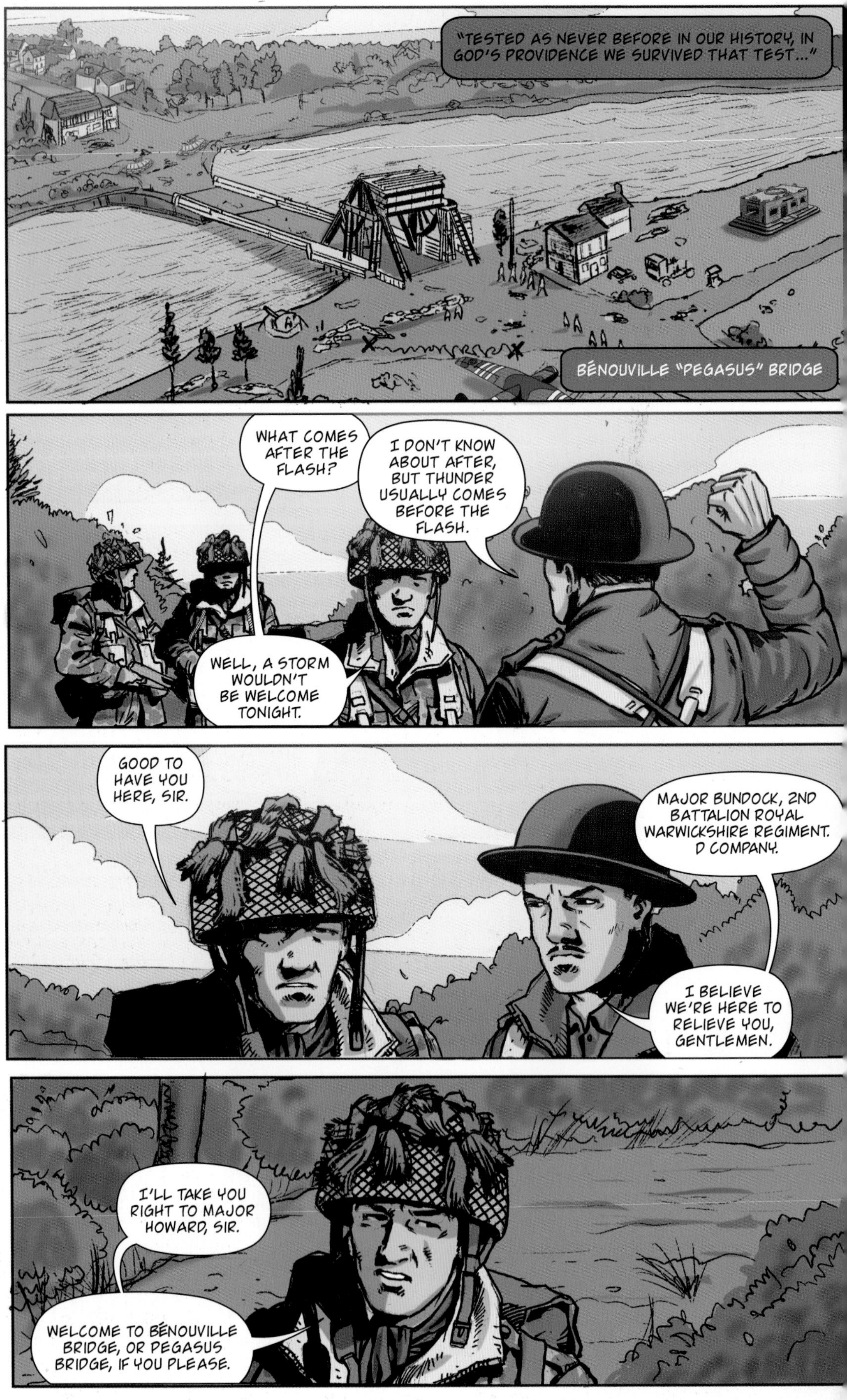
"TESTED AS NEVER BEFORE IN OUR HISTORY, IN GOD'S PROVIDENCE WE SURVIVED THAT TEST..."
BÉNOUVILLE "PEGASUS" BRIDGE
WHAT COMES AFTER THE FLASH?
I DON'T KNOW ABOUT AFTER, BUT THUNDER USUALLY COMES BEFORE THE FLASH.
WELL, A STORM WOULDN'T BE WELCOME TONIGHT.
GOOD TO HAVE YOU HERE, SIR.
MAJOR BUNDOCK, 2ND BATTALION ROYAL WARWICKSHIRE REGIMENT. D COMPANY.
I BELIEVE WE'RE HERE TO RELIEVE YOU, GENTLEMEN.
I'LL TAKE YOU RIGHT TO MAJOR HOWARD, SIR.
WELCOME TO BÉNOUVILLE BRIDGE, OR PEGASUS BRIDGE, IF YOU PLEASE.

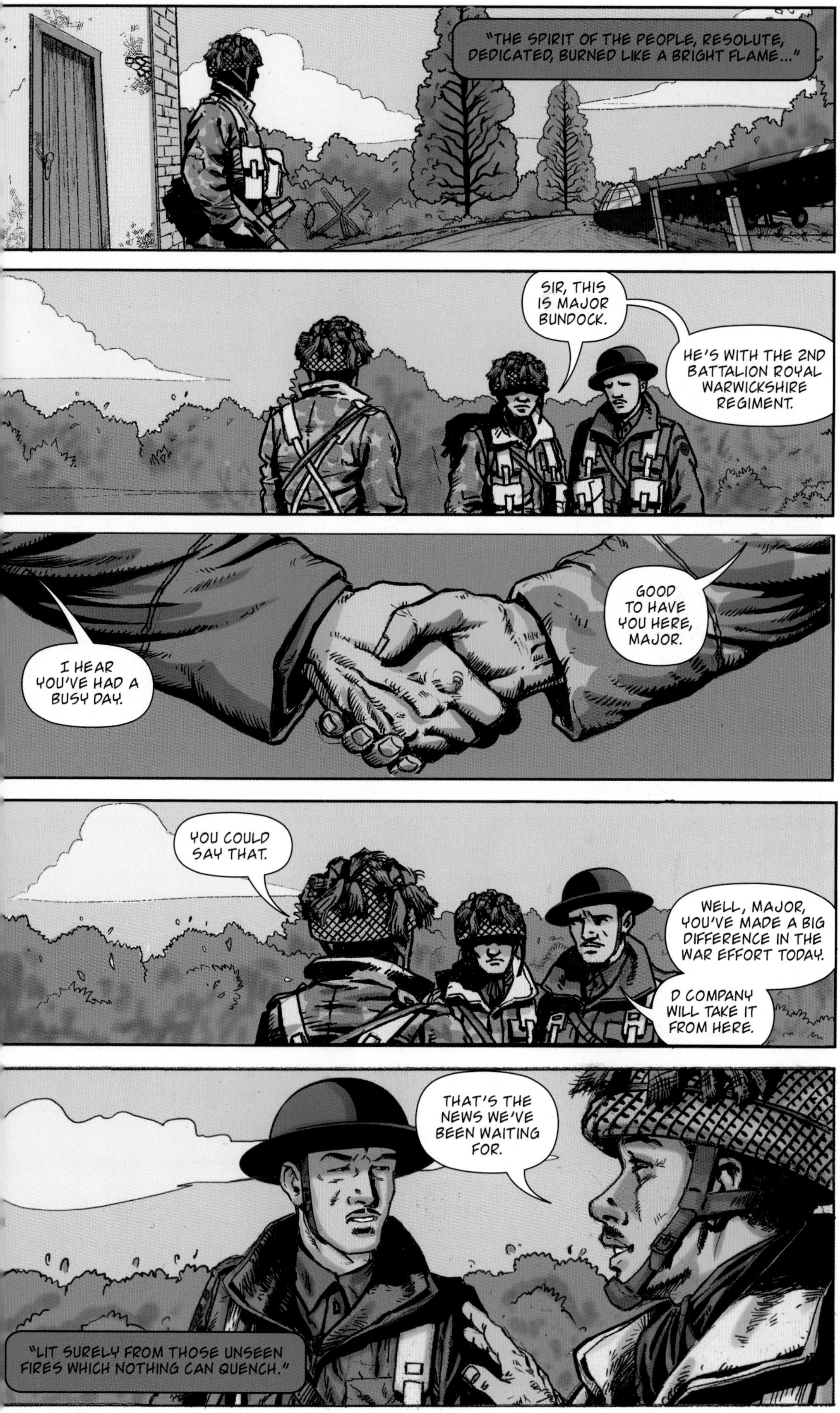
"THE SPIRIT OF THE PEOPLE, RESOLUTE, DEDICATED, BURNED LIKE A BRIGHT FLAME..."
SIR, THIS IS MAJOR BUNDOCK.
HE'S WITH THE 2ND BATTALION ROYAL WARWICKSHIRE REGIMENT.
GOOD TO HAVE YOU HERE, MAJOR.
I HEAR YOU'VE HAD A BUSY DAY.
YOU COULD SAY THAT.
WELL, MAJOR, YOU'VE MADE A BIG DIFFERENCE IN THE WAR EFFORT TODAY.
D COMPANY WILL TAKE IT FROM HERE.
THAT'S THE NEWS WE'VE BEEN WAITING FOR.
"LIT SURELY FROM THOSE UNSEEN FIRES WHICH NOTHING CAN QUENCH."

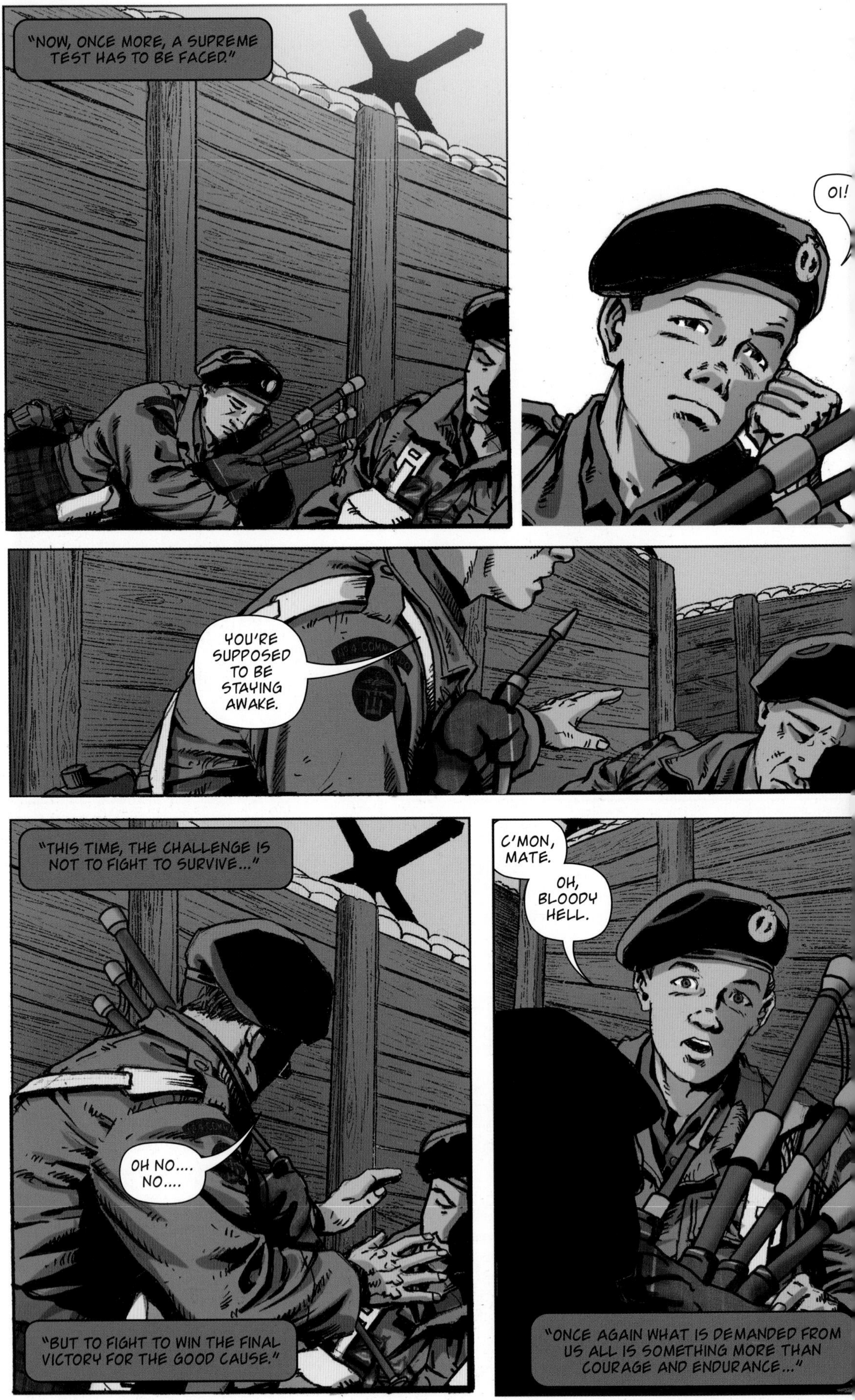

"NOW, ONCE MORE, A SUPREME TEST HAS TO BE FACED."
OI!
YOU'RE SUPPOSED TO BE STAYING AWAKE.
"THIS TIME, THE CHALLENGE IS NOT TO FIGHT TO SURVIVE..."
OH NO.... NO....
"BUT TO FIGHT TO WIN THE FINAL VICTORY FOR THE GOOD CAUSE."
C'MON, MATE.
OH, BLOODY HELL.
"ONCE AGAIN WHAT IS DEMANDED FROM US ALL IS SOMETHING MORE THAN COURAGE AND ENDURANCE..."

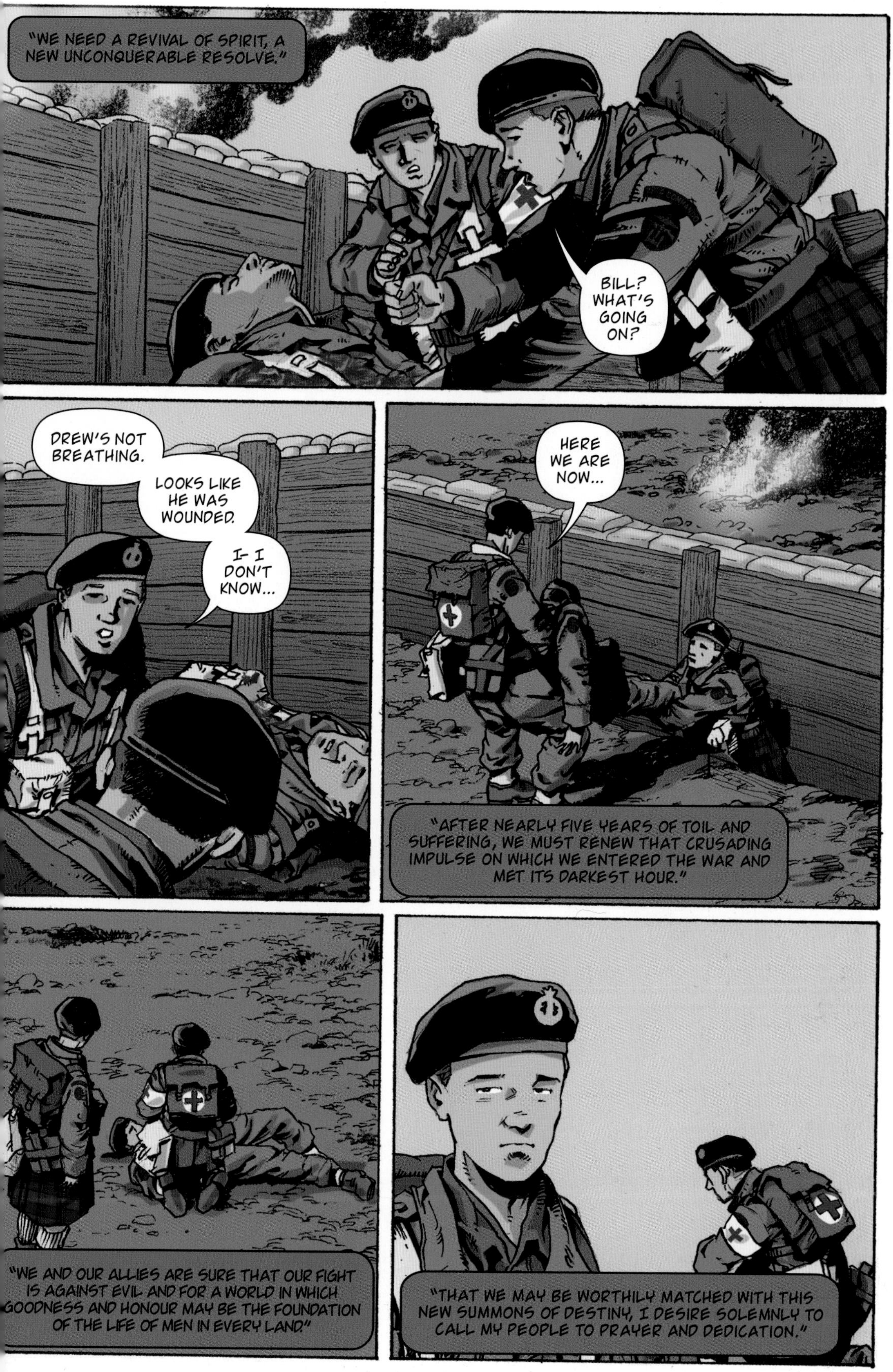
"WE NEED A REVIVAL OF SPIRIT, A NEW UNCONQUERABLE RESOLVE."
BILL? WHAT'S GOING ON?
DREW'S NOT BREATHING.
LOOKS LIKE HE WAS WOUNDED.
I- I DON'T KNOW...
HERE WE ARE NOW...
"AFTER NEARLY FIVE YEARS OF TOIL AND SUFFERING, WE MUST RENEW THAT CRUSADING IMPULSE ON WHICH WE ENTERED THE WAR AND MET ITS DARKEST HOUR."
"WE AND OUR ALLIES ARE SURE THAT OUR FIGHT IS AGAINST EVIL AND FOR A WORLD IN WHICH GOODNESS AND HONOUR MAY BE THE FOUNDATION OF THE LIFE OF MEN IN EVERY LAND."
"THAT WE MAY BE WORTHILY MATCHED WITH THIS NEW SUMMONS OF DESTINY, I DESIRE SOLEMNLY TO CALL MY PEOPLE TO PRAYER AND DEDICATION."

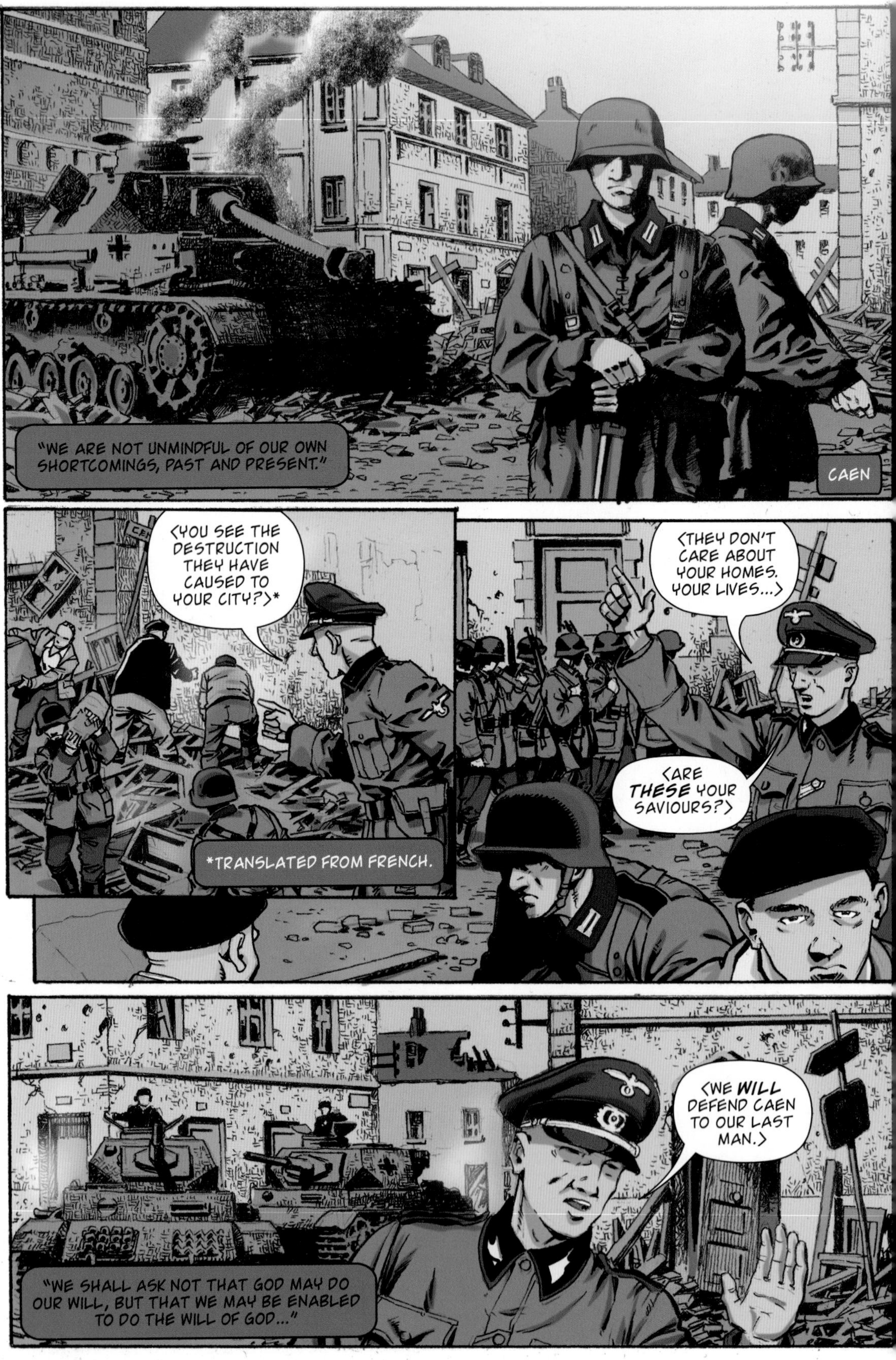
"WE ARE NOT UNMINDFUL OF OUR OWN SHORTCOMINGS, PAST AND PRESENT."
CAEN
<YOU SEE THE DESTRUCTION THEY HAVE CAUSED TO YOUR CITY?>*
*TRANSLATED FROM FRENCH.
<THEY DON'T CARE ABOUT YOUR HOMES. YOUR LIVES...>
<ARE **THESE** YOUR SAVIOURS?>
<WE **WILL** DEFEND CAEN TO OUR LAST MAN.>
"WE SHALL ASK NOT THAT GOD MAY DO OUR WILL, BUT THAT WE MAY BE ENABLED TO DO THE WILL OF GOD..."

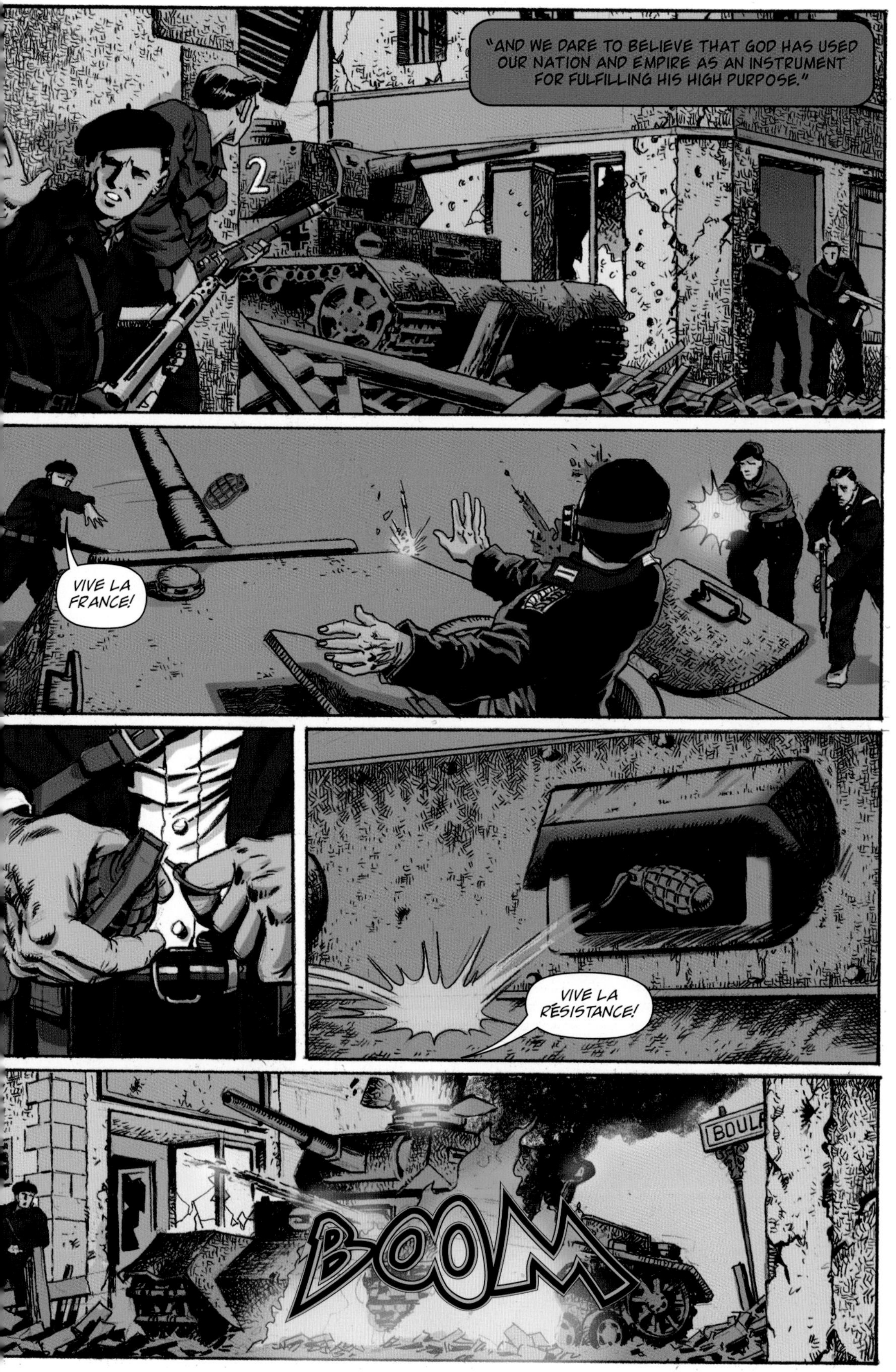
"AND WE DARE TO BELIEVE THAT GOD HAS USED OUR NATION AND EMPIRE AS AN INSTRUMENT FOR FULFILLING HIS HIGH PURPOSE."
VIVE LA FRANCE!
VIVE LA RÉSISTANCE!
BOUL
BOOM

"I HOPE THAT THROUGHOUT THE PRESENT CRISIS OF THE LIBERATION OF EUROPE THERE MAY BE OFFERED UP EARNEST, CONTINUOUS AND WIDESPREAD PRAYER."

WE'RE GOING TO NEED A FEW OF YOU IN THE BARN.

FIVE UPSTAIRS, TOO.

LIEUTENANT-COLONEL TERENCE OTWAY

CHÂTEAU D'AMFREVILLE

BEFORE WE REST THIS EVENING, LET US PRAY.

"WE WHO REMAIN IN THIS LAND CAN MOST EFFECTIVELY ENTER INTO THE SUFFERINGS OF SUBJUGATED EUROPE BY PRAYER..."

DEAR LORD.

GIVE US STRENGTH ON THIS DARK DAY.

TAKE CARE OF OUR BROTHERS, WHO HAVE FALLEN.

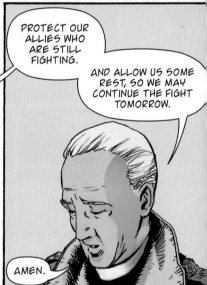

PROTECT OUR ALLIES WHO ARE STILL FIGHTING.

AND ALLOW US SOME REST, SO WE MAY CONTINUE THE FIGHT TOMORROW.

AMEN.

AMEN.

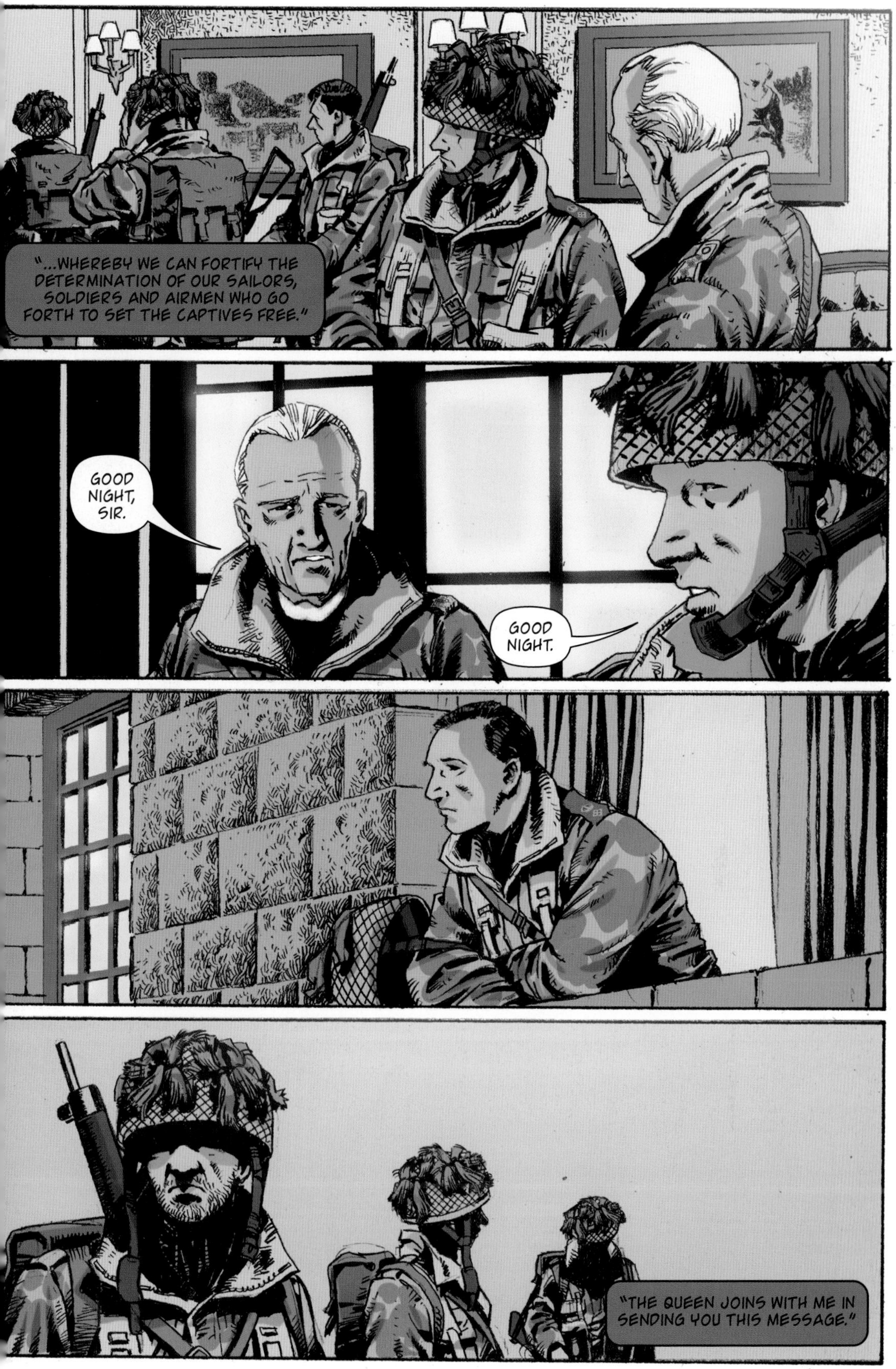
"...WHEREBY WE CAN FORTIFY THE DETERMINATION OF OUR SAILORS, SOLDIERS AND AIRMEN WHO GO FORTH TO SET THE CAPTIVES FREE."
GOOD NIGHT, SIR.
GOOD NIGHT.
"THE QUEEN JOINS WITH ME IN SENDING YOU THIS MESSAGE."

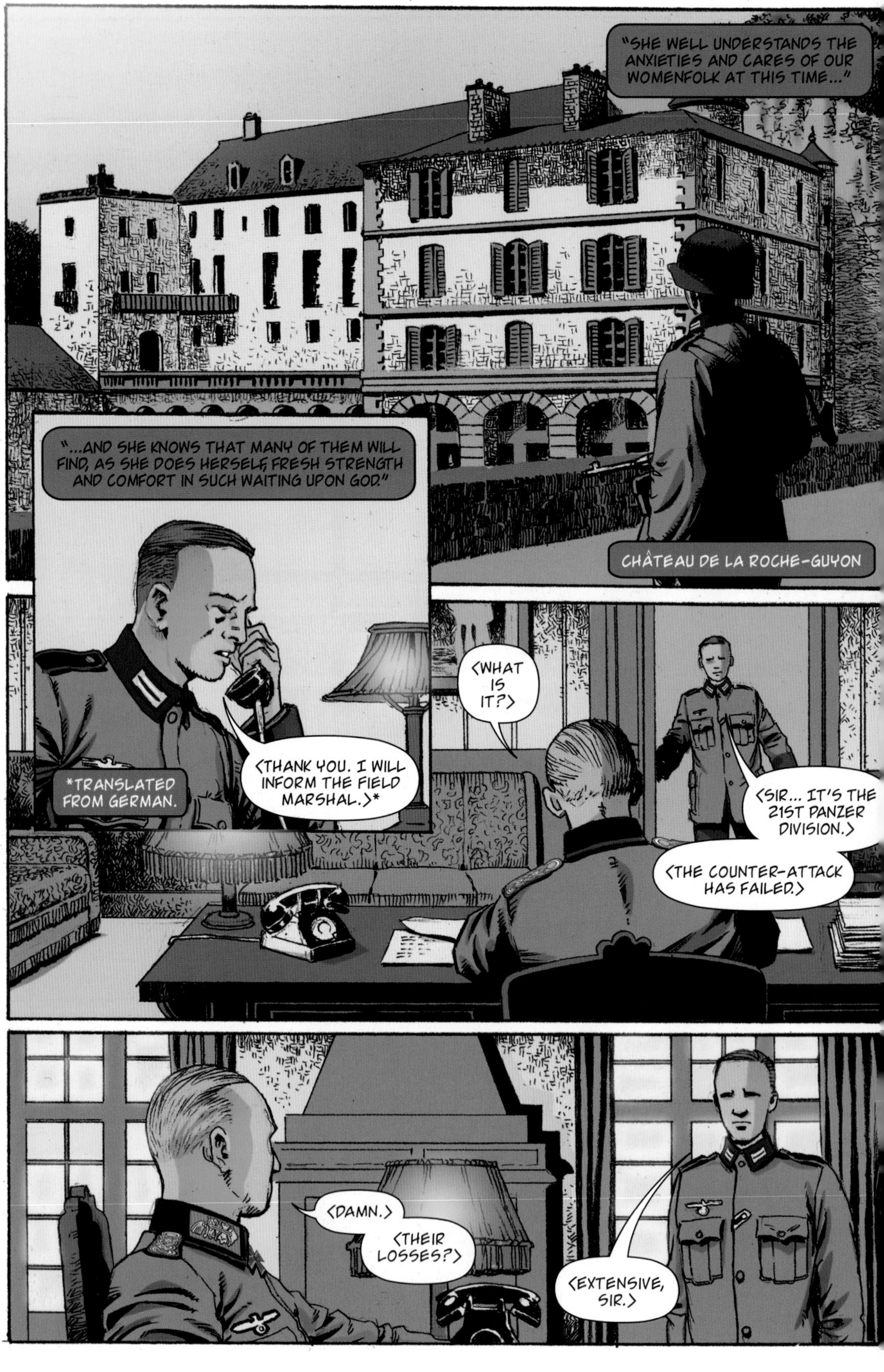
"SHE WELL UNDERSTANDS THE ANXIETIES AND CARES OF OUR WOMENFOLK AT THIS TIME..."
CHÂTEAU DE LA ROCHE-GUYON
"...AND SHE KNOWS THAT MANY OF THEM WILL FIND, AS SHE DOES HERSELF, FRESH STRENGTH AND COMFORT IN SUCH WAITING UPON GOD."
<THANK YOU. I WILL INFORM THE FIELD MARSHAL.>*
*TRANSLATED FROM GERMAN.
<WHAT IS IT?>
<SIR... IT'S THE 21ST PANZER DIVISION.>
<THE COUNTER-ATTACK HAS FAILED.>
<DAMN.>
<THEIR LOSSES?>
<EXTENSIVE, SIR.>

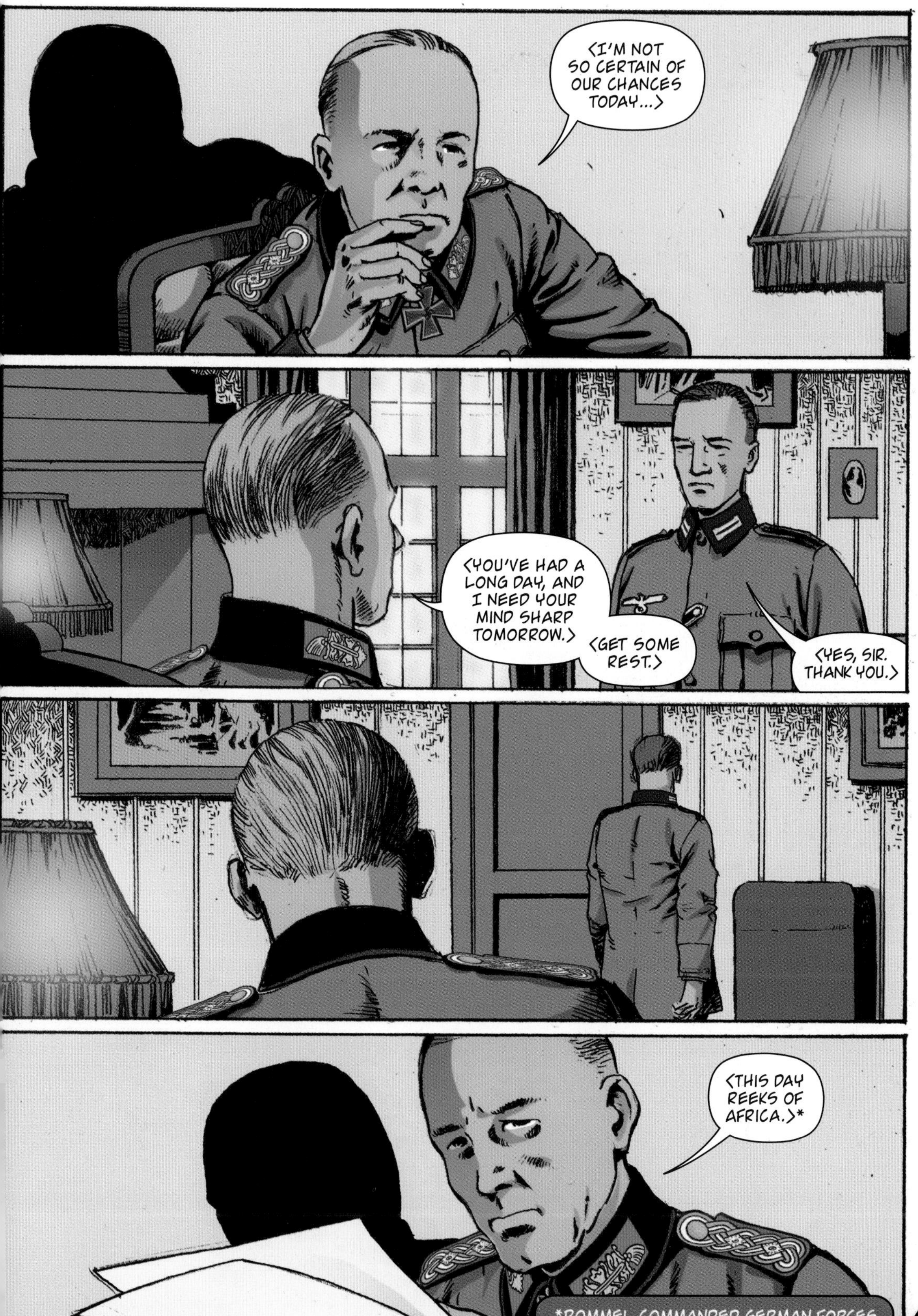

<I'M NOT SO CERTAIN OF OUR CHANCES TODAY...>
<YOU'VE HAD A LONG DAY, AND I NEED YOUR MIND SHARP TOMORROW.>
<GET SOME REST.>
<YES, SIR. THANK YOU.>
<THIS DAY REEKS OF AFRICA.>*
*ROMMEL COMMANDED GERMAN FORCES IN NORTH AFRICA– A MAJOR DEFEAT IN THE NORTH AFRICA CAMPAIGN.

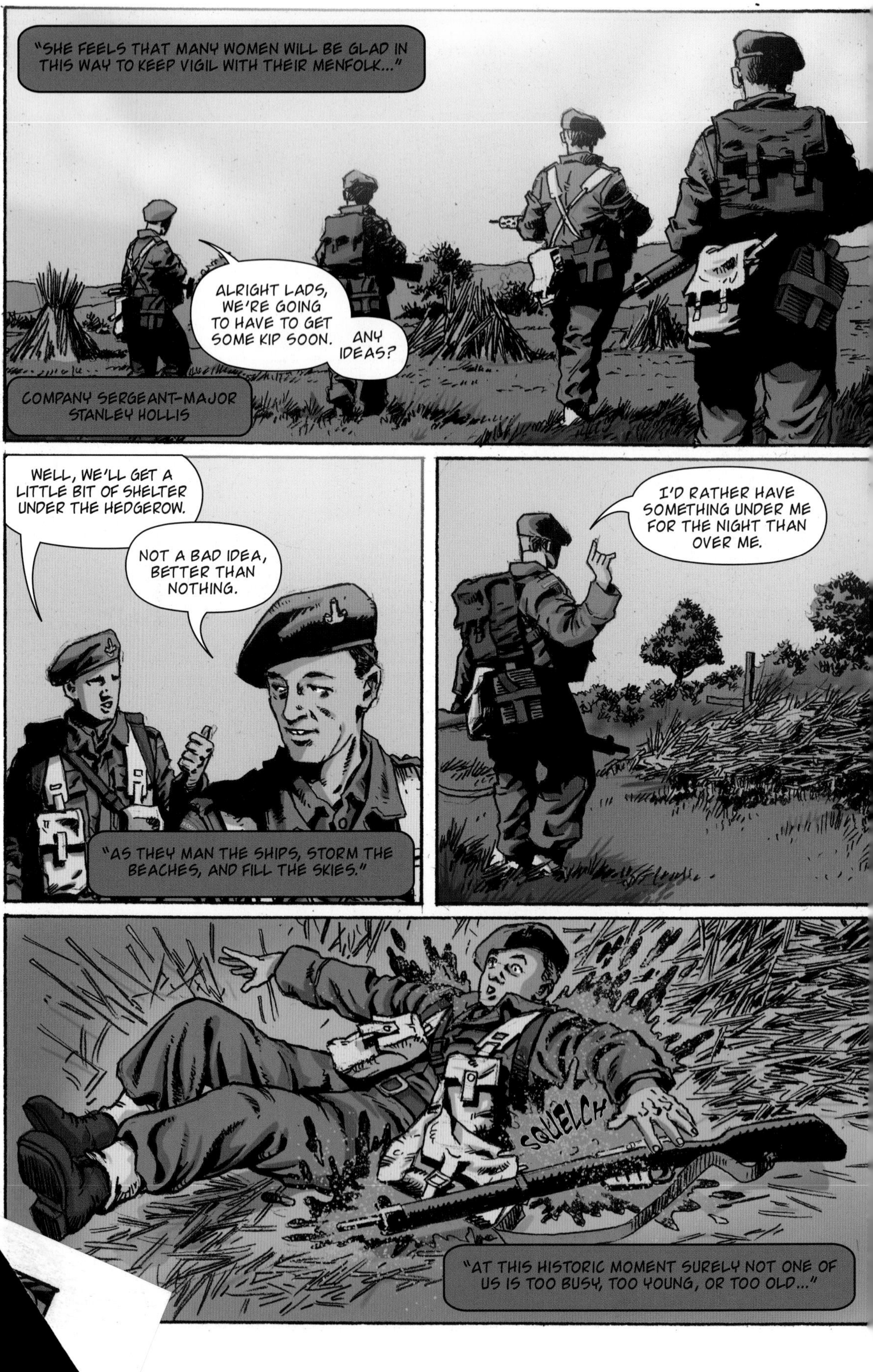
"SHE FEELS THAT MANY WOMEN WILL BE GLAD IN THIS WAY TO KEEP VIGIL WITH THEIR MENFOLK..."
ALRIGHT LADS, WE'RE GOING TO HAVE TO GET SOME KIP SOON.
ANY IDEAS?
COMPANY SERGEANT-MAJOR STANLEY HOLLIS
WELL, WE'LL GET A LITTLE BIT OF SHELTER UNDER THE HEDGEROW.
NOT A BAD IDEA, BETTER THAN NOTHING.
"AS THEY MAN THE SHIPS, STORM THE BEACHES, AND FILL THE SKIES."
I'D RATHER HAVE SOMETHING UNDER ME FOR THE NIGHT THAN OVER ME.
SQUELCH
"AT THIS HISTORIC MOMENT SURELY NOT ONE OF US IS TOO BUSY, TOO YOUNG, OR TOO OLD..."

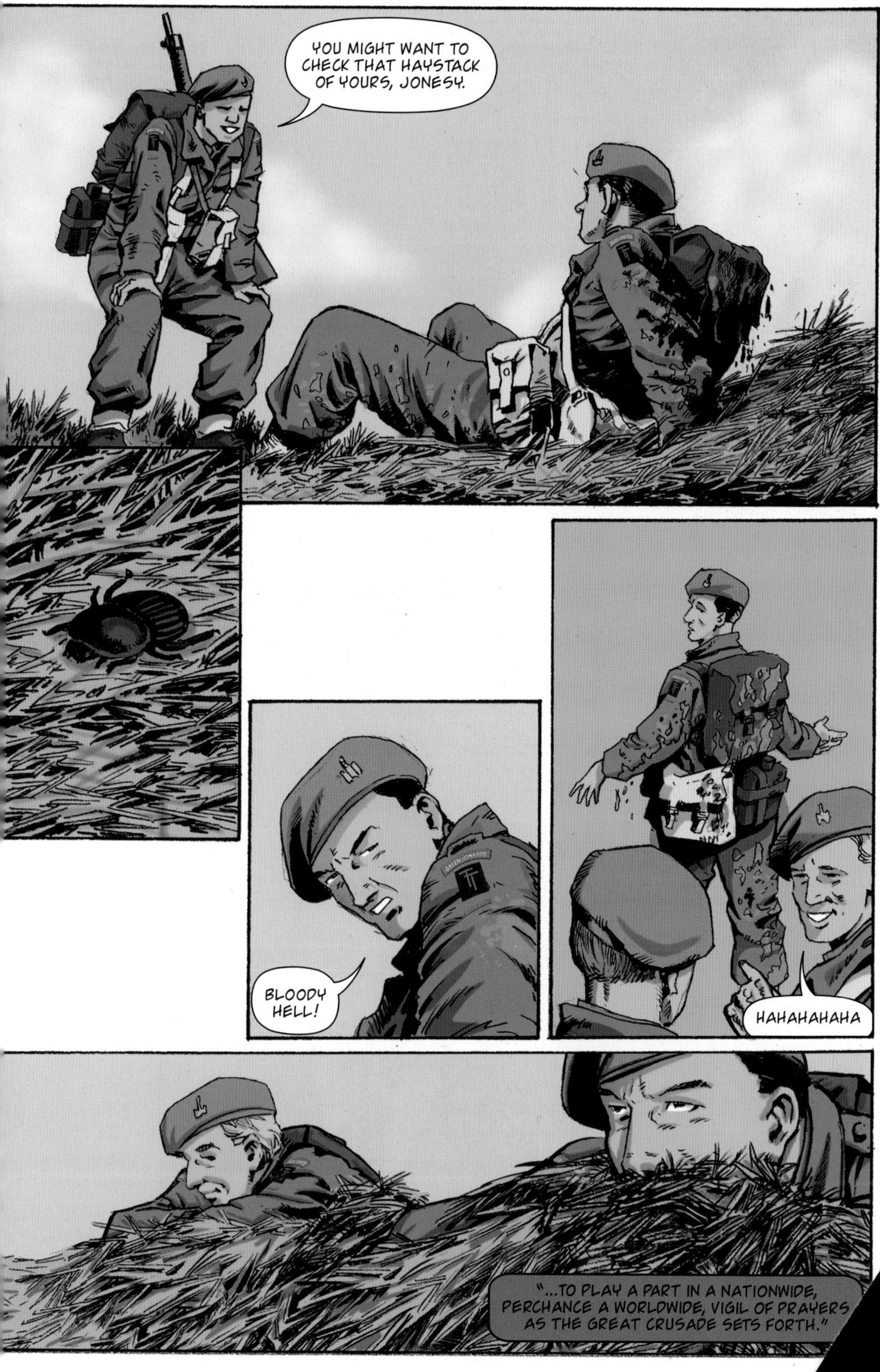

YOU MIGHT WANT TO CHECK THAT HAYSTACK OF YOURS, JONESY.
GREEN HOWARDS
BLOODY HELL!
HAHAHAHAHA
"...TO PLAY A PART IN A NATIONWIDE, PERCHANCE A WORLDWIDE, VIGIL OF PRAYERS AS THE GREAT CRUSADE SETS FORTH."

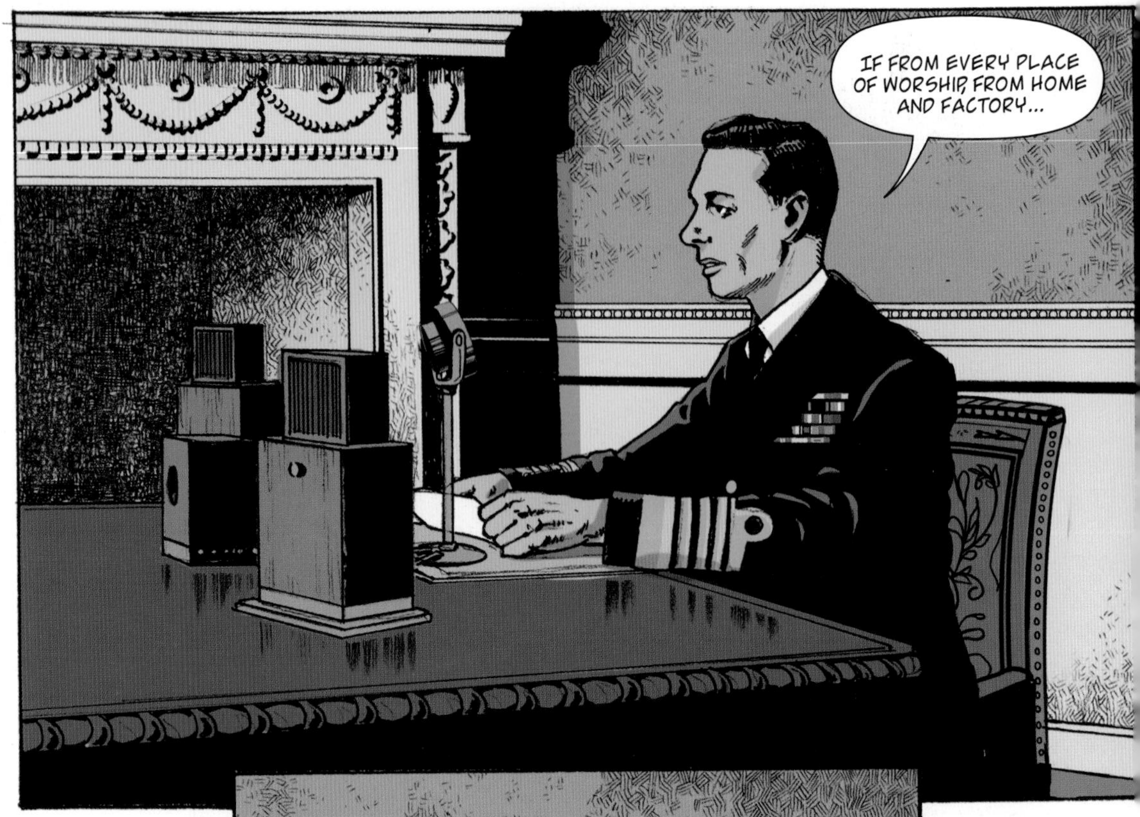
IF FROM EVERY PLACE OF WORSHIP, FROM HOME AND FACTORY...

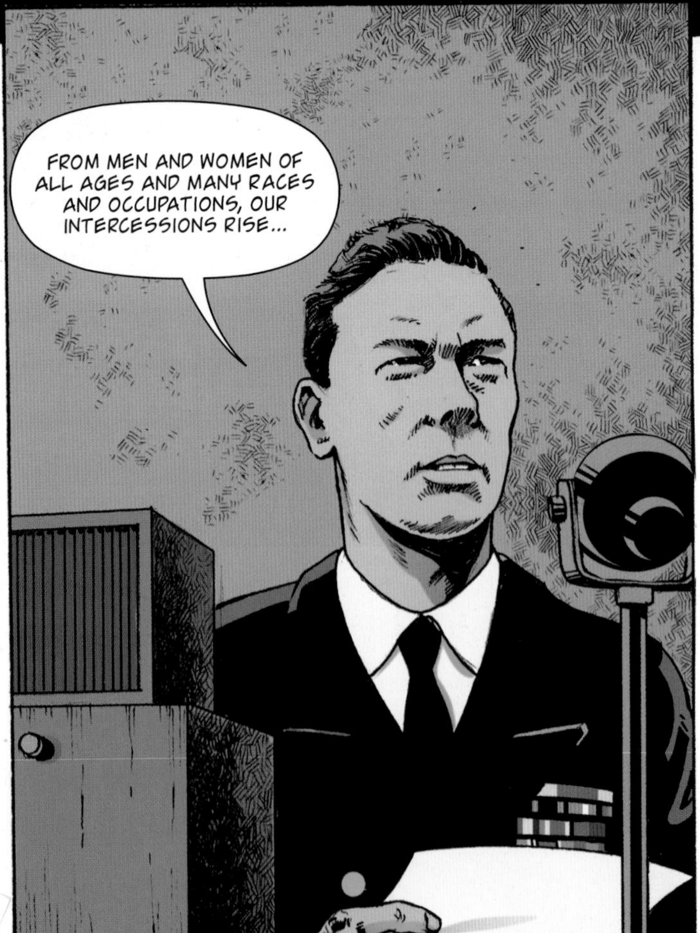
FROM MEN AND WOMEN OF ALL AGES AND MANY RACES AND OCCUPATIONS, OUR INTERCESSIONS RISE...

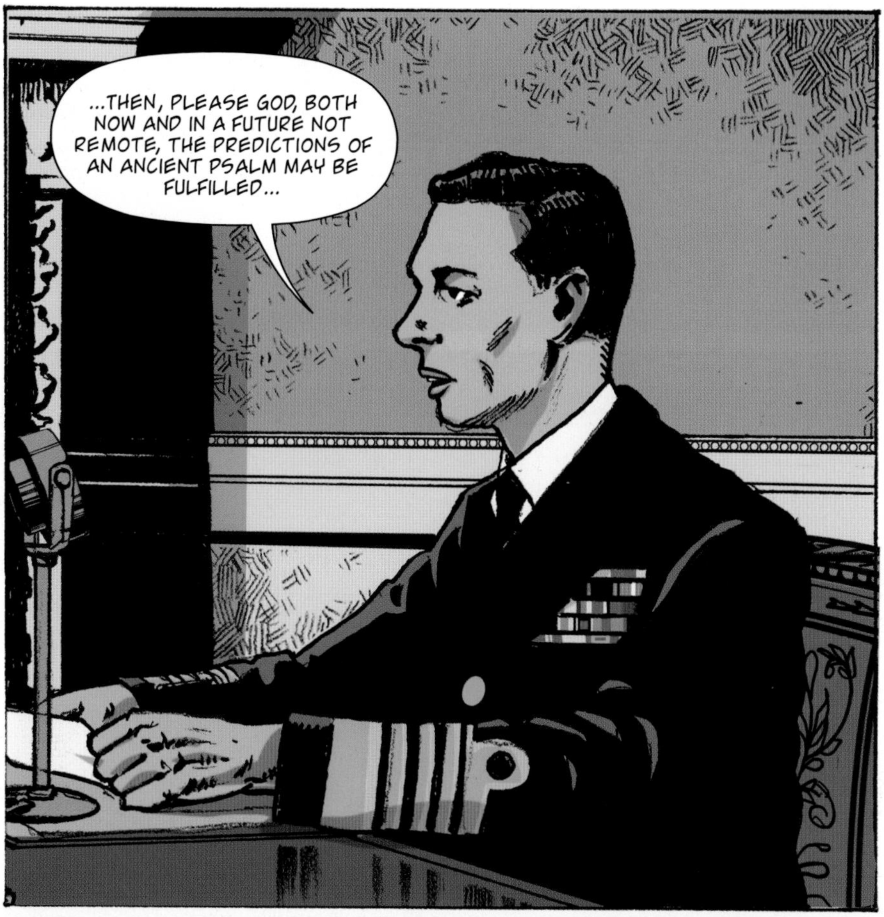
...THEN, PLEASE GOD, BOTH NOW AND IN A FUTURE NOT REMOTE, THE PREDICTIONS OF AN ANCIENT PSALM MAY BE FULFILLED...

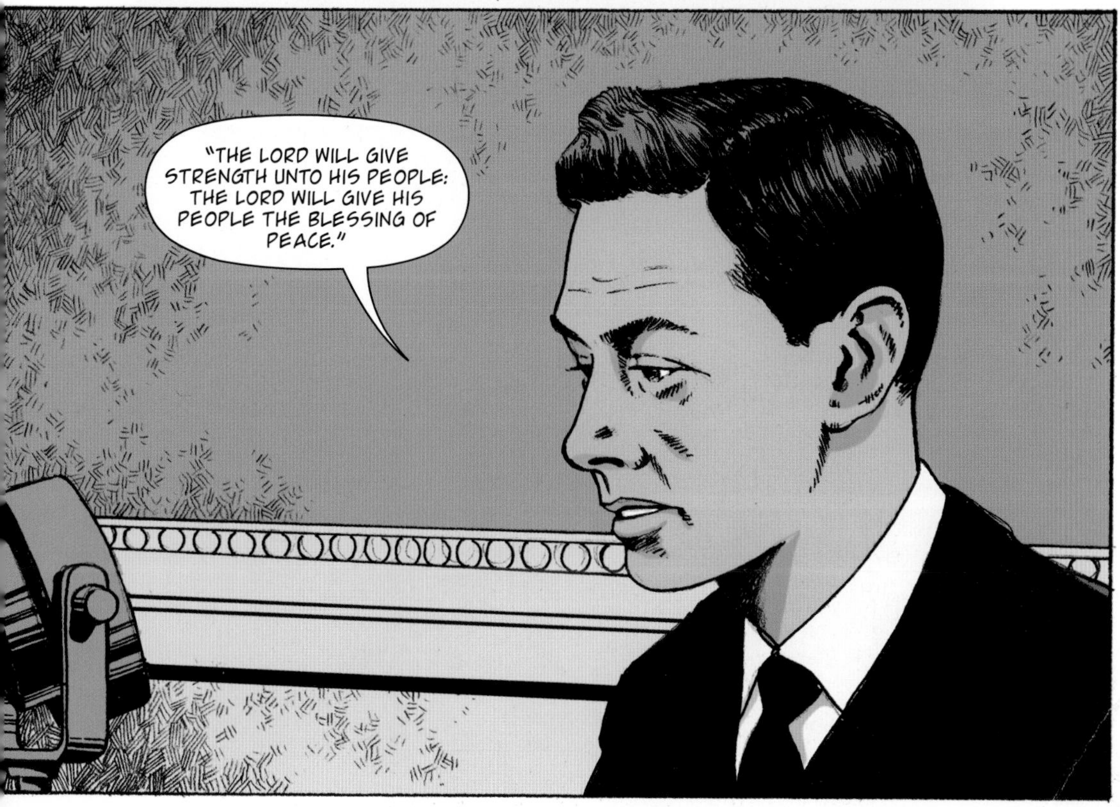
"THE LORD WILL GIVE STRENGTH UNTO HIS PEOPLE: THE LORD WILL GIVE HIS PEOPLE THE BLESSING OF PEACE."

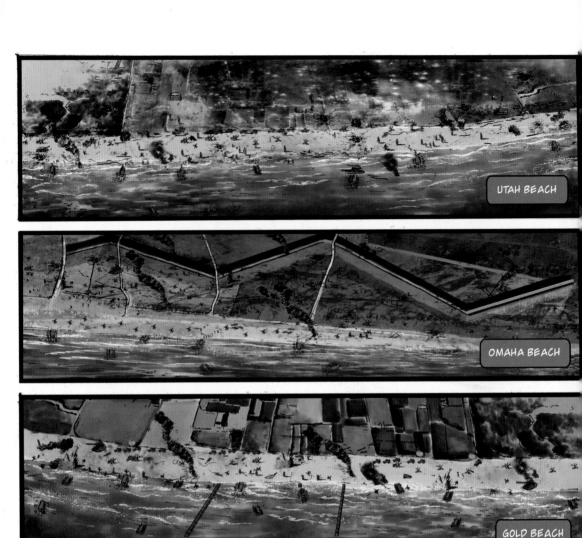

UTAH BEACH

OMAHA BEACH

GOLD BEACH

JUNO BEACH

SWORD BEACH

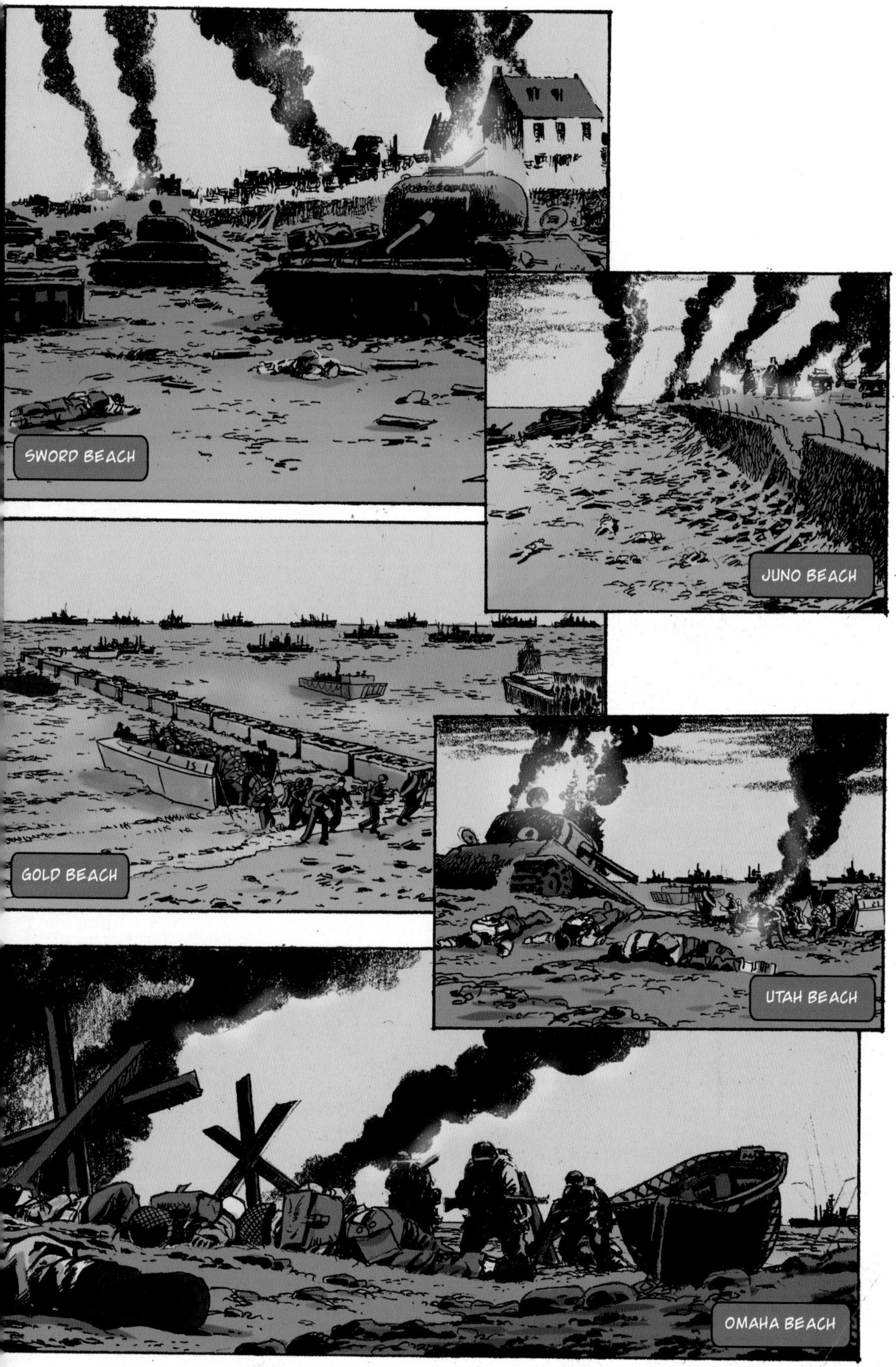
SWORD BEACH
JUNO BEACH
GOLD BEACH
UTAH BEACH
OMAHA BEACH

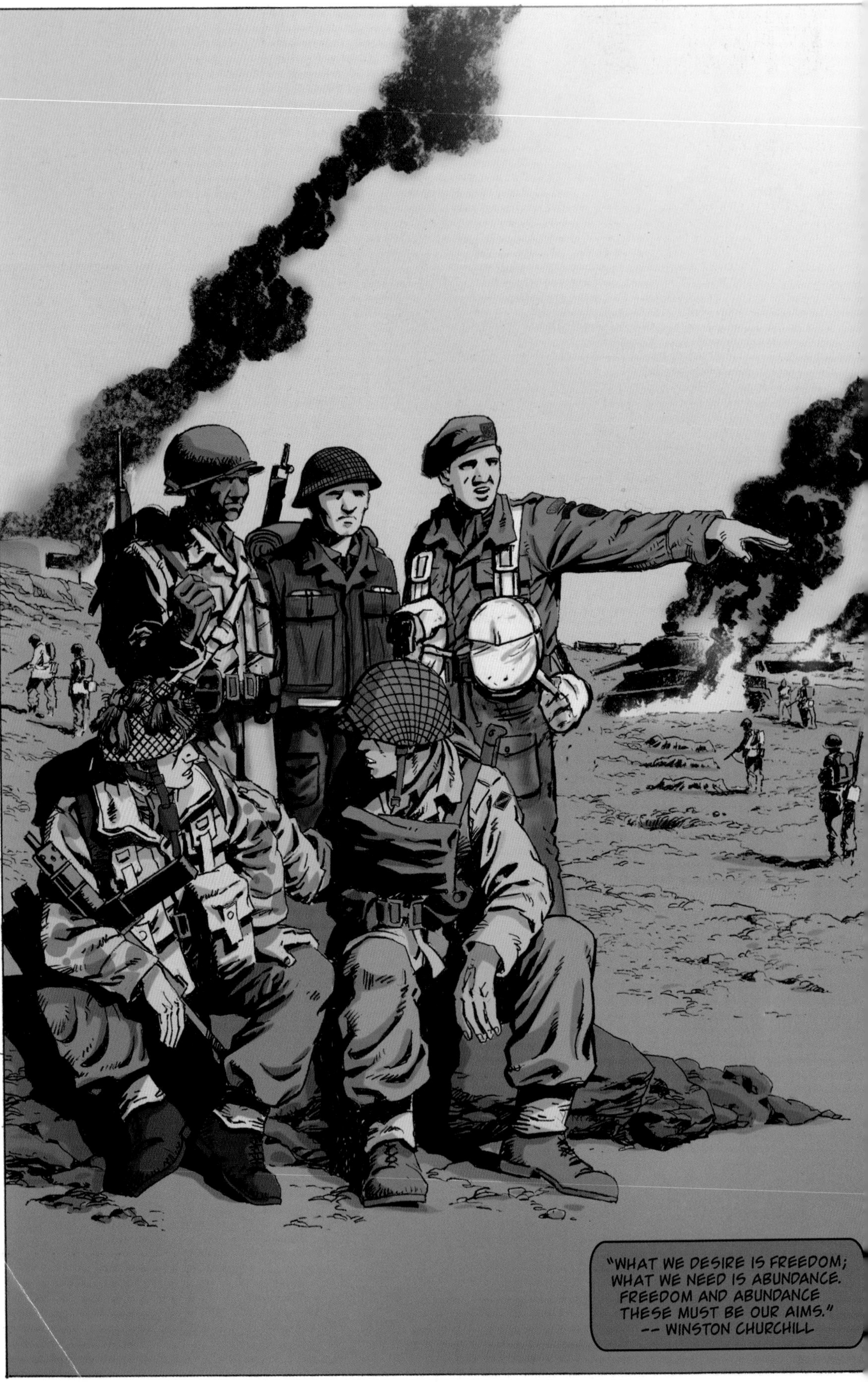
"WHAT WE DESIRE IS FREEDOM; WHAT WE NEED IS ABUNDANCE. FREEDOM AND ABUNDANCE THESE MUST BE OUR AIMS."
-- WINSTON CHURCHILL

UNDER FIRE

A NEW GRAPHIC NOVEL SERIES EXPLORING HISTORY'S MOST DRAMATIC BATTLES THROUGH THE EYES OF THE MEN WHO WERE THERE

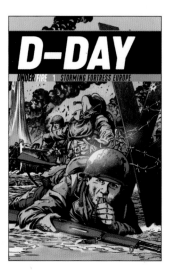

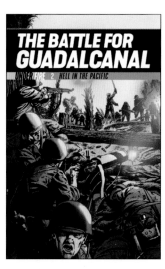

THE GREAT CAMPAIGN FOR
THE LIBERATION OF EUROPE

HIGH-STAKES COMBAT IN
A HOSTILE JUNGLE

A DESPERATE STRUGGLE FOR
CONTROL OF THE SKIES

Each graphic novel combines authentic historical detail with vivid illustration and expert storytelling to capture the heroism and despair, loss and comradeship of bold offensives and desperate last stands.

LOOK OUT FOR UNDER FIRE VOLUME 2:
THE BATTLE FOR GUADALCANAL
HELL IN THE PACIFIC

On 7 August, 1942, US Marines stormed the Japanese-held island of Guadalcanal, signalling the beginning of a campaign which would last over six months. This colourful graphic novel follows the stories of the troops on the ground, bringing the campaign vividly to life through the eyes of the soldiers, sailors, and pilots who fought on both sides. Combining an authentic historical story with striking visuals and expert storytelling, *The Battle for Guadalcanal* reveals a campaign that changed the course of the War in the Pacific.

More information can be found on our website:
WWW.OSPREYPUBLISHING.COM